Learn Bit Python

by masara

Learn Bit Python

masara

Learn Bit Python

1. Learn Bit Python
2. Table of Contents

    1. 00 Welcome
    2. 02 How
    3. 03 Builtin
    4. 04 Input
    5. 05 File
    6. 06 Path
    7. 07 Block
    8. 08 String
    9. 09 Sequence
    10. 10 Heap
    11. 11 Cython
    12. 12 Function
    13. 13 Class
    14. 14 Project
    15. 15 Package
    16. 16 pandas
    17. 17 regex
    18. 18 Les Temps

19. 19 XML
20. 20 Scikit Learn
21. 21 list
22. 22 logging
23. 23 Gibbys
24. 24 PDB
25. 25 timing
26. 26 urllib
27. 27 selenium
28. 28 requests
29. 29 flask
30. 30 sqlite
31. 31 render
32. 32 sys
33. 33 sympy
34. 34 Sale
35. 35 pybroker
36. 36 Price
37. 37 Minute
38. 38 mplfinance
39. 39 stockstats
40. 40 qpython
41. 41 qsl4a
42. 42 espeakng
43. 43 UNINSTALL
44. 44 kivy
45. 45 CPU
46. 46 Uniapp

47. 47 p4a
48. 48 git
49. 49 SHA
50. 50 efinance
51. 51 Gann
52. 52 MP3
53. 53 Tarot
54. 54 random
55. 55 argparse
56. 56 unittest
57. 57 lilypond
58. 58 mingus
59. 59 threading
60. 60 multiprocessing
61. 61 asyncio
62. 62 numpy
63. 63 Oneliner

First edition

Learn Bit Python

00 Welcome

This is the 4th book I wrote, it is about Python lauguage, very basic things. The reason I wrote it is not to teach, nor to communicate, I myself just know basic things, so I wrote it because of managment. Some words I think I use maybe wrong, I seldom do auto correction, since they will interfere my typing and thinking, which again proves me not a good writer as well.

Since I already have 3 books, so I have a feeling of pages if published, around 208 to 280. Sometimes I feel emotions are just gone, I myself now am no longer young, and writing probably is a proof that I ever lived. Last two years I have fixed many wrong opinions, and many harmful relationships are abandonned. For me this is hard, since I always hope the world be in a peace. 嫌われる勇気：自己啓発の源流「アドラー」の教え is a 300 days best seller on amazon Japan in 2014. The book is inspired by Alfred Adler, who is so famous now and died 90 years ago. Adler says it is easier to fight for one's principles than to live up to them.

Does that make sense?

When people are young, meaning is very important, then people getting old, or les gens vieillissent in French, meaning is no longer important and is forgotten. The earth has 200+ countries, combien en savons-nous? And how many langueges are there on earth? Do you notice it is wrong because the article the is missing? Should it be missing or missed? Why do we care? Or we just cant care? Why missed atstrophe '?

Nonsense.

We really live in a different world today, based on the fast growing technology, especially Internet. And what is Internet? Why I in big letter? Why dont you ask P is big in Python too? If I tell you the network is larger and lareger, in the order of NANO, BAN, PAN, LAN, CAN, MAN, RAN, WAN, does this make sense to you? The thing you do not sense is not sensive? Why you can be in the center of sense? It is just because you are controlling yourself.

Life is short, use Python, such slogan T-shirt is famous among programmers, especially those who use Python. Python was initially designed by Guido van Rossum in 1991 and now is under Python Software Foundation's control. When we say control, it does not refer to anything bad, it is just a big orgnization, has goal and has process. Control for better, not for bidden. In software world, version control is a very common idea, and it usually goes like x.xx.xxx.xxxx, x means the version in version, so the most left represents the biggest version, and others version in version. 01.1994 Python 1.0, 10.2000 Python 2.0, 12.2008 Python 3.0, 10.2020 Python 3.9. Will there be a Python 4.0? Check out https://www.youtube.com/watch?v=aYbNh3NS7jA.

When we were young, we admire the top people in a system. How do they become success? How much money do they earn? How big their houses are? Howerver, nous vieillissons, nous nous en moquons, et ce qui nous préoccupe devrait nous être bénéfique. Si vous pouvez acheter un programme, pourquoi écrire? Si vous avez de l'argent, pourquoi ouvrir une entreprise? Si vous parlez anglais, vous n'allez jamais en France? On apprend donc un nouveau langage parce qu'on doit l'utiliser à l'occasion. If we all use Python, do we have communication problem? Can we train everyone be able to use Python? What is the best path to learn Python? Or anything? Can we transfer from Python to Android? All the questions are open, and I can't answer them, but I would like to introduce my path, which I wrote here, exchanging opinions, with Pythoners.

OK, talk is cheap, show you the code.

f"{datetime(2024,9,1)} in Corcadia, Montreal, Canada"

01 Hello

There are two ways to install Python on comupters, one via market using GUI, the other via command line. The important thing is to make sure the version you want. Though there is full explaination of each version's coverage, no one would really read, like no one would read the agreement when download X.

Check out https://www.python.org/downloads/ for the versions, and I will use cmd-line, which is just self habit. There are two commands I think are useful, as below,

```
python --version
python -c "help('modules')"
```

Python can also go into an interactive mode, as below,

```
C:\Users\Lenovo>python
Python 3.12.5 (tags/v3.12.5:ff3bc82, Aug  6 2024, 20:45:27) [MSC v.1940 64 bit
(AMD64)] on win32
Type "help", "copyright", "credits" or "license" for more information.
>>> print('hello')
hello
>>> exit()
```

```
C:\Users\Lenovo>
```

Python can also go with a .py file in excutive mode, as below,

```
C:\Users\Lenovo>notepad hello.py

print('hello')
print('안녕하세요')
print('bonjour')
print('ciao')
print('درود')
print('сёлём')
print('สวัสดีครับ/คะ')
print('Xin chào')

C:\Users\Lenovo>python hello.py
hello
안녕하세요
bonjour
ciao
درود
сёлём
สวัสดีครับ/คะ
Xin chào

C:\Users\Lenovo>
```

Python can also run a module, as below,

```
C:\Users\Lenovo>python -m pip show pip
Name: pip
Version: 24.2
Summary: The PyPA recommended tool for installing Python packages.
Home-page: https://pip.pypa.io/
Author:
Author-email: The pip developers <distutils-sig@python.org>
License: MIT
Location:                                                                 C:\Program
Files\WindowsApps\PythonSoftwareFoundation.Python.3.12_3.12.1520.0_x64__qbz5n2kfra8p
0\Lib\site-packages
Requires:
Required-by:

C:\Users\Lenovo>python -m pip list
Package            Version
------------------ -----------
akracer            0.0.13
akshare            1.13.86
appdirs            1.4.4
attrs              23.2.0
beautifulsoup4     4.12.3
```

```
certifi             2024.2.2
cffi                1.16.0
charset-normalizer  3.3.2
colorama            0.4.6
contourpy           1.2.0
cycler              0.12.1
decorator           5.1.1
efinance            0.5.1
et-xmlfile          1.1.0
fonttools           4.49.0
frozendict          2.4.1
futu-api            8.1.4108
h11                 0.14.0
html5lib            1.1
idna                3.6
inputimeout         1.0.4
jsonpath            0.82.2
kiwisolver          1.4.5
lxml                5.2.1
markdown-it-py      3.0.0
MarkupSafe          2.1.5
matplotlib          3.8.3
mdurl               0.1.2
multitasking        0.0.11
numpy               1.26.4
openpyxl            3.1.2
outcome             1.3.0.post0
packaging           24.0
pandas              2.2.1
peewee              3.17.1
pillow              10.2.0
pip                 24.2
protobuf            3.20.3
psutil              5.9.8
py                  1.11.0
py-mini-racer       0.6.0
pycparser           2.21
pycryptodome        3.20.0
Pygments            2.17.2
pyparsing           3.1.2
PySocks             1.7.1
python-dateutil     2.9.0.post0
pytz                2024.1
requests            2.31.0
retry               0.9.2
rich                13.7.1
selenium            4.18.1
simplejson          3.19.2
six                 1.16.0
sniffio             1.3.1
sortedcontainers    2.4.0
soupsieve           2.5
tabulate            0.9.0
```

```
tqdm                4.66.2
trio                0.24.0
trio-websocket      0.11.1
typing_extensions   4.10.0
tzdata              2024.1
urllib3             2.2.1
webencodings        0.5.1
wsproto             1.2.0
xlrd                2.0.1

C:\Users\Lenovo>
```

PIP is a python package manager, some useful commands, as below,

```
pip list
pip inspect
pip install pygame
pip uninstall pygame
```

Pygame is just an example, it can be any module or library, one can also build by self for sure. To do a useful hello by pygame, type below,

```
C:\Users\Lenovo>python -m pygame.examples.aliens
pygame 2.6.0 (SDL 2.28.4, Python 3.12.5)
Hello from the pygame community. https://www.pygame.org/contribute.html

C:\Users\Lenovo>
```

Check out pygame/examples/README.rst at main · pygame/pygame · GitHub for the full pygame examples.

02 How

Create a file called display.py, as below,

```
import sys
import pygame

pygame.init()
screen = pygame.display.set_mode((400, 400))
clock = pygame.time.Clock()

dialogue_font = pygame.font.SysFont('arial', 15)
name_font = pygame.font.SysFont('Helvetica', 20)
game_over_font = pygame.font.SysFont('Verdana', 60)

dialogue = dialogue_font.render("Hey there, let's try font!",
                                True, (0,0,0))
name = name_font.render("masara", True, (0,0,255))
game_over = game_over_font.render("Game Over", True, (255,0,0))
```

```
while True:
    for event in pygame.event.get():
        if event.type == pygame.QUIT:
            pygame.quit()
            sys.exit()

    screen.fill((255, 255, 255))

    screen.blit(dialogue, (40,40))
    screen.blit(name, (40,140))
    screen.blit(game_over, (40,240))

    pygame.display.flip()
    clock.tick(60)
```

Run display.py to see the displayed fonts. And next try another file arrow.py, as below,

```
import pygame, sys, random
from pygame.locals import *

# Init
pygame.init()

# Colours
BACKGROUND = (255, 255, 255)
TEXTCOLOUR = (200, 100, 0)

# Game Setup
FPS = 60
fpsClock = pygame.time.Clock()
WINDOW_WIDTH = 400
WINDOW_HEIGHT = 300

WINDOW = pygame.display.set_mode((WINDOW_WIDTH, WINDOW_HEIGHT))
pygame.display.set_caption('My Game!')

# Set up fonts
fontObj = pygame.font.Font(None, 32)
rightText = fontObj.render('Right', True, TEXTCOLOUR, None)
leftText = fontObj.render('Left', True, TEXTCOLOUR, None)
rightTextRectObj = rightText.get_rect()
leftTextRectObj = leftText.get_rect()
# Center the text on the window
rightTextRectObj.center = (WINDOW_WIDTH // 2, WINDOW_HEIGHT //2)
leftTextRectObj.center = (WINDOW_WIDTH // 2, WINDOW_HEIGHT //2)


# Selects ramdomly either Left or Right
def select_side () :
  side = ''
```

```
  chosen = random.randint(0,1)
  if chosen == 1 :
    side = 'Right'
  else :
    side = 'Left'

  return side


# The main function that controls the game
def main () :
  looping = True

  target = select_side() # Prime the target before the main loop
  goes = 0 # How many goes the user has had
  score = 0
  rounds = 10 # How many rounds in the game
  active = True # Used so that the next target won't be set until the user releases
the key on the keyboard

  # The main game loop
  while looping :
    sideChosen = ''

    # Get inputs
    for event in pygame.event.get() :
      if event.type == QUIT :
        pygame.quit()
        sys.exit()

    pressed = pygame.key.get_pressed()
    if pressed[K_RIGHT] :
      sideChosen = 'Right'
    elif pressed[K_LEFT] :
      sideChosen = 'Left'


    # Processing
    if sideChosen != '' and sideChosen != target and active == True :
      print ('Correct')
      goes = goes + 1
      score = score + 1
      active = False
    elif sideChosen == target and active == True :
      print ('Incorrect')
      goes = goes + 1
      active = False
    elif active == False and sideChosen == '' : # Enable the next round
      active = True
      target = select_side()

    if goes == rounds :
      looping = False
```

```
    # Render elements of the game
    WINDOW.fill(BACKGROUND)
    if target == 'Right' and active == True :
      WINDOW.blit(rightText, rightTextRectObj)
    elif target == 'Left' and active == True :
      WINDOW.blit(leftText, leftTextRectObj)
    pygame.display.update()
    fpsClock.tick(FPS)

  print ('Game Over')
  print (f'Your score was : {score}')

main()
```

And we can also make a simple animation, as below,

```
import pygame, sys
from pygame.locals import *

pygame.init()

FPS = 30 # frames per second setting
fpsClock = pygame.time.Clock()

# set up the window
DISPLAYSURF = pygame.display.set_mode((400, 300), 0, 32)
pygame.display.set_caption('Animation')

WHITE = (255, 255, 255)
catImg = pygame.image.load('univ.jpg')
catx = 10
caty = 10
direction = 'right'

while True: # the main game loop
    DISPLAYSURF.fill(WHITE)

    if direction == 'right':
        catx += 5
        if catx == 280:
            direction = 'down'
    elif direction == 'down':
        caty += 5
        if caty == 220:
            direction = 'left'
    elif direction == 'left':
        catx -= 5
        if catx == 10:
            direction = 'up'
    elif direction == 'up':
        caty -= 5
```

```
        if caty == 10:
            direction = 'right'

    DISPLAYSURF.blit(catImg, (catx, caty))

    for event in pygame.event.get():
        if event.type == QUIT:
            pygame.quit()
            sys.exit()

    pygame.display.update()
    fpsClock.tick(FPS)
```

These three examples are just something demo, and not so deep, the thing is to get a flavor, to notice the typing style of Python. We see there are tabs, newlines, spaces, and english words(yes, Python can use other languege for varible now), it is really human readable writing and just calculations. But how come I do not know how to write? Is it because I am stupid? Definitely no! Remember when we learn a second languege? How long does it take to really speak using it? Years? And for writing? Especially academic how long?

English is the most widely used languege in the world, but not the universe. Math is. So we should really know numbers and how numbers represent in computer languege, in this case, Python.

03 Builtin

There are three types of Python numbers, int, float, and complex.

```
C:\Users\Lenovo>more check.py
print("=>start check the data type")
print(type(1))
print(type(2.8))
print(type(1+2j))
print("=>finish")

C:\Users\Lenovo>python check.py
=>start check the data type
<class 'int'>
<class 'float'>
<class 'complex'>
=>finish

C:\Users\Lenovo>
```

For complex, we can also use function, for example,

```
# file
print("=>start check the data type")
z = complex(1, 2)
print(type(z))
print("=>finish")

# output
=>start check the data type
<class 'complex'>
=>finish
```

function, or builtin, is something Python self defined, or high frequently used method, just like in math, particular in primary school, if we do not care about the complexity. How many builtins? See below,

```
# file
print("=>start check the data type")
import builtins
for e in dir(builtins): print(e),
print("=>finish")

# output
=>start check the data type
ArithmeticError
AssertionError
AttributeError
BaseException
BaseExceptionGroup
BlockingIOError
BrokenPipeError
BufferError
BytesWarning
ChildProcessError
ConnectionAbortedError
ConnectionError
ConnectionRefusedError
ConnectionResetError
DeprecationWarning
EOFError
Ellipsis
EncodingWarning
EnvironmentError
Exception
ExceptionGroup
False
FileExistsError
FileNotFoundError
FloatingPointError
FutureWarning
GeneratorExit
IOError
ImportError
```

```
ImportWarning
IndentationError
IndexError
InterruptedError
IsADirectoryError
KeyError
KeyboardInterrupt
LookupError
MemoryError
ModuleNotFoundError
NameError
None
NotADirectoryError
NotImplemented
NotImplementedError
OSError
OverflowError
PendingDeprecationWarning
PermissionError
ProcessLookupError
RecursionError
ReferenceError
ResourceWarning
RuntimeError
RuntimeWarning
StopAsyncIteration
StopIteration
SyntaxError
SyntaxWarning
SystemError
SystemExit
TabError
TimeoutError
True
TypeError
UnboundLocalError
UnicodeDecodeError
UnicodeEncodeError
UnicodeError
UnicodeTranslateError
UnicodeWarning
UserWarning
ValueError
Warning
WindowsError
ZeroDivisionError
__build_class__
__debug__
__doc__
__import__
__loader__
__name__
__package__
```

```
__spec__
abs
aiter
all
anext
any
ascii
bin
bool
breakpoint
bytearray
bytes
callable
chr
classmethod
compile
complex
copyright
credits
delattr
dict
dir
divmod
enumerate
eval
exec
exit
filter
float
format
frozenset
getattr
globals
hasattr
hash
help
hex
id
input
int
isinstance
issubclass
iter
len
license
list
locals
map
max
memoryview
min
next
object
```

```
oct
open
ord
pow
print
property
quit
range
repr
reversed
round
set
setattr
slice
sorted
staticmethod
str
sum
super
tuple
type
vars
zip
=>finish
```

Depends on different version, the builtins are different, but the ideas are same, builtins save repeating work, that is to say, save the time to rebuild tire. Notice that print is one of the builtins, and buitins is a kind of a module. In Python, import usually goes with a module. The order goes variable, function, library in math, in Python too. Math related function as below,

Function	**Description**
`abs()`	Calculates the absolute value of a number
`divmod()`	Computes the quotient and remainder of integer division
`max()`	Finds the largest of the given arguments or items in an iterable
`min()`	Finds the smallest of the given arguments or items in an iterable
`pow()`	Raises a number to a power
`round()`	Rounds a floating-point value
`sum()`	Sums the values in an iterable

Basic variables type as below,

Function	**Description**
`int()`	Constructs an integer object from a number or string
`bin()`	Converts an integer to a binary string

Function	Description
`oct()`	Converts an integer to an octal string
`hex()`	Converts an integer to a hexadecimal string
`float()`	Constructs a floating-point object from a number or string
`complex()`	Constructs a complex number from arguments
`str()`	Creates a string object
`repr()`	Creates a developer-friendly string representation of an object
`bool()`	Converts an argument to a Boolean value
`ord()`	Looks up the integer code point of a character
`chr()`	Looks up the character for the given integer code point
`bytes()`	Creates a `bytes` object (similar to `bytearray`, but immutable)
`bytearray()`	Creates an object of the bytearray class

Notice we can represent a integer in different digits, as below,

```
print("=>start check the data type")
print(42)
print(bin(42))
print(oct(42))
print(hex(42))
print("=>finish")

=>start check the data type
42
0b101010
0o52
0x2a
=>finish
```

We can also represent an integer in other form, as below,

```
print("=>start check the data type")
print(str(42))
print(repr(42))
print(repr('42'))
print("=>finish")

=>start check the data type
42
42
'42'
=>finish
```

function str() converts into string, repr() converts any object into discrption, discription is in terms of Python interpreter, not human, so human feel the same.

Object is a larger thing, than variable, that is to say, a variable, and a class, and see below,

```
num = 10
type(num) #<class 'int'>

amount = 78.50
type(amount) #<class 'float'>

greet='Hello World'
type(greet) #<class 'str'>

isActive = True
type(isActive) #<class 'bool'>
```

In Python, each object has an id, see below,

```
id(num) #140723813747416

id(amount) #2786120779088

id(greet) #2786122381488

id(isActive) #140723812946448
```

The value of a variable or object is called assignment, see below,

```
a = 10
b = 5

sum = a + b
difference = a - b
product = a * b
quotient = a / b

print(sum, difference, product, quotient) #15 5 50 2.0

# Modulus operation
remainder = a % b
print(remainder) #0

# Exponentiation
power = a ** b
print(power) #100000
```

We can also do comparision, as below,

```
print(x < y) #False
print(x > y) #True
print(x == y) #True
print(x != y) #False
```

We all hear computer is binary, so why we see not only 0 and 1? It is because when we type the code, we use english, but in fact all these are binary code essentially, and some people just prefer to write binary directly, or most people will do this during debug, and that time, they miss varibles so much.

So for naming varibles in Python, we need to remember, three rules, 1. Variable names must start with a letter or an underscore _ character. 2. Variable names can only contain letters, numbers, and underscores. 3. Variable names cannot contain spaces or special characters.

04 Input

We know function print can output our coding to screen, and we are eager to input for interaction so much, and see a guess game below,

```
from random import randint

LOW, HIGH = 1, 10

secret_number = randint(LOW, HIGH)
clue = ""

while True:
    guess = input(f"Guess a number between {LOW} and {HIGH} {clue} ")
    number = int(guess)
    if number > secret_number:
        clue = f"(less than {number})"
    elif number < secret_number:
        clue = f"(greater than {number})"
    else:
        break

print(f"You guessed it! The secret number is {number}")
```

The game is just a game, with cool color or just in white black, the **f"()"** use brackets to take the varible name into use other than just a string. **while** loop and **if** statement are process control in Python, and the logic is straitforward, by using a function from module **random**. Notice the **if** statement has a tab right aligned to the **while** loop. All the process control is formatted as such, see below,

```
from time import sleep
from progress import progress

for percent in range(101):
    sleep(0.2)
    progress(percent) #[###########                   ] 38%
```

If you see, ModuleNotFoundError: No module named 'progress', please, pip install progeress, and a progress bar is done. We can also write our own, by lagging the time for the bar, see below,

```
import time
import sys

def display_progress_bar(iteration, total, bar_length=50):
    progress = (iteration / total)
    arrow = '#' * int(round(progress * bar_length) - 1)
    spaces = ' ' * (bar_length - len(arrow))

    sys.stdout.write(f'\rProgress: [{arrow + spaces}] {int(progress * 100)}%')
    sys.stdout.flush()

# Test the progress bar
total = 100
for i in range(total + 1):
    time.sleep(0.1)  #simulate some work
    display_progress_bar(i, total) #[###########                       ] 38%
```

range() is to make percetage from 1 to 100, and **time.sleep()** has a 0.1 lag, calling self defined function display_progress_bar to output the bar, and **stdout()** is compositing write() and flush() to make it. The input is hidden but in fact is time elapsed, we should really think about this.

Time is the most valueble input in the world. Anything that can not go back is priceless. Program is all about efficiency, precisely time and space complexity. We don't want rebuild the tire, but we also don't want use a bad tire. That's why some big projects do not import too many outside functions, because it enlarges the study path for different modules, and it kills to much time to do the adaption.

A self written function is easy to modify, see below,

```
def progress(percent=0, width=30):
    end = "" if percent < 100 else "\n"
    left = width * percent // 100
    right = width - left
    print(
        "\r[",
        "#" * left,
        " " * right,
        "]",
        f" {percent:.0f}%",
        sep="",
        end=end,
        flush=True,
    )
```

```
progress(38) #[###########                    ] 38%
```

The progress bar is taking a number as input, you see why you stuck at a program? The seeing maybe not believing in some case, as when you know deeper. To know is also an emotion thing, there are many things we just do not want to know. How a woman think? How a mayer elected? How a man grow up? How a looser give up? Everything at the beginning, can be too rush to new learners. What is the best way to learn? How much practice one need? What is the final acheivement? Where can I use it? So learners really need a guide, see how to make a calculator as below,

```
print('Type "help", "exit", "add a [b [c ...]]"')
while True:
    command, *arguments = input('~ ').split(' ')
    if len(command) > 0:
        if command.lower() == 'exit':
            break
        elif command.lower() == 'help':
            print('you can only add integers now.')
        elif command.lower() == 'add':
            print(sum(map(int, arguments)))
        else:
            print('Unknown command')
```

With this structure, we can add minus, multiply, and divide later. So programm is all about variable and structure, together called design. How you think is the most important thing, and coding is just a demostration. So P2P, B2B, C2C, B2C, C2B and other fancy names are important, since they are business models, and they are the real input, to markets. And similar to markets, if we make a Python module, and if it is good to use, never wrong, then this module is going to be imported by many people. And such module can be operator, see below,

```
import operator

n=5+5
print(n)

n=operator.add(5, 5)
print(n)

n=operator.__add__(5, 5)
print(n)

A = int(input('A=?'))
print(A)
B = int(input('B=?'))
print(B)
```

```
res = operator.add(A, B)
print(f"A+B={res}")
```

The above input would fail if one use non integer, so that explains why we have so many stuck program, because we can not cover all the cases. That is life. We are human beings.

05 File

We mostly have a PC now, even not using after school. PC is just files in a folder, and folders in folders, can you believe that? We do not believe things because we can't. It does not matter with what we see, and because we do not see files in a PC, we think the program is binary code, which stored in memories, yet it's not true.

One may also ask what excatly is Python? Is it an app? If not why I can download at software market? After installation Python has a folder, so it is an app. But app is a languege? How to understand this? When we run python files, we type in python plus the .py, and what excatly this does?

We have tried input function, which can interact with keyboards, but it can be tedious when data is managed, for example two columns of intgers looking for sum, see below,

```
# file.txt
1 43
23 67
35 47
23 49
31 34
24 56
63 78
90 22
```

If we input, then 20 times same action, therefore we try read the file, as below,

```
with open("file.txt", "r") as file:
    print(file.read())
```

Python function **open()** is short for **open(file, mode="r",buffering=-1,encoding=None,errors=None,newline=None,closefd=True,opener=None)**, there are many modes,

Mode	Description
`"r"`	Opens the file for reading and is the default value

Mode	Description
`"w"`	Opens the file for writing, truncating the file first
`"x"`	Opens the file for exclusive creation, failing if the file already exists
`"a"`	Opens the file for writing, appending the new data to the end of the file if it already exists
`"b"`	Opens the file in binary mode
`"t"`	Opens the file in text mode, which is the default mode
`"+"`	Opens the file for updating, which allows reading and writing operations

In fact, **print()** is short for **print(objects, sep=" ", end="\", file=None, flush=False)**,

Argument	Description
`*objects`	An arbitrary number of Python objects
`sep`	The string you want to use to separate input objects from one another
`end`	The string to use after the last input object
`file`	The open file object where you want to write the input objects
`flush`	A Boolean value that defines whether you want to flush the output buffer

recall the previous function progress(), it has two arguments, so if you want write a fruit list, you should use open() in "w" mode,

```
with open("fruits.txt", mode="w") as text_file:
    print("apple", file=text_file)
    print("banana", file=text_file)
    print("cherry", file=text_file)
    print("orange", file=text_file)
    print("mango", file=text_file)
```

The arguments not specified are using the default setting, which saved people a lot time. In this world, many things are in default, like people eat, drink and learn. Learn is really mimic at very beginning, especailly language, and Python is just a language in terms of computer.

with in english is a preception, in Python it is a keyword. The keywords in Python is some words that have sole meanings, for linkage or for structure, as below,

Keyword	Description
False	instance of class bool.

Keyword	Description
class	keyword to define a class.
from	clause to import class from module
or	Boolean operator
None	instance of NoneType object
continue	continue statement, used in the nested for and while loop. It continues with the next cycle of the nearest enclosing loop.
global	global statement allows us to modify the variables outside the current scope.
pass	Python pass statement is used to do nothing. It is useful when we require some statement but we don't want to execute any code.
True	instance of bool class.
def	keyword used to define a function.
if	if statement is used to write conditional code block.
raise	The raise statement is used to throw exceptions in the program.
and	Boolean operator for and operation.
del	The del keyword is used to delete objects such as variables, list, objects, etc.
import	The import statement is used to import modules and classes into our program.
return	The return statement is used in the function to return a value.
as	Python as keyword is used to provide name for import, except, and with statement.
elif	The elif statement is always used with if statement for "else if" operation.
in	Python in keyword is used to test membership.
try	Python try statement is used to write exception handling code.
assert	The assert statement allows us to insert debugging assertions in the program. If the assertion is True, the program continues to run. Otherwise AssertionError is thrown.
else	The else statement is used with if-elif conditions. It is used to execute statements when none of the earlier conditions are True.
is	Python is keyword is used to test if two variables refer to the same object. This is same as using == operator.
while	The while statement is used to run a block of statements till the expression is True.
async	New keyword introduced in Python 3.5. This keyword is always used in couroutine function body. It's used with asyncio module and await

Keyword	Description
	keywords.
await	New keyword in Python 3.5 for asynchronous processing.
lambda	The lambda keyword is used to create lambda expressions.
with	Python with statement is used to wrap the execution of a block with methods defined by a context manager. The object must implement **enter**() and **exit**() functions.
except	Python except keyword is used to catch the exceptions thrown in try block and process it.
finally	The finally statement is used with try-except statements. The code in finally block is always executed. It's mainly used to close resources.
nonlocal	The nonlocal keyword is used to access the variables defined outside the scope of the block. This is always used in the nested functions to access variables defined outside.
yield	Python yield keyword is a replacement of return keyword. This is used to return values one by one from the function.
break	The break statement is used with nested "for" and "while" loops. It stops the current loop execution and passes the control to the start of the loop.
for	Python for keyword is used to iterate over the elements of a sequence or iterable object.
not	The not keyword is used for boolean not operation.

So if we do not want to squeeze **enter()** and **exit()** for file open, we can also do that, see below,

```
path = 'file.txt'

f = open(path)

print(type(f))
# <class '_io.TextIOWrapper'>

f.close()
```

06 Path

What is the Python path? It is where Python search program to run on the PC, as below,

```
C:\Users\Lenovo>python -c "import sys; print('\n'.join(sys.path))"
```

```
C:\Program
Files\WindowsApps\PythonSoftwareFoundation.Python.3.12_3.12.1520.0_x64__qbz5n2kfra8p
0\python312.zip
C:\Program
Files\WindowsApps\PythonSoftwareFoundation.Python.3.12_3.12.1520.0_x64__qbz5n2kfra8p
0\DLLs
C:\Program
Files\WindowsApps\PythonSoftwareFoundation.Python.3.12_3.12.1520.0_x64__qbz5n2kfra8p
0\Lib
C:\Program
Files\WindowsApps\PythonSoftwareFoundation.Python.3.12_3.12.1520.0_x64__qbz5n2kfra8p
0
C:\Users\Lenovo\AppData\Local\Packages\PythonSoftwareFoundation.Python.3.12_qbz5n2kf
ra8p0\LocalCache\local-packages\Python312\site-packages
C:\Program
Files\WindowsApps\PythonSoftwareFoundation.Python.3.12_3.12.1520.0_x64__qbz5n2kfra8p
0\Lib\site-packages
```

We can also enter interactive mode and import pathlib module, then the PC's operating system is not a big deal, see below,

```
C:\Users\Lenovo>python
Python 3.12.5 (tags/v3.12.5:ff3bc82, Aug  6 2024, 20:45:27) [MSC v.1940 64 bit
(AMD64)] on win32
Type "help", "copyright", "credits" or "license" for more information.
>>> from pathlib import Path
>>> Path.cwd()
WindowsPath('C:/Users/Lenovo')
>>> Path.home()
WindowsPath('C:/Users/Lenovo')
>>> path = Path('file.txt'); path.exists()
True
>>> with open("file.txt", "r") as file: print(file.read())
...
1 43
23 67
35 47
23 49
31 34
24 56
63 78
90 22
>>> path.stem
'file'
>>> path.suffix
'.txt'
>>> path.is_dir()
False
>>> path.is_file()
True
```

So the path is really a path, it can be a folder, or it can be a file. If it was a file, then four things can be done, as below,

```
>>> path.read_text()
'1 43\n23 67\n35 47\n23 49\n31 34\n24 56\n63 78\n90 22'
>>> path.unlink()
>>> path
WindowsPath('file.txt')
>>> path.touch()
>>> path.write_text('# Path is awesome')
17
>>> path.read_text()
'# Path is awesome'
```

If the path was a folder, listing is the most important things, see below

```
>>> current_path = Path.cwd()
>>> paths = [path for path in current_path.iterdir() if path.is_dir()]
>>> print(paths)
[WindowsPath('C:/Users/Lenovo/.cache'), WindowsPath('C:/Users/Lenovo/.matplotlib'),
WindowsPath('C:/Users/Lenovo/AppData'), WindowsPath('C:/Users/Lenovo/Application
Data'), WindowsPath('C:/Users/Lenovo/Contacts'),
WindowsPath('C:/Users/Lenovo/Cookies'), WindowsPath('C:/Users/Lenovo/Desktop'),
WindowsPath('C:/Users/Lenovo/Documents'), WindowsPath('C:/Users/Lenovo/Downloads'),
WindowsPath('C:/Users/Lenovo/Favorites'), WindowsPath('C:/Users/Lenovo/Links'),
WindowsPath('C:/Users/Lenovo/Local Settings'), WindowsPath('C:/Users/Lenovo/Music'),
WindowsPath('C:/Users/Lenovo/My Documents'), WindowsPath('C:/Users/Lenovo/NetHood'),
WindowsPath('C:/Users/Lenovo/OneDrive'), WindowsPath('C:/Users/Lenovo/Pictures'),
WindowsPath('C:/Users/Lenovo/PrintHood'), WindowsPath('C:/Users/Lenovo/Recent'),
WindowsPath('C:/Users/Lenovo/Saved Games'), WindowsPath('C:/Users/Lenovo/Searches'),
WindowsPath('C:/Users/Lenovo/SendTo'), WindowsPath('C:/Users/Lenovo/Templates'),
WindowsPath('C:/Users/Lenovo/Videos'), WindowsPath('C:/Users/Lenovo/Start Menu')]
```

Put everything in one line is called Pythonic Style, and we should try to be adapted to that. The path for python to search modules are set during installation, but we can also add our modules via writing, as below,

```
# my_module.py
def module_func():
    print("You just imported the user-defined module")

# run_my_module.py
import my_module
my_module.module_func() #You just imported the user-defined module
```

If we write many modules, and bound like a package, we can even upload to PIP, checkout https://packaging.python.org/en/latest/tutorials/packaging-projects/ for the entire steps to submit a package.

07 Block

PIP is mamaging packages for Python, in almost 20 years. The mainainers are acsbidoul, pf_moore, uranusjr, and so on, and we can contact with them via distutils-sig@python.org.

For some computers, PIP is seperate from Python, so we need add them soly, as below,

```
python -c "exec('try: from urllib2 import urlopen \nexcept: from urllib.request import urlopen');f=urlopen('https://bootstrap.pypa.io/get-pip.py').read();exec(f)"
```

Try Catch is a control block, and there are three more kinds, **While**, **For**, and **If**. We say block because they are fixed, the way to use them are straight forward.

Try Catch means there might be some errors or unexpected behavior, why is that? Maybe accident or unknown, see below,

Errors	Description
AssertionError	Raised when the assert statement fails.
AttributeError	Raised on the attribute assignment or reference fails.
EOFError	Raised when the input() function hits the end-of-file condition.
FloatingPointError	Raised when a floating point operation fails.
GeneratorExit	Raised when a generator's close() method is called.
ImportError	Raised when the imported module is not found.
IndexError	Raised when the index of a sequence is out of range.
KeyError	Raised when a key is not found in a dictionary.
KeyboardInterrupt	Raised when the user hits the interrupt key (Ctrl+c or delete).
MemoryError	Raised when an operation runs out of memory.
NameError	Raised when a variable is not found in the local or global scope.
NotImplementedError	Raised by abstract methods.
OSError	Raised when a system operation causes a system-related error.
OverflowError	Raised when the result of an arithmetic operation is too large to be represented.
ReferenceError	Raised when a weak reference proxy is used to access a garbage collected referent.

Errors	Description
RuntimeError	Raised when an error does not fall under any other category.
StopIteration	Raised by the next() function to indicate that there is no further item to be returned by the iterator.
SyntaxError	Raised by the parser when a syntax error is encountered.
IndentationError	Raised when there is an incorrect indentation.
TabError	Raised when the indentation consists of inconsistent tabs and spaces.
SystemError	Raised when the interpreter detects internal error.
SystemExit	Raised by the sys.exit() function.
TypeError	Raised when a function or operation is applied to an object of an incorrect type.
UnboundLocalError	Raised when a reference is made to a local variable in a function or method, but no value has been bound to that variable.
UnicodeError	Raised when a Unicode-related encoding or decoding error occurs.
UnicodeEncodeError	Raised when a Unicode-related error occurs during encoding.
UnicodeDecodeError	Raised when a Unicode-related error occurs during decoding.
UnicodeTranslateError	Raised when a Unicode-related error occurs during translation.
ValueError	Raised when a function gets an argument of correct type but improper value.
ZeroDivisionError	Raised when the second operand of a division or module operation is zero.

So some very usual errors are the wrong name, as below,

```
>>> import mumodule
ModuleNotFoundError: No module named 'mumodule'

>>> age
Traceback (most recent call last):
File "<pyshell#6>", line 1, in <module>

age
NameError: name 'age' is not defined

>>> x=100/0
```

```
Traceback (most recent call last):
File "<pyshell#8>", line 1, in <module>

x=100/0
ZeroDivisionError: division by zero
```

So we should write a Try Catch block to make the program not crash out, as below,

```
try:
    a=100
    b='0'
    print(a/b)
except:
    print('Some error occurred.') ###
print("Out of try except blocks.")
```

We can even specify the error, as below,

```
try:
    a=100
    b=0
    print (a/b)
except TypeError:
    print('Unsupported operation')
except ZeroDivisionError:
    print ('Division by zero not allowed') ###
except:
  print('Some error occurred.')
print ('Out of try except blocks')
```

We can also use raise to announce the error, as below,

```
try:
  x,y=100,2
  z=x/2
  if z > 10:
    raise ValueError(z)
except ValueError:
  print(z, "is out of allowed range") ###
else:
  print(z, "is within the allowed range")
```

So treat except as a branch, more like **if**, as below,

```
price = 100

if price > 100:
 print("price is greater than 100")

if price == 100:
```

```
  print("price is 100")

if price < 100:
    print("price is less than 100")
```

We can also use elif, as below,

```
price = 100

if price > 100:
    print("price is greater than 100")
elif price == 100:
    print("price is 100")
elif price < 100:
    print("price is less than 100")
```

Or else, as below,

```
price = 100

if price > 100:
    print("price is greater than 100")
elif price == 100:
    print("price is 100")
else:
    print("price is less than 100")
```

And we can nest if, as below,

```
price = 50
quantity = 5
amount = price*quantity

if amount > 100:
    if amount > 500:
      print("Amount is greater than 500")
    else:
      if amount <= 500 and amount >= 400:
        print("Amount is between 400 and 500")
      elif amount <= 400 and amount >= 300:
        print("Amount is between 300 and 400")
      else:
        print("Amount is between 200 and 300") ###
elif amount == 100:
    print("Amount is 100")
else:
    print("Amount is less than 100")
```

Besides we have loop in two kinds, one for, the other while. The difference is one is in a range, the other not. What is a range? See below,

```
>>> range(10)
range(0, 10)
>>> list(range(10))
[0, 1, 2, 3, 4, 5, 6, 7, 8, 9]
>>> for i in list(range(10)): print(i, end=',')
0,1,2,3,4,5,6,7,8,9,
```

list a range is called list comprehension, list is a compound type in Python. It is the group of values or variables in a list,

Data Types	Classes	Description
Single		
Numeric	int, float, complex	holds numeric values
String	str	holds sequence of characters
None	None	holds none
Boolean	bool	ture or false
Compound		
Sequence	range, list, tuple	holds collection of items
Mapping	dict	holds data in key-value pair form
Set	set, frozenset	hold collection of unique items
Binary	bytes, bytearray, memoryview	advanced use...

To print 1 to 10, we can also use while, as below,

```
number = 1

while number <= 10:
    print(number, end=',')
    number += 1
```

The difference is one uses list, the other no.

08 String

In real life, the very outer interface is string, so we will go into the real life string. There are 200 more countries in the world, how do we really type their words or their charaters? And how do those display on the screen?

Strings are made up with characters, as below,

```
string = "Strings are made up with characters"
print(string[0]) # S
```

To get a character is called indexing, where index is the number of the characters in the string. String splite is another thing, it cut out the words, in a list, see below,

```
string.split() # ['Strings', 'are', 'made', 'up', 'with', 'characters']
```

We can replace word in a string, as below,

```
string.replace("up with ", "of")

print(string) # Strings are made of characters
```

All input are strings, and we must be careful with numbers, if we want use them, see below,

```
marks = input("Enter marks ")

print(marks/100) # this would fail with out converting

Traceback (most recent call last):
  File "<stdin>", line 1, in <module>
TypeError: unsupported operand type(s) for /: 'str' and 'int'

print(float(marks)/100) # this would pass
```

An AI bot example can be as below,

```
data = []
print("=>Tell me about yourself")
while True:
    line = input()
    if line: data.append(line)
    else: break
finalText = '\n'.join(data)
print("\n")
print("=>Final text input")
print(finalText)
```

We can also do a input system for students' marks, as below,

```
name = input("Enter Name ")
marks = input("Enter marks ")
print("\n")

print('Student:  Name:  {firstName},  Marks:  {percentage}%'.format(firstName=name,
percentage=marks))
```

Notice **format** is actually substitute, there are many places we just can't use the rgith word, but the meaning is that, so remember and use it. And for strings, you can use double column or single column, it is only important when you want multiplines, see below,

```
sentence = """This is a long sentence that goes over three

lines so it's easier to read. This is useful for writing

docstrings for your functions"""
```

And we can add a exclamation point.

```
final_index = '!'
print(sentence + final_index)
```

Nowadays, there are many emojis, see below,

```
# _Grinning_ _face__
print("\U0001F600")
# _Beaming_ _face__
print("\U0001F601")
```

What is this `\U`? It is unicode, and what is Unicode? Unicode is a standard, to encode characters from various writing systems around the world. Checkout https://symbl.cc/en/unicode-table/, and the reason for unicode is at the very beginning computer only support ascii https://www.ascii-code.com/, so if we want to print a spade 10, it is impossible before, as below,

```
ascii_unsupported = "\U0001F0AA"
print(ascii_unsupported)
# Using 'ignore', 'replace', and 'xmlcharrefreplace' to handle errors
print(ascii_unsupported.encode('ascii', errors='ignore'))
print(ascii_unsupported.encode('ascii', errors='replace'))
print(ascii_unsupported.encode('ascii', errors='xmlcharrefreplace'))

🂪
b''
b'?'
b'&#127146;'
```

In fact, printing is not same as encoding, see below,

```
>>> s1 =  'hôtel'
>>> s2 = 'ho\u0302tel'
>>> len(s1) == len(s2) # False
```

To solve it, we need to normalize, as below,

```
from unicodedata import normalize
print(normalize('NFD', s2))
print(normalize('NFKD', s2))
```

```
print(normalize('NFC', s2))
print(normalize('NFKC', s2))
```

And do not think merge unicode equals the unmerge, as below,

```
print('\u0001\uF40D')
print('\u0001')
print('\uF40D')
print('\u0001F40D') # not equal
```

Why is unicode so useful? See below,

```
try:
    with open('tmp.txt', 'r') as f:
        print("If open, then do...")
except OSError:
    # 'File not found' error message.
    print("Fichier non trouvé")
```

If we have no French installed, we just use `\u00E9`, and we can find its decimal value, as below,

```
print("\u00E9") # é
print(ord('\u00E9')) # 233
print(chr(233)) # é
```

That is to say, if you know the symbol number, you do not need to worry about languege installed or not, see below,

```
s = "a\xac\u1234\u20ac\U00008000"
#     ^^^^ two-digit hex escape
#          ^^^^^^ four-digit Unicode escape
#                      ^^^^^^^^^^ eight-digit Unicode escape
print(s)
print([ord(c) for c in s]) # [97, 172, 4660, 8364, 32768]
```

We can write in file too, see below,

```
with open('tmp.txt', encoding='utf-8', mode='w+') as f:
    f.write('\u4500 blah blah blah\n')
    f.seek(0)
    print(repr(f.readline()[:1]))
```

So the unicode is written in the tmp file, and encoded in utf-8, that is to say the file can be encoded in many formats, and the format makes the content different.

Codec	Aliases	Languages
ascii	646, us-ascii	English
big5	big5-tw, csbig5	Traditional Chinese

Codec	Aliases	Languages
big5hkscs	big5-hkscs, hkscs	Traditional Chinese
cp037	IBM037, IBM039	English
cp273	273, IBM273, csIBM273	German Added in version 3.4.
cp424	EBCDIC-CP-HE, IBM424	Hebrew
cp437	437, IBM437	English
cp500	EBCDIC-CP-BE, EBCDIC-CP-CH, IBM500	Western Europe
cp720		Arabic
cp737		Greek
cp775	IBM775	Baltic languages
cp850	850, IBM850	Western Europe
cp852	852, IBM852	Central and Eastern Europe
cp855	855, IBM855	Bulgarian, Byelorussian, Macedonian, Russian, Serbian
cp856		Hebrew
cp857	857, IBM857	Turkish
cp858	858, IBM858	Western Europe
cp860	860, IBM860	Portuguese
cp861	861, CP-IS, IBM861	Icelandic
cp862	862, IBM862	Hebrew
cp863	863, IBM863	Canadian
cp864	IBM864	Arabic
cp865	865, IBM865	Danish, Norwegian
cp866	866, IBM866	Russian
cp869	869, CP-GR, IBM869	Greek
cp874		Thai
cp875		Greek
cp932	932, ms932, mskanji, ms-kanji	Japanese
cp949	949, ms949, uhc	Korean
cp950	950, ms950	Traditional Chinese
cp1006		Urdu
cp1026	ibm1026	Turkish

Codec	Aliases	Languages
cp1125	1125, ibm1125, cp866u, ruscii	Ukrainian Added in version 3.4.
cp1140	ibm1140	Western Europe
cp1250	windows-1250	Central and Eastern Europe
cp1251	windows-1251	Bulgarian, Byelorussian, Macedonian, Russian, Serbian
cp1252	windows-1252	Western Europe
cp1253	windows-1253	Greek
cp1254	windows-1254	Turkish
cp1255	windows-1255	Hebrew
cp1256	windows-1256	Arabic
cp1257	windows-1257	Baltic languages
cp1258	windows-1258	Vietnamese
euc_jp	eucjp, ujis, u-jis	Japanese
euc_jis_2004	jisx0213, eucjis2004	Japanese
euc_jisx0213	eucjisx0213	Japanese
euc_kr	euckr, korean, ksc5601, ks_c-5601, ks_c-5601-1987, ksx1001, ks_x-1001	Korean
gb2312	chinese, csiso58gb231280, euc-cn, euccn, eucgb2312-cn, gb2312-1980, gb2312-80, iso-ir-58	Simplified Chinese
gbk	936, cp936, ms936	Unified Chinese
gb18030	gb18030-2000	Unified Chinese
hz	hzgb, hz-gb, hz-gb-2312	Simplified Chinese
iso2022_jp	csiso2022jp, iso2022jp, iso-2022-jp	Japanese
iso2022_jp_1	iso2022jp-1, iso-2022-jp-1	Japanese
iso2022_jp_2	iso2022jp-2, iso-2022-jp-2	Japanese, Korean, Simplified Chinese, Western Europe, Greek
iso2022_jp_2004	iso2022jp-2004, iso-2022-jp-2004	Japanese
iso2022_jp_3	iso2022jp-3, iso-2022-jp-3	Japanese
iso2022_jp_ext	iso2022jp-ext, iso-2022-jp-ext	Japanese
iso2022_kr	csiso2022kr, iso2022kr, iso-2022-kr	Korean

Codec	Aliases	Languages
latin_1	iso-8859-1, iso8859-1, 8859, cp819, latin, latin1, L1	Western Europe
iso8859_2	iso-8859-2, latin2, L2	Central and Eastern Europe
iso8859_3	iso-8859-3, latin3, L3	Esperanto, Maltese
iso8859_4	iso-8859-4, latin4, L4	Baltic languages
iso8859_5	iso-8859-5, cyrillic	Bulgarian, Byelorussian, Macedonian, Russian, Serbian
iso8859_6	iso-8859-6, arabic	Arabic
iso8859_7	iso-8859-7, greek, greek8	Greek
iso8859_8	iso-8859-8, hebrew	Hebrew
iso8859_9	iso-8859-9, latin5, L5	Turkish
iso8859_10	iso-8859-10, latin6, L6	Nordic languages
iso8859_11	iso-8859-11, thai	Thai languages
iso8859_13	iso-8859-13, latin7, L7	Baltic languages
iso8859_14	iso-8859-14, latin8, L8	Celtic languages
iso8859_15	iso-8859-15, latin9, L9	Western Europe
iso8859_16	iso-8859-16, latin10, L10	South-Eastern Europe
johab	cp1361, ms1361	Korean
koi8_r		Russian
koi8_t		Tajik Added in version 3.5.
koi8_u		Ukrainian
kz1048	kz_1048, strk1048_2002, rk1048	Kazakh Added in version 3.5.
mac_cyrillic	maccyrillic	Bulgarian, Byelorussian, Macedonian, Russian, Serbian
mac_greek	macgreek	Greek
mac_iceland	maciceland	Icelandic
mac_latin2	maclatin2, maccentraleurope, mac_centeuro	Central and Eastern Europe
mac_roman	macroman, macintosh	Western Europe
mac_turkish	macturkish	Turkish

Codec	Aliases	Languages
ptcp154	csptcp154, pt154, cp154, cyrillic-asian	Kazakh
shift_jis	csshiftjis, shiftjis, sjis, s_jis	Japanese
shift_jis_2004	shiftjis2004, sjis_2004, sjis2004	Japanese
shift_jisx0213	shiftjisx0213, sjisx0213, s_jisx0213	Japanese
utf_32	U32, utf32	all languages
utf_32_be	UTF-32BE	all languages
utf_32_le	UTF-32LE	all languages
utf_16	U16, utf16	all languages
utf_16_be	UTF-16BE	all languages
utf_16_le	UTF-16LE	all languages
utf_7	U7, unicode-1-1-utf-7	all languages
utf_8	U8, UTF, utf8, cp65001	all languages
utf_8_sig		all languages

Idealy we should use the same file reader to decode the file encoded, otherwise we are just not going to be able to read. That is why Python ruled its file in format of utf-8, see the header in a standard py file, as below,

```
#!/usr/bin/env python
# -*- coding: utf-8 -*-

# fow windows change the shebang, with the python.exe location
```

So it is good to know the encoding required, since it would save the direction, and direction is always more important than effort.

09 Sequence

String itself has no sequence, but words have, and sentence have, and many things have. Or the world at least the human world, wants things in a sequence, so it's easier to manage. The professional term for this is called entropy. Rudolf Clausius is the first one talked about this term, and the term is now used to measure the amount of missing information before reception.

Python has 6 types of sequence, 1. Strings 2. Lists 3. Tuples 4. Bytes Sequences 5. Bytes Arrays 6. range() objects

Recall we talked a string, s, as below,

```
s = "a\xac\u1234\u20ac\U00008000"
print(s) # a¬ሴ€耀
```

```
print(len(s)) # 5
```

len() function is to measure the length, and we know string are made of chars. `\x` is hex, `\u` is unicode, `\U` is unicode in 16, so if we make a equal list, it is going to use the same number, as below,

```
sList = [97, 172, 4660, 8364, 32768]
s = ''.join(chr(char) for char in sList)
print(s)
```

And tuple, only the bracket difference, round, as below,

```
sTuple = (97, 172, 4660, 8364, 32768)
s = ''.join(chr(char) for char in sTuple)
print(s)
```

Byte in sequence is just hex numbers, see below,

```
for h in [97, 172, 4660, 8364, 32768]: print(hex(h))
s = "\x61\xac\u1234\u20ac\u8000" # cant use "\x61\xac\x1234\x20ac\x8000"
print(s)
```

Notice In Python, a bytes object is used to store a mutable sequence of integers in the range 0 to 255. Indexing a bytes object outside the range 0 to 255 will cause exceptions, bytearray is the same.

```
ba = bytearray([50, 100, 76, 72, 88]) print(ba)  # bytearray(b'2dLHX')
b = bytes([50, 100, 76, 72, 88]) print(b)  # b'2dLHX'
```

Bytes are important when we face pure bin file, as below,

```
# Writing binary data to a file
with open("example.bin", "wb") as file:
    file.write(b"Python bytes example")

# Reading binary data from a file
with open("example.bin", "rb") as file:
    data = file.read()
    print(data)  # b'Python bytes example'
```

Notice that memory in computer is binary and usually put in hex form, so we should convert to hex for data study. See below,

```
s = 'Join our freelance network'
print(s)
print(repr(s.encode('utf-8')))
for h in (s): print(ord(h), end=',')
print("\n", len(s), "\n")
for h in (s): print(hex(ord(h))[2:], end=' ', ) # 4a 6f 69 6e 20 6f 75 72 20 66 72
65 65 6c 61 6e 63 65 20 6e 65 74 77 6f 72 6b
```

Notice that `"\n"` is nextline, but the `len(s)` can't go the very left, so we need add another argument, as below,

```
print("\n", len(s), sep="")
```

Let's try a counting on a simple txt, as below,

```
Active code page: 437

C:\Users\Lenovo>type file.txt
"check out the bytes"

C:\Users\Lenovo>dir file.txt
 Volume in drive C is Windows-SSD
 Volume Serial Number is 5286-8C92

 Directory of C:\Users\Lenovo

2024/08/14  11:05                24 file.txt
               1 File(s)             24 bytes
               0 Dir(s)  75,955,843,072 bytes free

C:\Users\Lenovo>
```

Compared with Python Path, they are same, as below,

```
C:\Users\Lenovo>python
Python 3.12.5 (tags/v3.12.5:ff3bc82, Aug  6 2024, 20:45:27) [MSC v.1940 64 bit
(AMD64)] on win32
Type "help", "copyright", "credits" or "license" for more information.
>>> from pathlib import Path
>>> Path('file.txt').stat()
os.stat_result(st_mode=33206, st_ino=5629499534370972, st_dev=8093679649504529554,
st_nlink=1, st_uid=0, st_gid=0, st_size=24, st_atime=1723605186,
st_mtime=1723604718, st_ctime=1723499809)
>>> Path('file.txt').stat().st_size
24
>>>
```

Read the content, by keyword `with` and function `open()`, as below,

```
>>> with  open(r'file.txt') as size:
...     #size.seek(0, os.SEEK_END)
...     num = 6
...     for _ in range(num): size.read(4)
...     #print('File size:', size.tell(), 'bytes')
...
'"che'
'ck o'
'ut t'
'he b'
```

```
'ytes'
'" \n'
```

And convert to hex, as below,

```
with  open(r'file.txt') as size:
    content = size.read()
    content.encode().hex() # 22636865636b206f757420746865206279746573222200a
```

And convert the hex to string, as below,

```
bytes.fromhex('22636865636b206f757420746865206279746573222200a').decode()   #   '"check
out the bytes" \n'
```

So there are three things, str to hex, hex to bytes, see one more example below,

```
>>> "hello".encode().hex()
'68656c6c6f'

>>> bytes.fromhex("68656c6c6f")
b'hello'

>>> b"hello".hex()
'68656c6c6f'

>>> bytes.fromhex("68656c6c6f").decode()
'hello'
```

There are some other operations for sequence as below,

```
test = [2, 4, 6, 8, 10, 10]

print(len(test))

print(test.index(6))

print(min(test))

print(max(test))

print(test.count(10))

test.append(11)
print(test) # [2, 4, 6, 8, 10, 10, 11]

test.clear()
print(test) # []

test = [2, 4, 6, 8, 10, 10]
test.insert(9,4)
print(test) # [2, 4, 6, 8, 10, 10, 4]
```

```
print(test.pop()) 4

test.remove(10)
print(test) # [2, 4, 6, 8, 10]

test.reverse()
print(test) # [10, 8, 6, 4, 2]

print(test[:5]) # [10, 8, 6, 4, 2]

print(test[2:4]) # [6, 4]

print(test[-1:]) # [2]
```

And a sum() of tuple is going to make a new tuple, as below,

```
tuple_before = ([2,3,4], [8,9],[20])

# Combination of sum() and tuple() function

tuple_after = tuple(sum(tuple_before, []))

print(tuple_after) # (2,3,4,8,9,20)
```

Why do we need tuple? Because, it can contain items of any data type so can mix different types, as below,

```
tuple = ("masara", 34, True, 40, "male")
```

Also, remember tuple cannot be modified, it is immutable, so we can not add, change, or delete items of a tuple. But the tuple itself can be deleted, as below,

```
del tuple
```

What is **del**? It is a keyword used to delete the variable, object, and so on. Recall del is the last ASCII character, as below,

ASCII	Hexadecimal	Binary
NUL	00	00000000
SOH	01	00000001
STX	02	00000010
ETX	03	00000011
EOT	04	00000100
ENQ	05	00000101
ACK	06	00000110
BEL	07	00000111

ASCII	Hexadecimal	Binary
BS	08	00001000
HT	09	00001001
LF	0A	00001010
VT	0B	00001011
FF	0C	00001100
CR	0D	00001101
SO	0E	00001110
SI	0F	00001111
DLE	10	00010000
DC1	11	00010001
DC2	12	00010010
DC3	13	00010011
DC4	14	00010100
NAK	15	00010101
SYN	16	00010110
ETB	17	00010111
CAN	18	00011000
EM	19	00011001
SUB	1A	00011010
ESC	1B	00011011
FS	1C	00011100
GS	1D	00011101
RS	1E	00011110
US	1F	00011111
Space	20	00100000
!	21	00100001
″	22	00100010
#	23	00100011
$	24	00100100
%	25	00100101
&	26	00100110
′	27	00100111
(	28	00101000
)	29	00101001
*	2A	00101010

ASCII	Hexadecimal	Binary
+	2B	00101011
,	2C	00101100
-	2D	00101101
.	2E	00101110
/	2F	00101111
0	30	00110000
1	31	00110001
2	32	00110010
3	33	00110011
4	34	00110100
5	35	00110101
6	36	00110110
7	37	00110111
8	38	00111000
9	39	00111001
:	3A	00111010
;	3B	00111011
<	3C	00111100
=	3D	00111101
>	3E	00111110
?	3F	00111111
@	40	01000000
A	41	01000001
B	42	01000010
C	43	01000011
D	44	01000100
E	45	01000101
F	46	01000110
G	47	01000111
H	48	01001000
I	49	01001001
J	4A	01001010
K	4B	01001011
L	4C	01001100
M	4D	01001101

ASCII	Hexadecimal	Binary
N	4E	01001110
O	4F	01001111
P	50	01010000
Q	51	01010001
R	52	01010010
S	53	01010011
T	54	01010100
U	55	01010101
V	56	01010110
W	57	01010111
X	58	01011000
Y	59	01011001
Z	5A	01011010
[	5B	01011011
|5C	01011100	
]	5D	01011101
^	5E	01011110
_	5F	01011111
`	60	01100000
a	61	01100001
b	62	01100010
c	63	01100011
d	64	01100100
e	65	01100101
f	66	01100110
g	67	01100111
h	68	01101000
i	69	01101001
j	6A	01101010
k	6B	01101011
l	6C	01101100
m	6D	01101101
n	6E	01101110
o	6F	01101111
p	70	01110000

ASCII	Hexadecimal	Binary
q	71	01110001
r	72	01110010
s	73	01110011
t	74	01110100
u	75	01110101
v	76	01110110
w	77	01110111
x	78	01111000
y	79	01111001
z	7A	01111010
{	7B	01111011
|	7C	01111100
}	7D	01111101
~	7E	01111110
DEL	7F	01111111

This is actually how the keyboard works, and how the program works, that is to say, all the program is a big while loop with break, as below,

```
# interrupt.py
import time
try:
    num = 11
    while True:
        if num % 2 == 0:
            break
        print(num)
        num = num + 2
        time.sleep(1)
except KeyboardInterrupt: # Ctrl + C
    pass
print("Continuing with the program")

# python interrupt.py
11
13
15
17
19
21
23
25
27
29
```

```
31
33
35
37
39
41
43
Continuing with the program
```

So computer is a huge while loop, waiting for interruption and gives response, it is very like our lives. Whose life is not a loop? You think you work hard, but you are actually interrupted. By work, by people, by government, you can't even pick where you born, and you suffer since you born. Not only you, all people like you, all suffer, and in a whatever sequence, only if some are in a priority queue.

What is a queue? See below,

```
queue = []
queue.append('a')
queue.append('b')
queue.append('c')
print("Initial queue")
print(queue)
print("\nELements dequeued from queue")
print(queue.pop(0))
print(queue.pop(0))
print(queue.pop(0))
print("\nQueue after removing elements")
print(queue)
```

So queue is a first in firt out data structure, that's why we can only append, to the end, and remove from the begining, it is very easy to understand it if you go to SAAQ. Python also has a built-in queue, see below,

```
# queue.py
from queue import Queue
q = Queue(maxsize = 3)
print(q.qsize())
q.put('a')
q.put('b')
q.put('c')
print("\nFull: ", q.full())
print("\nElements dequeued from the queue")
print(q.get())
print(q.get())
print(q.get())
print("\nEmpty: ", q.empty())
print("="*24)
q.put(1)
print("\nEmpty: ", q.empty())
```

```
print("Full: ", q.full())

# python queue.py
0

Full:  True

Elements dequeued from the queue
a
b
c

Empty:  True
========================
Empty:  False
Full:  False
```

queue module also provides a last in first out data structure, see below,

```
# queueLifo.py
from queue import LifoQueue
stack = LifoQueue(maxsize = 3)
print(stack.qsize())
stack.put('a')
stack.put('b')
stack.put('c')
print("Full: ", stack.full())
print("Size: ", stack.qsize())
print('\nElements popped from the stack')
print(stack.get())
print(stack.get())
print(stack.get())
print("\nEmpty: ", stack.empty())

# python queueLifo.py
0
Full:  True
Size:  3

Elements popped from the stack
c
b
a

Empty:  True
```

The LIFO is important since it is one of the two memory types in computer, or even in human brain. When we learn things we usually put them into a LIFO structer, to index and to manage. Don't believe? See below,

Présent	Passé composé	Imparfait	Futur simple
Je sais	J'ai su	Je savais	Je saurai
Tu sais	Tu as su	Tu savais	Tu sauras
Il/elle sait	Il/elle a su	Il/elle savait	Il/elle saura
Nous savons	Nous avons su	Nous savions	Nous saurons
Vous savez	Vous avez su	Vous saviez	Vous saurez
Ils/elles savent	Ils/elles ont su	Ils/elles savaient	Ils/elles sauron

So when we first learn the four basic tense for French word Savoir, we put them in rows and columns. When we try to pull out vous, how do we do? Usually from Je something to vous, and it is stacked. That is to say, computer is really no other than an electric brain.

10 Heap

Besides stack, there is another memory type, heap, in comupter, and it is not dimensional managed. When we say dimension, it means an axis to an extent. It has range, and usually continuous. Python also has a builtin library for heap, as below,

```
# heap.py
import heapq
heap = [21, 1, 45, 78, 3, 5]
print(type(heap))
heapq.heapify(heap)
print(heap)
print(type(heap))

# python heap.py
<class 'list'>
[1, 3, 5, 78, 21, 45]
<class 'list'>
```

So **heapq.heapify()** function put the list into a heap, by putting the smallest number at beginning. The very straitforward heap is as below,

```
# arr in heap
arr = [0] * 5
print(id(arr))
print(id(arr[0]))
print(id(arr[1]))
print(id(arr[2]))
print(id(arr[3]))
print(id(arr[4]))
print(id(arr[5]))
```

```
# output
1775823274304
140711749814680
140711749814680
140711749814680
140711749814680
140711749814680
Traceback (most recent call last):
  File "C:\Users\Lenovo\hi.py", line 8, in <module>
    print(id(arr[5]))
             ~~~^^^
IndexError: list index out of range
```

So the array is in fact just one, and the 6th does not exit. And if we put them in a list,

```
# arr in stack
arr = [0, 1, 2, 3, 4]
print(id(arr))
print(id(arr[0]))
print(id(arr[1]))
print(id(arr[2]))
print(id(arr[3]))
print(id(arr[4]))
print(id(arr[5]))

# output
1909851886144
140711720716696
140711720716728
140711720716760
140711720716792
140711720716824
Traceback (most recent call last):
  File "C:\Users\Lenovo\hi.py", line 8, in <module>
    print(id(arr[5]))
             ~~~^^^
IndexError: list index out of range
```

And it is usually hex when present address, as below,

```
# 5 index array
arr = [0, 1, 2, 3, 4]
print(id(arr))
print(id(arr(i))) for i in arr

# output address
2433562120768 # decimal
0x7ffa00210998 # hexdecimal
0x7ffa002109b8
0x7ffa002109d8
```

```
0x7ffa002109f8
0x7ffa00210a18
```

You probably see the address so similar in stack and heap, and you doubt if it is really stack? And you are right, it is not. Python only uese heap, if it is CPython. What is CPython?

Features	**Python**	**Cpython**
Scope	Python is a language specification, defining syntax, keywords, and core concepts.	Cpython is an **interpreter** that executes Python code.
Implementation	Language-agnostic, meaning it can be implemented in various languages.	Specifically implemented in C, making it efficient but tying it to C's ecosystem.
Portability	Designed to be portable across different platforms.	Portability depends on C compilers and libraries being available on the target system.
Performance	Varies depending on implementation	Generally slower due to interpreted nature but can be optimized with C extensions
Compatibility	Broadly compatible across different platforms and implementations	Specifically tailored to work with C extensions
Usage	General-purpose programming	Used when performance optimization is required or when integrating with C libraries

So we mostly use CPython, which means the Python code is interpereted as C, as below,

```
# Python Code Example
arr = [0, 1, 2, 3, 4]
squared = []

# Squaring each number using a loop
for num in arr:
    squared.append(num ** 2)

print(f"Squared Numbers: {squared}")

# C Code Interepreter
#include <Python.h>

int main()
{
```

```
    // Initialize the Python interpreter
    Py_Initialize();

    // Create a Python list: numbers = [1, 2, 3, 4, 5]
    PyObject* numbers = PyList_New(5);
    for (int i = 0; i < 5; i++) {
        PyList_SetItem(numbers, i, PyLong_FromLong(i + 1));
    }

    // Create an empty list: squared_numbers = []
    PyObject* squared_numbers = PyList_New(0);

    // Squaring each number using a loop
    for (int i = 0; i < 5; i++) {
        PyObject* num = PyList_GetItem(numbers, i);
        PyObject* squared = PyNumber_Power(
            num, PyLong_FromLong(2), Py_None);
        PyList_Append(squared_numbers, squared);
        Py_DECREF(squared);
    }

    // Convert the result list to a string and print it
    PyObject* squared_numbers_str
        = PyObject_Str(squared_numbers);
    const char* squared_numbers_cstr
        = PyUnicode_AsUTF8(squared_numbers_str);
    printf("Squared Numbers: %s\n", squared_numbers_cstr);

    // Clean up
    Py_DECREF(numbers);
    Py_DECREF(squared_numbers);
    Py_DECREF(squared_numbers_str);

    // Finalize the Python interpreter
    Py_Finalize();

    return 0;
}
```

Now you see that Python makes life easier?

11 Cython

```
import ctypes
a = 69
b = ctypes.c_int(a)
print(ctypes.addressof(b), id(b)) # 3019741457816 3019741457744
```

So the address in CPython is different from Python, why CPython? Because there are something Python want to embed, and it is those not implemented in Python. Generally CPython compiles .py files to .pyc files in the background, .pyc files contain the Python bytecode. Python bytecode is then interpreted by the Python Virtual Machine – PVM, which later to execute Python. And what is Cython? Cython is the compiler that understands both C and Python specifications, except for a few limitations. Do you believe that the popular package SciPy and Pandas are written in Cython? Like Cython, Nuitka is another Python to c compiler, and it utilizes **libpython** for execution. One can build oneslef a complier with a certain demand, for instance, Python -> RustPython -> WebAssembly.

In reality, it is hard to say which compiler is better, but we can choose the best one after seeing the benchmark result. Let us write a Fibonacci series, as below,

```
# program.py
def fib(n):
    n1, n2 = 0, 1
    for i in range(1, n + 1):
        temp = n1 + n2
        n1 = n2
        n2 = temp
    return n2

# setup.py
from setuptools import setup

from Cython.Build import cythonize

setup(

    ext_modules=cythonize("program1.pyx",

    compiler_directives = { "language_level" : "3"}),

)

# program1_cy.pyx
def fib(n):
    n1, n2 = 0, 1
    for i in range(1, n + 1):
        temp = n1 + n2
        n1 = n2
        n2 = temp
    return n2


# run python setup.py build_ext --inplace
# and check the file
C:\Users\Lenovo>dir
 Volume in drive C is Windows-SSD
 Volume Serial Number is 5286-8C92

 Directory of C:\Users\Lenovo
```

```
2024/08/16  08:52    <DIR>          .
2024/08/16  08:21    <DIR>          ..
2024/08/16  08:52    <DIR>          build
2024/08/16  08:14               142 program.py
2024/08/16  08:22           245,322 program1_cy.c
2024/08/16  08:52            34,816 program1_cy.cp312-win_amd64.pyd
2024/08/16  08:14               142 program1_cy.pyx
2024/08/16  08:22               179 setup.py
2024/08/16  08:23         4,419,488 vs_BuildTools.exe

# test.py
import timeit

python= timeit.timeit('program.fib(10000)',
       setup='import program1',number=100)
cython= timeit.timeit('program1_cy.fib(10000)',
       setup='import program1_cy',number=100)

print("Python Time: ", python)
print("Cython Time: ", cython)
print(f"{python/cython}x times faster")

# run test.py
Python Time:  0.1410401000175625
Cython Time:  0.13240040000528097
1.0652543346692074x times faster
```

How to make Cython faster? See below,

```
# program2_cy.pyx
cpdef int fib(int n):
    cdef int n1 = 0
    cdef int n2 = 1
    cdef int temp, i

    for i in range(1, n + 1):
        temp = n1 + n2
        n1 = n2
        n2 = temp
    return n2
# rerun test.py
Python Time:  0.12709729999187402
Cython Time:  0.0002880000101868063
441.3100538067152x times faster
```

Checkout more examples of Cython on https://cython.readthedocs.io/en/latest/src/tutorial/cython_tutorial.html, and rememeber the code is forever can be optimized.

12 Function

We already used many functions, so we are sure on calling so far, yet maybe not sure on defining. With the keyword **def**, we can make many more functions our own, and then bundle to a module, then package.

The simplest function is just bundling print, see below,

```
# function
def message():
    print("Learn Function")
# call function using its name
message()
```

Add parameter inside the bracket, as below,

```
# function
def course_func(name, course_name):
    print("Hello", name)
    print("Your course name is", course_name)

# call function
course_func('masara', 'Python')
```

We can also make block inside a function, as below,

```
# function
def even_odd(n):
    # check numne ris even or odd
    if n % 2 == 0:
        print('Even number')
    else:
        print('Odd Number')

# calling function by its name
even_odd(19)
# Output Odd Number
```

And the most common way to call a function is from a module, as below,

```
# import randint function
from random import randint

# call randint function to get random number
print(randint(10, 20))
# Output 14
```

We can make return so the function called will have a value, as below,

```
def is_even(list1):
    even_num = []
    for n in list1:
        if n % 2 == 0:
            even_num.append(n)
    # return a list
    return even_num

# Pass list to the function
even_num = is_even([2, 3, 42, 51, 62, 70, 5, 9])
print("Even numbers are:", even_num)
```

We can even return many values, as below,

```
def arithmetic(num1, num2):
    add = num1 + num2
    sub = num1 - num2
    multiply = num1 * num2
    division = num1 / num2
    # return four values
    return add, sub, multiply, division

# read four return values in four variables
a, b, c, d = arithmetic(10, 2)

print("Addition: ", a)
print("Subtraction: ", b)
print("Multiplication: ", c)
print("Division: ", d)
```

So now the variable inside the function is called local variable, and we also have global varible, as below,

```
global_var = 999

def function1():
    print("Value in 1nd function :", global_var - 1)

def function2():
    print("Value in 2nd function :", global_var - 2)

function1()
function2()
```

Keyword **nonlocal** is used for uplevel the local to global, as below,

```
def outer_func():
    x = 777

    def inner_func():
        # local variable now acts as global variable
        nonlocal x
```

```
        x = 700
        print("value of x inside inner function is :", x)

    inner_func()
    print("value of x inside outer function is :", x)

outer_func()
```

We can put a star to represent many arguments, as below,

```
def addition(*numbers):
    total = 0
    for no in numbers:
        total = total + no
    print("Sum is:", total)


# 0 arguments
addition()

# 5 arguments
addition(10, 5, 2, 5, 4)


# 3 arguments
addition(78, 7, 2.5)
```

And lamda function is so fun, see below,

```
l = [10, 5, 12, 78, 6, 1, 7, 9]
even_nos = list(filter(lambda x: x % 2 == 0, l))
print("Even numbers are: ", even_nos) # Even numbers are: [10, 12, 78, 6]
```

Use keyword filter to get the postive numbers, as below,

```
l = [-10, 5, 12, -78, 6, -1, -7, 9]
positive_nos = list(filter(lambda x: x > 0, l))
print("Positive numbers are: ", positive_nos)
```

And use keyword map to do power, as below,

```
l = [-10, 5, 12, -78, 6, -1, -7, 9]
l2 = list(map(lambda x: x*x*x, l))
print("Cube values are:", l2)
```

A very strange kind function is recursive, see below,

```
def count_down(start):
    """ Count down from a number """
    print(start)
    # call the count_down if the next
```

```
    # number is greater than 0
    next = start - 1
    if next > 0:
        count_down(next)

count_down(3)
```

When Carl Gauss was 7 years old, a teacher gave the class a homework to add from 1 to 100, so everyone worked so hard, but...

Gauss quickly wrote down 5050, and all shocked.

How did Gauss add natural numbers from 1 to 100? The idea is as below,

```
The series is 1+2+3+4+5+…+96+97+98+99+100

Add the first number of the series (1) and the last number of the series (100) - we get 101.

Add the second number of the series (2) and second-last number of the series (99) - we get 101.

Add the third number of the series (3) and third-last number of the series (98) - we get 101.

And so on… we get 101 everytime (50 times).

So we have 50 * 101 which is equal to 5050.
```

But this smart way is not useful in computer world now, see below,

```
def sum(n):
    total = 0
    for index in range(n+1):
        total += index
    return total

print(sum(100)) # 5050
```

The reason is because there is sometimes we don't know the number to put, but we know the next one, and this is the real life, if you set up a plan, how would you know the next one before you finish this one? So the formula is not that useful in prediction, you can not write a formulat, as below,

```
def sum(n):
    total = n*(n+1)/2
    return total

print(sum(100)) # 5050.0
```

Function can also be written in a Pythonic Way, one line as below,

```
def compress(a): return [a[i] for i in range(len(a)) if i == 0 or a[i] != a[i-1]]

print(compress([4, 0, 0, 5, 0, 9]))
```

It is short in Pythonic Way, but only use it when logic clear, as below,

```
my_num = 50
result = 10 if my_num > 100 else 20 if my_num < 100 else 0
print(result)  # 20
```

13 Class

A class is a user-defined blueprint or prototype from which objects are created. A class has many attributes, and a real object is of a class, called an instance. Let's try make a dog class, as below,

```
# class
class Dog:

    # A simple class
    # attribute
    attr1 = "mammal"
    attr2 = "dog"

    # A sample method
    def fun(self):
        print("I'm a", self.attr1)
        print("I'm a", self.attr2)

# instantiation
Rodger = Dog()

# accessing class attributes
# and method through objects
print(Rodger.attr1)
Rodger.fun()

# output
ammal
I'm a mammal
I'm a dog
```

More commonly, we write the class with underline string, as below,

```
class GFG:
    def __init__(self, name, company):
        self.name = name
        self.company = company
```

```
    def __str__(self):
        return f"My name is {self.name} and I work as a {self.company}."

my_obj = GFG("masara", "Writer")
print(my_obj) # My name is masara and I work as a Writer.
```

We can even make the output in color, as below,

```
class bcolors:
    HEADER = '\033[95m'
    OKBLUE = '\033[94m'
    OKCYAN = '\033[96m'
    OKGREEN = '\033[92m'
    WARNING = '\033[93m'
    FAIL = '\033[91m'
    ENDC = '\033[0m'
    BOLD = '\033[1m'
    UNDERLINE = '\033[4m'

class GFG:
    def __init__(self, name, company):
        self.name = name
        self.company = company

    def __str__(self):
            return (f"{bcolors.WARNING}My name is {self.name} and I work as a
{self.company}.{bcolors.ENDC}")

my_obj = GFG("masara", "Writer")
print(my_obj) # My name is masara and I work as a Writer.
```

We can even add the blinking for the option, as below,

```
class bcolors:
    HEADER = '\033[95m'
    OKBLUE = '\033[94m'
    OKCYAN = '\033[96m'
    OKGREEN = '\033[92m'
    WARNING = '\033[93m'
    FAIL = '\033[91m'
    ENDC = '\033[0m'
    BOLD = '\033[1m'
    UNDERLINE = '\033[4m'
    BLINKING = '\033[5m'


class GFG:
    def __init__(self, name, company):
        self.name = name
        self.company = company
```

```
    def __str__(self):
            return (f"{bcolors.WARNING}My name is {bcolors.BLINKING}{self.name}
{bcolors.ENDC} and I work as a {bcolors.BLINKING}{self.company}{bcolors.ENDC}.")

my_obj = GFG("masara", "Writer")
print(my_obj) # My name is masara and I work as a Writer.
```

We can also try a flash card for yes and no question, as below,

```
# flash.py
import random

class flashcard:
    def __init__(self):

        self.fruits={'apple':'red',
                     'orange':'orange',
                     'watermelon':'green',
                     'banana':'yellow'}

    def quiz(self):
        while (True):

            fruit, color = random.choice(list(self.fruits.items()))

            print("What is the color of {}".format(fruit))
            user_answer = input()

            if(user_answer.lower() == color):
                print("Correct answer")
            else:
                print("Wrong answer")

            option = int(input("enter 0 , if you want to play again : "))
            if (option):
                break

print("welcome to fruit quiz ")
fc=flashcard()
fc.quiz()

# output
welcome to fruit quiz
What is the color of apple
green
Wrong answer
enter 0 , if you want to play again : 0
What is the color of orange
orange
Correct answer
enter 0 , if you want to play again : 1
```

The very big reason we make class, is when we want to monarch our package, so it goes like package, module, class, function, and we can easily to add a new method, or delete, or comment out a method. Let's try download some real packages, and discover how it arranges the lots of method. See math below,

```
C:\Users\Lenovo>
Python 3.12.5 (tags/v3.12.5:ff3bc82, Aug  6 2024, 20:45:27) [MSC v.1940 64 bit (AMD64)] on win32
Type "help", "copyright", "credits" or "license" for more information.
>>> import math
>>> dir(math)
['__doc__', '__loader__', '__name__', '__package__', '__spec__', 'acos', 'acosh', 'asin', 'asinh', 'atan', 'atan2', 'atanh', 'cbrt', 'ceil', 'comb', 'copysign', 'cos', 'cosh', 'degrees', 'dist', 'e', 'erf', 'erfc', 'exp', 'exp2', 'expm1', 'fabs', 'factorial', 'floor', 'fmod', 'frexp', 'fsum', 'gamma', 'gcd', 'hypot', 'inf', 'isclose', 'isfinite', 'isinf', 'isnan', 'isqrt', 'lcm', 'ldexp', 'lgamma', 'log', 'log10', 'log1p', 'log2', 'modf', 'nan', 'nextafter', 'perm', 'pi', 'pow', 'prod', 'radians', 'remainder', 'sin', 'sinh', 'sqrt', 'sumprod', 'tan', 'tanh', 'tau', 'trunc', 'ulp']
>>> print(math.__doc__)
This module provides access to the mathematical functions
defined by the C standard.
```

So from the doc, we can recall that math class should have 5 underline string method, and other calculation method,

Method	**Description**
ceil(x)	Returns the smallest integer greater than or equal to x.
copysign(x, y)	Returns x with the sign of y
fabs(x)	Returns the absolute value of x
factorial(x)	Returns the factorial of x
floor(x)	Returns the largest integer less than or equal to x
fmod(x, y)	Returns the remainder when x is divided by y
frexp(x)	Returns the mantissa and exponent of x as the pair (m, e)
fsum(iterable)	Returns an accurate floating point sum of values in the iterable
isfinite(x)	Returns True if x is neither an infinity nor a NaN (Not a Number)
isinf(x)	Returns True if x is a positive or negative infinity
isnan(x)	Returns True if x is a NaN
ldexp(x, i)	Returns x * (2**i)
modf(x)	Returns the fractional and integer parts of x
trunc(x)	Returns the truncated integer value of x
exp(x)	Returns e**x

Method	Description
expm1(x)	Returns e**x - 1
log(x[, b])	Returns the logarithm of x to the base b (defaults to e)
log1p(x)	Returns the natural logarithm of 1+x
log2(x)	Returns the base-2 logarithm of x
log10(x)	Returns the base-10 logarithm of x
pow(x, y)	Returns x raised to the power y
sqrt(x)	Returns the square root of x
acos(x)	Returns the arc cosine of x
asin(x)	Returns the arc sine of x
atan(x)	Returns the arc tangent of x
atan2(y, x)	Returns atan(y / x)
cos(x)	Returns the cosine of x
hypot(x, y)	Returns the Euclidean norm, sqrt(x*x + y*y*)
sin(x)	Returns the sine of x
tan(x)	Returns the tangent of x
degrees(x)	Converts angle x from radians to degrees
radians(x)	Converts angle x from degrees to radians
acosh(x)	Returns the inverse hyperbolic cosine of x
asinh(x)	Returns the inverse hyperbolic sine of x
atanh(x)	Returns the inverse hyperbolic tangent of x
cosh(x)	Returns the hyperbolic cosine of x
sinh(x)	Returns the hyperbolic cosine of x
tanh(x)	Returns the hyperbolic tangent of x
erf(x)	Returns the error function at x
erfc(x)	Returns the complementary error function at x
gamma(x)	Returns the Gamma function at x
lgamma(x)	Returns the natural logarithm of the absolute value of the Gamma function at x
pi	Mathematical constant, the ratio of circumference of a circle to it's diameter (3.14159...)
e	mathematical constant e (2.71828...)

We can debug or enter a verbose mode for Python, as below,

```
C:\Users\Lenovo>python -v
>>> print(type(math))
<class 'module'>
```

```
>>> print(dir(math))
['__doc__', '__loader__', '__name__', '__package__', '__spec__', 'acos', 'acosh',
'asin', 'asinh', 'atan', 'atan2', 'atanh', 'cbrt', 'ceil', 'comb', 'copysign',
'cos', 'cosh', 'degrees', 'dist', 'e', 'erf', 'erfc', 'exp', 'exp2', 'expm1',
'fabs', 'factorial', 'floor', 'fmod', 'frexp', 'fsum', 'gamma', 'gcd', 'hypot',
'inf', 'isclose', 'isfinite', 'isinf', 'isnan', 'isqrt', 'lcm', 'ldexp', 'lgamma',
'log', 'log10', 'log1p', 'log2', 'modf', 'nan', 'nextafter', 'perm', 'pi', 'pow',
'prod', 'radians', 'remainder', 'sin', 'sinh', 'sqrt', 'sumprod', 'tan', 'tanh',
'tau', 'trunc', 'ulp']
>>> print(math.exp())
Traceback (most recent call last):
  File "<stdin>", line 1, in <module>
TypeError: math.exp() takes exactly one argument (0 given)
>>> print(math.exp)
<built-in function exp>
```

If we write ourself a math class, what can it be?

14 Project

To write ourself a math class, it can be just one file, as below,

```
C:\Users\Lenovo\Project>dir
 Volume in drive C is Windows-SSD
 Volume Serial Number is 5286-8C92

 Directory of C:\Users\Lenovo\Project

2024/08/16  12:53    <DIR>          .
2024/08/16  12:53    <DIR>          ..
2024/08/16  12:53                 5 ourmath.py
               1 File(s)              5 bytes
               2 Dir(s)  76,510,617,600 bytes free
```

We wil make two methods, one show the two values, the other get the product of the two values, as below,

```
# create ourmath class
class ourmath:
    x = 0.0
    y = 0.0

    # method to show values
    def show(self):
        print("x, y =>", self.x, self.y)

    # method to calculate product
    def product(self):
        print("product =>", self.x * self.y)
```

```
# create object of ourmath
study_ourmath = ourmath()

# assign values to all the properties
study_ourmath.x = 1.32
study_ourmath.y = 0.47

# show values
study_ourmath.show()

# access product method
study_ourmath.product()
```

We can seperate the class file and the run file, as below,

```
# ourmath.py
class ourmath:
    x = 0.0
    y = 0.0

    # method to show values
    def show(self):
        print("x, y =>", self.x, self.y)

    # method to calculate product
    def product(self):
        print("product =>", self.x * self.y)

# run.py
import ourmath
study_ourmath = ourmath.ourmath()

# assign values to all the properties
study_ourmath.x = 1.32
study_ourmath.y = 0.47

# show values
study_ourmath.show()

# access product method
study_ourmath.product()
```

Then we can coutinue to modify the method, imagine you buy a stock at two times, you then want the average, and when are you going to sell? Not below the average price, as below,

```
# ourmath.py
class ourmath:
    x1 = 0.0
    y1 = 0.0
    x2 = 0.0
    y2 = 0.0
```

```
    # method to show values
    def show(self):
        print("x1, y1, x2, y2 =>", self.x1, self.y1, self.x2, self.y2)

    # method to calculate total
    def total(self):
        print("product =>", self.y1 + self.y2)

    # method to calculate average
    def average(self):
          print("average =>", (self.x1 * self.y1 + self.x2 * self.y2) / (self.y1 +
self.y2))

# run.py
import ourmath
study_ourmath = ourmath.ourmath()

# assign values to all the properties
study_ourmath.x1 = 1.32
study_ourmath.y1 = 1000

study_ourmath.x2 = 0.47
study_ourmath.y2 = 4000

# show values
study_ourmath.show()

# access total method
study_ourmath.total() # 5000

# access average method
study_ourmath.average() # 0.264
```

So you may also want to know the gain if you sell at a higer a price, as below,

```
# ourmath.py
class ourmath:
    x1 = 0.0
    y1 = 0.0
    x2 = 0.0
    y2 = 0.0
    s = 0.0

    # method to show values
    def show(self):
        print("x1, y1, x2, y2 =>", self.x1, self.y1, self.x2, self.y2)

    # method to calculate total
    def total(self):
        print("product =>", self.y1 + self.y2)

    # method to calculate average
```

```
    def average(self):
          print("average =>", (self.x1 * self.y1 + self.x2 * self.y2) / (self.y1 +
self.y2))

    # method to sell
    def sell(self):
        print("s =>", self.s)

    # method to caluclate gain
    def gain(self):
          print("gain =>", - (self.x1 * self.y1 + self.x2 * self.y2) + (self.y1 +
self.y2) * s)

# run.py
import ourmath
study_ourmath = ourmath.ourmath()

# assign values to all the properties
study_ourmath.x1 = 1.32
study_ourmath.y1 = 1000

study_ourmath.x2 = 0.47
study_ourmath.y2 = 4000

# show values
study_ourmath.show()

# access total method
study_ourmath.total() # 5000

# access average method
study_ourmath.average() # 0.264

# gain
study_ourmath.s = 3
study_ourmath.gain() #  11800.0
```

You may find the program not interactive, and tired of changing the value inside the run file, so you want modify with **input()**, as below,

```
class ourmath:
    def __init__(self,last,this,gain,money):
        self.last = last
        self.this = this
        self.gain = gain
        self.money = money

    def show(self):
        print("last time you buy", self.last.split())
        print("this time you buy", self.this.split())

        x1 = float(self.last.split()[0])
```

```
        y1 = float(self.last.split()[1])
        x2 = float(self.this.split()[0])
        y2 = float(self.this.split()[1])

        s = (x1 * y1+ x2 * y2 - self.gain) / (y1 + y2)
        print("if you want to gain {0} you should sell at {1},\nbecause you buy {2}
at {3}, and {4} at {5}".format(self.gain, s, y1, x1, y2, x2))
        result = self.money - x2 * y2
        ring = "good" if result > 0 else "not enough"
        print(ring + " to go because you have {0} != {1}".format(self.money, y2 *
x2))

# run.py
import ourmath

study = ourmath.ourmath(input("last buy: "), input("this buy: "), double(input("want
gain: ")), double(input("have money: ")))

study.show()
```

So we notice that there are two very important pattern, one `self`, the other `__init__()`, the method has underline is different from those without. There are more kinds, `__add__()`, `__len__()`, `__new()__`, `__dict__()`, these are called builtin methods. Let's recall the keyword **del**, as below,

```
class Student:
  def __init__(self, name, age):
    self.name = name
    self.age = age
  def displayInfo(self): # class method
    print('Student Name: ', self.name,', Age: ', self.age)

std = Student('Steve', 25)
std.displayInfo()

del std.name # deleting attribute
print(std.name) #error

del std
print(std.name) #error

del Student  # deleting class
std = Student('Steve', 25) #error
```

So the class has property, and method, and after the initialization, an object will be created, and object has attribute, and function. Make them private with __ only on the leftside, so they can't be deleted. And the class can even be the class's subgroup, see below,

```
class quadriLateral:
  def __init__(self, a, b, c, d):
    self.side1=a
    self.side2=b
    self.side3=c
    self.side4=d

  def perimeter(self):
    p=self.side1 + self.side2 + self.side3 + self.side4
    print("perimeter=",p)

class rectangle(quadriLateral):
    def __init__(self, a, b):
      super().__init__(a, b, a, b)


r1=rectangle(10, 20)
r1.perimeter() # perimeter= 60
```

And there are two method operations that are used often. Overloading is a type of Compile-time Polymorphism, which wehave multiple methods in the same class with the same name but with a different parameter list, as below,

```
def sum_number(*args):
    # variable to store the sum of numbers
    result = 0

    # accessing the arguments
    for num in args:
        result += num

    # Output
    print("Sum : ", result)


# Driver Code
if(__name__ == "__main__"):
    print("Similar to Method Overloading\n")
    print("Single Argument    ->", end = " ")
    sum_number(10)

    print("Two Arguments      ->", end = " ")
    sum_number(30, 2)

    print("Multiple Arguments ->", end = " ")
    sum_number(1, 2, 3, 4, 5)
```

And overriding is to redefine a parent class method in the derived class, as below,

```
# Parent Class
class A:
    def first(self):
        print("First function of class A")

    def second(self):
        print('Second function of class A')

# Derived Class
class B(A):
    # Overriden Function
    def first(self):
        print("Redefined function of class A in class B")

    def display(self):
        print('Display Function of Child class')

# Driver Code
if(__name__ == "__main__"):
    # Creating child class object
    child_obj = B()

    # Calling the overridden method
    print("Method Overriding\n")
    child_obj.first()

    # Calling the original Parent class method
    # Using parent class object.
    A().first()
```

And there are @methods in class, which can make us mad, as below,

```
import datetime

class Movie:
    def __init__(self, name, release_year, genre):
        self.name = name
        self.release_year = release_year
        self.genre = genre

    def get_description(self):
        print(f"The value of self is {self}.")
              print(f"The  {self.genre.lower()}  movie  {self.name}  was  released  in
{self.release_year}.")

    @staticmethod
    def get_years_from_release(release_year):
        return datetime.datetime.now().year - int(release_year)

    @classmethod
    def action_movie(cls, name, release_year):
        print(f"The value of cls is {cls}.")
        return cls(name, release_year, "Action")
```

```
movie = Movie.action_movie("Rambo", "1982")
movie.get_description()
print(f"The {movie.genre.lower()} movie {movie.name} is get_years_from_release {movie.release_year} years old.")
```

@classmethod takes class as argument, @staticmethod is just a function, but inside the class, see below,

```
import datetime

def get_years_from_release(release_year): return datetime.datetime.now().year - int(release_year)

class Movie:
    def __init__(self, name, release_year, genre):
        self.name = name
        self.release_year = release_year
        self.genre = genre

    def get_description(self):
        print(f"The value of self is {self}.")
            print(f"The {self.genre.lower()} movie {self.name} was released in {self.release_year}.")

    @classmethod
    def action_movie(cls, name, release_year):
        print(f"The value of cls is {cls}.")
        return cls(name, release_year, "Action")

movie = Movie.action_movie("Rambo", "1982")
movie.get_description()
print(f"The {movie.genre.lower()} movie {movie.name} is get_years_from_release {movie.release_year} years old.")
```

We see the troublesome to build the class in these fancy ways. Recall PIP, do you feel that download can be a good way for us now?

15 Package

Mature project can be package, for example mathplotlib, see below,

```
import matplotlib.pyplot as plt
plt.plot([1, 2, 3, 4], [1, 4, 9, 16], 'ro')
plt.axis((0, 6, 0, 20))
plt.ylabel('some points')
plt.show()
```

Notice that axis parameters are xmin, xmax, ymin, ymax, and we can also link the points if we do not use 'ro',

character	description
'.'	point marker
','	pixel marker
'o'	circle marker
'v'	triangle_down marker
'^'	triangle_up marker
'<'	triangle_left marker
'>'	triangle_right marker
'1'	tri_down marker
'2'	tri_up marker
'3'	tri_left marker
'4'	tri_right marker
'8'	octagon marker
's'	square marker
'p'	pentagon marker
'P'	plus (filled) marker
'*'	star marker
'h'	hexagon1 marker
'H'	hexagon2 marker
'+'	plus marker
'x'	x marker
'X'	x (filled) marker
'D'	diamond marker
'd'	thin_diamond marker
'|'	vline marker
'_'	hline marker

And for line and color,

haracter	
'b'	blue
'g'	green
'r'	red
'c'	cyan
'm'	magenta

haracter	
'y'	yellow
'k'	black
'w'	white
line	
'-'	solid line style
'--'	dashed line style
'-.'	dash-dot line style
':'	dotted line style

So we can try make two stock lines, as below,

```
import matplotlib.pyplot as plt
plt.plot([1, 2], [1.125, 0.46],label="02515")
plt.plot([1, 2], [1.733, 1.38],label="02559")
plt.axis((0, 6, 0, 20))
plt.ylabel('two stocks')
plt.legend()
plt.show()
```

Stocks are now in so many markets, HK is just one of them, and there are many big companies to collect the data for us, which saves our time to input the data. That is to say, the price we were using for "02515.HK" and "02559.HK" can be grabbed via data companies. We will try use Yahoo, see below,

```
c:\Users\Lenovo\Finance>pip install yfinance
c:\Users\Lenovo\Finance>python
>>> import yfinance as yf
>>> stock = yf.Ticker("2515.HK")
>>> stock.info
{'address1': 'No. 112, Dongting Road', 'address2': 'Economic and Technological Development Zone', 'city': 'Tianjin', 'country': 'China', 'phone': '86 22 2536 1111', 'website': 'https://www.tjcdg.com', 'industry': 'Engineering & Construction', 'industryKey': 'engineering-construction', 'industryDisp': 'Engineering & Construction', 'sector': 'Industrials', 'sectorKey': 'industrials', 'sectorDisp': 'Industrials', 'longBusinessSummary': 'Tianjin Construction Development Group Co., Ltd. engages in the engineering construction business in Tianjin. It primary undertakes municipal public works, foundation projects, construction projects, and petrochemical projects. The company was founded in 2010 and is based in Tianjin, China. Tianjin Construction Development Group Co., Ltd. operates as a subsidiary of Shengyuan Group Holdings (Tianjin) Co., Ltd.', 'fullTimeEmployees': 133, 'companyOfficers': [{'maxAge': 1, 'name': 'Mr. Kuanghua  Zhao', 'age': 39, 'title': 'President & Executive Director', 'yearBorn': 1984, 'fiscalYear': 2023, 'totalPay': 441533, 'exercisedValue': 0, 'unexercisedValue': 0}, {'maxAge': 1, 'name': 'Mr. Youhua  Yang', 'age': 33, 'title': 'Assistant President, Manager of the Marketing Department & Executive Director', 'yearBorn': 1990, 'fiscalYear': 2023, 'totalPay': 212066, 'exercisedValue': 0, 'unexercisedValue': 0}, {'maxAge': 1, 'name': 'Ms.
```

```
Xiaorong  Zhao', 'age': 41, 'title': 'VP & Executive Director', 'yearBorn': 1982,
'fiscalYear': 2023, 'totalPay': 197928, 'exercisedValue': 0, 'unexercisedValue': 0},
{'maxAge': 1, 'name': 'Mr. Baqun  Ni', 'age': 37, 'title': 'Assistant president,
Manager of the Procurement Department & Executive Director', 'yearBorn': 1986,
'fiscalYear': 2023, 'totalPay': 165303, 'exercisedValue': 0, 'unexercisedValue': 0},
{'maxAge': 1, 'name': 'Mr. Kai  Li', 'age': 48, 'title': 'CFO, Joint Company
Secretary & Executive Director', 'yearBorn': 1975, 'fiscalYear': 2023,
'exercisedValue': 0, 'unexercisedValue': 0}, {'maxAge': 1, 'name': 'Mr. Wing Yat
Lui', 'age': 33, 'title': 'Joint Company Secretary', 'yearBorn': 1990, 'fiscalYear':
2023, 'exercisedValue': 0, 'unexercisedValue': 0}], 'compensationAsOfEpochDate':
1703980800, 'maxAge': 86400, 'priceHint': 3, 'previousClose': 0.49, 'open': 0.49,
'dayLow': 0.45, 'dayHigh': 0.5, 'regularMarketPreviousClose': 0.49,
'regularMarketOpen': 0.49, 'regularMarketDayLow': 0.45, 'regularMarketDayHigh': 0.5,
'trailingPE': 2.2380953, 'volume': 660000, 'regularMarketVolume': 660000,
'averageVolume': 1993741, 'averageVolume10days': 9223800, 'averageDailyVolume10Day':
9223800, 'bid': 0.45, 'ask': 0.47, 'marketCap': 101423656, 'fiftyTwoWeekLow': 0.435,
'fiftyTwoWeekHigh': 2.18, 'priceToSalesTrailing12Months': 0.31750754,
'fiftyDayAverage': 1.1244, 'twoHundredDayAverage': 1.2159259, 'currency': 'HKD',
'enterpriseValue': 115224536, 'profitMargins': 0.12849, 'floatShares': 53950845,
'sharesOutstanding': 53950000, 'impliedSharesOutstanding': 215795008, 'bookValue':
1.391, 'priceToBook': 0.3378864, 'lastFiscalYearEnd': 1703980800,
'nextFiscalYearEnd': 1735603200, 'mostRecentQuarter': 1703980800,
'earningsQuarterlyGrowth': -0.316, 'netIncomeToCommon': 41045000, 'trailingEps':
0.21, 'enterpriseToRevenue': 0.361, 'enterpriseToEbitda': 2.379, '52WeekChange':
-0.6776316, 'SandP52WeekChange': 0.26174653, 'exchange': 'HKG', 'quoteType':
'EQUITY', 'symbol': '2515.HK', 'underlyingSymbol': '2515.HK', 'shortName': 'TJCD',
'longName': 'Tianjin Constr Dvlp Grp Co Ltd', 'firstTradeDateEpochUtc': 1713835800,
'timeZoneFullName': 'Asia/Hong_Kong', 'timeZoneShortName': 'HKT', 'uuid': 'd1376872-
aeac-37e8-9c16-385d632fbe73', 'messageBoardId': 'finmb_1866316057',
'gmtOffSetMilliseconds': 28800000, 'currentPrice': 0.47, 'recommendationKey':
'none', 'totalCash': 6422000, 'totalCashPerShare': 0.03, 'ebitda': 48436000,
'totalDebt': 20223000, 'quickRatio': 1.397, 'currentRatio': 1.484, 'totalRevenue':
319436992, 'debtToEquity': 8.981, 'revenuePerShare': 2.093, 'returnOnAssets':
0.05609, 'returnOnEquity': 0.21485001, 'freeCashflow': -46736624,
'operatingCashflow': -33600000, 'earningsGrowth': -0.339, 'revenueGrowth': -0.075,
'grossMargins': 0.2514, 'ebitdaMargins': 0.15163, 'operatingMargins': 0.10979,
'financialCurrency': 'CNY', 'trailingPegRatio': None}
>>> stock.get_shares_full(start="2024-07-01", end=None)
2024-07-04 00:00:00+08:00    215795008
2024-07-08 00:00:00+08:00    206803008
2024-07-09 00:00:00+08:00    215795008
2024-07-11 00:00:00+08:00    215795008
2024-07-11 00:00:00+08:00    205436992
2024-07-15 00:00:00+08:00    219304000
2024-07-16 00:00:00+08:00    215795008
2024-07-16 00:00:00+08:00    214054000
2024-07-18 00:00:00+08:00    215795008
2024-07-18 00:00:00+08:00    212198000
2024-07-19 00:00:00+08:00    215795008
2024-07-22 00:00:00+08:00    222486000
2024-07-23 00:00:00+08:00    215795008
2024-07-25 00:00:00+08:00    221235008
2024-07-26 00:00:00+08:00    215795008
```

```
2024-07-29 00:00:00+08:00    215795008
2024-07-31 00:00:00+08:00    215795008
2024-08-03 00:00:00+08:00    215795008
2024-08-05 00:00:00+08:00    215795008
2024-08-07 00:00:00+08:00    215795008
2024-08-09 00:00:00+08:00    199927008
2024-08-10 00:00:00+08:00    215795008
2024-08-12 00:00:00+08:00    266800992
2024-08-13 00:00:00+08:00    215795008
2024-08-14 00:00:00+08:00    215795008
2024-08-19 00:00:00+08:00    215795008
2024-08-20 00:00:00+08:00    200380992
2024-08-21 00:00:00+08:00    215795008
dtype: int64
>>> stock.cashflow
                                  2023-12-31  2022-12-31  2021-12-31  2020-
12-31
Free Cash Flow                       -35042000.0   2807000.0   7669000.0
-1751000.0
Repurchase Of Capital Stock        -13452000.0  -2239000.0         0.0
0.0
Repayment Of Debt                  -10000000.0         0.0         0.0
NaN
Issuance Of Debt                    30000000.0         0.0         0.0
0.0
Issuance Of Capital Stock           10000000.0         0.0    998000.0
0.0
Capital Expenditure                  -1442000.0  -8343000.0  -3498000.0
-8722000.0
End Cash Position                     6422000.0  20200000.0  11312000.0
12202000.0
Beginning Cash Position              20200000.0  11312000.0  12202000.0
3702000.0
Changes In Cash                     -13778000.0   8888000.0   -890000.0
8500000.0
Financing Cash Flow                  10522000.0  -3010000.0    615000.0
-164000.0
Net Other Financing Charges          -5605000.0   -771000.0   -383000.0
-164000.0
Interest Paid Cff                      -366000.0         0.0         0.0
0.0
Net Common Stock Issuance            -3452000.0  -2239000.0    998000.0
0.0
Common Stock Payments              -13452000.0  -2239000.0         0.0
0.0
Common Stock Issuance               10000000.0         0.0    998000.0
0.0
Net Issuance Payments Of Debt      20000000.0         0.0         0.0
0.0
Net Short Term Debt Issuance       20000000.0         0.0         0.0
0.0
Short Term Debt Payments          -10000000.0         0.0         0.0
NaN
```

```
Short Term Debt Issuance                         30000000.0           0.0            0.0
0.0
Investing Cash Flow                               9300000.0      748000.0   -12672000.0
1693000.0
Net Other Investing Changes                      2558000.0           NaN            NaN
NaN
Net PPE Purchase And Sale                        -1442000.0    -8263000.0    -3498000.0
-8722000.0
Sale Of PPE                                             0.0       80000.0           0.0
0.0
Purchase Of PPE                                  -1442000.0    -8343000.0    -3498000.0
-8722000.0
Operating Cash Flow                             -33600000.0    11150000.0    11167000.0
6971000.0
Taxes Refund Paid                                -6865000.0    -6579000.0     -380000.0
-296000.0
Change In Working Capital                       -82950000.0   -34227000.0   -42612000.0
-2291000.0
Change In Other Current Assets                  -3791000.0      381000.0    -1581000.0
1371000.0
Change In Accrued Expense                        7503000.0     4349000.0     7021000.0
5935000.0
Change In Payable                               44315000.0    90658000.0    89029000.0
14367000.0
Change In Prepaid Assets                         1286000.0     -666000.0     5747000.0
778000.0
Change In Inventory                                -88000.0      -19000.0     -136000.0
-39000.0
Change In Receivables                          -132175000.0 -128930000.0 -142692000.0
-24703000.0
Other Non Cash Items                              -168000.0     -550000.0     -565000.0
-198000.0
Depreciation And Amortization                    4091000.0     3260000.0     3249000.0
2297000.0
Depreciation                                      4091000.0     3260000.0     3249000.0
2297000.0
Gain Loss On Sale Of PPE                               0.0      -80000.0           0.0
0.0
Net Income From Continuing Operations     46948000.0    39177000.0    47622000.0
7621000.0
>>> stock.recommendations
404 Client Error: Not Found for url:
https://query2.finance.yahoo.com/v10/finance/quoteSummary/2515.HK?
modules=recommendationTrend&corsDomain=finance.yahoo.com&formatted=false&symbol=2515
.HK&crumb=IzfigUJLR2V
Empty DataFrame
Columns: []
Index: []
>>> stock.insider_transactions
Traceback (most recent call last):
                                                                                  File
"C:\Users\Lenovo\AppData\Local\Packages\PythonSoftwareFoundation.Python.3.12_qbz5n2k
fra8p0\LocalCache\local-packages\Python312\site-
```

```
packages\yfinance\scrapers\holders.py", line 99, in _fetch_and_parse
    self._parse_institution_ownership(data["institutionOwnership"])
                                     ~~~~^^^^^^^^^^^^^^^^^^^^^^^^
KeyError: 'institutionOwnership'

During handling of the above exception, another exception occurred:

Traceback (most recent call last):
  File "<stdin>", line 1, in <module>
                                                                                File
"C:\Users\Lenovo\AppData\Local\Packages\PythonSoftwareFoundation.Python.3.12_qbz5n2k
fra8p0\LocalCache\local-packages\Python312\site-packages\yfinance\ticker.py",   line
125, in insider_transactions
    return self.get_insider_transactions()
           ^^^^^^^^^^^^^^^^^^^^^^^^^^^^^^^
                                                                                File
"C:\Users\Lenovo\AppData\Local\Packages\PythonSoftwareFoundation.Python.3.12_qbz5n2k
fra8p0\LocalCache\local-packages\Python312\site-packages\yfinance\base.py",     line
207, in get_insider_transactions
    data = self._holders.insider_transactions
           ^^^^^^^^^^^^^^^^^^^^^^^^^^^^^^^^^^
                                                                                File
"C:\Users\Lenovo\AppData\Local\Packages\PythonSoftwareFoundation.Python.3.12_qbz5n2k
fra8p0\LocalCache\local-packages\Python312\site-
packages\yfinance\scrapers\holders.py", line 56, in insider_transactions
    self._fetch_and_parse()
                                                                                File
"C:\Users\Lenovo\AppData\Local\Packages\PythonSoftwareFoundation.Python.3.12_qbz5n2k
fra8p0\LocalCache\local-packages\Python312\site-
packages\yfinance\scrapers\holders.py", line 107, in _fetch_and_parse
    raise YFDataException("Failed to parse holders json data.")
yfinance.exceptions.YFDataException: Failed to parse holders json data.
```

So we face a problem on inside transactions, there are no holders, let's try "AAPL", see below,

```
>>> stock = yf.Ticker("AAPL")
>>> stock.info
{'address1': 'One Apple Park Way', 'city': 'Cupertino', 'state': 'CA', 'zip':
'95014', 'country': 'United States', 'phone': '408 996 1010', 'website':
'https://www.apple.com', 'industry': 'Consumer Electronics', 'industryKey':
'consumer-electronics', 'industryDisp': 'Consumer Electronics', 'sector':
'Technology', 'sectorKey': 'technology', 'sectorDisp': 'Technology',
'longBusinessSummary': 'Apple Inc. designs, manufactures, and markets smartphones,
personal computers, tablets, wearables, and accessories worldwide. The company
offers iPhone, a line of smartphones; Mac, a line of personal computers; iPad, a
line of multi-purpose tablets; and wearables, home, and accessories comprising
AirPods, Apple TV, Apple Watch, Beats products, and HomePod. It also provides
AppleCare support and cloud services; and operates various platforms, including the
App Store that allow customers to discover and download applications and digital
content, such as books, music, video, games, and podcasts. In addition, the company
offers various services, such as Apple Arcade, a game subscription service; Apple
```

Fitness+, a personalized fitness service; Apple Music, which offers users a curated listening experience with on-demand radio stations; Apple News+, a subscription news and magazine service; Apple TV+, which offers exclusive original content; Apple Card, a co-branded credit card; and Apple Pay, a cashless payment service, as well as licenses its intellectual property. The company serves consumers, and small and mid-sized businesses; and the education, enterprise, and government markets. It distributes third-party applications for its products through the App Store. The company also sells its products through its retail and online stores, and direct sales force; and third-party cellular network carriers, wholesalers, retailers, and resellers. Apple Inc. was founded in 1976 and is headquartered in Cupertino, California.', 'fullTimeEmployees': 161000, 'companyOfficers': [{'maxAge': 1, 'name': 'Mr. Timothy D. Cook', 'age': 62, 'title': 'CEO & Director', 'yearBorn': 1961, 'fiscalYear': 2023, 'totalPay': 16239562, 'exercisedValue': 0, 'unexercisedValue': 0}, {'maxAge': 1, 'name': 'Mr. Luca Maestri', 'age': 60, 'title': 'CFO & Senior VP', 'yearBorn': 1963, 'fiscalYear': 2023, 'totalPay': 4612242, 'exercisedValue': 0, 'unexercisedValue': 0}, {'maxAge': 1, 'name': 'Mr. Jeffrey E. Williams', 'age': 59, 'title': 'Chief Operating Officer', 'yearBorn': 1964, 'fiscalYear': 2023, 'totalPay': 4637585, 'exercisedValue': 0, 'unexercisedValue': 0}, {'maxAge': 1, 'name': 'Ms. Katherine L. Adams', 'age': 59, 'title': 'Senior VP, General Counsel & Secretary', 'yearBorn': 1964, 'fiscalYear': 2023, 'totalPay': 4618064, 'exercisedValue': 0, 'unexercisedValue': 0}, {'maxAge': 1, 'name': "Ms. Deirdre O'Brien", 'age': 56, 'title': 'Senior Vice President of Retail', 'yearBorn': 1967, 'fiscalYear': 2023, 'totalPay': 4613369, 'exercisedValue': 0, 'unexercisedValue': 0}, {'maxAge': 1, 'name': 'Mr. Chris Kondo', 'title': 'Senior Director of Corporate Accounting', 'fiscalYear': 2023, 'exercisedValue': 0, 'unexercisedValue': 0}, {'maxAge': 1, 'name': 'Mr. James Wilson', 'title': 'Chief Technology Officer', 'fiscalYear': 2023, 'exercisedValue': 0, 'unexercisedValue': 0}, {'maxAge': 1, 'name': 'Suhasini Chandramouli', 'title': 'Director of Investor Relations', 'fiscalYear': 2023, 'exercisedValue': 0, 'unexercisedValue': 0}, {'maxAge': 1, 'name': 'Mr. Greg Joswiak', 'title': 'Senior Vice President of Worldwide Marketing', 'fiscalYear': 2023, 'exercisedValue': 0, 'unexercisedValue': 0}, {'maxAge': 1, 'name': 'Mr. Adrian Perica', 'age': 49, 'title': 'Head of Corporate Development', 'yearBorn': 1974, 'fiscalYear': 2023, 'exercisedValue': 0, 'unexercisedValue': 0}], 'auditRisk': 6, 'boardRisk': 1, 'compensationRisk': 2, 'shareHolderRightsRisk': 1, 'overallRisk': 1, 'governanceEpochDate': 1722470400, 'compensationAsOfEpochDate': 1703980800, 'irWebsite': 'http://investor.apple.com/', 'maxAge': 86400, 'priceHint': 2, 'previousClose': 226.51, 'open': 226.49, 'dayLow': 225.191, 'dayHigh': 227.98, 'regularMarketPreviousClose': 226.51, 'regularMarketOpen': 226.49, 'regularMarketDayLow': 225.191, 'regularMarketDayHigh': 227.98, 'dividendRate': 1.0, 'dividendYield': 0.0044, 'exDividendDate': 1723420800, 'payoutRatio': 0.1476, 'fiveYearAvgDividendYield': 0.68, 'beta': 1.244, 'trailingPE': 34.459663, 'forwardPE': 30.267378, 'volume': 33246786, 'regularMarketVolume': 33246786, 'averageVolume': 64926977, 'averageVolume10days': 43870630, 'averageDailyVolume10Day': 43870630, 'bid': 226.38, 'ask': 226.47, 'bidSize': 200, 'askSize': 100, 'marketCap': 3442208145408, 'fiftyTwoWeekLow': 164.08, 'fiftyTwoWeekHigh': 237.23, 'priceToSalesTrailing12Months': 8.926819, 'fiftyDayAverage': 218.8466, 'twoHundredDayAverage': 192.2743, 'trailingAnnualDividendRate': 0.97, 'trailingAnnualDividendYield': 0.004282372, 'currency': 'USD', 'enterpriseValue': 3483392016384, 'profitMargins': 0.26441, 'floatShares': 15179810381, 'sharesOutstanding': 15204100096, 'sharesShort': 117696224, 'sharesShortPriorMonth': 132235437, 'sharesShortPreviousMonthDate': 1719532800, 'dateShortInterest': 1722384000, 'sharesPercentSharesOut': 0.0077, 'heldPercentInsiders': 0.02703, 'heldPercentInstitutions': 0.60867, 'shortRatio':

```
2.25, 'shortPercentOfFloat': 0.0077, 'impliedSharesOutstanding': 15410899968,
'bookValue': 4.382, 'priceToBook': 51.665905, 'lastFiscalYearEnd': 1696032000,
'nextFiscalYearEnd': 1727654400, 'mostRecentQuarter': 1719619200,
'earningsQuarterlyGrowth': 0.079, 'netIncomeToCommon': 101956001792, 'trailingEps':
6.57, 'forwardEps': 7.48, 'pegRatio': 3.05, 'lastSplitFactor': '4:1',
'lastSplitDate': 1598832000, 'enterpriseToRevenue': 9.034, 'enterpriseToEbitda':
26.433, '52WeekChange': 0.25060737, 'SandP52WeekChange': 0.26174653,
'lastDividendValue': 0.25, 'lastDividendDate': 1723420800, 'exchange': 'NMS',
'quoteType': 'EQUITY', 'symbol': 'AAPL', 'underlyingSymbol': 'AAPL', 'shortName':
'Apple Inc.', 'longName': 'Apple Inc.', 'firstTradeDateEpochUtc': 345479400,
'timeZoneFullName': 'America/New_York', 'timeZoneShortName': 'EDT', 'uuid':
'8b10e4ae-9eeb-3684-921a-9ab27e4d87aa', 'messageBoardId': 'finmb_24937',
'gmtOffSetMilliseconds': -14400000, 'currentPrice': 226.4, 'targetHighPrice': 300.0,
'targetLowPrice': 183.86, 'targetMeanPrice': 235.58, 'targetMedianPrice': 240.0,
'recommendationMean': 2.0, 'recommendationKey': 'buy', 'numberOfAnalystOpinions':
39, 'totalCash': 61801000960, 'totalCashPerShare': 4.065, 'ebitda': 131781001216,
'totalDebt': 101304000512, 'quickRatio': 0.798, 'currentRatio': 0.953,
'totalRevenue': 385603010560, 'debtToEquity': 151.862, 'revenuePerShare': 24.957,
'returnOnAssets': 0.22612, 'returnOnEquity': 1.60583, 'freeCashflow': 86158123008,
'operatingCashflow': 113040998400, 'earningsGrowth': 0.111, 'revenueGrowth': 0.049,
'grossMargins': 0.45962003, 'ebitdaMargins': 0.34175, 'operatingMargins': 0.29556,
'financialCurrency': 'USD', 'trailingPegRatio': 2.2029}
>>> stock.recommendations
  period  strongBuy  buy  hold  sell  strongSell
0     0m         11   21     6     0           0
1    -1m         12   21    10     1           0
2    -2m         12   19    12     1           0
3    -3m         10   24     7     1           0
>>> stock.insider_transactions
      Shares        Value URL                                              Text  ...
Position Transaction Start Date Ownership
0       8706    1958850.0                     Sale at price 225.00 per share.  ...
Officer             2024-08-15         D
1       5178    1121037.0                     Sale at price 216.50 per share.  ...
Officer             2024-08-09         D
2      4500          0.0          Stock Gift at price 0.00 per share.  ...  General
Counsel             2024-08-07         D
3     100000  20643512.0      Sale at price 206.42 - 207.05 per share.  ...  General
Counsel             2024-08-05         D
4      75000   14368500.0                     Sale at price 191.58 per share.  ...
Director             2024-05-30         D
..       ...          ...  ..                                                  ...  ...
...         ...         ...        ...
145     3416           NaN                                                       ...
Director             2021-02-01         D
146   17000   2273749.0      Sale at price 131.79 - 134.56 per share.  ...  General
Counsel             2021-02-01         D
147      408           0.0               Stock Gift at price 0.00 per share.  ...
Director             2020-12-02         D
148   57480          NaN                                                 ...  General
Counsel             2020-11-13         D
149   17000   1877109.0      Sale at price 109.22 - 110.99 per share.  ...  General
Counsel             2020-11-03         D
```

```
[150 rows x 9 columns]
>>> stock.isin
'US0378331005'
>>> stock.option_chain('2024-08-30')
Options(calls=            contractSymbol             lastTradeDate  strike  ...
inTheMoney  contractSize  currency
0      AAPL240830C00100000  2024-07-25  15:10:43+00:00     100.0   ...            True
REGULAR        USD
1      AAPL240830C00125000  2024-08-02  19:09:41+00:00     125.0   ...            True
REGULAR        USD
2      AAPL240830C00135000  2024-08-20  18:52:51+00:00     135.0   ...            True
REGULAR        USD
3      AAPL240830C00140000  2024-08-15  17:54:27+00:00     140.0   ...            True
REGULAR        USD
4      AAPL240830C00145000  2024-08-16  17:54:20+00:00     145.0   ...            True
REGULAR        USD
5      AAPL240830C00150000  2024-08-14  14:07:22+00:00     150.0   ...            True
REGULAR        USD
6      AAPL240830C00160000  2024-08-21  15:26:44+00:00     160.0   ...            True
REGULAR        USD
7      AAPL240830C00165000  2024-08-21  15:58:27+00:00     165.0   ...            True
REGULAR        USD
8      AAPL240830C00170000  2024-08-21  16:56:28+00:00     170.0   ...            True
REGULAR        USD
9      AAPL240830C00175000  2024-08-21  15:52:57+00:00     175.0   ...            True
REGULAR        USD
10    AAPL240830C00180000  2024-08-21  19:59:30+00:00     180.0   ...            True
REGULAR        USD
11    AAPL240830C00185000  2024-08-20  19:08:20+00:00     185.0   ...            True
REGULAR        USD
12    AAPL240830C00190000  2024-08-21  19:22:40+00:00     190.0   ...            True
REGULAR        USD
13    AAPL240830C00192500  2024-08-21  14:31:22+00:00     192.5   ...            True
REGULAR        USD
14    AAPL240830C00195000  2024-08-21  14:19:06+00:00     195.0   ...            True
REGULAR        USD
15    AAPL240830C00197500  2024-08-21  17:18:53+00:00     197.5   ...            True
REGULAR        USD
16    AAPL240830C00200000  2024-08-21  19:01:24+00:00     200.0   ...            True
REGULAR        USD
17    AAPL240830C00202500  2024-08-21  17:18:53+00:00     202.5   ...            True
REGULAR        USD
18    AAPL240830C00205000  2024-08-21  19:33:49+00:00     205.0   ...            True
REGULAR        USD
19    AAPL240830C00207500  2024-08-21  19:17:20+00:00     207.5   ...            True
REGULAR        USD
20    AAPL240830C00210000  2024-08-21  19:21:30+00:00     210.0   ...            True
REGULAR        USD
21    AAPL240830C00212500  2024-08-21  19:54:49+00:00     212.5   ...            True
REGULAR        USD
22    AAPL240830C00215000  2024-08-21  19:50:00+00:00     215.0   ...            True
REGULAR        USD
```

```
23   AAPL240830C00217500  2024-08-21  19:54:49+00:00     217.5   ...            True
REGULAR        USD
24   AAPL240830C00220000  2024-08-21  19:58:14+00:00     220.0   ...            True
REGULAR        USD
25   AAPL240830C00222500  2024-08-21  19:59:50+00:00     222.5   ...            True
REGULAR        USD
26   AAPL240830C00225000  2024-08-21  19:59:22+00:00     225.0   ...            True
REGULAR        USD
27   AAPL240830C00227500  2024-08-21  19:59:41+00:00     227.5   ...           False
REGULAR        USD
28   AAPL240830C00230000  2024-08-21  19:59:45+00:00     230.0   ...           False
REGULAR        USD
29   AAPL240830C00232500  2024-08-21  19:59:54+00:00     232.5   ...           False
REGULAR        USD
30   AAPL240830C00235000  2024-08-21  19:59:05+00:00     235.0   ...           False
REGULAR        USD
31   AAPL240830C00237500  2024-08-21  19:59:25+00:00     237.5   ...           False
REGULAR        USD
32   AAPL240830C00240000  2024-08-21  19:59:12+00:00     240.0   ...           False
REGULAR        USD
33   AAPL240830C00242500  2024-08-21  19:43:21+00:00     242.5   ...           False
REGULAR        USD
34   AAPL240830C00245000  2024-08-21  19:54:09+00:00     245.0   ...           False
REGULAR        USD
35   AAPL240830C00247500  2024-08-21  19:46:08+00:00     247.5   ...           False
REGULAR        USD
36   AAPL240830C00250000  2024-08-21  19:07:48+00:00     250.0   ...           False
REGULAR        USD
37   AAPL240830C00252500  2024-08-21  19:41:29+00:00     252.5   ...           False
REGULAR        USD
38   AAPL240830C00255000  2024-08-21  17:49:08+00:00     255.0   ...           False
REGULAR        USD
39   AAPL240830C00257500  2024-08-21  16:27:57+00:00     257.5   ...           False
REGULAR        USD
40   AAPL240830C00260000  2024-08-21  19:14:11+00:00     260.0   ...           False
REGULAR        USD
41   AAPL240830C00265000  2024-08-21  19:01:36+00:00     265.0   ...           False
REGULAR        USD
42   AAPL240830C00270000  2024-08-21  14:51:55+00:00     270.0   ...           False
REGULAR        USD
43   AAPL240830C00275000  2024-08-21  13:30:02+00:00     275.0   ...           False
REGULAR        USD
44   AAPL240830C00280000  2024-08-20  17:48:58+00:00     280.0   ...           False
REGULAR        USD
45   AAPL240830C00285000  2024-08-20  17:19:52+00:00     285.0   ...           False
REGULAR        USD
46   AAPL240830C00290000  2024-08-19  13:45:14+00:00     290.0   ...           False
REGULAR        USD
47   AAPL240830C00295000  2024-08-20  18:46:34+00:00     295.0   ...           False
REGULAR        USD
48   AAPL240830C00300000  2024-08-16  13:36:48+00:00     300.0   ...           False
REGULAR        USD
```

```
[49 rows x 14 columns], puts=           contractSymbol              lastTradeDate
strike  ...  inTheMoney  contractSize  currency
0     AAPL240830P00100000  2024-08-06  13:54:56+00:00     100.0     ...          False
REGULAR        USD
1     AAPL240830P00105000  2024-08-06  17:28:18+00:00     105.0     ...          False
REGULAR        USD
2     AAPL240830P00110000  2024-08-06  14:05:55+00:00     110.0     ...          False
REGULAR        USD
3     AAPL240830P00115000  2024-08-19  17:24:36+00:00     115.0     ...          False
REGULAR        USD
4     AAPL240830P00120000  2024-08-12  19:30:21+00:00     120.0     ...          False
REGULAR        USD
5     AAPL240830P00125000  2024-08-12  14:55:28+00:00     125.0     ...          False
REGULAR        USD
6     AAPL240830P00130000  2024-08-15  13:30:05+00:00     130.0     ...          False
REGULAR        USD
7     AAPL240830P00135000  2024-08-14  17:24:43+00:00     135.0     ...          False
REGULAR        USD
8     AAPL240830P00140000  2024-08-16  19:55:58+00:00     140.0     ...          False
REGULAR        USD
9     AAPL240830P00145000  2024-08-16  19:55:53+00:00     145.0     ...          False
REGULAR        USD
10    AAPL240830P00150000  2024-08-19  14:33:09+00:00     150.0     ...          False
REGULAR        USD
11    AAPL240830P00155000  2024-08-20  18:05:27+00:00     155.0     ...          False
REGULAR        USD
12    AAPL240830P00160000  2024-08-21  17:45:03+00:00     160.0     ...          False
REGULAR        USD
13    AAPL240830P00165000  2024-08-21  18:48:48+00:00     165.0     ...          False
REGULAR        USD
14    AAPL240830P00170000  2024-08-21  19:49:14+00:00     170.0     ...          False
REGULAR        USD
15    AAPL240830P00175000  2024-08-21  19:18:35+00:00     175.0     ...          False
REGULAR        USD
16    AAPL240830P00180000  2024-08-21  19:33:35+00:00     180.0     ...          False
REGULAR        USD
17    AAPL240830P00185000  2024-08-21  19:33:35+00:00     185.0     ...          False
REGULAR        USD
18    AAPL240830P00190000  2024-08-21  19:25:29+00:00     190.0     ...          False
REGULAR        USD
19    AAPL240830P00192500  2024-08-21  17:55:43+00:00     192.5     ...          False
REGULAR        USD
20    AAPL240830P00195000  2024-08-21  19:59:14+00:00     195.0     ...          False
REGULAR        USD
21    AAPL240830P00197500  2024-08-21  19:41:16+00:00     197.5     ...          False
REGULAR        USD
22    AAPL240830P00200000  2024-08-21  19:59:10+00:00     200.0     ...          False
REGULAR        USD
23    AAPL240830P00202500  2024-08-21  19:49:06+00:00     202.5     ...          False
REGULAR        USD
24    AAPL240830P00205000  2024-08-21  19:52:14+00:00     205.0     ...          False
REGULAR        USD
25    AAPL240830P00207500  2024-08-21  19:44:08+00:00     207.5     ...          False
```

```
REGULAR        USD
26    AAPL240830P00210000  2024-08-21  19:47:55+00:00     210.0    ...             False
REGULAR        USD
27    AAPL240830P00212500  2024-08-21  19:57:49+00:00     212.5    ...             False
REGULAR        USD
28    AAPL240830P00215000  2024-08-21  19:58:10+00:00     215.0    ...             False
REGULAR        USD
29    AAPL240830P00217500  2024-08-21  19:59:27+00:00     217.5    ...             False
REGULAR        USD
30    AAPL240830P00220000  2024-08-21  19:59:57+00:00     220.0    ...             False
REGULAR        USD
31    AAPL240830P00222500  2024-08-21  19:59:59+00:00     222.5    ...             False
REGULAR        USD
32    AAPL240830P00225000  2024-08-21  19:59:54+00:00     225.0    ...             False
REGULAR        USD
33    AAPL240830P00227500  2024-08-21  19:59:00+00:00     227.5    ...              True
REGULAR        USD
34    AAPL240830P00230000  2024-08-21  19:59:56+00:00     230.0    ...              True
REGULAR        USD
35    AAPL240830P00232500  2024-08-21  19:43:20+00:00     232.5    ...              True
REGULAR        USD
36    AAPL240830P00235000  2024-08-21  19:50:00+00:00     235.0    ...              True
REGULAR        USD
37    AAPL240830P00237500  2024-08-21  19:21:06+00:00     237.5    ...              True
REGULAR        USD
38    AAPL240830P00240000  2024-08-21  18:10:20+00:00     240.0    ...              True
REGULAR        USD
39    AAPL240830P00245000  2024-08-21  19:26:59+00:00     245.0    ...              True
REGULAR        USD
40    AAPL240830P00250000  2024-08-20  16:23:20+00:00     250.0    ...              True
REGULAR        USD
41    AAPL240830P00255000  2024-08-15  19:38:29+00:00     255.0    ...              True
REGULAR        USD
42    AAPL240830P00260000  2024-08-02  19:27:46+00:00     260.0    ...              True
REGULAR        USD
43    AAPL240830P00265000  2024-07-24  14:44:01+00:00     265.0    ...              True
REGULAR        USD
44    AAPL240830P00275000  2024-07-16  15:37:32+00:00     275.0    ...              True
REGULAR        USD
45    AAPL240830P00285000  2024-08-19  14:16:26+00:00     285.0    ...              True
REGULAR        USD
46    AAPL240830P00300000  2024-07-15  13:34:12+00:00     300.0    ...              True
REGULAR        USD

[47 rows x 14 columns], underlying={'language': 'en-US', 'region': 'US', 'quoteType': 'EQUITY', 'typeDisp': 'Equity', 'quoteSourceName': 'Nasdaq Real Time Price', 'triggerable': True, 'customPriceAlertConfidence': 'HIGH', 'currency': 'USD', 'gmtOffSetMilliseconds': -14400000, 'esgPopulated': False, 'regularMarketChangePercent': -0.04856325, 'regularMarketPrice': 226.4, 'exchange': 'NMS', 'shortName': 'Apple Inc.', 'longName': 'Apple Inc.', 'messageBoardId': 'finmb_24937', 'exchangeTimezoneName': 'America/New_York', 'exchangeTimezoneShortName': 'EDT', 'market': 'us_market', 'marketState': 'POST', 'hasPrePostMarketData': True, 'firstTradeDateMilliseconds': 345479400000,
```

```
'priceHint': 2, 'postMarketChangePercent': 0.079508804, 'postMarketTime': 1724277978, 'postMarketPrice': 226.58, 'postMarketChange': 0.18000793, 'regularMarketChange': -0.11000061, 'regularMarketTime': 1724270401, 'regularMarketDayHigh': 227.98, 'regularMarketDayRange': '225.191 - 227.98', 'regularMarketDayLow': 225.191, 'regularMarketVolume': 33246786, 'regularMarketPreviousClose': 226.51, 'bid': 226.38, 'ask': 226.47, 'bidSize': 2, 'askSize': 1, 'fullExchangeName': 'NasdaqGS', 'financialCurrency': 'USD', 'regularMarketOpen': 226.49, 'averageDailyVolume3Month': 64926977, 'averageDailyVolume10Day': 43870630, 'fiftyTwoWeekLowChange': 62.319992, 'fiftyTwoWeekLowChangePercent': 0.37981468, 'fiftyTwoWeekRange': '164.08 - 237.23', 'fiftyTwoWeekHighChange': -10.830002, 'fiftyTwoWeekHighChangePercent': -0.04565191, 'fiftyTwoWeekLow': 164.08, 'fiftyTwoWeekHigh': 237.23, 'fiftyTwoWeekChangePercent': 25.060738, 'dividendDate': 1723680000, 'earningsTimestamp': 1722544200, 'earningsTimestampStart': 1730372340, 'earningsTimestampEnd': 1730721600, 'earningsCallTimestampStart': 1722546000, 'earningsCallTimestampEnd': 1722546000, 'isEarningsDateEstimate': True, 'trailingAnnualDividendRate': 0.97, 'trailingPE': 34.459663, 'dividendRate': 1.0, 'trailingAnnualDividendYield': 0.004282372, 'dividendYield': 0.44, 'epsTrailingTwelveMonths': 6.57, 'epsForward': 7.48, 'epsCurrentYear': 6.7, 'priceEpsCurrentYear': 33.791046, 'sharesOutstanding': 15204100096, 'bookValue': 4.382, 'fiftyDayAverage': 218.8466, 'fiftyDayAverageChange': 7.5533905, 'fiftyDayAverageChangePercent': 0.034514543, 'twoHundredDayAverage': 192.2743, 'twoHundredDayAverageChange': 34.125687, 'twoHundredDayAverageChangePercent': 0.17748438, 'marketCap': 3442208145408, 'forwardPE': 30.267378, 'priceToBook': 51.665905, 'sourceInterval': 15, 'exchangeDataDelayedBy': 0, 'averageAnalystRating': '2.0 - Buy', 'tradeable': False, 'cryptoTradeable': False, 'displayName': 'Apple', 'symbol': 'AAPL'})
```

So if you goto https://finance.yahoo.com/quote/AAPL/options/=1724976000, the data are very same. How to get the function usage? Checkout https://github.com/ranaroussi/yfinance, all the data and functions are designed as shown. So we can draw the price line, as below,

```
>>> data = yf.download('aapl', period='1mo')
>>> data
[*********************100%%***********************]  1 of 1 completed
                  Open        High         Low       Close   Adj Close     Volume
Date
2024-07-22  227.009995  227.779999  223.089996  223.960007  223.701080   48201800
2024-07-23  224.369995  226.940002  222.679993  225.009995  224.749847   39960300
2024-07-24  224.000000  224.800003  217.130005  218.539993  218.287323   61777600
2024-07-25  218.929993  220.850006  214.619995  217.490005  217.238556   51391200
2024-07-26  218.699997  219.490005  216.009995  217.960007  217.708008   41601300
2024-07-29  216.960007  219.300003  215.750000  218.240005  217.987686   36311800
2024-07-30  219.190002  220.330002  216.119995  218.800003  218.547043   41643800
2024-07-31  221.440002  223.820007  220.630005  222.080002  221.823242   50036300
2024-08-01  224.369995  224.479996  217.020004  218.360001  218.107544   62501000
2024-08-02  219.149994  225.600006  217.710007  219.860001  219.605804  105568600
2024-08-05  199.089996  213.500000  196.000000  209.270004  209.028061  119548600
2024-08-06  205.300003  209.990005  201.070007  207.229996  206.990402   69660500
2024-08-07  206.899994  213.639999  206.389999  209.820007  209.577423   63516400
2024-08-08  213.110001  214.199997  208.830002  213.309998  213.063385   47161100
2024-08-09  212.100006  216.779999  211.970001  216.240005  215.990005   42201600
```

```
2024-08-12  216.070007  219.509995  215.600006  217.529999  217.529999   38028100
2024-08-13  219.009995  221.889999  219.009995  221.270004  221.270004   44155300
2024-08-14  220.570007  223.029999  219.699997  221.720001  221.720001   41960600
2024-08-15  224.600006  225.350006  222.759995  224.720001  224.720001   46414000
2024-08-16  223.919998  226.830002  223.649994  226.050003  226.050003   44340200
2024-08-19  225.720001  225.990005  223.039993  225.889999  225.889999   40687800
2024-08-20  225.770004  227.169998  225.449997  226.509995  226.509995   30299000
2024-08-21  226.490005  227.979996  225.190994  226.399994  226.399994   33246786

>>>
>>>
plt.plot(data['Close'], label='Close Price') # [<matplotlib.lines.Line2D object at 0x0000023406FEF7D0>]
data['20_MA'] = data['Close'].rolling(window=20).mean()
plt.plot(data['20_MA'], label='20 Day MA')
plt.title('AAPL Stock Price and 20 Day Moving Averages')
plt.xlabel('Date')
plt.ylabel('Price')
plt.legend()
plt.show()
```

And we can draw the daily return as below,

```
data['Daily_Return'] = data['Close'].pct_change()
plt.figure(figsize=(12, 6))
plt.plot(data['Daily_Return'], label='Daily Return')
plt.title('AAPL Daily Returns')
plt.xlabel('Date')
plt.ylabel('Daily Return')
plt.legend()
plt.show()
```

And we can draw cumulative returns, as below,

```
data['Cumulative_Return'] = (1 + data['Daily_Return']).cumprod()
plt.figure(figsize=(12, 6))
plt.plot(data['Cumulative_Return'], label='Cumulative Return')
plt.title('AAPL Cumulative Returns')
plt.xlabel('Date')
plt.ylabel('Cumulative Return')
plt.legend()
plt.show()
```

And we can try draw together, as below,

```
stock_data = data

# Calculate MACD and Signal Line
stock_data['MACD'] = stock_data['Close'].ewm(span=12, adjust=False).mean() - stock_data['Close'].ewm(span=26, adjust=False).mean()
stock_data['Signal_Line'] = stock_data['MACD'].ewm(span=9, adjust=False).mean()
```

```
# Plot MACD and Signal Line
plt.figure(figsize=(12, 6))
plt.plot(stock_data['MACD'], label='MACD')
plt.plot(stock_data['Signal_Line'], label='Signal Line')
plt.title('AAPL MACD and Signal Line')
plt.xlabel('Date')
plt.ylabel('Value')
plt.legend()
plt.show()
```

Can we draw the line in real time? See below,

```
# stock.py
import streamlit as st
import yfinance as yf
import matplotlib.pyplot as plt
import time

st.title("Real-time Apple Stock Prices")

# Define the ticker symbol for Apple
ticker_symbol = 'AAPL'

# Get the data of the stock
apple_stock = yf.Ticker(ticker_symbol)

# Create a matplotlib figure
fig, ax = plt.subplots()

# Use st.pyplot to display the plot
plot = st.pyplot(fig)

# Loop to fetch and update stock values
while True:
    # Get the historical prices for Apple stock
    historical_prices = apple_stock.history(period='1d', interval='1m')

    # Get the latest price and time
    latest_price = historical_prices['Close'].iloc[-1]
    latest_time = historical_prices.index[-1].strftime('%H:%M:%S')

    # Clear the plot and plot the new data
    ax.clear()
         ax.plot(historical_prices.index,  historical_prices['Close'],  label='Stock
Value')
    ax.set_xlabel('Time')
    ax.set_ylabel('Stock Value')
    ax.set_title('Apple Stock Value')
    ax.legend(loc='upper left')
    ax.tick_params(axis='x', rotation=45)

    # Update the plot in the Streamlit app
```

```
    plot.pyplot(fig)

    # Show the latest stock value in the app
    st.write(f"Latest Price ({latest_time}): {latest_price}")

    # Sleep for 1 minute before fetching new data
    time.sleep(60)

# python -m streamlit run stock.py
```

Also, matplotlib is bundled with in some packages to make fancy effects, see below,

```
import yfinance as yf
import mplfinance as mpf

ticker_symbol = 'AAPL'

df = yf.download(ticker_symbol, period='6mo')

mpf.plot(df, type='candle')
```

And we draw moving average, as below,

```
import yfinance as yf
import mplfinance as mpf

ticker_symbol = 'AAPL'

df = yf.download(ticker_symbol, period='1mo')

mpf.plot(df, type='candle', mav=(5,20), volume=False)
```

And we can change the drawing color, as below,

```
# import required packages
import matplotlib.pyplot as plt
import yfinance as yf
from mplfinance.original_flavor import candlestick_ohlc
import pandas as pd
import matplotlib.dates as mpdates

plt.style.use('dark_background')

# extracting Data for plotting

ticker_symbol = 'AAPL'
df = yf.download(ticker_symbol, period='1mo')

df['Date'] = df.index
#print(df['Date'])
#df = pd.read_csv('data.csv')
```

```
df = df[['Date', 'Open', 'High', 'Low', 'Close']]

# convert into datetime object
df['Date'] = pd.to_datetime(df['Date'])

# apply map function
df['Date'] = df['Date'].map(mpdates.date2num)

# creating Subplots
fig, ax = plt.subplots()

# plotting the data
candlestick_ohlc(ax, df.values, width = 0.6,
                 colorup = 'green', colordown = 'red',
                 alpha = 0.8)

# allow grid
ax.grid(True)

# Setting labels
ax.set_xlabel('Date')
ax.set_ylabel('Price')

# setting title
plt.title('Prices For the Period in One Month')

# Formatting Date
date_format = mpdates.DateFormatter('%d-%m-%Y')
ax.xaxis.set_major_formatter(date_format)
fig.autofmt_xdate()

fig.tight_layout()

# show the plot
plt.show()
```

So here we see dataFrame from pandas, what is that?

16 pandas

Pandas are not animals, it is a table, or variable type of Dataframe, which includes row and columns, as below,

```
import pandas as pd

# intialise data of lists.
data = {'Name':['masara', 'nick', 'krish', 'jack'],
        'Age':[20, 21, 19, 18]}

# Create DataFrame
df = pd.DataFrame(data)
```

```
# Print the output.
print(df)
```

Since it is a table, so we can save it as `csv`, as below,

```
# Save
df.to_csv('people.csv', index=False)
```

To read, as below,

```
import pandas as pd

# making data frame from csv file
data = pd.read_csv("people.csv", index_col ="Name")

# retrieving rows by iloc method
row2 = data.iloc[3]
print(row2)
```

Notice that Dataframe is actually dict of lists, see below,

```
# importing pandas as pd
import pandas as pd

# dictionary of lists
dict = {'name':["aparna", "pankaj", "sudhir", "Geeku"],
        'degree': ["MBA", "BCA", "M.Tech", "MBA"],
        'score':[90, 40, 80, 98]}

# creating a dataframe from a dictionary
df = pd.DataFrame(dict)

print(df)
```

That means we can iter through line by line, as below,

```
# iterating over rows using iterrows() function
for i, j in df.iterrows():
    print(i, j)
    print()
```

Or column by column, as below,

```
# importing pandas as pd
import pandas as pd

# dictionary of lists
dict = {'name':["aparna", "pankaj", "sudhir", "Geeku"],
        'degree': ["MBA", "BCA", "M.Tech", "MBA"],
        'score':[90, 40, 80, 98]}
```

```
# creating a dataframe from a dictionary
df = pd.DataFrame(dict)

#print(df)

# creating a list of dataframe columns
columns = list(df)

for i in columns:

    # printing the third element of the column
    print (df[i])
```

Bit is a fun website, and we can read some data there, as below,

```
import pandas as pd
# url bit.ly
url = 'http://bit.ly/uforeports'

# read csv file
df = pd.read_csv(url)
df.head()
```

And we can do some basic operations for Dataframe, as below,

```
import pandas as pd

url = 'http://bit.ly/uforeports'

# read csv file
df = pd.read_csv(url)
d = df.head()
print(type(d))
new_index =['U', 'A', 'B', 'C', 'Z']
print(d.reindex(new_index))
d.columns = ['V', 'W', 'X', 'Y', 'Z']
print(d)
d.iat[1, 1]="22"
print(d)
d.at[1,'W']="40"
print(d)
d = d.replace(
    to_replace=r'\b\w{7}\b',
    value='7 letters',
    regex=True)
print(d)
```

So what is the regex?

17 regex

The first time I used regex is for my IP address checker, see below,

```
import re

def is_valid_ipv4(ip):
    ipv4_regex = re.compile(r'^(?:[0-9]{1,3}\.){3}[0-9]{1,3}$')
    return bool(ipv4_regex.match(ip))

def main():
    while True:
        test_ip = input("Please enter IP or type 'exit' to exit the program: ")
        if test_ip=="exit":
            break
        else:

            print(f"Is '{test_ip}' a valid IPv4 address? {is_valid_ipv4(test_ip)}")

if __name__=="__main__":
    main()
```

So, the **re** package offers the **match()** function for compare a pattern to a string, the pattern would be like the group description of the string format. In this case, IPv4, it would be the number in between 0 to 255, and four of them seperated by dot, as below,

```
import re

def is_valid_ipv4(ip):
      ipv4_regex = re.compile(r'^((25[0-5]|2[0-4][0-9]|[01]?[0-9][0-9]?)\.){3}(25[0-
5]|2[0-4][0-9]|[01]?[0-9][0-9]?)$')
    return bool(ipv4_regex.match(ip))

def main():
    while True:
        test_ip = input("Please enter IP or type 'exit' to exit the program: ")
        if test_ip=="exit":
            break
        else:
            print(f"Is '{test_ip}' a valid IPv4 address? {is_valid_ipv4(test_ip)}")

if __name__=="__main__":
    main()
```

It is not necassry to compile in **search()** funciton, see below,

```
import re
statement = 'Please contact us at: support@datacamp.com'
match       =       re.search(r'(?P<email>(?P<username>[\w\.-]+)@(?P<host>[\w\.-]+))',
statement)
```

```
if statement:
    print("Email address:", match.group('email'))
    print("Username:", match.group('username'))
    print("Host:", match.group('host'))
```

And we can also find the repeating patterns, see below,

```
import re
# Compile the regex pattern
pattern = re.compile(r'\bapple\b')
# The input text
text = "I have an apple, and he has an apple too. Apples are delicious."
# Search for the pattern
matches = pattern.findall(text)
# Print the matches
print("Matches:", matches)
```

And if add IPv6, see below,

```
import re

def is_valid_ipv6(ip):

    pattern = re.compile(r'^((([0-9]|[1-9][0-9]|1[0-9]{2}|2[0-4][0-9]|25[0-5])\.){3}
([0-9]|[1-9][0-9]|1[0-9]{2}|2[0-4][0-9]|25[0-5])$|^(([a-fA-F]|[a-fA-F][a-fA-F0-9\-]*
[a-fA-F0-9])\.)*([A-Fa-f]|[A-Fa-f][A-Fa-f0-9\-]*[A-Fa-f0-9])$|^(?:(?:(?:(?:(?:(?:(?:
[0-9a-fA-F]{1,4})):){6})(?:(?:(?:(?:(?:[0-9a-fA-F]{1,4})):(?:(?:[0-9a-fA-F]{1,4})))|
(?:(?:(?:(?:(?:25[0-5]|(?:[1-9]|1[0-9]|2[0-4])?[0-9]))\.){3}(?:(?:25[0-5]|(?:[1-
9]|1[0-9]|2[0-4])?[0-9])))))))|(?:(?:::(?:(?:(?:[0-9a-fA-F]{1,4})):){5})(?:(?:(?:(?:
(?:[0-9a-fA-F]{1,4})):(?:(?:[0-9a-fA-F]{1,4})))|(?:(?:(?:(?:(?:25[0-5]|(?:[1-9]|1[0-
9]|2[0-4])?[0-9]))\.){3}(?:(?:25[0-5]|(?:[1-9]|1[0-9]|2[0-4])?[0-9])))))))|(?:(?:(?:
(?:(?:[0-9a-fA-F]{1,4})))?::(?:(?:(?:[0-9a-fA-F]{1,4})):){4})(?:(?:(?:(?:(?:[0-9a-
fA-F]{1,4})):(?:(?:[0-9a-fA-F]{1,4})))|(?:(?:(?:(?:(?:25[0-5]|(?:[1-9]|1[0-9]|2[0-
4])?[0-9]))\.){3}(?:(?:25[0-5]|(?:[1-9]|1[0-9]|2[0-4])?[0-9])))))))|(?:(?:(?:(?:(?:
(?:[0-9a-fA-F]{1,4})):){0,1}(?:(?:[0-9a-fA-F]{1,4})))?::(?:(?:(?:[0-9a-fA-F]
{1,4})):){3})(?:(?:(?:(?:(?:[0-9a-fA-F]{1,4})):(?:(?:[0-9a-fA-F]{1,4})))|(?:(?:(?:
(?:(?:25[0-5]|(?:[1-9]|1[0-9]|2[0-4])?[0-9]))\.){3}(?:(?:25[0-5]|(?:[1-9]|1[0-
9]|2[0-4])?[0-9])))))))|(?:(?:(?:(?:(?:(?:[0-9a-fA-F]{1,4})):){0,2}(?:(?:[0-9a-fA-F]
{1,4})))?::(?:(?:(?:[0-9a-fA-F]{1,4})):){2})(?:(?:(?:(?:(?:[0-9a-fA-F]{1,4})):(?:(?:
[0-9a-fA-F]{1,4})))|(?:(?:(?:(?:(?:25[0-5]|(?:[1-9]|1[0-9]|2[0-4])?[0-9]))\.){3}(?:
(?:25[0-5]|(?:[1-9]|1[0-9]|2[0-4])?[0-9])))))))|(?:(?:(?:(?:(?:(?:[0-9a-fA-F]
{1,4})):){0,3}(?:(?:[0-9a-fA-F]{1,4})))?::(?:(?:[0-9a-fA-F]{1,4})):)(?:(?:(?:(?:(?:
[0-9a-fA-F]{1,4})):(?:(?:[0-9a-fA-F]{1,4})))|(?:(?:(?:(?:(?:25[0-5]|(?:[1-9]|1[0-
9]|2[0-4])?[0-9]))\.){3}(?:(?:25[0-5]|(?:[1-9]|1[0-9]|2[0-4])?[0-9])))))))|(?:(?:(?:
(?:(?:(?:[0-9a-fA-F]{1,4})):){0,4}(?:(?:[0-9a-fA-F]{1,4})))?::)(?:(?:(?:(?:(?:[0-9a-
fA-F]{1,4})):(?:(?:[0-9a-fA-F]{1,4})))|(?:(?:(?:(?:(?:25[0-5]|(?:[1-9]|1[0-9]|2[0-
4])?[0-9]))\.){3}(?:(?:25[0-5]|(?:[1-9]|1[0-9]|2[0-4])?[0-9])))))))|(?:(?:(?:(?:(?:
(?:[0-9a-fA-F]{1,4})):){0,5}(?:(?:[0-9a-fA-F]{1,4})))?::)(?:(?:[0-9a-fA-F]{1,4})))|
(?:(?:(?:(?:(?:(?:[0-9a-fA-F]{1,4})):){0,6}(?:(?:[0-9a-fA-F]{1,4})))?::)))))$')

    ipv6_regex = re.compile(pattern)
    return bool(ipv6_regex.match(ip))
```

```
def main():
    while True:
        test_ip = input("Please enter IPv6 or type 'exit' to exit the program: ")
        if test_ip=="exit":
            break
        else:

            print(f"Is '{test_ip}' a valid IPv6 address? {is_valid_ipv6(test_ip)}")

if __name__=="__main__":
    main()
```

Ok, one must be shocked with the long regex, but yes that is not avoidable. Can we use the regex in real life? See below,

```
import re
import requests
the_idiot_url = 'https://www.gutenberg.org/cache/epub/1184/pg1184-images.html'

def get_book(url):
    # Sends a http request to get the text from project Gutenberg
    raw = requests.get(url).text
    text = re.search(r"hus,.*\n",raw ).group(0)
    return text

def preprocess(sentence):
    return re.sub('[^A-Za-z0-9.]+' , ' ', sentence).lower()

book = get_book(the_idiot_url)
print(book)
processed_book = preprocess(book)
print(processed_book)
```

So we just removed the colon, and we learned the **requests** package for get action. **sub()** is substitute the searched pattern with the new pattern. **lower()** is change to small letters.

18 Les Temps

But regex is not always a good solution for strings, take a loot at the French verbs.

Tense	Time	Mood	English	French	Use
Présent	Present	Indicative	I wash	Je lave	Most Common
Imparfait	Past	Indicative	I was washing	Je lavais	Common

Tense	Time	Mood	English	French	Use
Passé Simple	Past	Indicative	I washed (formal)	Je lavai	Literary
Passé Composé	Past	Indicative	I washed, I have washed	J'ai lavé	Most Common
Plus-Que-Parfait	Past	Indicative	I had washed	J'avais lavé	Common
Passé Antérieur	Past	Indicative	I had washed (formal)	J'eus lavé	Literary
Futur Porche	Future	Indicative	I am going to wash	Je vais laver	Common
Futur Simple	Future	Indicative	I will wash	Je laverai	Most Common
Futur Antérieur	Future	Indicative	I will have washed	J'aurai lavé	Uncommon
Subjonctif Présent	Present	Subjunctive	That I wash	Que je lave	Common
Subjonctif Passé	Past	Subjunctive	That I had washed	Que j'aie lavé	Common
Subjonctif Imparfait	Past	Subjunctive	That I washed	Que je lavasse	Literary
Subjonctif Plus-Que-Parfait	Past	Subjunctive	That I had washed	Que j'eusse lavé	Literary
Conditionnel Présent	Present	Conditional	I would wash	Je laverais	Common
Conditionnel Passé	Past	Conditional	I would have washed	J'aurais lavé	Common
Conditionnel Passé II (Formal)	Past	Conditional	I would have washed (formal)	J'eusse lavé	Literary
L'impératif présent	Present	Imperative	(You) wash!	(Tu) lave!	Common
L'impératif passé	Past	Imperative	Have washed!	Aie lavé!	Extremely uncommon
L'infinitif présent	Present	Infinitive / Impersonal	To wash	laver	Most Common
L'infinitif passé	Past	Infinitive / Impersonal	To have washed	Avoir lavé	Uncommon
Le participe présent	Present	Impersonal	Washing	Lavant	Common

Tense	Time	Mood	English	French	Use
Le participe passé	Past	Impersonal	Washed	Lavé	Most Common

There are 22 tenses, so we can write a class for the verb, as below,

```
import random

class bcolors:
    HEADER = '\033[95m'
    OKBLUE = '\033[94m'
    OKCYAN = '\033[96m'
    OKGREEN = '\033[92m'
    WARNING = '\033[93m'
    FAIL = '\033[91m'
    ENDC = '\033[0m'
    BOLD = '\033[1m'
    UNDERLINE = '\033[4m'

class flashcard:
    def __init__(self):

        self.fruits={'Présent':' lave',
                     'Imparfait':' lavais',
                     'Passé Composé':"'ai lavé",
                     'Plus-Que-Parfait':"'avais lavé"}

    def quiz(self):
        while (True):

            fruit, color = random.choice(list(self.fruits.items()))

            print("What is the {} of laver for je".format(fruit))
            user_answer = input()

            if(user_answer.lower() == color):
                print(f"Correct answer")
            else:
                                print(f"Wrong  answer\nje"+f"{bcolors.OKGREEN}"+color+f"
{bcolors.ENDC}")

             option = input(f"{bcolors.OKBLUE}enter laver , if you want to quit play
: {bcolors.ENDC}")
            if (option == "laver"):
                break

print(f"{bcolors.OKBLUE}welcome to laver quiz {bcolors.ENDC}")
fc=flashcard()
fc.quiz()
```

Here we see that we missed other person pronouns, and we only have one verb, that is to say the verbs are in three orders, we need to specify the pronoun, then the verb, and the tense, as below,

```
import random

class bcolors:
    HEADER = '\033[95m'
    OKBLUE = '\033[94m'
    OKCYAN = '\033[96m'
    OKGREEN = '\033[92m'
    WARNING = '\033[93m'
    FAIL = '\033[91m'
    ENDC = '\033[0m'
    BOLD = '\033[1m'
    UNDERLINE = '\033[4m'

class flashcard:
    def __init__(self):

                      self.pronoun=['je', 'tu', 'il', 'elle', 'on', 'nous', 'vous',
'ills', 'elles']

                 self.verb=['laver', 'manger']#, 'boir', 'acheter', 'venir', 'denir',
'voir', 'avoir', 'devoir']

                     self.tense=['Présent', 'Imparfait', 'Passé Composé', 'Plus-Que-
Parfait']

                      self.laver=[{'Présent':' lave', 'Imparfait':' lavais', 'Passé
Composé':"'ai lavé", 'Plus-Que-Parfait':"'avais lavé"}, #je
{'Présent':' lave', 'Imparfait':' lavais', 'Passé Composé':"'ai lavé", 'Plus-Que-
Parfait':"'avais lavé"}, #tu
{'Présent':' lave', 'Imparfait':' lavais', 'Passé Composé':"'ai lavé", 'Plus-Que-
Parfait':"'avais lavé"}, #il
{'Présent':' lave', 'Imparfait':' lavais', 'Passé Composé':"'ai lavé", 'Plus-Que-
Parfait':"'avais lavé"}, #el
{'Présent':' lave', 'Imparfait':' lavais', 'Passé Composé':"'ai lavé", 'Plus-Que-
Parfait':"'avais lavé"}, #on
{'Présent':' lave', 'Imparfait':' lavais', 'Passé Composé':"'ai lavé", 'Plus-Que-
Parfait':"'avais lavé"}, #nous
{'Présent':' lave', 'Imparfait':' lavais', 'Passé Composé':"'ai lavé", 'Plus-Que-
Parfait':"'avais lavé"}, #vous
{'Présent':' lave', 'Imparfait':' lavais', 'Passé Composé':"'ai lavé", 'Plus-Que-
Parfait':"'avais lavé"}, #ills
{'Présent':' lave', 'Imparfait':' lavais', 'Passé Composé':"'ai lavé", 'Plus-Que-
Parfait':"'avais lavé"}] #ells

        self.manger=[{'Présent':' mange', 'Imparfait':' mange', 'Passé Composé':"'ai
mange", 'Plus-Que-Parfait':"'avais mange"}, {}, {}, {}, {}, {}, {}, {}, {}]
```

```
        def quiz(self):
        while (True):
            p = random.choice(self.pronoun)
            v = random.choice(self.verb)
            t = random.choice(self.tense)
            print("What is the {} of {} {}".format(t, p, v))
            user_answer = input()
            pro = user_answer.split()[0]
                        ver = user_answer.split()[1]
            if v == 'laver':
                if pro == 'je':
                    print(self.jelaver[t])
                else:
                    print('laver')
            if v == 'manger':
                print('manger')
                      option = input(f"{bcolors.OKBLUE}Enter ., if you want to quit
play : {bcolors.ENDC}")
            if (option == "."):
                break

print(f"{bcolors.OKBLUE}welcome to verb quiz {bcolors.ENDC}")
fc=flashcard()
fc.quiz()
```

The reason we not using the French verb group rules is because there are always exception, and this is exactly the real wolrd solution, checkout https://github.com/Ars-Linguistica/mlconjug3/blob/master/mlconjug3/verbs/verbs.py, where data are stored in xml foramt.

To use `mlconjug3`, we need to install prerequisite packages, as below,

```
pip install scikit-learn==1.3.0
pip install tomlkit, defusedxml, joblib, pyyaml
pip install mlconjug3
```

Notice that double equal specifies the exact version, and due to maintainance reason, the packages are not always the updated ones. And we can check if the the verb tense is correct, as below,

```
from mlconjug3 import Conjugator

# initialize the conjugator
conjugator = Conjugator()

# conjugate the verb "manger"
verb = conjugator.conjugate("manger")
```

```
# check if the form "tu manges" is in the conjugated forms. Prints False.
print("tu manges" not in verb) # False
```

What does the conjugate do? Checkout https://github.com/Ars-Linguistica/mlconjug3/blob/master/mlconjug3/mlconjug.py#L94, it takes a verb and goto https://github.com/Ars-Linguistica/mlconjug3/blob/master/mlconjug3/mlconjug.py#L117, and method `_conjugate` will form the verb into a verb object with all tenses, that is why we then can check if `"tu manges" not in verb`.

And the verb tense format is in a group and subgroup order, as below,

```
print(verb.conjug_info["Indicatif"]["Présent"]["tu"]) # manges
```

How many verbs we can check? Many as in https://github.com/Ars-Linguistica/mlconjug3/blob/master/mlconjug3/data/conjug_manager/conjugation-fr.xml, that is to say, if we have written our own French verb xml, we can just continue build our tense checker. Notice that MLConjug does not combine the vowels too good, so we have to do a substitution ourselves if making sentence, as below,

```
from mlconjug3 import Conjugator

# initialize the conjugator
conjugator = Conjugator()

# conjugate the verb "avoir"
verb = conjugator.conjugate("avoir")

# making sentence
print("j'"+verb.conjug_info["Indicatif"]["Présent"]["je"]+" un livre") # j'ai un
livre
```

And for `[Impartif]`, we can even try a list of verbs, as below,

```
from mlconjug3 import Conjugator

# initialize the conjugator
conjugator = Conjugator()

a='''
Être Conjugation (To be)
Avoir Conjugation (To have)
Pouvoir Conjugation (Can, to be able to)
Vouloir Conjugation (To want)
Faire Conjugation (To do, to make)
Aller Conjugation (To go)
Venir Conjugation (To come)
Devenir Conjugation (To become)
```

Prendre Conjugation (To take)
Comprendre Conjugation (To understand)
Apprendre Conjugation (To learn)
Voir Conjugation (To see)
Devoir Conjugation (Must)
Recevoir Conjugation (To receive)
Croire Conjugation (To believe)
Boire Conjugation (To drink)
Acheter Conjugation (To buy)
Vivre Conjugation (To live)
Dire Conjugation (To say)
Lire Conjugation (To read)
Écrire Conjugation (To write)
Rire Conjugation (To laugh)
Sourire Conjugation (To smile)
Suivre Conjugation (To follow)
Savoir Conjugation (To know)
Connaître Conjugation (To know)
Naître Conjugation (To be born)
Mourir Conjugation (To die)
Dormir Conjugation (To sleep)
Ouvrir Conjugation (To open)
Couvrir Conjugation (To cover)
Découvrir Conjugation (To discover)
Mettre Conjugation (To put)
Permettre Conjugation (To allow)
Promettre Conjugation (To promise)
Manger Conjugation (To eat)
Partager Conjugation (To share)
Partir Conjugation (To leave)
Sortir Conjugation (To go out)
Tenir Conjugation (To hold)
Obtenir Conjugation (To get)
Produire Conjugation (To produce)
Détruire Conjugation (To destroy)
Traduire Conjugation (To translate)
Conduire Conjugation (To drive)
Cuire Conjugation (To cook)
Courir Conjugation (To run)
Appeler Conjugation (To call, to be called)
Intéresser Conjugation (To interest)
Inquiéter Conjugation (To worry)
Souvenir Conjugation (To remember)
Lever Conjugation (To get up)
Parler Conjugation (To speak)
Aimer Conjugation (To like, to love)
Donner Conjugation (To give)
Demander Conjugation (To ask)
Trouver Conjugation (To find)
Passer Conjugation (To pass)
Porter Conjugation (To wear)
Penser Conjugation (To think)
Écouter Conjugation (To listen)

```
Rester Conjugation (To stay)
Étudier Conjugation (To study)
Montrer Conjugation (To show)
Arriver Conjugation (To arrive)
Laisser Conjugation (To leave )
Payer Conjugation (To pay)
Jouer Conjugation (To play)
Changer Conjugation (To change)
Décider Conjugation (To decide)
Commencer Conjugation (To begin)
Compter Conjugation (To count)
Expliquer Conjugation (To explain)
Gagner Conjugation (To win)
Exister Conjugation (To exist)
Travailler Conjugation (To work)
Rencontrer Conjugation (To meet)
Chercher Conjugation (To search)
Entrer Conjugation (To enter)
Préparer Conjugation (To prepare)
Vendre Conjugation (To sell)
Attendre Conjugation (To wait)
Perdre Conjugation (To lose)
Entendre Conjugation (To hear)
Répondre Conjugation (To respond)
Rendre Conjugation (To return sth)
Prétendre Conjugation (To claim)
Défendre Conjugation (To defend)
Fondre Conjugation (To melt)
Descendre Conjugation (To descend)
Finir Conjugation (To finish)
Réussir Conjugation (To succeed)
Choisir Conjugation (To choose)
Agir Conjugation (To act)
Investir Conjugation (To invest)
Obéir Conjugation (To obey)
Grossir Conjugation (To gain weight)
Grandir Conjugation (To grow up)
Vieillir Conjugation (To grow old)
Réfléchir Conjugation (To think)
'''

aa = a.split("\n")
for i in aa:
    ii = i.split(" ")
    aaa = (ii[0])
    if aaa != "":
        verb = conjugator.conjugate(aaa)
        b=(verb.conjug_info["Imperatif"].values())
        for k in b:
            print("|", ii[0], "|", k[''], "|")
```

19 XML

Let's write a test.xml first, see below,

```
# test.py

from xml.etree import ElementTree as et
import xml.dom.minidom as minidom

root = et.Element('school')
names = ['don', 'tom']
genders = ['male', 'male']
ages = ['20', '18']

student1 = et.SubElement(root, 'student')
student2 = et.SubElement(root, 'student')
et.SubElement(student1, 'name').text = names[0]
et.SubElement(student1, 'gender').text = genders[0]
et.SubElement(student1, 'age').text = ages[0]
et.SubElement(student2, 'name').text = names[1]
et.SubElement(student2, 'gender').text = genders[1]
et.SubElement(student2, 'age').text = ages[1]

tree = et.ElementTree(root)
rough_str = et.tostring(root, 'utf-8')

reparsed = minidom.parseString(rough_str)
new_str = reparsed.toprettyxml(indent='\t')
f = open('test.xml', 'w', encoding='utf-8')

f.write(new_str)
f.close()

# test.xml
<?xml version="1.0" ?>
<school>
	<student>
		<name>don</name>
		<gender>male</gender>
		<age>20</age>
	</student>
	<student>
		<name>tom</name>
		<gender>male</gender>
		<age>18</age>
	</student>
</school>
```

And read as below,

```
# test.py
import xml.etree.ElementTree as et
```

```
tree = et.parse('test.xml')

root = tree.getroot()
for stu in root:
    print('name:', stu[0].text, ', gender:', stu[1].text, ', age:', stu[2].text)

# output
name: don , gender: male , age: 20
name: tom , gender: male , age: 18
```

XML is really a tree, with many branches and leaves. Each point for new branch is called node, and we can add, delete, modify. The starting node is called root, and all nodes have name, value, type. Let's check with French verbs, as below,

```
# tense.py
import xml.etree.ElementTree as et

tree = et.parse('tense.xml')

root = tree.getroot()
i=0
for child in root:
    i += 1
    print(child.tag, child.text, child.attrib)
    print(i) # to 149
    for c in child:
        print(c.tag, c.text) # 6
```

That is to say there are only 149 verbs, which really shocks us, because there are much more in reality, how could this be possible? Well, it is because the package embeds learning technique to predict, and it just works like a charm, see below,

```
from mlconjug3 import Conjugator

# initialize the conjugator
conjugator = Conjugator()

# conjugate the verb "mourir"
verb = conjugator.conjugate("mourir")

# info
print(verb.verb_info)
print(verb.iterate())
```

So how does it learn? Based on the template verbs, as below,

```
# template.py
import xml.etree.ElementTree as et

tree = et.parse('tense.xml')
```

```
root = tree.getroot()

for name in root.iter('template'):
    print(name.attrib)

# output
{'name': 'pla:cer'}
{'name': 'référenci:er'}
{'name': 'dép:ecer'}
{'name': 'man:ger'}
{'name': 'pa:yer'}
{'name': 'netto:yer'}
{'name': 'grasse:yer'}
{'name': 'app:eler'}
{'name': 'p:eler'}
{'name': 'harc:eler'}
{'name': 'j:eter'}
{'name': 'ach:eter'}
{'name': 'héb:éter'}
{'name': 's:emer'}
{'name': 'l:éguer'}
{'name': 'diss:équer'}
{'name': 'rév:éler'}
{'name': 'imp:étrer'}
{'name': 'r:égler'}
{'name': 'r:égner'}
{'name': 'cél:ébrer'}
{'name': 'int:égrer'}
{'name': 'décr:éter'}
{'name': 'ali:éner'}
{'name': 'm:ener'}
{'name': 'l:ever'}
{'name': 'p:eser'}
{'name': 's:écher'}
{'name': 'réf:érer'}
{'name': 's:evrer'}
{'name': 'c:éder'}
{'name': 'rec:éper'}
{'name': 'rec:eper'}
{'name': 'l:éser'}
{'name': 'cr:émer'}
{'name': 'abr:éger'}
{'name': 'aim:er'}
{'name': 'enfi:évrer'}
{'name': 'ex:écrer'}
{'name': 'acqu:érir'}
{'name': 'qu:érir'}
{'name': 'ha:ïr'}
{'name': 'amu:ïr'}
{'name': 'fl:eurir'}
{'name': 'ouv:rir'}
{'name': 'dor:mir'}
```

```
{'name': 'men:tir'}
{'name': 'ser:vir'}
{'name': 'bou:illir'}
{'name': 'assaill:ir'}
{'name': 'saill:ir'}
{'name': 'cueill:ir'}
{'name': 't:enir'}
{'name': 'adv:enir'}
{'name': 'fu:ir'}
{'name': 'm:ourir'}
{'name': 'vêt:ir'}
{'name': 'cour:ir'}
{'name': 'fin:ir'}
{'name': 'chauv:ir'}
{'name': 'maud:ire'}
{'name': 'fa:illir'}
{'name': 'g:ésir'}
{'name': 'dé:cevoir'}
{'name': 'd:evoir'}
{'name': 'm:ouvoir'}
{'name': 'prom:ouvoir'}
{'name': 's:avoir'}
{'name': 'v:ouloir'}
{'name': 'va:loir'}
{'name': 'préva:loir'}
{'name': 'p:ouvoir'}
{'name': 'v:oir'}
{'name': 'prév:oir'}
{'name': 'ass:eoir'}
{'name': 'ass:oir'}
{'name': 'surs:eoir'}
{'name': 'surs:oir'}
{'name': 's:eoir'}
{'name': 'pl:euvoir'}
{'name': 'fa:lloir'}
{'name': 'déch:oir'}
{'name': 'pourv:oir'}
{'name': 'ch:oir'}
{'name': 'éch:oir'}
{'name': 'ten:dre'}
{'name': 'vain:cre'}
{'name': 'bat:tre'}
{'name': 'fou:tre'}
{'name': 'm:ettre'}
{'name': 'pr:endre'}
{'name': 'rom:pre'}
{'name': 'mou:dre'}
{'name': 'cou:dre'}
{'name': 'réso:udre'}
{'name': 'abso:udre'}
{'name': 'disso:udre'}
{'name': 'crai:ndre'}
{'name': 'poi:ndre'}
```

```
{'name': 'sui:vre'}
{'name': 'v:ivre'}
{'name': 'rep:aître'}
{'name': 'p:aître'}
{'name': 'par:aître'}
{'name': 'n:aître'}
{'name': 'ren:aître'}
{'name': 'cr:oître'}
{'name': 'recr:oître'}
{'name': 'accr:oître'}
{'name': 'r:ire'}
{'name': 'circonc:ire'}
{'name': 'concl:ure'}
{'name': 'incl:ure'}
{'name': 'nui:re'}
{'name': 'lu:ire'}
{'name': 'condui:re'}
{'name': 'écri:re'}
{'name': 'cr:oire'}
{'name': 'suff:ire'}
{'name': 'd:ire'}
{'name': 'interd:ire'}
{'name': 'méd:ire'}
{'name': 'préd:ire'}
{'name': 'l:ire'}
{'name': 'b:oire'}
{'name': 't:aire'}
{'name': 'pl:aire'}
{'name': 'f:aire'}
{'name': 'extra:ire'}
{'name': 'bra:ire'}
{'name': 's:ourdre'}
{'name': 'cl:ore'}
{'name': 'éclo:re'}
{'name': 'forclo:re'}
{'name': 'fri:re'}
{'name': 'brui:re'}
{'name': 'oi:ndre'}
{'name': 'env:oyer'}
{'name': ':avoir'}
{'name': ':être'}
{'name': ':aller'}
{'name': 'app:aroir'}
{'name': 'cha:loir'}
{'name': ':ravoir'}
{'name': 'est:er'}
{'name': 'fér:ir'}
{'name': 'o:uïr'}
{'name': 'occi:re'}
{'name': 'brumass:er'}
```

Do classification to similarize the format, as below,

```
# tense.py
from mlconjug3 import Conjugator

# initialize the conjugator
conjugator = Conjugator()

# input

verb = conjugator.conjugate(input("Enter: "))

# info
print(verb.verb_info)
print(verb.iterate())

# output
Enter: baxer
mlconjug3.verbs.verbs.VerbInfo(baxer, bax, aim:er)
[('Infinitif', 'Infinitif Présent', 'baxer'), ('Indicatif', 'Présent', 'je', 'baxe'), ('Indicatif', 'Présent', 'tu', 'baxes'), ('Indicatif', 'Présent', 'il (elle, on)', 'baxe'), ('Indicatif', 'Présent', 'nous', 'baxons'), ('Indicatif', 'Présent', 'vous', 'baxez'), ('Indicatif', 'Présent', 'ils (elles)', 'baxent'), ('Indicatif', 'Imparfait', 'je', 'baxais'), ('Indicatif', 'Imparfait', 'tu', 'baxais'), ('Indicatif', 'Imparfait', 'il (elle, on)', 'baxait'), ('Indicatif', 'Imparfait', 'nous', 'baxions'), ('Indicatif', 'Imparfait', 'vous', 'baxiez'), ('Indicatif', 'Imparfait', 'ils (elles)', 'baxaient'), ('Indicatif', 'Futur', 'je', 'baxerai'), ('Indicatif', 'Futur', 'tu', 'baxeras'), ('Indicatif', 'Futur', 'il (elle, on)', 'baxera'), ('Indicatif', 'Futur', 'nous', 'baxerons'), ('Indicatif', 'Futur', 'vous', 'baxerez'), ('Indicatif', 'Futur', 'ils (elles)', 'baxeront'), ('Indicatif', 'Passé Simple', 'je', 'baxai'), ('Indicatif', 'Passé Simple', 'tu', 'baxas'), ('Indicatif', 'Passé Simple', 'il (elle, on)', 'baxa'), ('Indicatif', 'Passé Simple', 'nous', 'baxâmes'), ('Indicatif', 'Passé Simple', 'vous', 'baxâtes'), ('Indicatif', 'Passé Simple', 'ils (elles)', 'baxèrent'), ('Conditionnel', 'Présent', 'je', 'baxerais'), ('Conditionnel', 'Présent', 'tu', 'baxerais'), ('Conditionnel', 'Présent', 'il (elle, on)', 'baxerait'), ('Conditionnel', 'Présent', 'nous', 'baxerions'), ('Conditionnel', 'Présent', 'vous', 'baxeriez'), ('Conditionnel', 'Présent', 'ils (elles)', 'baxeraient'), ('Subjonctif', 'Présent', 'je', 'baxe'), ('Subjonctif', 'Présent', 'tu', 'baxes'), ('Subjonctif', 'Présent', 'il (elle, on)', 'baxe'), ('Subjonctif', 'Présent', 'nous', 'baxions'), ('Subjonctif', 'Présent', 'vous', 'baxiez'), ('Subjonctif', 'Présent', 'ils (elles)', 'baxent'), ('Subjonctif', 'Imparfait', 'je', 'baxasse'), ('Subjonctif', 'Imparfait', 'tu', 'baxasses'), ('Subjonctif', 'Imparfait', 'il (elle, on)', 'baxât'), ('Subjonctif', 'Imparfait', 'nous', 'baxassions'), ('Subjonctif', 'Imparfait', 'vous', 'baxassiez'), ('Subjonctif', 'Imparfait', 'ils (elles)', 'baxassent'), ('Imperatif', 'Imperatif Présent', '', 'baxez'), ('Participe', 'Participe Présent', 'baxant'), ('Participe', 'Participe Passé', 'masculin singulier', 'baxé'), ('Participe', 'Participe Passé', 'masculin pluriel', 'baxés'), ('Participe', 'Participe Passé', 'feminin singulier', 'baxée'), ('Participe', 'Participe Passé', 'feminin pluriel', 'baxées')]
```

So now you see the learning process nature, mimic and correct.

20 Scikit Learn

A common use for SL is regression, and hand writing recongininition is now very useful, see below,

```
import matplotlib.pyplot as plt

from sklearn import datasets

# Load the digits dataset
digits = datasets.load_digits()

# Display the last digit
plt.figure(figsize=(3, 3))
image = digits.images[4]
print(image)
plt.imsave("digit4.png", image, cmap='gray')

# output
[[ 0.  0.  0.  1. 11.  0.  0.  0.]
 [ 0.  0.  0.  7.  8.  0.  0.  0.]
 [ 0.  0.  1. 13.  6.  2.  2.  0.]
 [ 0.  0.  7. 15.  0.  9.  8.  0.]
 [ 0.  5. 16. 10.  0. 16.  6.  0.]
 [ 0.  4. 15. 16. 13. 16.  1.  0.]
 [ 0.  0.  0.  3. 15. 10.  0.  0.]
 [ 0.  0.  0.  2. 16.  4.  0.  0.]]
```

To predict the `digit4.png`, we need first train our data to build the learning machine, as below,

```
from sklearn import datasets
digits = datasets.load_digits()

# flatten the images
n_samples = len(digits.images)
data = digits.images.reshape((n_samples, -1))

from sklearn import svm
# Create a classifier: a support vector classifier
clf = svm.SVC(gamma=0.001)
from sklearn.model_selection import train_test_split
# Split data into 50% train and 50% test subsets
X_train, X_test, y_train, y_test = train_test_split(
    data, digits.target, test_size=0.5, shuffle=False
)

# Learn the digits on the train subset
clf.fit(X_train, y_train)

# Predict the value of the digit on the test subset
```

```
predicted = clf.predict(X_test)
print(X_test, predicted)
```

Then we will replace our `digit4.png` with `X_test`, and do prediction, as below,

```
#importing required modules
import matplotlib.pyplot as plt
import matplotlib.image as mpimg

#read the original image
img_rgb = mpimg.imread('digit4.png')
plt.imshow(img_rgb)
#display the original image
plt.show()
print('Type:', type(img_rgb))
print('dtype:', img_rgb.dtype)
print('shape:', img_rgb.shape) # (8,8,4)
```

The tricky thing is `digit4.png` is made of a 3D numpy array, but made from a 2D numpy array. When is the array changed? `imsave`.

Image type	Coordinates
2D grayscale	(row, column)
2D multichannel	(row, column, channel)
3D grayscale (or volumetric)	(plane, row, column)
3D multichannel	(plane, row, column, channel)

So the `digit4.png` is a 3D grayscale graph, and the `shape` means it is a 8 plane, 8 row, 4 column graph. That is to say, it will be in a list of 8 index, and the 8 index each is a list of 8 row and 4 column, as below,

```
print(img_rgb)

# output
[[[0.        0.        0.        1.        ]
  [0.        0.        0.        1.        ]
  [0.        0.        0.        1.        ]
  [0.0627451 0.0627451 0.0627451 1.        ]
  [0.6901961 0.6901961 0.6901961 1.        ]
  [0.        0.        0.        1.        ]
  [0.        0.        0.        1.        ]
  [0.        0.        0.        1.        ]] # plane 0

 [[0.        0.        0.        1.        ]  # row 0
  [0.        0.        0.        1.        ]
  [0.        0.        0.        1.        ]
  [0.4392157 0.4392157 0.4392157 1.        ]
  [0.5019608 0.5019608 0.5019608 1.        ]
```

```
 [0.         0.         0.         1.        ]
 [0.         0.         0.         1.        ]
 [0.         0.         0.         1.        ]]
  #column 0
[[0.         0.         0.         1.        ]
 [0.         0.         0.         1.        ]
 [0.0627451  0.0627451  0.0627451  1.        ]
 [0.8156863  0.8156863  0.8156863  1.        ]
 [0.3764706  0.3764706  0.3764706  1.        ]
 [0.1254902  0.1254902  0.1254902  1.        ]
 [0.1254902  0.1254902  0.1254902  1.        ]
 [0.         0.         0.         1.        ]]

[[0.         0.         0.         1.        ]
 [0.         0.         0.         1.        ]
 [0.4392157  0.4392157  0.4392157  1.        ]
 [0.9411765  0.9411765  0.9411765  1.        ]
 [0.         0.         0.         1.        ]
 [0.5647059  0.5647059  0.5647059  1.        ]
 [0.5019608  0.5019608  0.5019608  1.        ]
 [0.         0.         0.         1.        ]]

[[0.         0.         0.         1.        ]
 [0.3137255  0.3137255  0.3137255  1.        ]
 [1.         1.         1.         1.        ]
 [0.627451   0.627451   0.627451   1.        ]
 [0.         0.         0.         1.        ]
 [1.         1.         1.         1.        ]
 [0.3764706  0.3764706  0.3764706  1.        ]
 [0.         0.         0.         1.        ]]

[[0.         0.         0.         1.        ]
 [0.2509804  0.2509804  0.2509804  1.        ]
 [0.9411765  0.9411765  0.9411765  1.        ]
 [1.         1.         1.         1.        ]
 [0.8156863  0.8156863  0.8156863  1.        ]
 [1.         1.         1.         1.        ]
 [0.0627451  0.0627451  0.0627451  1.        ]
 [0.         0.         0.         1.        ]]

[[0.         0.         0.         1.        ]
 [0.         0.         0.         1.        ]
 [0.         0.         0.         1.        ]
 [0.1882353  0.1882353  0.1882353  1.        ]
 [0.9411765  0.9411765  0.9411765  1.        ]
 [0.627451   0.627451   0.627451   1.        ]
 [0.         0.         0.         1.        ]
 [0.         0.         0.         1.        ]]

[[0.         0.         0.         1.        ]
 [0.         0.         0.         1.        ]
 [0.         0.         0.         1.        ]
 [0.1254902  0.1254902  0.1254902  1.        ]
```

```
  [1.        1.        1.        1.        ]
  [0.2509804 0.2509804 0.2509804 1.        ]
  [0.        0.        0.        1.        ]
  [0.        0.        0.        1.        ]]]
```

The graph can be reshaped, see below,

```
# reshape
b = img_rgb.reshape(4,8,8)
print(b)

# output
[[[0.        0.        0.        1.        0.        0.        0.
   1.       ]
  [0.        0.        0.        1.        0.0627451 0.0627451 0.0627451
   1.       ]
  [0.6901961 0.6901961 0.6901961 1.        0.        0.        0.
   1.       ]
  [0.        0.        0.        1.        0.        0.        0.
   1.       ]
  [0.        0.        0.        1.        0.        0.        0.
   1.       ]
  [0.        0.        0.        1.        0.4392157 0.4392157 0.4392157
   1.       ]
  [0.5019608 0.5019608 0.5019608 1.        0.        0.        0.
   1.       ]
  [0.        0.        0.        1.        0.        0.        0.
   1.       ]]

 [[0.        0.        0.        1.        0.        0.        0.
   1.       ]
  [0.0627451 0.0627451 0.0627451 1.        0.8156863 0.8156863 0.8156863
   1.       ]
  [0.3764706 0.3764706 0.3764706 1.        0.1254902 0.1254902 0.1254902
   1.       ]
  [0.1254902 0.1254902 0.1254902 1.        0.        0.        0.
   1.       ]
  [0.        0.        0.        1.        0.        0.        0.
   1.       ]
  [0.4392157 0.4392157 0.4392157 1.        0.9411765 0.9411765 0.9411765
   1.       ]
  [0.        0.        0.        1.        0.5647059 0.5647059 0.5647059
   1.       ]
  [0.5019608 0.5019608 0.5019608 1.        0.        0.        0.
   1.       ]]

 [[0.        0.        0.        1.        0.3137255 0.3137255 0.3137255
   1.       ]
  [1.        1.        1.        1.        0.627451  0.627451  0.627451
   1.       ]
  [0.        0.        0.        1.        1.        1.        1.
   1.       ]
  [0.3764706 0.3764706 0.3764706 1.        0.        0.        0.
```

```
  1.        ]
 [0.        0.        0.        1.        0.2509804 0.2509804 0.2509804
  1.        ]
 [0.9411765 0.9411765 0.9411765 1.        1.        1.        1.
  1.        ]
 [0.8156863 0.8156863 0.8156863 1.        1.        1.        1.
  1.        ]
 [0.0627451 0.0627451 0.0627451 1.        0.        0.        0.
  1.        ]]

[[0.        0.        0.        1.        0.        0.        0.
  1.        ]
 [0.        0.        0.        1.        0.1882353 0.1882353 0.1882353
  1.        ]
 [0.9411765 0.9411765 0.9411765 1.        0.627451  0.627451  0.627451
  1.        ]
 [0.        0.        0.        1.        0.        0.        0.
  1.        ]
 [0.        0.        0.        1.        0.        0.        0.
  1.        ]
 [0.        0.        0.        1.        0.1254902 0.1254902 0.1254902
  1.        ]
 [1.        1.        1.        1.        0.2509804 0.2509804 0.2509804
  1.        ]
 [0.        0.        0.        1.        0.        0.        0.
  1.        ]]]
```

And the two arrays are not the same, see below,

```
import numpy as np
print(np.array_equal(b, img_rgb)) # False
```

So how to convert back the rgb to grayscale, and normalized to 0 to 16? Use the equation,

```
'''
norm1 = (non1 - min_val) / (max_val - min_val)
gray = 0.299*rgb[:,:,0] + 0.587*rgb[:,:,1] + 0.114*rgb[:,:,2]
'''

gray = 0.299*rgb[:,:,0] + 0.587*rgb[:,:,1] + 0.114*rgb[:,:,2]
org_digits = gray * (max_val - min_val) + min_val
print(np.round(org_digits))

# output
[[ 0.  0.  0.  1. 11.  0.  0.  0.]
 [ 0.  0.  0.  7.  8.  0.  0.  0.]
 [ 0.  0.  1. 13.  6.  2.  2.  0.]
 [ 0.  0.  7. 15.  0.  9.  8.  0.]
 [ 0.  5. 16. 10.  0. 16.  6.  0.]
 [ 0.  4. 15. 16. 13. 16.  1.  0.]
```

```
 [ 0.  0.  0.  3. 15. 10.  0.  0.]
 [ 0.  0.  0.  2. 16.  4.  0.  0.]]
```

Now we can use this 8 x 8 array to predict the number, and it is just 4, as below,

```
digit4 = np.round(org_digits)
imgdata = np.reshape(digit4, (1,64)) # reshape to fit in
t = [(imgdata[0])]

class bcolors:
    HEADER = '\033[95m'
    OKBLUE = '\033[94m'
    OKCYAN = '\033[96m'
    OKGREEN = '\033[92m'
    WARNING = '\033[93m'
    FAIL = '\033[91m'
    ENDC = '\033[0m'
    BOLD = '\033[1m'
    UNDERLINE = '\033[4m'

print(f"{bcolors.OKBLUE}{t}{bcolors.ENDC} {clf.predict(t)}")

# output
[array([ 0.,  0.,  0.,  1., 11.,  0.,  0.,  0.,  0.,  0.,  0.,  7.,  8.,
         0.,  0.,  0.,  0.,  0.,  1., 13.,  6.,  2.,  2.,  0.,  0.,  0.,
         7., 15.,  0.,  9.,  8.,  0.,  0.,  5., 16., 10.,  0., 16.,  6.,
         0.,  0.,  4., 15., 16., 13., 16.,  1.,  0.,  0.,  0.,  0.,  3.,
        15., 10.,  0.,  0.,  0.,  0.,  0.,  2., 16.,  4.,  0.,  0.],
       dtype=float32)] [4]
```

So the essential thing is that we must provide a 1 x 64 numpy array, float but with no decimals, and the SVC would do the trick, see below,

```
img=np.random.randint(0,16,size=[1,8,8])
img=(img[0])*1.0
imgdata = np.reshape(img, (1,64))
t=[(imgdata[0])]
print(t, clf.predict(t))

imgdata = np.random.randint(16, size=(1, 64))
t=[(imgdata[0])]
print(t, clf.predict(t))

imgdata = np.random.gamma(2, 2, 64)
digit=np.round(imgdata)
imgdata = np.reshape(digit, (1,64))
t = [(imgdata[0])]
print(t, clf.predict(t))
```

Checkout https://numpy.org/doc/1.16/reference/routines.random.html for more distributions, or one can really random input, as below,

```
print("Enter the array in a single line (separated by space): ")

# User input of entries in a
# single line separated by space
entries = list(map(int, input().split()))

# For printing the array
imgdata = np.array(entries).reshape(1, 64)
print(imgdata)
t=[(imgdata[0])]
print(t, clf.predict(t))
```

And we don't really need to save the array in a graph, see below,

```
from sklearn import datasets

# Load the digits dataset
digits = datasets.load_digits()

image = digits.images[4]
print(image)
import numpy as np
# save
np.save("digit.npy", image)
```

And to read and predict, as below,

```
import numpy as np

data = np.load("digit.npy")
print(data, type(data), data.shape)
imgdata = np.reshape(data, (1,64))
t=[(imgdata[0])]

from sklearn import datasets
digits = datasets.load_digits()

# flatten the images
n_samples = len(digits.images)
data = digits.images.reshape((n_samples, -1))

from sklearn import svm
# Create a classifier: a support vector classifier
clf = svm.SVC(gamma=0.001)
from sklearn.model_selection import train_test_split
# Split data into 50% train and 50% test subsets
X_train, X_test, y_train, y_test = train_test_split(
    data, digits.target, test_size=0.5, shuffle=False
)

# Learn the digits on the train subset
clf.fit(X_train, y_train)
```

```
# Predict the value of the digit on the test subset
print(t, clf.predict(t))
```

And we can also configure the array inside the file, as below,

```
import numpy as np

d='''
[[ 0.   0.   0.   1. 11.   0.   0.   0.]
 [ 0.   0.   0.   7.   8.   0.   0.   0.]
 [ 0.   0.   1. 13.   6.   2.   2.   0.]
 [ 0.   0.   7. 15.   0.   9.   8.   0.]
 [ 0.   5. 16. 10.   0. 16.   6.   0.]
 [ 0.   4. 15. 16. 13. 16.   1.   0.]
 [ 0.   0.   0.   3. 15. 10.   0.   0.]
 [ 0.   0.   0.   2. 16.   4.   0.   0.]]
'''
print(d)

import re

org_string = d

pattern = r'[\[\]\n\.]'

mod_string = re.sub(pattern, '', org_string)
mod_string=mod_string.split()
r = [float(ele) for ele in mod_string]

def split_list(list_object, chunk_size):
    chunks = []
    for start in range(0, len(list_object), chunk_size):
        stop = start + chunk_size
        chunks.append(list_object[start:stop])
    return chunks

m = split_list(r, 8)

data = np.array(m)

print(data, type(data), data.shape)
imgdata = np.reshape(data, (1,64))
t=[(imgdata[0])]

from sklearn import datasets
digits = datasets.load_digits()

# flatten the images
n_samples = len(digits.images)
data = digits.images.reshape((n_samples, -1))

from sklearn import svm
```

```
# Create a classifier: a support vector classifier
clf = svm.SVC(gamma=0.001)
from sklearn.model_selection import train_test_split
# Split data into 50% train and 50% test subsets
X_train, X_test, y_train, y_test = train_test_split(
    data, digits.target, test_size=0.5, shuffle=False
)

# Learn the digits on the train subset
clf.fit(X_train, y_train)

# Predict the value of the digit on the test subset
print(clf.predict(t))
```

21 list

Python list is a collection of items, closed by square brackets, seperated by comma. List is commonly used to arrange data, and many other data is built from list, so we do a summary here for the list.

21.1 Creation

```
my_list = [1, 'a', True, 3.14]
```

21.2 Len Keyword

```
len(my_list)
```

21.3 Access Item

```
first_item = my_list[0]
last_item = my_list[-1]
```

21.4 List Keyword

```
thislist = list(("apple", "banana", "cherry")) # note the double round-brackets
print(thislist)
```

21.5 Append Method

```
thislist = ["apple", "banana", "cherry"]
thislist.append("orange")
```

21.6 Extend Method

```
thislist = ["apple", "banana", "cherry"]
tropical = ["mango", "pineapple", "papaya"]
thislist.extend(tropical)
```

21.7 Pop Method

```
thislist = ["apple", "banana", "cherry"]
thislist.pop(1)
```

21.8 Clear Method

```
thislist = ["apple", "banana", "cherry"]
thislist.clear()
```

21.9 Delete Keyword

```
thislist = ["apple", "banana", "cherry"]
del thislist[0]
```

21.10 List Comprehension

```
fruits = ["apple", "banana", "cherry", "kiwi", "mango"]
newlist = [x for x in fruits if "a" in x]

ints = [1, 2, 3, 4, 5]
floats = [float(ele) for ele in ints]
```

21.11 Remove Method

```
thislist = ["apple", "banana", "cherry", "banana", "kiwi"]
thislist.remove("banana")
```

21.12 Join List

```
list1 = ["a", "b", "c"]
list2 = [1, 2, 3]
list3 = list1 + list2
print(list3)
```

21.13 Scalarize List

```
a = [[1,2,3],[4,5,6],[7],[8,9]]
t = []
for i in a: t.extend(i)
print(t)
```

21.14 Shallow Copy List

```
countries = ["United States", "Canada", "Poland", "Germany", "Austria"]
nations = countries[:]
id(countries) == id(nations) # False
id(nations[1]) == id(countries[1]) # True
```

and we can use the copy function

```
>>> from copy import copy

>>> countries = ["United States", "Canada", "Poland", "Germany", "Austria"]

>>> nations = copy(countries)
>>> nations
['United States', 'Canada', 'Poland', 'Germany', 'Austria']

>>> id(countries) == id(nations)
False
>>> id(countries[0]) == id(nations[0])
True
```

21.15 Deep Copy List

```
>>> from copy import deepcopy

>>> matrix = [[1, 2, 3], [4, 5, 6], [7, 8, 9]]
>>> matrix_copy = deepcopy(matrix)

>>> id(matrix) == id(matrix_copy)
False
>>> id(matrix[0]) == id(matrix_copy[0])
False
>>> id(matrix[1]) == id(matrix_copy[1])
False
```

21.16 Slice Method

```
a = ["a", "b", "c", "d", "e", "f", "g", "h"]
x = slice(0, 8, 3)

letters = ["A", "a", "B", "b", "C", "c", "D", "d"]
upper_letters = letters[slice(0, None, 2)]
lower_letters = letters[slice(1, None, 2)]
```

21.16 List Plus

```
[0, 1, 2, 3] + [4, 5, 6] + [7, 8, 9] # [0, 1, 2, 3, 4, 5, 6, 7, 8, 9]
```

21.17 List Multiplication

```
[0, 1, 2, 3] * 3
```

21.18 Map Keyword

Use Map to change the string into numbers,

```
numbers = ["1", "2", "3", "4", "5"]

numbers = list(map(int, numbers))
```

Faster than,

```
numbers = [int(i) for i in numbers]
```

Equivelant to,

```
for i, number in enumerate(numbers):
    numbers[i] = int(number)
```

21.19 Index Method

```
usernames = ["john", "jane", "bob", "david", "eve"]

usernames.index("eve") # 4
```

21.20 Min and Max

```
min([3, 5, 9, 1, -5]) # -5

max([3, 5, 9, 1, -5]) # 9
```

21.21 ND Matrix

Matrix is a more complex list, build 5 x 5 zeros,

```
matrix = []
for row in range(5):
    matrix.append([])
    for _ in range(5):
        matrix[row].append(0)
```

List comprehension,

```
[[0 for _ in range(5)] for _ in range(5)]
```

Multiplication,

```
matrix = [[0] * 5] * 5
```

21.22 Change column

```
matrix[0][0] = 1

# output
print(matrix) # in one line
for i in matrix: print(i) # in multiple line
```

21.23 Flatten matrix

```
flattened = []
for row in matrix: flattened.extend(row)
print(flattened) # [0, 1, 2, 10, 11, 12, 20, 21, 22]
```

21.24 Chunk List

```
def split_list(list_object, chunk_size):
    chunks = []
    for start in range(0, len(list_object), chunk_size):
        stop = start + chunk_size
        chunks.append(list_object[start:stop])
    return chunks

def prows(list_object):
    for i in list_object: print(i)

chunks = split_list([0, 1, 2, 10, 11, 12, 20, 21, 22], 3)
prows(chunks)

# output
[0, 1, 2]
[10, 11, 12]
[20, 21, 22]
```

21.25 Matrix Transpose

```
def prows(list_object):
    for i in list_object: print(i)
T = [[1, 2, 3], [4, 5, 6]]
prows(T)
T = list(map(list, zip(*T)))
prows(T)
T = [[row[i] for row in T] for i in range(len(T[0]))]
prows(T)
```

21.26 Matrix Inverse

Given two matrixes **A** and **B**, if there is an unknown matrix **X** in the form **AX=B**, we can multiply both sides by the inverse of A, provided the inverse exists.

We get **inv(A).A.X=inv(A).B**, where **inv(A).A=I**, **I** is the identity matrix. Also, **IX=X**, because the multiplication of any matrix with an identity matrix leaves it unaltered.

So we get, **X=inv(A).B**. This way X can be found by multiplying B with the inverse of matrix A.

```
def prows(list_object):
    for i in list_object: print(i)
```

```
# This function returns the transpose of a matrix
def transposeMatrix(m):
    transpose=list(map(list,zip(*m)))
    print('transpose of cofactor matrix->',transpose)
    return transpose

# This function returns the minor matrix of the element
# at postion i,j
def getMatrixMinor(m,i,j):
    minor_matrix = [row[:j] + row[j+1:] for row in (m[:i]+m[i+1:])]
    return minor_matrix

# This function find the determinant of the matrix
def getMatrixDeternminant(m):
    #base case for 2x2 matrix
    if len(m) == 2:
        return m[0][0]*m[1][1]-m[0][1]*m[1][0]
    determinant = 0
    for c in range(len(m)):
                                                determinant      +=      ((-1)**c)*m[0]
[c]*getMatrixDeternminant(getMatrixMinor(m,0,c))
    print('determinant=',determinant)
    return determinant

def getMatrixInverse(m):
    determinant = getMatrixDeternminant(m)
    if(determinant==0):
        print('Error! Determinant of the matrix is zero')
        print('Inverse cannot be calculated')
        return

    #special case for 2x2 matrix:
    if len(m) == 2:
        return [[m[1][1]/determinant, -1*m[0][1]/determinant],
                [-1*m[1][0]/determinant, m[0][0]/determinant]]

    #find matrix of cofactors
    cofactors = []
    for r in range(len(m)):
        cofactorRow = []
        for c in range(len(m)):
            minor = getMatrixMinor(m,r,c)
            cofactorRow.append(((-1)**(r+c)) * getMatrixDeternminant(minor))
        cofactors.append(cofactorRow)

    # Transposing the cofactor matrix to get disjoint
    Disjoint = transposeMatrix(cofactors)

    # Dividing each element of the adjoint matrix by the determinant
    for r in range(len(Disjoint)):
        for c in range(len(Disjoint)):
            Disjoint[r][c] = Disjoint[r][c]/determinant
```

```
    return Disjoint

# Input matrix as a list of lists
a=[[1,2,3],[0,1,4],[5,6,0]]
a = [[5, -2, 2, 7], [1, 0, 0, 3], [-3, 1, 5, 0], [3, -1, -9, 4]]
print("the matrix->")
prows((a))

# Print the inverse
print("Inverse of the matrix->")
prows(getMatrixInverse(a))
```

22 logging

Sometimes we wish to switch the print, or change the style, as below,

```
def prows(list_object, style):
    if style == 0:
        for i in list_object: print(i)
    if style == 1:
        print(list_object)
    if style == 2:
        for i, j in enumerate(list_object): print(i, j)
    if style == 3:
        pass
T = [[1, 2, 3], [4, 5, 6]]
prows(T, 0)
prows(T, 1)
prows(T, 2)
prows(T, 3)
```

Python has a logging module to quickly get this job done, in 5 levels, debug, info, warning, error, critical. The only thing we need to do is select the level, and we can even give a format, as below,

```
import logging

from logging.handlers import HTTPHandler

import sys

logger = logging.getLogger(__name__)

logger.setLevel(level=logging.DEBUG)

# StreamHandler

stream_handler = logging.StreamHandler(sys.stdout)

stream_handler.setLevel(level=logging.DEBUG)
```

```
logger.addHandler(stream_handler)

# FileHandler

file_handler = logging.FileHandler('output.log')

file_handler.setLevel(level=logging.INFO)

formatter = logging.Formatter('%(asctime)s - %(name)s - %(levelname)s - %
(message)s')

file_handler.setFormatter(formatter)

logger.addHandler(file_handler)

# HTTPHandler

http_handler = HTTPHandler(host='localhost:8001', url='example', method='POST')

logger.addHandler(http_handler)

#handler close
# Log

logger.info('>>This is a log info')

logger.debug('>>Debugging')

logger.warning('>>Warning exists')

logger.info('>>Finish')
```

Notice the HTTP handler is a server opened on port 8001, and waiting for POST request, as below,

```
from http.server import BaseHTTPRequestHandler, HTTPServer
import time

hostName = "localhost"
serverPort = 8001

class MyServer(BaseHTTPRequestHandler):
    def do_GET(self):
        self.send_response(200)
        self.send_header("Content-type", "text/html")
        self.end_headers()
           self.wfile.write(bytes("<html><head><title>example</title></head>", "utf-
8"))
        self.wfile.write(bytes("<p>Request: %s</p>" % self.path, "utf-8"))
        self.wfile.write(bytes("<body>", "utf-8"))
        self.wfile.write(bytes("<p>This is an example for get.</p>", "utf-8"))
```

```
        self.wfile.write(bytes("</body></html>", "utf-8"))

    def do_POST(self):
        self.send_response(200)
        self.send_header('Content-type','text/html')
        self.end_headers()

        message = "Hello, World! Here is a POST response"

        print('>> post:', self.path, self.client_address, message)
        self.wfile.write(bytes("<p>This is an example for get.</p>", "utf-8"))

if __name__ == "__main__":
    webServer = HTTPServer((hostName, serverPort), MyServer)
    print("Server started http://%s:%s" % (hostName, serverPort))

    try:
        webServer.serve_forever()
    except KeyboardInterrupt:
        webServer.server_close()
    print("Server stopped.")
```

Now, let's do logging for the previous matrix inverse, through HTTP POST, see below,

```
C:\Users\Lenovo\Project>dir
 Volume in drive C is Windows-SSD
 Volume Serial Number is 5286-8C92

 Directory of C:\Users\Lenovo\Project

2024/09/08  14:15    <DIR>          .
2024/09/08  14:03    <DIR>          ..
2024/09/08  12:47    <DIR>          cgi-bin
2024/09/08  14:58               325 index.html
2024/09/08  14:59               543 server.py
               2 File(s)            868 bytes
               3 Dir(s)  42,140,762,112 bytes free

# server.py
from http.server import HTTPServer, CGIHTTPRequestHandler

if __name__ == '__main__':
    try:
        handler = CGIHTTPRequestHandler
        handler.cgi_directories = ['/cgi-bin', '/htbin']
        #port = int(sys.argv[1])
        port = 8001
        print('port is %d' % port)
        server = HTTPServer(('', port), handler)
        print('Welcome to my website -> localhost:8001')
        server.serve_forever()
```

```
    except KeyboardInterrupt:
        print('^C received, shutting down server')
        server.socket.close()

# index.html
<html>
<head>
<title>Matrix</title>
</head>


<body>
<h1>Matrix
</h1>
<p>eg. -> [[1,2,3],[0,1,4],[5,6,0]]</p>

<div><form action="cgi-bin/setup.py", method="POST">

  <input type="text" id="matrix" name="matrix" value=""><br>

  <input type="submit" value="Submit">
</form></div>
</body>
</html>

# cgi-bin\setup.py
import cgi
# Create instance of FieldStorage
form = cgi.FieldStorage()
# Get data from form
matrix = form.getvalue('matrix')

import sys
import logging
logger = logging.getLogger(__name__)
logger.setLevel(level=logging.DEBUG)

# StreamHandler
stream_handler = logging.StreamHandler(sys.stdout)
stream_handler.setLevel(level=logging.DEBUG)
logger.addHandler(stream_handler)

# Input matrix as a list of lists
logger.info('>>the matrix was: '+matrix)
#[[1,2,3],[0,1,4],[5,6,0]]

ls = len(matrix.split('],'))

import re

pattern = r'[\[\]\']'
```

```
ms = re.sub(pattern, '', matrix)
ms=ms.split(',')

ms = [int(ele) for ele in ms]

def split_list(list_object, chunk_size):
    chunks = []
    for start in range(0, len(list_object), chunk_size):
        stop = start + chunk_size
        chunks.append(list_object[start:stop])
    return chunks

matrix = split_list(ms, ls)


# This function returns the transpose of a matrix
def transposeMatrix(m):
    transpose=list(map(list,zip(*m)))
    logger.debug('transpose of cofactor matrix->',str(transpose))
    return transpose

# This function returns the minor matrix of the element
# at postion i,j
def getMatrixMinor(m,i,j):
    minor_matrix = [row[:j] + row[j+1:] for row in (m[:i]+m[i+1:])]
    return minor_matrix

# This function find the determinant of the matrix
def getMatrixDeternminant(m):
    #base case for 2x2 matrix
    if len(m) == 2:
        return m[0][0]*m[1][1]-m[0][1]*m[1][0]
    determinant = 0
    for c in range(len(m)):
                                            determinant      +=       ((-1)**c)*m[0]
[c]*getMatrixDeternminant(getMatrixMinor(m,0,c))
    logger.debug('>>determinant = '+str(determinant))

    return determinant

def getMatrixInverse(m):
    determinant = getMatrixDeternminant(m)
    if(determinant==0):
        logger.error('Error! Determinant of the matrix is zero')
        return

    #special case for 2x2 matrix:
    if len(m) == 2:
        return [[m[1][1]/determinant, -1*m[0][1]/determinant],
                [-1*m[1][0]/determinant, m[0][0]/determinant]]

    #find matrix of cofactors
    cofactors = []
```

```
    for r in range(len(m)):
        cofactorRow = []
        for c in range(len(m)):
            minor = getMatrixMinor(m,r,c)
            cofactorRow.append(((-1)**(r+c)) * getMatrixDeternminant(minor))
        cofactors.append(cofactorRow)

    # Transposing the cofactor matrix to get disjoint
    Disjoint = transposeMatrix(cofactors)

    # Dividing each element of the adjoint matrix by the determinant
    for r in range(len(Disjoint)):
        for c in range(len(Disjoint)):
            Disjoint[r][c] = Disjoint[r][c]/determinant

    return Disjoint


# Print the inverse
inverse = []
inverse = getMatrixInverse(matrix)

# Generate response
print("Content-Type: text/html")    # HTML is following
print()                             # blank line, end of headers
print(f"")
print(f"<h1>Matrix</h1>")
print(f"<p>Your input matrix was\n {matrix}</p>")
print(f"")
print(f"<p>Your inverse matrix is\n {inverse}</p>")
```

The 5 levels, debug, info, warning, error, critical maps to 10, 20, 30, 40, 50. Setting the basic config to info, basicly means debug is off, as below,

```
import logging
logging.basicConfig(level=logging.WARNING)

def hypotenuse(a, b):
    """Compute the hypotenuse"""
    return (a**2 + b**2)**0.5

kwargs = {'a':3, 'b':4, 'c':hypotenuse(3, 4)}

logging.debug("a = {a}, b = {b}".format(**kwargs))
logging.info("Hypotenuse of {a}, {b} is {c}".format(**kwargs))
logging.warning("a={a} and b={b} are equal".format(**kwargs))
logging.error("a={a} and b={b} cannot be negative".format(**kwargs))
logging.critical("Hypotenuse of {a}, {b} is {c}".format(**kwargs))

#> WARNING:root:a=3 and b=3 are equal
#> ERROR:root:a=-1 and b=4 cannot be negative
#> CRITICAL:root:Hypotenuse of a, b is 5.0
```

If we do not want the program to be stopped, we can also log the exception, as below,

```
import logging

# Create or get the logger
logger = logging.getLogger(__name__)

# set log level
logger.setLevel(logging.INFO)

def divide(x, y):
    try:
        out = x / y
    except ZeroDivisionError:
        logger.exception("Division by zero problem")
    else:
        return out

# Logs
logger.error("Divide {x} / {y} = {c}".format(x=10, y=0, c=divide(10,0)))

#> ERROR:__main__:Division by zero problem
#> Traceback (most recent call last):
#>   File "<ipython-input-16-a010a44fdc0a>", line 12, in divide
#>     out = x / y
#> ZeroDivisionError: division by zero
#> ERROR:__main__:None
```

We can also formatter our logging with color, as below,

```
import logging
import datetime

class CustomFormatter(logging.Formatter):

    grey = '\x1b[38;21m'
    blue = '\x1b[38;5;39m'
    yellow = '\x1b[38;5;226m'
    red = '\x1b[38;5;196m'
    bold_red = '\x1b[31;1m'
    reset = '\x1b[0m'

    def __init__(self, fmt):
        super().__init__()
        self.fmt = fmt
        self.FORMATS = {
            logging.DEBUG: self.grey + self.fmt + self.reset,
            logging.INFO: self.blue + self.fmt + self.reset,
            logging.WARNING: self.yellow + self.fmt + self.reset,
            logging.ERROR: self.red + self.fmt + self.reset,
            logging.CRITICAL: self.bold_red + self.fmt + self.reset
```

```
        }

    def format(self, record):
        log_fmt = self.FORMATS.get(record.levelno)
        formatter = logging.Formatter(log_fmt)
        return formatter.format(record)



# Create custom logger logging all five levels
logger = logging.getLogger(__name__)
logger.setLevel(logging.DEBUG)

# Define format for logs
fmt = '%(asctime)s | %(levelname)8s | %(message)s'

# Create stdout handler for logging to the console (logs all five levels)
stdout_handler = logging.StreamHandler()
stdout_handler.setLevel(logging.DEBUG)
stdout_handler.setFormatter(CustomFormatter(fmt))

# Create file handler for logging to a file (logs all five levels)
today = datetime.date.today()
file_handler                                                              =
logging.FileHandler('my_app_{}.log'.format(today.strftime('%Y_%m_%d')))
file_handler.setLevel(logging.DEBUG)
file_handler.setFormatter(logging.Formatter(fmt))

# Add both handlers to the logger
logger.addHandler(stdout_handler)
logger.addHandler(file_handler)

logger.debug('This is a debug-level message')
logger.info('This is an info-level message')
logger.warning('This is a warning-level message')
logger.error('This is an error-level message')
logger.critical('This is a critical-level message')

# output
2024-09-09 19:28:06,907 |    DEBUG | This is a debug-level message
2024-09-09 19:28:06,909 |     INFO | This is an info-level message
2024-09-09 19:28:06,910 |  WARNING | This is a warning-level message
2024-09-09 19:28:06,910 |    ERROR | This is an error-level message
2024-09-09 19:28:06,910 | CRITICAL | This is a critical-level message
```

The most useful logging function is the function and line number, see below,

```
import logging
import sys
from logging.handlers import TimedRotatingFileHandler
FORMATTER  =  logging.Formatter("%(asctime)s  —  %(name)s  —  %(levelname)s  —  %
(funcName)s:%(lineno)d — %(message)s")
LOG_FILE = "my_app.log"
```

```
def get_console_handler():
   console_handler = logging.StreamHandler(sys.stdout)
   console_handler.setFormatter(FORMATTER)
   return console_handler
def get_file_handler():
   file_handler = TimedRotatingFileHandler(LOG_FILE, when='midnight')
   file_handler.setFormatter(FORMATTER)
   return file_handler
def get_logger(logger_name):
   logger = logging.getLogger(logger_name)
   logger.setLevel(logging.DEBUG) # better to have too much log than not enough
   logger.addHandler(get_console_handler())
   logger.addHandler(get_file_handler())
   # with this pattern, it's rarely necessary to propagate the error up to parent
   logger.propagate = False
   return logger

my_logger = get_logger("my module name")
my_logger.debug("a debug message")

# output
2024-09-09 19:34:58,936 — my module name — DEBUG — <module>:25 — a debug message
```

23 Gibbys

In montreal, there are many steak houses, and the most advanced one is Gibbys. One can have a perfect dinner with high class red wine, after walking around the old port, the old town and the old market. Life is slow when people are young, and finally all belong to death. We find ourselves are animals at last, so we better shut up. A mouth is only used to eat for old adults. No more talk, since no more to say. In montreal, it is good to be silent, since French is the first language. I do not want to say anything, for I am already too too too old. I wasted a lot, money, emotion, energy, and life.

Very often, I find myself is a waste. Waste food, waste drink, waste time, waste life. There are few memories I feel joy, and maybe it is the bad experience during my early growing years. Many times I look forward to freedom, and I need a stubborn support. Until these years, I find all these are meaningless. What really can be used is just the thing support living, so food is essential, and that's it. Do not think, just eat!

If a Python developer wants to order a food, what is the non-waste way? See below,

```
# import tkinter module
from tkinter import *
```

```
# make a window
window = Tk()

# specify it's size
window.geometry("872x691")

# take a image for background
bg = PhotoImage(file='bg.png')

# label it in the background
label1 = Label(window, image=bg)

# position the image as well
label1.place(x=0, y=0)

# closing the main loop
window.mainloop()
```

And it would be nice to have dishes price calculated, as below,

```
# import tkinter module
from tkinter import *

# make a window
window = Tk()

# specify it's size
window.geometry("872x691")

# take a image for background
bg = PhotoImage(file='bg.png')

# label it in the background
label = Label(window, image=bg)

# position the image as well
label.place(x=0, y=0)

window.counter = 0
label1 = Label(window, text="Click below to order.\nOr click this to pay")
label1.pack()

def clicked(p):
    window.counter += 1*p
    label1['text'] = 'Total Price: .' + str(window.counter)

label2 = Label(window,text="Rib Steak 22 oz......79",font="times 12")
label2.place(x=20,y=400+(0+1)*20)
label2.bind("<Button-1>", lambda e:clicked(79))

label3 = Label(window,text="Rib Eye Steak 15 oz......77",font="times 12")
label3.place(x=20,y=400+(1+1)*20)
```

```
label3.bind("<Button-1>", lambda e:clicked(77))

label4 = Label(window,text="Sirloin 16 oz......77",font="times 12")
label4.place(x=20,y=400+(2+1)*20)
label4.bind("<Button-1>", lambda e:clicked(77))

label5 = Label(window,text="Cowboy Steak 36 oz......155",font="times 12")
label5.place(x=20,y=400+(3+1)*20)
label5.bind("<Button-1>", lambda e:clicked(155))

label6 = Label(window,text="Filet Mignon 8 oz......75",font="times 12")
label6.place(x=20,y=400+(4+1)*20)
label6.bind("<Button-1>", lambda e:clicked(75))

label7 = Label(window,text="Filet Mignon 12 oz......82",font="times 12")
label7.place(x=20,y=400+(5+1)*20)
label7.bind("<Button-1>", lambda e:clicked(82))

label8 = Label(window,text="Filet Mignon Kebab Style......65",font="times 12")
label8.place(x=20,y=400+(6+1)*20)
label8.bind("<Button-1>", lambda e:clicked(65))

label9 = Label(window,text="Eggplant Parmesan......42",font="times 12")
label9.place(x=20,y=400+(7+1)*20)
label9.bind("<Button-1>", lambda e:clicked(42))

label10 = Label(window,text="Rack of Lamb......Youville......65",font="times 12")
label10.place(x=20,y=400+(8+1)*20)
label10.bind("<Button-1>", lambda e:clicked(65))

label11 = Label(window,text="Roasted Cornish Hen......54",font="times 12")
label11.place(x=20,y=400+(9+1)*20)
label11.bind("<Button-1>", lambda e:clicked(54))

label12 = Label(window,text="Filet Mignon of Beef WELLINGTON 8
oz......85",font="times 12")
label12.place(x=20,y=400+(10+1)*20)
label12.bind("<Button-1>", lambda e:clicked(85))

label13 = Label(window,text="Mignons of Beef Diane 12 oz......83",font="times 12")
label13.place(x=20,y=400+(11+1)*20)
label13.bind("<Button-1>", lambda e:clicked(83))


label14 = Label(window,text="CLOS STE-CROIX......74",font="times 12")
label14.place(x=340,y=400+(0+1)*20)
label14.bind("<Button-1>", lambda e:clicked(74))

label15 = Label(window,text="MALIVOIRE......77",font="times 12")
label15.place(x=340,y=400+(1+1)*20)
label15.bind("<Button-1>", lambda e:clicked(77))

label16 = Label(window,text="DOMAINE QUEYLUS.....87",font="times 12")
```

```
label16.place(x=340,y=400+(2+1)*20)
label16.bind("<Button-1>", lambda e:clicked(87))

label17 = Label(window,text="OSOYOOS LAROSE......128",font="times 12")
label17.place(x=340,y=400+(3+1)*20)
label17.bind("<Button-1>", lambda e:clicked(128))

label18 = Label(window,text="J. LOHR......66",font="times 12")
label18.place(x=340,y=400+(4+1)*20)
label18.bind("<Button-1>", lambda e:clicked(66))

label19 = Label(window,text="FREI BROTHERS RESERVE......73",font="times 12")
label19.place(x=340,y=400+(5+1)*20)
label19.bind("<Button-1>", lambda e:clicked(73))

label20 = Label(window,text="FRANCIS FORD COPPOLA......87",font="times 12")
label20.place(x=340,y=400+(6+1)*20)
label20.bind("<Button-1>", lambda e:clicked(87))

label21 = Label(window,text="BERINGER......108",font="times 12")
label21.place(x=340,y=400+(7+1)*20)
label21.bind("<Button-1>", lambda e:clicked(108))

label22 = Label(window,text="DRY CREEK VINEYARD......118",font="times 12")
label22.place(x=340,y=400+(8+1)*20)
label22.bind("<Button-1>", lambda e:clicked(118))

label23 = Label(window,text="NEYERS......251",font="times 12")
label23.place(x=340,y=400+(9+1)*20)
label23.bind("<Button-1>", lambda e:clicked(251))

label24 = Label(window,text="GHOST PINES......60",font="times 12")
label24.place(x=340,y=400+(10+1)*20)
label24.bind("<Button-1>", lambda e:clicked(60))

label25 = Label(window,text="MEIOMI......64",font="times 12")
label25.place(x=340,y=400+(11+1)*20)
label25.bind("<Button-1>", lambda e:clicked(64))

label26 = Label(window,text="OMEN......85",font="times 12")
label26.place(x=340,y=400+(12+1)*20)
label26.bind("<Button-1>", lambda e:clicked(85))

label27 = Label(window,text="Gibbys Salad......19",font="times 12")
label27.place(x=600,y=400+(0+1)*20)
label27.bind("<Button-1>", lambda e:clicked(19))

label28 = Label(window,text="Blue Cheese Wedge Salad......20",font="times 12")
label28.place(x=600,y=400+(1+1)*20)
label28.bind("<Button-1>", lambda e:clicked(20))

label29 = Label(window,text="Burrata D'amore......26",font="times 12")
label29.place(x=600,y=400+(2+1)*20)
```

```
label29.bind("<Button-1>", lambda e:clicked(26))

label30 = Label(window,text="Arugula Salad.....21",font="times 12")
label30.place(x=600,y=400+(3+1)*20)
label30.bind("<Button-1>", lambda e:clicked(21))

label31 = Label(window,text="Crab Cake......38",font="times 12")
label31.place(x=600,y=400+(4+1)*20)
label31.bind("<Button-1>", lambda e:clicked(38))

label32 = Label(window,text="Octopus Salad......31",font="times 12")
label32.place(x=600,y=400+(5+1)*20)
label32.bind("<Button-1>", lambda e:clicked(31))

label33 = Label(window,text="Beef Carpaccio......29",font="times 12")
label33.place(x=600,y=400+(6+1)*20)
label33.bind("<Button-1>", lambda e:clicked(29))

label34 = Label(window,text="Shrimp Cocktail......38",font="times 12")
label34.place(x=600,y=400+(7+1)*20)
label34.bind("<Button-1>", lambda e:clicked(38))

label35 = Label(window,text="Wild Shrimps......38",font="times 12")
label35.place(x=600,y=400+(8+1)*20)
label35.bind("<Button-1>", lambda e:clicked(38))

label36 = Label(window,text="Escargots Bourguignonne......28",font="times 12")
label36.place(x=600,y=400+(9+1)*20)
label36.bind("<Button-1>", lambda e:clicked(28))

label37 = Label(window,text="Seafood Tower......195",font="times 12")
label37.place(x=600,y=400+(10+1)*20)
label37.bind("<Button-1>", lambda e:clicked(195))

label38 = Label(window,text="New England-Style Clam Chowder......23",font="times 12")
label38.place(x=600,y=400+(11+1)*20)
label38.bind("<Button-1>", lambda e:clicked(23))

label39 = Label(window,text="French Onion Soup......24",font="times 12")
label39.place(x=600,y=400+(12+1)*20)
label39.bind("<Button-1>", lambda e:clicked(24))


# closing the main loop
window.mainloop()
```

And to order, we need the link, which have to cooperate with the restaurant, as below,

```
import webbrowser
# Define the order web api

```

```
url= 'https://www.gibbys.com/menus/'
def open_url(url):
   webbrowser.open_new_tab(url)
# Bind the label with the URL to open in a new tab
label1.bind("<Button-1>", lambda e:open_url(url))
```

But why don't we use for loop for the labels?

24 PDB

Simply put the label into three lists in a list, and making variables adding by one, as below,

```
# import tkinter module
from tkinter import *

# make a window
window = Tk()

# specify it's size
window.geometry("872x691")

# take a image for background
bg = PhotoImage(file='bg.png')

# label it in the background
label = Label(window, image=bg)

# position the image as well
label.place(x=0, y=0)

window.counter = 0
label1 = Label(window, text="Click below to order.\nOr click this to pay")
label1.pack()

import logging
import sys
from logging.handlers import TimedRotatingFileHandler
FORMATTER = logging.Formatter("%(asctime)s — %(name)s — %(levelname)s — %
(funcName)s:%(lineno)d — %(message)s")
LOG_FILE = "Gibbys_menu.log"

def get_console_handler():
   console_handler = logging.StreamHandler(sys.stdout)
   console_handler.setFormatter(FORMATTER)
   return console_handler
def get_file_handler():
   file_handler = TimedRotatingFileHandler(LOG_FILE, when='midnight')
   file_handler.setFormatter(FORMATTER)
   return file_handler
def get_logger(logger_name):
```

```
    logger = logging.getLogger(logger_name)
    logger.setLevel(logging.DEBUG) # better to have too much log than not enough
    logger.addHandler(get_console_handler())
    logger.addHandler(get_file_handler())
    # with this pattern, it's rarely necessary to propagate the error up to parent
    logger.propagate = False
    return logger




def clicked(f):
     my_logger = get_logger("Gibbys menu")
     my_logger.debug("a debug message: "+f)
     p = f.split("......")[1]
     window.counter += 1*int(p)
     label1['text'] = 'Total Price: .' + str(window.counter)

menu = [[
"Rib Steak 22 oz......79",
"Rib Eye Steak 15 oz......77",
"Sirloin 16 oz......77",
"Cowboy Steak 36 oz......155",
"Filet Mignon 8 oz......75",
"Filet Mignon 12 oz......82",
"Filet Mignon Kebab Style......65",
"Eggplant Parmesan......42",
"Rack of Lamb......Youville......65",
"Mignons of Beef Diane 12 oz......83",
"Filet Mignon of Beef WELLINGTON 8 oz......85",
"Roasted Cornish Hen......54"
],
["CLOS STE-CROIX......74",
"MALIVOIRE......77",
"Sirloin 16 oz......75",
"DOMAINE QUEYLUS.....87",
"J. LOHR......66",
"FREI BROTHERS RESERVE......73",
"FRANCIS FORD COPPOLA......87",
"BERINGER......108",
"DRY CREEK VINEYARD......118",
"NEYERS......251",
"GHOST PINES......60",
"MEIOMI......64",
"OMEN......85",
],
["Gibbys Salad......19",
"Blue Cheese Wedge Salad......20",
"Burrata D'amore......26",
"Arugula Salad.....21",
"Crab Cake......38",
"Octopus Salad......31",
"Beef Carpaccio......29",
```

```
"Shrimp Cocktail......38",
"Wild Shrimps......38",
"Escargots Bourguignonne......28",
"Seafood Tower......195",
"New England-Style Clam Chowder......23",
"French Onion Soup......24",
]]

n = 2
for row in menu:
  for m, item in enumerate(row):

    globals()[f"label{n}"] = Label(window,text=item,font="times 12")

    if n <= 13:
        globals()[f"label{n}"].place(x=20,y=400+(m+1)*20)
    if n >= 14 and n <= 26:
        globals()[f"label{n}"].place(x=340,y=400+(m+1)*20)
    if n >= 27:
        globals()[f"label{n}"].place(x=600,y=400+(m+1)*20)
    globals()[f"label{n}"].bind("<Button-1>", lambda e:clicked(item))


    n += 1

# closing the main loop
window.mainloop()

# output
2024-09-10 12:46:47,520 — Gibbys menu — DEBUG — clicked:51 — a debug message: French
Onion Soup......24
```

Here we are faceing a problem, the lambda function gives the wrong item "French Onion Soup......24", why is that? We can add PDB around line 51 to find out, as below,

```
# import tkinter module
from tkinter import *

# make a window
window = Tk()

# specify it's size
window.geometry("872x691")

# take a image for background
bg = PhotoImage(file='bg.png')

# label it in the background
label = Label(window, image=bg)

# position the image as well
```

```
label.place(x=0, y=0)

window.counter = 0
label1 = Label(window, text="Click below to order.\nOr click this to pay")
label1.pack()

import logging
import sys
from logging.handlers import TimedRotatingFileHandler
FORMATTER = logging.Formatter("%(asctime)s — %(name)s — %(levelname)s — %(funcName)s:%(lineno)d — %(message)s")
LOG_FILE = "Gibbys_menu.log"

def get_console_handler():
   console_handler = logging.StreamHandler(sys.stdout)
   console_handler.setFormatter(FORMATTER)
   return console_handler
def get_file_handler():
   file_handler = TimedRotatingFileHandler(LOG_FILE, when='midnight')
   file_handler.setFormatter(FORMATTER)
   return file_handler
def get_logger(logger_name):
   logger = logging.getLogger(logger_name)
   logger.setLevel(logging.DEBUG) # better to have too much log than not enough
   logger.addHandler(get_console_handler())
   logger.addHandler(get_file_handler())
   # with this pattern, it's rarely necessary to propagate the error up to parent
   logger.propagate = False
   return logger

def clicked(f):
    my_logger = get_logger("Gibbys menu")
    my_logger.debug("a debug message: "+f)
    p = f.split("......")[1]
    window.counter += 1*int(p)
    label1['text'] = 'Total Price: .' + str(window.counter)

menu = [[
"Rib Steak 22 oz......79",
"Rib Eye Steak 15 oz......77",
"Sirloin 16 oz......77",
"Cowboy Steak 36 oz......155",
"Filet Mignon 8 oz......75",
"Filet Mignon 12 oz......82",
"Filet Mignon Kebab Style......65",
"Eggplant Parmesan......42",
"Rack of Lamb......Youville......65",
"Mignons of Beef Diane 12 oz......83",
"Filet Mignon of Beef WELLINGTON 8 oz......85",
"Roasted Cornish Hen......54"
],
["CLOS STE-CROIX......74",
"MALIVOIRE......77",
```

```
"Sirloin 16 oz......75",
"DOMAINE QUEYLUS.....87",
"J. LOHR......66",
"FREI BROTHERS RESERVE......73",
"FRANCIS FORD COPPOLA......87",
"BERINGER......108",
"DRY CREEK VINEYARD......118",
"NEYERS......251",
"GHOST PINES......60",
"MEIOMI......64",
"OMEN......85",
],
["Gibbys Salad......19",
"Blue Cheese Wedge Salad......20",
"Burrata D'amore......26",
"Arugula Salad.....21",
"Crab Cake......38",
"Octopus Salad......31",
"Beef Carpaccio......29",
"Shrimp Cocktail......38",
"Wild Shrimps......38",
"Escargots Bourguignonne......28",
"Seafood Tower......195",
"New England-Style Clam Chowder......23",
"French Onion Soup......24",
]]

n = 2
for row in menu:
  for m, item in enumerate(row):

    globals()[f"label{n}"] = Label(window,text=item,font="times 12")

    if n <= 13:
        globals()[f"label{n}"].place(x=20,y=400+(m+1)*20)
    if n >= 14 and n <= 26:
        globals()[f"label{n}"].place(x=340,y=400+(m+1)*20)
    if n >= 27:
        globals()[f"label{n}"].place(x=600,y=400+(m+1)*20)
    print("pdb invoking for lambda")
    import pdb;pdb.set_trace()
    globals()[f"label{n}"].bind("<Button-1>", lambda e:clicked(item))
    print("lambda invoked")
    n += 1

# closing the main loop
window.mainloop()

# output
C:\Users\Lenovo\PDB>python Gibbys.py
.!label3 Rib Steak 22 oz......79
pdb invoking for lambda
> c:\users\lenovo\PDB\Gibbys.py(118)<module>()
```

```
-> print("lambda invoked")
(Pdb) n
lambda invoked
> c:\users\lenovo\PDB\Gibbys.py(119)<module>()
-> n += 1
(Pdb)
> c:\users\lenovo\PDB\Gibbys.py(104)<module>()
-> for m, item in enumerate(row):
(Pdb)
> c:\users\lenovo\PDB\Gibbys.py(106)<module>()
-> globals()[f"label{n}"] = Label(window,text=item,font="times 12")
(Pdb)
> c:\users\lenovo\PDB\Gibbys.py(107)<module>()
-> globals()[f"label{n}"].bind("<Button-1>", clickok(globals()[f"label{n}"], item))
(Pdb)
.!label4 Rib Eye Steak 15 oz......77
> c:\users\lenovo\PDB\Gibbys.py(109)<module>()
-> if n <= 13:
(Pdb)
> c:\users\lenovo\PDB\Gibbys.py(110)<module>()
-> globals()[f"label{n}"].place(x=20,y=400+(m+1)*20)
(Pdb)
> c:\users\lenovo\PDB\Gibbys.py(111)<module>()
-> if n >= 14 and n <= 26:
(Pdb)
> c:\users\lenovo\PDB\Gibbys.py(113)<module>()
-> if n >= 27:
(Pdb)
> c:\users\lenovo\PDB\Gibbys.py(115)<module>()
-> print("pdb invoking for lambda")
(Pdb)
pdb invoking for lambda
> c:\users\lenovo\PDB\Gibbys.py(116)<module>()
-> import pdb;pdb.set_trace()
(Pdb)
> c:\users\lenovo\PDB\Gibbys.py(118)<module>()
-> print("lambda invoked")
(Pdb)
(Pdb) n
lambda invoked
> c:\users\lenovo\PDB\Gibbys.py(119)<module>()
-> n += 1
(Pdb)
> c:\users\lenovo\PDB\Gibbys.py(104)<module>()
-> for m, item in enumerate(row):
(Pdb)
> c:\users\lenovo\PDB\Gibbys.py(106)<module>()
-> globals()[f"label{n}"] = Label(window,text=item,font="times 12")
(Pdb)
> c:\users\lenovo\PDB\Gibbys.py(107)<module>()
-> globals()[f"label{n}"].bind("<Button-1>", clickok(globals()[f"label{n}"], item))
(Pdb)
.!label5 Sirloin 16 oz......77
```

```
> c:\users\lenovo\PDB\Gibbys.py(109)<module>()
-> if n <= 13:
(Pdb)
> c:\users\lenovo\PDB\Gibbys.py(110)<module>()
-> globals()[f"label{n}"].place(x=20,y=400+(m+1)*20)
(Pdb)
> c:\users\lenovo\PDB\Gibbys.py(111)<module>()
-> if n >= 14 and n <= 26:
(Pdb)
> c:\users\lenovo\PDB\Gibbys.py(113)<module>()
-> if n >= 27:
(Pdb)
> c:\users\lenovo\PDB\Gibbys.py(115)<module>()
-> print("pdb invoking for lambda")
(Pdb)
pdb invoking for lambda
> c:\users\lenovo\PDB\Gibbys.py(116)<module>()
-> import pdb;pdb.set_trace()
(Pdb)
> c:\users\lenovo\PDB\Gibbys.py(118)<module>()
-> print("lambda invoked")
(Pdb)
(Pdb) n
lambda invoked
> c:\users\lenovo\PDB\Gibbys.py(119)<module>()
-> n += 1
(Pdb)
> c:\users\lenovo\PDB\Gibbys.py(104)<module>()
-> for m, item in enumerate(row):
(Pdb)
> c:\users\lenovo\PDB\Gibbys.py(106)<module>()
-> globals()[f"label{n}"] = Label(window,text=item,font="times 12")
(Pdb)
> c:\users\lenovo\PDB\Gibbys.py(107)<module>()
-> globals()[f"label{n}"].bind("<Button-1>", clickok(globals()[f"label{n}"], item))
(Pdb)
.!label6 Cowboy Steak 36 oz......155
> c:\users\lenovo\PDB\Gibbys.py(109)<module>()
-> if n <= 13:
(Pdb)
> c:\users\lenovo\PDB\Gibbys.py(110)<module>()
-> globals()[f"label{n}"].place(x=20,y=400+(m+1)*20)
(Pdb)
> c:\users\lenovo\PDB\Gibbys.py(111)<module>()
-> if n >= 14 and n <= 26:
(Pdb)
> c:\users\lenovo\PDB\Gibbys.py(113)<module>()
-> if n >= 27:
(Pdb)
> c:\users\lenovo\PDB\Gibbys.py(115)<module>()
-> print("pdb invoking for lambda")
(Pdb)
pdb invoking for lambda
```

```
> c:\users\lenovo\PDB\Gibbys.py(116)<module>()
-> import pdb;pdb.set_trace()
(Pdb)
> c:\users\lenovo\PDB\Gibbys.py(118)<module>()
-> print("lambda invoked")
(Pdb)
(Pdb)
```

We then find the clicked part is binding to each, but click just goes to the end, so that means we may need click list, to handle the different labels.

We use print for PDB, and logger for log, just make debug easy, as below,

```
# import tkinter module
from tkinter import *

# make a window
window = Tk()
```

```
# specify it's size
window.geometry("872x691")

# take a image for background
bg = PhotoImage(file='bg.png')

# label it in the background
label = Label(window, image=bg)

# position the image as well
label.place(x=0, y=0)

window.counter = 0
label1 = Label(window, text="Click below to order.\nOr click this to pay")
label1.pack()

import logging
import sys
from logging.handlers import TimedRotatingFileHandler
FORMATTER = logging.Formatter("%(asctime)s — %(name)s — %(levelname)s — %
(funcName)s:%(lineno)d — %(message)s")
LOG_FILE = "Gibbys_menu.log"

def get_console_handler():
   console_handler = logging.StreamHandler(sys.stdout)
   console_handler.setFormatter(FORMATTER)
   return console_handler
def get_file_handler():
   file_handler = TimedRotatingFileHandler(LOG_FILE, when='midnight')
   file_handler.setFormatter(FORMATTER)
   return file_handler
def get_logger(logger_name):
   logger = logging.getLogger(logger_name)
   logger.setLevel(logging.DEBUG) # better to have too much log than not enough
   logger.addHandler(get_console_handler())
   logger.addHandler(get_file_handler())
   # with this pattern, it's rarely necessary to propagate the error up to parent
   logger.propagate = False
   return logger




def clicked(f):



    p = f.split("......")[1]
    window.counter += 1*int(p)
    label1['text'] = 'Total Price: .' + str(window.counter)
```

```
menu = [[
"Rib Steak 22 oz......79",
"Rib Eye Steak 15 oz......77",
"Sirloin 16 oz......77",
"Cowboy Steak 36 oz......155",
"Filet Mignon 8 oz......75",
"Filet Mignon 12 oz......82",
"Filet Mignon Kebab Style......65",
"Eggplant Parmesan......42",
"Rack of Lamb......65",
"Mignons of Beef Diane 12 oz......83",
"Filet Mignon of Beef WELLINGTON 8 oz......85",
"Roasted Cornish Hen......54"
],
["CLOS STE-CROIX......74",
"MALIVOIRE......77",
"Sirloin 16 oz......75",
"DOMAINE QUEYLUS......87",
"J. LOHR......66",
"FREI BROTHERS RESERVE......73",
"FRANCIS FORD COPPOLA......87",
"BERINGER......108",
"DRY CREEK VINEYARD......118",
"NEYERS......251",
"GHOST PINES......60",
"MEIOMI......64",
"OMEN......85",
],
["Gibbys Salad......19",
"Blue Cheese Wedge Salad......20",
"Burrata D'amore......26",
"Arugula Salad......21",
"Crab Cake......38",
"Octopus Salad......31",
"Beef Carpaccio......29",
"Shrimp Cocktail......38",
"Wild Shrimps......38",
"Escargots Bourguignonne......28",
"Seafood Tower......195",
"New England-Style Clam Chowder......23",
"French Onion Soup......24",
]]

def bindok(l, f):

    test_str = f

    res = None
    temp = (test_str + test_str).find(test_str, 1, -1)
    if temp != -1:
        res = test_str[:temp]
```

```
    if res == None: res = f


    l.bind("<Button-1>", lambda e:clicked(res))


n = 2
for row in menu:
  for m, item in enumerate(row):

    globals()[f"label{n}"] = Label(window,text=item,font="times 12")
    if n <= 13:
        globals()[f"label{n}"].place(x=20,y=400+(m+1)*20)
    if n >= 14 and n <= 26:
        globals()[f"label{n}"].place(x=340,y=400+(m+1)*20)
    if n >= 27:
        globals()[f"label{n}"].place(x=600,y=400+(m+1)*20)
    #print("pdb invoking for lambda")
    #import pdb;pdb.set_trace()
    #print("lambda invoked")
    print(item)
    bindok(globals()[f"label{n}"], item)

    n += 1

import webbrowser
# Define the order web api
url= 'https://www.gibbys.com/menus/'
def open_url(url):
   webbrowser.open_new_tab(url)
# Bind the label with the URL to open in a new tab
label1.bind("<Button-1>", lambda e:open_url(url))

# closing the main loop
window.mainloop()
```

Besides the basic `n` command, there are other common ones.

Command	**Description**
`h` or `help`	Show a list of available commands
`q` or `quit`	Quit PDB
`n` or `next`	Execute the current line and move to the next line
`s` or `step`	Execute the current line and step into any function calls
`c` or `continue`	Continue execution until the next breakpoint
`r` or `return`	Continue execution until the current function returns
`l` or `list`	Show the current line and surrounding lines of code
`w` or `where`	Show the current stack trace

Command	Description
`p` or `print`	Evaluate and print an expression
`pp` or `pprint`	Evaluate and pretty-print an expression
`a` or `args`	Show the arguments of the current function
`u` or `up`	Move up the stack trace
`d` or `down`	Move down the stack trace
`b` or `break`	Set a breakpoint at the current line
`b file.py:line`	Set a breakpoint at `file.py:line`
`b function`	Set a breakpoint at the start of `function`
`b function:line`	Set a breakpoint at `function:line`
`b` with no arguments	List all breakpoints
`cl` or `clear`	Clear a breakpoint
`cl file.py:line`	Clear the breakpoint at `file.py:line`
`cl bpnumber`	Clear the breakpoint with number `bpnumber`
`watch expression`	Set a watchpoint on `expression`
`watch -r expression`	Set a reverse watchpoint on `expression`
`watch` with no arguments	List all watchpoints
`rwatch expression`	Set a watchpoint on `expression` that only triggers when it is read
`rwatch -r expression`	Set a reverse watchpoint on `expression` that only triggers when it is read
`rwatch` with no arguments	List all reverse watchpoints
`awatch expression`	Set an automatic watchpoint on `expression` that is deleted after it triggers
`awatch -r expression`	Set a reverse automatic watchpoint on `expression` that is deleted after it triggers
`awatch` with no arguments	List all automatic watchpoints
`s` or `step`	Step into the current line

Command	Description
`n` or `next`	Step over the current line
`unt` or `until`	Continue execution until the current function returns or reaches a line greater than the current line
`j` or `jump`	Jump to a different line in the current function
`w` or `where`	Show the current stack trace
`u` or `up`	Move up the stack trace
`d` or `down`	Move down the stack trace
`bt` or `backtrace`	Show the full stack trace
`p` or `print`	Print the value of a variable or expression
`pp` or `pprint`	Pretty-print the value of a variable or expression
`a` or `args`	Show the arguments of the current function
`l` or `locals`	Show the local variables of the current function
`g` or `globals`	Show the global variables
`whatis expression`	Show the type of `expression`
`source expression`	Show the source code of `expression`
`interact`	Start an interactive interpreter with access to the current frame
`h` or `help`	Show a list of available commands
`!`	Execute a Python statement in the current context
`alias`	Define an alias for a command
`unalias`	Remove an alias
`pdbrc`	Load a configuration file
`run`	Restart the program from the beginning

And we wil use the simple arithmetic interactive mode to demo, as below,

```
# arit.py
operators = ['+', '-', '*', '/']
numbers = [10, 20]
def calculator():
    print("Operators available: ")
    for op in operators:
        print(op)
        print("Numbers to be used: ")
    for num in numbers:
        print(num)

def main():
```

```
        calculator()

main()
```

List is to show the file lines

```
C:\Users\Lenovo>python -m pdb arit.py
> c:\users\lenovo\arit.py(1)<module>()
-> operators = ['+', '-', '*', '/']
(Pdb) l
  1  -> operators = ['+', '-', '*', '/']
  2     numbers = [10, 20]
  3     def calculator():
  4             print("Operators available: ")
  5             for op in operators:
  6                     print(op)
  7                     print("Numbers to be used: ")
  8             for num in numbers:
  9                     print(num)
 10
 11     def main():
(Pdb) l15
*** NameError: name 'l15' is not defined
(Pdb) l+15
 10
 11     def main():
 12                     calculator()
 13
 14     main()
[EOF]
(Pdb) l4, 6
*** NameError: name 'l4' is not defined
(Pdb) l
[EOF]
(Pdb) l 4, 6
  4             print("Operators available: ")
  5             for op in operators:
  6                     print(op)
```

Set a breakpoint at a line,

```
(Pdb) b 8
Breakpoint 1 at c:\users\lenovo\arit.py:8
(Pdb) r
Operators available:
+
Numbers to be used:
-
Numbers to be used:
*
Numbers to be used:
/
```

```
Numbers to be used:
> c:\users\lenovo\arit.py(8)calculator()
-> for num in numbers:
(Pdb) exit

C:\Users\Lenovo\arit.py>
```

We can also disable the breakpoint,

```
C:\Users\Lenovo>python -m pdb arit.py
> c:\users\lenovo\arit.py(1)<module>()
-> operators = ['+', '-', '*', '/']
(Pdb) break calc.calculator
Breakpoint 1 at c:\users\lenovo\arit.py:3
(Pdb) b
Num Type         Disp Enb   Where
1   breakpoint   keep yes   at c:\users\lenovo\arit.py:3
(Pdb) b 10
*** Blank or comment
(Pdb) b9
*** NameError: name 'b9' is not defined
(Pdb) b 9
Breakpoint 2 at c:\users\lenovo\arit.py:9
(Pdb) b
Num Type         Disp Enb   Where
1   breakpoint   keep yes   at c:\users\lenovo\arit.py:3
2   breakpoint   keep yes   at c:\users\lenovo\arit.py:9
(Pdb) dis b 2
*** SyntaxError: invalid syntax
(Pdb) dis 2
*** SyntaxError: invalid syntax
(Pdb) disable 2
Disabled breakpoint 2 at c:\users\lenovo\arit.py:9
(Pdb) b
Num Type         Disp Enb   Where
1   breakpoint   keep yes   at c:\users\lenovo\arit.py:3
2   breakpoint   keep no    at c:\users\lenovo\arit.py:9
```

Run and continue,

```
(Pdb) r
> c:\users\lenovo\arit.py(4)calculator()
-> print("Operators available: ")
(Pdb) c
Operators available:
+
Numbers to be used:
-
Numbers to be used:
*
Numbers to be used:
/
```

```
Numbers to be used:
10
20
The program finished and will be restarted
> c:\users\lenovo\arit.py(1)<module>()
-> operators = ['+', '-', '*', '/']
(Pdb) b
Num Type         Disp Enb   Where
1   breakpoint   keep yes   at c:\users\lenovo\arit.py:3
        breakpoint already hit 2 times
2   breakpoint   keep no    at c:\users\lenovo\arit.py:9
```

And we can jump into PDB by using a `post_mortem` method, as below,

```
# post_mortem.py
import pdb
def faulty_function(x):
    return 5 / x
try:
    print(faulty_function(0))
except Exception:
    pdb.post_mortem()

# output
> c:\users\lenovo\ttt\hi.py(3)faulty_function()
-> return 5 / x
(Pdb) r
```

25 timing

A program can be written in many ways, because thinking are different, and writing are different, how do we know which way is better?

Usually we check the speed, that is to say, which one runs faster, which one is better. To do this, there are different levels, file, function, loop, or other parts. A timing tool is used outside the level, that is to say, the tool better be independent of the invesgated logic parts.

Recall timeit module, as below,

```
# fib.py
def fib(n):
    n1, n2 = 0, 1
    for i in range(1, n + 1):
        temp = n1 + n2
        n1 = n2
        n2 = temp
    return n2
```

```
# test.py
import timeit
python= timeit.timeit('fib.fib(10000)',
       setup='import fib',number=100)
print("Python Time: ", python)

# output
Python Time:  0.1410401000175625
```

Now move the number outside test.py, as below,

```
# test.py
import timeit
number=int(input("times: "))
python= timeit.timeit('fib.fib(10000)',
       setup='import fib', number=number)
print("Python %d Time: " % number, python)

# output
times: 100
Python 100 Time:  0.3160902000090573

times: 100
Python 100 Time:  0.31869000001461245

times: 1000
Python 1000 Time:  3.741279999987455

times: 1000
Python 1000 Time:  3.0232329000136815
```

We see do the fibnacci from 0 to 10000, 1000 times are approximately 10 times of 100 times. And if we move the number input in, as below,

```
import timeit
python= timeit.timeit('fib.fib(10000)',
       setup='import fib', number=int(input("times: ")))
print("Python Time: ", python)

# output
times: 100
Python Time:  0.3206812999851536

times: 1000
Python Time:  2.9670487999974284

times: 1000
Python Time:  2.9964145999983884

times: 1000
Python Time:  3.085216199979186
```

So the time can be less, and in fact, we count the time is really not a one time thing, all the data in science is a distribution, which means in a range, and most likely be which ones, at a certain condition. That is why we use approximately, the word represents the likely chance.

If we doubt the timeit module consume unnecassary time, we have to think about how timing work. Start, and end, the thing is just like that, so why don't we write ourselves? How do we count time in computer?

We then see the right bottom time display of the computer, format in seconds, and compare the timeit module, it is less precise. So how precise can computer be? What is the clock in a computer? See below,

```
>>> import time
>>> time.get_clock_info('monotonic')
namespace(implementation='GetTickCount64()', monotonic=True, adjustable=False, resolution=0.015625)
>>> time.get_clock_info('perf_counter')
namespace(implementation='QueryPerformanceCounter()', monotonic=True, adjustable=False, resolution=1e-07)
>>> time.get_clock_info('process_time')
namespace(implementation='GetProcessTimes()', monotonic=True, adjustable=False, resolution=1e-07)
>>> time.get_clock_info('thread_time')
namespace(implementation='GetThreadTimes()', monotonic=True, adjustable=False, resolution=1e-07)
>>> time.get_clock_info('time')
namespace(implementation='GetSystemTimeAsFileTime()', monotonic=False, adjustable=True, resolution=0.015625)
>>> time.localtime()
time.struct_time(tm_year=2024, tm_mon=9, tm_mday=12, tm_hour=11, tm_min=52, tm_sec=36, tm_wday=3, tm_yday=256, tm_isdst=0)
>>> time.ctime()
'Thu Sep 12 11:52:38 2024'
```

Python can read clock, but it is also a software clock, what is the hardware clock? Why do we need that? Because we want precise. But why less precise is not ok?

It is ok. And most people's life are just ok with what are offered. Who will go to Zenith to say your clock is bad? No one. So we just use the module, we have to. And use it, as below,

```
import time

def fib(n):
    n1, n2 = 0, 1
    for i in range(1, n + 1):
        temp = n1 + n2
        n1 = n2
```

```
        n2 = temp
    return n2

start = time.time()
[fib(10000) for x in range(0, 100)]
end = time.time()
print(f'Python time: {end - start}')

# output
times: 100
Python time: 0.12054896354675293
```

And 1000 tims, as below,

```
import time

def fib(n):
    n1, n2 = 0, 1
    for i in range(1, n + 1):
        temp = n1 + n2
        n1 = n2
        n2 = temp
    return n2

start = time.time()
[fib(10000) for x in range(0, 1000)]
end = time.time()
print(f'Python time: {end - start}')

# output
times: 1000
Python time: 1.2072255611419678
```

And to make the times from input, as below,

```
import time

def fib(n):
    n1, n2 = 0, 1
    for i in range(1, n + 1):
        temp = n1 + n2
        n1 = n2
        n2 = temp
    return n2

start = time.perf_counter()
[fib(10000) for x in range(0, int(input("times:")))]
end = time.perf_counter()
print(f'Python time: {end - start}')

# output
```

```
times:1000
Python time: 3.232925400000113
```

Then the time is close to timeit module, so we know timeit is counting more than just the fib() function, and it can be seen from the code, so do not waste time on the unnecassary functions when doing timing. Print itself may also consume time, so it just can not be precise. And do not even try in a software level. What is the print function time usage? See below,

```
import time
from functools import wraps
def func_time(f):
    """
    :param f:
    :return:
    """

    @wraps(f)
    def wrapper(*args, **kwargs):
        start = time.time()
        result = f(*args, **kwargs)
        end = time.time()
        print(f'Python time: {end - start}')
        return result

    return wrapper

@func_time
def test():
    for x in range(10000000):
        pass

test()

# output
Python time: 0.11257290840148926
```

So print 10 million apporximately 0.11 seconds, one time can really be ignored. Wrap is a good way to adding other functions into one funcion, and we can add cProfile function to each line of our function, as below,

```
import cProfile
import time
from functools import wraps
def func_cprofile(f):
    @wraps(f)
    def wrapper(*args, **kwargs):
        profile = cProfile.Profile()
        try:
            profile.enable()
            result = f(*args, **kwargs)
```

```
            profile.disable()
            return result
        finally:
            profile.print_stats(sort='time')
    return wrapper

@func_cprofile
def fib(n):
    n1, n2 = 0, 1
    for i in range(1, n + 1):
        temp = n1 + n2
        n1 = n2
        n2 = temp
    return n2

def func_time(f):
    """
    :param f:
    :return:
    """

    @wraps(f)
    def wrapper(*args, **kwargs):
        start = time.time()
        result = f(*args, **kwargs)
        end = time.time()
        print(f'Python time: {end - start}')
        return result

    return wrapper

@func_time
def test(n):
    for x in range(n):
        (fib(10000))

(test(1))

# output
 2 function calls in 0.001 seconds

   Ordered by: internal time

   ncalls  tottime  percall  cumtime  percall filename:lineno(function)
        1    0.001    0.001    0.001    0.001 test.py:17(fib)
             1        0.000        0.000        0.000        0.000 {method 'disable' of
'_lsprof.Profiler' objects}


Python time: 0.0319976806640625
```

And we can use profile module from outside, as below,

```
# test.py
def fib(n):
    n1, n2 = 0, 1
    for i in range(1, n + 1):
        temp = n1 + n2
        n1 = n2
        n2 = temp
    return n2

def test(n):
    for x in range(n):
        (fib(10000))

(test(1))

# python -m profile test.py

# output
6 function calls in 0.016 seconds

   Ordered by: standard name

   ncalls  tottime  percall  cumtime  percall filename:lineno(function)
        1    0.000    0.000    0.000    0.000 :0(exec)
        1    0.000    0.000    0.000    0.000 :0(setprofile)
         1     0.016     0.016     0.016     0.016 profile:0(<code object <module> at 
0x00000179A87C2F70, file "test.py", line 1>)
        0    0.000             0.000          profile:0(profiler)
        1    0.000    0.000    0.000    0.000 test.py:1(<module>)
        1    0.000    0.000    0.000    0.000 test.py:1(fib)
        1    0.000    0.000    0.000    0.000 test.py:9(test)
```

Notice the line 1 is the most time cosuming line, and that is not what we can do when we import others module, so are we going to build our own? See below,

```
# test.py
#coding:utf-8
import re,time,random,os,datetime
import urllib.request

def print_run_time(func):
    def wrapper(*args, **kw):
        local_time = time.time()
        func(*args, **kw)
        print('current Function [%s] run time is %.2f' % (func.__name__ ,time.time() 
- local_time))
    return wrapper

class test:
    def __init__(self):
        self.url=''
    #get web
```

```
    @print_run_time
    def get_html(self,url):
        try:
            html = urllib.request.urlopen(url=url)


        except:
            print('fail')
            return None
        return html

    @print_run_time
    def run(self):
        self.url='http://www.bing.com'
        self.get_html(self.url)
        print('end')

@print_run_time
def get_current_dir(spath):
    #spath=os.getcwd()
    #spath=os.path.abspath(os.curdir)

    for schild in os.listdir(spath):
        schildpath=spath+'/'+schild
        if os.path.isdir(schildpath):
            get_current_dir(schildpath)
        else:
            print(schildpath)

if __name__ == '__main__':
    my_test=test()
    my_test.run()
    spath=os.path.abspath('.')
    get_current_dir(spath)

# output
C:\Users\Lenovo\Project>python test.py
current Function [get_html] run time is 1.43
end
current Function [run] run time is 1.43
C:\Users\Lenovo\Project/cgi-bin/setup.py
current Function [get_current_dir] run time is 0.00
C:\Users\Lenovo\Project/index.html
C:\Users\Lenovo\Project/server.py
C:\Users\Lenovo\Project/test.py
current Function [get_current_dir] run time is 0.01
```

Don't rebuild the wheel, that is the most important thing in Python. Any thing that can be used, or imported, just use, it can save a lot time, and a project is good enough if it can run.

```
# import tkinter module
from tkinter import *

# make a window
window = Tk()

# specify it's size
window.geometry("872x691")

# take a image for background
bg = PhotoImage(file='bg.png')

# label it in the background
label = Label(window, image=bg)

# position the image as well
label.place(x=0, y=0)
window.counter = 0
label1 = Label(window, text="Click below to order,\nor click this to pay.")
label1.pack()

import webbrowser
# Define the order web api
url= 'https://www.gibbys.com/menus/'
def open_url(url):
   webbrowser.open_new_tab(url)
# Bind the label with the URL to open in a new tab
label1.bind("<Button-1>", lambda e:open_url(url))
def clicked(p):
    window.counter += 1*p
    label1['text'] = 'Total Price: .' + str(window.counter)

# closing the main loop
window.mainloop()
```

26 urllib

Anything written into a class is a module, and is exported, or partially exported. Built-in fucntion **dir()** can be used to check the available functions of a module. Let's try see what urllib has and how to use, as below,

```
>>> import urllib.error
>>> dir()
['__annotations__', '__builtins__', '__doc__', '__loader__', '__name__',
'__package__', '__spec__', 'urllib']
>>> dir(urllib.error)
['ContentTooShortError', 'HTTPError', 'URLError', '__all__', '__builtins__',
'__cached__', '__doc__', '__file__', '__loader__', '__name__', '__package__',
'__spec__', 'io', 'urllib']
>>> del('urllib')
>>> import urllib
```

```
>>> dir(urllib)
['__builtins__', '__cached__', '__doc__', '__file__', '__loader__', '__name__',
'__package__', '__path__', '__spec__']
>>> dir()
['__annotations__', '__builtins__', '__doc__', '__loader__', '__name__',
'__package__', '__spec__', 'urllib']
```

How come urllib has error, but not showing? Checkout https://github.com/python/cpython/tree/3.12/Lib/urllib/, there is no line in `__init__.py`, is this really? See below,

```
>>> help('urllib')
Help on package urllib:

NAME
    urllib

MODULE REFERENCE
    https://docs.python.org/3.12/library/urllib.html

    The following documentation is automatically generated from the Python
    source files.  It may be incomplete, incorrect or include features that
    are considered implementation detail and may vary between Python
    implementations.  When in doubt, consult the module reference at the
    location listed above.

PACKAGE CONTENTS
    error
    parse
    request
    response
    robotparser

FILE
                                                                   c:\program
files\windowsapps\pythonsoftwarefoundation.python.3.12_3.12.1776.0_x64__qbz5n2kfra8p
0\lib\urllib\__init__.py
```

It is true, and we can build our own, `kkk`, as below,

```
C:\Users\Lenovo\Project>dir kkk
 Volume in drive C is Windows-SSD
 Volume Serial Number is 5286-8C92

 Directory of C:\Users\Lenovo\Project\kkk

2024/09/12  14:41    <DIR>          .
2024/09/12  14:34    <DIR>          ..
2024/09/10  11:41                 0 __init__.py
2024/09/12  14:41    <DIR>          __pycache__
               1 File(s)              0 bytes
               3 Dir(s)  67,576,848,384 bytes free
```

And we are going to use the same `error.py`, as below,

```
C:\Users\Lenovo\Project>dir kkk
 Volume in drive C is Windows-SSD
 Volume Serial Number is 5286-8C92

 Directory of C:\Users\Lenovo\Project\kkk

2024/09/12  14:41    <DIR>          .
2024/09/12  14:34    <DIR>          ..
2024/09/10  11:41                 0 __init__.py
2024/3/1    23:04              2489 error.py
2024/09/12  14:41    <DIR>          __pycache__
               1 File(s)              0 bytes
               3 Dir(s)  67,576,848,384 bytes free

C:\Users\Lenovo\Project>more kkk\error.py
"""Exception classes raised by urllib.

The base exception class is URLError, which inherits from OSError.  It
doesn't define any behavior of its own, but is the base class for all
exceptions defined in this package.

HTTPError is an exception class that is also a valid HTTP response
instance.  It behaves this way because HTTP protocol errors are valid
responses, with a status code, headers, and a body.  In some contexts,
an application may want to handle an exception like a regular
response.
"""
import io
import urllib.response

__all__ = ['URLError', 'HTTPError', 'ContentTooShortError']


class URLError(OSError):
    # URLError is a sub-type of OSError, but it doesn't share any of
    # the implementation.  need to override __init__ and __str__.
    # It sets self.args for compatibility with other OSError
    # subclasses, but args doesn't have the typical format with errno in
    # slot 0 and strerror in slot 1.  This may be better than nothing.
    def __init__(self, reason, filename=None):
        self.args = reason,
        self.reason = reason
        if filename is not None:
            self.filename = filename

    def __str__(self):
        return '<urlopen error %s>' % self.reason


class HTTPError(URLError, urllib.response.addinfourl):
```

```
    """Raised when HTTP error occurs, but also acts like non-error return"""
    __super_init = urllib.response.addinfourl.__init__

    def __init__(self, url, code, msg, hdrs, fp):
        self.code = code
        self.msg = msg
        self.hdrs = hdrs
        self.fp = fp
        self.filename = url
        if fp is None:
            fp = io.BytesIO()
        self.__super_init(fp, hdrs, url, code)

    def __str__(self):
        return 'HTTP Error %s: %s' % (self.code, self.msg)

    def __repr__(self):
        return '<HTTPError %s: %r>' % (self.code, self.msg)

    # since URLError specifies a .reason attribute, HTTPError should also
    #  provide this attribute. See issue13211 for discussion.
    @property
    def reason(self):
        return self.msg

    @property
    def headers(self):
        return self.hdrs

    @headers.setter
    def headers(self, headers):
        self.hdrs = headers


class ContentTooShortError(URLError):
    """Exception raised when downloaded size does not match content-length."""
    def __init__(self, message, content):
        URLError.__init__(self, message)
        self.content = content

Python 3.12.6 (tags/v3.12.6:a4a2d2b, Sep  6 2024, 20:11:23) [MSC v.1940 64 bit (AMD64)] on win32
Type "help", "copyright", "credits" or "license" for more information.
>>> import kkk.error
>>> dir()
['__annotations__', '__builtins__', '__doc__', '__loader__', '__name__', '__package__', '__spec__', 'kkk']
>>> dir(kkk)
['__builtins__', '__cached__', '__doc__', '__file__', '__loader__', '__name__', '__package__', '__path__', '__spec__', 'error']
```

'__builtins__', '__cached__', '__doc__', '__file__', '__loader__', '__name__', '__package__', '__path__', '__spec__' are the default properties for a class, which means Python declared.

```
>>> print(kkk.__spec__)
ModuleSpec(name='kkk', loader=<_frozen_importlib_external.SourceFileLoader object at 0x0000028BBCEC0200>, origin='C:\\Users\\Lenovo\\kkk\\__init__.py', submodule_search_locations=['C:\\Users\\Lenovo\\kkk'])
>>> print(kkk.error.__doc__)
Exception classes raised by urllib.

The base exception class is URLError, which inherits from OSError.  It
doesn't define any behavior of its own, but is the base class for all
exceptions defined in this package.

HTTPError is an exception class that is also a valid HTTP response
instance.  It behaves this way because HTTP protocol errors are valid
responses, with a status code, headers, and a body.  In some contexts,
an application may want to handle an exception like a regular
response.
>>> print(kkk.error.URLError.__doc__)
None
>>> print(kkk.error.HTTPError.__doc__)
Raised when HTTP error occurs, but also acts like non-error return
>>>
```

so `__doc__` is the part in between the three '', and `HTTPError` has superinit and three properties. `@property` is the read-only operation of a method.

```
>>> dir(kkk.error.HTTPError)
['_HTTPError__super_init', '__cause__', '__class__', '__context__', '__delattr__', '__dict__', '__dir__', '__doc__', '__enter__', '__eq__', '__exit__', '__format__', '__ge__', '__getattr__', '__getattribute__', '__getstate__', '__gt__', '__hash__', '__init__', '__init_subclass__', '__iter__', '__le__', '__lt__', '__module__', '__ne__', '__new__', '__reduce__', '__reduce_ex__', '__repr__', '__setattr__', '__setstate__', '__sizeof__', '__str__', '__subclasshook__', '__suppress_context__', '__traceback__', '__weakref__', 'add_note', 'args', 'characters_written', 'close', 'errno', 'filename', 'filename2', 'getcode', 'geturl', 'headers', 'info', 'reason', 'status', 'strerror', 'winerror', 'with_traceback']
```

`__getattr__` and `__setattr__` are two default method in Python class,

```
>>> kkk.error.HTTPError.__getattr__()
Traceback (most recent call last):
  File "<stdin>", line 1, in <module>
TypeError: _TemporaryFileWrapper.__getattr__() missing 2 required positional arguments: 'self' and 'name'
>>> getattr(kkk.error.HTTPError, 'msg', 'NA')
'NA'
>>> vars(kkk.error.HTTPError)
mappingproxy({'__module__': 'kkk.error', '__doc__': 'Raised when HTTP error occurs,
```

```
but also acts like non-error return', '_HTTPError__super_init': <function addinfourl.__init__ at 0x0000028BBCF1F600>, '__init__': <function HTTPError.__init__ at 0x0000028BBCF1F920>, '__str__': <function HTTPError.__str__ at 0x0000028BBCF1F9C0>, '__repr__': <function HTTPError.__repr__ at 0x0000028BBCF1FA60>, 'reason': <property object at 0x0000028BBCEC8A90>, 'headers': <property object at 0x0000028BBCF0AA20>})
>>> getattr(kkk.error.HTTPError, '__repr__', 'NA')
<function HTTPError.__repr__ at 0x0000028BBCF1FA60>
```

Imagine when we are in debug mode, and we want to add a certain value for the class,

```
>>> setattr(kkk.error.HTTPError, '__myname__', 'masara')
>>> getattr(kkk.error.HTTPError, '__myname__', 'NA')
'masara'
```

Notice HTTPError is inherent two classes, **URLError**, **urllib.response.addinfourl**, see below,

```
class Root:
    pass

class A(Root):
    pass

class B(Root):
    pass

class C(A, B):
    pass

print(C.__mro__)

# (<class '__main__.C'>, <class '__main__.A'>, <class '__main__.B'>, <class '__main__.Root'>, <class 'object'>)
```

`__MRO__` gives the C inherent order, C from A, B, A, B from Root, and Root from object, which means class. In fact calling default function can be very tricky,

```
>>> print(kkk.error.HTTPError())
Traceback (most recent call last):
  File "<stdin>", line 1, in <module>
TypeError: HTTPError.__init__() missing 5 required positional arguments: 'url', 'code', 'msg', 'hdrs', and 'fp'
>>> e = open("e.txt", "w")
>>> print(kkk.error.HTTPError("a","b","c","d", e))
HTTP Error b: c
>>> e.close()
```

In fact, Python itself is a big class, checkout https://github.com/python/cpython/blob/main/Programs/python.c, and the corresponding headers,

```
// Entry point of the Python C API.
// C extensions should only #include <Python.h>, and not include directly
// the other Python header files included by <Python.h>.

#ifndef Py_PYTHON_H
#define Py_PYTHON_H

// Since this is a "meta-include" file, no #ifdef __cplusplus / extern "C" {

// Include Python header files
#include "patchlevel.h"
#include "pyconfig.h"
#include "pymacconfig.h"

#if defined(__sgi) && !defined(_SGI_MP_SOURCE)
#  define _SGI_MP_SOURCE
#endif

// stdlib.h, stdio.h, errno.h and string.h headers are not used by Python
// headers, but kept for backward compatibility. They are excluded from the
// limited C API of Python 3.11.
#if !defined(Py_LIMITED_API) || Py_LIMITED_API+0 < 0x030b0000
#  include <stdlib.h>
#  include <stdio.h>              // FILE*
#  include <errno.h>              // errno
#  include <string.h>             // memcpy()
#endif
#ifndef MS_WINDOWS
#  include <unistd.h>
#endif
#ifdef HAVE_STDDEF_H
#  include <stddef.h>             // size_t
#endif

#include <assert.h>               // assert()
#include <wchar.h>                // wchar_t

#include "pyport.h"
#include "pymacro.h"
#include "pymath.h"
#include "pymem.h"
#include "pytypedefs.h"
#include "pybuffer.h"
#include "object.h"
#include "objimpl.h"
#include "typeslots.h"
#include "pyhash.h"
#include "cpython/pydebug.h"
```

```
#include "bytearrayobject.h"
#include "bytesobject.h"
#include "unicodeobject.h"
#include "cpython/initconfig.h"
#include "pystate.h"
#include "pyerrors.h"
#include "longobject.h"
#include "cpython/longintrepr.h"
#include "boolobject.h"
#include "floatobject.h"
#include "complexobject.h"
#include "rangeobject.h"
#include "memoryobject.h"
#include "tupleobject.h"
#include "listobject.h"
#include "dictobject.h"
#include "cpython/odictobject.h"
#include "enumobject.h"
#include "setobject.h"
#include "methodobject.h"
#include "moduleobject.h"
#include "cpython/funcobject.h"
#include "cpython/classobject.h"
#include "fileobject.h"
#include "pycapsule.h"
#include "cpython/code.h"
#include "pyframe.h"
#include "traceback.h"
#include "sliceobject.h"
#include "cpython/cellobject.h"
#include "iterobject.h"
#include "cpython/genobject.h"
#include "descrobject.h"
#include "genericaliasobject.h"
#include "warnings.h"
#include "weakrefobject.h"
#include "structseq.h"
#include "cpython/picklebufobject.h"
#include "cpython/pytime.h"
#include "codecs.h"
#include "pythread.h"
#include "cpython/context.h"
#include "modsupport.h"
#include "compile.h"
#include "pythonrun.h"
#include "pylifecycle.h"
#include "ceval.h"
#include "sysmodule.h"
#include "osmodule.h"
#include "intrcheck.h"
#include "import.h"
#include "abstract.h"
#include "bltinmodule.h"
```

```
#include "cpython/pyctype.h"
#include "pystrtod.h"
#include "pystrcmp.h"
#include "fileutils.h"
#include "cpython/pyfpe.h"
#include "tracemalloc.h"

#endif /* !Py_PYTHON_H */
```

It can be much easier to find the class relation if we build, instead of install, since we can see the configure and make on the computer, directly from the source,

```
PCbuild\build.bat -e -d -p x64
```

So we can see the interactive Python uses the class `InteractiveConsole`, which inherent from `InteractiveInterpreter`,

```
"""Utilities needed to emulate Python's interactive interpreter.

"""

# Inspired by similar code by Jeff Epler and Fredrik Lundh.


import builtins
import sys
import traceback
from codeop import CommandCompiler, compile_command

__all__ = ["InteractiveInterpreter", "InteractiveConsole", "interact",
           "compile_command"]

class InteractiveInterpreter:
    """Base class for InteractiveConsole.

    This class deals with parsing and interpreter state (the user's
    namespace); it doesn't deal with input buffering or prompting or
    input file naming (the filename is always passed in explicitly).

    """

    def __init__(self, locals=None):
        """Constructor.

        The optional 'locals' argument specifies a mapping to use as the
        namespace in which code will be executed; it defaults to a newly
        created dictionary with key "__name__" set to "__console__" and
        key "__doc__" set to None.

        """
        if locals is None:
            locals = {"__name__": "__console__", "__doc__": None}
```

```
        self.locals = locals
        self.compile = CommandCompiler()

    def runsource(self, source, filename="<input>", symbol="single"):
        """Compile and run some source in the interpreter.

        Arguments are as for compile_command().

        One of several things can happen:

        1) The input is incorrect; compile_command() raised an
        exception (SyntaxError or OverflowError).  A syntax traceback
        will be printed by calling the showsyntaxerror() method.

        2) The input is incomplete, and more input is required;
        compile_command() returned None.  Nothing happens.

        3) The input is complete; compile_command() returned a code
        object.  The code is executed by calling self.runcode() (which
        also handles run-time exceptions, except for SystemExit).

        The return value is True in case 2, False in the other cases (unless
        an exception is raised).  The return value can be used to
        decide whether to use sys.ps1 or sys.ps2 to prompt the next
        line.

        """
        try:
            code = self.compile(source, filename, symbol)
        except (OverflowError, SyntaxError, ValueError):
            # Case 1
            self.showsyntaxerror(filename, source=source)
            return False

        if code is None:
            # Case 2
            return True

        # Case 3
        self.runcode(code)
        return False

    def runcode(self, code):
        """Execute a code object.

        When an exception occurs, self.showtraceback() is called to
        display a traceback.  All exceptions are caught except
        SystemExit, which is reraised.

        A note about KeyboardInterrupt: this exception may occur
        elsewhere in this code, and may not always be caught.  The
        caller should be prepared to deal with it.
```

```
        """
        try:
            exec(code, self.locals)
        except SystemExit:
            raise
        except:
            self.showtraceback()

    def showsyntaxerror(self, filename=None, **kwargs):
        """Display the syntax error that just occurred.

        This doesn't display a stack trace because there isn't one.

        If a filename is given, it is stuffed in the exception instead
        of what was there before (because Python's parser always uses
        "<string>" when reading from a string).

        The output is written by self.write(), below.

        """
        try:
            typ, value, tb = sys.exc_info()
            if filename and issubclass(typ, SyntaxError):
                value.filename = filename
            source = kwargs.pop('source', "")
            self._showtraceback(typ, value, None, source)
        finally:
            typ = value = tb = None

    def showtraceback(self):
        """Display the exception that just occurred.

        We remove the first stack item because it is our own code.

        The output is written by self.write(), below.

        """
        try:
            typ, value, tb = sys.exc_info()
            self._showtraceback(typ, value, tb.tb_next, "")
        finally:
            typ = value = tb = None

    def _showtraceback(self, typ, value, tb, source):
        sys.last_type = typ
        sys.last_traceback = tb
        value = value.with_traceback(tb)
        # Set the line of text that the exception refers to
        lines = source.splitlines()
        if (source and typ is SyntaxError
                and not value.text and len(lines) >= value.lineno):
            value.text = lines[value.lineno - 1]
        sys.last_exc = sys.last_value = value
```

```
        if sys.excepthook is sys.__excepthook__:
            self._excepthook(typ, value, tb)
        else:
            # If someone has set sys.excepthook, we let that take precedence
            # over self.write
            try:
                sys.excepthook(typ, value, tb)
            except SystemExit:
                raise
            except BaseException as e:
                e.__context__ = None
                e = e.with_traceback(e.__traceback__.tb_next)
                print('Error in sys.excepthook:', file=sys.stderr)
                sys.__excepthook__(type(e), e, e.__traceback__)
                print(file=sys.stderr)
                print('Original exception was:', file=sys.stderr)
                sys.__excepthook__(typ, value, tb)

    def _excepthook(self, typ, value, tb):
        # This method is being overwritten in
        # _pyrepl.console.InteractiveColoredConsole
        lines = traceback.format_exception(typ, value, tb)
        self.write(''.join(lines))

    def write(self, data):
        """Write a string.

        The base implementation writes to sys.stderr; a subclass may
        replace this with a different implementation.

        """
        sys.stderr.write(data)


class InteractiveConsole(InteractiveInterpreter):
    """Closely emulate the behavior of the interactive Python interpreter.

    This class builds on InteractiveInterpreter and adds prompting
    using the familiar sys.ps1 and sys.ps2, and input buffering.

    """

    def __init__(self, locals=None, filename="<console>", *, local_exit=False):
        """Constructor.

        The optional locals argument will be passed to the
        InteractiveInterpreter base class.

        The optional filename argument should specify the (file)name
        of the input stream; it will show up in tracebacks.

        """
        InteractiveInterpreter.__init__(self, locals)
```

```
        self.filename = filename
        self.local_exit = local_exit
        self.resetbuffer()

    def resetbuffer(self):
        """Reset the input buffer."""
        self.buffer = []

    def interact(self, banner=None, exitmsg=None):
        """Closely emulate the interactive Python console.

        The optional banner argument specifies the banner to print
        before the first interaction; by default it prints a banner
        similar to the one printed by the real Python interpreter,
        followed by the current class name in parentheses (so as not
        to confuse this with the real interpreter -- since it's so
        close!).

        The optional exitmsg argument specifies the exit message
        printed when exiting. Pass the empty string to suppress
        printing an exit message. If exitmsg is not given or None,
        a default message is printed.

        """
        try:
            sys.ps1
        except AttributeError:
            sys.ps1 = ">>> "
        try:
            sys.ps2
        except AttributeError:
            sys.ps2 = "... "
            cprt = 'Type "help", "copyright", "credits" or "license" for more
information.'
        if banner is None:
            self.write("Python %s on %s\n%s\n(%s)\n" %
                       (sys.version, sys.platform, cprt,
                        self.__class__.__name__))
        elif banner:
            self.write("%s\n" % str(banner))
        more = 0

        # When the user uses exit() or quit() in their interactive shell
        # they probably just want to exit the created shell, not the whole
        # process. exit and quit in builtins closes sys.stdin which makes
        # it super difficult to restore
        #
        # When self.local_exit is True, we overwrite the builtins so
        # exit() and quit() only raises SystemExit and we can catch that
        # to only exit the interactive shell

        _exit = None
        _quit = None
```

```
        if self.local_exit:
            if hasattr(builtins, "exit"):
                _exit = builtins.exit
                builtins.exit = Quitter("exit")

            if hasattr(builtins, "quit"):
                _quit = builtins.quit
                builtins.quit = Quitter("quit")

        try:
            while True:
                try:
                    if more:
                        prompt = sys.ps2
                    else:
                        prompt = sys.ps1
                    try:
                        line = self.raw_input(prompt)
                    except EOFError:
                        self.write("\n")
                        break
                    else:
                        more = self.push(line)
                except KeyboardInterrupt:
                    self.write("\nKeyboardInterrupt\n")
                    self.resetbuffer()
                    more = 0
                except SystemExit as e:
                    if self.local_exit:
                        self.write("\n")
                        break
                    else:
                        raise e
        finally:
            # restore exit and quit in builtins if they were modified
            if _exit is not None:
                builtins.exit = _exit

            if _quit is not None:
                builtins.quit = _quit

            if exitmsg is None:
                self.write('now exiting %s...\n' % self.__class__.__name__)
            elif exitmsg != '':
                self.write('%s\n' % exitmsg)

    def push(self, line, filename=None, _symbol="single"):
        """Push a line to the interpreter.

        The line should not have a trailing newline; it may have
        internal newlines.  The line is appended to a buffer and the
        interpreter's runsource() method is called with the
```

```
        concatenated contents of the buffer as source.  If this
        indicates that the command was executed or invalid, the buffer
        is reset; otherwise, the command is incomplete, and the buffer
        is left as it was after the line was appended.  The return
        value is 1 if more input is required, 0 if the line was dealt
        with in some way (this is the same as runsource()).

        """
        self.buffer.append(line)
        source = "\n".join(self.buffer)
        if filename is None:
            filename = self.filename
        more = self.runsource(source, filename, symbol=_symbol)
        if not more:
            self.resetbuffer()
        return more

    def raw_input(self, prompt=""):
        """Write a prompt and read a line.

        The returned line does not include the trailing newline.
        When the user enters the EOF key sequence, EOFError is raised.

        The base implementation uses the built-in function
        input(); a subclass may replace this with a different
        implementation.

        """
        return input(prompt)


class Quitter:
    def __init__(self, name):
        self.name = name
        if sys.platform == "win32":
            self.eof = 'Ctrl-Z plus Return'
        else:
            self.eof = 'Ctrl-D (i.e. EOF)'

    def __repr__(self):
        return f'Use {self.name} or {self.eof} to exit'

    def __call__(self, code=None):
        raise SystemExit(code)


def interact(banner=None, readfunc=None, local=None, exitmsg=None,
local_exit=False):
    """Closely emulate the interactive Python interpreter.

    This is a backwards compatible interface to the InteractiveConsole
    class.  When readfunc is not specified, it attempts to import the
    readline module to enable GNU readline if it is available.
```

```
    Arguments (all optional, all default to None):

    banner -- passed to InteractiveConsole.interact()
    readfunc -- if not None, replaces InteractiveConsole.raw_input()
    local -- passed to InteractiveInterpreter.__init__()
    exitmsg -- passed to InteractiveConsole.interact()
    local_exit -- passed to InteractiveConsole.__init__()

    """
    console = InteractiveConsole(local, local_exit=local_exit)
    if readfunc is not None:
        console.raw_input = readfunc
    else:
        try:
            import readline  # noqa: F401
        except ImportError:
            pass
    console.interact(banner, exitmsg)


if __name__ == "__main__":
    import argparse

    parser = argparse.ArgumentParser()
    parser.add_argument('-q', action='store_true',
                       help="don't print version and copyright messages")
    args = parser.parse_args()
    if args.q or sys.flags.quiet:
        banner = ''
    else:
        banner = None
    interact(banner)
```

Notice urllib.parse is embedded in Python, so we can copy into `kkk` as well, see below,

```
>>> for i in dir(kkk.parse): ((i))
...
'DefragResult'
'DefragResultBytes'
'ParseResult'
'ParseResultBytes'
'ResultBase'
'SplitResult'
'SplitResultBytes'
'_ALWAYS_SAFE'
'_ALWAYS_SAFE_BYTES'
'_DefragResultBase'
'_NetlocResultMixinBase'
'_NetlocResultMixinBytes'
'_NetlocResultMixinStr'
```

```
'_ParseResultBase'
'_Quoter'
'_ResultMixinBytes'
'_ResultMixinStr'
'_SplitResultBase'
'_UNSAFE_URL_BYTES_TO_REMOVE'
'_WHATWG_C0_CONTROL_OR_SPACE'
'__all__'
'__builtins__'
'__cached__'
'__doc__'
'__file__'
'__getattr__'
'__loader__'
'__name__'
'__package__'
'__spec__'
'_asciire'
'_byte_quoter_factory'
'_check_bracketed_host'
'_checknetloc'
'_coerce_args'
'_decode_args'
'_encode_result'
'_generate_unquoted_parts'
'_hexdig'
'_hextobyte'
'_hostprog'
'_implicit_encoding'
'_implicit_errors'
'_noop'
'_portprog'
'_splitattr'
'_splithost'
'_splitnetloc'
'_splitnport'
'_splitparams'
'_splitpasswd'
'_splitport'
'_splitquery'
'_splittag'
'_splittype'
'_splituser'
'_splitvalue'
'_to_bytes'
'_typeprog'
'_unquote_impl'
'clear_cache'
'functools'
'ipaddress'
'math'
'namedtuple'
'non_hierarchical'
```

```
'parse_qs'
'parse_qsl'
'quote'
'quote_from_bytes'
'quote_plus'
're'
'scheme_chars'
'splitattr'
'splithost'
'splitnport'
'splitpasswd'
'splitport'
'splitquery'
'splittag'
'splittype'
'splituser'
'splitvalue'
'to_bytes'
'types'
'unquote'
'unquote_plus'
'unquote_to_bytes'
'unwrap'
'urldefrag'
'urlencode'
'urljoin'
'urlparse'
'urlsplit'
'urlunparse'
'urlunsplit'
'uses_fragment'
'uses_netloc'
'uses_params'
'uses_query'
'uses_relative'
'warnings'
>>>
```

To map with how to use, checkout https://github.com/python/cpython/blob/main/Lib/urllib/parse.py, or read the docs, and we find the url parse is cutting into 6 parts, as below,

```
>>> kkk.parse.urlparse('https://docs.python.org/3/library/urllib.parse.html#module-urllib.parse')
ParseResult(scheme='https', netloc='docs.python.org', path='/3/library/urllib.parse.html', params='', query='', fragment='module-urllib.parse')
>>>
```

And we can join, as below,

```
>>> base_url = 'https://docs.python.org'
>>> addition = '3/library/urllib.parse.html#module-urllib.parse'
>>> url = kkk.parse.urljoin(base_url, addition)
>>> url
'https://docs.python.org/3/library/urllib.parse.html#module-urllib.parse'
```

So we should get used to use single quote for the upper level from now on, and we not afraid of quote, see below,

```
>>> kkk.parse.quote('á á')
'%C3%A1%20%C3%A1'
>>> kkk.parse.urlencode({'type': 'customer foo','client_id': 123})
'type=customer+foo&client_id=123'
```

We can also upper the level for functions, as below,

```
>>> from kkk.parse import *
>>> dir()
['DefragResult', 'DefragResultBytes', 'ParseResult', 'ParseResultBytes',
'SplitResult', 'SplitResultBytes', '__annotations__', '__builtins__', '__doc__',
'__loader__', '__name__', '__package__', '__spec__', 'parse_qs', 'parse_qsl',
'quote', 'quote_from_bytes', 'quote_plus', 'unquote', 'unquote_plus',
'unquote_to_bytes', 'urldefrag', 'urlencode', 'urljoin', 'urlparse', 'urlsplit',
'urlunparse', 'urlunsplit']
>>> from kkk.error import *
>>> dir()
['ContentTooShortError', 'DefragResult', 'DefragResultBytes', 'HTTPError',
'ParseResult', 'ParseResultBytes', 'SplitResult', 'SplitResultBytes', 'URLError',
'__annotations__', '__builtins__', '__doc__', '__loader__', '__name__',
'__package__', '__spec__', 'parse_qs', 'parse_qsl', 'quote', 'quote_from_bytes',
'quote_plus', 'unquote', 'unquote_plus', 'unquote_to_bytes', 'urldefrag',
'urlencode', 'urljoin', 'urlparse', 'urlsplit', 'urlunparse', 'urlunsplit']
```

We really need to be careful if import functions to the same level, because it is easier to overlap, and that will drag us to do the set calculation, which is another topic.

27 selenium

Nowadays there are many websites, and browsers can be very tedious to scroll if we already know the location we want. Or it can be impossible on no screen computers to see the information. However back to HTTP protocol, it is just request and response.

Request Method	Description
CONNECT	This specification reserves the method name CONNECT for use with a proxy that can dynamically switch to being a tunnel (e.g. SSL tunneling).
DELETE	The DELETE method requests that the origin server delete the resource identified by the Request-URI.
GET	The GET method retrieves whatever information (in the form of an entity) is identified by the Request-URI.
HEAD	The HEAD method is identical to GET except that the server MUST NOT return a message-body in the response.
OPTIONS	The OPTIONS method represents a request for information about the communication options available on the request/response chain identified by the Request-URI.
POST	The POST method is used to request that the origin server accept the entity enclosed in the request as a new subordinate of the resource identified by the Request-URI in the Request-Line.
PUT	The PUT method requests that the enclosed entity be stored under the supplied Request-URI.
TRACE	The TRACE method is used to invoke a remote, application-layer loop-back of the request message.
Response code	**Description**
100	An initial part of the request was received, and the client should continue.
101	The server is changing protocols, as specified by the client, to one listed in the Upgrade header.
200	The request is okay.
201	The resource was created (for requests that create server objects).
202	The request was accepted, but the server has not yet performed any action with it.
203	The transaction was okay, except the information contained in the entity headers was not from the origin server, but from a copy of the resource.
204	The response message contains headers and a status line, but no entity body.
205	Another code primarily for browsers; basically means that the browser should clear any HTML form elements on the current page.
206	A partial request was successful.

Request Method	Description
300	A client has requested a URL that actually refers to multiple resources. This code is returned along with a list of options; the user can then select which one he wants.
301	The requested URL has been moved. The response should contain a Location URL indicating where the resource now resides.
302	Like the 301 status code, but the move is temporary. The client should use the URL given in the Location header to locate the resource temporarily.
303	Tells the client that the resource should be fetched using a different URL. This new URL is in the Location header of the response message.
304	Clients can make their requests conditional by the request headers they include. This code indicates that the resource has not changed.
305	The resource must be accessed through a proxy, the location of the proxy is given in the Location header.
306	This status code currently is not used.
307	Like the 301 status code; however, the client should use the URL given in the Location header to locate the resource temporarily.
400	Tells the client that it sent a malformed request.
401	Returned along with appropriate headers that ask the client to authenticate itself before it can gain access to the resource.
402	Currently this status code is not used, but it has been set aside for future use.
403	The request was refused by the server.
404	The server cannot find the requested URL.
405	A request was made with a method that is not supported for the requested URL. The Allow header should be included in the response to tell the client what methods are allowed on the requested resource.
406	Clients can specify parameters about what types of entities they are willing to accept. This code is used when the server has no resource matching the URL that is acceptable for the client.
407	Like the 401 status code, but used for proxy servers that require authentication for a resource.
408	If a client takes too long to complete its request, a server can send back this status code and close down the connection.
409	The request is causing some conflict on a resource.

Request Method	Description
410	Like the 404 status code, except that the server once held the resource.
411	Servers use this code when they require a Content-Length header in the request message. The server will not accept requests for the resource without the Content-Length header.
412	If a client makes a conditional request and one of the conditions fails, this response code is returned.
413	The client sent an entity body that is larger than the server can or wants to process.
414	The client sent a request with a request URL that is larger than what the server can or wants to process.
415	The client sent an entity of a content type that the server does not understand or support.
416	The request message requested a range of a given resource, and that range either was invalid or could not be met.
417	The request contained an expectation in the Expect request header that could not be satisfied by the server.
500	The server encountered an error that prevented it from servicing the request.
501	The client made a request that is beyond the server's capabilities.
502	A server acting as a proxy or gateway encountered a bogus response from the next link in the request response chain.
503	The server cannot currently service the request but will be able to in the future.
504	Similar to the 408 status code, except that the response is coming from a gateway or proxy that has timed out waiting for a response to its request from another server.
505	The server received a request in a version of the protocol that it can't or won't support.

Recall the Python server, which has the matrix form to submit, we can just use `urllib` to fill it, as below,

```
import urllib.request

url = 'http://localhost:8001'

print("GET")
```

```
response = urllib.request.urlopen(url)
print(response.read().decode('utf-8'))

url = 'http://localhost:8001/cgi-bin/setup.py'
print("POST")
form_data = {
'matrix' = '[[1,2,3],[0,1,4],[5,6,0]]'
}
data = urllib.parse.urlencode(form_data).encode('utf-8')
req = urllib.request.Request(url, data)
response = urllib.request.urlopen(req)
print(response.read().decode('utf-8'))

# output
GET
<html>
<head>
<title>Matrix</title>
</head>


<body>
<h1>Matrix
</h1>
<p>eg. -> [[1,2,3],[0,1,4],[5,6,0]]</p>

<div><form action="cgi-bin/setup.py", method="POST">

  <input type="text" id="matrix" name="matrix" value=""><br>

  <input type="submit" value="Submit">
</form></div>
</body>
</html>
POST

<h1>Matrix</h1>
<p>Your input matrix was
 [[1,2,3],[0,1,4],[5,6,0]]</p>
>>the matrix was: [[1,2,3],[0,1,4],[5,6,0]]
>>determinant = 1

<p>Your inverse matrix is
 [[-24.0, 18.0, 5.0], [20.0, -15.0, -4.0], [-5.0, 4.0, 1.0]]</p>
```

And would it be better if we can just use some package to not only grab data, from web, but also manage? Even draw? See below,

```
import pandas_datareader.data as web
from datetime import datetime

stocks = ['ORCL', 'TSLA', 'IBM','YELP', 'MSFT']
```

```
ls_key = 'Adj Close'
start = datetime(2014,1,1)
end = datetime(2014,3,28)
f = web.DataReader(stocks, 'yahoo',start,end)


cleanData = f.ix[ls_key]
dataFrame = pd.DataFrame(cleanData)
```

But it can't work! Why is that? Checkout https://query1.finance.yahoo.com/v7/finance/quote,


```
{

    "finance": {
        "result": null,
        "error": {
            "code": "Unauthorized",
                    "description": "User is unable to access this feature - https://bit.ly/yahoo-finance-api-feedback"
        }
    }

}
```


So there is very high risk to use 3rd party API, whenever it is disabled, the whole package is useless. But how about build our own API? From the web, e.g. https://stockanalysis.com/list/hong-kong-stock-exchange/, notice that only 500 index shown, and there are 4 more pages,

```
from selenium import webdriver

from selenium.webdriver.edge.options import Options

options = Options()
options.add_argument("headless")
options.add_argument("--start-maximized")
options.add_argument("--disable-notifications")

options.binary_location = r"C:\Program Files (x86)\Microsoft\Edge\Application\128.0.2739.79\msedge.exe"
driver = webdriver.Edge(options = options) # Modify the path here...

from selenium.webdriver.common.by import By
import time

u="https://stockanalysis.com/list/hong-kong-stock-exchange/"

driver.get(u)
print(driver.title)
print(driver.current_window_handle)
```

```
print(driver.window_handles)
time.sleep(5)

data_list = []

xpath = '//*[@id="main-table"]/tbody'

table = driver.find_element(By.XPATH, xpath)

rows = table.find_elements(By.XPATH, xpath+'//tr')

for row in rows:
    data_list.append(row.text)

driver.execute_script("window.scrollTo(0,document.body.scrollHeight)");

#2
'''
xpath = '//*[@id="main"]/div/div/div/nav/button[2]'
button = driver.find_element(By.XPATH, xpath)
print((button.text))
button.click()
'''

xpath = '//*[@id="main"]/div/div/div/nav/button[2]'
element = driver.find_element(By.XPATH, xpath)
driver.execute_script("arguments[0].click();", element)


time.sleep(15)
xpath = '//*[@id="main-table"]/tbody'
table = driver.find_element(By.XPATH, xpath)
rows = table.find_elements(By.XPATH, xpath+'//tr')
for row in rows:
    data_list.append(row.text)

#3
xpath = '//*[@id="main"]/div/div/div/nav/button[2]'
element = driver.find_element(By.XPATH, xpath)
driver.execute_script("arguments[0].click();", element)
time.sleep(15)
xpath = '//*[@id="main-table"]/tbody'
table = driver.find_element(By.XPATH, xpath)
rows = table.find_elements(By.XPATH, xpath+'//tr')
for row in rows:
    data_list.append(row.text)

#4
xpath = '//*[@id="main"]/div/div/div/nav/button[2]'
element = driver.find_element(By.XPATH, xpath)
driver.execute_script("arguments[0].click();", element)
time.sleep(15)
xpath = '//*[@id="main-table"]/tbody'
```

```
table = driver.find_element(By.XPATH, xpath)
rows = table.find_elements(By.XPATH, xpath+'//tr')
for row in rows:
    data_list.append(row.text)

#5
xpath = '//*[@id="main"]/div/div/div/nav/button[2]'
element = driver.find_element(By.XPATH, xpath)
driver.execute_script("arguments[0].click();", element)
time.sleep(15)
xpath = '//*[@id="main-table"]/tbody'
table = driver.find_element(By.XPATH, xpath)
rows = table.find_elements(By.XPATH, xpath+'//tr')
for row in rows:
    data_list.append(row.text)

driver.quit()

import json

# convert to Json
#json_str = json.dumps(data_list)
#print("Json List:", json_str)

# save file
with open("HKStock.json", "w") as final:
    json.dump(data_list, final)
```

So the daily price is saved in file, format in json, the three ' part for button click is just not working, which is really killing programmer, and we even have the trace, as below,

```
Traceback (most recent call last):
  File "C:\Users\Lenovo\kkk\bing.py", line 41, in <module>
    button.click()
                                                                                File
"C:\Users\Lenovo\AppData\Local\Packages\PythonSoftwareFoundation.Python.3.12_qbz5n2k
fra8p0\LocalCache\local-packages\Python312\site-
packages\selenium\webdriver\remote\webelement.py", line 94, in click
    self._execute(Command.CLICK_ELEMENT)
                                                                                File
"C:\Users\Lenovo\AppData\Local\Packages\PythonSoftwareFoundation.Python.3.12_qbz5n2k
fra8p0\LocalCache\local-packages\Python312\site-
packages\selenium\webdriver\remote\webelement.py", line 395, in _execute
    return self._parent.execute(command, params)
           ^^^^^^^^^^^^^^^^^^^^^^^^^^^^^^^^^^^^^^

                                                                                File
"C:\Users\Lenovo\AppData\Local\Packages\PythonSoftwareFoundation.Python.3.12_qbz5n2k
fra8p0\LocalCache\local-packages\Python312\site-
packages\selenium\webdriver\remote\webdriver.py", line 347, in execute
    self.error_handler.check_response(response)
```

```
                                                                                   File
"C:\Users\Lenovo\AppData\Local\Packages\PythonSoftwareFoundation.Python.3.12_qbz5n2k
fra8p0\LocalCache\local-packages\Python312\site-
packages\selenium\webdriver\remote\errorhandler.py", line 229, in check_response
    raise exception_class(message, screen, stacktrace)
selenium.common.exceptions.ElementClickInterceptedException: Message: element click
intercepted: Element <button class="controls-btn xs:pl-1 xs:pr-1.5 bp:text-sm sm:pl-
3 sm:pr-1">...</button> is not clickable at point (802, 92). Other element would
receive the click: <div class="px-5 py-8 xs:px-8 md:px-32 md:py-20">...</div>
  (Session info: MicrosoftEdge=128.0.2739.79)
Stacktrace:
        GetHandleVerifier [0x00F476E3+37459]
                         Microsoft::Applications::Events::time_ticks_t::time_ticks_t
[0x00E04046+386102]
                       Microsoft::Applications::Events::ILogConfiguration::operator*
[0x00C157DA+3578]
        Microsoft::Applications::Events::GUID_t::GUID_t [0x00C4DC05+124805]
        Microsoft::Applications::Events::GUID_t::GUID_t [0x00C4C827+119719]
        Microsoft::Applications::Events::GUID_t::GUID_t [0x00C4B28F+114191]
        Microsoft::Applications::Events::GUID_t::GUID_t [0x00C4AAC6+112198]
        Microsoft::Applications::Events::GUID_t::GUID_t [0x00C435A8+82216]
        Microsoft::Applications::Events::GUID_t::GUID_t [0x00C613FC+204668]
        Microsoft::Applications::Events::GUID_t::GUID_t [0x00C430E1+80993]
        Microsoft::Applications::Events::GUID_t::GUID_t [0x00C43060+80864]
        Microsoft::Applications::Events::GUID_t::GUID_t [0x00C61724+205476]
        Microsoft::Applications::Events::GUID_t::GUID_t [0x00C430E1+80993]
        Microsoft::Applications::Events::GUID_t::GUID_t [0x00C75C5A+288730]
        Microsoft::Applications::Events::GUID_t::GUID_t [0x00C61066+203750]
        Microsoft::Applications::Events::GUID_t::GUID_t [0x00C4292F+79023]
        Microsoft::Applications::Events::GUID_t::GUID_t [0x00C41997+75031]
        Microsoft::Applications::Events::GUID_t::GUID_t [0x00C4237D+77565]
        GetHandleVerifier [0x0104F8BC+1119276]
        Microsoft::Applications::Events::FromJSON [0x01126DDC+150780]
        Microsoft::Applications::Events::FromJSON [0x011266E3+148995]
        Microsoft::Applications::Events::FromJSON [0x01117154+86132]
        Microsoft::Applications::Events::FromJSON [0x01127587+152743]
                         Microsoft::Applications::Events::time_ticks_t::time_ticks_t
[0x00E19F2D+475933]
                         Microsoft::Applications::Events::time_ticks_t::time_ticks_t
[0x00E0D448+423992]
                         Microsoft::Applications::Events::time_ticks_t::time_ticks_t
[0x00E0D633+424483]
                         Microsoft::Applications::Events::time_ticks_t::time_ticks_t
[0x00DF55BA+326058]
        BaseThreadInitThunk [0x758D7BA9+25]
        RtlInitializeExceptionChain [0x7741C10B+107]
        RtlClearBits [0x7741C08F+191]
```

Why is it not clickable? Because it is not focused, and to focus,

```
driver.execute_script("arguments[0].scrollIntoView();", element)
element.click()
```

The selenium wait function has two types, but they are less real than `time.sleep()`,

```
# implicit

from selenium.webdriver.common.by import By

driver.implicitly_wait(10)

# explicit

from selenium.webdriver.support.wait import WebDriverWait
from selenium.webdriver.support import expected_conditions as EC

try:
    login_modal = WebDriverWait(driver, 10).until(
    EC.presence_of_element_located((By.XPATH, xpath))
    )

finally:
    print(login_modal.text)
```

And we can also do a frequency wait,

```
# try once, timeout in 10 seconds

wait = WebDriverWait(driver, timeout=10, poll_frequency=1)

login_modal = wait.until(EC.presence_of_element_located((By.XPATH, xpath)))

print(login_modal.text)
```

We can also use javascript to wait,

```
from selenium import webdriver
from selenium.webdriver.edge.options import Options
from selenium.webdriver.common.by import By

options = Options()
#options.add_argument("headless")
options.add_argument("--start-maximized")
options.add_argument("--disable-notifications")
options.binary_location = r"C:\Program Files (x86)\Microsoft\Edge\Application\128.0.2739.79\msedge.exe"
driver = webdriver.Edge(options = options) # Modify the path here...

#set the script timeout to 3 seconds
driver.set_script_timeout(3)
#save our url as a variable
url = "https://www.amazon.com"
#navigate to the url
driver.get(url)
```

```
#save our selector as a variable
css_selector = "#nav-link-accountList > span"
#find the modal
login_modal = driver.find_element(By.CSS_SELECTOR, css_selector)
#print the text of the modal
print(login_modal.text)
```

Wait is very important, because in real life, everything needs loading, and automation is all about timing, and life is all about timing. You find an element too early, or too late, you neither can find the element.

One reason we do the automation is, we can go over the language, the human language, see below,

```
#!/usr/bin/env python
# -- coding: utf-8 --
from selenium import webdriver
import time
from selenium.webdriver.edge.options import Options
from selenium.webdriver.common.by import By

options = Options()
#options.add_argument("headless")
options.add_argument("--start-maximized")
options.add_argument("--disable-notifications")
options.binary_location = r"C:\Program Files (x86)\Microsoft\Edge\Application\128.0.2739.79\msedge.exe"
browser = webdriver.Edge(options = options) # Modify the path here...
email = input("your email")
password = input("your password")

#save our url as a variable
url = "http://mail.163.com/"
browser.get(url)
time.sleep(3)
# iframe
iframe = browser.find_elements(By.TAG_NAME,'iframe')[0]
browser.switch_to.frame(iframe)
browser.find_element(By.NAME, "email").send_keys(email)
browser.find_element(By.NAME, "password").send_keys(password)
browser.find_element(By.ID, "dologin").click()
time.sleep(3)
input("Enter after reading the emails")
browser.quit()
```

And the most important thing to use Selenium is just be confident with the element, most time retry until it appears,

```
from selenium.common.exceptions import TimeoutException
max_attempts = 3
for _ in range(max_attempts):
```

```
    try:
        element = WebDriverWait(driver,5).until(
          EC.presence_of_element_located((By.ID, "dologin")))
        # Perform actions on the element
        break # Exit the loop if successful

    except TimeoutException:
        continue # Retry if a timeout occurs
```

If really can't find the element, then we have to handle the Error, at least print the error,

```
from selenium.common.exceptions import TimeoutException
try:
    element = WebDriverWait(driver,10).until(
        EC.presence_of_element_located((By.ID, "dologin")))
    # Perform actions on the element
    except TimeoutException:
    # Handle the timeout error here (e.g.log the error or take alternative actions)
        print("this error is...")
```

Notice 163 is a big company in NASDAQ, and it offers music as well, most are free, and it is a huge benefit, so why no try?

```
#!/usr/bin/env python
# -- coding: utf-8 --
from selenium import webdriver
from selenium.webdriver.common.by import By
import time

options = webdriver.EdgeOptions()

options.add_argument('--enable-chrome-browser-cloud-management')
options.add_argument('log-level=INT')
options.add_argument('-ignore-certificate-errors')
options.add_argument('--ignore-certificate-errors-spki-list')
options.add_argument('--ignore-ssl-errors')
options.add_argument('--disable-infobars')
options.add_argument('--disable-extensions')
options.add_argument('--disable-popup-blocking')
options.add_argument('--disable-javascript')
options.add_argument('--disable-blink-features=AutomationControlled')

options.add_experimental_option("detach", True)

options.page_load_strategy = 'eager'

driver = webdriver.Edge(options = options)

driver.get("https://music.163.com/")
driver.implicitly_wait(1)
driver.maximize_window()
```

```
time.sleep(10)

driver.find_element(By.CSS_SELECTOR, '.link.s-fc3').click()
driver.implicitly_wait(10)

driver.find_element(By.CSS_SELECTOR, '._3xIXD0Q6').click()
driver.implicitly_wait(10)

driver.find_element(By.ID, 'j-official-terms').click() # checkbox

driver.find_element(By.XPATH,
'/html/body/div[7]/div/div[2]/div/div/div[2]/div/div/div/div[1]/div[2]/ul/li[4]/a').
click()

iframe = driver.find_elements(By.TAG_NAME, "iframe")
#print(iframe)

driver.switch_to.frame(driver.find_element(By.XPATH,  "//iframe[starts-with(@id,  'x-
URS-iframe')]"))

driver.find_element(By.XPATH,
'/html/body/div[2]/div[2]/div[2]/form/div/div[1]/div[2]/input').send_keys(username)

driver.find_element(By.XPATH,
'/html/body/div[2]/div[2]/div[2]/form/div/div[3]/div[2]/input[2]').send_keys(passwor
d)

driver.find_element(By.ID, 'dologin').click() # login
driver.implicitly_wait(10)

driver.find_element(By.XPATH,
"/html/body/div[1]/div[1]/div/ul/li[2]/span/a").click()
driver.implicitly_wait(10)
print("===============task one===================")
#print(driver.page_source)
iframe = driver.find_elements(By.TAG_NAME, "iframe")
print(iframe)
driver.switch_to.frame("contentFrame")
time.sleep(3)
driver.find_element(By.ID, 'flag_play').click()
# two hours till here
print("===============well done===================")

print("===============task two===================")
driver.execute_script('window.open("https://www.github.com/")')
time.sleep(3)
window = driver.window_handles
print(window)
print("===============well done===================")
#driver.switch_to.window(window[0])

#driver.quit()
```

28 requests

In fact, http requests have 9 types, we already know POST, GET, and we familiar with PUT, PATCH, DELETE. A PUT request is used to modify the data on the server, its function is upload or update. PATCH is similar to PUT, but just a part of the data. A DELETE request is used to delete the data on the server at a specified location.

Let's try GET using requests package, as below,

```
import requests

response = requests.get('https://www.httpbin.org')
print(response.status_code)
print(response.content)
```

and POST as below,

```
import requests

response = requests.post('https://httpbin.org/post', data={'text': 'Hello HTTP #1
**cool**, and #1!'})
print(response.status_code)
print(response.text)
```

Notice `text` is more formatted than `content`, and we can upload a file via POST as below,

```
import requests


url = "https://httpbin.org/post"
files = {'file': open('report.xls', 'rb')}

r = requests.post(url, files=files)
print(r.text)
```

And for PUT as below,

```
import requests


url = "https://httpbin.org/put"
r = requests.put(url, data={'key': 'value'})
print(r.text)
```

And for DELETE as below,

```
import requests


url = "https://httpbin.org/delete"
payload = {'key1': 'value1', 'key2': ['value2', 'value3']}
r = requests.delete(url, data=payload)
print(r.text)
```

So can we find a user from Github? See below,

```
import requests

r = requests.get('https://api.github.com/users')
data = (r.json())

count = len(data)
print("Number of JSON objects:", count) # 30
```

This only gives us 30, which apparently is not big enough. The users are in the second level, as below,

```
import requests

r = requests.get('https://api.github.com/users/python')
data = (r.json())
print(data)

# output
{'login': 'python', 'id': 1525981, 'node_id': 'MDEyOk9yZ2FuaXphdGlvbjE1MjU5ODE=', 'avatar_url': 'https://avatars.githubusercontent.com/u/1525981?v=4', 'gravatar_id': '', 'url': 'https://api.github.com/users/python', 'html_url': 'https://github.com/python', 'followers_url': 'https://api.github.com/users/python/followers', 'following_url': 'https://api.github.com/users/python/following{/other_user}', 'gists_url': 'https://api.github.com/users/python/gists{/gist_id}', 'starred_url': 'https://api.github.com/users/python/starred{/owner}{/repo}', 'subscriptions_url': 'https://api.github.com/users/python/subscriptions', 'organizations_url': 'https://api.github.com/users/python/orgs', 'repos_url': 'https://api.github.com/users/python/repos', 'events_url': 'https://api.github.com/users/python/events{/privacy}', 'received_events_url': 'https://api.github.com/users/python/received_events', 'type': 'Organization', 'site_admin': False, 'name': 'Python', 'company': None, 'blog': 'https://www.python.org/', 'location': None, 'email': None, 'hireable': None, 'bio': 'Repositories related to the Python Programming language', 'twitter_username': None, 'public_repos': 82, 'public_gists': 0, 'followers': 22350, 'following': 0, 'created_at': '2012-03-11T15:56:37Z', 'updated_at': '2023-06-09T11:16:41Z'}
```

Can we delete?

Nasdaq has 3331 stock companies, and trading company is one of them, isn't this fun? 2019 futu has reached on board and can you imagine buying a stock inside the stock company?

29 flask

We can't.

Because we do not know the url to delete, the server is out of our control. In fact we are not able to know if the web page is interactive or not, as below,

```
<!DOCTYPE html>
<html lang="en">
<head>
   <title>myObject</title>
</head>
<body>
   <script>
      let myObject = {
      "name": "masara",
      "department": {
        "name": "Engineering",
        "location": "Syria"
      },
      "projects": [
        { "name": "Project A", "status": "In Progress" },
        { "name": "Project B", "status": "Completed" }
      ]
      };

      document.write("<pre>"+JSON.stringify(myObject, null, '\t')+"</pre>");

   </script>
</body>
</html>
```

If we do not know how the data shows, we would just get it as below,

```
import requests

r = requests.get('http://localhost:8001/myObject.html')
#print(r.text)
data = (r.json())
print(data)

# output
Traceback (most recent call last):
  File "C:\Users\Lenovo\Project\test.py", line 5, in <module>
    data = (r.json())
           ^^^^^^^^
                                                                                 File
"C:\Users\Lenovo\AppData\Local\Packages\PythonSoftwareFoundation.Python.3.12_qbz5n2k
```

```
fra8p0\LocalCache\local-packages\Python312\site-packages\requests\models.py",    line
975, in json
    raise RequestsJSONDecodeError(e.msg, e.doc, e.pos)
requests.exceptions.JSONDecodeError: Expecting value: line 1 column 1 (char 0)
```

It is just a javascrript mimic json file, but it is not real, so we need a real file, `myObject.json`, as below,

```
{
      "name": "masara",
      "department": {
        "name": "Engineering",
        "location": "Syria"
      },
      "projects": [
        { "name": "Project A", "status": "In Progress" },
        { "name": "Project B", "status": "Completed" }
      ]
}
```

And we can parse it, as below,

```
import requests

r = requests.get('http://localhost:8001/myObject.json')

data = (r.json())
print(data)
count = len(data)
print("Number of JSON objects:", count) # 3
```

And can we delete an object?

Again no, as below,

```
import requests

r = requests.delete('http://localhost:8001/myObject.json')
print(r.text)

# output
<!DOCTYPE HTML>
<html lang="en">
    <head>
        <meta charset="utf-8">
        <title>Error response</title>
    </head>
    <body>
        <h1>Error response</h1>
        <p>Error code: 501</p>
        <p>Message: Unsupported method ('DELETE').</p>
```

```
        <p>Error code explanation: 501 - Server does not support this operation.</p>
    </body>
</html>
```

That is to say we have no delete handler, so we try to make this handler on server, as below,

```
import logging
logging.basicConfig(level=logging.WARNING)

import cgi
params = cgi.FieldStorage()
#logging.warning('\033[93m'+params+'\033[0m')

logging.warning(params)

for query in params.getlist("delete"):
    logging.warning(query) #
# output
501
b'<!DOCTYPE HTML>\n<html lang="en">\n     <head>\n          <meta charset="utf-8">\n
<title>Error response</title>\n      </head>\n      <body>\n              <h1>Error
response</h1>\n          <p>Error code: 501</p>\n          <p>Message: Unsupported
method (\'DELETE\').</p>\n         <p>Error code explanation: 501 - Server does not
support this operation.</p>\n    </body>\n</html>\n'
```

And we are refused, that is to say we have to adapt the cgi entirely, not just the storage part. So it is really about how to handle the query and map to the file. `requests.delete('http://localhost:8001/myObject.json/1')` or `requests.post('http://localhost:8001/myObject.json/delete/1')`?

And on client, we can decide want we want to do when facing error,

```
import requests

response = requests.delete('http://localhost:8001/cgi-bin/myObject.py/1')
print(response.status_code)

if response.status_code == 403:
    print('Unauthorized to delete this resource')
elif response.status_code == 404:
    print('Resource not found')
elif response.status_code == 429:
    print('Rate limited - slow down deletes')
else:
    print(response.content)
```

Notice the error code starts from 5 is special,

```
for i in range(3):
    response = requests.delete(url)
    if response.status_code // 100 != 5:
        break

    print('Server error, retrying...{}'.format(i))
```

The http.client can also send HTTP requests delete, and aiohttp can send non-blocking delete, and httplib2, httpx, treq and others also can send delete. Or we can use the built API, and even Flask uses REST, so why not?

REST = representational state transfer, it is a software architecture style that defines a pattern for client and server, within HTTP mainly. Flask is developed by Armin Ronacher, and uses REST idea to deploy fast server. How fast?

```
#!/usr/bin/env python
# encoding: utf-8
import json
from flask import Flask
app = Flask(__name__)
@app.route('/')
def index():
    return json.dumps({ "name": "masara", "department": { "name": "Engineering",
"location": "Syria" }, "projects": [ { "name": "Project A", "status": "In Progress"
}, { "name": "Project B", "status": "Completed" } ] })
app.run()
```

The default route is GET, how to set up PUT, DELETE, POST?

```
#!/usr/bin/env python
# encoding: utf-8
import json
from flask import Flask, request, jsonify

app = Flask(__name__)

@app.route('/', methods=['GET'])
def query_records():
    name = request.args.get('name')

    with open("data.txt", 'r') as f:
        data = f.read()
        records = json.loads(data)
        for record in records:
            #print(type(record), record)
            if record['name'] == name:
                return jsonify(record)
        return jsonify({'error': 'data not found'})

@app.route('/', methods=['PUT'])
def create_record():
```

```
    record = json.loads(request.data)
    with open("data.txt", 'r') as f:
        data = f.read()
    if not data:
        records = [record]
    else:
        records = json.loads(data)
        records.append(record)
    with open("data.txt", 'w') as f:
        f.write(json.dumps(records, indent=2))
    return jsonify(record)

@app.route('/', methods=['DELETE'])
def delete_record():
    record = json.loads(request.data)
    new_records = []
    with open("data.txt", 'r') as f:
        data = f.read()
        records = json.loads(data)
        for r in records:
            if r['name'] == record['name']:
                continue
            new_records.append(r)
    with open("data.txt", 'w') as f:
        f.write(json.dumps(new_records, indent=2))
    return jsonify(record)

@app.route('/', methods=['POST'])
def update_record():
    record = json.loads(request.data)
    new_records = []
    with open("data.txt", 'r') as f:
        data = f.read()
        records = json.loads(data)
    for r in records:
        if r['name'] == record['name']:
            r['email'] = record['email']
        new_records.append(r)
    with open("data.txt", 'w') as f:
        f.write(json.dumps(new_records, indent=2))
    return jsonify(record)

app.run(debug=True)
```

the IO for get,

```
# input is data.txt
[{"name": "alice", "email": "alice@outlook.com"}]

# and the getdata.py
import requests
response = requests.get('http://localhost:5000/?name=alice')
print(response.text)
```

```
# output is on screen
127.0.0.1 - - [22/Sep/2024 16:25:14] "GET /?name=alice HTTP/1.1" 200 -
```

the IO for put, equivalent to add,

```
# putdata.py
import requests

r = requests.put('http://localhost:5000', '{"name": "bob", "email": "bob@outlook.com"}')
print(r.text)

response = requests.get('http://localhost:5000?name=bob')
print(response.text)

# output from server
127.0.0.1 - - [22/Sep/2024 16:58:50] "PUT / HTTP/1.1" 200 -
127.0.0.1 - - [22/Sep/2024 16:58:52] "GET /?name=bob HTTP/1.1" 200 -
```

the IO for delete,

```
import requests
r = requests.delete('http://localhost:5000/', '{"name": "bob", "email": "bob@outlook.com"}')
print(r.text)

# output
Traceback (most recent call last):
  File "C:\Users\Lenovo\Flask\test.py", line 7, in <module>
        r = requests.delete('http://localhost:5000/', {"email": "bob@outlook.com", "name": "bob"})

^^^^^^^^^^^^^^^^^^^^^^^^^^^^^^^^^^^^^^^^^^^^^^^^^^^^^^^^^^^^^^^^^^^^^^^^^^^^^^^^^^^^^^^^^^^
TypeError: delete() takes 1 positional argument but 2 were given
```

What is the problem? Recall `httpbin.org`,

```
import requests
url = "https://httpbin.org/delete"
payload = {"email": "bob@outlook.com", "name": "bob"}
r = requests.delete(url, data=payload)
print(r.text)

# output
{
  "args": {},
  "data": "",
  "files": {},
  "form": {
    "email": "bob@outlook.com",
```

```
    "name": "bob"
  },
  "headers": {
    "Accept": "*/*",
    "Accept-Encoding": "gzip, deflate",
    "Content-Length": "32",
    "Content-Type": "application/x-www-form-urlencoded",
    "Host": "httpbin.org",
    "User-Agent": "python-requests/2.31.0",
    "X-Amzn-Trace-Id": "Root=1-66efecee-0ab625704bb829b375f0b785"
  },
  "json": null,
  "origin": "112.97.57.68",
  "url": "https://httpbin.org/delete"
}
```


So...

The problem is the slash? Redo a friends kv list, as below,

```
#!/usr/bin/env python
# encoding: utf-8
import json

from flask import Flask, request

app = Flask(__name__)

model = []

@app.route('/friends', methods=['GET'])
def get_friends():
    return model

@app.route('/friend/<int:id>', methods=['GET'])
def get_one_friend(id):
    return model[id], 200

@app.route('/friend', methods=['POST'])
def create_friend():
    request_data = request.get_json()
    new_friend = {"name": request_data["name"], "id": len(model)}
    model.append(new_friend)
    return new_friend, 201

@app.route('/friend/<int:id>', methods=['DELETE'])
def delete_friend(id):
    del model[id]
    return {"success": "data successfully deleted from the server"}, 200

@app.route('/friend', methods=['PUT'])
def add_friend():
```

```
    print(request.data)
    new_friend = json.loads(request.data)
    model.append(new_friend)
    return {"success": "data successfully added to the server"}, 201

app.run(debug=True)
```

and we test to add the friend and delete it, as below,

```
import requests

r = requests.get('http://localhost:5000/friends')
print(r.text)

r = requests.put('http://localhost:5000/friend', '{"name": "bob", "email": "bob@outlook.com"}')
print(r.text)

r = requests.get('http://localhost:5000/friends')
print(r.text)

r = requests.delete('http://localhost:5000/friend/0')
print(r.text)

r = requests.get('http://localhost:5000/friends')
print(r.text)

# server output
127.0.0.1 - - [22/Sep/2024 18:49:08] "GET /friends HTTP/1.1" 200 -
b'{"name": "bob", "email": "bob@outlook.com"}'
127.0.0.1 - - [22/Sep/2024 18:49:10] "PUT /friend HTTP/1.1" 201 -
127.0.0.1 - - [22/Sep/2024 18:49:12] "GET /friends HTTP/1.1" 200 -
127.0.0.1 - - [22/Sep/2024 18:49:14] "DELETE /friend/0 HTTP/1.1" 200 -
127.0.0.1 - - [22/Sep/2024 18:49:17] "GET /friends HTTP/1.1" 200 -

# client ouput
[]

{
  "success": "data successfully added to the server"
}

[
  {
    "email": "bob@outlook.com",
    "name": "bob"
  }
]

{
  "success": "data successfully deleted from the server"
}
```

```
[]
```

We do not save the friends into a file, not because of just one, but we are going to use sqlite, a type of database, and much more concise than json file, even though itself is also a file.

30 sqlite

Since we notice that the data to add and to delete can be seperated from the layout, on the web, we then think of using database, like sqlite, to make Flask more structured.

```
C:\Users\Lenovo\Flask\app>dir
 Volume in drive C is Windows-SSD
 Volume Serial Number is 5286-8C92

 Directory of C:\Users\Lenovo\Flask\app

2024/09/27  14:56    <DIR>          .
2024/09/27  14:44    <DIR>          ..
2024/09/27  14:52               446 posts.py
2024/09/27  14:48            12,288 database.db
2024/09/27  14:40               490 init_db.py
2024/09/27  14:40               210 schema.sql
2024/09/27  14:56    <DIR>          templates
               4 File(s)         13,434 bytes
               3 Dir(s)  63,770,755,072 bytes free
```

The `schema.sql` is the title of our posts,

```
DROP TABLE IF EXISTS posts;

CREATE TABLE posts (
    id INTEGER PRIMARY KEY AUTOINCREMENT,
    created TIMESTAMP NOT NULL DEFAULT CURRENT_TIMESTAMP,
    title TEXT NOT NULL,
    content TEXT NOT NULL
);
```

Run `init_db.py` to create the default database,

```
import sqlite3

connection = sqlite3.connect('database.db')


with open('schema.sql') as f:
    connection.executescript(f.read())
```

```
cur = connection.cursor()

cur.execute("INSERT INTO posts (title, content) VALUES (?, ?)",
            ('First Post', 'Content for the first post')
            )

cur.execute("INSERT INTO posts (title, content) VALUES (?, ?)",
            ('Second Post', 'Content for the second post')
            )

connection.commit()
connection.close()
```

`database.db` can be accessed by sqlite command line too, but here we are just using Python, and the `posts.py` will make the web for us,

```
import sqlite3
from flask import Flask, render_template

app = Flask(__name__)

def get_db_connection():
    conn = sqlite3.connect('database.db')
    conn.row_factory = sqlite3.Row
    return conn


@app.route('/')
def index():
    conn = get_db_connection()
    posts = conn.execute('SELECT * FROM posts').fetchall()
    print(posts)
    conn.close()
    return render_template('index.html', posts=posts)

app.run(debug=True)
```

Attention! The html should be put under `templates` folder, this is how Flask works,

```
C:\Users\Lenovo\Flask\app>more templates\index.html
{% extends 'base.html' %}

{% block content %}
    <h1>{% block title %} Posts {% endblock %}</h1>
    {% for post in posts %}
        <div class='post'>
            <p>{{ post['created'] }}</p>
            <h2>{{ post['title'] }}</h2>
            <p>{{ post['content'] }}</p>
        </div>
    {% endfor %}
```

```
{% endblock %}

C:\Users\Lenovo\Flask\app>more templates\base.html
<!DOCTYPE html>
<html lang="en">
<head>
    <meta charset="UTF-8">
    <title>{% block title %} {% endblock %}- FlaskApp</title>
    <style>
        .post {
            padding: 10px;
            margin: 5px;
            background-color: #f3f3f3
        }

        nav a {
            color: #d64161;
            font-size: 3em;
            margin-left: 50px;
            text-decoration: none;
        }
    </style>
</head>
<body>
    <nav>
        <a href="{{ url_for('index') }}">FlaskApp</a>
        <a href="#">About</a>
    </nav>
    <hr>
    <div class="content">
        {% block content %} {% endblock %}
    </div>
</body>
</html>
```

And type http://127.0.0.1:5000/# on browser, we can get,

```
<!DOCTYPE html>
<html lang="en">
<head>
    <meta charset="UTF-8">
    <title> Posts - FlaskApp</title>
    <style>
        .post {
            padding: 10px;
            margin: 5px;
            background-color: #f3f3f3
        }

        nav a {
            color: #d64161;
            font-size: 3em;
```

```
            margin-left: 50px;
            text-decoration: none;
        }
    </style>
</head>
<body>
    <nav>
        <a href="/">FlaskApp</a>
        <a href="#">About</a>
    </nav>
    <hr>
    <div class="content">

    <h1> Posts </h1>

        <div class='post'>
            <p>2024-09-27 06:48:40</p>
            <h2>First Post</h2>
            <p>Content for the first post</p>
        </div>

        <div class='post'>
            <p>2024-09-27 06:48:40</p>
            <h2>Second Post</h2>
            <p>Content for the second post</p>
        </div>


    </div>
</body>
</html>
```

We can add `about.html` under templates,

```
C:\Users\Lenovo\Flask\app>more templates\about.html
{% extends 'base.html' %}

{% block content %}
    <h1>{% block title %} About {% endblock %}</h1>
    <h3>FlaskApp is a Flask web application written in Python.</h3>
{% endblock %}
```

and don't forget adapt `posts.py`,

```

import sqlite3
from flask import Flask, render_template

app = Flask(__name__)

def get_db_connection():
    conn = sqlite3.connect('database.db')
```

```
    conn.row_factory = sqlite3.Row
    return conn


@app.route('/')
def index():
    conn = get_db_connection()
    posts = conn.execute('SELECT * FROM posts').fetchall()
    print(posts)
    conn.close()
    return render_template('index.html', posts=posts)

@app.route('/about/')
def about():
    return render_template('about.html')

app.run(debug=True)
```

also `base.html`,

```
<!DOCTYPE html>
<html lang="en">
<head>
    <meta charset="UTF-8">
    <title>{% block title %} {% endblock %}- FlaskApp</title>
    <style>
        .post {
            padding: 10px;
            margin: 5px;
            background-color: #f3f3f3
        }

        nav a {
            color: #d64161;
            font-size: 3em;
            margin-left: 50px;
            text-decoration: none;
        }
    </style>
</head>
<body>
    <nav>
        <a href="{{ url_for('index') }}">FlaskApp</a>
        <a href="{{ url_for('about') }}">About</a>
    </nav>
    <hr>
    <div class="content">
        {% block content %} {% endblock %}
    </div>
</body>
</html>
```

so `url_for()` can change the routes and the links, let's add `comments.html` as well,

```
{% extends 'base.html' %}

{% block content %}
    <h1>{% block title %} Comments {% endblock %}</h1>
    <div style="width: 50%; margin: auto">
        {% for comment in comments %}
            {% if loop.index % 2 == 0 %}
                {% set bg_color = '#e6f9ff' %}
            {% else %}
                {% set bg_color = '#eee' %}
            {% endif %}

                <div style="padding: 10px; background-color: {{ bg_color }}; margin:
20px">
                 <p>#{{ loop.index }}</p>
                 <p style="font-size: 24px">{{ comment }}</p>
            </div>
        {% endfor %}
    </div>
{% endblock %}
```

and modify the `base.html`,

```
<!DOCTYPE html>
<html lang="en">
<head>
    <meta charset="UTF-8">
    <title>{% block title %} {% endblock %}- FlaskApp</title>
    <style>
        .post {
            padding: 10px;
            margin: 5px;
            background-color: #f3f3f3
        }

        nav a {
            color: #d64161;
            font-size: 3em;
            margin-left: 50px;
            text-decoration: none;
        }
    </style>
</head>
<body>
    <nav>
        <a href="{{ url_for('index') }}">FlaskApp</a>
        <a href="{{ url_for('about') }}">About</a>
        <a href="{{ url_for('comments') }}">Comments</a>

    </nav>
```

```
    <hr>
    <div class="content">
        {% block content %} {% endblock %}
    </div>
</body>
</html>
```

We may want to control comments, add, edit, or delete,

```
# posts.py
import sqlite3
from flask import Flask, render_template, request, url_for, flash, redirect, abort

app = Flask(__name__)

app.config['SECRET_KEY'] = 'delete_must_have_this'

def get_db_connection():
    conn = sqlite3.connect('database.db')
    conn.row_factory = sqlite3.Row
    return conn

def get_post(post_id):
    conn = get_db_connection()
    post = conn.execute('SELECT * FROM posts WHERE id = ?',
                        (post_id,)).fetchone()
    conn.close()
    if post is None:
        abort(404)
    return post

@app.route('/')
def index():
    conn = get_db_connection()

    posts = conn.execute('SELECT * FROM posts').fetchall()
    conn.commit()

    conn.close()
    return render_template('index.html', len = len(posts), posts=posts)

@app.route('/about/')
def about():
    return render_template('about.html')

@app.route('/comments/')
def comments():
    comments = ['This is the first comment.',
                'This is the second comment.',
                'This is the third comment.',
                'This is the fourth comment.'
                ]
```

```
    return render_template('comments.html', comments=comments)

@app.route('/add/', methods=('GET', 'POST'))
def create():
    if request.method == 'POST':
        title = request.form['title']
        content = request.form['content']

        if not title:
            flash('Title is required!')
        elif not content:
            flash('Content is required!')
        else:
            conn = get_db_connection()

            number = conn.cursor()

            i = "SELECT * FROM posts order by posts.created"
            number.execute(i)
            l = len(number.fetchall())

            conn.execute('INSERT INTO posts (id, title, content) VALUES (?, ?, ?)',
                         (l+1, title, content))
            conn.commit()

            conn.close()

            return redirect(url_for('index'))

    return render_template('add.html')

@app.route('/<int:id>/edit/', methods=('GET', 'POST'))
def edit(id):
    post = get_post(id)

    if request.method == 'POST':
        title = request.form['title']
        content = request.form['content']

        if not title:
            flash('Title is required!')

        elif not content:
            flash('Content is required!')

        else:
            conn = get_db_connection()
            conn.execute('UPDATE posts SET title = ?, content = ?'
                         ' WHERE id = ?',
                         (title, content, id))
            conn.commit()
            conn.close()
            return redirect(url_for('index'))
```

```
    return render_template('edit.html', post=post)

@app.route('/<int:id>/delete/', methods=('POST',))
def delete(id):
    post = get_post(id)
    conn = get_db_connection()
    conn.execute('DELETE FROM posts WHERE id = ?', (id,))
    conn.commit()
    conn.execute('update posts set id = id -1 where id > ?', (id,))
    conn.commit()
    conn.close()
    flash('"{}" was successfully deleted!'.format(post['title']))
    return redirect(url_for('index'))

app.run(debug=True)

# templates\base.html
<!DOCTYPE html>
<html lang="en">
<head>
    <meta charset="UTF-8">
    <title>{% block title %} {% endblock %}- FlaskApp</title>
    <style>
        .post {
            padding: 10px;
            margin: 5px;
            background-color: #f3f3f3
        }

        nav a {
            color: #d64161;
            font-size: 3em;
            margin-left: 50px;
            text-decoration: none;
        }
    </style>
</head>
<body>
    <nav>
        <a href="{{ url_for('index') }}">FlaskApp</a>
        <a href="{{ url_for('about') }}">About</a>
        <a href="{{ url_for('comments') }}">Comments</a>

    </nav>
    <hr>
    <div class="content">

        {% for message in get_flashed_messages() %}
            <div class="alert">{{ message }}</div>
        {% endfor %}

        {% block content %} {% endblock %}
```

```
    </div>
</body>
</html>

# templates\index.html
{% extends 'base.html' %}

{% block content %}
      <h2>{% block title %} Posts {% endblock %}     <a
href="../add"><button>add</button></a></h2>
    {% for i in range(0, len) %}
        <div class='post'>
            <p>{{ posts[i]['created'] }}</p>
             <h2>{{ posts[i]['title'] }}     <a href="../{{
i + 1 }}/edit"><button>edit or delete</button></a>
            <p>{{ posts[i]['content'] }}</p>
        </div>
    {% endfor %}
{% endblock %}

# templates\add.html
{% extends 'base.html' %}

{% block content %}
    <h1>{% block title %} Add a New Post {% endblock %}</h1>
    <form method="post">
        <label for="title">Post Title</label>
        <br>
        <input type="text" name="title"
               placeholder="Post title"
               value="{{ request.form['title'] }}"></input>
        <br>

        <label for="content">Post Content</label>
        <br>
        <textarea name="content"
                  placeholder="Post content"
                  rows="15"
                  cols="60"
                  >{{ request.form['content'] }}</textarea>
        <br>
        <button type="submit">Submit</button>
    </form>
{% endblock %}

# templates\edit.html
{% extends 'base.html' %}

{% block content %}
    <h1>{% block title %} Edit "{{ post['title'] }}" {% endblock %}</h1>
    <form method="POST">
        <label for="title">Title</label>
        <br>
```

```
        <input type="text" name="title"
               placeholder="Post title"
               value="{{ request.form['title'] or post['title'] }}"></input>
        <br>

        <label for="content">Post Content</label>
        <br>
        <textarea name="content"
                  placeholder="Post content"
                  rows="15"
                  cols="60"
                  >{{ request.form['content'] or post['content'] }}</textarea>
        <br>
        <button type="submit">Submit</button>
    </form>

<hr>
    <form action="{{ url_for('delete', id=post['id']) }}" method="POST">
        <input type="submit" value="Delete Post"
                     onclick="return confirm('Are you sure you want to delete this
post?')">
    </form>
{% endblock %}
```

So the hard thing is how to reorder the `id` after deletion and addition, it is so hard, since `sqlite` just do not offer this, and that is why we use Python to go up a level, to count the length of the rows, and we reset the row number from 1, again and again...

And for delete, it is `get` of request, which we fail with the button, so we make the delete page same in `edit.html`, with a horizontal line.

Apparently if we look at the code in `posts.py`, the router part, we may feel inconsistent, and we feel the db connection troublesome, but that is what we always face in reality, and the important thing is make it run, that is why we always have dirty code...

31 render

Sqlite is really a table database, and we can use python to create, modify, display, or convert it.

```
# create.py

import sqlite3

conn = sqlite3.connect('flight.db')
```

```
cursor = conn.cursor()

cursor.execute("CREATE TABLE IF NOT EXISTS users ( flight_number TEXT PRIMARY KEY
NOT NULL, origin TEXT NOT NULL, destination TEXT NOT NULL )")

cursor.execute("DELETE FROM users")

data = [
    ("BD36457", "New York", "Los Angeles"),
    ("SZ37486", "Milan", "London"),
    ("BT34567", "Oslo", "Copenhagen"),
    ("RS25690", "Madrid", "Turin")
]

cursor.executemany("INSERT INTO users (flight_number, origin, destination) VALUES
(?, ?, ?)", data)

conn.commit()

conn.close()


# show.py
import sqlite3


conn = sqlite3.connect("flight.db")
cursor = conn.cursor()

i = "SELECT * FROM users"
cursor.execute(i)
rows = cursor.fetchall()

#conn.commit()
conn.close()

for row in rows:
   print(row)

# output
('BD36457', 'New York', 'Los Angeles')
('SZ37486', 'Milan', 'London')
('BT34567', 'Oslo', 'Copenhagen')
('RS25690', 'Madrid', 'Turin')
```

`executemany` is mapping the data line compared to `execute`, and use `commit` when saving the change, like renaming the table,

```
import sqlite3

# Connecting to sqlite
```

```
conn = sqlite3.connect('flight.db')

# cursor object
cursor = conn.cursor()

# select from sqlite_flights
cursor.execute("SELECT * FROM flights")

table = cursor.fetchall()
print("Before changing the name of Table")
print("The row 0 col 2 of the table:", table[0][2])

# Rename the SQLite Table
renameTable = "ALTER TABLE flights RENAME TO users"
cursor.execute(renameTable)


# select from sqlite
cursor.execute("SELECT * FROM users")

table = cursor.fetchall()

print("After changing the name of Table")
print("The row 0 col 2 of the table:", table[0][2])

conn.commit()

conn.close()
```

In order to dump the db, we can also `execute` the sentence,

```
set = '''.output ./backup_users.sql
.dump users
.exit'''

for i in set.split('\n'):
    cursor.execute(i)
```

and inversely,

```
set = '''.read ./backup.sql
.exit'''
```

and we can dump the db into Pandas df,

```
# dump.py
import sqlite3

conn = sqlite3.connect("flight.db")

import pandas as pd

```

```
users_df = pd.read_sql_query("SELECT * FROM users", conn) # Display the DataFrame
conn.close()
print(users_df.head())

# output
  flight_number    origin  destination
0       BD36457  New York  Los Angeles
1       SZ37486     Milan       London
2       BT34567      Oslo   Copenhagen
3       RS25690    Madrid        Turin
```

The reason to use pandas is because of sqlite is so hard draw, and analysis, for we add passangers' gender and age,

```
import sqlite3

sqlite_file = 'flight.db'    # name of the sqlite database file
table_name = 'users'   # name of the table to be created
id_column = 'flight_number' # name of the PRIMARY KEY column
new_column1 = 'gender'  # name of the new column
column1_type = 'TEXT' # E.g., INTEGER, TEXT, NULL, REAL, BLOB
new_column2 = 'age'  # name of the new column
column2_type = 'INTEGER' # E.g., INTEGER, TEXT, NULL, REAL, BLOB

# Connecting to the database file
conn = sqlite3.connect(sqlite_file)
cursor = conn.cursor()

cursor.execute("ALTER TABLE {tn} ADD COLUMN '{cn}' {ct}"\
        .format(tn=table_name, cn=new_column1, ct=column1_type))

cursor.execute("ALTER TABLE {tn} ADD COLUMN '{cn}' {ct}"\
        .format(tn=table_name, cn=new_column2, ct=column2_type))

cursor.execute("UPDATE {tn} SET {cn1}=('Male') {cn2} = (40) WHERE {idf}=(1)".\
        format(tn=table_name, cn1=new_column1, cn2=new_column2, idf='rowid'))
cursor.execute("UPDATE {tn} SET {cn1}=('Female') {cn2} = (20) WHERE {idf}=(2)".\
        format(tn=table_name, cn1=new_column1, cn2=new_column2, idf='rowid'))
cursor.execute("UPDATE {tn} SET {cn1}=('Female') {cn2} = (60) WHERE {idf}=(3)".\
        format(tn=table_name, cn1=new_column1, cn2=new_column2, idf='rowid'))
cursor.execute("UPDATE {tn} SET {cn1}=('Male') {cn2} = (30) WHERE {idf}=(4)".\
        format(tn=table_name, cn1=new_column1, cn2=new_column2, idf='rowid'))

# Committing changes and closing the connection to the database file
conn.commit()
conn.close()

# output
  flight_number    origin  destination  gender  age
0       BD36457  New York  Los Angeles    Male   40
1       SZ37486     Milan       London  Female   20
```

```
2       BT34567      Oslo   Copenhagen  Female   60
3       RS25690    Madrid        Turin    Male   30
```

and finally we can use `matplot`,

```
import sqlite3

conn = sqlite3.connect("flight.db")

# this part is the fetchall print
'''
cursor = conn.cursor()

i = "SELECT * FROM users"
cursor.execute(i)
rows = cursor.fetchall()

for row in rows:
   print(row)
'''

# this part is the pandas print
import pandas as pd

users_df = pd.read_sql_query("SELECT * FROM users", conn) # Display the DataFrame
conn.close()
print(users_df.head())

# this part is the matplot print
import matplotlib.pyplot as plt

# Perform a basic analysis: Average user age by gender
average_age_by_gender = users_df.groupby('gender')['age'].mean()

# Visualization
average_age_by_gender.plot(kind='bar')
plt.title('Average Age by Gender')
plt.xlabel('Gender')
plt.ylabel('Average Age')
plt.show()
```

Let's try make our stock analysis table, with the price we buy and sell. First we build a database for the stock.

```
# build.py
import sqlite3

# Connect to an SQLite database (or create it if it doesn't exist)
conn = sqlite3.connect('stock.db')

# Create a cursor object using the cursor() method
cursor = conn.cursor()
```

```
# Drop table
cursor.execute("DROP TABLE stocks")

# Create table
cursor.execute("CREATE TABLE IF NOT EXISTS stocks
             (date text, trans text, symbol text, qty real, price real)")

# Insert
cursor.execute("INSERT INTO stocks VALUES ('2023-02-06','BUY','FFIE',100,7700)")
cursor.execute("INSERT INTO stocks VALUES ('2023-03-06','BUY','FFIE',100,5600)")
cursor.execute("INSERT INTO stocks VALUES ('2023-04-06','WATCH','FFIE',100,2740)")

# Or modify
#cursor.execute("INSERT INTO stocks VALUES ('2006-01-05','SELL','RHAT',100,35.14)")
#cursor.execute("DELETE FROM stocks where rowid = 2")
#cursor.execute("UPDATE stocks SET symbol = ('KEEP') where rowid = 1")

# Save (commit) the changes
conn.commit()

# Close the connection
conn.close()
```

and to see,

```
# show.py
import sqlite3

conn = sqlite3.connect("stock.db")

cursor = conn.cursor()

i = "SELECT * FROM stocks"
cursor.execute(i)
rows = cursor.fetchall()

#conn.commit()

conn.close()
for row in rows:
   print(row)
```

and to render in HTML, by Flask,

```
# index.html
{% extends 'base.html' %}

{% block content %}
    <h1>{% block title %} Stocks <mark>{{ products }}</mark> USD{% endblock %}</h1>

    {% for stock in stocks %}
```

```
<h3>{{ stock['date'] }}</h3>

        <div class='stock'>

{% if stock['trans'] == "BUY": %}
            <h2 style='color: green; display:inline;'>{{ stock['trans'] }}</h2>

{% elif stock['trans'] == "SELL": %}
            <h2 style='color: red; display:inline;'>{{ stock['trans'] }}</h2>

{% else %}
            <h2 style='display:inline;'>{{ stock['trans'] }}</h2>

{% endif %}

                         <p  style="display:inline;">     {{
stock['symbol']    }}     {{    stock['qty']    }}    x    {{
stock['price'] }} USD</p>
        </div>
    {% endfor %}
{% endblock %}

# base.html
<!DOCTYPE html>
<html lang="en">
<head>
    <meta charset="UTF-8">
    <title>{% block title %} {% endblock %}- Stocks</title>

    <style>
        .stock {
              width: 80%;
  margin: 15px auto;
  border-collapse: collapse;
  font-family: Arial, sans-serif;
  color: #333;
  background-color: lightgray;

        }

        nav a {

            color: #d64161;
            font-size: 24px;
            margin-left: 50px;
            text-decoration: none;
        }
    </style>
</head>
<body>
    <nav>
        <a href="{{ url_for('index') }}">Stocks</a>
```

```
    </nav>
    <hr>
    <div class="content">
        {% block content %} {% endblock %}
    </div>
</body>
</html>
```

and run the Flask,

```
# stock.py

app = Flask(__name__)

def get_db_connection():
    conn = sqlite3.connect('stock.db')
    conn.row_factory = sqlite3.Row
    return conn

@app.route('/')
def index():
    conn = get_db_connection()
    stocks = conn.execute('SELECT * FROM stocks').fetchall()

      #stocks = pd.read_sql_query("SELECT * FROM stocks", conn) # Display the
DataFrame
          plus = conn.execute('SELECT qty, price FROM stocks where
trans="BUY"').fetchall()
    products = 0
    for product in plus:
        products = product[0]*product[1] + products

          minus = conn.execute('SELECT qty, price FROM stocks where
trans="SELL"').fetchall()
    for product in minus:
        products = - product[0]*product[1] + products

    conn.close()
    return render_template('index.html', stocks=stocks, products=products)

app.run(debug=True)
```

So, the annoying thing is we need to pass a products to `index.html`, which we go through the table once, but we go again in Flask, just to display, to optimize, we really need once, and this is always the reaility, especially the huge system, and it is usually hard to get update with all the teamwork, so for loop just go over and over... Notice that Flask can render the df data directly into HTML, so it can save us time to write the HTML file, which really helps. Using `akshare` to check the effect.

```
import akshare as ak
@app.route('/watch')
def watch():
    stock = "ffie"
    df = ak.stock_us_daily(symbol=stock.upper(), adjust="")
    return df.to_html()
```

Before `return` we can also give some column colors, by define some formatter,

```
def format_color_groups(df):
    colors = ['gold', 'lightblue']
    x = df.copy()
    factors = list(x['open'].unique())
    i = 0
    for factor in factors:
        style = f'background-color: {colors[i]}'
        x.loc[x['open'] == factor, :] = style
        i = not i
    return x

df.sort_values(by='open').style.apply(format_color_groups, axis=None)
```

What exactly is a table?

32 sys

In math, a table is used to solve matrix problem, what is matrix?

```
x + y = 5
x - y = 5
```

Aren't these two equations?

Maybe no...

```
[ 1 1                    [5
          *    [x y] =
  1 -1]                   5]
```

So the matrix is from equations, fancy?

Sometimes, but math is really about solving problems, or at least simplifying problems...

And programming is really about simplifying problems...

But sometimes, programming makes problem more complex, since too many choices, and it is just because the languege not fit in the problem...

At least two problems in programming, showing and solving, and it just can't combined as one, since usually these are two langueges, two system langueges, one showing, and the other solving...

It is not same as what we use with a paper, solution is obtained and the output is printed. And when we want to store, computer is so different from paper, because all things are seperate in memory and storage, so it comes to the third languege, database, like `sqlite`,

```
import sqlite3

# Connect to an SQLite database (or create it if it doesn't exist)
conn = sqlite3.connect('eqation.db')

# Create a cursor object using the cursor() method
cursor = conn.cursor()

# Create table
cursor.execute('''CREATE TABLE IF NOT EXISTS equations
             (date text, calc text, symbol text, result real)''')

# Insert a row of data
cursor.execute("INSERT INTO equations VALUES ('2024-01-01','x + y','=', 1)")
cursor.execute("INSERT INTO equations VALUES ('2024-01-01','x - y','=', 1)")

# Show
i = "SELECT calc, symbol, result FROM equations"
cursor.execute(i)
rows = cursor.fetchall()

# Save (commit) the changes
conn.commit()

# Close the connection
conn.close()

# Print
for row in rows:
   print(row)

###### output ######
#('x + y', '=', 1.0)
#('x - y', '=', 1.0)
```

We find the `calc` column is annoying, and in fact the last three columns can be grouped as one,

```
import sqlite3

# Connect to an SQLite database (or create it if it doesn't exist)
```

```
conn = sqlite3.connect('eqation.db')

# Create a cursor object using the cursor() method
cursor = conn.cursor()

# Drop table
cursor.execute('''DROP TABLE IF EXISTS equations ''')

# Create table
cursor.execute('''CREATE TABLE IF NOT EXISTS equations
             (date text, equation text)''')

# Insert a row of data
cursor.execute("INSERT INTO equations VALUES ('2024-01-02','x + y = 1')")
cursor.execute("INSERT INTO equations VALUES ('2024-01-02','x - y = 1')")

# Show
i = "SELECT equation FROM equations"
cursor.execute(i)
rows = cursor.fetchall()

# Save (commit) the changes
conn.commit()

# Print
for row in rows:
   print(row)

# Or convert to df
users_df = pd.read_sql_query("SELECT equation FROM equations", conn)

# Display the DataFrame
print(users_df.head())

# Close the connection
conn.close()

###### output ######
('x + y = 1',)
('x - y = 1',)
    equation
0  x + y = 1
1  x - y = 1
```

So if we use df to link with HTML, the database needs more columns, alternatively we can use df,

```
import pandas as pd
df = pd.DataFrame({
    "first":         ["x","+","y","=", "1"],
    "second" :    ["x","-","y","=", "1"]
    })
```

```
def maximum_value_in_column(column):

    highlight = 'background-color: palegreen;'
    default = ''

    maximum_in_column = column.max()

    # must return one string per cell in this column
    return [highlight if v == maximum_in_column else default for v in column]

df.style.apply(maximum_value_in_column, subset=['num_children', 'num_pets'], axis=0)

print(df.transpose().head().to_html())
```

notice we have to do a transpose to make our code human readable, since pd columns are now five, and not meanningfun, or hard to name...

```
<table border="1" class="dataframe">
  <thead>
    <tr style="text-align: right;">
      <th></th>
      <th>0</th>
      <th>1</th>
      <th>2</th>
      <th>3</th>
      <th>4</th>
    </tr>
  </thead>
  <tbody>
    <tr>
      <th>first</th>
      <td>x</td>
      <td>+</td>
      <td>y</td>
      <td>=</td>
      <td>1</td>
    </tr>
    <tr>
      <th>second</th>
      <td>x</td>
      <td>-</td>
      <td>y</td>
      <td>=</td>
      <td>1</td>
    </tr>
  </tbody>
</table>
```

Copy the table to HTML, then we will have the equation well displayed, but it is still not solved, and it is really hard to solve now, or at least we have to convert the data forth and back twice. One time string to number, and one time back. So the logic is inefficient, but this is really what we face in reality, and most times we will just use string as input and ouptut, and convert them to numbers during calculation.

```
A = [[1, 1], [1, -1]]
b = [5, 5]
from sympy import symbols
x, y = symbols("x, y")
import numpy as np
A = np.array(A)
b = np.array(b)
solution = np.linalg.solve(A, b)
print("solution", {x: solution[0], y: solution[1]})
print("checked", np.allclose(np.dot(A, solution), b))
```

So `A` and `B` are two list, converted to array and using `numpy` and `sympy` to calculate the solution matrix, but when we want to type in outside the Python file, how do we convert it?

```
# the arg.py
import sys
print(sys.argv[0], sys.argv[1])


ini_list = sys.argv[1]


# Converting string to list
res = list(map(str, ini_list[1:-1].split('],')))


res[0] = list(map(int, res[0][1:].split(',')))
res[1] = list(map(int, res[1][2:-1].split(',')))

# printing final result and its type
print ("final list", res)
print (type(res))


ini_list = sys.argv[2]


# Converting string to list
res = list(map(int, ini_list[1:-1].split(',')))

# printing final result and its type
print ("final list", res)
print (type(res))
```

```
# python arg.py "[[1,1], [1, -1]]" "[1, -1]"

# output
final list [[1, 1], [1, -1]]
<class 'list'>
final list [1, -1]
<class 'list'>
```

What does `map` do here?

```
def addition(n):
    return n + n

# numbers * 2 using map()
numbers = (1, 2, 3, 4)
result = map(addition, numbers)
print(list(result))
```

Or,

```
numbers = (1, 2, 3, 4)
result = map(lambda x: x + x, numbers)
print(list(result))
```

What does `lambda` do here?

```
numbers1 = [1, 2, 3]
numbers2 = [4, 5, 6]

result = map(lambda x, y: x + y, numbers1, numbers2)
print(list(result)) # 5, 7, 9
```

That is how we use super variables for list, and it is a sign of Pythonic way to solve problem.

And what is the significance?

`for` loop... is saved by `map`,

```
list_of_strings = ["5","6","7","8","9", "10"]

result = map(int,list_of_strings)

print(list(result))
```

So if you have a dictionary { k1: v1, k2: v2 ... } you can use map fucntion to do the calculation on keys,

```
my_dictionary = {k: f(v) for k, v in my_dictionary.items()}
```

```
# Or

my_dictionary = dict(map(lambda kv: (kv[0], f(kv[1])), my_dictionary.items()))
```

OK, back to the sys, how do we control the numer of arguments?

```
import sys
# Check if the required number of arguments is provided
required_arguments = 2
if len(sys.argv) - 1 < required_arguments:
    print("This script requires at least 2 arguments.")
    sys.exit(1)  # Exit the script with an error status
# Continue with the processing if enough arguments are provided
first_argument = sys.argv[1]
second_argument = sys.argv[2]
```

Or,

```
import sys

if len(sys.argv) != 3:
    print("Usage: python script.py arg1 arg2")
    sys.exit(1)

first_argument = sys.argv[1]
second_argument = sys.argv[2]

# Do something with the arguments
print(f'First argument is: {first_argument}')
print(f'Second argument is: {second_argument}')
```

0 and 1 are the exit codes. Usually, exit(0) means a clean exit without any errors / problems, exit(1) means there was some issue / error / problem and that is why the program is exiting. This is important for automation, but code is not strict, can be not numbers.

```
import sys
age = 17
if age < 18:
    sys.exit("Age less than 18")
else:
    print("Age is not less than 18")
```

and a program now has the enter and exit part, so we can make modes selection,

```
import sys
if len(sys.argv) > 1:
    if sys.argv[1] == "verbose":
        print("Running in verbose mode")
    elif sys.argv[1] == "silent":
        print("Running in silent mode")
```

```
    else: print("Unknown mode")
else:
    sys.exit("No mode selected")
```

How do Python handle error?

```
import sys
try:
    x = 1 / 0
except Exception:
    print(sys.exc_info())
```

In fact all program is in a loop, with multiple tries or ifs, what are the difference?

```
def iffindVal(dictionary, key):
    print('key item:', key)
    if key in mydict:
        print('Colour related to key item:', dictionary[key])
    else:
        print("key '{}' is not present in dictionary!".format(key))
    print()

mydict = {'rose': 'red', 'cream': 'white', 'chocolate': 'brown'}

# calling function with key 'rose'
iffindVal(mydict, 'rose')
# calling function with key 'vanilla'
iffindVal(mydict, 'vanilla')

def tryfindVal(dictionary, key):
    print('key item:', key)
    try:
        print('Colour related to key item:', dictionary[key])
    except KeyError:
        print("KeyError: '{}' is not present in dictionary!".format(key))
    print()

mydict = {'rose': 'red', 'cream': 'white', 'chocolate': 'brown'}

# calling function with key 'rose'
tryfindVal(mydict, 'rose')
# calling function with key 'vanilla'
tryfindVal(mydict, 'vanilla')


# output
key item: rose
Colour related to key item: red

key item: vanilla
key 'vanilla' is not present in dictionary!
```

```
key item: rose
Colour related to key item: red

key item: vanilla
KeyError: 'vanilla' is not present in dictionary!
```

Looks no difference, really?

```
x = 1
try:
    print(5 / x)
except ZeroDivisionError:
    print("I am the except clause!")
else:
    print("I am the else clause!")
finally:
    print("I am the finally clause!")

print("I am executing after the try clause!")

# 5.0 # change x = 0, this line not show
# I am the else clause!
# I am the finally clause!
# I am executing after the try clause!
```

If you don't want stop the program, you better use `try`, that's why it is called `try`, and the common word is just `else`, which confuses writing, but the keyword is really `try`, or `if`.

Besides, we can create error, by `raise`,

```
class FooError(Exception):
    def __init__(self, message):
        self.message = message

    def foo(self):
        print("bar")

try:
    raise FooError("This is a test error")
except FooError as e:
    e.foo()
print("ok")
# output
bar
ok
```

What is `raise`? It is like the `alert` in javascript...

```
<html>
<head>
```

```
<script type="text/javascript">
  function myFunction(){
    alert("hello");
  }
</script>
 </head>
<body>
<center style="position: relative; top: 50%; transform: translateY(-50%);">
<input type="submit" onClick="myFunction()">
</center>
</body>
</html>
```

and similiarly confirm button click in Python,

```
def confirm():
    confirm = input("[c]Confirm or [v]Void: ")
    while True:
        if confirm.strip().lower() in ("c", "v"):
            return confirm
        else:
            print("\n Invalid Option. Please Enter a Valid Option.")
            break
confirm()
```

How many other functions in `sys`?

```
import pandas as pd

data = [{'functions': i} for i in dir(sys)]

df = pd.DataFrame(data)

df.to_markdown()
```

sys	functions
0	breakpointhook
1	displayhook
2	doc
3	excepthook
4	interactivehook
5	loader
6	name
7	package
8	spec
9	stderr
10	stdin

sys	functions
11	stdout
12	unraisablehook
13	_base_executable
14	_clear_type_cache
15	_current_exceptions
16	_current_frames
17	_debugmallocstats
18	_enablelegacywindowsfsencoding
19	_framework
20	_getframe
21	_getframemodulename
22	_git
23	_home
24	_setprofileallthreads
25	_settraceallthreads
26	_stdlib_dir
27	_vpath
28	_xoptions
29	activate_stack_trampoline
30	addaudithook
31	api_version
32	argv
33	audit
34	base_exec_prefix
35	base_prefix
36	breakpointhook
37	builtin_module_names
38	byteorder
39	call_tracing
40	copyright
41	deactivate_stack_trampoline
42	displayhook
43	dllhandle
44	dont_write_bytecode
45	exc_info

sys	functions
46	excepthook
47	exception
48	exec_prefix
49	executable
50	exit
51	flags
52	float_info
53	float_repr_style
54	get_asyncgen_hooks
55	get_coroutine_origin_tracking_depth
56	get_int_max_str_digits
57	getallocatedblocks
58	getdefaultencoding
59	getfilesystemencodeerrors
60	getfilesystemencoding
61	getprofile
62	getrecursionlimit
63	getrefcount
64	getsizeof
65	getswitchinterval
66	gettrace
67	getunicodeinternedsize
68	getwindowsversion
69	hash_info
70	hexversion
71	implementation
72	int_info
73	intern
74	is_finalizing
75	is_stack_trampoline_active
76	last_exc
77	last_traceback
78	last_type
79	last_value
80	maxsize

sys	functions
81	maxunicode
82	meta_path
83	modules
84	monitoring
85	orig_argv
86	path
87	path_hooks
88	path_importer_cache
89	platform
90	platlibdir
91	prefix
92	ps1
93	ps2
94	pycache_prefix
95	set_asyncgen_hooks
96	set_coroutine_origin_tracking_depth
97	set_int_max_str_digits
98	setprofile
99	setrecursionlimit
100	setswitchinterval
101	settrace
102	stderr
103	stdin
104	stdlib_module_names
105	stdout
106	thread_info
107	unraisablehook
108	version
109	version_info
110	warnoptions
111	winver

we see stdin and stdout, the two are samiliar from `c`, and in reality name just borrowed around, that is how we learm, and that is why we confuse...

33 sympy

If we treat unknow x, y, z as equations, we are actually solving symbolics,

```
x + y = a
x - y = b
```

Python has a `sympy` module to solve such problem,

```
import sympy

x, y = sympy.symbols("x, y")

a = x + y
b = x - y
print("{} = 5\n{} = 5".format(a, b))

f = sympy.Function('f')
a = x + f(x)
b = x - f(x)
print("{} = 5\n{} = 5".format(a, b))

#output
x + y = 5
x - y = 5
x + f(x) = 5
x - f(x) = 5
```

Use `eq` to solve, with the `a` and `b` assigned,

```
from sympy import Eq, solve
a = x + y
b = x - y
equation_1 = Eq((a), 5)
equation_2 = Eq((b), 5)
print("Equation 1:", equation_1)
print("Equation 2:", equation_2)
solution = solve((equation_1, equation_2), (x, y))
print("Solution:", solution)

# output
Equation 1: Eq(x + y, 5)
Equation 2: Eq(x - y, 5)
Solution: {x: 5, y: 0}
```

We can also use linear list,

```
from sympy import linear_eq_to_matrix
eqs = [x + y -5, x - y - 5]
A, b = linear_eq_to_matrix(eqs, [x, y])
print(A.solve(b))
```

Or matrix,

```
from sympy.matrices import Matrix
A = Matrix([[1, 1], [1, -1]])
b = Matrix([5, 5])
print(A.solve(b))

from sympy import linsolve
x = sympy.Symbol("x")
y = sympy.Symbol("y")
z = sympy.Symbol("z")
A = Matrix([[1, 1], [1, -1]])
b = Matrix([5, 5])
print(linsolve((A, b), [x, y]))
```

and we can check,

```
A = Matrix([ [1, 1], [1, -1] ])
x = Matrix(2,1,[5, 0])
b = A*x
soln = A.LUsolve(b)
print("x =", soln) # Matrix([[5], [0]])
```

Or with inverse,

```
print("x :", A.inv(method="LU")*b) # Matrix([[5], [0]])
```

and we can find gcd,

```
from sympy.abc import x, y
from sympy import gcd
from sympy.matrices import zeros, ones
m = Matrix([[x, y], [x, -y]])
print(m)
gm = gcd(tuple(m))
print(gm, ones(2)/gm)
```

Or with lambda,

```
A = Matrix([ [x, y], [x, -y] ])
f = lambda i: i/x if i == x else i/y
print(A.applyfunc(f))
```

We can use real calue for `x` and `y`,

```
from sympy import sympify
exp = (x + y)
exp = exp.subs(x, 5)
val = exp.subs(y, 0)
print(val)
```

in a list,

```
expr = x+y
val = expr.subs([(x, 5), (y, 0)])
print(val)
```

and we can also convert string,

```
from sympy import sympify
str_expr = "x - y"
expr = sympify(str_expr)
print(expr.subs([(x, 5), (y, 0)]))
```

and to `float`,

```
expr = x - y
print(expr.evalf(subs={x: 5, y: 0}))
```

Notice `solve` is not `subs`,

```
# Find a numerical solution to cos(x) = x
solution = nsolve(cos(x) - x, x, 1)
print(solution)

solution = solve(3.1124 * 40000 + 2.324 * x - y * (40000 + x))
print('solution:', solution[0]) # solution: {x: 4000.0*(7781.0 - 2500.0*y)/(250.0*y
- 581.0)}
```

and it is always `subs` after `solve`, just like the calculation on paper, double check,

```
eq = 3.1124 * 40000 + 2.324 * x - y * (40000 + x)
print("equation", eq, "= 0")
solution = solve(eq)
print('solution:', solution[0]) # solution: {x: 4000.0*(7781.0 - 2500.0*y)/(250.0*y
- 581.0)}
quantity = (solution[0][x].subs(y, 2.5))
print("solution: {", eq.subs([(x, quantity), (y, 2.5)]))
```

So we are solving a reality problem, the last time we buy 40000@3.1124, and now the price is 2.324, if we want to sell at 2.5 later, how can we benefit?

```
from sympy import sympify
str_expr = "y * (40000 + x) - (3.1124 * 40000 + 2.324 * x)"
print(str_expr, "= 0")
eq = sympify(str_expr)

solution = solve(eq)
print('solution:', solution[0]) # solution: {x: 4000.0*(7781.0 - 2500.0*y)/(250.0*y
- 581.0)}
price = 2.5
```

```
quantity = (solution[0][x].subs(y, price))
print("solution: {x:", quantity, "y:", price, "z:", eq.subs([(x, quantity), (y, 2.5)]), "}")
print(quantity*3.1124)

# output
y * (40000 + x) - (3.1124 * 40000 + 2.324 * x) = 0
solution: {x: 4000.0*(7781.0 - 2500.0*y)/(250.0*y - 581.0)}
solution: {x: 139181.818181818 y: 2.5 z: 0 }
433189.490909091
```

So it is better to just wait, 433189 that is too too much, and that only balance the buy...

```
from sympy import Eq
quantity = 0
price = 3.2
z = int(10000)
print(str_expr, "=", z)
eq1 = sympify(str_expr)
eq2 = Eq((eq1), z);
solution = solve((eq2), (x, y, z))
print("solution: {x:", quantity, "y:", price, "z:", eq.subs([(x, quantity), (y, price)]), "}")

# output
y * (40000 + x) - (3.1124 * 40000 + 2.324 * x) = 10000
solution: {x: 0 y: 3.2 z: 3504.00000000000 }
```

but how long can this be? If it is 5 years, do we wait?

```
print(3.1124 * 40000, 2.324 * 40000, (2.324 - 3.1124) * 40000))
print(2.324 * 40000 * 5 * 4 / 100)
# output
124496.0 92960.0 -31536.000000000007
18592.0
```

To summary, the condition is knowing previously buy price and quantity, and the current price, we may have an expect price later in a time, maybe part of a year, how do we decide, and what is the equation to solve?

```
from sympy import Eq
known_price = 3.1124
known_quantity = 40000
current_price = 2.324
unknown_quantity = 0
expect_price = 3
expect_quantity = unknow_quantity + known_quantity
benefit = 0

unknow_quantity = 'x'
```

```
z = int(benefit)
current_price = 'y'
str_expr = f"{current_price} * ({known_quantity} + {unknown_quantity}) - ({known_price} * {known_quantity} + {current_price} * {unknown_quantity})"

print(str_expr, "=", z)
eq1 = sympify(str_expr)
eq2 = Eq((eq1), z);
solution = solve((eq2), (x, y, z))
x = unknown_quantity
y = current_price
print("solution: {x:", unkown_quantity, "y:", current_price, "z:", eq.subs([(x, quantity), (y, price)]), "}")
```

There are three unkonwn, x for how much to buy now, y for what price to sell, z for benefit to gain,

```
from sympy import Eq
known_price = 3.1124
known_quantity = 40000
current_price = 2.324
unknown_quantity = 0
expect_price = 3
expect_quantity = unknown_quantity + known_quantity
benefit = 0

unknown_quantity = 'x'
expect_price = 'y'
z = benefit

str_expr = f"{expect_price} * ({known_quantity} + {unknown_quantity}) - ({known_price} * {known_quantity} + {current_price} * {unknown_quantity})"

print("current: {x:", known_quantity, "y:", current_price, "z:", (current_price - known_price) * known_quantity, "}")
print("stuck:", known_price * known_quantity, "left:", (current_price - known_price) * known_quantity, "lose:", current_price * known_quantity)
print("solve:", str_expr, "=", z)
eq1 = sympify(str_expr)
eq2 = Eq((eq1), z);
solution = solve((eq2), (x, y, z))

print("solution:", solution)
print(solution[0])
#x = unknown_quantity
#y = current_price
print(current_price)
print("unstuck:", (solution[0][0]).subs(y, current_price))

# output
current: {x: 40000 y: 2.324 z: -31536.000000000007 }
stuck: 124496.0 left: -31536.000000000007 lose: 92960.0
```

```
solve: y * (40000 + x) - (3.1124 * 40000 + 2.324 * x) - 0
solution: [(250.0*(124496.0 - 40000.0*y)/(250.0*y - 581.0), y, 0)]
(250.0*(124496.0 - 40000.0*y)/(250.0*y - 581.0), y, 0)
2.324
unstuck: zoo
```

What does `zoo` mean?

```
print("solution:", solution)
print(solution[0])
#x = unknown_quantity
#y = current_price
print(type(solution[0][0]))
#print(dir(solution[0][0]))
expr = solution[0][0]
print(expr, type(expr))
print("unstuck:", expr.evalf(subs={y: current_price}))
print(current_price)

# output
(250.0*(124496.0 - 40000.0*y)/(250.0*y - 581.0), y, 0)
<class 'sympy.core.mul.Mul'>
250.0*(124496.0 - 40000.0*y)/(250.0*y - 581.0) <class 'sympy.core.mul.Mul'>
unstuck: -2.01740792398801e+20
2.324
```

So it means too too large, and negative... means solve `y * (40000 + x) - (3.1124 * 40000 + 2.324 * x) = 0` is impossible.

```
expr = y * (40000 + x) - (3.1124 * 40000 + 2.324 * x)
print(expr.evalf(subs={x: 0, y: 2.324})) # -31536.0000000000
```

and we can also use `lambdify`, which gives integer result.

```
from sympy import lambdify
f = lambdify((x, y), expr)
print(f(0, 2.324)) # -31536.0
```

There are more ways to substitute, we can choose based on system reqirements,

Tool	Speed	Qualities	Dependencies
subs/evalf	50us	Simple	None
lambdify	1us	Scalar functions	math
lambdify-numpy	10ns	Vector functions	numpy
ufuncify	10ns	Complex vector expressions	f2py, Cython
lambdify-cupy	10ns	Vector functions on GPUs	cupy

Tool	Speed	Qualities	Dependencies
lambdify-jax	10ns	Vector functions on CPUs, GPUs and TPUs	jax
Aesara	10ns	Many outputs, CSE, GPUs	Aesara

So if we treat expr as the benefit, we can substitue many different values, x for how much buy now, y for what price sell later, we want the benefit > 0,

```
expr = y * (40000 + x) - (3.1124 * 40000 + 2.324 * x)
print(expr.evalf(subs={x: 10000, y: 3})) # 2264
```

the average and quantity can be estimated too,

```
avg = (3.1124 * 40000 + 2.324 * x) / (40000 + x) # the avg price
qty = (40000 + x)
print(avg.evalf(subs={x: 10000, y: 3}), qty.evalf(subs={x: 10000})) # 2.95, 50000
```

the benefit ratio,

```
ratio = (y - ((3.1124 * 40000 + 2.324 * x) / (40000 + x))) * (40000 + x) / (3.1124 * 
40000 + 2.324 * x)
print(ratio.evalf(subs={x: 10000, y: 3})*100) # 1.5
```

How about adding the fee? so we will take the trade amount, which is a positive number, does not matter with sell or buy, it will have many sections and will plus together.

```
def fee(pos):
    a = pos * 0.03 * 0.01 if pos * 0.03 * 0.01 >= 3 else 3
    b = 15
    c = 0.002 * 0.01 * pos
    c = c if c >= 2 else 2
    c = c if c <= 100 else 100
    d = math.ceil(0.1 * 0.01 * pos)
    e = 0.00565 * 0.01 * pos if 0.00565 * 0.01 * pos >= 0.01 else 0.01
    f = 0.0027 * 0.01 * pos if 0.0027 * 0.01 * pos >= 0.01 else 0.01
    g = 0.00015 * 0.01 * pos
    fee = a + b + c + d + e + f + g
    fee = math.ceil(fee * 100) / 100
    return fee
```

Let's see the range,

```
import math
def fee(pos):
    a = pos * 0.03 * 0.01 if pos * 0.03 * 0.01 >= 3 else 3
    b = 15
    c = 0.002 * 0.01 * pos
    c = c if c >= 2 else 2
```

```
    c = c if c <= 100 else 100
    d = math.ceil(0.1 * 0.01 * pos)
    e = 0.00565 * 0.01 * pos if 0.00565 * 0.01 * pos >= 0.01 else 0.01
    f = 0.0027 * 0.01 * pos if 0.0027 * 0.01 * pos >= 0.01 else 0.01
    g = 0.00015 * 0.01 * pos
    fee = a + b + c + d + e + f + g
    fee = math.ceil(fee * 100) / 100
    return fee

l = [100, 1000, 5000, 10000, 20000, 50000, 100000]

for i in l: print(i, "=>", fee(i))

# output
100 => 21.03
1000 => 21.09
5000 => 25.43
10000 => 30.85
20000 => 44.7
50000 => 86.25
100000 => 155.5
```

We can put our estimate together,

```
import math
def fee(pos):
    a = pos * 0.03 * 0.01 if pos * 0.03 * 0.01 >= 3 else 3
    b = 15
    c = 0.002 * 0.01 * pos
    c = c if c >= 2 else 2
    c = c if c <= 100 else 100
    d = math.ceil(0.1 * 0.01 * pos)
    e = 0.00565 * 0.01 * pos if 0.00565 * 0.01 * pos >= 0.01 else 0.01
    f = 0.0027 * 0.01 * pos if 0.0027 * 0.01 * pos >= 0.01 else 0.01
    g = 0.00015 * 0.01 * pos
    fee = a + b + c + d + e + f + g
    fee = math.ceil(fee * 100) / 100
    return fee

known_price = 3.1124
known_quantity = 40000
current_price = 2.324
unknown_quantity = known_quantity * (1/4)
expect_price = 3.0
expect_quantity = unknown_quantity + known_quantity
cash =  current_price * unknown_quantity
print("Notice our avg not include trade fee:", fee(known_price * known_quantity),
fee(cash))
new_avg = (known_price * known_quantity + cash) / (expect_quantity)
stuck = known_price * known_quantity + cash
goal_benefit = (expect_price - new_avg) * expect_quantity

import pandas as pd
```

```
dict = {
    "avg": [known_price],
    "qty": [known_quantity],
    "stuck": [known_price * known_quantity],
    "z": [(current_price - known_price) * known_quantity],
    "x": [current_price],
    "xq": [unknown_quantity],
    "xavg": [new_avg],
    "cash": [cash],
    "qty+xq": [expect_quantity],
    "stuck+": [stuck],
    "z-": [(current_price - new_avg) * expect_quantity],
    "y": [expect_price],
    "z+": [goal_benefit],
    #"z+%": [f"{goal_benefit/stuck:.2f}"],

}

df = pd.DataFrame(dict)
gfg = df.to_markdown(
        numalign="left",
        stralign="left",
    )

print(gfg)

unknown_quantity = 'x'
expect_price = 'y'
z = goal_benefit
str_expr   =   f"{expect_price}   *   ({known_quantity}   +   {unknown_quantity})   -
({known_price} * {known_quantity} + {current_price} * {unknown_quantity})"

print("the above table is same as we sell at y, buy how many at x, can we benefit z?
\n   ", str_expr, "=", z)

from sympy import sympify, symbols
eq1 = sympify(str_expr)
x, y = symbols("x, y")

from sympy import Eq, solve
eq2 = Eq((eq1), z);
solution = solve((eq2), (x, y, z))

print("and x =", solution[0][0])

from sympy import lambdify
expect_price = new_avg+0.01
print("and y =", expect_price)
f = lambdify((y), str(solution[0][0]))
print("    x =", f(expect_price))

expect_price = 3.0
print("and y =", expect_price)
```

```
f = lambdify((y), str(solution[0][0]))
q = f(expect_price)
print("    x =", q)

z = 0
print("if you want set xavg as y, that means z+ = 0, what is y?\n    ", str_expr,
"=", z)

avg = (known_price * known_quantity + current_price * x) / (known_quantity + x) #
the new avg price
f = lambdify((x), avg)
print("and x =", q)
print("    y =", f(q))
```

34 Sale

So the trade has fee, no matter buy or sell, based on the amount, and we know the trade can be call or put, so we make a calculator, a clever one which can give us a hint on how much we gain and how much we waste.

```
import pandas as pd
import sys

dict = {
    "trade": ["quantity@price"],
    "fee": [0],
    "waste": [0],
    "quantity": [0],
    "#assets": [0],
    "costs": [0],
    "avg": [0],
    "cash": [0],
    "benefit": "percentage",
}
df = pd.DataFrame(dict)
assets = 0
quantity = 0
costs = 0
waste = 0
benefit = "0%"
cash = 0
times = 0

last = {
    "trade": [""],
    "fee": [0],
    "waste": [0],
    "quantity": [0],
    "#assets": [0],
    "costs": [0],
    "avg": [0],
```

```
    "cash": [0],
    "benefit": "",
}

import math

def payhk(pos):
    a = pos * 0.03 * 0.01 if pos * 0.03 * 0.01 >= 3 else 3
    b = 15
    c = 0.002 * 0.01 * pos
    c = c if c >= 2 else 2
    c = c if c <= 100 else 100
    d = math.ceil(0.1 * 0.01 * pos)
    e = 0.00565 * 0.01 * pos if 0.00565 * 0.01 * pos >= 0.01 else 0.01
    f = 0.0027 * 0.01 * pos if 0.0027 * 0.01 * pos >= 0.01 else 0.01
    g = 0.00015 * 0.01 * pos
    fee = a + b + c + d + e + f + g
    fee = math.ceil(fee * 100) / 100
    return fee

def call():
    print("################estimate call with fee################################")
    transaction = yourinput.split(",")
    aptab = ""
    aplst = []
    for i in transaction:
        q, p = i.split("@")
         global waste; global costs; global cash; global assets; global df; global
quantity; global last; global times
        aplst.append([q, p])
        times = times + 1
        if q[0] == "-":
            T = q[1:].isnumeric() and p.replace(".", "0").isnumeric()
        else:
            T = q.isnumeric() and p.replace(".", "0").isnumeric()
        if T:

            trade = float(p) * int(q)  # postive if buy, negtive if sell
            pos = abs(trade)
            fee = payhk(pos)  # but fee is always postive, and postive means spent
            waste = waste + fee
            quantity = quantity + (int(q))
            assets = float(p) * quantity
            cash = cash + trade + fee
            if trade > 0:
                costs = costs + trade + fee

            else:
                costs = costs + fee

            if quantity == 0:
                avg = 0
```

```
            else:

                if cash < 0:
                    avg = (assets + fee) / quantity
                else:
                    avg = (costs) / quantity

            if costs != 0:
                benefit = f"{-cash / costs:.2%}"

            last = {
                "trade": i,
                "fee": fee,
                "waste": waste,
                "quantity": quantity,
                "#assets": assets,
                "costs": costs,
                "avg": avg,
                "cash": -cash,
                "benefit": benefit,
            }

            df = df._append(last, ignore_index=True)

        else:
            aptab = aptab + (f"| {times}  | {q} @ {p}\n")

    gfg = df.to_markdown(
        numalign="left",
        stralign="left",
    )

    print(gfg)

from random import random

import math
def payus(qty, prc): # for number
    pos = abs(qty)
    a = pos * 0.0049 if pos * 0.0049 >= 0.99 else 0.99
    a = a if a <= pos * prc * 0.5 * 0.01 else pos * prc * 0.5 * 0.01
    b = pos * 0.005 if pos * 0.005 >= 1 else 1
    b = b if b <= pos * prc * 0.5 * 0.01 else pos * prc * 0.5 * 0.01
    c = 0.003 * pos
    d = 0
    e = 0
    if qty < 0:
        d = 0.0000278 * prc * pos; d = 0.01 if d <= 0.01 else d; e = 0.000166 * pos;
e = 8.3 if d >= 8.3 else d; e = 0.01 if d <= 0.01 else d
    fee = a + b + c + d + e
    fee = math.ceil(fee * 100) / 100
    return fee
```

```
def put():
    print("################estimate put with fee###############################")
    transaction = yourinput.split(",")

    aptab = ""
    aplst = []
    T = 1
    ttlq = 0
    ttll = 0
    prc = 0

    for n, i in enumerate(transaction):
        q, p = i.split("@")
         global waste; global costs; global cash; global assets; global df; global
quantity; global last; global times

        aplst.append([q, p])
        times = times + 1
        buyq = int(q)
        buyp = float(p)
        if buyq < 0:
            ttlq = ttlq + abs(buyq)
            quantity = ttlq
            prc = buyp
            ttll = ttll + buyp * buyq
        else:
            quantity = quantity - buyq
        avgprc = -ttll / ttlq


        trade = buyq * buyp  # postive if sell negtive if buy
        #pos = abs(trade)
          fee = payus(buyq, buyp)  # but fee is always postive, and postive means
spent
        waste = waste + fee
        if trade < 0:
            costs = costs - trade + fee
            cash = trade - fee + cash

        else:
            costs = costs + fee

            # cash = cash - buyq * (buyp - avgprc) - waste # oh, the cash not useful
here
            assets = assets - buyq * (buyp - avgprc)
            cash = assets - waste
        if quantity == 0:  # this is the ending point
            avg = 0
        else:
            if trade < 0:
                avg = (cash) / quantity
            else:
                avg = (cash) / quantity - prc
```

```
        if costs != 0:
            benefit = f"{cash / costs:.2%}"

        last = {
            "trade": i,
            "fee": fee,
            "waste": waste,
            "quantity": quantity,
            "#assets": assets,
            "costs": costs,
            "avg": -avg,
            "cash": cash,
            "benefit": benefit,
        }

        df = df._append(last, ignore_index=True)
    gfg = df.to_markdown(
        numalign="left",
        stralign="left",
    )
    # df.to_excel("save.xlsx", sheet_name='save')
    print(gfg)

yourinput = sys.argv[1]

if yourinput[0] == "-": put()
else: call()
```

Notice trade fee is different for different market, compare the range, for US and HK,

quantity	price	USD	HKD
100	1	1.3	21.03
1000	1	12.9	21.09
5000	1	64.5	25.43
10000	1	129.0	30.85
20000	1	258.0	44.7
50000	1	645.0	86.25
100000	1	1290.0	155.5

and plus the currency rate, US stocks are really expensive, though US has more stocks for short sale.

trade AAPL	fee	waste	quantity	no fee	costs	avg	cash	benefit
quantity@price	0	0	0	0	0	0	0	percentage

trade AAPL	fee	waste	quantity	no fee	costs	avg	cash	benefit
-100@221.69	3.53	3.53	100	0	22172.5	221.725	-22172.5	-100.00%
100@220	2.29	5.82	0	169	22174.8	0	163.18	0.74%

Let's compare the long sale, the other side,

trade AAPL	fee	waste	quantity	assets	costs	avg	cash	benefit
quantity@price	0	0	0	0	0	0	0	percentage
100@220	2.84	2.84	100	22000	22002.8	220.028	-22002.8	-100.00%
-100@221.69	2.86	5.7	0	0	22005.7	0	163.3	0.74%

and in reality there is interest loan in short sale, so it is much better to do long sale, unless you can catch the huge drop.

The sale is not only a stock problem, even for a market, as long as there are many products, and different price, we give discount is for buy back, not for lose.

```
import math
def payus(qty, prc): # for number
    pos = abs(qty)
    a = pos * 0.0049 if pos * 0.0049 >= 0.99 else 0.99
    a = a if a <= pos * prc * 0.5 * 0.01 else pos * prc * 0.5 * 0.01
    b = pos * 0.005 if pos * 0.005 >= 1 else 1
    b = b if b <= pos * prc * 0.5 * 0.01 else pos * prc * 0.5 * 0.01
    c = 0.003 * pos
    d = 0
    e = 0
    if qty < 0:
        d = 0.0000278 * prc * pos; d = 0.01 if d <= 0.01 else d; e = 0.000166 * pos;
e = 8.3 if d >= 8.3 else d; e = 0.01 if d <= 0.01 else d
    fee = a + b + c + d + e
    fee = math.ceil(fee * 100) / 100
    return fee

known_price = 1.12
known_quantity = 5000
current_price = 0.6
unknown_quantity = known_quantity * (5)
expect_price = 1

expect_quantity = unknown_quantity + known_quantity
cash =  current_price * unknown_quantity
print("and  fee:[",  payus(known_quantity,  known_price),  payus(unknown_quantity,
current_price), payus(expect_quantity, expect_price), "]")
new_avg = (known_price * known_quantity + cash) / (expect_quantity)
stuck = known_price * known_quantity + cash
goal_benefit = (expect_price - new_avg) * expect_quantity
```

```
import pandas as pd
dict = {
    "avg": [known_price],
    "qty": [known_quantity],
    "stuck": [known_price * known_quantity],
    "z": [(current_price - known_price) * known_quantity],
    "x": [current_price],
    "xq": [unknown_quantity],
    "xavg": [new_avg],
    "cash": [cash],
    "qty+xq": [expect_quantity],
    "stuck+": [stuck],
    "z-": [(current_price - new_avg) * expect_quantity],
    "y": [expect_price],
    "z+": [goal_benefit],
    #"z+%": [f"{goal_benefit/stuck:.2f}"],

}

df = pd.DataFrame(dict)
gfg = df.to_markdown(
        numalign="left",
        stralign="left",
    )

print(gfg)
```

Regardless of the fee, the first time we buy 5000@1.12, and then we buy 25000@0.6, we then sell all the quantity 30000@1, we just earned 9400, benefit ratio nearly 50%.

avg	qty	stuck	z	x	xq	xavg	cash	qty+xq	stuck+	z-	y	z+
1.12	5000	5600	-2600	0.6	25000	0.686667	15000	30000	20600	-2600	1	**9400**

and compare to the fee, 64.5 225.0 387.0,

trade	fee	waste	quantity	assets	costs	avg	cash	benefi
quantity@price	0	0	0	0	0	0	0	percent
5000@1.12	64.5	64.5	5000	5600	5664.5	1.1329	-5664.5	-100.0
25000@0.6	225	289.5	30000	18000	20889.5	0.696317	-20889.5	-100.0
-30000@1	388.67	678.17	0	0	21278.2	0	**8721.83**	40.99%

10% is off... we can also use the `sys.argv`,

```
import math
def payus(qty, prc): # for number
    pos = abs(qty)
```

```
    a = pos * 0.0049 if pos * 0.0049 >= 0.99 else 0.99
    a = a if a <= pos * prc * 0.5 * 0.01 else pos * prc * 0.5 * 0.01
    b = pos * 0.005 if pos * 0.005 >= 1 else 1
    b = b if b <= pos * prc * 0.5 * 0.01 else pos * prc * 0.5 * 0.01
    c = 0.003 * pos
    d = 0
    e = 0
    if qty < 0:
        d = 0.0000278 * prc * pos; d = 0.01 if d <= 0.01 else d; e = 0.000166 * pos;
e = 8.3 if d >= 8.3 else d; e = 0.01 if d <= 0.01 else d
    fee = a + b + c + d + e
    fee = math.ceil(fee * 100) / 100
    return fee

import sys
#print(sys.argv)
l = sys.argv[1]
# 5000@1.12,x@0.55,y@1.2

lll = l.split(',')
print(lll)

[known_quantity, known_price] = lll[0].split('@')
known_quantity = int(known_quantity)
known_price = float(known_price)

[unknown_quantity, current_price] = lll[1].split('@')
unknown_quantity = known_quantity * (1)
current_price = float(current_price)
if current_price == 0.0: unknown_quantity = 0
[expect_quantity, expect_price] = lll[2].split('@')
expect_quantity = unknown_quantity + known_quantity
expect_price = float(expect_price)
org_expect_price = expect_price

expect_quantity = unknown_quantity + known_quantity
cash =  current_price * unknown_quantity
print("and    fee:[",    fee(known_quantity,    known_price),    fee(unknown_quantity,
current_price), fee(expect_quantity, expect_price), "]")
new_avg = (known_price * known_quantity + cash) / (expect_quantity)
stuck = known_price * known_quantity + cash
goal_benefit = (expect_price - new_avg) * expect_quantity

import pandas as pd
dict = {
    "avg": [known_price],
    "qty": [known_quantity],
    "stuck": [known_price * known_quantity],
    "z": [(current_price - known_price) * known_quantity],
    "x": [current_price],
    "xq": [unknown_quantity],
    "xavg": [new_avg],
    "cash": [cash],
```

```
    "qty+xq": [expect_quantity],
    "stuck+": [stuck],
    "z-": [(current_price - new_avg) * expect_quantity],
    "y": [expect_price],
    "z+": [goal_benefit],
    #"z+%": [f"{goal_benefit/stuck:.2f}"],

}

df = pd.DataFrame(dict)
gfg = df.to_markdown(
        numalign="left",
        stralign="left",
    )

print(gfg)
```

avg	qty	stuck	z	x	xq	xavg	cash	qty+xq	stuck+	z-	y	z+
1.12	5000	5600	-2850	0.55	5000	0.835	2750	10000	8350	-2850	1.2	3650

The `sys.argv` simply splits by ',' and takeout the two parts besides '@', 5000@1.12,x@0.55,y@1.2, means at price 0.55, buy again 5000, and sell at price 1.2 later, how much can we benefit? 3650.

We find it is actually solve the equation, y * (5000 + x) - (1.12 * 5000 + 0.55 * x) = 3650.

```
unknown_quantity = 'x'
expect_price = 'y'
z = goal_benefit
str_expr = f"{expect_price} * ({known_quantity} + {unknown_quantity}) - ({known_price} * {known_quantity} + {current_price} * {unknown_quantity})"

print("the above table is same as we sell at y, buy how many at x, can we benefit z?\n  ", str_expr, "=", z)

from sympy import sympify, symbols
eq1 = sympify(str_expr)
x, y = symbols("x, y")

from sympy import Eq, solve
eq2 = Eq((eq1), z);
solution = solve((eq2), (x, y, z))

print("and x =", solution[0][0])

from sympy import lambdify
expect_price = new_avg#+0.01
print("and y =", expect_price)
f = lambdify((y), str(solution[0][0]))
```

```
print("    xq =", f(expect_price))

# output
the above table is same as we sell at y, buy how many at x, can we benefit z?
    y * (5000 + x) - (1.12 * 5000 + 0.55 * x) = 3650.0
and x = 20.0*(9250.0 - 5000.0*y)/(20.0*y - 11.0)
and y = 0.835
    xq = 17807.017543859653
```

so the avg really does not mean much.

```
import sys
#print(sys.argv)
l = sys.argv[1]
#l = "100@3.19,x@price,y@4" for xq
#or xq@2 for x

lll = l.split(',')
print(lll)

[known_quantity, known_price] = lll[0].split('@')
known_quantity = int(known_quantity)
known_price = float(known_price)

[unknown_quantity, current_price] = lll[1].split('@')
[expect_quantity, expect_price] = lll[2].split('@')

#unknown_quantity = 'x'
#expect_price = 'y'
z = 0

str_expr = f"{expect_price} * ({known_quantity} + {unknown_quantity}) - ({known_price} * {known_quantity} + {current_price} * {unknown_quantity})"

print("from the avg y to solve x...\n    ", str_expr, "=", z)
from sympy import symbols, Eq, solve, sympify

eq1 = sympify(str_expr)
x, y = symbols("x, y")

eq2 = Eq((eq1), z);
solution = solve((eq2), (x, y, z))

print("and x =", solution[0][0])
```

and we can add z for benefit, to find how much we buy,

```
import sys
#print(sys.argv)
l = sys.argv[1]
#l = "5000@1.12,x@1.1,y@6,4000@z"
```

```
lll = l.split(',')
print(lll)

[known_quantity, known_price] = lll[0].split('@')
known_quantity = int(known_quantity)
known_price = float(known_price)

[unknown_quantity, current_price] = lll[1].split('@')
[expect_quantity, expect_price] = lll[2].split('@')
[expect_benefit, expect_ratio] = lll[3].split('@')

#unknown_quantity = 'x'
#expect_price = 'y'
z = int(expect_benefit)

str_expr = f"{expect_price} * ({known_quantity} + {unknown_quantity}) -
({known_price} * {known_quantity} + {current_price} * {unknown_quantity})"

print("from the avg y to solve x...\n    ", str_expr, "=", z)
from sympy import symbols, Eq, solve, sympify

eq1 = sympify(str_expr)
x, y = symbols("x, y")


eq2 = Eq((eq1), z);
solution = solve((eq2), (x, y, z))

print("and x =", solution[0][0])

# output
['5000@1.12', 'x@1.1', 'y@6', '4000@z']
from the avg y to solve x...
    6 * (5000 + x) - (1.12 * 5000 + 1.1 * x) = 4000
and x = -4163.26530612245
```

you see, some solution is just meanningless...

```
# output
['5000@1.12', 'x@1.1', 'y@6', '400000@z']
from the avg y to solve x...
    6 * (5000 + x) - (1.12 * 5000 + 1.1 * x) = 400000
and x = 76653.0612244898
```

this solution is too much, kind of meanningless too, and if we want to switch x quantity and price,

```
# output
['5000@1.12', '6000@x', 'y@6', '400000@z']
from the avg y to solve x...
    6 * (5000 + 6000) - (1.12 * 5000 + x * 6000) = 400000
and x = -56.6000000000000
```

```
Traceback (most recent call last):
  File "C:\Users\Lenovo\Flask\stock\bsc.py", line 79, in <module>
    current_price = float(current_price)
                    ^^^^^^^^^^^^^^^^^^^^
ValueError: could not convert string to float: 'x'
```

It is because we follows the reality, that price is always given, so we convert it into `float`, but switch makes it a string `x`, so traceback. Add a check for if the price is float,

```
try:
    float(current_price)
except:
    sys.exit("price can't concert to float...")
# add the above
current_price = float(current_price)
if current_price == 0.0: unknown_quantity = 0
```

`futu-api` is a real time trade system, with the help of OpenD client, https://openapi.futunn.com/futu-api-doc/en/intro/intro.html, it offers three parts, login, quote, trade. Select the right version of OpenD and `pip install futu-api` to start use.

```
# openfutu.py

import time;
import os;
import sys;
from futu import *
import subprocess
import psutil

#-----------------------------------------------

def is_process_running(process_name):
        for process in psutil.process_iter(['name']):
                if process.info['name'] == process_name:
                        return True
        return False

#-----------------------------------------------

def main( ) :
        process_name = 'FutuOpenD.exe'
        if is_process_running(process_name):
                print(f"Don't close the windoe of {process_name}")
                futu()

        else:
                #print(f"{process_name}' needs verification code")
                        command = r'.\Futu_OpenD_8.6.4608_Windows\FutuOpenD.exe -
```

```
login_account=yourphone -login_pwd=youpassword -lang=en'
                p = subprocess.Popen(command, shell=False)

                try:
                        p.wait(timeout=5);
                        print( 'stdout:', p.stdout );

                except subprocess.TimeoutExpired:
                        #p.kill()
                        print("timeout...")
                finally:
                        print(f"keep the window of {process_name} open")


        return 0;

#-----------------------------------------------#

main( );

#-----------------------------------------------#

# taskkill /F /IM python.exe
```

to check AAPL quote,

```
# quotefutu.py

import time;
import os;
import sys;
from futu import *
import subprocess
import psutil

def is_process_running(process_name):
    for process in psutil.process_iter(['name']):
        if process.info['name'] == process_name:
            return True
    return False

#-----------------------------------------------

def futu( ):

    quote_ctx = OpenQuoteContext(host='127.0.0.1', port=11111)

    print(quote_ctx.get_market_snapshot('US.AAPL'))

    quote_ctx.close()

    return 0;
```

```
#---------------------------------------------
def main( ) :
    process_name = 'FutuOpenD.exe'
    if is_process_running(process_name):
        print(f"don't close {process_name} window")
#---------------------------------------------
        futu( );
#---------------------------------------------

    else:
                      command   =   r'.\Futu_OpenD_8.6.4608_Windows\FutuOpenD.exe   -
login_account=yourphone -login_pwd=yourpassword -lang=en'
        print(f"you need run {process_name}first")

    return 0;

#---------------------------------------------
main( );
#---------------------------------------------

# taskkill /F /IM python.exe

# output
(-1, 'No right to get the quote for US.AAPL, please check the Stocks of US Market
quote right')
```

why is that?

From the OpenD window, we can see...

```
Futu OpenD is running
Load configuration file successfully
Server startup
API Listening Address: 127.0.0.1:11111
API RSA Enable: No
Login Method: Account password login
Logging in
Quote Connection: Conn06-HK
Login Account: 231760246
Login successful
User Quota: Subscription Quota: 1000, Historical Candlestick Quota: 1000
HK Securities: LV2, Permission Status: Normal
HK Options: LV2, Permission Status: Normal
HK Futures: LV2, Permission Status: Normal
US Securities: No Authority, Permission Status: Normal
US Options: LV1, Permission Status: Normal
CME Futures: No Authority, Permission Status: Normal
CBOT Futures: No Authority, Permission Status: Normal
NYMEX Futures: No Authority, Permission Status: Normal
COMEX Futures: No Authority, Permission Status: Normal
```

```
CBOE Futures: No Authority, Permission Status: Normal
SSE: LV1, Permission Status: Normal
SZSE: LV1, Permission Status: Normal
US Index: No Authority, Permission Status: Normal
US OTC: No Authority, Permission Status: Normal
SG Futures: No Authority, Permission Status: Normal
JP Futures: No Authority, Permission Status: Normal
Trade Connection1: 119.91.243.37-HK
The necessary data is ready
```

No authority, https://openapi.futunn.com/futu-api-doc/en/qa/quote.html, well, that is the reality, and some quotes can be bought by https://qtcardfthk.futufin.com/, but it is so annoying... so we change to IB, we download TWS, https://www.interactivebrokers.com/campus/ibkr-quant-news/interactive-brokers-python-api-native-a-step-by-step-guide/, and connect again...

```
# ib_api_demo.py

if __name__ == "__main__":
    # Connect to the Trader Workstation (TWS) running on the
    # usual port of 7496, with a clientId of 100
    # (The clientId is chosen by us and we will need
    # separate IDs for both the execution connection and
    # market data connection)
    tws_conn = Connection.create(port=7496, clientId=100)
    tws_conn.connect()

    # Assign the error handling function defined above
    # to the TWS connection
    tws_conn.register(error_handler, 'Error')

    # Assign all of the server reply messages to the
    # reply_handler function defined above
    tws_conn.registerAll(reply_handler)

    # Create an order ID which is 'global' for this session. This
    # will need incrementing once new orders are submitted.
    order_id = 1

    # Create a contract in GOOG stock via SMART order routing
    goog_contract = create_contract('GOOG', 'AAPL', 'FFIE')

    # Go long 100 shares of Google
    goog_order = create_order('MKT', 100, 'BUY')

    # Use the connection to the send the order to IB
    tws_conn.placeOrder(order_id, goog_contract, goog_order)

    # Disconnect from TWS
    tws_conn.disconnect()
```

35 pybroker

The important thing is to get the candles, or the data, so that we can analysis and expect, basicly the price, drop we short, go up we long. If we do by futu,

```
from futu import *
quote_ctx = OpenQuoteContext(host='127.0.0.1', port=11111)
ret, data, page_req_key = quote_ctx.request_history_kline('HK.07588', start='2024-08-09', end='2024-09-09', max_count=5) # 5 per page, request the first page
if ret == RET_OK:
    print(data)
    #print(data['code'][0]) # Take the first stock code
     #print(data['close'].values.tolist()) # The closing price of the first page is converted to a list
else:
    print('error:', data)
while page_req_key != None: # Request all results after
    print('*************************************')
          ret, data, page_req_key = quote_ctx.request_history_kline('HK.07588', start='2024-09-09', end='2024-10-09', max_count=5, page_req_key=page_req_key) # Request the page after turning data
    if ret == RET_OK:
        print(data)
    else:
        print('error:', data)
print('All pages are finished!')
quote_ctx.close()
```

and we can use the `datetime` module,

```
from futu import *
from datetime import date, datetime, timedelta

tday = date.today()
#daytoday = tday.ctime()
onem = (datetime.now() - timedelta(days=20, hours=-5))
onemday = onem.date()
twom = (datetime.now() - timedelta(days=40, hours=-5))
twomday = onem.date()
threem = (datetime.now() - timedelta(days=60, hours=-5))
threemday = threem.date()

[tday, onemday, twomday, threemday] = map(str, [tday, onemday, twomday, threemday])

print("The date today is ", tday)
print("The date info. is ", str(onemday))
stock = 'HK.07588'
quote_ctx = OpenQuoteContext(host='127.0.0.1', port=11111)
ret, data, page_req_key = quote_ctx.request_history_kline(stock, start=threemday, end=twomday, max_count=5) # 5 per page, request the first page
if ret == RET_OK:
```

```
    print(data)
    #print(data['code'][0]) # Take the first stock code
     #print(data['close'].values.tolist()) # The closing price of the first page is
converted to a list
else:
    print('error:', data)
while page_req_key != None: # Request all results after
    print('*************************************')
     ret, data, page_req_key = quote_ctx.request_history_kline(stock, start=twomday,
end=tday, max_count=5, page_req_key=page_req_key) # Request the page after turning
data
    if ret == RET_OK:
        print(data)
    else:
        print('error:', data)
print('All pages are finished!')
quote_ctx.close()

# output
        code              name               time_key   open  ...   volume   turnover
change_rate  last_close
0  HK.07588  FI2 CSOP HSCEI  2024-08-12 00:00:00  4.714  ...   769200  3624329.0
-0.042481      4.708
1  HK.07588  FI2 CSOP HSCEI  2024-08-13 00:00:00  4.692  ...    65000   305686.0
-0.594985      4.706
2  HK.07588  FI2 CSOP HSCEI  2024-08-14 00:00:00  4.616  ...   378400  1764232.0
0.726806      4.678
3  HK.07588  FI2 CSOP HSCEI  2024-08-15 00:00:00  4.800  ...   390600  1821007.0
-0.254669      4.712
4  HK.07588  FI2 CSOP HSCEI  2024-08-16 00:00:00  4.598  ...   742200  3353368.0
-4.297872      4.700

[5 rows x 13 columns]
*************************************
        code              name               time_key   open  ...   volume   turnover
change_rate  last_close
0  HK.07588  FI2 CSOP HSCEI  2024-08-19 00:00:00  4.400  ...   585300  2562264.0
-3.068030      4.498
1  HK.07588  FI2 CSOP HSCEI  2024-08-20 00:00:00  4.376  ...   981600  4328100.0
2.201835      4.360
2  HK.07588  FI2 CSOP HSCEI  2024-08-21 00:00:00  4.500  ...  1037400  4741047.0
1.615799      4.456
3  HK.07588  FI2 CSOP HSCEI  2024-08-22 00:00:00  4.470  ...  1278200  5728154.0
-2.738516      4.528
4  HK.07588  FI2 CSOP HSCEI  2024-08-23 00:00:00  4.480  ...   396800  1766550.0
0.136240      4.404

[5 rows x 13 columns]
*************************************
        code              name               time_key   open  ...   volume   turnover
change_rate  last_close
0  HK.07588  FI2 CSOP HSCEI  2024-08-26 00:00:00  4.336  ...   731200  3169202.0
-1.859410      4.410
```

```
1  HK.07588  FI2 CSOP HSCEI  2024-08-27 00:00:00  4.380  ...  1167100   5029387.0
-1.016636      4.328
2  HK.07588  FI2 CSOP HSCEI  2024-08-28 00:00:00  4.310  ...  3166600  13936998.0
2.661064      4.284
3  HK.07588  FI2 CSOP HSCEI  2024-08-29 00:00:00  4.448  ...  1162500   5143485.0
-0.773079      4.398
4  HK.07588  FI2 CSOP HSCEI  2024-08-30 00:00:00  4.340  ...  1431800   6027472.0
-2.887259      4.364

[5 rows x 13 columns]
************************************
       code             name             time_key   open  ...   volume   turnover
change_rate  last_close
0  HK.07588  FI2 CSOP HSCEI  2024-09-02 00:00:00  4.330  ...  1847200  8078161.0
2.265219      4.238
1  HK.07588  FI2 CSOP HSCEI  2024-09-03 00:00:00  4.384  ...  1432100  6307047.0
1.845870      4.334
2  HK.07588  FI2 CSOP HSCEI  2024-09-04 00:00:00  4.414  ...  1708200  7703847.0
1.721794      4.414
3  HK.07588  FI2 CSOP HSCEI  2024-09-05 00:00:00  4.490  ...  1555800  7049163.0
1.247216      4.490
4  HK.07588  FI2 CSOP HSCEI  2024-09-09 00:00:00  4.620  ...  2024100  9469071.0
3.431588      4.546

[5 rows x 13 columns]
************************************
       code             name             time_key   open  ...   volume   turnover
change_rate  last_close
0  HK.07588  FI2 CSOP HSCEI  2024-09-10 00:00:00  4.668  ...   433200  2021404.0
-1.105912      4.702
1  HK.07588  FI2 CSOP HSCEI  2024-09-11 00:00:00  4.750  ...   997400  4754488.0
1.419355      4.650
2  HK.07588  FI2 CSOP HSCEI  2024-09-12 00:00:00  4.668  ...   324300  1503507.0
-1.526718      4.716
3  HK.07588  FI2 CSOP HSCEI  2024-09-13 00:00:00  4.580  ...  1149000  5230878.0
-1.722653      4.644
4  HK.07588  FI2 CSOP HSCEI  2024-09-16 00:00:00  4.660  ...   333600  1537023.0
-0.613497      4.564

[5 rows x 13 columns]
************************************
       code             name             time_key   open  ...   volume    turnover
change_rate  last_close
0  HK.07588  FI2 CSOP HSCEI  2024-09-17 00:00:00  4.530  ...   548300   2417226.0
-2.910053      4.536
1  HK.07588  FI2 CSOP HSCEI  2024-09-19 00:00:00  4.416  ...  2337600  10115456.0
-4.223433      4.404
2  HK.07588  FI2 CSOP HSCEI  2024-09-20 00:00:00  4.220  ...   968800   3992461.0
-2.086297      4.218
3  HK.07588  FI2 CSOP HSCEI  2024-09-23 00:00:00  4.116  ...   799000   3254442.0
-0.290557      4.130
4  HK.07588  FI2 CSOP HSCEI  2024-09-24 00:00:00  4.036  ...  4896200  18824173.0
-10.539097      4.118
```

```
[5 rows x 13 columns]
************************************
        code              name                time_key  open  ...    volume    turnover
change_rate  last_close
0  HK.07588  FI2 CSOP HSCEI  2024-09-25 00:00:00  3.60  ...  3342400  11651247.0
-1.248643     3.684
1  HK.07588  FI2 CSOP HSCEI  2024-09-26 00:00:00  3.56  ...  3380950  11651928.0
-9.840572     3.638
2  HK.07588  FI2 CSOP HSCEI  2024-09-27 00:00:00  3.24  ...  4938200  15455526.0
-5.670732     3.280
3  HK.07588  FI2 CSOP HSCEI  2024-09-30 00:00:00  3.00  ...  3376100   9802549.0
-5.817712     3.094
4  HK.07588  FI2 CSOP HSCEI  2024-10-02 00:00:00  2.89  ...  8300000  21473641.0
-14.275909     2.914

[5 rows x 13 columns]
************************************
        code              name                time_key   open  ...    volume    turnover
change_rate  last_close
0  HK.07588  FI2 CSOP HSCEI  2024-10-03 00:00:00  2.498  ...   5837500  15338837.0
3.362690     2.498
1  HK.07588  FI2 CSOP HSCEI  2024-10-04 00:00:00  2.624  ...   3054600   7630849.0
-5.886909     2.582
2  HK.07588  FI2 CSOP HSCEI  2024-10-07 00:00:00  2.388  ...   3498500   8278637.0
-4.362140     2.430
3  HK.07588  FI2 CSOP HSCEI  2024-10-08 00:00:00  2.280  ...   8575300  22720497.0
20.912220     2.324
4  HK.07588  FI2 CSOP HSCEI  2024-10-09 00:00:00  2.810  ...  21600900  60681940.0
2.633452     2.810

[5 rows x 13 columns]
All pages are finished!
```

and if we do by akshare

```
import akshare as ak

#version 1.13.86

hkstock = "07588"

ak.stock_hk_hist_min_em
stock_hk_hist_hfq_df     =     ak.stock_hk_hist(symbol=hkstock,     period="daily",
start_date="2024-08-12", end_date="2024-10-09", adjust="qfq")
stocks = (stock_hk_hist_hfq_df)

#print(stocks.iloc[4])
#select date

df = stocks.iloc[:, [0, 1, 2, 5, 7]]
column_index_to_rename = 0  # Index of the 'name' column
new_column_name = 'date'
```

```
df.rename(columns={df.columns[column_index_to_rename]:                new_column_name},
inplace=True)

column_index_to_rename = 1  # Index of the 'name' column
new_column_name = 'open'
df.rename(columns={df.columns[column_index_to_rename]:                new_column_name},
inplace=True)

column_index_to_rename = 2  # Index of the 'name' column
new_column_name = 'close'
df.rename(columns={df.columns[column_index_to_rename]:                new_column_name},
inplace=True)

column_index_to_rename = 3  # Index of the 'name' column
new_column_name = 'volume'
df.rename(columns={df.columns[column_index_to_rename]:                new_column_name},
inplace=True)

column_index_to_rename = 4  # Index of the 'name' column
new_column_name = 'bias'
df.rename(columns={df.columns[column_index_to_rename]:                new_column_name},
inplace=True)
print(df.to_markdown())
```

	date	**open**	**close**	**volume**	**bias**
1	2024-08-13	4.692	4.678	65000	2.04
2	2024-08-14	4.616	4.712	378400	2.86
3	2024-08-15	4.8	4.7	390600	4.46
4	2024-08-16	4.598	4.498	742200	2.85
5	2024-08-19	4.4	4.36	585300	1.65
6	2024-08-20	4.376	4.456	981600	2.39
7	2024-08-21	4.5	4.528	1037400	2.65
8	2024-08-22	4.47	4.404	1278200	3.31
9	2024-08-23	4.48	4.41	396800	1.95
10	2024-08-26	4.336	4.328	731200	1.54
11	2024-08-27	4.38	4.284	1167100	2.73
12	2024-08-28	4.31	4.398	3166600	2.57
13	2024-08-29	4.448	4.364	1162500	3.46
14	2024-08-30	4.34	4.238	1431800	4.63
15	2024-09-02	4.33	4.334	1847200	2.12
16	2024-09-03	4.384	4.414	1432100	1.71
17	2024-09-04	4.414	4.49	1708200	3.4
18	2024-09-05	4.49	4.546	1555800	2.32
19	2024-09-09	4.62	4.702	2024100	3.26

	date	open	close	volume	bias
20	2024-09-10	4.668	4.65	433200	1.91
21	2024-09-11	4.75	4.716	997400	1.85
22	2024-09-12	4.668	4.644	324300	2.76
23	2024-09-13	4.58	4.564	1149000	2.2
24	2024-09-16	4.66	4.536	333600	2.89
25	2024-09-17	4.53	4.404	548300	3.35
26	2024-09-19	4.416	4.218	2337600	5.99
27	2024-09-20	4.22	4.13	968800	3.89
28	2024-09-23	4.116	4.118	799000	2.42
29	2024-09-24	4.036	3.684	4896200	8.79
30	2024-09-25	3.6	3.638	3342400	6.03
31	2024-09-26	3.56	3.28	3380950	9.35
32	2024-09-27	3.24	3.094	4938200	6.34
33	2024-09-30	3	2.914	3376100	7.43
34	2024-10-02	2.89	2.498	8300000	15.99
35	2024-10-03	2.498	2.582	5837500	10.33
36	2024-10-04	2.624	2.43	3054600	8.99
37	2024-10-07	2.388	2.324	3498500	5.02
38	2024-10-08	2.28	2.81	8575300	23.84
39	2024-10-09	2.81	2.884	21600900	13.02

To find the detail for 5 days,

```
import akshare as ak

hkstock = "07588"

stocks = ak.stock_hk_hist_min_em(symbol=hkstock, period='1', adjust='',
                                                    start_date="2024-10-06 9:32:00",
                                                    end_date="2024-10-10 16:32:00")

df = stocks.iloc[:, [0, 1, 2, 5, 7]]
column_index_to_rename = 0  # Index of the 'name' column
new_column_name = 'date'
df.rename(columns={df.columns[column_index_to_rename]:              new_column_name},
inplace=True)

column_index_to_rename = 1  # Index of the 'name' column
new_column_name = 'open'
df.rename(columns={df.columns[column_index_to_rename]:              new_column_name},
inplace=True)
```

```
column_index_to_rename = 2  # Index of the 'name' column
new_column_name = 'close'
df.rename(columns={df.columns[column_index_to_rename]:                    new_column_name},
inplace=True)

column_index_to_rename = 3  # Index of the 'name' column
new_column_name = 'volume'
df.rename(columns={df.columns[column_index_to_rename]:                    new_column_name},
inplace=True)

column_index_to_rename = 4  # Index of the 'name' column
new_column_name = 'price'
df.rename(columns={df.columns[column_index_to_rename]:                    new_column_name},
inplace=True)
print(df.to_markdown())
```

The data has 1315 rows,

...	date	open	close	volume	price
1315	2024-10-10 15:52:00	2.668	2.664	0	2.6635
1316	2024-10-10 15:53:00	2.666	2.67	14000	2.6635
1317	2024-10-10 15:54:00	2.672	2.672	0	2.6635
1318	2024-10-10 15:55:00	2.674	2.672	0	2.6635
1319	2024-10-10 15:56:00	2.674	2.672	15000	2.6635
1320	2024-10-10 15:57:00	2.674	2.672	18300	2.6635
1321	2024-10-10 15:58:00	2.67	2.67	5000	2.6635
1322	2024-10-10 15:59:00	2.668	2.664	9400	2.6635
1323	2024-10-10 16:00:00	2.666	2.672	57800	2.6635

So, is it possible to do any strategy?

```
import pybroker as pb
from pybroker import Strategy, ExecContext
from pybroker.ext.data import AKShare

pb.param(name='stock_code', value='07588')



akshare = AKShare()


df    =   akshare.query(symbols=[pb.param(name='stock_code')],   start_date='20241006',
end_date='20241010')

print(df.to_markdown())

# output
```

```
Loading bar data...
Traceback (most recent call last):
  File "C:\Users\Lenovo\Flask\stock\quotefutu.py", line 8, in <module>
    df = akshare.query(
         ^^^^^^^^^^^^^^
                                                                                          File
"C:\Users\Lenovo\AppData\Local\Packages\PythonSoftwareFoundation.Python.3.12_qbz5n2k
fra8p0\LocalCache\local-packages\Python312\site-packages\pybroker\data.py",      line
231, in query
    df = self._fetch_data(
         ^^^^^^^^^^^^^^^^^
                                                                                          File
"C:\Users\Lenovo\AppData\Local\Packages\PythonSoftwareFoundation.Python.3.12_qbz5n2k
fra8p0\LocalCache\local-packages\Python312\site-packages\pybroker\ext\data.py",  line
47, in _fetch_data
    temp_df = akshare.stock_zh_a_hist(
              ^^^^^^^^^^^^^^^^^^^^^^^^
                                                                                          File
"C:\Users\Lenovo\AppData\Local\Packages\PythonSoftwareFoundation.Python.3.12_qbz5n2k
fra8p0\LocalCache\local-packages\Python312\site-
packages\akshare\stock_feature\stock_hist_em.py", line 1051, in stock_zh_a_hist
    "secid": f"{code_id_dict[symbol]}.{symbol}",
                ~~~~~~~~~~~~^^^^^^^^
KeyError: '07588'
```

It is so sad that we have to change the py file if we want to use, since the function it uses is not HK, so we have to try, change the line as the error says,

```
#
C:\Users\Lenovo\AppData\Local\Packages\PythonSoftwareFoundation.Python.3.12_qbz5n2kf
ra8p0\LocalCache\local-packages\Python312\site-packages\pybroker\ext\data.py
                temp_df = akshare.stock_hk_hist(#zh_a_hist(
# output
Loading bar data...
Loaded bar data: 0:00:01
```

	date	symbol	open	high	low	close	volume
0	2024-10-07 00:00:00	07588	2.388	2.422	2.3	2.324	3498500
1	2024-10-08 00:00:00	07588	2.28	2.834	2.28	2.81	8575300
2	2024-10-09 00:00:00	07588	2.81	3.008	2.642	2.884	21600900
3	2024-10-10 00:00:00	07588	2.862	2.862	2.558	2.672	11287600

Backtesting: 2024-10-06 00:00:00 to 2024-10-10 00:00:00

Let's move on to the buy part,

```
pb.param(name='percent', value=1)
pb.param(name='stop_loss_pct', value=10)
pb.param(name='stop_profit_pct', value=10)
```

```
def buy_with_stop_loss(ctx: ExecContext):
    pos = ctx.long_pos()
    if not pos:

        ctx.buy_shares = ctx.calc_target_shares(pb.param(name='percent'))
        ctx.hold_bars = 100
    else:
        ctx.sell_shares = pos.shares

        ctx.stop_profit_pct = pb.param(name='stop_profit_pct')



my_config = pb.StrategyConfig(initial_cash=30000)

strategy    =    Strategy(akshare,    start_date='20241006',    end_date='20241010',
config=my_config)

strategy.add_execution(fn=buy_with_stop_loss, symbols=[pb.param(name='stock_code')])

result = strategy.backtest()
print(result.metrics_df.round(4))

# output
Finished backtest: 0:00:09
                      name       value
0              trade_count      1.0000
1     initial_market_value  30000.0000
2         end_market_value  32611.2800
3                total_pnl   3046.6800
4           unrealized_pnl   -435.4000
5         total_return_pct     10.1556
6             total_profit   3046.6800
7               total_loss      0.0000
8               total_fees      0.0000
9             max_drawdown   -435.4000
10        max_drawdown_pct     -1.3175
11                win_rate    100.0000
12               loss_rate      0.0000
13          winning_trades      1.0000
14           losing_trades      0.0000
15                 avg_pnl   3046.6800
16          avg_return_pct     10.1600
17          avg_trade_bars      1.0000
18              avg_profit   3046.6800
19          avg_profit_pct     10.1600
20  avg_winning_trade_bars      1.0000
21                avg_loss      0.0000
22            avg_loss_pct      0.0000
23   avg_losing_trade_bars      0.0000
24             largest_win   3046.6800
25         largest_win_pct     10.1600
```

```
26       largest_win_bars       1.0000
27           largest_loss       0.0000
28       largest_loss_pct       0.0000
29      largest_loss_bars       0.0000
30               max_wins       1.0000
31             max_losses       0.0000
32                 sharpe       0.5908
33                sortino       0.0000
34          profit_factor       6.9974
35            ulcer_index       0.0000
36                    upi       0.0000
37              equity_r2       0.5060
38              std_error    1249.6895
```

Notice the stratergy only has some estimate on the percent to stop loss or win, which has no information about what price do trade, do how much, so it is the next step we have to complete.

For M5,

```
import pybroker as pb
from pybroker import Strategy, ExecContext
from pybroker.ext.data import AKShare

pb.param(name='stock_code', value='07588')

akshare = AKShare()

df  =  akshare.query(symbols=[pb.param(name='stock_code')],  start_date='20241006',
end_date='20241010')

print(df.to_markdown())
import numpy as np
from numba import njit

def cmma(bar_data, lookback):

    @njit  # Enable Numba JIT.
    def vec_cmma(values):
        # Initialize the result array.
        n = len(values)
        out = np.array([np.nan for _ in range(n)])

        # For all bars starting at lookback:
        for i in range(lookback, n):
            # Calculate the moving average for the lookback.
            ma = 0
            for j in range(i - lookback, i):
                ma += values[j]
            ma /= lookback
            # Subtract the moving average from value.
            out[i] = values[i] - ma
```

```
        return out

    # Calculate with close prices.
    return vec_cmma(bar_data.close)

cmma_5 = pb.indicator('cmma_5', cmma, lookback=5)

print(cmma_5.iqr(df), cmma_5.relative_entropy(df)) # 0 0.0
```

It is because days too few, give it 3 months,

```
df   =   akshare.query(symbols=[pb.param(name='stock_code')],   start_date='20240706',
end_date='20241010')

# output
0.2816000000000001 0.890411471649109
```

	date	symbol	open	high	low	close	volume
0	2024-07-08 00:00:00	07588	4.32	4.4	4.284	4.38	763800
1	2024-07-09 00:00:00	07588	4.42	4.45	4.32	4.4	550400
2	2024-07-10 00:00:00	07588	4.336	4.43	4.25	4.43	488700
3	2024-07-11 00:00:00	07588	4.316	4.334	4.23	4.232	538200
4	2024-07-12 00:00:00	07588	4.2	4.2	4.02	4.046	1259200
5	2024-07-15 00:00:00	07588	4.08	4.2	4.07	4.176	1367400
6	2024-07-16 00:00:00	07588	4.232	4.306	4.224	4.306	1286200
7	2024-07-17 00:00:00	07588	4.284	4.358	4.284	4.32	132300
8	2024-07-18 00:00:00	07588	4.344	4.41	4.276	4.31	353800
9	2024-07-19 00:00:00	07588	4.4	4.544	4.352	4.52	1421400
10	2024-07-22 00:00:00	07588	4.476	4.566	4.36	4.376	580500
11	2024-07-23 00:00:00	07588	4.37	4.486	4.37	4.458	718700
12	2024-07-24 00:00:00	07588	4.482	4.57	4.454	4.548	1101000
13	2024-07-25 00:00:00	07588	4.6	4.748	4.588	4.714	890400
14	2024-07-26 00:00:00	07588	4.672	4.768	4.6	4.736	446200
15	2024-07-29 00:00:00	07588	4.646	4.676	4.56	4.628	139200
16	2024-07-30 00:00:00	07588	4.708	4.8	4.692	4.792	237800
17	2024-07-31 00:00:00	07588	4.692	4.692	4.544	4.558	336200
18	2024-08-01 00:00:00	07588	4.598	4.65	4.574	4.614	843200
19	2024-08-02 00:00:00	07588	4.75	4.842	4.742	4.8	966300
20	2024-08-05 00:00:00	07588	4.9	5.11	4.794	4.958	1292300
21	2024-08-06 00:00:00	07588	4.828	5	4.828	4.982	471500
22	2024-08-07 00:00:00	07588	4.858	4.904	4.772	4.878	482100

	date	symbol	open	high	low	close	volume
23	2024-08-08 00:00:00	07588	4.946	4.968	4.756	4.852	475100
24	2024-08-09 00:00:00	07588	4.7	4.72	4.62	4.708	768600
25	2024-08-12 00:00:00	07588	4.714	4.768	4.69	4.706	769200
26	2024-08-13 00:00:00	07588	4.692	4.726	4.63	4.678	65000
27	2024-08-14 00:00:00	07588	4.616	4.75	4.616	4.712	378400
28	2024-08-15 00:00:00	07588	4.8	4.804	4.594	4.7	390600
29	2024-08-16 00:00:00	07588	4.598	4.6	4.466	4.498	742200
30	2024-08-19 00:00:00	07588	4.4	4.41	4.336	4.36	585300
31	2024-08-20 00:00:00	07588	4.376	4.48	4.376	4.456	981600
32	2024-08-21 00:00:00	07588	4.5	4.618	4.5	4.528	1037400
33	2024-08-22 00:00:00	07588	4.47	4.542	4.392	4.404	1278200
34	2024-08-23 00:00:00	07588	4.48	4.486	4.4	4.41	396800
35	2024-08-26 00:00:00	07588	4.336	4.368	4.3	4.328	731200
36	2024-08-27 00:00:00	07588	4.38	4.4	4.282	4.284	1167100
37	2024-08-28 00:00:00	07588	4.31	4.42	4.31	4.398	3166600
38	2024-08-29 00:00:00	07588	4.448	4.51	4.358	4.364	1162500
39	2024-08-30 00:00:00	07588	4.34	4.34	4.138	4.238	1431800
40	2024-09-02 00:00:00	07588	4.33	4.42	4.33	4.334	1847200
41	2024-09-03 00:00:00	07588	4.384	4.45	4.376	4.414	1432100
42	2024-09-04 00:00:00	07588	4.414	4.564	4.414	4.49	1708200
43	2024-09-05 00:00:00	07588	4.49	4.594	4.49	4.546	1555800
44	2024-09-09 00:00:00	07588	4.62	4.756	4.608	4.702	2024100
45	2024-09-10 00:00:00	07588	4.668	4.71	4.62	4.65	433200
46	2024-09-11 00:00:00	07588	4.75	4.8	4.714	4.716	997400
47	2024-09-12 00:00:00	07588	4.668	4.71	4.58	4.644	324300
48	2024-09-13 00:00:00	07588	4.58	4.58	4.478	4.564	1149000
49	2024-09-16 00:00:00	07588	4.66	4.668	4.536	4.536	333600
50	2024-09-17 00:00:00	07588	4.53	4.53	4.378	4.404	548300
51	2024-09-19 00:00:00	07588	4.416	4.454	4.19	4.218	2337600
52	2024-09-20 00:00:00	07588	4.22	4.22	4.056	4.13	968800
53	2024-09-23 00:00:00	07588	4.116	4.126	4.026	4.118	799000
54	2024-09-24 00:00:00	07588	4.036	4.036	3.674	3.684	4896200
55	2024-09-25 00:00:00	07588	3.6	3.642	3.42	3.638	3342400
56	2024-09-26 00:00:00	07588	3.56	3.6	3.26	3.28	3380950
57	2024-09-27 00:00:00	07588	3.24	3.24	3.032	3.094	4938200

	date	symbol	open	high	low	close	volume
58	2024-09-30 00:00:00	07588	3	3.03	2.8	2.914	3376100
59	2024-10-02 00:00:00	07588	2.89	2.89	2.424	2.498	8300000
60	2024-10-03 00:00:00	07588	2.498	2.756	2.498	2.582	5837500
61	2024-10-04 00:00:00	07588	2.624	2.662	2.43	2.43	3054600
62	2024-10-07 00:00:00	07588	2.388	2.422	2.3	2.324	3498500
63	2024-10-08 00:00:00	07588	2.28	2.834	2.28	2.81	8575300
64	2024-10-09 00:00:00	07588	2.81	3.008	2.642	2.884	21600900
65	2024-10-10 00:00:00	07588	2.862	2.862	2.558	2.672	11287600

If you want US stock, you can change the line hk to us again from `C:\Users\Lenovo\AppData\Local\Packages\PythonSoftwareFoundation.Python.3.12_qbz5n2kfra8p0\LocalCache\local-packages\Python312\site-packages\pybroker\ext\data.py`

```
import pybroker as pb
from pybroker import Strategy, ExecContext
from pybroker.ext.data import AKShare

pb.param(name='stock_code', value='AAPL')

akshare = AKShare()

df = akshare.query(symbols=[pb.param(name='stock_code')], start_date='20240706',
end_date='20241010')

print(df.to_markdown())

# output
Traceback (most recent call last):
  File "C:\Users\Lenovo\Flask\stock\quotefutu.py", line 9, in <module>
    df = akshare.query(symbols=[pb.param(name='stock_code')], start_date='20240706',
end_date='20241010')

^^^^^^^^^^^^^^^^^^^^^^^^^^^^^^^^^^^^^^^^^^^^^^^^^^^^^^^^^^^^^^^^^^^^^^^^^^^^^^^^^^^^
^^^^^^^^^^^^
                                                                                File
"C:\Users\Lenovo\AppData\Local\Packages\PythonSoftwareFoundation.Python.3.12_qbz5n2k
fra8p0\LocalCache\local-packages\Python312\site-packages\pybroker\data.py",      line
231, in query
    df = self._fetch_data(
         ^^^^^^^^^^^^^^^^^
                                                                                File
"C:\Users\Lenovo\AppData\Local\Packages\PythonSoftwareFoundation.Python.3.12_qbz5n2k
fra8p0\LocalCache\local-packages\Python312\site-packages\pybroker\ext\data.py",  line
47, in _fetch_data
    temp_df = akshare.stock_us_hist(#zh_a_hist(
```

```
                ^^^^^^^^^^^^^^^^^^^^^^^^^^^^^^^^^^
                                                                                 File
"C:\Users\Lenovo\AppData\Local\Packages\PythonSoftwareFoundation.Python.3.12_qbz5n2k
fra8p0\LocalCache\local-packages\Python312\site-
packages\akshare\stock_feature\stock_hist_em.py", line 1797, in stock_us_hist
    if not data_json["data"]["klines"]:
           ~~~~~~~~~~~~~~~~~^^^^^^^^^^
TypeError: 'NoneType' object is not subscriptable
```

So the problem is realy "AAPL" not found, and go to the `data.py`, we find the symbol it uses is a list, which we have to assign value before use...

```
symbols_simple = [item.split(".")[0] for item in symbols_list]
        result = pd.DataFrame(); symbols_simple = ["105.AAPL"]
        formatted_tf = self._format_timeframe(timeframe)
        if formatted_tf in AKShare._tf_to_period:
            period = AKShare._tf_to_period[formatted_tf]
            for i in range(len(symbols_list)):
                temp_df = akshare.stock_us_hist(#zh_a_hist(
```

Finally, we get the data for AAPL, and this is the reality, just do not believe any data is correct, because all the work is man made...

	date	symbol	open	high	low	close	volume
0	2024-07-08 00:00:00	105.AAPL	227.09	227.85	223.25	227.82	59085861
1	2024-07-09 00:00:00	105.AAPL	227.93	229.4	226.372	228.68	48169822
2	2024-07-10 00:00:00	105.AAPL	229.3	233.08	229.25	232.98	62627687
3	2024-07-11 00:00:00	105.AAPL	231.39	232.39	225.77	227.57	64710617
4	2024-07-12 00:00:00	105.AAPL	228.92	232.64	228.68	230.54	53046527
5	2024-07-15 00:00:00	105.AAPL	236.48	237.23	233.09	234.4	62631252
6	2024-07-16 00:00:00	105.AAPL	235	236.27	232.33	234.82	43234278
7	2024-07-17 00:00:00	105.AAPL	229.45	231.46	226.64	228.88	57345884
8	2024-07-18 00:00:00	105.AAPL	230.28	230.44	222.27	224.18	66034585
9	2024-07-19 00:00:00	105.AAPL	224.82	226.8	223.275	224.31	49151453
10	2024-07-22 00:00:00	105.AAPL	227.01	227.78	223.09	223.96	48201835
11	2024-07-23 00:00:00	105.AAPL	224.365	226.94	222.68	225.01	39960260
12	2024-07-24 00:00:00	105.AAPL	224	224.8	217.13	218.54	61777576
13	2024-07-25 00:00:00	105.AAPL	218.93	220.85	214.62	217.49	51391199
14	2024-07-26 00:00:00	105.AAPL	218.7	219.49	216.01	217.96	41601345
15	2024-07-29 00:00:00	105.AAPL	216.96	219.3	215.75	218.24	36311778
16	2024-07-30 00:00:00	105.AAPL	219.19	220.325	216.12	218.8	41643840
17	2024-07-31 00:00:00	105.AAPL	221.44	223.82	220.63	222.08	50036262

	date	symbol	open	high	low	close	volume
18	2024-08-01 00:00:00	105.AAPL	224.37	224.48	217.02	218.36	62500996
19	2024-08-02 00:00:00	105.AAPL	219.15	225.6	217.71	219.86	105568560
20	2024-08-05 00:00:00	105.AAPL	199.09	213.5	196	209.27	119548589
21	2024-08-06 00:00:00	105.AAPL	205.3	209.99	201.07	207.23	69660488
22	2024-08-07 00:00:00	105.AAPL	206.9	213.64	206.39	209.82	63516417
23	2024-08-08 00:00:00	105.AAPL	213.11	214.2	208.83	213.31	47161149
24	2024-08-09 00:00:00	105.AAPL	212.1	216.78	211.97	216.24	42201646
25	2024-08-12 00:00:00	105.AAPL	216.07	219.51	215.6	217.53	38028092
26	2024-08-13 00:00:00	105.AAPL	219.01	221.89	219.01	221.27	44155331
27	2024-08-14 00:00:00	105.AAPL	220.57	223.03	219.7	221.72	41960574
28	2024-08-15 00:00:00	105.AAPL	224.6	225.35	222.76	224.72	46414013
29	2024-08-16 00:00:00	105.AAPL	223.92	226.827	223.65	226.05	44340240
30	2024-08-19 00:00:00	105.AAPL	225.72	225.99	223.04	225.89	40687813
31	2024-08-20 00:00:00	105.AAPL	225.77	227.17	225.45	226.51	30299033
32	2024-08-21 00:00:00	105.AAPL	226.52	227.98	225.05	226.4	34765480
33	2024-08-22 00:00:00	105.AAPL	227.79	228.34	223.9	224.53	43695321
34	2024-08-23 00:00:00	105.AAPL	225.659	228.22	224.33	226.84	38677250
35	2024-08-26 00:00:00	105.AAPL	226.76	227.28	223.891	227.18	30602208
36	2024-08-27 00:00:00	105.AAPL	225.995	228.85	224.89	228.03	35934559
37	2024-08-28 00:00:00	105.AAPL	227.92	229.86	225.68	226.49	38052167
38	2024-08-29 00:00:00	105.AAPL	230.1	232.92	228.88	229.79	51906297
39	2024-08-30 00:00:00	105.AAPL	230.19	230.4	227.48	229	52990770
40	2024-09-03 00:00:00	105.AAPL	228.55	229	221.17	222.77	50190574
41	2024-09-04 00:00:00	105.AAPL	221.66	221.78	217.48	220.85	43840196
42	2024-09-05 00:00:00	105.AAPL	221.625	225.48	221.52	222.38	36615398
43	2024-09-06 00:00:00	105.AAPL	223.95	225.24	219.77	220.82	48423011
44	2024-09-09 00:00:00	105.AAPL	220.82	221.27	216.71	220.91	67179965
45	2024-09-10 00:00:00	105.AAPL	218.92	221.48	216.73	220.11	51591033
46	2024-09-11 00:00:00	105.AAPL	221.455	223.09	217.89	222.66	44587072
47	2024-09-12 00:00:00	105.AAPL	222.5	223.55	219.82	222.77	37498225
48	2024-09-13 00:00:00	105.AAPL	223.58	224.04	221.91	222.5	36766619
49	2024-09-16 00:00:00	105.AAPL	216.54	217.22	213.92	216.32	59357427
50	2024-09-17 00:00:00	105.AAPL	215.75	216.9	214.5	216.79	45519339
51	2024-09-18 00:00:00	105.AAPL	217.55	222.71	217.54	220.69	59894928
52	2024-09-19 00:00:00	105.AAPL	224.99	229.82	224.63	228.87	66781315

	date	symbol	open	high	low	close	volume
53	2024-09-20 00:00:00	105.AAPL	229.97	233.09	227.62	228.2	318679888
54	2024-09-23 00:00:00	105.AAPL	227.34	229.45	225.81	226.47	54146023
55	2024-09-24 00:00:00	105.AAPL	228.645	229.35	225.73	227.37	43556068
56	2024-09-25 00:00:00	105.AAPL	224.93	227.29	224.02	226.37	42308715
57	2024-09-26 00:00:00	105.AAPL	227.3	228.5	225.41	227.52	36636707
58	2024-09-27 00:00:00	105.AAPL	228.46	229.52	227.3	227.79	34025967
59	2024-09-30 00:00:00	105.AAPL	230.04	233	229.65	233	54793391
60	2024-10-01 00:00:00	105.AAPL	229.52	229.65	223.74	226.21	63285048
61	2024-10-02 00:00:00	105.AAPL	225.89	227.37	223.02	226.78	32880605
62	2024-10-03 00:00:00	105.AAPL	225.14	226.805	223.32	225.67	34044158
63	2024-10-04 00:00:00	105.AAPL	227.9	228	224.13	226.8	37345098
64	2024-10-07 00:00:00	105.AAPL	224.5	225.69	221.33	221.69	39505354
65	2024-10-08 00:00:00	105.AAPL	224.3	225.98	223.25	225.77	31855693
66	2024-10-09 00:00:00	105.AAPL	225.23	229.75	224.83	229.54	33591091
67	2024-10-10 00:00:00	105.AAPL	227.78	229.5	227.17	229.04	28183544

Big risk? How to judge the price?

```
import pybroker as pb
from pybroker import Strategy, ExecContext
from pybroker.ext.data import AKShare

pb.param(name='stock_code', value='105.AAPL')

akshare = AKShare()

df = akshare.query(symbols=[pb.param(name='stock_code')], start_date='20240706', end_date='20241010')

import numpy as np
from numba import njit

def cmma(bar_data, lookback):

    @njit  # Enable Numba JIT.
    def vec_cmma(values):
        # Initialize the result array.
        n = len(values)
        out = np.array([np.nan for _ in range(n)])

        # For all bars starting at lookback:
        for i in range(lookback, n):
            # Calculate the moving average for the lookback.
            ma = 0
```

```
            for j in range(i - lookback, i):
                ma += values[j]
            ma /= lookback
            # Subtract the moving average from value.
            out[i] = values[i] - ma
        return out

    # Calculate with close prices.
    return vec_cmma(bar_data.close)

cmma_5 = pb.indicator('cmma_5', cmma, lookback=5)

print(cmma_5(df).to_markdown())
```

date	cmma_5
2024-07-08 00:00:00	nan
2024-07-09 00:00:00	nan
2024-07-10 00:00:00	nan
2024-07-11 00:00:00	nan
2024-07-12 00:00:00	nan
2024-07-15 00:00:00	4.882
2024-07-16 00:00:00	3.986
2024-07-17 00:00:00	-3.182
2024-07-18 00:00:00	-7.062
2024-07-19 00:00:00	-6.254
2024-07-22 00:00:00	-5.358
2024-07-23 00:00:00	-2.22
2024-07-24 00:00:00	-6.728
2024-07-25 00:00:00	-5.71
2024-07-26 00:00:00	-3.902
2024-07-29 00:00:00	-2.352
2024-07-30 00:00:00	-0.648
2024-07-31 00:00:00	3.874
2024-08-01 00:00:00	-0.554
2024-08-02 00:00:00	0.772
2024-08-05 00:00:00	-10.198
2024-08-06 00:00:00	-10.444
2024-08-07 00:00:00	-5.54
2024-08-08 00:00:00	0.402
2024-08-09 00:00:00	4.342

date	cmma_5
2024-08-12 00:00:00	6.356
2024-08-13 00:00:00	8.444
2024-08-14 00:00:00	6.086
2024-08-15 00:00:00	6.706
2024-08-16 00:00:00	5.754
2024-08-19 00:00:00	3.632
2024-08-20 00:00:00	2.58
2024-08-21 00:00:00	1.422
2024-08-22 00:00:00	-1.384
2024-08-23 00:00:00	0.964
2024-08-26 00:00:00	1.146
2024-08-27 00:00:00	1.738
2024-08-28 00:00:00	-0.106
2024-08-29 00:00:00	3.176
2024-08-30 00:00:00	1.334
2024-09-03 00:00:00	-5.328
2024-09-04 00:00:00	-6.366
2024-09-05 00:00:00	-3.4
2024-09-06 00:00:00	-4.138
2024-09-09 00:00:00	-2.254
2024-09-10 00:00:00	-1.436
2024-09-11 00:00:00	1.646
2024-09-12 00:00:00	1.394
2024-09-13 00:00:00	1.046
2024-09-16 00:00:00	-5.47
2024-09-17 00:00:00	-4.082
2024-09-18 00:00:00	0.482
2024-09-19 00:00:00	9.056
2024-09-20 00:00:00	7.166
2024-09-23 00:00:00	4.296
2024-09-24 00:00:00	3.166
2024-09-25 00:00:00	0.05
2024-09-26 00:00:00	0.064
2024-09-27 00:00:00	0.604
2024-09-30 00:00:00	5.896

date	cmma_5
2024-10-01 00:00:00	-2.2
2024-10-02 00:00:00	-1.398
2024-10-03 00:00:00	-2.59
2024-10-04 00:00:00	-1.09
2024-10-07 00:00:00	-6.002
2024-10-08 00:00:00	0.34
2024-10-09 00:00:00	4.198
2024-10-10 00:00:00	3.146

With the MA20, we can just set up a buy stratergy, and to see the long time goal, if in three years,

```
import pybroker as pb
from pybroker import Strategy, ExecContext
from pybroker.ext.data import AKShare

pb.param(name='stock_code', value='105.AAPL')

akshare = AKShare()

df = akshare.query(symbols=[pb.param(name='stock_code')], start_date='20201006', end_date='20241010')

print(df.to_markdown())
import numpy as np
from numba import njit

def cmma(bar_data, lookback):

    @njit  # Enable Numba JIT.
    def vec_cmma(values):
        # Initialize the result array.
        n = len(values)
        out = np.array([np.nan for _ in range(n)])

        # For all bars starting at lookback:
        for i in range(lookback, n):
            # Calculate the moving average for the lookback.
            ma = 0
            for j in range(i - lookback, i):
                ma += values[j]
            ma /= lookback
            # Subtract the moving average from value.
            out[i] = values[i] - ma
        return out

    # Calculate with close prices.
```

```
    return vec_cmma(bar_data.close)

cmma_20 = pb.indicator('cmma_20', cmma, lookback=20)

print(cmma_20(df).to_markdown())

def buy_cmma(ctx):
    if ctx.long_pos():
        return
    # Place a buy order if the most recent value of the 20 day CMMA is < 0:
    if ctx.indicator('cmma_20')[-1] < 0:
        ctx.buy_shares = ctx.calc_target_shares(1)
        ctx.hold_bars = 3

strategy = Strategy(akshare, start_date='20201006', end_date='20241010')

strategy.add_execution(buy_cmma, 'AAPL', indicators=cmma_20)

result = strategy.backtest(warmup=20)

print(result.metrics_df.round(4))

# output
|                     |          0 |
|:--------------------|----------:|
| 2020-10-06 00:00:00 | nan        |
| 2020-10-07 00:00:00 | nan        |
| 2020-10-08 00:00:00 | nan        |
| 2020-10-09 00:00:00 | nan        |
| 2020-10-12 00:00:00 | nan        |
| 2020-10-13 00:00:00 | nan        |
| 2020-10-14 00:00:00 | nan        |
| 2020-10-15 00:00:00 | nan        |
| 2020-10-16 00:00:00 | nan        |
| 2020-10-19 00:00:00 | nan        |
| 2020-10-20 00:00:00 | nan        |
| 2020-10-21 00:00:00 | nan        |
| 2020-10-22 00:00:00 | nan        |
| 2020-10-23 00:00:00 | nan        |
| 2020-10-26 00:00:00 | nan        |
| 2020-10-27 00:00:00 | nan        |
| 2020-10-28 00:00:00 | nan        |
| 2020-10-29 00:00:00 | nan        |
| 2020-10-30 00:00:00 | nan        |
| 2020-11-02 00:00:00 | nan        |
| 2020-11-03 00:00:00 |   -5.7375  |
| 2020-11-04 00:00:00 |   -1.0915  |
| 2020-11-05 00:00:00 |    2.995   |
| 2020-11-06 00:00:00 |    2.452   |
| 2020-11-09 00:00:00 |   -0.004   |
| 2020-11-10 00:00:00 |    0.05    |
| 2020-11-11 00:00:00 |    3.8265  |
| 2020-11-12 00:00:00 |    3.6315  |
```

2020-11-13 00:00:00	3.7565
2020-11-16 00:00:00	4.7845
2020-11-17 00:00:00	3.6585
2020-11-18 00:00:00	2.2045
2020-11-19 00:00:00	2.7565
2020-11-20 00:00:00	1.312
2020-11-23 00:00:00	-2.293
2020-11-24 00:00:00	-0.913
2020-11-25 00:00:00	0.0185
2020-11-27 00:00:00	0.337
2020-11-30 00:00:00	2.7335
2020-12-01 00:00:00	5.894
2020-12-02 00:00:00	5.5565
2020-12-03 00:00:00	4.7845
2020-12-04 00:00:00	3.695
2020-12-07 00:00:00	5.034
2020-12-08 00:00:00	5.411
2020-12-09 00:00:00	2.408
2020-12-10 00:00:00	3.5775
2020-12-11 00:00:00	2.56
2020-12-14 00:00:00	1.77
2020-12-15 00:00:00	7.744
2020-12-16 00:00:00	7.295
2020-12-17 00:00:00	7.764
2020-12-18 00:00:00	5.1905
2020-12-21 00:00:00	6.3595
2020-12-22 00:00:00	9.465
2020-12-23 00:00:00	7.6435
2020-12-24 00:00:00	7.864
2020-12-28 00:00:00	11.787
2020-12-29 00:00:00	8.962
2020-12-30 00:00:00	7.021
2020-12-31 00:00:00	5.441
2021-01-04 00:00:00	1.6805
2021-01-05 00:00:00	2.957
2021-01-06 00:00:00	-1.891
2021-01-07 00:00:00	2.2865
2021-01-08 00:00:00	3.0895
2021-01-11 00:00:00	-0.494
2021-01-12 00:00:00	-0.961
2021-01-13 00:00:00	0.8095
2021-01-14 00:00:00	-1.626
2021-01-15 00:00:00	-3.4475
2021-01-19 00:00:00	-2.724
2021-01-20 00:00:00	1.5195
2021-01-21 00:00:00	6.091
2021-01-22 00:00:00	7.859
2021-01-25 00:00:00	11.3495
2021-01-26 00:00:00	10.9915
2021-01-27 00:00:00	9.332
2021-01-28 00:00:00	4.0935
2021-01-29 00:00:00	-1.1475
2021-02-01 00:00:00	1.1205

2021-02-02 00:00:00	1.898
2021-02-03 00:00:00	0.569
2021-02-04 00:00:00	3.8725
2021-02-05 00:00:00	2.703
2021-02-08 00:00:00	2.561
2021-02-09 00:00:00	1.418
2021-02-10 00:00:00	0.4465
2021-02-11 00:00:00	-0.143
2021-02-12 00:00:00	-0.115
2021-02-16 00:00:00	-2.618
2021-02-17 00:00:00	-5.2705
2021-02-18 00:00:00	-6.551
2021-02-19 00:00:00	-6.275
2021-02-22 00:00:00	-9.795
2021-02-23 00:00:00	-9.2815
2021-02-24 00:00:00	-8.9385
2021-02-25 00:00:00	-12.408
2021-02-26 00:00:00	-11.0845
2021-03-01 00:00:00	-3.763
2021-03-02 00:00:00	-6.2245
2021-03-03 00:00:00	-8.8335
2021-03-04 00:00:00	-10.117
2021-03-05 00:00:00	-8.1365
2021-03-08 00:00:00	-12.398
2021-03-09 00:00:00	-6.653
2021-03-10 00:00:00	-6.96675
2021-03-11 00:00:00	-4.18525
2021-03-12 00:00:00	-4.44375
2021-03-15 00:00:00	-0.77875
2021-03-16 00:00:00	1.37025
2021-03-17 00:00:00	0.94125
2021-03-18 00:00:00	-2.98475
2021-03-19 00:00:00	-3.06575
2021-03-22 00:00:00	0.82825
2021-03-23 00:00:00	0.10875
2021-03-24 00:00:00	-2.17525
2021-03-25 00:00:00	-1.41225
2021-03-26 00:00:00	-0.77225
2021-03-29 00:00:00	-0.58975
2021-03-30 00:00:00	-1.75975
2021-03-31 00:00:00	0.75125
2021-04-01 00:00:00	1.59675
2021-04-05 00:00:00	4.35325
2021-04-06 00:00:00	4.43925
2021-04-07 00:00:00	5.63675
2021-04-08 00:00:00	7.756
2021-04-09 00:00:00	9.872
2021-04-12 00:00:00	7.56525
2021-04-13 00:00:00	10.2447
2021-04-14 00:00:00	7.32275
2021-04-15 00:00:00	9.46975
2021-04-16 00:00:00	8.64275
2021-04-19 00:00:00	8.64125

2021-04-20 00:00:00	6.16875
2021-04-21 00:00:00	6.07275
2021-04-22 00:00:00	3.96475
2021-04-23 00:00:00	5.75225
2021-04-26 00:00:00	5.46575
2021-04-27 00:00:00	4.46025
2021-04-28 00:00:00	3.00025
2021-04-29 00:00:00	2.21625
2021-04-30 00:00:00	-0.37025
2021-05-03 00:00:00	0.28675
2021-05-04 00:00:00	-4.73525
2021-05-05 00:00:00	-4.56725
2021-05-06 00:00:00	-2.93725
2021-05-07 00:00:00	-2.43625
2021-05-10 00:00:00	-5.657
2021-05-11 00:00:00	-6.3775
2021-05-12 00:00:00	-9.0915
2021-05-13 00:00:00	-6.4285
2021-05-14 00:00:00	-3.472
2021-05-17 00:00:00	-4.3165
2021-05-18 00:00:00	-5.308
2021-05-19 00:00:00	-5.055
2021-05-20 00:00:00	-1.9945
2021-05-21 00:00:00	-3.643
2021-05-24 00:00:00	-1.5285
2021-05-25 00:00:00	-1.3475
2021-05-26 00:00:00	-1.023
2021-05-27 00:00:00	-2.2565
2021-05-28 00:00:00	-2.5165
2021-06-01 00:00:00	-2.504
2021-06-02 00:00:00	-1.311
2021-06-03 00:00:00	-2.6915
2021-06-04 00:00:00	-0.1135
2021-06-07 00:00:00	0.089
2021-06-08 00:00:00	1.1445
2021-06-09 00:00:00	1.54
2021-06-10 00:00:00	0.459
2021-06-11 00:00:00	1.532
2021-06-14 00:00:00	4.543
2021-06-15 00:00:00	3.5515
2021-06-16 00:00:00	3.893
2021-06-17 00:00:00	5.268
2021-06-18 00:00:00	3.583
2021-06-21 00:00:00	5.2655
2021-06-22 00:00:00	6.602
2021-06-23 00:00:00	5.978
2021-06-24 00:00:00	5.348
2021-06-25 00:00:00	4.72
2021-06-28 00:00:00	5.9985
2021-06-29 00:00:00	7.04
2021-06-30 00:00:00	7.0675
2021-07-01 00:00:00	6.7825
2021-07-02 00:00:00	8.786

2021-07-06 00:00:00	10.1425
2021-07-07 00:00:00	11.8865
2021-07-08 00:00:00	9.665
2021-07-09 00:00:00	10.7295
2021-07-12 00:00:00	9.1695
2021-07-13 00:00:00	9.452
2021-07-14 00:00:00	12.204
2021-07-15 00:00:00	10.5585
2021-07-16 00:00:00	7.552
2021-07-19 00:00:00	2.882
2021-07-20 00:00:00	5.9825
2021-07-21 00:00:00	4.54
2021-07-22 00:00:00	5.369
2021-07-23 00:00:00	6.474
2021-07-26 00:00:00	6.1465
2021-07-27 00:00:00	3.1325
2021-07-28 00:00:00	0.743
2021-07-29 00:00:00	0.9705
2021-07-30 00:00:00	0.7565
2021-08-02 00:00:00	-0.013
2021-08-03 00:00:00	1.549
2021-08-04 00:00:00	0.872
2021-08-05 00:00:00	0.863
2021-08-06 00:00:00	-0.248
2021-08-09 00:00:00	-0.3495
2021-08-10 00:00:00	-0.919
2021-08-11 00:00:00	-0.657
2021-08-12 00:00:00	2.5375
2021-08-13 00:00:00	2.727
2021-08-16 00:00:00	4.6115
2021-08-17 00:00:00	3.248
2021-08-18 00:00:00	-0.784
2021-08-19 00:00:00	-0.492
2021-08-20 00:00:00	1.003
2021-08-23 00:00:00	2.5415
2021-08-24 00:00:00	2.4155
2021-08-25 00:00:00	1.013
2021-08-26 00:00:00	0.024
2021-08-27 00:00:00	0.989
2021-08-30 00:00:00	5.372
2021-08-31 00:00:00	3.702
2021-09-01 00:00:00	4.1585
2021-09-02 00:00:00	5.0205
2021-09-03 00:00:00	5.341
2021-09-07 00:00:00	7.323
2021-09-08 00:00:00	5.213
2021-09-09 00:00:00	3.6975
2021-09-10 00:00:00	-1.813
2021-09-13 00:00:00	-1.237
2021-09-14 00:00:00	-2.6895
2021-09-15 00:00:00	-1.6295
2021-09-16 00:00:00	-1.8115
2021-09-17 00:00:00	-4.663

2021-09-20 00:00:00	-7.751
2021-09-21 00:00:00	-6.9985
2021-09-22 00:00:00	-4.2645
2021-09-23 00:00:00	-3.096
2021-09-24 00:00:00	-2.9295
2021-09-27 00:00:00	-4.4485
2021-09-28 00:00:00	-7.747
2021-09-29 00:00:00	-6.2665
2021-09-30 00:00:00	-7.1465
2021-10-01 00:00:00	-5.446
2021-10-04 00:00:00	-8.406
2021-10-05 00:00:00	-5.678
2021-10-06 00:00:00	-4.009
2021-10-07 00:00:00	-2.0635
2021-10-08 00:00:00	-1.9145
2021-10-11 00:00:00	-1.701
2021-10-12 00:00:00	-2.664
2021-10-13 00:00:00	-2.9335
2021-10-14 00:00:00	0.3225
2021-10-15 00:00:00	1.654
2021-10-18 00:00:00	3.425
2021-10-19 00:00:00	5.4545
2021-10-20 00:00:00	5.688
2021-10-21 00:00:00	5.7375
2021-10-22 00:00:00	4.815
2021-10-25 00:00:00	4.6765
2021-10-26 00:00:00	5.193
2021-10-27 00:00:00	4.3525
2021-10-28 00:00:00	7.7715
2021-10-29 00:00:00	4.448
2021-11-01 00:00:00	3.2505
2021-11-02 00:00:00	3.8195
2021-11-03 00:00:00	4.844
2021-11-04 00:00:00	3.8395
2021-11-05 00:00:00	3.776
2021-11-08 00:00:00	2.517
2021-11-09 00:00:00	2.5055
2021-11-10 00:00:00	-0.8495
2021-11-11 00:00:00	-1.25
2021-11-12 00:00:00	0.6645
2021-11-15 00:00:00	0.417
2021-11-16 00:00:00	1.2445
2021-11-17 00:00:00	3.6225
2021-11-18 00:00:00	7.791
2021-11-19 00:00:00	10.0515
2021-11-22 00:00:00	9.9285
2021-11-23 00:00:00	9.6995
2021-11-24 00:00:00	9.625
2021-11-26 00:00:00	3.8405
2021-11-29 00:00:00	7.0585
2021-11-30 00:00:00	11.5965
2021-12-01 00:00:00	10.2495
2021-12-02 00:00:00	8.502

2021-12-03 00:00:00	5.9685
2021-12-06 00:00:00	8.9045
2021-12-07 00:00:00	14.0625
2021-12-08 00:00:00	16.9255
2021-12-09 00:00:00	15.192
2021-12-10 00:00:00	18.75
2021-12-13 00:00:00	13.461
2021-12-14 00:00:00	10.7635
2021-12-15 00:00:00	14.517
2021-12-16 00:00:00	6.062
2021-12-17 00:00:00	4.0035
2021-12-20 00:00:00	1.95
2021-12-21 00:00:00	4.73
2021-12-22 00:00:00	6.7815
2021-12-23 00:00:00	6.71
2021-12-27 00:00:00	10.043
2021-12-28 00:00:00	7.827
2021-12-29 00:00:00	6.9645
2021-12-30 00:00:00	5.0805
2021-12-31 00:00:00	3.779
2022-01-03 00:00:00	7.5285
2022-01-04 00:00:00	4.21
2022-01-05 00:00:00	-1.289
2022-01-06 00:00:00	-4.396
2022-01-07 00:00:00	-4.072
2022-01-10 00:00:00	-3.9325
2022-01-11 00:00:00	-0.6795
2022-01-12 00:00:00	-0.1965
2022-01-13 00:00:00	-3.5965
2022-01-14 00:00:00	-2.361
2022-01-18 00:00:00	-5.6715
2022-01-19 00:00:00	-9.1745
2022-01-20 00:00:00	-10.7185
2022-01-21 00:00:00	-12.3945
2022-01-24 00:00:00	-12.523
2022-01-25 00:00:00	-13.63
2022-01-26 00:00:00	-12.6925
2022-01-27 00:00:00	-12.1825
2022-01-28 00:00:00	-0.0645
2022-01-31 00:00:00	4.779
2022-02-01 00:00:00	4.7485
2022-02-02 00:00:00	6.3485
2022-02-03 00:00:00	3.6015
2022-02-04 00:00:00	3.1925
2022-02-07 00:00:00	2.443
2022-02-08 00:00:00	5.6385
2022-02-09 00:00:00	6.9565
2022-02-10 00:00:00	2.7365
2022-02-11 00:00:00	-0.573
2022-02-14 00:00:00	-0.1555
2022-02-15 00:00:00	3.964
2022-02-16 00:00:00	3.5745
2022-02-17 00:00:00	-0.4115

2022-02-18 00:00:00	-2.21
2022-02-22 00:00:00	-5.4345
2022-02-23 00:00:00	-9.8195
2022-02-24 00:00:00	-7.164
2022-02-25 00:00:00	-5.2065
2022-02-28 00:00:00	-5.218
2022-03-01 00:00:00	-6.8775
2022-03-02 00:00:00	-2.9385
2022-03-03 00:00:00	-2.866
2022-03-04 00:00:00	-5.4455
2022-03-07 00:00:00	-8.829
2022-03-08 00:00:00	-10.0345
2022-03-09 00:00:00	-3.8135
2022-03-10 00:00:00	-7.6495
2022-03-11 00:00:00	-10.5515
2022-03-14 00:00:00	-13.792
2022-03-15 00:00:00	-8.421
2022-03-16 00:00:00	-3.2315
2022-03-17 00:00:00	-1.5415
2022-03-18 00:00:00	2.415
2022-03-21 00:00:00	4.06
2022-03-22 00:00:00	7.596
2022-03-23 00:00:00	8.761
2022-03-24 00:00:00	12.114
2022-03-25 00:00:00	12.1975
2022-03-28 00:00:00	12.584
2022-03-29 00:00:00	15.42
2022-03-30 00:00:00	13.442
2022-03-31 00:00:00	9.7215
2022-04-01 00:00:00	9.0025
2022-04-04 00:00:00	12.5755
2022-04-05 00:00:00	8.2385
2022-04-06 00:00:00	4.1275
2022-04-07 00:00:00	3.9935
2022-04-08 00:00:00	1.2625
2022-04-11 00:00:00	-3.8455
2022-04-12 00:00:00	-2.692
2022-04-13 00:00:00	-0.5805
2022-04-14 00:00:00	-6.231
2022-04-18 00:00:00	-6.6845
2022-04-19 00:00:00	-4.409
2022-04-20 00:00:00	-4.68
2022-04-21 00:00:00	-5.4105
2022-04-22 00:00:00	-9.851
2022-04-25 00:00:00	-8.147
2022-04-26 00:00:00	-13.635
2022-04-27 00:00:00	-12.925
2022-04-28 00:00:00	-4.7355
2022-04-29 00:00:00	-10.019
2022-05-02 00:00:00	-8.861
2022-05-03 00:00:00	-6.5235
2022-05-04 00:00:00	0.9645
2022-05-05 00:00:00	-7.8335

2022-05-06 00:00:00	-6.5705
2022-05-09 00:00:00	-11.0475
2022-05-10 00:00:00	-7.696
2022-05-11 00:00:00	-15.144
2022-05-12 00:00:00	-18.026
2022-05-13 00:00:00	-12.084
2022-05-16 00:00:00	-12.745
2022-05-17 00:00:00	-8.0685
2022-05-18 00:00:00	-15.5805
2022-05-19 00:00:00	-17.73
2022-05-20 00:00:00	-16.0365
2022-05-23 00:00:00	-9.3065
2022-05-24 00:00:00	-11.068
2022-05-25 00:00:00	-10.086
2022-05-26 00:00:00	-6.0235
2022-05-27 00:00:00	0.8295
2022-05-31 00:00:00	0.43
2022-06-01 00:00:00	0.756
2022-06-02 00:00:00	3.7945
2022-06-03 00:00:00	-1.295
2022-06-06 00:00:00	0.0345
2022-06-07 00:00:00	3.1615
2022-06-08 00:00:00	2.579
2022-06-09 00:00:00	-2.4135
2022-06-10 00:00:00	-7.7305
2022-06-13 00:00:00	-12.709
2022-06-14 00:00:00	-11.0675
2022-06-15 00:00:00	-7.7585
2022-06-16 00:00:00	-12.438
2022-06-17 00:00:00	-10.4
2022-06-21 00:00:00	-5.8005
2022-06-22 00:00:00	-6.2345
2022-06-23 00:00:00	-2.9265
2022-06-24 00:00:00	0.568
2022-06-27 00:00:00	0.511
2022-06-28 00:00:00	-3.603
2022-06-29 00:00:00	-1.203
2022-06-30 00:00:00	-3.2325
2022-07-01 00:00:00	-0.423
2022-07-05 00:00:00	2.821
2022-07-06 00:00:00	4.372
2022-07-07 00:00:00	7.963
2022-07-08 00:00:00	8.771
2022-07-11 00:00:00	6.647
2022-07-12 00:00:00	7.5255
2022-07-13 00:00:00	6.719
2022-07-14 00:00:00	9.0185
2022-07-15 00:00:00	9.933
2022-07-18 00:00:00	6.096
2022-07-19 00:00:00	9.1755
2022-07-20 00:00:00	10.2435
2022-07-21 00:00:00	11.695
2022-07-22 00:00:00	9.435

2022-07-25 00:00:00	7.504
2022-07-26 00:00:00	5.5895
2022-07-27 00:00:00	10.2825
2022-07-28 00:00:00	9.875
2022-07-29 00:00:00	14.129
2022-08-01 00:00:00	11.8395
2022-08-02 00:00:00	9.2105
2022-08-03 00:00:00	14.408
2022-08-04 00:00:00	12.9275
2022-08-05 00:00:00	11.4945
2022-08-08 00:00:00	10.099
2022-08-09 00:00:00	9.149
2022-08-10 00:00:00	12.516
2022-08-11 00:00:00	10.5785
2022-08-12 00:00:00	13.1875
2022-08-15 00:00:00	13.181
2022-08-16 00:00:00	11.715
2022-08-17 00:00:00	12.1335
2022-08-18 00:00:00	10.658
2022-08-19 00:00:00	7.088
2022-08-22 00:00:00	2.2665
2022-08-23 00:00:00	1.1955
2022-08-24 00:00:00	0.714
2022-08-25 00:00:00	2.677
2022-08-26 00:00:00	-4.367
2022-08-29 00:00:00	-6.6625
2022-08-30 00:00:00	-9.126
2022-08-31 00:00:00	-10.761
2022-09-01 00:00:00	-9.5755
2022-09-02 00:00:00	-11.333
2022-09-06 00:00:00	-12.136
2022-09-07 00:00:00	-10.189
2022-09-08 00:00:00	-11.241
2022-09-09 00:00:00	-7.592
2022-09-12 00:00:00	-0.976
2022-09-13 00:00:00	-10.1325
2022-09-14 00:00:00	-7.695
2022-09-15 00:00:00	-9.749
2022-09-16 00:00:00	-10.31
2022-09-19 00:00:00	-5.3575
2022-09-20 00:00:00	-2.0855
2022-09-21 00:00:00	-4.732
2022-09-22 00:00:00	-5.0365
2022-09-23 00:00:00	-6.607
2022-09-26 00:00:00	-5.287
2022-09-27 00:00:00	-3.6545
2022-09-28 00:00:00	-5.0935
2022-09-29 00:00:00	-12
2022-09-30 00:00:00	-15.543
2022-10-03 00:00:00	-10.305
2022-10-04 00:00:00	-5.987
2022-10-05 00:00:00	-5.2655
2022-10-06 00:00:00	-5.7575

2022-10-07 00:00:00	-10.646
2022-10-10 00:00:00	-9.452
2022-10-11 00:00:00	-9.7415
2022-10-12 00:00:00	-9.6385
2022-10-13 00:00:00	-4.14
2022-10-14 00:00:00	-8.281
2022-10-17 00:00:00	-3.635
2022-10-18 00:00:00	-1.6915
2022-10-19 00:00:00	-0.924
2022-10-20 00:00:00	-0.901
2022-10-21 00:00:00	3.4465
2022-10-24 00:00:00	5.7845
2022-10-25 00:00:00	8.7405
2022-10-26 00:00:00	5.7215
2022-10-27 00:00:00	1.196
2022-10-28 00:00:00	12.02
2022-10-31 00:00:00	8.743
2022-11-01 00:00:00	5.5085
2022-11-02 00:00:00	-0.339
2022-11-03 00:00:00	-6.4205
2022-11-04 00:00:00	-6.593
2022-11-07 00:00:00	-5.9675
2022-11-08 00:00:00	-5.3125
2022-11-09 00:00:00	-9.9685
2022-11-10 00:00:00	2.205
2022-11-11 00:00:00	4.841
2022-11-14 00:00:00	2.855
2022-11-15 00:00:00	4.3215
2022-11-16 00:00:00	2.757
2022-11-17 00:00:00	4.4405
2022-11-18 00:00:00	4.644
2022-11-21 00:00:00	1.163
2022-11-22 00:00:00	3.405
2022-11-23 00:00:00	4.403
2022-11-25 00:00:00	1.357
2022-11-28 00:00:00	-2.6985
2022-11-29 00:00:00	-5.1725
2022-11-30 00:00:00	2.296
2022-12-01 00:00:00	2.707
2022-12-02 00:00:00	2.043
2022-12-05 00:00:00	0.4165
2022-12-06 00:00:00	-3.716
2022-12-07 00:00:00	-5.8855
2022-12-08 00:00:00	-4.2475
2022-12-09 00:00:00	-5.1265
2022-12-12 00:00:00	-2.561
2022-12-13 00:00:00	-1.3205
2022-12-14 00:00:00	-3.44
2022-12-15 00:00:00	-9.8085
2022-12-16 00:00:00	-11.184
2022-12-19 00:00:00	-12.5135
2022-12-20 00:00:00	-11.6375
2022-12-21 00:00:00	-7.702

2022-12-22 00:00:00	-10.1855
2022-12-23 00:00:00	-9.6135
2022-12-27 00:00:00	-10.631
2022-12-28 00:00:00	-13.9115
2022-12-29 00:00:00	-9.585
2022-12-30 00:00:00	-8.344
2023-01-03 00:00:00	-12.285
2023-01-04 00:00:00	-9.858
2023-01-05 00:00:00	-10.1845
2023-01-06 00:00:00	-4.69
2023-01-09 00:00:00	-3.594
2023-01-10 00:00:00	-2.389
2023-01-11 00:00:00	0.9425
2023-01-12 00:00:00	1.4125
2023-01-13 00:00:00	3.3655
2023-01-17 00:00:00	4.968
2023-01-18 00:00:00	4.266
2023-01-19 00:00:00	4.291
2023-01-20 00:00:00	6.746
2023-01-23 00:00:00	9.7075
2023-01-24 00:00:00	10.8445
2023-01-25 00:00:00	9.6595
2023-01-26 00:00:00	11.2595
2023-01-27 00:00:00	12.533
2023-01-30 00:00:00	8.6085
2023-01-31 00:00:00	9.229
2023-02-01 00:00:00	9.651
2023-02-02 00:00:00	14.023
2023-02-03 00:00:00	16.48
2023-02-06 00:00:00	12.236
2023-02-07 00:00:00	14.0505
2023-02-08 00:00:00	10.0955
2023-02-09 00:00:00	7.986
2023-02-10 00:00:00	7.257
2023-02-13 00:00:00	9.217
2023-02-14 00:00:00	7.6125
2023-02-15 00:00:00	8.8795
2023-02-16 00:00:00	6.2535
2023-02-17 00:00:00	4.1715
2023-02-21 00:00:00	-0.6325
2023-02-22 00:00:00	-0.571
2023-02-23 00:00:00	-0.4
2023-02-24 00:00:00	-3.467
2023-02-27 00:00:00	-2.3945
2023-02-28 00:00:00	-3.004
2023-03-01 00:00:00	-5.3245
2023-03-02 00:00:00	-4.7755
2023-03-03 00:00:00	0.3205
2023-03-06 00:00:00	3.11
2023-03-07 00:00:00	0.9135
2023-03-08 00:00:00	2.19
2023-03-09 00:00:00	-0.001
2023-03-10 00:00:00	-2.0245

2023-03-13 00:00:00	0.064
2023-03-14 00:00:00	2.211
2023-03-15 00:00:00	2.674
2023-03-16 00:00:00	5.5445
2023-03-17 00:00:00	4.6685
2023-03-20 00:00:00	7.004
2023-03-21 00:00:00	8.6415
2023-03-22 00:00:00	6.6515
2023-03-23 00:00:00	7.3055
2023-03-24 00:00:00	8.149
2023-03-27 00:00:00	5.502
2023-03-28 00:00:00	4.354
2023-03-29 00:00:00	6.962
2023-03-30 00:00:00	7.779
2023-03-31 00:00:00	9.4965
2023-04-03 00:00:00	10.073
2023-04-04 00:00:00	8.916
2023-04-05 00:00:00	6.3445
2023-04-06 00:00:00	6.7
2023-04-10 00:00:00	3.3665
2023-04-11 00:00:00	1.46
2023-04-12 00:00:00	0.2435
2023-04-13 00:00:00	5.328
2023-04-14 00:00:00	4.3495
2023-04-17 00:00:00	3.9015
2023-04-18 00:00:00	4.63
2023-04-19 00:00:00	5.3365
2023-04-20 00:00:00	3.939
2023-04-21 00:00:00	1.868
2023-04-24 00:00:00	1.8735
2023-04-25 00:00:00	0.0595
2023-04-26 00:00:00	-0.225
2023-04-27 00:00:00	4.1195
2023-04-28 00:00:00	5.0075
2023-05-01 00:00:00	4.5515
2023-05-02 00:00:00	3.267
2023-05-03 00:00:00	2.0585
2023-05-04 00:00:00	0.3075
2023-05-05 00:00:00	7.986
2023-05-08 00:00:00	7.4705
2023-05-09 00:00:00	5.167
2023-05-10 00:00:00	6.4035
2023-05-11 00:00:00	5.92575
2023-05-12 00:00:00	4.33625
2023-05-15 00:00:00	3.46825
2023-05-16 00:00:00	3.12625
2023-05-17 00:00:00	3.46625
2023-05-18 00:00:00	5.57325
2023-05-19 00:00:00	5.26325
2023-05-22 00:00:00	3.79625
2023-05-23 00:00:00	0.71275
2023-05-24 00:00:00	0.60325
2023-05-25 00:00:00	1.34925

2023-05-26 00:00:00	3.56025
2023-05-30 00:00:00	5.14275
2023-05-31 00:00:00	4.70725
2023-06-01 00:00:00	7.11175
2023-06-02 00:00:00	7.33975
2023-06-05 00:00:00	5.21175
2023-06-06 00:00:00	4.54125
2023-06-07 00:00:00	2.86575
2023-06-08 00:00:00	5.31325
2023-06-09 00:00:00	5.3525
2023-06-12 00:00:00	7.822
2023-06-13 00:00:00	6.781
2023-06-14 00:00:00	6.859
2023-06-15 00:00:00	8.325
2023-06-16 00:00:00	6.569
2023-06-20 00:00:00	6.1655
2023-06-21 00:00:00	4.623
2023-06-22 00:00:00	7.175
2023-06-23 00:00:00	6.083
2023-06-26 00:00:00	3.931
2023-06-27 00:00:00	6.107
2023-06-28 00:00:00	6.6655
2023-06-29 00:00:00	6.408
2023-06-30 00:00:00	10.171
2023-07-03 00:00:00	7.967
2023-07-05 00:00:00	6.2615
2023-07-06 00:00:00	6.154
2023-07-07 00:00:00	4.394
2023-07-10 00:00:00	1.681
2023-07-11 00:00:00	0.749
2023-07-12 00:00:00	2.083
2023-07-13 00:00:00	2.554
2023-07-14 00:00:00	2.3425
2023-07-17 00:00:00	5.3055
2023-07-18 00:00:00	4.6465
2023-07-19 00:00:00	5.576
2023-07-20 00:00:00	3.1015
2023-07-21 00:00:00	1.453
2023-07-24 00:00:00	2.016
2023-07-25 00:00:00	2.5825
2023-07-26 00:00:00	3.045
2023-07-27 00:00:00	1.443
2023-07-28 00:00:00	3.8545
2023-07-31 00:00:00	4.1625
2023-08-01 00:00:00	3.1935
2023-08-02 00:00:00	0.01125
2023-08-03 00:00:00	-1.46125
2023-08-04 00:00:00	-10.6092
2023-08-07 00:00:00	-13.3147
2023-08-08 00:00:00	-11.8767
2023-08-09 00:00:00	-13.0727
2023-08-10 00:00:00	-12.7138
2023-08-11 00:00:00	-12.2653

2023-08-14 00:00:00	-9.95025
2023-08-15 00:00:00	-11.2337
2023-08-16 00:00:00	-11.2998
2023-08-17 00:00:00	-12.9432
2023-08-18 00:00:00	-11.4967
2023-08-21 00:00:00	-9.27425
2023-08-22 00:00:00	-7.03875
2023-08-23 00:00:00	-2.32925
2023-08-24 00:00:00	-6.40025
2023-08-25 00:00:00	-3.32825
2023-08-28 00:00:00	-0.88725
2023-08-29 00:00:00	3.85575
2023-08-30 00:00:00	7.96
2023-08-31 00:00:00	8.4265
2023-09-01 00:00:00	10.1815
2023-09-05 00:00:00	10.048
2023-09-06 00:00:00	2.7155
2023-09-07 00:00:00	-2.79
2023-09-08 00:00:00	-2.1385
2023-09-11 00:00:00	-0.969
2023-09-12 00:00:00	-4.1075
2023-09-13 00:00:00	-6.0395
2023-09-14 00:00:00	-4.3475
2023-09-15 00:00:00	-5.036
2023-09-18 00:00:00	-2.1265
2023-09-19 00:00:00	-1.2005
2023-09-20 00:00:00	-4.942
2023-09-21 00:00:00	-6.415
2023-09-22 00:00:00	-5.1955
2023-09-25 00:00:00	-3.826
2023-09-26 00:00:00	-7.8195
2023-09-27 00:00:00	-8.938
2023-09-28 00:00:00	-7.9935
2023-09-29 00:00:00	-6.6255
2023-10-02 00:00:00	-3.2525
2023-10-03 00:00:00	-3.817
2023-10-04 00:00:00	-1.692
2023-10-05 00:00:00	0.0205
2023-10-06 00:00:00	2.733
2023-10-09 00:00:00	4.2675
2023-10-10 00:00:00	3.686
2023-10-11 00:00:00	4.9915
2023-10-12 00:00:00	5.622
2023-10-13 00:00:00	3.5135
2023-10-16 00:00:00	3.1915
2023-10-17 00:00:00	1.584
2023-10-18 00:00:00	0.37
2023-10-19 00:00:00	-0.0275
2023-10-20 00:00:00	-2.684
2023-10-23 00:00:00	-2.4685
2023-10-24 00:00:00	-1.8745
2023-10-25 00:00:00	-4.2885
2023-10-26 00:00:00	-8.532

2023-10-27 00:00:00	-7.012
2023-10-30 00:00:00	-4.7925
2023-10-31 00:00:00	-4.1395
2023-11-01 00:00:00	-0.858
2023-11-02 00:00:00	2.7265
2023-11-03 00:00:00	1.6735
2023-11-06 00:00:00	4.2955
2023-11-07 00:00:00	6.8735
2023-11-08 00:00:00	7.772
2023-11-09 00:00:00	7.1375
2023-11-10 00:00:00	11.0425
2023-11-13 00:00:00	9.065
2023-11-14 00:00:00	11.401
2023-11-15 00:00:00	11.4565
2023-11-16 00:00:00	12.548
2023-11-17 00:00:00	11.8155
2023-11-20 00:00:00	12.735
2023-11-21 00:00:00	11.0025
2023-11-22 00:00:00	10.8125
2023-11-24 00:00:00	8.462
2023-11-27 00:00:00	7.128
2023-11-28 00:00:00	6.6595
2023-11-29 00:00:00	4.624
2023-11-30 00:00:00	4.274
2023-12-01 00:00:00	4.765
2023-12-04 00:00:00	2.2715
2023-12-05 00:00:00	5.6225
2023-12-06 00:00:00	3.813
2023-12-07 00:00:00	5.238
2023-12-08 00:00:00	6.109
2023-12-11 00:00:00	2.914
2023-12-12 00:00:00	4.105
2023-12-13 00:00:00	6.8595
2023-12-14 00:00:00	6.4835
2023-12-15 00:00:00	5.4385
2023-12-18 00:00:00	3.3655
2023-12-19 00:00:00	4.1055
2023-12-20 00:00:00	1.721
2023-12-21 00:00:00	1.3615
2023-12-22 00:00:00	0.113
2023-12-26 00:00:00	-0.6185
2023-12-27 00:00:00	-0.6815
2023-12-28 00:00:00	-0.389
2023-12-29 00:00:00	-1.6495
2024-01-02 00:00:00	-8.6685
2024-01-03 00:00:00	-9.7785
2024-01-04 00:00:00	-11.8595
2024-01-05 00:00:00	-12.014
2024-01-08 00:00:00	-7.077
2024-01-09 00:00:00	-7.0615
2024-01-10 00:00:00	-5.483
2024-01-11 00:00:00	-5.7335
2024-01-12 00:00:00	-4.9475

2024-01-16 00:00:00	-6.6355
2024-01-17 00:00:00	-6.8615
2024-01-18 00:00:00	-0.167
2024-01-19 00:00:00	3.126
2024-01-22 00:00:00	5.725
2024-01-23 00:00:00	7.062
2024-01-24 00:00:00	6.357
2024-01-25 00:00:00	5.982
2024-01-26 00:00:00	4.176
2024-01-29 00:00:00	3.5225
2024-01-30 00:00:00	-0.075
2024-01-31 00:00:00	-3.4905
2024-02-01 00:00:00	-0.9685
2024-02-02 00:00:00	-2.109
2024-02-05 00:00:00	-0.476
2024-02-06 00:00:00	0.819
2024-02-07 00:00:00	0.742
2024-02-08 00:00:00	-0.5615
2024-02-09 00:00:00	-0.138
2024-02-12 00:00:00	-2.001
2024-02-13 00:00:00	-4.1725
2024-02-14 00:00:00	-5.133
2024-02-15 00:00:00	-5.4965
2024-02-16 00:00:00	-6.808
2024-02-20 00:00:00	-7.0955
2024-02-21 00:00:00	-5.719
2024-02-22 00:00:00	-3.026
2024-02-23 00:00:00	-4.3695
2024-02-26 00:00:00	-5.147
2024-02-27 00:00:00	-3.114
2024-02-28 00:00:00	-3.869
2024-02-29 00:00:00	-4.208
2024-03-01 00:00:00	-5.1155
2024-03-04 00:00:00	-9.3155
2024-03-05 00:00:00	-13.758
2024-03-06 00:00:00	-13.88
2024-03-07 00:00:00	-12.991
2024-03-08 00:00:00	-10.2405
2024-03-11 00:00:00	-7.341
2024-03-12 00:00:00	-6.056
2024-03-13 00:00:00	-7.46
2024-03-14 00:00:00	-4.8945
2024-03-15 00:00:00	-4.717
2024-03-18 00:00:00	-3.055
2024-03-19 00:00:00	-0.2655
2024-03-20 00:00:00	2.5985
2024-03-21 00:00:00	-4.519
2024-03-22 00:00:00	-2.959
2024-03-25 00:00:00	-3.877
2024-03-26 00:00:00	-4.5015
2024-03-27 00:00:00	-0.2555
2024-03-28 00:00:00	-1.68
2024-04-01 00:00:00	-2.6665

2024-04-02 00:00:00	-3.375
2024-04-03 00:00:00	-2.252
2024-04-04 00:00:00	-3.0585
2024-04-05 00:00:00	-2.2835
2024-04-08 00:00:00	-3.4425
2024-04-09 00:00:00	-2.1085
2024-04-10 00:00:00	-3.8445
2024-04-11 00:00:00	3.688
2024-04-12 00:00:00	5.0025
2024-04-15 00:00:00	0.965
2024-04-16 00:00:00	-2.3485
2024-04-17 00:00:00	-3.5115
2024-04-18 00:00:00	-4.0675
2024-04-19 00:00:00	-5.526
2024-04-22 00:00:00	-4.3675
2024-04-23 00:00:00	-2.9855
2024-04-24 00:00:00	-0.668
2024-04-25 00:00:00	0.2365
2024-04-26 00:00:00	-0.1825
2024-04-29 00:00:00	4.1265
2024-04-30 00:00:00	0.783
2024-05-01 00:00:00	-0.3215
2024-05-02 00:00:00	3.426
2024-05-03 00:00:00	13.5655
2024-05-06 00:00:00	11.2055
2024-05-07 00:00:00	11.2325
2024-05-08 00:00:00	10.936
2024-05-09 00:00:00	12.018
2024-05-10 00:00:00	10.0215
2024-05-13 00:00:00	12.9265
2024-05-14 00:00:00	13.397
2024-05-15 00:00:00	14.7845
2024-05-16 00:00:00	13.8185
2024-05-17 00:00:00	12.7085
2024-05-20 00:00:00	12.635
2024-05-21 00:00:00	12.685
2024-05-22 00:00:00	9.9625
2024-05-23 00:00:00	4.8485
2024-05-24 00:00:00	7.099
2024-05-28 00:00:00	6.075
2024-05-29 00:00:00	5.5505
2024-05-30 00:00:00	5.5525
2024-05-31 00:00:00	5.413
2024-06-03 00:00:00	6.232
2024-06-04 00:00:00	6.0195
2024-06-05 00:00:00	6.9075
2024-06-06 00:00:00	4.844
2024-06-07 00:00:00	6.667
2024-06-10 00:00:00	2.281
2024-06-11 00:00:00	15.8075
2024-06-12 00:00:00	20.684
2024-06-13 00:00:00	20.572
2024-06-14 00:00:00	17.596

2024-06-17 00:00:00	20.6435
2024-06-18 00:00:00	16.9235
2024-06-20 00:00:00	11.151
2024-06-21 00:00:00	8.0945
2024-06-24 00:00:00	7.915
2024-06-25 00:00:00	7.782
2024-06-26 00:00:00	11.0075
2024-06-27 00:00:00	10.6945
2024-06-28 00:00:00	6.024
2024-07-01 00:00:00	11.1875
2024-07-02 00:00:00	13.4825
2024-07-03 00:00:00	13.4505
2024-07-05 00:00:00	16.8805
2024-07-08 00:00:00	16.837
2024-07-09 00:00:00	16.03
2024-07-10 00:00:00	18.7405
2024-07-11 00:00:00	11.3375
2024-07-12 00:00:00	13.2865
2024-07-15 00:00:00	16.273
2024-07-16 00:00:00	15.685
2024-07-17 00:00:00	8.6285
2024-07-18 00:00:00	3.318
2024-07-19 00:00:00	2.9535
2024-07-22 00:00:00	1.872
2024-07-23 00:00:00	2.0985
2024-07-24 00:00:00	-5.215
2024-07-25 00:00:00	-6.7385
2024-07-26 00:00:00	-6.4805
2024-07-29 00:00:00	-6.3935
2024-07-30 00:00:00	-6.2145
2024-07-31 00:00:00	-3.037
2024-08-01 00:00:00	-6.8475
2024-08-02 00:00:00	-5.188
2024-08-05 00:00:00	-15.454
2024-08-06 00:00:00	-16.5665
2024-08-07 00:00:00	-12.904
2024-08-08 00:00:00	-8.256
2024-08-09 00:00:00	-4.613
2024-08-12 00:00:00	-2.608
2024-08-13 00:00:00	1.9755
2024-08-14 00:00:00	3.103
2024-08-15 00:00:00	6.461
2024-08-16 00:00:00	7.764
2024-08-19 00:00:00	7.517
2024-08-20 00:00:00	8.0405
2024-08-21 00:00:00	7.8555
2024-08-22 00:00:00	5.5925
2024-08-23 00:00:00	7.5505
2024-08-26 00:00:00	7.4465
2024-08-27 00:00:00	7.8495
2024-08-28 00:00:00	5.848
2024-08-29 00:00:00	8.9275
2024-08-30 00:00:00	7.566

```
| 2024-09-03 00:00:00 |   0.879   |
| 2024-09-04 00:00:00 |  -1.716   |
| 2024-09-05 00:00:00 |  -0.867   |
| 2024-09-06 00:00:00 |  -3.055   |
| 2024-09-09 00:00:00 |  -3.3405  |
| 2024-09-10 00:00:00 |  -4.374   |
| 2024-09-11 00:00:00 |  -1.953   |
| 2024-09-12 00:00:00 |  -1.9125  |
| 2024-09-13 00:00:00 |  -2.235   |
| 2024-09-16 00:00:00 |  -8.304   |
| 2024-09-17 00:00:00 |  -7.3475  |
| 2024-09-18 00:00:00 |  -2.9925  |
| 2024-09-19 00:00:00 |   5.4785  |
| 2024-09-20 00:00:00 |   4.685   |
| 2024-09-23 00:00:00 |   2.7715  |
| 2024-09-24 00:00:00 |   3.69    |
| 2024-09-25 00:00:00 |   2.6805  |
| 2024-09-26 00:00:00 |   3.9135  |
| 2024-09-27 00:00:00 |   4.132   |
| 2024-09-30 00:00:00 |   9.442   |
| 2024-10-01 00:00:00 |   2.452   |
| 2024-10-02 00:00:00 |   2.85    |
| 2024-10-03 00:00:00 |   1.4435  |
| 2024-10-04 00:00:00 |   2.409   |
| 2024-10-07 00:00:00 |  -3       |
| 2024-10-08 00:00:00 |   1.041   |
| 2024-10-09 00:00:00 |   4.528   |
| 2024-10-10 00:00:00 |   3.684   |
Backtesting: 2020-10-06 00:00:00 to 2024-10-10 00:00:00

Loading bar data...
Loaded bar data: 0:00:09

Computing indicators...
100%  (1  of  1)  |##############################################################|
Elapsed Time: 0:00:00 Time:  0:00:00

Test split: 2020-10-06 00:00:00 to 2024-10-10 00:00:00
100%  (1010  of  1010)  |########################################################|
Elapsed Time: 0:00:00 Time:  0:00:00

Finished backtest: 0:00:21
                     name        value
0             trade_count     120.0000
1     initial_market_value  100000.0000
2         end_market_value   94117.7000
3                total_pnl   -7694.5000
4           unrealized_pnl    1812.2000
5         total_return_pct      -7.6945
6             total_profit  133557.1000
7               total_loss -141251.6000
8               total_fees       0.0000
9             max_drawdown  -39502.4100
```

```
10        max_drawdown_pct     -32.9044
11                win_rate      48.3333
12               loss_rate      51.6667
13          winning_trades      58.0000
14           losing_trades      62.0000
15                 avg_pnl     -64.1208
16          avg_return_pct      -0.0152
17          avg_trade_bars       3.0000
18              avg_profit    2302.7086
19          avg_profit_pct       2.4902
20  avg_winning_trade_bars       3.0000
21                avg_loss   -2278.2516
22            avg_loss_pct      -2.3590
23   avg_losing_trade_bars       3.0000
24             largest_win    8549.0000
25         largest_win_pct       7.8900
26        largest_win_bars       3.0000
27            largest_loss   -7678.9300
28        largest_loss_pct      -7.7600
29       largest_loss_bars       3.0000
30                max_wins       4.0000
31              max_losses       4.0000
32                  sharpe      -0.0059
33                 sortino      -0.0061
34           profit_factor       0.9766
35             ulcer_index       2.8886
36                     upi      -0.0002
37               equity_r2       0.5265
38               std_error    7502.7808
```

So we do 120 trades, and we will benefit likely lose, this is the estimate from MA20, how about MA5?

```
import pybroker as pb
from pybroker import Strategy, ExecContext
from pybroker.ext.data import AKShare

pb.param(name='stock_code', value='105.AAPL')

akshare = AKShare()

df  =  akshare.query(symbols=[pb.param(name='stock_code')],  start_date='20240706',
end_date='20241010')

print(df.to_markdown())
import numpy as np
from numba import njit

def cmma(bar_data, lookback):

    @njit  # Enable Numba JIT.
    def vec_cmma(values):
```

```
        # Initialize the result array.
        n = len(values)
        out = np.array([np.nan for _ in range(n)])

        # For all bars starting at lookback:
        for i in range(lookback, n):
            # Calculate the moving average for the lookback.
            ma = 0
            for j in range(i - lookback, i):
                ma += values[j]
            ma /= lookback
            # Subtract the moving average from value.
            out[i] = values[i] - ma
        return out

    # Calculate with close prices.
    return vec_cmma(bar_data.close)

cmma_5 = pb.indicator('cmma_5', cmma, lookback=5)

print(cmma_5(df).to_markdown())

def buy_cmma(ctx):
    if ctx.long_pos():
        return
    # Place a buy order if the most recent value of the 5 day CMMA is < 0:
    if ctx.indicator('cmma_5')[-1] < 0:
        ctx.buy_shares = ctx.calc_target_shares(1)
        ctx.hold_bars = 3

strategy = Strategy(akshare, start_date='20240706', end_date='20241010')

strategy.add_execution(buy_cmma, 'AAPL', indicators=cmma_5)

result = strategy.backtest(warmup=5)

print(result.metrics_df.round(4))

# output
|                     |       0 |
|:--------------------|--------:|
| 2024-07-08 00:00:00 | nan     |
| 2024-07-09 00:00:00 | nan     |
| 2024-07-10 00:00:00 | nan     |
| 2024-07-11 00:00:00 | nan     |
| 2024-07-12 00:00:00 | nan     |
| 2024-07-15 00:00:00 |   4.882 |
| 2024-07-16 00:00:00 |   3.986 |
| 2024-07-17 00:00:00 |  -3.182 |
| 2024-07-18 00:00:00 |  -7.062 |
| 2024-07-19 00:00:00 |  -6.254 |
| 2024-07-22 00:00:00 |  -5.358 |
| 2024-07-23 00:00:00 |  -2.22  |
```

2024-07-24 00:00:00	-6.728
2024-07-25 00:00:00	-5.71
2024-07-26 00:00:00	-3.902
2024-07-29 00:00:00	-2.352
2024-07-30 00:00:00	-0.648
2024-07-31 00:00:00	3.874
2024-08-01 00:00:00	-0.554
2024-08-02 00:00:00	0.772
2024-08-05 00:00:00	-10.198
2024-08-06 00:00:00	-10.444
2024-08-07 00:00:00	-5.54
2024-08-08 00:00:00	0.402
2024-08-09 00:00:00	4.342
2024-08-12 00:00:00	6.356
2024-08-13 00:00:00	8.444
2024-08-14 00:00:00	6.086
2024-08-15 00:00:00	6.706
2024-08-16 00:00:00	5.754
2024-08-19 00:00:00	3.632
2024-08-20 00:00:00	2.58
2024-08-21 00:00:00	1.422
2024-08-22 00:00:00	-1.384
2024-08-23 00:00:00	0.964
2024-08-26 00:00:00	1.146
2024-08-27 00:00:00	1.738
2024-08-28 00:00:00	-0.106
2024-08-29 00:00:00	3.176
2024-08-30 00:00:00	1.334
2024-09-03 00:00:00	-5.328
2024-09-04 00:00:00	-6.366
2024-09-05 00:00:00	-3.4
2024-09-06 00:00:00	-4.138
2024-09-09 00:00:00	-2.254
2024-09-10 00:00:00	-1.436
2024-09-11 00:00:00	1.646
2024-09-12 00:00:00	1.394
2024-09-13 00:00:00	1.046
2024-09-16 00:00:00	-5.47
2024-09-17 00:00:00	-4.082
2024-09-18 00:00:00	0.482
2024-09-19 00:00:00	9.056
2024-09-20 00:00:00	7.166
2024-09-23 00:00:00	4.296
2024-09-24 00:00:00	3.166
2024-09-25 00:00:00	0.05
2024-09-26 00:00:00	0.064
2024-09-27 00:00:00	0.604
2024-09-30 00:00:00	5.896
2024-10-01 00:00:00	-2.2
2024-10-02 00:00:00	-1.398
2024-10-03 00:00:00	-2.59
2024-10-04 00:00:00	-1.09
2024-10-07 00:00:00	-6.002

```
| 2024-10-08 00:00:00 |   0.34  |
| 2024-10-09 00:00:00 |   4.198 |
| 2024-10-10 00:00:00 |   3.146 |
Backtesting: 2024-07-06 00:00:00 to 2024-10-10 00:00:00

Loading bar data...
Loaded bar data: 0:00:07

Computing indicators...
100% (1 of 1) |##################################################################|
Elapsed Time: 0:00:00 Time:  0:00:00

Test split: 2024-07-08 00:00:00 to 2024-10-10 00:00:00
100% (68 of 68) |################################################################|
Elapsed Time: 0:00:00 Time:  0:00:00

Finished backtest: 0:00:18
                      name        value
0              trade_count      10.0000
1     initial_market_value  100000.0000
2         end_market_value  102686.1200
3                total_pnl     705.9600
4           unrealized_pnl    1980.1600
5         total_return_pct       0.7060
6             total_profit   12852.6900
7               total_loss  -12146.7300
8               total_fees       0.0000
9             max_drawdown   -9315.5900
10        max_drawdown_pct      -8.9279
11                win_rate      40.0000
12               loss_rate      60.0000
13          winning_trades       4.0000
14           losing_trades       6.0000
15                 avg_pnl      70.5960
16          avg_return_pct       0.1280
17          avg_trade_bars       3.0000
18              avg_profit    3213.1725
19          avg_profit_pct       3.3375
20  avg_winning_trade_bars       3.0000
21                avg_loss   -2024.4550
22            avg_loss_pct      -2.0117
23   avg_losing_trade_bars       3.0000
24             largest_win    6435.7400
25         largest_win_pct       6.8000
26        largest_win_bars       3.0000
27            largest_loss   -5082.7700
28        largest_loss_pct      -4.8800
29       largest_loss_bars       3.0000
30                max_wins       3.0000
31              max_losses       3.0000
32                  sharpe       0.0425
33                 sortino       0.0480
34           profit_factor       1.1576
```

```
35          ulcer_index       3.0689
36                  upi       0.0144
37            equity_r2       0.0290
38            std_error    2291.7741
```

Aww, likely win…

So we are really not sure what should we do? And based on what MA is better? Or even HHV?

```
import pybroker as pb

from pybroker.ext.data import AKShare

pb.param(name='stock_code', value='105.AAPL')

akshare = AKShare()

df  =  akshare.query(symbols=[pb.param(name='stock_code')],  start_date='20240706', end_date='20241010')

print(df.to_markdown())

from pybroker import highv

def hhv(bar_data, period):
    return highv(bar_data.high, period)

hhv_5 = pb.indicator('hhv_5', hhv, period=5)
print(hhv_5(df).to_markdown())
```

	0
2024-07-08 00:00:00	nan
2024-07-09 00:00:00	nan
2024-07-10 00:00:00	nan
2024-07-11 00:00:00	nan
2024-07-12 00:00:00	233.08
2024-07-15 00:00:00	237.23
2024-07-16 00:00:00	237.23
2024-07-17 00:00:00	237.23
2024-07-18 00:00:00	237.23
2024-07-19 00:00:00	237.23
2024-07-22 00:00:00	236.27
2024-07-23 00:00:00	231.46
2024-07-24 00:00:00	230.44

	0
2024-07-25 00:00:00	227.78
2024-07-26 00:00:00	227.78
2024-07-29 00:00:00	226.94
2024-07-30 00:00:00	224.8
2024-07-31 00:00:00	223.82
2024-08-01 00:00:00	224.48
2024-08-02 00:00:00	225.6
2024-08-05 00:00:00	225.6
2024-08-06 00:00:00	225.6
2024-08-07 00:00:00	225.6
2024-08-08 00:00:00	225.6
2024-08-09 00:00:00	216.78
2024-08-12 00:00:00	219.51
2024-08-13 00:00:00	221.89
2024-08-14 00:00:00	223.03
2024-08-15 00:00:00	225.35
2024-08-16 00:00:00	226.827
2024-08-19 00:00:00	226.827
2024-08-20 00:00:00	227.17
2024-08-21 00:00:00	227.98
2024-08-22 00:00:00	228.34
2024-08-23 00:00:00	228.34
2024-08-26 00:00:00	228.34
2024-08-27 00:00:00	228.85
2024-08-28 00:00:00	229.86
2024-08-29 00:00:00	232.92
2024-08-30 00:00:00	232.92
2024-09-03 00:00:00	232.92
2024-09-04 00:00:00	232.92
2024-09-05 00:00:00	232.92
2024-09-06 00:00:00	230.4
2024-09-09 00:00:00	229
2024-09-10 00:00:00	225.48
2024-09-11 00:00:00	225.48
2024-09-12 00:00:00	225.24

	0
2024-09-13 00:00:00	224.04
2024-09-16 00:00:00	224.04
2024-09-17 00:00:00	224.04
2024-09-18 00:00:00	224.04
2024-09-19 00:00:00	229.82
2024-09-20 00:00:00	233.09
2024-09-23 00:00:00	233.09
2024-09-24 00:00:00	233.09
2024-09-25 00:00:00	233.09
2024-09-26 00:00:00	233.09
2024-09-27 00:00:00	229.52
2024-09-30 00:00:00	233
2024-10-01 00:00:00	233
2024-10-02 00:00:00	233
2024-10-03 00:00:00	233
2024-10-04 00:00:00	233
2024-10-07 00:00:00	229.65
2024-10-08 00:00:00	228
2024-10-09 00:00:00	229.75
2024-10-10 00:00:00	229.75

Checkout https://www.pybroker.com/en/dev/reference/pybroker.indicator.html, these are the most useful parts, indicators, or the calculation for prices, otherwise we have to caluculate ourselfves, that is crazy, let's just use 10 days,

date	symbol	open	high	low	close	volume
2024-10-01 00:00:00	105.AAPL	229.52	229.65	223.74	226.21	63285048
2024-10-02 00:00:00	105.AAPL	225.89	227.37	223.02	226.78	32880605
2024-10-03 00:00:00	105.AAPL	225.14	226.805	223.32	225.67	34044158
2024-10-04 00:00:00	105.AAPL	227.9	228	224.13	226.8	37345098
2024-10-07 00:00:00	105.AAPL	224.5	225.69	221.33	221.69	39505354
2024-10-08 00:00:00	105.AAPL	224.3	225.98	223.25	225.77	31855693
2024-10-09 00:00:00	105.AAPL	225.23	229.75	224.83	229.54	33591091
2024-10-10 00:00:00	105.AAPL	227.78	229.5	227.17	229.04	28183544

```
import pybroker as pb
from pybroker import Strategy, ExecContext
```

```
from pybroker.ext.data import AKShare

pb.param(name='stock_code', value='105.AAPL')

akshare = AKShare()

df              =              akshare.query(symbols=[pb.param(name='stock_code')],
start_date='20241001000930', end_date='20241010000430')
print(df.columns)
from pybroker import lowv, highv

def lwv(bar_data, period):
    print(dir(bar_data))
    return lowv(bar_data.low, period)

lwv_5 = pb.indicator('lwv_5', lwv, period=5)

def hhv(bar_data, period):
    return highv(bar_data.high, period)

hhv_5 = pb.indicator('hhv_5', hhv, period=5)

from pybroker import IndicatorSet

indicator_set = IndicatorSet()
indicator_set.add(lwv_5, hhv_5)
caldf = indicator_set(df)

print(caldf.to_markdown())

# output
Loading bar data...
Loaded bar data: 0:00:11

Index(['date', 'symbol', 'open', 'high', 'low', 'close', 'volume'], dtype='object')
Computing indicators...
  0% (0 of 2) |                                                                  |
Elapsed  Time:  0:00:00  ETA:   --:--:--['__class__',  '__delattr__',  '__dict__',
'__dir__',   '__doc__',   '__eq__',   '__format__',   '__ge__',   '__getattr__',
'__getattribute__',   '__getstate__',   '__gt__',   '__hash__',   '__init__',
'__init_subclass__',  '__le__',  '__lt__',  '__module__',  '__ne__',  '__new__',
'__reduce__', '__reduce_ex__', '__repr__', '__setattr__', '__sizeof__', '__str__',
'__subclasshook__',  '__weakref__',  '_custom_col_data',  'close',  'date',  'high',
'low', 'open', 'volume', 'vwap']
100%  (2  of  2)  |################################################################|
Elapsed Time: 0:00:03 Time:  0:00:03

|    | symbol    | date                |   hhv_5 |   lwv_5 |
|---:|:----------|:--------------------|--------:|--------:|
|  0 | 105.AAPL  | 2024-10-01 00:00:00 |  nan    |  nan    |
|  1 | 105.AAPL  | 2024-10-02 00:00:00 |  nan    |  nan    |
|  2 | 105.AAPL  | 2024-10-03 00:00:00 |  nan    |  nan    |
|  3 | 105.AAPL  | 2024-10-04 00:00:00 |  nan    |  nan    |
```

```
|   4 | 105.AAPL | 2024-10-07 00:00:00 |  229.65 |  221.33 |
|   5 | 105.AAPL | 2024-10-08 00:00:00 |  228    |  221.33 |
|   6 | 105.AAPL | 2024-10-09 00:00:00 |  229.75 |  221.33 |
|   7 | 105.AAPL | 2024-10-10 00:00:00 |  229.75 |  221.33 |
```

And with the close price, volume,

```
import pybroker as pb
from pybroker import Strategy, ExecContext
from pybroker.ext.data import AKShare

pb.param(name='stock_code', value='105.AAPL')

akshare = AKShare()

df = akshare.query(symbols=[pb.param(name='stock_code')], start_date='20241001000930', end_date='20241010000430')
print(df.columns)
from pybroker import lowv, highv

def lwv(bar_data, period):
    return lowv(bar_data.low, period)

lwv_5 = pb.indicator('lwv_5', lwv, period=5)

def hhv(bar_data, period):
    return highv(bar_data.high, period)

hhv_5 = pb.indicator('hhv_5', hhv, period=5)

from pybroker.vect import aroon_diff

def adiff(bar_data, period):
    return aroon_diff(bar_data.high, bar_data.low, period)

adiff_5 = pb.indicator('aroon_diff_5', adiff, period=5)

from pybroker.vect import intraday_intensity

def inin(bar_data, period):
    return intraday_intensity(bar_data.high, bar_data.low, bar_data.close, bar_data.volume, period)

intraday_intensity_5 = pb.indicator('intraday_intensity_5', inin, period=5)

from pybroker.vect import macd

def macd57(bar_data, short_length, long_length):
    return macd(bar_data.high, bar_data.low, bar_data.close, short_length, long_length)

macd_5_7 = pb.indicator('macd_5_7', macd57, short_length=5, long_length=7)
```

```
from pybroker import IndicatorSet

indicator_set = IndicatorSet()
indicator_set.add(lwv_5, hhv_5, adiff_5, intraday_intensity_5, macd_5_7)
caldf = indicator_set(df)

print(caldf.to_markdown())
```

symbol	date	aroon_diff_5	hhv_5	intraday_intensity_5	lwv_5	macd_5_
105.AAPL	2024-10-01 00:00:00	0	nan	0	nan	
105.AAPL	2024-10-02 00:00:00	0	nan	0	nan	0.435
105.AAPL	2024-10-03 00:00:00	0	nan	0	nan	-0.2567
105.AAPL	2024-10-04 00:00:00	0	nan	0	nan	0.3548
105.AAPL	2024-10-07 00:00:00	0	229.65	1.32945e+08	221.33	-3.378
105.AAPL	2024-10-08 00:00:00	0	228	8.79779e+08	221.33	-1.793
105.AAPL	2024-10-09 00:00:00	20	229.75	1.01502e+09	221.33	2.018
105.AAPL	2024-10-10 00:00:00	100	229.75	1.11875e+09	221.33	3.591

There is also some analysis model we can just import and use,

```
import numpy as np
import pandas as pd
import pybroker
from numba import njit
from pybroker import Strategy, StrategyConfig

def cmma(bar_data, lookback):
```

```
    @njit  # Enable Numba JIT.
    def vec_cmma(values):
        # Initialize the result array.
        n = len(values)
        out = np.array([np.nan for _ in range(n)])

        # For all bars starting at lookback:
        for i in range(lookback, n):
            # Calculate the moving average for the lookback.
            ma = 0
            for j in range(i - lookback, i):
                ma += values[j]
            ma /= lookback
            # Subtract the moving average from value.
            out[i] = values[i] - ma
        return out

    # Calculate for close prices.
    return vec_cmma(bar_data.close)

cmma_20 = pybroker.indicator('cmma_20', cmma, lookback=20)

from sklearn.linear_model import LinearRegression
from sklearn.metrics import r2_score

def train_slr(symbol, train_data, test_data):
    # Train
    # Previous day close prices.
    train_prev_close = train_data['close'].shift(1)
    # Calculate daily returns.
        train_daily_returns = (train_data['close'] - train_prev_close) /
train_prev_close
    # Predict next day's return.
    train_data['pred'] = train_daily_returns.shift(-1)
    train_data = train_data.dropna()
    # Train the LinearRegession model to predict the next day's return
    # given the 20-day CMMA.
    X_train = train_data[['cmma_20']]
    y_train = train_data[['pred']]
    model = LinearRegression()
    model.fit(X_train, y_train)

    # Test
    test_prev_close = test_data['close'].shift(1)
    test_daily_returns = (test_data['close'] - test_prev_close) / test_prev_close
    test_data['pred'] = test_daily_returns.shift(-1)
    test_data = test_data.dropna()
    X_test = test_data[['cmma_20']]
    y_test = test_data[['pred']]
    # Make predictions from test data.
    y_pred = model.predict(X_test)
    # Print goodness of fit.
    r2 = r2_score(y_test, np.squeeze(y_pred))
```

```
    print(symbol, f'R^2={r2}')

    # Return the trained model and columns to use as input data.
    return model, ['cmma_20']

model_slr = pybroker.model('slr', train_slr, indicators=[cmma_20])

from pybroker.ext.data import AKShare

config = StrategyConfig(bootstrap_sample_size=100)
strategy = Strategy(AKShare(), '1/1/2024', '10/10/2024', config)
strategy.add_execution(None, ['105.AAPL'], models=model_slr)
strategy.backtest(train_size=0.5)

# output
Backtesting: 2024-01-01 00:00:00 to 2024-10-10 00:00:00

Loading bar data...
Loaded bar data: 0:00:01

Computing indicators...
100%  (1  of  1) |##################################################################|
Elapsed Time: 0:00:00 Time:  0:00:00

Train split: 2024-01-02 00:00:00 to 2024-05-21 00:00:00
105.AAPL R^2=-0.01772720602397171
Finished training models: 0:00:00

Finished backtest: 0:00:02
```

and continue to do the walkforward,

```
def hold_long(ctx):
    if not ctx.long_pos():
        # Buy if the next bar is predicted to have a positive return:
        if ctx.preds('slr')[-1] > 0:
            ctx.buy_shares = 100
    else:
        # Sell if the next bar is predicted to have a negative return:
        if ctx.preds('slr')[-1] < 0:
            ctx.sell_shares = 100

strategy.clear_executions()
strategy.add_execution(hold_long, ['105.AAPL'], models=model_slr)

result = strategy.walkforward(
    warmup=20,
    windows=3,
    train_size=0.5,
    lookahead=1,
    calc_bootstrap=True
)
```

```
print(result.metrics_df)

# output
Calculating bootstrap metrics: sample_size=100, samples=10000...
Calculated bootstrap metrics: 0:00:17

Finished backtest: 0:00:30
                     name          value
0             trade_count       2.000000
1    initial_market_value  100000.000000
2        end_market_value  101912.000000
3               total_pnl    1644.000000
4          unrealized_pnl     268.000000
5        total_return_pct       1.644000
6            total_profit    1644.000000
7              total_loss       0.000000
8              total_fees       0.000000
9            max_drawdown   -1923.000000
10       max_drawdown_pct      -1.891711
11               win_rate     100.000000
12              loss_rate       0.000000
13         winning_trades       2.000000
14          losing_trades       0.000000
15                avg_pnl     822.000000
16         avg_return_pct       3.800000
17         avg_trade_bars       4.500000
18             avg_profit     822.000000
19         avg_profit_pct       3.800000
20  avg_winning_trade_bars       4.500000
21               avg_loss       0.000000
22           avg_loss_pct       0.000000
23   avg_losing_trade_bars       0.000000
24            largest_win    1280.000000
25        largest_win_pct       6.020000
26       largest_win_bars       7.000000
27           largest_loss       0.000000
28       largest_loss_pct       0.000000
29      largest_loss_bars       0.000000
30               max_wins       2.000000
31             max_losses       0.000000
32                 sharpe       0.061027
33                sortino       0.051697
34          profit_factor       1.276181
35            ulcer_index       0.470827
36                    upi       0.028631
37              equity_r2       0.687523
38              std_error     733.732710
```

and the result bootstrap,

```
print(result.bootstrap.conf_intervals)

print(result.bootstrap.drawdown_conf)
```

```
# output
                           lower     upper
name           conf
Profit Factor 97.5%  0.450956  2.553732
              95%    0.536496  2.229487
              90%    0.655404  1.926319
Sharpe Ratio  97.5% -0.208252  0.200477
              95%   -0.167459  0.169299
              90%   -0.131255  0.133716
       amount   percent
conf
99.9% -6716.0 -6.423780
99%   -5088.0 -4.898960
95%   -3804.0 -3.693896
90%   -3216.0 -3.134925
```

What is bootstrap? It's just taking the samples in, and with the stratergy to give result.

```
from pybroker.ext.data import AKShare
import pybroker
from pybroker import Strategy, StrategyConfig

#pybroker.enable_data_source_cache('my_strategy')

def buy_low(ctx):
    if ctx.long_pos():
        return
    if ctx.bars >= 2 and ctx.close[-1] < ctx.low[-2]:
        ctx.buy_shares = ctx.calc_target_shares(0.25)
        ctx.buy_limit_price = ctx.close[-1] - 0.01
        ctx.hold_bars = 3

def sell_high(ctx):
    if ctx.short_pos():
        return
    if ctx.bars >= 2 and ctx.close[-1] > ctx.high[-2]:
        ctx.sell_shares = 100
        ctx.hold_bars = 2
config = StrategyConfig(initial_cash=500_000, bootstrap_sample_size=100)
strategy = Strategy(AKShare(), '1/1/2024', '10/10/2024', config)
strategy.add_execution(buy_low, ['105.AAPL'])
result = strategy.backtest(calc_bootstrap=True)

print(result.metrics_df)
print(result.bootstrap.conf_intervals)
print(result.bootstrap.drawdown_conf)

# output
Backtesting: 2024-01-01 00:00:00 to 2024-10-10 00:00:00
```

```
Loading bar data...
Loaded bar data: 0:00:05

Test split: 2024-01-02 00:00:00 to 2024-10-10 00:00:00
100% (196 of 196) |#################################################################|
Elapsed Time: 0:00:00 Time:  0:00:00

Calculating bootstrap metrics: sample_size=100, samples=10000...
Calculated bootstrap metrics: 0:00:18

Finished backtest: 0:00:37
                      name         value
0              trade_count  1.500000e+01
1     initial_market_value  5.000000e+05
2         end_market_value  5.169051e+05
3                total_pnl  1.690509e+04
4           unrealized_pnl  2.546585e-11
5         total_return_pct  3.381018e+00
6             total_profit  2.941513e+04
7               total_loss -1.251004e+04
8               total_fees  0.000000e+00
9             max_drawdown -1.057677e+04
10        max_drawdown_pct -2.070332e+00
11                win_rate  6.000000e+01
12               loss_rate  4.000000e+01
13          winning_trades  9.000000e+00
14           losing_trades  6.000000e+00
15                 avg_pnl  1.127006e+03
16          avg_return_pct  9.086667e-01
17          avg_trade_bars  3.000000e+00
18              avg_profit  3.268348e+03
19          avg_profit_pct  2.616667e+00
20  avg_winning_trade_bars  3.000000e+00
21                avg_loss -2.085007e+03
22            avg_loss_pct -1.653333e+00
23   avg_losing_trade_bars  3.000000e+00
24             largest_win  8.620080e+03
25         largest_win_pct  6.800000e+00
26        largest_win_bars  3.000000e+00
27            largest_loss -5.012910e+03
28        largest_loss_pct -3.950000e+00
29       largest_loss_bars  3.000000e+00
30                max_wins  2.000000e+00
31              max_losses  2.000000e+00
32                  sharpe  1.150108e-01
33                 sortino  1.514172e-01
34           profit_factor  1.792482e+00
35             ulcer_index  3.552160e-01
36                     upi  4.831871e-02
37               equity_r2  2.969878e-01
38               std_error  4.425839e+03
                        lower     upper
name           conf
```

```
Profit Factor 97.5%  0.211466  2.027164
              95%    0.303352  1.716510
              90%    0.350751  1.431039
Sharpe Ratio  97.5% -0.272848  0.135678
              95%   -0.227696  0.106329
              90%   -0.197323  0.070991
         amount   percent
conf
99.9% -14746.27 -2.868141
99%   -11756.38 -2.290103
95%    -8721.49 -1.705361
90%    -7343.60 -1.437948
```

and we can also draw the value,

```
import matplotlib.pyplot as plt

p = plt.subplot2grid((3, 2), (0, 0), rowspan=3, colspan=2)
p.plot(result.portfolio.index, result.portfolio['market_value'])

plt.show()
```

and the classification by our trade function,

```
print(result.trades)
```

id	type	symbol	entry_date	exit_date	entry	exit	shares	pnl	return_
1	long	105.AAPL	2024-01-05 00:00:00	2024-01-10 00:00:00	181.46	185.16	687	2541.9	2
2	long	105.AAPL	2024-01-17 00:00:00	2024-01-22 00:00:00	181.62	193.8	684	8331.12	6
3	long	105.AAPL	2024-01-26 00:00:00	2024-01-31 00:00:00	193.35	185.72	657	-5012.91	-3
4	long	105.AAPL	2024-02-13 00:00:00	2024-02-16 00:00:00	184.86	183.26	675	-1080	-(
5	long	105.AAPL	2024-03-05 00:00:00	2024-03-08 00:00:00	170.83	171.32	720	352.8	(
6	long	105.AAPL	2024-04-02 00:00:00	2024-04-05 00:00:00	168.78	169.67	742	660.38	(

id	type	symbol	entry_date	exit_date	entry	exit	shares	pnl	return_
7	long	105.AAPL	2024-04-16 00:00:00	2024-04-19 00:00:00	171.02	165.24	732	-4230.96	-3
8	long	105.AAPL	2024-05-23 00:00:00	2024-05-29 00:00:00	188.81	190.88	656	1357.92	
9	long	105.AAPL	2024-06-21 00:00:00	2024-06-26 00:00:00	209.5	212.75	599	1946.75	1
10	long	105.AAPL	2024-07-18 00:00:00	2024-07-23 00:00:00	226.36	224.81	551	-854.05	-0
11	long	105.AAPL	2024-07-25 00:00:00	2024-07-30 00:00:00	217.74	218.22	576	276.48	0
12	long	105.AAPL	2024-08-06 00:00:00	2024-08-09 00:00:00	205.53	214.38	602	5327.7	4
13	long	105.AAPL	2024-09-04 00:00:00	2024-09-09 00:00:00	219.63	218.99	571	-365.44	-0
14	long	105.AAPL	2024-09-17 00:00:00	2024-09-20 00:00:00	215.7	230.36	588	8620.08	
15	long	105.AAPL	2024-10-02 00:00:00	2024-10-07 00:00:00	225.2	223.51	572	-966.68	-0

36 Price

For trader, the most important thing is to judge if the price is right, low buy, high sell, sounds easy?

```
import pybroker as pb
from pybroker import Strategy, ExecContext
from pybroker.ext.data import AKShare

# version 1.14

pb.param(name='stock_code', value='TSLA')
```

```
akshare = AKShare()

df = akshare.query(symbols=[pb.param(name='stock_code')], start_date='20241007000000', end_date='20241010000000', timeframe='1m')

print(df.to_markdown())

# output
Loading bar data...
Loaded bar data: 0:00:00

| symbol    | date    | open    | high    | low    | close    | volume    |
|----------|--------|--------|--------|-------|---------|----------|
```

What?

No data?

```
import pybroker as pb
from pybroker import Strategy, ExecContext
from pybroker.ext.data import AKShare

pb.param(name='stock_code', value='TLSA')

akshare = AKShare()

df = akshare.query(symbols=[pb.param(name='stock_code')], start_date='20240706', end_date='20241010')

print(df.to_markdown())
```

	date	symbol	open	high	low	close	volume
0	2024-07-08 00:00:00	TLSA	227.09	227.85	223.25	227.82	59085861
1	2024-07-09 00:00:00	TLSA	227.93	229.4	226.372	228.68	48169822
2	2024-07-10 00:00:00	TLSA	229.3	233.08	229.25	232.98	62627687
3	2024-07-11 00:00:00	TLSA	231.39	232.39	225.77	227.57	64710617
4	2024-07-12 00:00:00	TLSA	228.92	232.64	228.68	230.54	53046527
5	2024-07-15 00:00:00	TLSA	236.48	237.23	233.09	234.4	62631252
6	2024-07-16 00:00:00	TLSA	235	236.27	232.33	234.82	43234278
7	2024-07-17 00:00:00	TLSA	229.45	231.46	226.64	228.88	57345884
8	2024-07-18 00:00:00	TLSA	230.28	230.44	222.27	224.18	66034585
9	2024-07-19 00:00:00	TLSA	224.82	226.8	223.275	224.31	49151453
10	2024-07-22 00:00:00	TLSA	227.01	227.78	223.09	223.96	48201835
11	2024-07-23 00:00:00	TLSA	224.365	226.94	222.68	225.01	39960260
12	2024-07-24 00:00:00	TLSA	224	224.8	217.13	218.54	61777576

	date	symbol	open	high	low	close	volume
13	2024-07-25 00:00:00	TLSA	218.93	220.85	214.62	217.49	51391199
14	2024-07-26 00:00:00	TLSA	218.7	219.49	216.01	217.96	41601345
15	2024-07-29 00:00:00	TLSA	216.96	219.3	215.75	218.24	36311778
16	2024-07-30 00:00:00	TLSA	219.19	220.325	216.12	218.8	41643840
17	2024-07-31 00:00:00	TLSA	221.44	223.82	220.63	222.08	50036262
18	2024-08-01 00:00:00	TLSA	224.37	224.48	217.02	218.36	62500996
19	2024-08-02 00:00:00	TLSA	219.15	225.6	217.71	219.86	105568560
20	2024-08-05 00:00:00	TLSA	199.09	213.5	196	209.27	119548589
21	2024-08-06 00:00:00	TLSA	205.3	209.99	201.07	207.23	69660488
22	2024-08-07 00:00:00	TLSA	206.9	213.64	206.39	209.82	63516417
23	2024-08-08 00:00:00	TLSA	213.11	214.2	208.83	213.31	47161149
24	2024-08-09 00:00:00	TLSA	212.1	216.78	211.97	216.24	42201646
25	2024-08-12 00:00:00	TLSA	216.07	219.51	215.6	217.53	38028092
26	2024-08-13 00:00:00	TLSA	219.01	221.89	219.01	221.27	44155331
27	2024-08-14 00:00:00	TLSA	220.57	223.03	219.7	221.72	41960574
28	2024-08-15 00:00:00	TLSA	224.6	225.35	222.76	224.72	46414013
29	2024-08-16 00:00:00	TLSA	223.92	226.827	223.65	226.05	44340240
30	2024-08-19 00:00:00	TLSA	225.72	225.99	223.04	225.89	40687813
31	2024-08-20 00:00:00	TLSA	225.77	227.17	225.45	226.51	30299033
32	2024-08-21 00:00:00	TLSA	226.52	227.98	225.05	226.4	34765480
33	2024-08-22 00:00:00	TLSA	227.79	228.34	223.9	224.53	43695321
34	2024-08-23 00:00:00	TLSA	225.659	228.22	224.33	226.84	38677250
35	2024-08-26 00:00:00	TLSA	226.76	227.28	223.891	227.18	30602208
36	2024-08-27 00:00:00	TLSA	225.995	228.85	224.89	228.03	35934559
37	2024-08-28 00:00:00	TLSA	227.92	229.86	225.68	226.49	38052167
38	2024-08-29 00:00:00	TLSA	230.1	232.92	228.88	229.79	51906297
39	2024-08-30 00:00:00	TLSA	230.19	230.4	227.48	229	52990770
40	2024-09-03 00:00:00	TLSA	228.55	229	221.17	222.77	50190574
41	2024-09-04 00:00:00	TLSA	221.66	221.78	217.48	220.85	43840196
42	2024-09-05 00:00:00	TLSA	221.625	225.48	221.52	222.38	36615398
43	2024-09-06 00:00:00	TLSA	223.95	225.24	219.77	220.82	48423011
44	2024-09-09 00:00:00	TLSA	220.82	221.27	216.71	220.91	67179965
45	2024-09-10 00:00:00	TLSA	218.92	221.48	216.73	220.11	51591033
46	2024-09-11 00:00:00	TLSA	221.455	223.09	217.89	222.66	44587072
47	2024-09-12 00:00:00	TLSA	222.5	223.55	219.82	222.77	37498225

	date	symbol	open	high	low	close	volume
48	2024-09-13 00:00:00	TLSA	223.58	224.04	221.91	222.5	36766619
49	2024-09-16 00:00:00	TLSA	216.54	217.22	213.92	216.32	59357427
50	2024-09-17 00:00:00	TLSA	215.75	216.9	214.5	216.79	45519339
51	2024-09-18 00:00:00	TLSA	217.55	222.71	217.54	220.69	59894928
52	2024-09-19 00:00:00	TLSA	224.99	229.82	224.63	228.87	66781315
53	2024-09-20 00:00:00	TLSA	229.97	233.09	227.62	228.2	318679888
54	2024-09-23 00:00:00	TLSA	227.34	229.45	225.81	226.47	54146023
55	2024-09-24 00:00:00	TLSA	228.645	229.35	225.73	227.37	43556068
56	2024-09-25 00:00:00	TLSA	224.93	227.29	224.02	226.37	42308715
57	2024-09-26 00:00:00	TLSA	227.3	228.5	225.41	227.52	36636707
58	2024-09-27 00:00:00	TLSA	228.46	229.52	227.3	227.79	34025967
59	2024-09-30 00:00:00	TLSA	230.04	233	229.65	233	54793391
60	2024-10-01 00:00:00	TLSA	229.52	229.65	223.74	226.21	63285048
61	2024-10-02 00:00:00	TLSA	225.89	227.37	223.02	226.78	32880605
62	2024-10-03 00:00:00	TLSA	225.14	226.805	223.32	225.67	34044158
63	2024-10-04 00:00:00	TLSA	227.9	228	224.13	226.8	37345098
64	2024-10-07 00:00:00	TLSA	224.5	225.69	221.33	221.69	39505354
65	2024-10-08 00:00:00	TLSA	224.3	225.98	223.25	225.77	31855693
66	2024-10-09 00:00:00	TLSA	225.23	229.75	224.83	229.54	33591091
67	2024-10-10 00:00:00	TLSA	227.78	229.5	227.17	229.04	28183544

Aww, it is so wrong, TLSA is not TSLA...

But continue with 1 week,

```
import pybroker as pb
from pybroker import Strategy, ExecContext
from pybroker.ext.data import AKShare

pb.param(name='stock_code', value='TSLA')

akshare = AKShare()

df                =                akshare.query(symbols=[pb.param(name='stock_code')],
start_date='20241007000000', end_date='20241010000000', timeframe='1w')

print(df.to_markdown())
```

	date	symbol	open	high	low	close	volume
0	2024-07-12 00:00:00	TLSA	227.09	233.08	223.25	230.54	287640514

	date	symbol	open	high	low	close	volume
1	2024-07-19 00:00:00	TLSA	236.48	237.23	222.27	224.31	278397452
2	2024-07-26 00:00:00	TLSA	227.01	227.78	214.62	217.96	242932215
3	2024-08-02 00:00:00	TLSA	216.96	225.6	215.75	219.86	296061436
4	2024-08-09 00:00:00	TLSA	199.09	216.78	196	216.24	342088289
5	2024-08-16 00:00:00	TLSA	216.07	226.827	215.6	226.05	214898250
6	2024-08-23 00:00:00	TLSA	225.72	228.34	223.04	226.84	188124897
7	2024-08-30 00:00:00	TLSA	226.76	232.92	223.891	229	209486001
8	2024-09-06 00:00:00	TLSA	228.55	229	217.48	220.82	179069179
9	2024-09-13 00:00:00	TLSA	220.82	224.04	216.71	222.5	237622914
10	2024-09-20 00:00:00	TLSA	216.54	233.09	213.92	228.2	550232897
11	2024-09-27 00:00:00	TLSA	227.34	229.52	224.02	227.79	210673480
12	2024-10-04 00:00:00	TLSA	230.04	233	223.02	226.8	222348300

however we can't put into minutes...

```
import pybroker as pb
from pybroker import Strategy, ExecContext
from pybroker.ext.data import AKShare

pb.param(name='stock_code', value='TSLA')

akshare = AKShare()

df                =                akshare.query(symbols=[pb.param(name='stock_code')],
start_date='20241007000000', end_date='20241010000000', timeframe='1m')

print(df.to_markdown())

# output
Loading bar data...
Loaded bar data: 0:00:00

| symbol    | date    | open    | high    | low    | close    | volume    |
|----------|--------|--------|--------|-------|---------|----------|
```

This is the reality, never think the tool is perfect, Python is just a computer language, it is not guarantee to be correct, all things are done by people, real people, and that's why mistakes around,

```
import akshare as ak

#us_stock_current_df = ak.stock_us_spot()
#print(us_stock_current_df)
```

```
stock_us_spot_em_df = ak.stock_us_spot_em()
#print(stock_us_spot_em_df)
df = stock_us_spot_em_df.iloc[:, [1, 2, -1]]
#print(df.columns)

column_index_to_rename = 0  # Index of the 'name' column
new_column_name = 'name'
df.rename(columns={df.columns[column_index_to_rename]:              new_column_name},
inplace=True)

column_index_to_rename = 1  # Index of the 'name' column
new_column_name = 'price'
df.rename(columns={df.columns[column_index_to_rename]:              new_column_name},
inplace=True)

column_index_to_rename = -1  # Index of the 'name' column
new_column_name = 'code'
df.rename(columns={df.columns[column_index_to_rename]:              new_column_name},
inplace=True)
mask = df['code'].values == '105.TLSA'
df_new = df.loc[mask]
print(df_new)

mask = df['code'].values == '105.TSLA'
df_new = df.loc[mask]
print(df_new.iloc[:, 1:])

# output
    name  price      code
10023  Tiziana Life Sciences Ltd  0.929  105.TLSA
       price      code
3597  219.16  105.TSLA
```

OK, so we have to use TLSA for TSLA...

```
import akshare as ak

stock_us_hist_min_em_df = ak.stock_us_hist_min_em(symbol="105.TSLA")
print(stock_us_hist_min_em_df)
```

and specify the date, otherwise it would be the recent 5 days, in 1m,

```
import akshare as ak

stock_us_hist_min_em_df          =          ak.stock_us_hist_min_em(symbol="105.TSLA",
start_date='20240706', end_date='20241010')
df = stock_us_hist_min_em_df.iloc[:, [0, 3, 4, 5, 7]]
df.columns.values[[0, 1, 2, 3, 4]] = ['date', 'high', 'low', 'volume', 'price']
print(df)

# output
```

```
              date     high      low   volume     price
0    2024-10-08 21:30:00  243.765  243.765        0  243.0317
1    2024-10-08 21:31:00  245.100  243.038  2724095  243.7127
2    2024-10-08 21:32:00  245.727  244.804   647288  244.0776
3    2024-10-08 21:33:00  245.980  245.150   600357  244.3649
4    2024-10-08 21:34:00  246.210  245.500   669394  244.6115
..                   ...      ...      ...      ...       ...
927  2024-10-10 23:55:00  239.760  238.713   395439  237.6499
928  2024-10-10 23:56:00  240.400  239.726   507568  237.6763
929  2024-10-10 23:57:00  240.660  240.267   269798  237.6945
930  2024-10-10 23:58:00  241.130  240.595   302007  237.7142
931  2024-10-10 23:59:00  241.270  240.855   423051  237.7482
```

So there is minute has no trade, and the date is not starting from 0706, how about in 1010 and 1011 two days?

```
import akshare as ak

stock_us_hist_min_em_df          =          ak.stock_us_hist_min_em(symbol="105.TSLA",
start_date='20241010', end_date='20241011')
df = stock_us_hist_min_em_df.iloc[:, [0, 3, 4, 5, 6, 7]]
df.columns.values[[0, 1, 2, 3, 4, 5]] = ['date', 'high', 'low', 'volume', 'trade',
'price']
print(df)

# output

 date    high      low  volume       trade     price
0    2024-10-10 00:00:00  244.93  244.750   77599  19001560.0  243.9632
1    2024-10-10 00:01:00  244.81  244.320  134445  32869359.0  243.9650
2    2024-10-10 00:02:00  244.70  244.190  109276  26701173.0  243.9662
3    2024-10-10 00:03:00  244.43  244.070  113717  27773886.0  243.9670
4    2024-10-10 00:04:00  244.23  243.710  170430  41568675.0  243.9667
..                   ...     ...      ...     ...         ...       ...
777  2024-10-11 23:55:00  220.40  219.941  274279  60406137.0  219.8457
778  2024-10-11 23:56:00  220.14  219.940  200175  44037565.0  219.8460
779  2024-10-11 23:57:00  220.31  219.970  165290  36391934.0  219.8466
780  2024-10-11 23:58:00  220.60  220.270  280909  61934290.0  219.8485
781  2024-10-11 23:59:00  220.38  220.070  163406  35993556.0  219.8493
```

and we can get the avg price for 1m,

```
import akshare as ak

stock_us_hist_min_em_df          =          ak.stock_us_hist_min_em(symbol="105.TSLA",
start_date='20241010', end_date='20241011')
df = stock_us_hist_min_em_df.iloc[:, [0, 3, 4, 5, 6, 7]]
df.columns.values[[0, 1, 2, 3, 4, 5]] = ['date', 'high', 'low', 'volume', 'trade',
'price']
# this avg means vwmp
df = df.assign(avg=df['trade'] / df['volume'])
```

```
print(df)

# output

  date     high       low  volume       trade      price          avg
0     2024-10-10 00:00:00  244.93  244.750   77599  19001560.0  243.9632  244.868619
1     2024-10-10 00:01:00  244.81  244.320  134445  32869359.0  243.9650  244.481825
2     2024-10-10 00:02:00  244.70  244.190  109276  26701173.0  243.9662  244.346178
3     2024-10-10 00:03:00  244.43  244.070  113717  27773886.0  243.9670  244.236886
4     2024-10-10 00:04:00  244.23  243.710  170430  41568675.0  243.9667  243.904682
..                    ...     ...      ...     ...         ...       ...         ...
777   2024-10-11 23:55:00  220.40  219.941  274279  60406137.0  219.8457  220.236099
778   2024-10-11 23:56:00  220.14  219.940  200175  44037565.0  219.8460  219.995329
779   2024-10-11 23:57:00  220.31  219.970  165290  36391934.0  219.8466  220.170210
780   2024-10-11 23:58:00  220.60  220.270  280909  61934290.0  219.8485  220.478126
781   2024-10-11 23:59:00  220.38  220.070  163406  35993556.0  219.8493  220.270712
```

If the price is smaller than avg, should we buy?

```
import akshare as ak

stock_us_hist_min_em_df          =          ak.stock_us_hist_min_em(symbol="105.TSLA", start_date='20241010', end_date='20241011')
df = stock_us_hist_min_em_df.iloc[:, [0, 3, 4, 5, 6, 7]]
df.columns.values[[0, 1, 2, 3, 4, 5]] = ['date', 'high', 'low', 'volume', 'trade', 'price']

df = df.assign(avg=df['trade'] / df['volume'])
df = df.assign(sub=df['price'] - df['avg'])
#print(df)

selected_rows = df[df['sub'] < -0.9]

print(selected_rows.iloc[:, [0, -3, -1]])

# output
 date      price        sub
0     2024-10-10 00:00:00  243.9632 -0.905419
32    2024-10-10 00:32:00  243.9496 -0.975092
33    2024-10-10 00:33:00  243.9542 -0.941326
34    2024-10-10 00:34:00  243.9581 -1.190629
38    2024-10-10 00:38:00  243.9711 -1.265322
..                    ...       ...       ...
728   2024-10-11 23:06:00  219.8513 -1.206350
729   2024-10-11 23:07:00  219.8543 -1.186751
730   2024-10-11 23:08:00  219.8569 -0.957549
731   2024-10-11 23:09:00  219.8596 -0.975677
732   2024-10-11 23:10:00  219.8650 -1.348315
```

Let's try just one day, 1010

```
import akshare as ak

stock_us_hist_min_em_df        =        ak.stock_us_hist_min_em(symbol="105.TSLA",
start_date='20241010', end_date='20241010')
df = stock_us_hist_min_em_df.iloc[:, [0, 3, 4, 5, 6, 7]]
df.columns.values[[0, 1, 2, 3, 4, 5]] = ['date', 'high', 'low', 'volume', 'trade',
'price']

start_date = '2024-10-10 00:00:00'
end_date = '2024-10-10 23:59:59'

filtered_df = df[(df['date'] >= start_date) & (df['date'] <= end_date)]
print(filtered_df)

df = df[(df['date'] <= end_date)]
print(df)


df = df.assign(avg=df['trade'] / df['volume'])
df = df.assign(sub=df['price'] - df['avg'])

selected_rows = df[df['sub'] < -2.1]

print(selected_rows.shape[0])
print(selected_rows.iloc[:, [0, -3, -1]])

# output
18
                    date     price       sub
300  2024-10-10 22:29:00  236.9928 -2.104842
315  2024-10-10 22:44:00  237.1405 -2.363831
316  2024-10-10 22:45:00  237.1644 -2.438965
319  2024-10-10 22:48:00  237.1964 -2.243419
329  2024-10-10 22:58:00  237.2972 -2.295070
341  2024-10-10 23:10:00  237.3858 -2.198860
342  2024-10-10 23:11:00  237.3982 -2.429909
343  2024-10-10 23:12:00  237.4115 -2.409581
344  2024-10-10 23:13:00  237.4229 -2.449015
346  2024-10-10 23:15:00  237.4394 -2.532278
347  2024-10-10 23:16:00  237.4474 -2.150822
348  2024-10-10 23:17:00  237.4593 -2.294274
370  2024-10-10 23:39:00  237.5725 -2.345178
371  2024-10-10 23:40:00  237.5799 -2.341568
387  2024-10-10 23:56:00  237.6763 -2.477892
388  2024-10-10 23:57:00  237.6945 -3.255874
389  2024-10-10 23:58:00  237.7142 -3.163617
390  2024-10-10 23:59:00  237.7482 -3.908444
```

It just has 18 rows, which is very very little chance to buy at the common price, and notice the timezone, the data we get is based on UTC+8,

```
import akshare as ak

stock_us_hist_min_em_df          =          ak.stock_us_hist_min_em(symbol="105.TSLA",
start_date='20241010', end_date='20241010')
df = stock_us_hist_min_em_df.iloc[:, [0, 3, 4, 5, 6, 7]]
df.columns.values[[0, 1, 2, 3, 4, 5]] = ['date', 'high', 'low', 'volume', 'trade',
'price']

start_date = '2024-10-10 00:00:00'
end_date = '2024-10-10 23:59:59'

filtered_df = df[(df['date'] >= start_date) & (df['date'] <= end_date)]
print(filtered_df.info())
import pandas as pd
filtered_df['date'] = pd.to_datetime(
                          filtered_df['date'],
                          format='%Y-%m-%d %H:%M:%S'
)
#print(filtered_df.info())

df = filtered_df
from pytz import timezone
df['date'] = df['date'].dt.tz_localize(timezone('Asia/Hong_Kong'))
print(df)

df['date'] = df['date'].dt.tz_convert(timezone('America/New_York'))
df = df.assign(avg=df['trade'] / df['volume'])
df = df.assign(sub=df['price'] - df['avg'])

selected_rows = df[df['sub'] < -2.1]
print(selected_rows.shape[0])
print(selected_rows.iloc[:, [0, -3, -1]])

# output
                         date    high      low  volume        trade     price
0   2024-10-10 00:00:00+08:00  244.93  244.750   77599   19001560.0  243.9632
1   2024-10-10 00:01:00+08:00  244.81  244.320  134445   32869359.0  243.9650
2   2024-10-10 00:02:00+08:00  244.70  244.190  109276   26701173.0  243.9662
3   2024-10-10 00:03:00+08:00  244.43  244.070  113717   27773886.0  243.9670
4   2024-10-10 00:04:00+08:00  244.23  243.710  170430   41568675.0  243.9667
..                        ...     ...      ...     ...          ...       ...
386 2024-10-10 23:55:00+08:00  239.76  238.713  395439   94761347.0  237.6499
387 2024-10-10 23:56:00+08:00  240.40  239.726  507568  121894583.0  237.6763
388 2024-10-10 23:57:00+08:00  240.66  240.267  269798   65007929.0  237.6945
389 2024-10-10 23:58:00+08:00  241.13  240.595  302007   72746787.0  237.7142
390 2024-10-10 23:59:00+08:00  241.27  240.855  423051  102233085.0  237.7482

[391 rows x 6 columns]
18
                         date     price       sub
300 2024-10-10 10:29:00-04:00  236.9928 -2.104842
315 2024-10-10 10:44:00-04:00  237.1405 -2.363831
316 2024-10-10 10:45:00-04:00  237.1644 -2.438965
```

```
319 2024-10-10 10:48:00-04:00  237.1964 -2.243419
329 2024-10-10 10:58:00-04:00  237.2972 -2.295070
341 2024-10-10 11:10:00-04:00  237.3858 -2.198860
342 2024-10-10 11:11:00-04:00  237.3982 -2.429909
343 2024-10-10 11:12:00-04:00  237.4115 -2.409581
344 2024-10-10 11:13:00-04:00  237.4229 -2.449015
346 2024-10-10 11:15:00-04:00  237.4394 -2.532278
347 2024-10-10 11:16:00-04:00  237.4474 -2.150822
348 2024-10-10 11:17:00-04:00  237.4593 -2.294274
370 2024-10-10 11:39:00-04:00  237.5725 -2.345178
371 2024-10-10 11:40:00-04:00  237.5799 -2.341568
387 2024-10-10 11:56:00-04:00  237.6763 -2.477892
388 2024-10-10 11:57:00-04:00  237.6945 -3.255874
389 2024-10-10 11:58:00-04:00  237.7142 -3.163617
390 2024-10-10 11:59:00-04:00  237.7482 -3.908444
```

The time implies the hotness of the trade, and mostly in the morning, in New York, because the NASDAQ is there. And `akshare` is based in Beijing, which market opens at 2130, and close 400.

```
from pytz import all_timezones
#for i in all_timezones: print(i)

import akshare as ak
#version 1.14
stock = "105.ASML"
st = '2024-10-15 21:30:00'
et = '2024-10-16 04:00:00'
print(stock, ":", st, "->", et, "HK")
stock_us_hist_min_em_df    =    ak.stock_us_hist_min_em(symbol=stock,    start_date=st,
end_date=et)
df = stock_us_hist_min_em_df.iloc[:, [0, 3, 4, 5, 6, 7]]
df.columns.values[[0, 1, 2, 3, 4, 5]] = ['date', 'high', 'low', 'volume', 'trade',
'price']
print(df)
convert_df = df
import pandas as pd
convert_df['date'] = pd.to_datetime(
                          df['date'],
                          format='%Y-%m-%d %H:%M:%S'
)

from pytz import timezone
df['date'] = convert_df['date'].dt.tz_localize(timezone('Asia/Hong_Kong'))
print(df)#.to_markdown())

df['date'] = df['date'].dt.tz_convert(timezone('America/New_York'))
print(df)#.to_markdown())


# output
105.ASML : 2024-10-15 21:30:00 -> 2024-10-16 04:00:00 HK
```

```
                    date     high      low  volume        trade     price
0     2024-10-15 21:30:00  867.220  867.220       0          0.0  866.1480
1     2024-10-15 21:31:00  869.850  867.000   82529   71575815.0  867.2808
2     2024-10-15 21:32:00  871.360  868.110    9884    8594639.0  867.5236
3     2024-10-15 21:33:00  872.855  870.015   17716   15426965.0  868.0495
4     2024-10-15 21:34:00  873.500  870.980   14556   12688206.0  868.4736
..                    ...      ...      ...     ...          ...       ...
386   2024-10-16 03:56:00  728.950  728.010   44090   31965896.0  753.2675
387   2024-10-16 03:57:00  728.875  728.010   32732   23818546.0  753.1720
388   2024-10-16 03:58:00  729.700  728.840   67083   48623115.0  752.9566
389   2024-10-16 03:59:00  729.990  729.210   52364   37857585.0  752.7798
390   2024-10-16 04:00:00  730.800  729.750  468032  337607600.0  751.2059

[391 rows x 6 columns]
C:\Users\Lenovo\Flask\stock\ak1_stock.py:30: SettingWithCopyWarning:
A value is trying to be set on a copy of a slice from a DataFrame.
Try using .loc[row_indexer,col_indexer] = value instead

See the caveats in the documentation: https://pandas.pydata.org/pandas-docs/stable/user_guide/indexing.html#returning-a-view-versus-a-copy
  convert_df['date'] = pd.to_datetime(
C:\Users\Lenovo\Flask\stock\ak1_stock.py:36: SettingWithCopyWarning:
A value is trying to be set on a copy of a slice from a DataFrame.
Try using .loc[row_indexer,col_indexer] = value instead

See the caveats in the documentation: https://pandas.pydata.org/pandas-docs/stable/user_guide/indexing.html#returning-a-view-versus-a-copy
  df['date'] = convert_df['date'].dt.tz_localize(timezone('Asia/Hong_Kong'))
                         date     high      low  volume        trade     price
0   2024-10-15 21:30:00+08:00  867.220  867.220       0          0.0  866.1480
1   2024-10-15 21:31:00+08:00  869.850  867.000   82529   71575815.0  867.2808
2   2024-10-15 21:32:00+08:00  871.360  868.110    9884    8594639.0  867.5236
3   2024-10-15 21:33:00+08:00  872.855  870.015   17716   15426965.0  868.0495
4   2024-10-15 21:34:00+08:00  873.500  870.980   14556   12688206.0  868.4736
..                        ...      ...      ...     ...          ...       ...
386 2024-10-16 03:56:00+08:00  728.950  728.010   44090   31965896.0  753.2675
387 2024-10-16 03:57:00+08:00  728.875  728.010   32732   23818546.0  753.1720
388 2024-10-16 03:58:00+08:00  729.700  728.840   67083   48623115.0  752.9566
389 2024-10-16 03:59:00+08:00  729.990  729.210   52364   37857585.0  752.7798
390 2024-10-16 04:00:00+08:00  730.800  729.750  468032  337607600.0  751.2059

[391 rows x 6 columns]
C:\Users\Lenovo\Flask\stock\ak1_stock.py:39: SettingWithCopyWarning:
A value is trying to be set on a copy of a slice from a DataFrame.
Try using .loc[row_indexer,col_indexer] = value instead

See the caveats in the documentation: https://pandas.pydata.org/pandas-docs/stable/user_guide/indexing.html#returning-a-view-versus-a-copy
  df['date'] = df['date'].dt.tz_convert(timezone('America/New_York'))
                         date     high      low  volume        trade     price
0   2024-10-15 09:30:00-04:00  867.220  867.220       0          0.0  866.1480
1   2024-10-15 09:31:00-04:00  869.850  867.000   82529   71575815.0  867.2808
2   2024-10-15 09:32:00-04:00  871.360  868.110    9884    8594639.0  867.5236
```

```
3   2024-10-15 09:33:00-04:00  872.855  870.015   17716   15426965.0  868.0495
4   2024-10-15 09:34:00-04:00  873.500  870.980   14556   12688206.0  868.4736
..                        ...      ...      ...     ...          ...       ...
386 2024-10-15 15:56:00-04:00  728.950  728.010   44090   31965896.0  753.2675
387 2024-10-15 15:57:00-04:00  728.875  728.010   32732   23818546.0  753.1720
388 2024-10-15 15:58:00-04:00  729.700  728.840   67083   48623115.0  752.9566
389 2024-10-15 15:59:00-04:00  729.990  729.210   52364   37857585.0  752.7798
390 2024-10-15 16:00:00-04:00  730.800  729.750  468032  337607600.0  751.2059

[391 rows x 6 columns]
```

continue to draw,

```
import matplotlib.pyplot as plt

plt.figure()
#print(df.index, df['date'])

plt.plot(df['date'], df['price'])
plt.gcf().autofmt_xdate()

plt.title('Prices For the Period in One Day (NYC)')

plt.show()
```

we can draw it into scatter too,

```
import matplotlib.pyplot as plt
import matplotlib.dates as mdates

# Plot the data
fig, ax = plt.subplots(figsize=(10,6))

date_format = mdates.DateFormatter('%H:%M')
ax.xaxis.set_major_formatter(date_format)
ax.grid(True)

ax.scatter(df['date'].dt.tz_convert(timezone('America/New_York'))

           df['price'],
           color='purple')
ax.set(xlabel="Date", ylabel="Price",
       title="Price in one day")
plt.xticks(rotation=45)
plt.title('Price in one day', fontweight ="bold")
plt.show()
```

But the time is in UTC, how to make it in NYC?

Aww, just remove the timezone...

```
# Create a datetime object with a timezone and remove it
dt = datetime(2021, 8, 10, 12, 0, 0, tzinfo=timezone('America/New_York'))
# Remove the timezone information
dt = dt.replace(tzinfo=None)
print(dt)

# Our part that timezone needs to be removed
import matplotlib.pyplot as plt
import matplotlib.dates as mdates

# Plot the data
fig, ax = plt.subplots(figsize=(10,6))

date_format = mdates.DateFormatter('%H:%M')
ax.xaxis.set_major_formatter(date_format)
ax.grid(True)
dt = df['date'].dt.tz_localize(None)
ax.scatter(dt,

           df['price'],
           color='purple')
ax.set(xlabel="Date", ylabel="Price",
       title="Price in one day")
plt.xticks(rotation=45)
plt.title('Price in one day', fontweight ="bold")
plt.show()
```

It takes a lot of time to find the matching function, which is really so tired sometimes, because it can take four or five hours, just try...

Can we make a try block for the function under?

```
dt = df['date'].dt.tz_localize(None)

for i in dir(df['date'].dt): print(i)

import sys
sys.exit("...trying...")
# just try before
ax.scatter(dt,
```

and can we just call?

```
for i in dir(df['date'].dt): print('df['date'].dt.'+i)
```

common way to do so is using `getattr`,

```
#for i in dir(df['date'].dt): print(i)
for i in dir(df['date'].dt): #print("df['date'].dt."+i)
    r = getattr(df['date'].dt, i)
```

```
    try:
        # calling the function and storing the result
        result = r()
        print("calling...", i, res)
    except:
        print("printing...", i, r)
    finally:
        print("but...", i, "is not callable")


import sys
sys.exit("...trying...")

# part of output
printing... tz America/New_York
but... tz is not callable
printing... tz_convert <bound method PandasDelegate._add_delegate_accessors.
<locals>._create_delegator_method.<locals>.f of
<pandas.core.indexes.accessors.DatetimeProperties object at 0x00000150A3361130>>
but... tz_convert is not callable
printing... tz_localize <bound method PandasDelegate._add_delegate_accessors.
<locals>._create_delegator_method.<locals>.f of
<pandas.core.indexes.accessors.DatetimeProperties object at 0x00000150A3361130>>
but... tz_localize is not callable
```

So from the output we can find three tz related vars, and we can use `eval` too,

```
for i in dir(df['date'].dt): #print()
    expression = "df['date'].dt."+i

    try:
        result = eval(expression)
        print(f"evalu... of {expression} is {result}")

    except:

        print(f"but... {expression} is not evaluable")


import sys
```

we finally can draw lines for high, average, low, and with a time cover,

```
import akshare as ak
stock = "105.ASML"
st = '2024-10-15 21:30:00'
et = '2024-10-16 04:00:00'
print(stock, ":", st, "->", et)
stock_us_hist_min_em_df = ak.stock_us_hist_min_em(symbol=stock, start_date=st,
end_date=et)
df = stock_us_hist_min_em_df.iloc[:, [0, 3, 4, 5, 6, 7]]
df.columns.values[[0, 1, 2, 3, 4, 5]] = ['date', 'high', 'low', 'volume', 'trade',
```

```
'price']

df = df.assign(avg=df['trade'] / df['volume'])
#print(vars(df['date']))
convert_df = df

import pandas as pd
convert_df['date'] = pd.to_datetime(
                          df['date'],
                          format='%Y-%m-%d %H:%M:%S'
)

print((convert_df['date'].dt.tz))

import matplotlib.pyplot as plt
import matplotlib.dates as mdates

# Plot the data
fig, ax = plt.subplots(figsize=(10,6))

date_format = mdates.DateFormatter('%H:%M')
ax.xaxis.set_major_formatter(date_format)
ax.grid(True)
dt = convert_df['date']
ax.plot(dt,

           convert_df['high'],
           color='red')
ax.plot(dt,

           convert_df['avg'],
           color='green')

ax.plot(dt,

           convert_df['low'],
           color='blue')
ax.set(xlabel="Date", ylabel="Price")
plt.xticks(rotation=45)
plt.title('Price in one day (HK)', fontweight ="bold")

plt.axvspan(datetime(2024, 10, 15, 22, 30, 0), datetime(2024, 10, 15, 23, 30, 0),
facecolor='yellow', alpha=0.5, hatch='/', edgecolor='red', linewidth=2)

plt.show()
```

and resample the data into hour, find the mean,

```
# can change the plot non block
plt.show(block=False)

df['change'] = df['high'] - df['low']
```

```
change = df.set_index('date').resample('h')['change'].mean()

print("hourly price change:\n", change)
```

sample has two kinds, up and down, because the library does not give us the every trade, so the price, newest one is just a sample, and the estimate can be dangerous, when dealing with real money! One minute has 60 seconds, that is a lot of money, and we are using the price, which is not really newest, laggy! Very dangerous with real money!、

```
import finnhub
finnhub_client = finnhub.Client(api_key="api_key")
d = (finnhub_client.symbol_lookup('ASML'))
for k in d['result']: print(k)
d = finnhub_client.quote('ASML')
from datetime import datetime
sse = d['t']
dtobject = datetime.fromtimestamp(sse)
print("The datetime object is :",dtobject)
#print(finnhub_client.company_peers('ASML'))

order = ["finnhub_client.company_profile(symbol='ASML')",
"finnhub_client.ownership('ASML', limit=5)",
"finnhub_client.stock_tick('ASML', '2024-10-15', 500, 0)"]
for i in order:
    try:
        print(eval(i))
    except Exception as e:
        print(f"Exception: {e}")

# output
{'description': 'ASML HOLDING NV', 'displaySymbol': 'ASML.AS', 'symbol': 'ASML.AS',
'type': 'Common Stock'}
{'description': 'ASML HOLDING NV-NY REG SHS', 'displaySymbol': 'ASML', 'symbol':
'ASML', 'type': 'NY Reg Shrs'}
{'description': 'ASML HOLDING NV', 'displaySymbol': 'ASML.SW', 'symbol': 'ASML.SW',
'type': 'Common Stock'}
{'description': 'ASML HOLDING NV', 'displaySymbol': 'ASML.WA', 'symbol': 'ASML.WA',
'type': 'Common Stock'}
{'description': 'ASML HOLDING NV', 'displaySymbol': 'ASML.VI', 'symbol': 'ASML.VI',
'type': 'Common Stock'}
{'description': 'ASML HOLDING NV', 'displaySymbol': 'ASMLF', 'symbol': 'ASMLF',
'type': 'Common Stock'}
{'description': 'ASMPT LTD', 'displaySymbol': 'ASMVF', 'symbol': 'ASMVF', 'type':
'Common Stock'}
{'description': 'ASMPT LTD', 'displaySymbol': 'AY7A.HA', 'symbol': 'AY7A.HA',
'type': 'Common Stock'}
{'description': 'ASMPT LTD', 'displaySymbol': 'AY7A.SG', 'symbol': 'AY7A.SG',
'type': 'Common Stock'}
{'description': 'ASMPT LTD', 'displaySymbol': '522.HK', 'symbol': '522.HK', 'type':
'Common Stock'}
{'description': 'ASMPT LTD', 'displaySymbol': 'AY7A.MU', 'symbol': 'AY7A.MU',
```

```
'type': 'Common Stock'}
{'description': 'ASMPT LTD', 'displaySymbol': 'AY7A.F', 'symbol': 'AY7A.F', 'type': 'Common Stock'}
{'description': 'ASMPT LTD', 'displaySymbol': 'AY7A.TG', 'symbol': 'AY7A.TG', 'type': 'Common Stock'}
{'description': 'ASMPT LTD', 'displaySymbol': 'AY7A.BE', 'symbol': 'AY7A.BE', 'type': 'Common Stock'}
{'description': 'ASMPT LTD', 'displaySymbol': 'AY7A.SW', 'symbol': 'AY7A.SW', 'type': 'Common Stock'}
{'description': 'ASMPT LTD', 'displaySymbol': 'AY7A.DU', 'symbol': 'AY7A.DU', 'type': 'Common Stock'}
{'description': 'ASHIMA LTD', 'displaySymbol': '514286.BO', 'symbol': '514286.BO', 'type': 'Common Stock'}
{'description': 'TASMEA LTD', 'displaySymbol': 'TEA.AX', 'symbol': 'TEA.AX', 'type': 'Common Stock'}
{'description': 'ASHIMA LTD', 'displaySymbol': 'ASHIMASYN.NS', 'symbol': 'ASHIMASYN.NS', 'type': 'Common Stock'}
{'description': 'ASML Holding', 'displaySymbol': 'A28T1T.HM', 'symbol': 'A28T1T.HM', 'type': ''}
{'description': 'ASML Holding', 'displaySymbol': 'A3LJG7.DU', 'symbol': 'A3LJG7.DU', 'type': ''}
{'description': 'ASML Holding', 'displaySymbol': 'A18304.MU', 'symbol': 'A18304.MU', 'type': ''}
{'description': 'ASML Holding', 'displaySymbol': 'A3K5LQ.HA', 'symbol': 'A3K5LQ.HA', 'type': ''}
The datetime object is : 2024-10-19 04:00:00
Exception: FinnhubAPIException(status_code: 403): You don't have access to this resource.
Exception: FinnhubAPIException(status_code: 403): You don't have access to this resource.
Exception: FinnhubAPIException(status_code: 403): You don't have access to this resource.
```

403 means we don’t have the right to pull data, so we must buy tick data if we really want every trade.

37 Minute

What we really want to do is trade, and the estimate price close to the real, to earn, not to lose.

```
import finnhub
finnhub_client = finnhub.Client(api_key="api key")

response = finnhub_client.stock_symbols('US')
import pandas as pd
response_df = pd.DataFrame.from_records(response)
print(response_df.shape)
#print(response_df.head())
```

```
response = finnhub_client.company_basic_financials('ASML', 'all')
response_df = pd.DataFrame.from_records(response)
#print(response_df.shape)
print(response_df)

response = finnhub_client.recommendation_trends('ASML')
response_df = pd.DataFrame.from_records(response)
print(response_df.head(6))

response = finnhub_client.company_earnings('ASML')
response_df = pd.DataFrame.from_records(response)
print(response_df)

# output
(27308, 10)
                                                           metric  metricType
series   symbol
10DayAverageTradingVolume                        1.01513                 all
NaN  ASML.AS
13WeekPriceReturnDaily                            -21.8695               all
NaN  ASML.AS
26WeekPriceReturnDaily                            -19.0621               all
NaN  ASML.AS
3MonthADReturnStd                                   54.976776            all
NaN  ASML.AS
3MonthAverageTradingVolume                      0.68057                  all
NaN  ASML.AS
...                                                      ...             ...
...       ...
totalDebt/totalEquityAnnual                      0.2998                  all
NaN  ASML.AS
totalDebt/totalEquityQuarterly               0.2581                      all
NaN  ASML.AS
yearToDatePriceReturnDaily                      -2.5231                  all
NaN  ASML.AS
annual                                  NaN         all  {'bookValue': [{'period':
'2023-12-31', 'v': 1...  ASML.AS
quarterly                                  NaN          all   {'assetTurnoverTTM':
[{'period': '2024-06-30',...  ASML.AS

[128 rows x 4 columns]
   buy  hold      period  sell  strongBuy  strongSell   symbol
0   24     7  2024-10-01     1         11           0  ASML.AS
1   25     6  2024-09-01     1         11           0  ASML.AS
2   24     5  2024-08-01     1         11           0  ASML.AS
3   24     6  2024-07-01     1         11           0  ASML.AS
   actual  estimate      period  quarter  surprise  surprisePercent   symbol  year
0    4.01    3.7634  2024-06-30        2    0.2466           6.5526  ASML.AS  2024
1    3.11    2.8166  2024-03-31        1    0.2934          10.4168  ASML.AS  2024
2    5.20    4.8555  2023-12-31        4    0.3445           7.0950  ASML.AS  2023
3    4.81    4.6826  2023-09-30        3    0.1274           2.7207  ASML.AS  2023
```

So there are 27308 stocks in US market, and if we want to just ASML, the trend, it shows only twenties buy? Can this be true?

There are too many data can be true or can be meaningless, how do we handle?

From the start, we should know a trade is made by two sides, one buy and one sell. It must have a time, and that is how tick form, a time and a price. Many ticks form a range of price in a time duration. If we select some ticks, then we are downsampling, in a certain time, maybe one minute, in fact there could be trade in second simultaneously.

Generally second is the smallest measurement, which is all people's common sense. And then minute, hour, day, week, month, year. Warren Buffet once said, if you aren't thinking about owning a stock for 10 years, don't even think about owning it for 10 minutes. Take three stocks for understanding, if you invested $1,000 Amazon before, in 2010, you'd have $21,121, if you invested $1,000 Apple, in 2008, you'd have $43,917, and $1,000 Netflix, in 2004, you'd have $370,844.

But there are many people doing short sale, less than 1 minutes some times, because the slope, is really jumping too too fast.

Besides, is the data really true?

5 min? 1 min?

```
from urllib.request import urlopen
import certifi
import json

def get_jsonparsed_data(url):
    response = urlopen(url, cafile=certifi.where())
    data = response.read().decode("utf-8")
    return json.loads(data)

bak = "https://financialmodelingprep.com/api/v3/stock/full/real-time-price/AMSL"
bak = "https://financialmodelingprep.com/api/v3/financial-statement-symbol-lists"
bak = "https://financialmodelingprep.com/api/v3/quote-short/ASML"
url = (bak + "?apikey=api key")
print(get_jsonparsed_data(url))

bak = "https://financialmodelingprep.com/api/v3/quote/ASML"
url = (bak + "?apikey=api key")
d = (get_jsonparsed_data(url))
for k, v in d[0].items(): print(k, v)
from datetime import datetime
sse = d[0]['timestamp']
dtobject = datetime.fromtimestamp(sse)
```

```
print("The datetime object is :",dtobject)

api = "apikey=api key"
bak = "https://financialmodelingprep.com/api/v3/stock/full/real-time-price/ASML"
url = (bak + "?"+api)
d = (get_jsonparsed_data(url))
#for k, v in d[0].items(): print(k, v)
print(d)

print("std")
bak = "https://financialmodelingprep.com/api/v3/technical_indicator/5min/ASML"
url = bak + "?" + "type=standardDeviation&period=10&" + api
d=(get_jsonparsed_data(url))
print(type(d), d.reverse())

print("chart")
bak = "https://financialmodelingprep.com/api/v3/historical-chart/1min/ASML"
url = bak + "?" + "from=2024-10-15&to=2024-10-16&" + api
d=(get_jsonparsed_data(url))
for i in d[::-1]:
    for k, v in i.items():
        print(k, v)
```

How to make sure?

```
from urllib.request import urlopen
import certifi
import json

def get_jsonparsed_data(url):
    response = urlopen(url, cafile=certifi.where())
    data = response.read().decode("utf-8")
    return json.loads(data)

api = "api key"

print("chart")
bak = "https://financialmodelingprep.com/api/v3/historical-chart/1min/ASML"
url = bak + "?" + "from=2024-10-15&to=2024-10-16&" + api
d=(get_jsonparsed_data(url))


print(type(d))
import pandas as pd
df = pd.DataFrame(d[::-1])

print(df)

import akshare as ak
#version 1.14
stock = "105.ASML"
st = '2024-10-16 21:30:00'
et = '2024-10-17 03:59:00'
```

```
print(stock, ":", st, "->", et, "HK")
stock_us_hist_min_em_df = ak.stock_us_hist_min_em(symbol=stock, start_date=st,
end_date=et)
#df = stock_us_hist_min_em_df

df2 = stock_us_hist_min_em_df.iloc[:, [0, 1, 4, 3, 2, 5]]
df2.columns.values[[0, 1, 2, 3, 4, 5]] = ['date', 'open', 'low', 'high', 'close',
'volume']
print(df2)

print(df.equals(df2)) # False
```

This is a big big problem...

How come two df does not equal? Notice the date...

```
st2 = '2024-10-16 09:30:00'
et2 = '2024-10-16 15:59:00'
print(stock, ":", st2, "->", et2, "NY")
filtered_df = df[(df['date'] >= st2) & (df['date'] <= et2)]

a = (filtered_df.tail(60)['volume'])
b = (df2.tail(59)['volume'])
print(pd.concat([d.reset_index(drop=True) for d in [a, b]], axis=1))
```

The last line even have a nan...

What is the last price?

```
from urllib.request import urlopen
import certifi
import json

def get_jsonparsed_data(url):
    response = urlopen(url, cafile=certifi.where())
    data = response.read().decode("utf-8")
    return json.loads(data)

bak = "https://financialmodelingprep.com/api/v3/quote-short/ASML"
url = (bak + "?apikey=api key")
print(get_jsonparsed_data(url))

url = "https://financialmodelingprep.com/api/v3/stock/full/real-time-price/ASML?
apikey=api key"
d=(get_jsonparsed_data(url))
print(d)

# output
[{'symbol': 'ASML', 'price': 723.26, 'volume': 4522898}]
[{'bidSize': 11, 'askPrice': 722.84, 'volume': 4531049, 'askSize': 3, 'bidPrice':
722, 'lastSalePrice': 722.9, 'lastSaleSize': 100, 'lastSaleTime': 1729293076308,
```

```
'fmpLast': 722.9, 'lastUpdated': 1729295971715, 'symbol': 'ASML'}]
The datetime object is : 2001-06-12 19:34:38
```

Ok, here is another problem, why is the 1729293076308? Not even a right time...

```
url = ("https://financialmodelingprep.com/api/v4/pre-post-market-trade/ASML?apikey=api key")
print(get_jsonparsed_data(url)) # fail because close...
```

We again see the dangerous by using the data from third party, it just can be wrong, and the real money will just gone...

So we better just do the test using third party, and we have to use IB or Futu, when we really want to trade, we can also use some tech or lib to combine, but the source data must be in good condition. Checkout https://www.eoddata.com/stockquote/NASDAQ/ASML.htm?e=NASDAQ&s=ASML, here we can download csv for different duration, but we have to pay for intraday too.

Checkout https://oneminutedata.com/aapl-intraday-data, here we can download some data, and we can compare with the day we want.

```
print("AAPL\n10.14 moring - 10.14 afternoon NY\n10.14 evening - 10.15 morning HK")
from urllib.request import urlopen
import certifi
import json
print("api")

def get_jsonparsed_data(url):
    response = urlopen(url, cafile=certifi.where())
    data = response.read().decode("utf-8")
    return json.loads(data)

url = ("https://financialmodelingprep.com/api/v3/historical-chart/1min/TSLA?from=2024-03-14&to=2024-03-15&apikey=api key")
d = (get_jsonparsed_data(url))

import pandas as pd
df = pd.DataFrame(d[::-1])
#print(df)
st = '2024-10-14 09:30:00'
et = '2024-10-14 15:59:00'
stock = "APPL"
print(stock, ":", st, "->", et, "NY")
filtered_df = df[(df['date'] >= st) & (df['date'] <= et)]

print(filtered_df.iloc[:, [0, 1, 3, 2, 4, 5]])

print("csv")
# Reading a CSV file
```

```
df = pd.read_csv('aapl_2024.csv')
st = '2024-10-14 09:30:00'
et = '2024-10-14 15:59:00'
stock = "AAPL"
print(stock, ":", st, "->", et, "NY")
filtered_df = df[(df['date'] >= st) & (df['date'] <= et)]
print(filtered_df)

print("ak")

import akshare as ak

#version 1.14
stock = "105.AAPL"
st = '2024-10-14 21:30:00'
et = '2024-10-15 03:59:00'
print(stock, ":", st, "->", et, "HK")
stock_us_hist_min_em_df    =    ak.stock_us_hist_min_em(symbol=stock,    start_date=st,
end_date=et)
#df = stock_us_hist_min_em_df

df2 = stock_us_hist_min_em_df.iloc[:, [0, 1, 3, 4, 2, 5]]
df2.columns.values[[0, 1, 2, 3, 4, 5]] = ['date', 'open', 'high', 'low', 'close',
'volume']
print(df2)
```

Checkout https://www.morningstar.com/stocks/xnas/aapl/chart, even volume are not same, we are so lost...

38 mplfinance

The common data catagories are open, high, low, close, for a particular time, can be minute, hour, day, week, let's continue use the csv, to draw the price graph.

```
import pandas as pd
print("csv")
# Reading a CSV file
df = pd.read_csv('aapl_2024.csv')
st = '2024-02-14 09:30:00'
et = '2024-03-14 15:59:00'
stock = "AAPL"
print(stock, ":", st, "->", et, "NY")
filtered_df = df[(df['date'] >= st) & (df['date'] <= et)]
#print(filtered_df)
print(8190/390)

stock_prices = filtered_df.reset_index()

import matplotlib.pyplot as plt
plt.figure()
```

```
# "up" dataframe will store the stock_prices
# when the closing stock price is greater
# than or equal to the opening stock prices
up = stock_prices[stock_prices.close >= stock_prices.open]

# "down" dataframe will store the stock_prices
# when the closing stock price is
# lesser than the opening stock prices
down = stock_prices[stock_prices.close < stock_prices.open]

# When the stock prices have decreased, then it
# will be represented by blue color candlestick
col1 = 'blue'

# When the stock prices have increased, then it
# will be represented by green color candlestick
col2 = 'green'

# Setting width of candlestick elements
width = .8
width2 = .08

# Plotting up prices of the stock
plt.bar(up.index, up.close-up.open, width, bottom=up.open, color=col1)
plt.bar(up.index, up.high-up.close, width2, bottom=up.close, color=col1)
plt.bar(up.index, up.low-up.open, width2, bottom=up.open, color=col1)

# Plotting down prices of the stock
plt.bar(down.index, down.close-down.open, width, bottom=down.open, color=col2)
plt.bar(down.index, down.high-down.open, width2, bottom=down.open, color=col2)
plt.bar(down.index, down.low-down.close, width2, bottom=down.close, color=col2)

# rotating the x-axis tick labels at 30degree
# towards right
plt.xticks(rotation=30, ha='right')

# displaying candlestick chart of stock data
# of a week
plt.show()
```

We can also draw just one day, by mpl,

```
import pandas as pd
print("csv")
# Reading a CSV file
df = pd.read_csv('aapl_2024.csv')
st = '2024-02-14 09:30:00'
et = '2024-02-14 15:59:00'
stock = "AAPL"
print(stock, ":", st, "->", et, "NY")
filtered_df = df[(df['date'] >= st) & (df['date'] <= et)]
#print(filtered_df)
```

```
print(8190/390)

data = filtered_df.reset_index()
df.set_index ('date', inplace= True)
data.index = pd.to_datetime(data.index)

import mplfinance as mpf

mpf.plot(data)
```

But the time axis, showing all 00:00 is not good, so we refresh the date index by select date,

```
import pandas as pd
print("csv")
# Reading a CSV file
data = pd.read_csv('aapl_2024.csv', index_col=0)
data.index = pd.to_datetime(data.index)
st = '2024-02-14 09:30:00'
et = '2024-02-14 15:59:00'
iday = data.loc[st:et,:]
import mplfinance as mpf

mpf.plot(iday, type="candle")
```

we can also directly set the index,

```
import pandas as pd
print("csv")
# Reading a CSV file
data = pd.read_csv('aapl_2024.csv', index_col=0)
data.index = pd.to_datetime(data.date)

import mplfinance as mpf

mpf.plot(data, type="candle")
```

The most convienient thing in mpf is quickly adding volume,

```
import pandas as pd
print("csv")
# Reading a CSV file
intraday = pd.read_csv('aapl_2024.csv', index_col=0)
intraday.index = pd.to_datetime(intraday.index)
st = '2024-02-14 09:30:00'
et = '2024-02-14 15:59:00'
iday = intraday.loc[st:et,:]
import mplfinance as mpf

mpf.plot(iday, type="candle", volume=True)
```

and moving average,

```
import pandas as pd
print("csv")
# Reading a CSV file
intraday = pd.read_csv('aapl_2024.csv', index_col=0)
intraday.index = pd.to_datetime(intraday.index)
st = '2024-02-14 09:30:00'
et = '2024-02-14 15:59:00'
iday = intraday.loc[st:et,:]
import mplfinance as mpf

mpf.plot(iday, type="candle", volume=True, mav=(7,12))
```

and for macd,

```
import pandas as pd
print("csv")
# Reading a CSV file
intraday = pd.read_csv('aapl_2024.csv', index_col=0)
intraday.index = pd.to_datetime(intraday.index)
st = '2024-02-14 09:30:00'
et = '2024-02-14 15:59:00'
iday = intraday.loc[st:et,:]
import mplfinance as mpf

#mpf.plot(iday, type="candle", volume=True, mav=(7,12))

def MACD(df, window_slow, window_fast, window_signal):
    macd = pd.DataFrame()
    macd['ema_slow'] = df['close'].ewm(span=window_slow).mean()
    macd['ema_fast'] = df['close'].ewm(span=window_fast).mean()
    macd['macd'] = macd['ema_slow'] - macd['ema_fast']
    macd['signal'] = macd['macd'].ewm(span=window_signal).mean()
    macd['diff'] = macd['macd'] - macd['signal']
    macd['bar_positive'] = macd['diff'].map(lambda x: x if x > 0 else 0)
    macd['bar_negative'] = macd['diff'].map(lambda x: x if x < 0 else 0)
    return macd

macd = MACD(iday, 12, 26, 9)
macd_plot = [
mpf.make_addplot((macd['macd']),     color='#606060',     panel=2,     ylabel='MACD', 
secondary_y=False),
mpf.make_addplot((macd['signal']), color='#1f77b4', panel=2, secondary_y=False),
mpf.make_addplot((macd['bar_positive']), type='bar', color='#4dc790', panel=2),
mpf.make_addplot((macd['bar_negative']), type='bar', color='#fd6b6c', panel=2),
]

mpf.plot(iday, type='candle', volume=True, addplot=macd_plot)
```

and for stochastic,

```
import pandas as pd
print("csv")
# Reading a CSV file
intraday = pd.read_csv('aapl_2024.csv', index_col=0)
intraday.index = pd.to_datetime(intraday.index)
st = '2024-02-14 09:30:00'
et = '2024-02-14 15:59:00'
iday = intraday.loc[st:et,:]
import mplfinance as mpf

def Stochastic(df, window, smooth_window):
    stochastic = pd.DataFrame()
    stochastic['%K'] = ((df['close'] - df['low'].rolling(window).min()) \
    / (df['high'].rolling(window).max() - df['low'].rolling(window).min())) * 100
    stochastic['%D'] = stochastic['%K'].rolling(smooth_window).mean()
    stochastic['%SD'] = stochastic['%D'].rolling(smooth_window).mean()
    stochastic['UL'] = 80
    stochastic['DL'] = 20
    return stochastic

stochastic = Stochastic(iday, 14, 3)
stochastic_plot = [
mpf.make_addplot((stochastic[['%K',  '%D',  '%SD',  'UL',  'DL']]),  ylim=[0,  100],
panel=2, ylabel='Stoch')
]

mpf.plot(iday, type='candle', volume=True, addplot=stochastic_plot)
```

we can also save the plot, so we can zoom,

```
import pandas as pd
print("csv")
# Reading a CSV file
intraday = pd.read_csv('aapl_2024.csv', index_col=0)
intraday.index = pd.to_datetime(intraday.index)
st = '2024-02-14 09:30:00'
et = '2024-02-14 15:59:00'
data = intraday.loc[st:et,:]
import mplfinance as mpf

mpf.plot(data, type='candle', style='charles',
            title='AAPL 2024-02-14',
            ylabel='Price ($)',
            ylabel_lower='Shares \nTraded',
            volume=True,
            mav=(3,6,9),
            savefig='aapl-mplfiance.png')
```

To draw ohlc, where ohlc means open, high, low, close,

```
import pandas as pd
print("csv")
# Reading a CSV file
intraday = pd.read_csv('aapl_2024.csv', index_col=0)
intraday.index = pd.to_datetime(intraday.index)
st = '2024-02-14 13:30:00'
et = '2024-02-14 15:59:00'
iday = intraday.loc[st:et,:]
import mplfinance as mpf

mpf.plot(iday, type='ohlc', mav=5, 10, 20) # green, purple, yellow
```

we can change a style and set ratio to make the figure larger,

```
import pandas as pd
print("csv")
# Reading a CSV file
intraday = pd.read_csv('aapl_2024.csv', index_col=0)
intraday.index = pd.to_datetime(intraday.index)
st = '2024-02-14 13:30:00'
et = '2024-02-14 15:59:00'
import mplfinance as mpf
afternoon = intraday.loc[st:et,:]
mpf.plot(afternoon, # the dataframe containing the OHLC (Open, High, Low and Close)
data
         type='ohlc', # use candlesticks
         volume=True, # also show the volume
         mav=(5,10,20), # use three different moving averages
         figratio=(3,1), # set the ratio of the figure
         style='yahoo',  # choose the yahoo style
         title='AAPL 2024-02-14 afternoon')
#from mplfinance import _styles
#_styles.available_styles() # ['binance', 'blueskies', 'brasil', 'charles',
'checkers', 'classic', 'default', 'ibd', 'kenan', 'mike', 'nightclouds',
'sas', 'starsandstripes', 'yahoo']
```

It is better to add self define function, than to directly use the plot embeded function, since we can print the data, and if we trade, we don't need the graph, number is good enough,

```
import pandas as pd
print("csv")
# Reading a CSV file
intraday = pd.read_csv('aapl_2024.csv', index_col=0)
intraday.index = pd.to_datetime(intraday.index)
st = '2024-02-14 13:30:00'
et = '2024-02-14 15:59:00'
import mplfinance as mpf
afternoon = intraday.loc[st:et,:]

def RSI(df, window):
```

```
    rsi = pd.DataFrame()
    change = df["close"].diff()
    change.dropna(inplace = True)
    up = change.copy()
    down = change.copy()
    up[up<0] = 0
    down[down>0] = 0
    rsi['up'] = up.rolling(14).mean()
    rsi['down'] = down.rolling(14).mean().abs()
    rsi['rsi'] = 100 * rsi['up'] / (rsi['up'] + rsi['down'] )

    return rsi

rsi = RSI(afternoon, 14)
#print(rsi)
#print(afternoon.iloc[1:])
#c = ['green' if val >= 80 else 'red' for val in rsi["rsi"]]
rsi_plot = [
mpf.make_addplot((rsi['rsi']), color='lime', panel=2, ylabel='RSI', ylim=(10, 90),
secondary_y=False)]
# since the rsi has one few row
mpf.plot(afternoon.iloc[1:], type='ohlc', volume=True, addplot=rsi_plot)
```

To add the legend, we need to use ax,

```
import mplfinance as mpf
import matplotlib.pyplot as plt

df["sma5"] = df["close"].rolling(window=5).mean()
df["sma20"] = df["close"].rolling(window=20).mean()

add_plot = [
    mpf.make_addplot(df["sma5"], panel=0, color="orange", width=0.8),
    mpf.make_addplot(df["sma20"], panel=0, color="blue", width=0.8),
]

# Setting the overall size of the graph
fig = mpf.figure()
#figsize=(12,10))

# Creating subplots for the main chart
ax_main = fig.add_subplot()

# Adjusting the spacing between subplots
fig.tight_layout()

added_plots = {
    'MA5': mpf.make_addplot(df.sma5, type='line', ax=ax_main, width=1.5),
    'MA20': mpf.make_addplot(df.sma20, type='line', ax=ax_main, width=1.5),
}

mc = mpf.make_marketcolors(up="#56B476", down="#E9544F", edge='black')
```

```
s = mpf.make_mpf_style(marketcolors=mc, gridcolor='#DDDDDD', gridstyle="--")

mpf.plot(df,
         style=s,
         type='candle',
         ax=ax_main,
         addplot=list(added_plots.values()),
         datetime_format='%H:%M',
         returnfig=True)

ax_main.set_ylabel('MA')
ax_main.set_title(stock+" "+st+"=>"+et, fontsize=12)
ax_main.legend([None] *(len(added_plots)+2))
handles = ax_main.get_legend().legend_handles
ax_main.legend(handles=handles[2:], labels=list(added_plots.keys()))
'''
tick_count = 10
step = (len(df) - 1) / (tick_count - 1)
ticks = [0 + int(step * i) for i in range(tick_count)]
ax_main.xaxis.set_ticks(ticks)
ax_main.xaxis.set_ticklabels([])
'''
# Configuring the grid
ax_main.grid(color='#dddddd', linestyle='--', linewidth=0.5)

# Displaying the graph
plt.show()
```

There are over 100 chart metrics based on stock ohlc, we can invent ourselves, it's just math,

```
def bias(df):
      df['bias_6'] = (df['close'] - df['close'].rolling(6, min_periods=1).mean())/
df['close'].rolling(6, min_periods=1).mean()*100
     df['bias_12'] = (df['close'] - df['close'].rolling(12, min_periods=1).mean())/
df['close'].rolling(12, min_periods=1).mean()*100
     df['bias_24'] = (df['close'] - df['close'].rolling(24, min_periods=1).mean())/
df['close'].rolling(24, min_periods=1).mean()*100
    df['bias_6'] = round(df['bias_6'], 2)
    df['bias_12'] = round(df['bias_12'], 2)
    df['bias_24'] = round(df['bias_24'], 2)
    return df
```

and we can think about converting math, to pesudo, then to code, in Python,

```
# what is KC?
'''
TR is below
**MAX** [ {**HIGH - LOW**}, {**HIGH - P.CLOSE**}, {**P.CLOSE - LOW**} ]

where,
MAX = Maximum values
```

```
HIGH = Market High
LOW = Market Low
P.CLOSE = Previous market close

and ATR is below
**ATR N** = **EMA N** [ **TR** ] **- 1** * **2**

where,
ATR N = Average True Range of 'N' period
SMA N = Simple Moving Average of 'N' period
TR = True Range

**MIDDLE LINE 20** = **EMA 20** [ **C.STOCK** ]
where,
EMA 20 = 20-day Exponential Moving Average
C.STOCK = Closing price of the stock

**UPPER BAND 20** = **EMA 20** [ **C.STOCK** ] + **MULTIPLIER** * **ATR 10
LOWER BAND 20** = **EMA 20** [ **C.STOCK** ] - **MULTIPLIER** * **ATR 10**
where,
EMA 20 = 20-day Exponential Moving Average
C.STOCK = Closing price of the stock
MULTIPLIER = 2
'''

def get_kc(df, kc_lookback, multiplier, atr_lookback):

    tr1 = df['high'] - df['low']
    tr2 = df['high'] - df['close'].shift()
    tr3 = df['low'] -  df['close'].shift()
    frames = [tr1, tr2, tr3]
    # can we not use pd?
    tr = pd.concat(frames, axis = 1, join = 'inner').max(axis = 1)
    atr = tr.ewm(alpha = 1/atr_lookback).mean()
    kc_middle = close.ewm(kc_lookback).mean()
    kc_upper = close.ewm(kc_lookback).mean() + multiplier * atr
    kc_lower = close.ewm(kc_lookback).mean() - multiplier * atr
    return kc_middle, kc_upper, kc_lower intc = intc.iloc[:,:4]
# try intel
intc['kc_middle'],   intc['kc_upper'],   intc['kc_lower']   =   get_kc(intc['high'],
intc['low'], intc['close'], 20, 2, 10)
#intc.tail()
```

a non-consistent thing is we have to import pd, and the join parameter can be crazy...

MERGE METHOD	JOIN NAME	DESCRIPTION
****left****	LEFT OUTER JOIN	Use keys from left frame only
****right****	RIGHT OUTER JOIN	Use keys from right frame only
****outer****	FULL OUTER JOIN	Use union of keys from both frames

MERGE METHOD	JOIN NAME	DESCRIPTION
****inner****	INNER JOIN	Use intersection of keys from both frames

To add a new column, we can also use `lambda`,

```
df['H_L'] = df.apply(lambda row: row['high'] - row['low'], axis=1)
```

The most important thing is to decide buy or sell,

```
def decide(prices, kc_upper, kc_lower):
    buy_price = []
    sell_price = []
    kc_signal = []
    signal = 0

    for i in range(len(prices)):
        if prices[i] < kc_lower[i] and prices[i+1] > prices[i]:
            if signal != 1:
                buy_price.append(prices[i])
                sell_price.append(np.nan)
                signal = 1
                kc_signal.append(signal)
            else:
                buy_price.append(np.nan)
                sell_price.append(np.nan)
                kc_signal.append(0)
        elif prices[i] > kc_upper[i] and prices[i+1] < prices[i]:
            if signal != -1:
                buy_price.append(np.nan)
                sell_price.append(prices[i])
                signal = -1
                kc_signal.append(signal)
            else:
                buy_price.append(np.nan)
                sell_price.append(np.nan)
                kc_signal.append(0)
        else:
            buy_price.append(np.nan)
            sell_price.append(np.nan)
            kc_signal.append(0)

    return buy_price, sell_price, kc_signal

buy_price,   sell_price,   kc_signal   =   decide(intc['close'],   intc['kc_upper'],
intc['kc_lower'])
```

That is to say from ohlc, we get kc, and from kc, we get the price to buy and sell.

39 stockstats

Before a decision made, it is indication, so how do we indicate? Using the KC we can even draw the buy, sell position,

```
import akshare as ak
stock = "105.INTC"

M=10
D=25
st = f'2024-{M}-{D}'
M=10
D=25
et = f'2024-{M}-{D+1}'
st = st + ' 21:30:00'
et = et + ' 04:00:00'
print(stock, ":", st, "->", et)

stock_us_hist_min_em_df = ak.stock_us_hist_min_em(symbol=stock, start_date=st,
end_date=et)
df = stock_us_hist_min_em_df.iloc[:, [0, 1, 3, 4, 2, 5]] #column
df.columns.values[[0, 1, 2, 3, 4, 5]] = ['date', 'open', 'high', 'low', 'close',
'volume']

#df = df.loc[st:et,:] #row
#print(df)


df_sorted_ascending = df.sort_values(by='high', ascending=False)
print(df_sorted_ascending.head(1)['high'])
df_sorted_descending = df.sort_values(by='low', ascending=True)
print(df_sorted_descending.head(1)['low'])
import pandas as pd
df.index = pd.to_datetime(df.date)

def get_kc(df, kc_lookback, multiplier, atr_lookback):
    tr1 = df['high'] - df['low']
    tr2 = df['high'] - df['close'].shift()
    tr3 = df['low'] -  df['close'].shift()
    frames = [tr1, tr2, tr3]
    tr = pd.concat(frames, axis = 1, join = 'inner').max(axis = 1)
    atr = tr.ewm(alpha = 1/atr_lookback).mean()

    kc_middle = df['close'].ewm(kc_lookback).mean()
    kc_upper = df['close'].ewm(kc_lookback).mean() + multiplier * atr
    kc_lower = df['close'].ewm(kc_lookback).mean() - multiplier * atr

    return kc_middle, kc_upper, kc_lower

intc = df.iloc[:,1:5]
intc['kc_middle'], intc['kc_upper'], intc['kc_lower'] = get_kc(intc, 20, 2, 10)
print(intc)
```

```
import numpy as np
def decide(prices, kc_upper, kc_lower):
    buy_price = []
    sell_price = []
    kc_signal = []
    signal = 0
    #print(len(prices), kc_upper, kc_lower)
    for i in range(len(prices)):
        if i < len(prices)-1: nextp = prices[i+1]
        else: nextp = 0
        #print(nextp)
        if prices[i] < kc_lower[i] and nextp > prices[i]:
            if signal != 1:
                buy_price.append(prices[i])
                sell_price.append(np.nan)
                signal = 1
                kc_signal.append(signal)
            else:
                buy_price.append(np.nan)
                sell_price.append(np.nan)
                kc_signal.append(0)
        elif prices[i] > kc_upper[i] and nextp < prices[i]:
            if signal != -1:
                buy_price.append(np.nan)
                sell_price.append(prices[i])
                signal = -1
                kc_signal.append(signal)
            else:
                buy_price.append(np.nan)
                sell_price.append(np.nan)
                kc_signal.append(0)
        else:
            buy_price.append(np.nan)
            sell_price.append(np.nan)
            kc_signal.append(0)

    return buy_price, sell_price, kc_signal

buy_price, sell_price, kc_signal = decide(intc['close'], intc['kc_upper'],
intc['kc_lower'])

import matplotlib.pyplot as plt
plt.plot(intc['close'], linewidth = 2, label = 'INTC')
plt.plot(intc['kc_upper'], linewidth = 2, color = 'orange', linestyle = '--', label
= 'KC UPPER 20')
plt.plot(intc['kc_middle'], linewidth = 1.5, color = 'grey', label = 'KC MIDDLE 20')
plt.plot(intc['kc_lower'], linewidth = 2, color = 'orange', linestyle = '--', label
= 'KC LOWER 20')
plt.plot(intc.index, buy_price, marker = '^', color = 'green', markersize = 15,
linewidth = 0, label = 'BUY SIGNAL')
plt.plot(intc.index, sell_price, marker = 'v', color= 'r', markersize = 15,
linewidth = 0, label = 'SELL SIGNAL')
```

```
plt.legend(loc = 'lower right')
plt.title('INTC KELTNER CHANNEL 20 TRADING SIGNALS')
plt.show()
```

So the first three signals are right, and we can see the high risk, and the trend is so hard to indicate....

```
import akshare as ak
stock = "105.INTC"

M=10
D=25
st = f'2024-{M}-{D}'
M=10
D=25
et = f'2024-{M}-{D+1}'
st = st + ' 21:30:00'
et = et + ' 04:00:00'
print(stock, ":", st, "->", et)

stock_us_hist_min_em_df   =   ak.stock_us_hist_min_em(symbol=stock,   start_date=st,
end_date=et)
df = stock_us_hist_min_em_df.iloc[:, [0, 1, 3, 4, 2, 5]] #column
df.columns.values[[0,  1,  2,  3,  4,  5]]  =  ['date',  'open',  'high',  'low',  'close',
'volume']

#df = df.loc[st:et,:] #select row
#print(df)

from stockstats import StockDataFrame
stock_data = StockDataFrame.retype(df)

# change this trend, to a criteria
stock_data['trend'] = stock_data['close_50_sma'] - stock_data['close_200_sma']
stock_data.reset_index(drop=False, inplace=True)
#print(stock_data.tail(50).to_markdown())
print(stock_data.iloc[:, [0, -1]])
ocur = 1; ocursell = 1;

for i in range(len(stock_data['trend'])):
    if stock_data['trend'][i] > 0:
        ocur = ocur - 1
              if  ocur  ==  0:  print(stock_data['date'][i],  "is  a  buy  signal  @",
stock_data['low'][i])

    elif stock_data['trend'][i] < 0:
        ocursell = ocursell -1
            if  ocursell  ==  0:  print(stock_data['date'][i],  "is  a  sell  signal  @",
stock_data['high'][i])
    else:
        pass#print(stock_data['date'][i], "a watch signal")
df = stock_data
```

```
df_sorted_ascending = df.sort_values(by='high', ascending=False)
print(df_sorted_ascending.head(1)['high'])
df_sorted_descending = df.sort_values(by='low', ascending=True)
print(df_sorted_descending.head(1)['low'])


# output
105.INTC : 2024-10-25 21:30:00 -> 2024-10-26 04:00:00
                    date     trend
0    2024-10-25 21:30:00  0.000000
1    2024-10-25 21:31:00  0.000000
2    2024-10-25 21:32:00  0.000000
3    2024-10-25 21:33:00  0.000000
4    2024-10-25 21:34:00  0.000000
..                   ...       ...
386  2024-10-26 03:56:00 -0.097815
387  2024-10-26 03:57:00 -0.098715
388  2024-10-26 03:58:00 -0.100275
389  2024-10-26 03:59:00 -0.101490
390  2024-10-26 04:00:00 -0.102415

[391 rows x 2 columns]
2024-10-25 22:20:00 is a buy signal @ 23.0
2024-10-26 01:18:00 is a sell signal @ 23.06
67    23.34
Name: high, dtype: float64
0    22.41
Name: low, dtype: float64
```

and if we see the full df for the highest and lowest,

```
df = stock_data
df_sorted_ascending = df.sort_values(by='high', ascending=False)
print(df_sorted_ascending.head(1))#['high'])
#print(h[['date','high']])

df_sorted_descending = df.sort_values(by='low', ascending=True)
print(df_sorted_descending.head(1))#['low'])

# output

                         date     open    high     low   close   volume   close_50_sma
close_200_sma     trend
67   2024-10-25  22:37:00   23.291   23.34   23.29   23.31   395908         23.05778
22.947044  0.110736
                         date    open    high     low   close   volume   close_50_sma
close_200_sma  trend
0   2024-10-25  21:30:00   22.42   22.43   22.41   22.42   837546               22.42
22.42   0.0
```

The lowest is in fact a watch action, which is really not a good action if we just watch...

How many metrics are there in stockstats?

- delta
- permutation (zero-based)
- log return
- max in range
- min in range
- middle = (close + high + low) / 3
- compare: le, ge, lt, gt, eq, ne
- count: both backward(c) and forward(fc)
- cross: including upward cross and downward cross
- SMA: Simple Moving Average
- EMA: Exponential Moving Average
- MSTD: Moving Standard Deviation
- MVAR: Moving Variance
- RSV: Raw Stochastic Value
- RSI: Relative Strength Index
- KDJ: Stochastic Oscillator
- Bolling: Bollinger Band
- MACD: Moving Average Convergence Divergence
- CR: Energy Index (Intermediate Willingness Index)
- WR: Williams Overbought/Oversold index
- CCI: Commodity Channel Index
- TR: True Range
- ATR: Average True Range
- DMA: Different of Moving Average (10, 50)
- DMI: Directional Moving Index, including
    - +DI: Positive Directional Indicator
    - -DI: Negative Directional Indicator
    - ADX: Average Directional Movement Index
    - ADXR: Smoothed Moving Average of ADX
- TRIX: Triple Exponential Moving Average
- TEMA: Another Triple Exponential Moving Average
- VR: Volume Variation Index
- MFI: Money Flow Index
- VWMA: Volume Weighted Moving Average
- CHOP: Choppiness Index
- KER: Kaufman's efficiency ratio
- KAMA: Kaufman's Adaptive Moving Average
- PPO: Percentage Price Oscillator
- StochRSI: Stochastic RSI
- WT: LazyBear's Wave Trend

- Supertrend: with the Upper Band and Lower Band
- Aroon: Aroon Oscillator
- Z: Z-Score
- AO: Awesome Oscillator
- BOP: Balance of Power
- MAD: Mean Absolute Deviation
- ROC: Rate of Change
- Coppock: Coppock Curve
- Ichimoku: Ichimoku Cloud
- CTI: Correlation Trend Indicator
- LRMA: Linear Regression Moving Average
- ERI: Elder-Ray Index
- FTR: the Gaussian Fisher Transform Price Reversals indicator
- RVGI: Relative Vigor Index
- Inertia: Inertia Indicator
- KST: Know Sure Thing
- PGO: Pretty Good Oscillator
- PSL: Psychological Line
- PVO: Percentage Volume Oscillator
- QQE: Quantitative Qualitative Estimation

Where are they?

```
>>> import stockstats
>>> dir()
['__annotations__', '__builtins__', '__doc__', '__loader__', '__name__',
'__package__', '__spec__', 'stockstats']
>>> dir(stockstats)
['Callable', 'Optional', 'StockDataFrame', 'StockStatsError', 'Union', '_Meta',
'__author__', '__builtins__', '__cached__', '__doc__', '__file__', '__loader__',
'__name__', '__package__', '__spec__', '_call_handler', '_dft_column',
'_dft_windows', 'as_strided', 'dft_column', 'dft_windows', 'functools', 'itertools',
'np', 'pd', 're', 'set_dft_window', 'unicode_literals', 'unwrap', 'wrap']
```

OK, so the function starts from wrap, let's try use `aapl` again,

```
import pandas as pd
from stockstats import wrap

df = pd.read_csv('aapl_2024.csv')
st = '2024-10-14 09:30:00'
et = '2024-10-14 15:59:00'
stock = "AAPL"
print(stock, ":", st, "->", et, "NY")
data = df[(df['date'] >= st) & (df['date'] <= et)]

df = wrap(data)
```

```
print(df)

from stockstats import StockDataFrame
stock_data = StockDataFrame.retype(df)

# change this trend, to a criteria
stock_data['trend'] = stock_data['close_50_sma'] - stock_data['close_200_sma']
stock_data.reset_index(drop=False, inplace=True)
#print(stock_data.tail(50).to_markdown())
print(stock_data.iloc[:, [0, -1]])
ocur = 1; ocursell = 1;

for i in range(len(stock_data['trend'])):
    if stock_data['trend'][i] > 0:
        ocur = ocur - 1
              if  ocur  ==  0:  print(stock_data['date'][i],  "is  a  buy  signal  @",
stock_data['low'][i])

    elif stock_data['trend'][i] < 0:
        ocursell = ocursell -1
            if  ocursell  ==  0:  print(stock_data['date'][i],  "is  a  sell  signal  @",
stock_data['high'][i])
    else:
        pass#print(stock_data['date'][i], "a watch signal")
df = stock_data
df_sorted_ascending = df.sort_values(by='high', ascending=False)
h = (df_sorted_ascending.head(1))
print(h[['date','high']])

df_sorted_descending = df.sort_values(by='low', ascending=True)
print(df_sorted_descending.head(1))#['low'])
```

and we can make the signal more significant,

```
df = stock_data
df_sorted_ascending = df.sort_values(by='high', ascending=False)
h = (df_sorted_ascending.head(1))
print(h[['date','high']])

df_sorted_descending = df.sort_values(by='low', ascending=True)
l = df_sorted_descending.head(1)
print(l[['date','low']])

dfs = h[['date','high']]
dfs.rename(columns={'high': 'price'}, inplace=True)
dfs2 = l[['date','low']]
dfs2.rename(columns={'low': 'price'}, inplace=True)

print(type(dfs))

print(type(dfs2))
```

```
print(dfs.append(dfs2))

# output
A value is trying to be set on a copy of a slice from a DataFrame

See the caveats in the documentation: https://pandas.pydata.org/pandas-docs/stable/user_guide/indexing.html#returning-a-view-versus-a-copy
  dfs.rename(columns={'high': 'price'}, inplace=True)
C:\Users\Lenovo\Flask\stock\test.py:46: SettingWithCopyWarning:
A value is trying to be set on a copy of a slice from a DataFrame

See the caveats in the documentation: https://pandas.pydata.org/pandas-docs/stable/user_guide/indexing.html#returning-a-view-versus-a-copy
  dfs2.rename(columns={'low': 'price'}, inplace=True)
<class 'pandas.core.frame.DataFrame'>
<class 'pandas.core.frame.DataFrame'>
Traceback (most recent call last):
  File "C:\Users\Lenovo\Flask\stock\test.py", line 52, in <module>
    print(dfs.append(dfs2))
          ^^^^^^^^^^
File "C:\Users\Lenovo\AppData\Local\Packages\PythonSoftwareFoundation.Python.3.12_qbz5n2kfra8p0\LocalCache\local-packages\Python312\site-packages\pandas\core\generic.py", line 6296, in __getattr__
    return object.__getattribute__(self, name)
           ^^^^^^^^^^^^^^^^^^^^^^^^^^^^^^^^^^^
AttributeError: 'DataFrame' object has no attribute 'append'. Did you mean: '_append'?
```

There is so many wrong things, some are warning, but the last one, is error.

Why is that? Because you can add a dict, not a pd. If you insist, you can use as suggested, prefix _, but it is not suggested, because it is private.

```
                     date   price
0     2024-02-14 09:30:00  185.53
5866  2024-03-07 09:46:00  168.49
```

So we see the price, highest and lowest, after 5866 trading minutes, and this is very direct, why?

We can estimate easily, if we buy 100, short sale, we can earn,

```
print((185.53 - 168.49) * 100) # 1703.999999999999
```

That's huge!

If we buy 1000, wow, wow, wow,

But how do we know if we can buy at 2024-02-14?

and,

put or call?

Is it indicatable? So we need go back one month,

```
import pandas as pd
from stockstats import wrap

csv = pd.read_csv('aapl_2024.csv')
st = '2024-01-14 09:30:00'
et = '2024-02-14 15:59:00'
stock = "AAPL"
print(stock, ":", st, "->", et, "NY")
data = csv[(csv['date'] >= st) & (csv['date'] <= et)]

df = wrap(data)

print(df)
from stockstats import StockDataFrame
stockStat = StockDataFrame.retype(df)
import matplotlib.pyplot as plt

stockStat[['volume','volume_delta']].plot(figsize=(10,6), grid=True)
plt.show()

stockStat[['close','close_delta']].plot(subplots=True, figsize=(10,6), grid=True)
plt.show()
```

Nothing we really can see from the two figures, but we can see the drawing is very simple, since all the columns are very easy to add, and figures can be easily put in one.

```
import pandas as pd
from stockstats import wrap

csv = pd.read_csv('aapl_2024.csv')
st = '2024-01-14 09:30:00'
et = '2024-02-14 15:59:00'
stock = "AAPL"
print(stock, ":", st, "->", et, "NY")
data = csv[(csv['date'] >= st) & (csv['date'] <= et)]


df = wrap(data)

print(df)
from stockstats import StockDataFrame
stockStat = StockDataFrame.retype(df)
import matplotlib.pyplot as plt
```

```
stockStat[['volume','volume_delta',     'close','close_delta']].plot(figsize=(10,6),
grid=True)
plt.show()
```

So if we use select price, we can see the graph comparing lines,

```
import pandas as pd
from stockstats import wrap

csv = pd.read_csv('aapl_2024.csv')
st = '2024-01-14 09:30:00'
et = '2024-02-14 15:59:00'
stock = "AAPL"
print(stock, ":", st, "->", et, "NY")
data = csv[(csv['date'] >= st) & (csv['date'] <= et)]

df = wrap(data)

#print(df)
from stockstats import StockDataFrame
stockStat = StockDataFrame.retype(df)
import matplotlib.pyplot as plt

p = stockStat[['low', 'close', 'low_5_sma', 'vwma_5']]
print(p)
p.plot(figsize=(10,6), grid=True)
plt.show()
```

MA is not useful for the short emotion,

```
import akshare as ak
stock = "105.UPXI"

M=10
D=25
st = f'2024-{M}-{D}'
M=10
D=25
et = f'2024-{M}-{D+1}'
st = st + ' 21:30:00'
et = et + ' 04:00:00'
print(stock, ":", st, "->", et)

stock_us_hist_min_em_df   =   ak.stock_us_hist_min_em(symbol=stock,   start_date=st,
end_date=et)
df = stock_us_hist_min_em_df.iloc[:, [0, 1, 3, 4, 2, 5]] #column
df.columns.values[[0, 1, 2, 3, 4, 5]] = ['date', 'open', 'high', 'low', 'close',
'volume']

from stockstats import wrap
df = wrap(df)
```

```
from stockstats import StockDataFrame
stockStat = StockDataFrame.retype(df)
import matplotlib.pyplot as plt

p = stockStat[['low', 'close', 'low_5_sma', 'vwma_5']]
print(p)
p.plot(figsize=(10,6), grid=True, subplots=True)
plt.gcf().autofmt_xdate()

plt.show()
```

What are the df column names we can use?

```
['open' 'high' 'close' 'low' 'volume' 'price_change' 'p_change' 'ma5'
 'ma10' 'ma20' 'v_ma5' 'v_ma10' 'v_ma20' 'turnover' 'volume_delta'
 u'open_2_s' u'open_2_d' u'open_-2_r' u'middle' u'cr' u'cr-ma1' u'cr-ma2'
 u'cr-ma3' u'volume_-3_s' u'volume_-1_s' u'volume_2_s'
 u'volume_-3,2,-1_max' u'volume_-2_s' u'volume_0_s' u'volume_1_s'
 u'volume_-3~1_min' u'rsv_9' u'kdjk_9' u'kdjk' u'kdjd_9' u'kdjd' u'kdjj_9'
 u'kdjj' u'rsv_3' u'kdjk_3' u'kdjd_3' 'kdjk_3_xu_kdjd_3' u'open_2_sma'
 u'close_26_ema' u'macd' u'macds' u'macdh' u'close_20_sma' u'close_20_mstd'
 u'boll' u'boll_ub' u'boll_lb' u'close_10.0_le' u'close_10.0_le_5_c'
 u'cr-ma1_20_c' 'cr-ma2_xu_cr-ma1_20_c' u'close_-1_s' u'close_-1_d' u'rs_6'
 u'rsi_6' u'rs_12' u'rsi_12' u'wr_10' u'wr_6' u'middle_14_sma' u'cci'
 u'middle_20_sma' u'cci_20' u'tr' u'atr' u'close_10_sma' u'close_50_sma'
 u'dma' u'high_delta' u'um' u'low_delta' u'dm' u'pdm' u'pdm_14_ema'
 u'pdm_14' u'atr_14' u'pdi_14' u'pdi' u'mdm' u'mdm_14_ema' u'mdm_14'
 u'mdi_14' u'mdi' u'dx_14' u'dx' u'dx_6_ema' u'adx' u'adx_6_ema' u'adxr'
 u'trix' u'trix_9_sma' u'change' u'vr' u'vr_6_sma']
```

40 qpython

We see matplotlib can be modified to adapt many different Python package, which is really convienient, can you imagine using it on your cellphone?

Do you know qpython? If you have an Android phone, you can chekcout https://github.com/qpython-android, this is a great tool to take advantage of Android phone CPU, into direct data analysis.

Recall we use flask before on Windows, now move on Android, first, open **settings** on your Android phone, scroll to the bottom, enter **system**, and tap **about phone**. Next, find the **build number** entry and tap it repeatedly. After seven taps, you should see a notification stating that you're now a developer. Go back to the main **settings** screen, unlock the **USB debugging**.

Then you can use download ADB, or scrcpy, https://github.com/Genymobile/scrcpy,

```
D:\scrcpy-win64-v2.7\scrcpy-win64-v2.7>scrcpy --select-usb
scrcpy 2.7 <https://github.com/Genymobile/scrcpy>
INFO: ADB device found:
INFO:     -->   (usb)  ZY22F47X6Q                     device  XT2175_2
D:\scrcpy-win64-v2.7\scrcpy-win64-v2.7\scrcpy-server: 1 file pushed, 0 skipped. 16.9
MB/s (71200 bytes in 0.004s)
[server] INFO: Device: [motorola] motorola XT2175-2 (Android 12)
INFO: Renderer: direct3d
INFO: Texture: 1080x2456
WARN: Device disconnected
```

Now you see a screen on your Windows, and if you use Mac, you can just use Android Studio, much easier...

You should have qpython.qpk ready, so in the Windows terminal, you can install it,

```
D:\scrcpy-win64-v2.7\scrcpy-win64-v2.7>adb install qpython.apk
```

To transfer files,

```
D:\scrcpy-win64-v2.7\scrcpy-win64-v2.7>adb push flaskdraw.py
/storage/emulated/0/qpython/scripts3

D:\scrcpy-win64-v2.7\scrcpy-win64-v2.7>adb pull
/storage/emulated/0/qpython/scripts3/webapp_hello.py .
```

To uninstall qpython,

```
adb uninstall org.qpython.qpy
```

To make the screen on, when it is black,

```
adb shell input keyevent 26
```

What is flaskdraw?

```
import base64

from io import BytesIO

from flask import Flask

from matplotlib.figure import Figure

app = Flask(__name__)

@app.route("/")
def hello():
    # Generate the figure **without using pyplot**.
    fig = Figure()
    ax = fig.subplots()
```

```
    ax.plot([1, 2])
    # Save it to a temporary buffer.
    buf = BytesIO()
    fig.savefig(buf, format="png")
    # Embed the result in the html output.
    data = base64.b64encode(buf.getbuffer()).decode("ascii")
    return f"<img src='data:image/png;base64,{data}'/>"

app.run()
```

It is drawing a graph on 127.0.0.1:5000, and what is webapp_hello?

```
#qpy:webapp:Hello QPython
#qpy://127.0.0.1:8080/
"""
This is a sample for qpython webapp
"""

from bottle import Bottle, ServerAdapter
from bottle import run, debug, route, error, static_file, template



######### QPYTHON WEB SERVER ###############

class MyWSGIRefServer(ServerAdapter):
    server = None

    def run(self, handler):
        from wsgiref.simple_server import make_server, WSGIRequestHandler
        if self.quiet:
            class QuietHandler(WSGIRequestHandler):
                def log_request(*args, **kw): pass
            self.options['handler_class'] = QuietHandler
        self.server = make_server(self.host, self.port, handler, **self.options)
        self.server.serve_forever()

    def stop(self):
        #sys.stderr.close()
        import threading
        threading.Thread(target=self.server.shutdown).start()
        #self.server.shutdown()
        self.server.server_close() #<--- alternative but causes bad fd exception
        print("# qpyhttpd stop")


######### BUILT-IN ROUTERS ###############
@route('/__exit', method=['GET','HEAD'])
def __exit():
    global server
    server.stop()

@route('/__ping')
```

```
def __ping():
    return "ok"


@route('/assets/<filepath:path>')
def server_static(filepath):
    return static_file(filepath, root='/sdcard')


######### WEBAPP ROUTERS ###############
@route('/')
def home():
    name='QPython'
    file=__file__[__file__.rfind('/qpython'):]
    cont=f'''
<h1>Hello {name} !</h1><a href="/assets{file}">View source</a><br><br>
<a href="__exit">>> Exit</a><br>
<a  href="http://wiki.qpython.org/doc/program_guide/web_app/">>>  About  QPython  Web
App</a>
'''
    return template(cont)


######### WEBAPP ROUTERS ###############
app = Bottle()
app.route('/', method='GET')(home)
app.route('/__exit', method=['GET','HEAD'])(__exit)
app.route('/__ping', method=['GET','HEAD'])(__ping)
app.route('/assets/<filepath:path>', method='GET')(server_static)

try:
    server = MyWSGIRefServer(host="127.0.0.1", port="8080")
    app.run(server=server,reloader=False)
except (Exception) as ex:
    print("Exception: %s" % repr(ex))
```

So we see it is a bottle server, why is bottle?

If you run, you will see it is adapted to WSGI, so it can show inside the qpython, with LOG button, but it is not a big deal, we can just use flask.

Or if we want to keep style, we just add ourself the flaskdraw part into this,

```
#qpy:webapp:Hello QPython
#qpy://127.0.0.1:8080/
"""
This is a sample for qpython webapp
"""

from bottle import Bottle, ServerAdapter
from bottle import run, debug, route, error, static_file, template
```

```
######### QPYTHON WEB SERVER ###############

class MyWSGIRefServer(ServerAdapter):
    server = None

    def run(self, handler):
        from wsgiref.simple_server import make_server, WSGIRequestHandler
        if self.quiet:
            class QuietHandler(WSGIRequestHandler):
                def log_request(*args, **kw): pass
            self.options['handler_class'] = QuietHandler
        self.server = make_server(self.host, self.port, handler, **self.options)
        self.server.serve_forever()

    def stop(self):
        #sys.stderr.close()
        import threading
        threading.Thread(target=self.server.shutdown).start()
        #self.server.shutdown()
        self.server.server_close() #<--- alternative but causes bad fd exception
        print("# qpyhttpd stop")


######### BUILT-IN ROUTERS ###############
@route('/__exit', method=['GET','HEAD'])
def __exit():
    global server
    server.stop()

@route('/__ping')
def __ping():
    return "ok"


@route('/assets/<filepath:path>')
def server_static(filepath):
    return static_file(filepath, root='/sdcard')


######### WEBAPP ROUTERS ###############
@route('/')
def home():
    name='QPython'
    file=__file__[__file__.rfind('/qpython'):]
    cont=f'''
<h1>Hello {name} !</h1><a href="/assets{file}">View source</a><br><br>
<a href="__exit">>> Exit</a><br>
<a  href="http://wiki.qpython.org/doc/program_guide/web_app/">>>  About  QPython  Web
App</a>
<br><br>
<a href="draw">>> Draw</a><br>
```

```
'''
    return template(cont)

import base64

from io import BytesIO

from matplotlib.figure import Figure

@route("/draw")
def draw():
    # Generate the figure **without using pyplot**.
    fig = Figure()
    ax = fig.subplots()
    ax.plot([1, 2])
    # Save it to a temporary buffer.
    buf = BytesIO()
    fig.savefig(buf, format="png")
    # Embed the result in the html output.
    data = base64.b64encode(buf.getbuffer()).decode("ascii")
    return f"<center><img src='data:image/png;base64,{data}'/></center>"

######### WEBAPP ROUTERS ###############
app = Bottle()
app.route('/', method='GET')(home)
app.route('/__exit', method=['GET','HEAD'])(__exit)
app.route('/__ping', method=['GET','HEAD'])(__ping)
app.route('/draw', method=['GET','HEAD'])(draw)
app.route('/assets/<filepath:path>', method='GET')(server_static)

try:
    server = MyWSGIRefServer(host="127.0.0.1", port="8080")
    app.run(server=server,reloader=False)
except (Exception) as ex:
    print("Exception: %s" % repr(ex))
```

Pretty easy? Now let's try to hold an upload server,

```
# bottle_up.py
#qpy:webapp
#qpy://127.0.0.1:9000/
"""
This is a sample for qpython webapp
"""
import os
from bottle import Bottle, ServerAdapter
from bottle import request, run, debug, route, error, static_file, template

import socket
# Get the hostname of the current system
hostname = socket.gethostname()
# Get the IP address associated with the hostname
ip = socket.gethostbyname(hostname)
```

```
ip = '0.0.0.0'
pt = 9000

######### QPYTHON WEB SERVER ###############

class MyWSGIRefServer(ServerAdapter):
    server = None

    def run(self, handler):
        from wsgiref.simple_server import make_server, WSGIRequestHandler
        if self.quiet:
            class QuietHandler(WSGIRequestHandler):
                def log_request(*args, **kw): pass
            self.options['handler_class'] = QuietHandler
        self.server = make_server(self.host, self.port, handler, **self.options)
        self.server.serve_forever()

    def stop(self):
        #sys.stderr.close()
        import threading
        threading.Thread(target=self.server.shutdown).start()
        #self.server.shutdown()
        self.server.server_close() #<--- alternative but causes bad fd exception
        print("# qpyhttpd stop")


######### BUILT-IN ROUTERS ###############
@route('/__exit', method=['GET','HEAD'])
def __exit():
    global server
    server.stop()
    return "stop"

@route('/__ping')
def __ping():
    return "ok"

# python /storag e/emulated/0/qpython/scripts3/mybottleapp.py
# qpython/scripts3/mybottleapp.py
@route('/assets/<filepath:path>')
def server_static(filepath):
    return static_file(filepath, root=os.path.dirname(os.path.abspath(__file__)))

#hello parts, just can't read files from folder
@route('/__hello')
def __hello():
#    return template ('/assets/hello.html')
    res = "<p>ip is: " + request.remote_addr + "</p>"
    return res

######### WEBAPP ROUTERS ###############
@route('/')
def home():
```

```
    name='QPython'
    file=os.path.basename(__file__)
    cont=f'''
<h1>Hello {name} !</h1>
<a href="/assets/{file}">View source</a><br><br>
<a href="__exit">>> Exit</a><br>
<a  href="http://wiki.qpython.org/doc/program_guide/web_app/">>>  About  QPython  Web
App</a><br>
<!-- hello parts -->
<a href="__hello">>> Hello</a><br>

<a href="/assets/up.html">>> File Upload</a><br><br>
<a href="/assets/hello.html">hello.html</a>

'''
    return template(cont)


# remember the qpython treat the current path as assets...
upload_path = '/assets/static/'
@route('/assets/upload')
def upload():

    upload_file = request.files.get('data')
    print("666")
    upload_file.save(upload_path, overwrite=True)

    return "uploaded"


######### WEBAPP ROUTERS ###############
app = Bottle()
app.route('/', method='GET')(home)
app.route('/__exit', method=['GET','HEAD'])(__exit)
app.route('/__ping', method=['GET','HEAD'])(__ping)
app.route('/assets/<filepath:path>', method='GET')(server_static)
#hello parts
app.route('/__hello', method=['GET','HEAD'])(__hello)

app.route('/assets/upload', method=['POST'])(upload)

try:
    server = MyWSGIRefServer(host=ip, port=pt)
    app.run(server=server,reloader=False)
except (Exception) as ex:
    print("Exception: %s" % repr(ex))

# up.html
<!DOCTYPE html>
<html>

<head>
  <title>Upload Test</title>
```

```
</head>

<body>
  <form action="upload" method="POST" enctype="multipart/form-data">
  <input type="file" name="data">

  <input type="submit" value="upload">
  </form>
  <script>

  </script>
</body>

</html>
```

Fail... via some key error, what?

Pretty hard!

Is it a permission problem? Since when we do `listdir`, we failed...

We see 500 internel error, which is realy internel, internal as maybe the qpython itself, are we going to solve it? If, then you actually join the community, https://github.com/qpython-android, you can just click the right button to send the log too.

Since we can use the `adb`, so we will just skip it, and continue to our stock analysis on Android phone. Are we going to use akshare?

Maybe no...

Because we already inside bottle, it is a http server, so we will just query some data from web, and continue,

What is query?

It can be just GET, we will try french first,

```
# french.py
#-*-coding:utf-8-*-
#check french verb
"""
french.py
index.html
assets/css
assets/font
assets/js
"""
```

```
from bottle import Bottle, ServerAdapter
from bottle import static_file, template, request

import urllib.request
import os,os.path
#### the files #########
ASSETS = "/assets/"
ROOT = os.path.dirname(os.path.abspath(__file__))

API_URL = 'wordreference.com/fren/{replacehere}'
API_URL2 = 'https://leconjugueur.lefigaro.fr/french/verb/{replacehere}.html'

##################### SL4A ##############
try:
    IS_SL4A = True
    #import androidhelper
    #Droid = androidhelper.Android()
    #Droid.startLocating()
except:
    IS_SL4A = False
    pass


######### QPYTHON WEB SERVER ###############

class MyWSGIRefServer(ServerAdapter):
    server = None

    def run(self, handler):
        from wsgiref.simple_server import make_server, WSGIRequestHandler
        print("server start")
        if self.quiet:
            class QuietHandler(WSGIRequestHandler):
                def log_request(*args, **kw): pass
            self.options['handler_class'] = QuietHandler
        self.server = make_server(self.host, self.port, handler, **self.options)
        self.server.serve_forever()

    def stop(self):
        #sys.stderr.close()
        import threading
        threading.Thread(target=self.server.shutdown).start()
        #self.server.shutdown()
        self.server.server_close()
        print("server stop")


######### BUILT-IN ROUTERS ###############
def __exit():
    global server
    server.stop()
    return "exit"
```

```
def __ping():
    return "ok"

def server_static(filepath):
    return static_file(filepath, root=ROOT+'/assets')

def home():
    #if IS_SL4A:
    #    location = Droid.getLastKnownLocation().result
    #    location = location.get('network', location.get('gps'))
    return template(ROOT+'/index.html', word='french')

######### WEBAPP ROUTERS ###############
app = Bottle()
app.route('/', method='GET')(home)
app.route('/__exit', method=['GET','HEAD'])(__exit)
app.route('/__ping', method=['GET','HEAD'])(__ping)
app.route('/assets/<filepath:path>', method='GET')(server_static)

try:
    server = MyWSGIRefServer(host="127.0.0.1", port="8081")
    app.run(server=server,reloader=False)
except Exception as ex:
    print( "Exception: %s" % repr(ex))

# index.html
<!doctype html>
<html class="no-js">
<head>
  <meta charset="utf-8">
  <meta http-equiv="X-UA-Compatible" content="IE=edge">
  <title></title>
  <meta name="description" content="">
  <meta name="keywords" content="">
    <meta name="viewport" content="width=device-width, initial-scale=1, maximum-scale=1, user-scalable=no">
  <meta name="renderer" content="webkit">
  <meta http-equiv="Cache-Control" content="no-siteapp" />
  <link rel="stylesheet" href="/assets/css/amazeui.min.css">
  <style>
     .get-title {
      font-size: 200%;
      border: 2px solid #fff;
      padding: 20px;
      display: inline-block;
    }
     .get {
      background: #1E5B94;
      color: #fff;
      text-align: center;
      padding: 70px 0;
    }
```

```
.get-title {
  font-size: 200%;
  border: 2px solid #fff;
  padding: 20px;
  display: inline-block;
}

.get-btn {
  background: #fff;
}

.detail {
  background: #fff;
}

.detail-h2 {
  text-align: center;
  font-size: 150%;
  margin: 40px 0;
}

.detail-h3 {
  color: #1f8dd6;
}

.detail-p {
  color: #7f8c8d;
}

.detail-mb {
  margin-bottom: 30px;
}

.hope {
  background: #fff37;
  padding: 50px 0;
}

.hope-img {
  text-align: center;
}

.hope-hr {
  border-color: #149C88;
}

.hope-title {
  font-size: 140%;
}

.about {
  background: #fff;
  padding: 40px 0;
```

```
        color: #7f8c8d;
      }

      .about-color {
        color: #34495e;
      }

      .about-title {
        font-size: 180%;
        padding: 30px 0 50px 0;
        text-align: center;
      }

      .footer p {
        color: #7f8c8d;
        margin: 0;
        padding: 15px 0;
        text-align: center;
        background: #2d3e50;
      }

      .no1{
      margin:50px;
      border:0;
      padding:0;
      }
    </style>
    <script type="text/javascript">
      function btnOnclick() {
          var keyword = $("#keyword").val();
          window.android.callDetailActivity(keyword);
      }
    </script>
</head>
<body>
<!-- Header -->
<header  data-am-widget="header"  class="am-header  am-header-default  .am-header-
fixed">
    <div class="am-header-left am-header-nav">
      <a href="#left-link" class="">
        <i class="am-header-icon am-icon-home"></i>
      </a>
    </div>
    <h1 class="am-header-title">
      <a href="#title-link" class="">Welcome</a>
    </h1>
    <div class="am-header-right am-header-nav">
      <a href="#right-link" class="">
        <i class="am-header-icon am-icon-bars"></i>
      </a>
    </div>
</header>
```

```
<div class="get">
  <div class="am-g">
    <div class="am-u-lg-12">
      <h1 class="get-title">french word search</h1>
    </div>
  </div>
</div>

<div data-am-widget="tabs" class="am-tabs am-tabs-default">
  <ul class="am-tabs-nav am-cf">
    <li class="am-active">
      <a href="[data-tab-panel-0]">word</a>
    </li>
    <li class="">
      <a href="[data-tab-panel-1]">conjugate</a>
    </li>
  </ul>

<div class="am-tabs-bd">
<div data-tab-panel-0 class="am-tab-panel am-active">
<div align="center" style="width:100%;padding:30px;padding-bottom:80px;">
     <input type="text" id="word" class="am-form-field am-round" placeholder="word"
style="width:50%;float:left;"/>
</div>
<div align="center"><button type="button" class="am-btn am-btn-primary am-round"
onclick="javascript:btnOnclick();"><i class="am-icon-search"></i> search</button>
</div>
</div>

<div data-tab-panel-1 class="am-tab-panel ">
<div align="center" style="width:100%;padding:30px;padding-bottom:80px;">
             <input type="text" id="keyword" class="am-form-field am-round"
placeholder="verb" style="width:50%;float:right;"/>
</div>
<div align="center"><button type="button" class="am-btn am-btn-primary am-round"
onclick="javascript:btnOnclick2();"><i class="am-icon-search"></i>search</button>
</div>
</div>

</div>
</div>


<div style="height:20px;"></div>

<script src="/assets/js/jquery.min.js"></script>
<script src="/assets/js/amazeui.min.js"></script>
<script type="text/javascript">

function btnOnclick() {
    var word = $("#word").val();

    location.href = "https://www.wordreference.com/fren/"+word
```

```
}
function btnOnclick2() {
    var verb = $("#keyword").val();
    location.href = "https://leconjugueur.lefigaro.fr/french/verb/"+verb+".html"

}
</script>


</body>
</html>
```

So the home render index.html, and we embed javascript to handle button click, the two pannels can uses two websites, one for the word, one for the verb. Let's try to query a stock, UPXI, from https://financialmodelingprep.com,

```
print("UPXI\n10.25 moring - 10.25 afternoon NY\n10.25 evening - 10.26 morning HK")
from urllib.request import urlopen
import certifi
import json
api = "api key"
#print(api)

def get_jsonparsed_data(url):
    response = urlopen(url, cafile=certifi.where())
    data = response.read().decode("utf-8")
    return json.loads(data)

url      =      ("https://financialmodelingprep.com/api/v3/historical-chart/1min/UPXI?
from=2024-10-25&to=2024-10-26&apikey="+api)
d = (get_jsonparsed_data(url))
#for i in d: print(i)
import pandas as pd
df = pd.DataFrame(d[::-1])
print(df)
```

to get the pre and post market,

```
url      =      ("https://financialmodelingprep.com/api/v4/pre-post-market-trade/UPXI?
apikey="+api)
d = (get_jsonparsed_data(url))
import pandas as pd
df = pd.DataFrame(d[::-1])
print(df)
```

and then we merge it with the french word search,

```
# main.py
"""
```

```
main.py
index.html
detail.html
assets/css
assets/font
assets/js
"""
from bottle import Bottle, ServerAdapter
from bottle import static_file, template, request

import os,os.path
ASSETS = "/assets/"
#ASSETS = "\\assets\\"

ROOT = os.path.dirname(os.path.abspath(__file__))
#ROOT = "127.0.0.1:8081"
#print(ROOT)
API_URL = 'https://financialmodelingprep.com/api/v3/historical-chart/1min'


#################### SL4A ##############
try:
    IS_SL4A = True
    #import androidhelper
    #Droid = androidhelper.Android()
    #Droid.startLocating()
except:
    IS_SL4A = False
    pass


######### QPYTHON WEB SERVER ###############

class MyWSGIRefServer(ServerAdapter):
    server = None

    def run(self, handler):
        from wsgiref.simple_server import make_server, WSGIRequestHandler
        if self.quiet:
            class QuietHandler(WSGIRequestHandler):
                def log_request(*args, **kw): pass
            self.options['handler_class'] = QuietHandler
        self.server = make_server(self.host, self.port, handler, **self.options)
        self.server.serve_forever()

    def stop(self):
        #sys.stderr.close()
        import threading
        threading.Thread(target=self.server.shutdown).start()
        #self.server.shutdown()
        self.server.server_close()
        print("# QWEBAPPEND")
```

```
######### BUILT-IN ROUTERS ###############
def __exit():
    global server
    server.stop()
    return "stop"

def __ping():
    return "ok"

def server_static(filepath):
    return static_file(filepath, root=ROOT+'/assets')


def home():
    #if IS_SL4A:
    #    location = Droid.getLastKnownLocation().result
    #    location = location.get('network', location.get('gps'))
    return template(ROOT+'/index.html', stock='UPXI')

from urllib.request import urlopen
import certifi

#print(api)
import json
def get_jsonparsed_data(url):

    #data = _get_json_content(API_URL+"&stock="+stock+"&start="+start+"&end="+end)

    response = urlopen(url, cafile=certifi.where())
    data = response.read().decode("utf-8")
    return json.loads(data)

def detail():
    stock = request.GET['stock']
    start = request.GET['start']
    end = request.GET['end']
    #d = "?stock="+stock+"&start="+start+"&end="+end
   #d = (get_jsonparsed_data())
    api = "uvjOS64tPdwai8mwwpKtDdfl1LpMFJ0T"
    url = (f"https://financialmodelingprep.com/api/v3/historical-chart/1min/{stock}?
from={start}&to={end}&apikey="+api)
    data = get_jsonparsed_data(url)
    data=data[::-1]
    return template(ROOT+'/detail.html',data=data)
    #return url

######### WEBAPP ROUTERS ###############
app = Bottle()
app.route('/', method='GET')(home)
app.route('/detail', method='GET')(detail)
app.route('/__exit', method=['GET','HEAD'])(__exit)
app.route('/__ping', method=['GET','HEAD'])(__ping)
```

```
app.route('/assets/<filepath:path>', method='GET')(server_static)

try:
    server = MyWSGIRefServer(host="127.0.0.1", port="8081")
    app.run(server=server,reloader=False)
except Exception as ex:
    print ("Exception: %s" % repr(ex))

# index.html
<!doctype html>
<html class="no-js">
<head>
  <meta charset="utf-8">
  <meta http-equiv="X-UA-Compatible" content="IE=edge">
  <title></title>
  <meta name="description" content="">
  <meta name="keywords" content="">
    <meta  name="viewport"  content="width=device-width,  initial-scale=1,  maximum-
scale=1, user-scalable=no">
  <meta name="renderer" content="webkit">
  <meta http-equiv="Cache-Control" content="no-siteapp" />
  <link rel="stylesheet" href="/assets/css/amazeui.min.css">
  <style>
     .get-title {
      font-size: 200%;
      border: 2px solid #fff;
      padding: 20px;
      display: inline-block;
    }
     .get {
      background: #1E5B94;
      color: #fff;
      text-align: center;
      padding: 70px 0;
    }

    .get-title {
      font-size: 200%;
      border: 2px solid #fff;
      padding: 20px;
      display: inline-block;
    }

    .get-btn {
      background: #fff;
    }

    .detail {
      background: #fff;
    }

    .detail-h2 {
      text-align: center;
```

```
  font-size: 150%;
  margin: 40px 0;
}

.detail-h3 {
  color: #1f8dd6;
}

.detail-p {
  color: #7f8c8d;
}

.detail-mb {
  margin-bottom: 30px;
}

.hope {
  background: #fff37;
  padding: 50px 0;
}

.hope-img {
  text-align: center;
}

.hope-hr {
  border-color: #149C88;
}

.hope-title {
  font-size: 140%;
}

.about {
  background: #fff;
  padding: 40px 0;
  color: #7f8c8d;
}

.about-color {
  color: #34495e;
}

.about-title {
  font-size: 180%;
  padding: 30px 0 50px 0;
  text-align: center;
}

.footer p {
  color: #7f8c8d;
  margin: 0;
  padding: 15px 0;
```

```
      text-align: center;
      background: #2d3e50;
    }

    .no1{
    margin:50px;
    border:0;
    padding:0;
    }
  </style>
  <script type="text/javascript">
    function btnOnclick() {
        var keyword = $("#keyword").val();
        window.android.callDetailActivity(keyword);
    }
  </script>
</head>
<body>
<!-- Header -->
<header  data-am-widget="header"  class="am-header  am-header-default  .am-header-fixed">
  <div class="am-header-left am-header-nav">
    <a href="#left-link" class="">
      <i class="am-header-icon am-icon-home"></i>
    </a>
  </div>
  <h1 class="am-header-title">
    <a href="#title-link" class="">Welcome</a>
  </h1>
  <div class="am-header-right am-header-nav">
    <a href="#right-link" class="">
      <i class="am-header-icon am-icon-bars"></i>
    </a>
  </div>
</header>

<div class="get">
  <div class="am-g">
    <div class="am-u-lg-12">
      <h1 class="get-title">stock search</h1>
    </div>
  </div>
</div>

<div data-am-widget="tabs" class="am-tabs am-tabs-default">
  <ul class="am-tabs-nav am-cf">

    <li class="">
      <a href="[data-tab-panel-1]">stock</a>
    </li>
  </ul>

<div class="am-tabs-bd">
```

```
<div data-tab-panel-1 class="am-tab-panel ">

<div align="center" style="width:100%;padding:30px;padding-bottom:80px;">
    <input type="text" id="stock" class="am-form-field am-round" placeholder="stock"
style="width:40%;float:left;"/>
      <input type="text" id="end" class="am-form-field am-round" placeholder="end"
style="width:30%;float:right;"/>
<input type="text" id="start" class="am-form-field am-round" placeholder="start"
style="width:30%;float:right;"/>

</div>

<div align="center"><button type="button" class="am-btn am-btn-primary am-round"
onclick="javascript:btnOnclick2();"><i class="am-icon-search"></i> search</button>
</div>
</div>


<div style="height:20px;"></div>

<script src="/assets/js/jquery.min.js"></script>
<script src="/assets/js/amazeui.min.js"></script>
<script type="text/javascript">
function btnOnclick2() {
    var stock = $("#stock").val();
    var start = $("#start").val();
    var end = $("#end").val();
   location.href = '/detail?stock='+stock+"&start="+start+"&end="+end;

//location.href = '/detail'
}

</script>


</body>
</html>

# detail.html
<!doctype html>
<html class="no-js">
<head>
  <meta charset="utf-8">
  <meta http-equiv="X-UA-Compatible" content="IE=edge">
  <title>stock detail</title>
  <meta name="description" content="">
  <meta name="keywords" content="">
    <meta name="viewport" content="width=device-width, initial-scale=1, maximum-
scale=1, user-scalable=no">
  <meta name="renderer" content="webkit">
  <meta http-equiv="Cache-Control" content="no-siteapp" />
```

```
  <link rel="stylesheet" href="assets/css/amazeui.min.css">
  <style>
  </style>
</head>
<body>
<!-- Header -->
<header data-am-widget="header" class="am-header am-header-default am-header-fixed">
  <div class="am-header-left am-header-nav">
    <a href="/" class="">
      <i class="am-header-icon am-icon-angle-left"></i>
    </a>
  </div>
  <h1 class="am-header-title">
    <a href="#title-link" id="title" class="">Loading ...</a>
  </h1>
  <div class="am-header-right am-header-nav">
    <a href="#right-link" class="">
      <i class="am-header-icon am-icon-bars"></i>
    </a>
  </div>
</header>


<section id="sectionId" data-am-widget="accordion" class="am-accordion am-accordion-
default"
data-am-accordion=''>

</section>

<div style="height:30px;"></div>

<script src="assets/js/jquery.min.js"></script>
<script src="assets/js/amazeui.min.js"></script>


<script type="text/javascript">

function appendDetail(date, low, close){

      $("#sectionId").append('<dl class="am-accordion-item"><dt class="am-accordion-
title">' + date +'</dt><dd class="am-accordion-bd am-collapse"><div class="am-
accordion-content"><code>low</code><br/>' + low + '<br/><hr><code>close</code><br/>'
+ close + '<br/></div></dd></dl>');

}

function resultCount(num) {

    $("#title").text("data "+num);

}

var data = {{ !data }}
```

```
var dl = data.length

resultCount(dl)

var b = (data[0])
document.write(b['date']+b['low']+b['close']);


if (dl==0) {

    $("#sectionId").append('<div style="padding:5px">no data found</div>');

} else {

    for (var i=0;i<dl;i++) {
        var b = data[i]
        var date = b['date']
        var low = b['low']
        var close = b['close']
        appendDetail(date, low, close);
        document.write();
    }
}

</script>
</body>
</html>


# assets
...
```

Now if we want to draw, we can just paste the draw part to the detail page, with a href, or with a button click location.href, the point is what kind of link we want to use.

It means we can make the link as processed in py, or we can make it processed in html. In fact someone already rendered it, https://lksfr.shinyapps.io/Shiny/, and there are many Javascript render the df too, https://gmousse.github.io/dataframe-js/, to use,

```
<!DOCTYPE html>
<html>

<head>
    <title>
    HTML Data Frame Render
    </title>
```

```
</head>

<body style="text-align:center;">
    <h1>
        df render
    </h1>

    <a href="https://gmousse.github.io/dataframe-js/">
         https://gmousse.github.io/dataframe-js/
    </a>
<script src="https://gmousse.github.io/dataframe-js/dist/dataframe.js">
</script>


<p id="df"></p>

<script type="module">
var DataFrame = dfjs.DataFrame;
const df = new DataFrame([
    {c1: 1, c2: 6}, // <------- A row
    {c4: 1, c3: 2}
], ['c1', 'c2', 'c3', 'c4']);
document.getElementById("df").innerHTML = df.show(1); //document.write(df.show(1));
document.write("<br>");

</script>

<p id="demo"></p>

<script type="text/javascript">
document.getElementById("demo").innerHTML = "ok";
</script>
</body>

</html>

# output
# df render

[https://gmousse.github.io/dataframe-js/](https://gmousse.github.io/dataframe-js/)

| c1 | c2 | c3 | c4 | ------------------------------------------------ | 1 | 6 |
undefined | undefined |

ok
```

The long dash is what?

Why it does not go to the next line? With a `<br>`?

That is very common when we use others' library, does not matter with what language, so how about read in original?

```
<script type="text/javascript">

document.write("read from str");
var DataFrame = dfjs.DataFrame;

var data = new DataFrame([
    {c1: 1, c2: 6}, // <------- A row
    {c4: 1, c3: 2}
], ['c1', 'c2', 'c3', 'c4']);


document.write(data.length+"<br><br>");

jstr = JSON.stringify(data);

var jcopy = JSON.parse(jstr, function(key, value){
    if(key == "c1"){
       // return new Date(value);
        document.write(value);
    } else {
        document.write("not c1: "+value);
    }
    document.write("<br>");
});
</script>

# output
read from strundefined

not c1: {"c1":[1,null],"c2":[6,null],"c3":[null,2],"c4":[null,1]}
```

OK, so the data.length is undefined.

And we can see why it is undefined, since the struct is key, value, but value is list...

This shows why we better direct use df.to_html() in py, since {{ data }} in javascript is not that fast,

```
<script type="text/javascript">

document.write("read from str");
var DataFrame = dfjs.DataFrame;

const data = new DataFrame({
    column1: [3, 6, 8], // <------ A column
    column2: [3, 4, 5],
}, ['column1', 'column2']);


document.write(data.length+"<br><br>");
```

```
jstr = JSON.stringify(data);

document.write(jstr);


</script>

# output
undefined


"{\"column1\":[3,6,8],\"column2\":[3,4,5]}"
```

and fast is the most important thing in daily life, since slow makes everything gone,

```
<script src="https://gmousse.github.io/dataframe-js/dist/dataframe.js">
</script>


<p id="df"></p>

<script type="module">
var DataFrame = dfjs.DataFrame;
const df = new DataFrame({
    column1: [3, 6, 8], // <------ A column
    column2: [3, 4, 5, 6],
}, ['column1', 'column2']);

document.getElementById("df").innerHTML = "<pre>"+df.show()+"</pre>";
document.write("<br>");
</script>
```

We can compare the pandas df and dataframe.js df, using the aapl csv data is the first 10 lines,

```
import pandas as pd

df = pd.read_csv('aapl_2024.csv')
print(df.head(10))

# output
                  date      open     high     low     close   volume
0  2024-01-02 09:30:00  187.1500  188.050  186.35  187.8300  2764965
1  2024-01-02 09:31:00  187.8300  188.120  187.63  187.7650   706809
2  2024-01-02 09:32:00  187.7700  188.440  187.73  188.2984   583340
3  2024-01-02 09:33:00  188.3050  188.310  187.81  188.1600   401818
4  2024-01-02 09:34:00  188.1500  188.150  187.67  187.7300   338270
5  2024-01-02 09:35:00  187.7600  188.070  187.66  188.0300   334993
6  2024-01-02 09:36:00  188.0400  188.050  187.66  187.6700   327928
7  2024-01-02 09:37:00  187.6700  187.810  187.56  187.5800   291625
```

```
8  2024-01-02 09:38:00  187.5848  187.625  187.13  187.3850   359752
9  2024-01-02 09:39:00  187.3800  187.590  187.36  187.5300   240877
```

40.1 Create

```
import pandas as pd

# initialize data of lists.
data = {'date': ['2024-01-02 09:30:00', '2024-01-02 09:31:00', '2024-01-02
09:32:00', '2024-01-02 09:33:00', '2024-01-02 09:34:00', '2024-01-02 09:35:00',
'2024-01-02 09:36:00', '2024-01-02 09:37:00', '2024-01-02 09:38:00', '2024-01-02
09:39:00'],
             'open': [187.1500, 187.8300, 187.7700, 187.3050, 188.1500, 187.7600,
188.0400, 187.6700, 187.5848, 187.3800],
           'high': [188.050, 188.120, 188.440, 188.310, 188.150, 188.070, 188.050,
187.810, 187.625, 187.590],
           'low': [186.35, 187.63, 187.73, 187.81, 187.67, 187.66, 187.66, 187.56,
187.13, 187.36],
             'close': [187.8300, 187.7650, 188.2984, 188.1600, 187.7300, 188.0300,
187.6700, 187.5800, 187.3850, 187.5300],
         'volume': [2764965, 706809, 583340, 401818, 338270, 334993, 327928, 291625,
359752, 240877]}

# Create DataFrame
df = pd.DataFrame(data)

print(df)

# js

<script src="https://gmousse.github.io/dataframe-js/dist/dataframe.js">
</script>

<p id="df"></p>

<script type="module">
var DataFrame = dfjs.DataFrame;
const data = new DataFrame(

{date: ['2024-01-02 09:30:00', '2024-01-02 09:31:00', '2024-01-02 09:32:00', '2024-
01-02 09:33:00', '2024-01-02 09:34:00', '2024-01-02 09:35:00', '2024-01-02
09:36:00', '2024-01-02 09:37:00', '2024-01-02 09:38:00', '2024-01-02 09:39:00'],
        open: [187.1500, 187.8300, 187.7700, 187.3050, 188.1500, 187.7600, 188.0400,
187.6700, 187.5848, 187.3800],
            high: [188.050, 188.120, 188.440, 188.310, 188.150, 188.070, 188.050,
187.810, 187.625, 187.590],
            low: [186.35, 187.63, 187.73, 187.81, 187.67, 187.66, 187.66, 187.56,
187.13, 187.36],
              close: [187.8300, 187.7650, 188.2984, 188.1600, 187.7300, 188.0300,
187.6700, 187.5800, 187.3850, 187.5300],
          volume: [2764965, 706809, 583340, 401818, 338270, 334993, 327928, 291625,
359752, 240877],
}, ['date', 'open', 'high', 'low', 'close', 'volume']
```

```
);

document.getElementById("df").innerHTML = "<pre>"+data.show()+"</pre>";
document.write("<br>");
</script>
```

We can also download the js in our folder, with requests,

```
import requests

url = 'https://gmousse.github.io/dataframe-js/dist/dataframe.js'
response = requests.get(url)

if response.status_code == 200:
    with open('dataframe.js', 'wb') as f:
        f.write(response.content)
```

We can try tuples to match the typing style,

```
import pandas as pd

date = ['2024-01-02 09:30:00', '2024-01-02 09:31:00', '2024-01-02 09:32:00', '2024-01-02 09:33:00', '2024-01-02 09:34:00', '2024-01-02 09:35:00', '2024-01-02 09:36:00', '2024-01-02 09:37:00', '2024-01-02 09:38:00', '2024-01-02 09:39:00']
open = [187.1500, 187.8300, 187.7700, 187.3050, 188.1500, 187.7600, 188.0400, 187.6700, 187.5848, 187.3800]
high = [188.050, 188.120, 188.440, 188.310, 188.150, 188.070, 188.050, 187.810, 187.625, 187.590]
low = [186.35, 187.63, 187.73, 187.81, 187.67, 187.66, 187.66, 187.56, 187.13, 187.36]
close = [187.8300, 187.7650, 188.2984, 188.1600, 187.7300, 188.0300, 187.6700, 187.5800, 187.3850, 187.5300]
volume = [2764965, 706809, 583340, 401818, 338270, 334993, 327928, 291625, 359752, 240877]

list_of_tuples = list(zip(date, open, high, low, close, volume))

df = pd.DataFrame(list_of_tuples, columns=['date', 'open', 'high', 'low', 'close', 'volume'])

print(df)
```

But be careful with the colon in py.

42.2 Convert to csv file format

```
print(df.to_csv('file.csv', index = True))

# js

<p id="df"></p>
```

```
<script type="module">
var DataFrame = dfjs.DataFrame;
const df = new DataFrame(

{date: ['2024-01-02 09:30:00', '2024-01-02 09:31:00', '2024-01-02 09:32:00', '2024-01-02 09:33:00', '2024-01-02 09:34:00', '2024-01-02 09:35:00', '2024-01-02 09:36:00', '2024-01-02 09:37:00', '2024-01-02 09:38:00', '2024-01-02 09:39:00'],
        open: [187.1500, 187.8300, 187.7700, 187.3050, 188.1500, 187.7600, 188.0400, 187.6700, 187.5848, 187.3800],
            high: [188.050, 188.120, 188.440, 188.310, 188.150, 188.070, 188.050, 187.810, 187.625, 187.590],
            low: [186.35, 187.63, 187.73, 187.81, 187.67, 187.66, 187.66, 187.56, 187.13, 187.36],
             close: [187.8300, 187.7650, 188.2984, 188.1600, 187.7300, 188.0300, 187.6700, 187.5800, 187.3850, 187.5300],
          volume: [2764965, 706809, 583340, 401818, 338270, 334993, 327928, 291625, 359752, 240877],
}, ['date', 'open', 'high', 'low', 'close', 'volume']
);

document.getElementById("df").innerHTML = "<pre>"+df.toCSV()+"</pre>";
document.write("<br>");

</script>
```

40.3 Add a row

```
df.loc[len(df.index)] = ['2024-01-02 09:40:00', 187.5400, 187.560, 187.02, 187.1300, 375997]

# js
var dff = df.push(['2024-01-02 09:40:00', 187.5400, 187.560, 187.02, 187.1300, 375997]);
document.getElementById("df").innerHTML = "<pre>"+dff.show(11)+"</pre>";
```

40.4 Add a column

```
withColumn = [0] * 11
print(withColumn)
df.loc[:, "index"] = withColumn

# js
var dff = df.push(['2024-01-02 09:40:00', 187.5400, 187.560, 187.02, 187.1300, 375997]);
dff = dff.withColumn('index', () => 0);
document.getElementById("df").innerHTML = "<pre>"+dff.show(11)+"</pre>";
```

40.5 Delete a column

```
df.drop(['index'], axis=1)
```

```
# js
dff = df.drop('index');
```

40.6 Delete multiple columns

```
df.drop(df.iloc[:, 1:5], inplace=True, axis=1) # delete these

# js
df.restructure(['date', 'volume']); //keep these
```

40.7 Delete rows by reassign

```
filtered_df = df.query('open >= 188')


# js
df.filter(row => row.get('open') >= 188);
```

40.8 Sort rows

```
df_sorted_ascending = df.sort_values(by='high', ascending=False)

# js
df.sortBy('high');
```

40.9 Replace values by column

```
df.loc[df["high"] == 188.440 "high"] = 0

# js
df.replace(188.440, 0, 'high');
```

41 qsl4a

What is the qsl4a? See the weather project,

```
# main.py
"""Display the weather report in a notification."""

__author__ = 'Damon Kohler <damonkohler@gmail.com>'
__copyright__ = 'Copyright (c) 2009, Google Inc.'
__license__ = 'Apache License, Version 2.0'

import androidhelper
import weather


def notify_weather(droid):
    """Display the weather at the current location in a notification."""
```

```
    msg = 'Failed to find location.'
    location = droid.getLastKnownLocation().result
    location = location.get('gps') or location.get('network')

    if location is not None:
        print('Finding ZIP code.')
                                addresses    =    droid.geocode(location['latitude'],
location['longitude']).result
        print("Location:")
        print(addresses[0])
        zip = addresses.result[0]['postal_code']
        if zip is not None:
            print('Fetching weather report.')
            result = weather.fetch_weather(zip)
                msg = '%(temperature)s degrees and %(conditions)s, in %(city)s.' %
result
    droid.notify('Weather Report', msg)
    droid.ttsSpeak(msg)


if __name__ == '__main__':
  droid = androidhelper.Android()
  notify_weather(droid)

# weather.py
"""Retrieve the weather report for the current location."""

__author__ = 'T.V. Raman <raman@google.com>'
__copyright__ = 'Copyright (c) 2009, Google Inc.'
__license__ = 'Apache License, Version 2.0'


import string
import urllib.request, urllib.parse, urllib.error
import urllib.request, urllib.error, urllib.parse
from xml.dom import minidom

WEATHER_URL = 'http://www.google.com/ig/api?weather=%s&hl=%s'


def extract_value(dom, parent, child):
  """Convenience function to dig out weather values."""
          return     dom.getElementsByTagName(parent)[0].getElementsByTagName(child)
[0].getAttribute('data')


def fetch_weather(location, hl=''):
  """Fetches weather report from Google

  Args:
    location: a zip code (94041); city name, state (weather=Mountain View,CA);...
    hl: the language parameter (language code)
```

```
    Returns:
      a dict of weather data.

    """
    url = WEATHER_URL % (urllib.parse.quote(location), hl)
    handler = urllib.request.urlopen(url)
    data = handler.read()
    dom = minidom.parseString(data)
    handler.close()

    data = {}
    weather_dom = dom.getElementsByTagName('weather')[0]
    data['city'] = extract_value(weather_dom, 'forecast_information','city')
    data['temperature'] = extract_value(weather_dom, 'current_conditions','temp_f')
    data['conditions'] = extract_value(weather_dom, 'current_conditions', 'condition')
    dom.unlink()
    return data
```

OK, so it analysis the tag from the google website, and returns the weather as data in a dict,

We can just put value, and this is why data encryption is important. Anyone who struggles from life, is because of cheat. You think the value from an orgnization, but it is manipulated.

```
                data['city']         =         'montreal'#extract_value(weather_dom,
'forecast_information','city')
                data['temperature']         =         '25'#extract_value(weather_dom,
'current_conditions','temp_f')
    data['conditions']   =   'good'#extract_value(weather_dom,   'current_conditions',
'condition')
```

The structure of this weather project is very cool, it hints us to make every find into as simple as two steps, find and report. Let's try find UPXI again,

```
# findx.py
import androidhelper
from urllib.request import urlopen
import certifi
import json
import pandas as pd
api_key = "uvjOS64tPdwai8mwwpKtDdfl1LpMFJ0T"

def find(stock):
    msg = stock + " not found"
    api = api_key
    url = (f"https://financialmodelingprep.com/api/v3/historical-chart/1min/{stock}?
apikey="+api)
    response = urlopen(url, cafile=certifi.where())
    data = response.read().decode("utf-8")
    d = json.loads(data);
```

```
    msg = d[0] # the df is in list... first index
    cl = msg['date']+str(msg['close'])
    return cl

def report(msg):
    droid = androidhelper.Android()
    droid.ttsSpeak(msg)

if __name__ == '__main__':
    stock = "UPXI"
    report("Try to find "+stock)
    msg = find(stock)
    report(msg)
```

and we can fit into bottle server,

```
from bottle import Bottle, ServerAdapter
from bottle import static_file, template, request

import os,os.path
ASSETS = "/assets/"
#ASSETS = "\\assets\\"

ROOT = os.path.dirname(os.path.abspath(__file__))
#ROOT = "127.0.0.1:8081"
#print(ROOT)
API_URL = 'https://financialmodelingprep.com/api/v3/historical-chart/1min'


##################### SL4A ##############
try:
    IS_SL4A = True
    #import androidhelper
    #Droid = androidhelper.Android()
    #Droid.startLocating()
except:
    IS_SL4A = False
    pass


######### QPYTHON WEB SERVER ###############

class MyWSGIRefServer(ServerAdapter):
    server = None

    def run(self, handler):
        from wsgiref.simple_server import make_server, WSGIRequestHandler
        if self.quiet:
            class QuietHandler(WSGIRequestHandler):
                def log_request(*args, **kw): pass
            self.options['handler_class'] = QuietHandler
        self.server = make_server(self.host, self.port, handler, **self.options)
```

```
        self.server.serve_forever()

    def stop(self):
        #sys.stderr.close()
        import threading
        threading.Thread(target=self.server.shutdown).start()
        #self.server.shutdown()
        self.server.server_close()
        print("# QWEBAPPEND")


######### BUILT-IN ROUTERS ###############
def __exit():
    global server
    server.stop()

def __ping():
    return "ok"

def server_static(filepath):
    return static_file(filepath, root=ROOT+'/assets')


def home():
    #if IS_SL4A:
    #    location = Droid.getLastKnownLocation().result
    #    location = location.get('network', location.get('gps'))
    return template(ROOT+'/index.html', stock='UPXI')



import androidhelper
from urllib.request import urlopen
import certifi
import json
import pandas as pd


def report (msg):
    droid = androidhelper.Android()
    droid.ttsSpeak(msg)


api_key = "your api"
def detail():
    api = api_key

    stock = request.GET['stock']
    start = request.GET['start']
    end = request.GET['end']

    #data = _get_json_content(API_URL+"&stock="+stock+"&start="+start+"&end="+end)
    url = (f"https://financialmodelingprep.com/api/v3/historical-chart/1min/{stock}?
```

```
from={start}&to={end}&apikey="+api)

    response = urlopen(url, cafile=certifi.where())
    data = response.read().decode("utf-8")
    d = json.loads(data);
    msg = d[0]#['close']
    cl = msg['date']+str(msg['close'])


    report(cl)
    return template(ROOT+'/detail.html',data=d)


######### WEBAPP ROUTERS ###############
app = Bottle()
app.route('/', method='GET')(home)
app.route('/detail', method=['GET','HEAD'])(detail)
app.route('/__exit', method=['GET','HEAD'])(__exit)
app.route('/__ping', method=['GET','HEAD'])(__ping)
app.route('/assets/<filepath:path>', method='GET')(server_static)

try:
    server = MyWSGIRefServer(host="127.0.0.1", port="8081")
    app.run(server=server,reloader=False)
except (Exception) as ex:
    print("Exception: %s" % repr(ex))

# index.html

<!doctype html>
<html class="no-js">
<head>
  <meta charset="utf-8">
  <meta http-equiv="X-UA-Compatible" content="IE=edge">
  <title></title>
  <meta name="description" content="">
  <meta name="keywords" content="">
    <meta  name="viewport"  content="width=device-width,  initial-scale=1,  maximum-
scale=1, user-scalable=no">
  <meta name="renderer" content="webkit">
  <meta http-equiv="Cache-Control" content="no-siteapp" />
  <link rel="stylesheet" href="/assets/css/amazeui.min.css">
  <style>
     .get-title {
      font-size: 200%;
      border: 2px solid #fff;
      padding: 20px;
      display: inline-block;
    }
     .get {
      background: #1E5B94;
      color: #fff;
      text-align: center;
```

```
  padding: 70px 0;
}

.get-title {
  font-size: 200%;
  border: 2px solid #fff;
  padding: 20px;
  display: inline-block;
}

.get-btn {
  background: #fff;
}

.detail {
  background: #fff;
}

.detail-h2 {
  text-align: center;
  font-size: 150%;
  margin: 40px 0;
}

.detail-h3 {
  color: #1f8dd6;
}

.detail-p {
  color: #7f8c8d;
}

.detail-mb {
  margin-bottom: 30px;
}

.hope {
  background: #fff37;
  padding: 50px 0;
}

.hope-img {
  text-align: center;
}

.hope-hr {
  border-color: #149C88;
}

.hope-title {
  font-size: 140%;
}
```

```
    .about {
      background: #fff;
      padding: 40px 0;
      color: #7f8c8d;
    }

    .about-color {
      color: #34495e;
    }

    .about-title {
      font-size: 180%;
      padding: 30px 0 50px 0;
      text-align: center;
    }

    .footer p {
      color: #7f8c8d;
      margin: 0;
      padding: 15px 0;
      text-align: center;
      background: #2d3e50;
    }

    .no1{
    margin:50px;
    border:0;
    padding:0;
    }
  </style>
  <script type="text/javascript">
    function btnOnclick() {
        var keyword = $("#keyword").val();
        window.android.callDetailActivity(keyword);
    }
  </script>
</head>
<body>
<!-- Header -->
<header  data-am-widget="header"  class="am-header  am-header-default  .am-header-
fixed">
  <div class="am-header-left am-header-nav">
    <a href="#left-link" class="">
      <i class="am-header-icon am-icon-home"></i>
    </a>
  </div>
  <h1 class="am-header-title">
    <a href="#title-link" class="">Welcome</a>
  </h1>
  <div class="am-header-right am-header-nav">
    <a href="#right-link" class="">
      <i class="am-header-icon am-icon-bars"></i>
    </a>
```

```
  </div>
</header>

<div class="get">
  <div class="am-g">
    <div class="am-u-lg-12">
      <h1 class="get-title">stock search</h1>
    </div>
  </div>
</div>

<div data-am-widget="tabs" class="am-tabs am-tabs-default">
  <ul class="am-tabs-nav am-cf">

    <li class="">
      <a href="[data-tab-panel-1]">stock</a>
    </li>
  </ul>

<div class="am-tabs-bd">


<div data-tab-panel-1 class="am-tab-panel ">

<div align="center" style="width:100%;padding:30px;padding-bottom:80px;">
    <input type="text" id="stock" class="am-form-field am-round" placeholder="stock"
style="width:40%;float:left;"/>
    <input type="text" id="start" class="am-form-field am-round" placeholder="start"
style="width:30%;float:right;"/>
      <input type="text" id="end" class="am-form-field am-round" placeholder="end"
style="width:30%;float:right;"/>
</div>

<div align="center"><button type="button" class="am-btn am-btn-primary am-round"
onclick="javascript:btnOnclick2();"><i class="am-icon-search"></i> search</button>
</div>
</div>


<div style="height:20px;"></div>

<script src="/assets/js/jquery.min.js"></script>
<script src="/assets/js/amazeui.min.js"></script>
<script type="text/javascript">
function btnOnclick2() {
    var stock = $("#stock").val();
    var start = $("#start").val();
    var end = $("#end").val();
    location.href = '/detail?stock='+stock+"&start="+start+"&end="+end;
}

</script>
```

```
</body>
</html>


# detail.html
<!doctype html>
<html class="no-js">
<head>
  <meta charset="utf-8">
  <meta http-equiv="X-UA-Compatible" content="IE=edge">
  <title>stock detail</title>
  <meta name="description" content="">
  <meta name="keywords" content="">
    <meta  name="viewport"  content="width=device-width,  initial-scale=1,  maximum-
scale=1, user-scalable=no">
  <meta name="renderer" content="webkit">
  <meta http-equiv="Cache-Control" content="no-siteapp" />
  <link rel="stylesheet" href="assets/css/amazeui.min.css">
  <style>
  </style>
</head>
<body>
<!-- Header -->
<header data-am-widget="header" class="am-header am-header-default am-header-fixed">
  <div class="am-header-left am-header-nav">
    <a href="/" class="">
      <i class="am-header-icon am-icon-angle-left"></i>
    </a>
  </div>
  <h1 class="am-header-title">
    <a href="#title-link" id="title" class="">Loading ...</a>
  </h1>
  <div class="am-header-right am-header-nav">
    <a href="#right-link" class="">
      <i class="am-header-icon am-icon-bars"></i>
    </a>
  </div>
</header>


<section id="sectionId" data-am-widget="accordion" class="am-accordion am-accordion-
default"
data-am-accordion=''>

</section>

<div style="height:30px;"></div>

<script src="assets/js/jquery.min.js"></script>
<script src="assets/js/amazeui.min.js"></script>
```

```
<script type="text/javascript">

function appendDetail(date, low, close){

      $("#sectionId").append('<dl class="am-accordion-item"><dt class="am-accordion-title">' + date +'</dt><dd class="am-accordion-bd am-collapse"><div class="am-accordion-content"><code>low</code><br/>' + low + '<br/><hr><code>close</code><br/>' + close + '<br/></div></dd></dl>');

}

function resultCount(num) {

    $("#title").text("data "+num);

}

var data = {{ !data }}

var dl = data.length

resultCount(dl)

var b = (data[0])
document.write(b['date']+b['low']+b['close']);


if (dl==0) {

    $("#sectionId").append('<div style="padding:5px">no data found</div>');

} else {

    for (var i=0;i<dl;i++) {
        var b = data[i]
        var date = b['date']
        var low = b['low']
        var close = b['close']
        appendDetail(date, low, close);
        document.write();
    }
}

</script>
</body>
</html>
```

So the report by ttsSpeak is one of the critical function of qsl4a, what else?

Notice that if put the py in project, it must be main.py, if in script, it can have the first two lines,

```
#qpy:webapp:Stock QPython
#qpy://127.0.0.1:8081/
```

Not a big deal, what else does qsl4a have?

- AndroidFacade
    - Clipboard APIs
    - Intent & startActivity APIs
    - SendBroadcast APIs
    - Vibrate
    - NetworkStatus
    - PackageVersion APIs
    - System APIs
    - SendEmail
    - Toast, getInput, getPassword, notify APIs
- ApplicationManagerFacade
    - Manager APIs
- CameraFacade
- CommonIntentsFacade
    - Barcode
    - View APIs
- ContactsFacade
- EventFacade
- LocationFacade
    - Providers APIs
    - Location APIs
    - GEO
- PhoneFacade
    - PhoneStat APIs
    - Call & Dia APIs
    - Get information APIs
- MediaRecorderFacade
    - Audio
    - Video APIs
    - Stop
- SensorManagerFacade
    - Start & Stop

    - Read data APIs
- SettingsFacade
    - Screen
    - AirplanerMode
    - Ringer Silent Mode
    - Vibrate Mode
    - Ringer & Media Volume
    - Screen Brightness
- SmsFacade
- SpeechRecognitionFacade
- ToneGeneratorFacade
- WakeLockFacade
- WifiFacade
- BatteryManagerFacade
- ActivityResultFacade
- MediaPlayerFacade
    - Control
    - Get Information
- PreferencesFacade
- QPyInterfaceFacade
- TextToSpeechFacade
- EyesFreeFacade
- BluetoothFacade
- SignalStrengthFacade
- WebCamFacade
- UiFacade
    - Dialog
    - NFC
    - Progress
    - Alert
    - Dialog Control
    - Layout
    - WebView
- USB Host Serial Facade
    - Requirements
    - Status
    - Author
    - APIs

Yes, tts is just one facade, and many android API is mapped to qsl4a, and it makes a qpython program looks like an android program,

```
#qpy:quiet
#-*-coding:utf8;-*-
"""
This is a sample project which use SL4A UI Framework,
There is another Sample project: https://github.com/qpython-android/qpy-calcount
"""
import qpy
import androidhelper
try:
    import urllib.request as ur
except:
    import urllib as ur
from qsl4ahelper.fullscreenwrapper2 import *

droid = androidhelper.Android()

class MainScreen(Layout):
    def __init__(self):
        super(MainScreen,self).__init__(str("""<?xml version="1.0" encoding="utf-8"?
>
<LinearLayout
    android:layout_width="fill_parent"
    android:layout_height="fill_parent"
    android:background="#ff0E4200"
    android:orientation="vertical"
    xmlns:android="http://schemas.android.com/apk/res/android">
    <ImageView
        android:id="@+id/logo"
        android:layout_width="fill_parent"
        android:layout_height="0px"
        android:layout_weight="10"
    />
    <LinearLayout
        android:layout_width="fill_parent"
        android:layout_height="0px"
        android:orientation="horizontal"
        android:layout_weight="20">

        <TextView
            android:layout_width="fill_parent"
            android:layout_height="fill_parent"
            android:textSize="8dp"
            android:text="Ask, Stock"
            android:textColor="#ffffffff"
            android:layout_weight="1"
            android:gravity="center"
        />
    </LinearLayout>
```

```
    <ListView
        android:id="@+id/data_list"
        android:layout_width="fill_parent"
        android:layout_height="0px"
        android:layout_weight="55"/>

    <LinearLayout
        android:layout_width="fill_parent"
        android:layout_height="0px"
        android:orientation="horizontal"
        android:layout_weight="8">
        <Button
            android:layout_width="fill_parent"
            android:layout_height="fill_parent"
            android:text="Ask"
            android:id="@+id/but_load"
            android:textSize="8dp"
            android:background="#ffEFC802"
            android:textColor="#ffffffff"
            android:layout_weight="1"
            android:gravity="center"/>
        <Button
            android:layout_width="fill_parent"
            android:layout_height="fill_parent"
            android:text="Exit"
            android:id="@+id/but_exit"
            android:textSize="8dp"
            android:background="#ff06AF00"
            android:textColor="#ffffffff"
            android:layout_weight="1"
            android:gravity="center"/>
    </LinearLayout>
</LinearLayout>
"""),"SL4AApp")

    def on_show(self):
               self.views.but_exit.add_event(click_EventHandler(self.views.but_exit,
self.exit))
               self.views.but_load.add_event(click_EventHandler(self.views.but_load,
self.load))

        pass

    def on_close(self):
        pass

    def load(self, view, dummy):
        droid = FullScreenWrapper2App.get_android_instance()
        #droid.makeToast("Stock")

        respond = droid.dialogGetInput("Hello", "What is your stock?")
        name = respond.result
        if name: message = 'Check, %s!' % name
```

```
        else: message = "Hey! You have no stock to check, %Username%!"
        droid.makeToast(message)

    def exit(self, view, dummy):
        droid = FullScreenWrapper2App.get_android_instance()
        droid.makeToast("Exit")
        FullScreenWrapper2App.close_layout()

if __name__ == '__main__':
    FullScreenWrapper2App.initialize(droid)
    FullScreenWrapper2App.show_layout(MainScreen())
    FullScreenWrapper2App.eventloop()
```

we can just repalce the makeToast to ttsSpeak, and with the query stock web, we just get a quick AI,

```
# qpy:quiet
# -*-coding:utf8;-*-
"""
This is a sample project which use SL4A UI Framework,
There is another Sample project: https://github.com/qpython-android/qpy-calcount
"""

from urllib.request import urlopen
import qpy
import certifi
import json
import pandas as pd
from qsl4ahelper.fullscreenwrapper2 import *
import androidhelper

droid = androidhelper.Android()


class MainScreen(Layout):
    def __init__(self):
        super(MainScreen, self).__init__(
            str(
                """<?xml version="1.0" encoding="utf-8"?>
<LinearLayout
    android:layout_width="fill_parent"
    android:layout_height="fill_parent"
    android:background="#ff0E4200"
    android:orientation="vertical"
    xmlns:android="http://schemas.android.com/apk/res/android">
    <ImageView
        android:id="@+id/logo"
        android:layout_width="fill_parent"
        android:layout_height="0px"
        android:layout_weight="10"
    />
```

```
    <LinearLayout
        android:layout_width="fill_parent"
        android:layout_height="0px"
        android:orientation="horizontal"
        android:layout_weight="20">

        <TextView
            android:layout_width="fill_parent"
            android:layout_height="fill_parent"
            android:textSize="8dp"
            android:text="Ask, Stock"
            android:textColor="#ffffffff"
            android:layout_weight="1"
            android:gravity="center"
        />
    </LinearLayout>

    <ListView
        android:id="@+id/data_list"
        android:layout_width="fill_parent"
        android:layout_height="0px"
        android:layout_weight="55"/>

    <LinearLayout
        android:layout_width="fill_parent"
        android:layout_height="0px"
        android:orientation="horizontal"
        android:layout_weight="8">
        <Button
            android:layout_width="fill_parent"
            android:layout_height="fill_parent"
            android:text="Ask"
            android:id="@+id/but_load"
            android:textSize="8dp"
            android:background="#ffEFC802"
            android:textColor="#ffffffff"
            android:layout_weight="1"
            android:gravity="center"/>
        <Button
            android:layout_width="fill_parent"
            android:layout_height="fill_parent"
            android:text="Exit"
            android:id="@+id/but_exit"
            android:textSize="8dp"
            android:background="#ff06AF00"
            android:textColor="#ffffffff"
            android:layout_weight="1"
            android:gravity="center"/>
    </LinearLayout>
</LinearLayout>
"""
            ),
            "SL4AApp",
```

```
        )

    def on_show(self):
        self.views.but_exit.add_event(
            click_EventHandler(self.views.but_exit, self.exit)
        )
        self.views.but_load.add_event(
            click_EventHandler(self.views.but_load, self.load)
        )

        pass

    def on_close(self):
        pass

    def report(msg):
        droid = androidhelper.Android()
        droid.ttsSpeak(msg)

    def detail(stock):
        api = "uvjOS64tPdwai8mwwpKtDdfl1LpMFJ0T"

        # stock = request.GET['stock']
        url = (
                               f"https://financialmodelingprep.com/api/v3/historical-
chart/1min/{stock}?apikey="
            + api
        )

        response = urlopen(url, cafile=certifi.where())
        data = response.read().decode("utf-8")
        d = json.loads(data)
        msg = d[0]  # ['close']
        cl = msg["date"] + str(msg["close"])

        report(cl)

    def load(self, view, dummy):
        droid = FullScreenWrapper2App.get_android_instance()
        # droid.makeToast("Stock")

        respond = droid.dialogGetInput("Hello", "What is your stock?")
        name = respond.result
        droid.makeToast(name)
        if name:
            detail(name)
        else:
            report("Hey! You have no stock to check")


    def exit(self, view, dummy):
        droid = FullScreenWrapper2App.get_android_instance()
        droid.makeToast("Exit")
```

```
        FullScreenWrapper2App.close_layout()


if __name__ == "__main__":
    FullScreenWrapper2App.initialize(droid)
    FullScreenWrapper2App.show_layout(MainScreen())
    FullScreenWrapper2App.eventloop()
```

The class MainScreen part is very similiar to what?

Kivy!

What is that?

A city?

That is Kyiv...

Speaking of city, can we get our location from qsl4a?

```
def load(self, view, dummy):
        droid = FullScreenWrapper2App.get_android_instance()

        location = droid.getLastKnownLocation().result
        location = location.get('network')

        droid.makeToast(location)
```

But why we click has no response? We need to toast the exception error,

```
def load(self, view, dummy):
        droid = FullScreenWrapper2App.get_android_instance()
        location = droid.getLastKnownLocation().result
        try:
            location = location.get('network')

            droid.makeToast(location)
        except (Exception) as ex:
            droid.makeToast("Exception: %s" % repr(ex))
```

so the location is just empty, means never get any known location, so result is empty, but error is ok, as long as we click exit, it can exit, means program logic is good, so always remember to add `try except` if you think it might has an error stuck the program.

So, what are the basic function that is ok in our phone?

```
import sys
import time
```

```
import types
import androidhelper
try:
  import gdata.docs.service
except ImportError:
  gdata = None

droid = androidhelper.Android()


def event_loop():
  for i in range(10):
    time.sleep(1)
    droid.eventClearBuffer()
    time.sleep(1)
    e = droid.eventPoll(1)
    if e.result is not None:
      return True
  return False

def test_imports():
  try:
    import termios
    import bs4 as BeautifulSoup
    import pyxmpp2 as xmpp
    from xml.dom import minidom
  except ImportError:
    return False
  return True

def test_clipboard():
  previous = droid.getClipboard().result
  msg = 'Hello, world!'
  droid.setClipboard(msg)
  echo = droid.getClipboard().result
  droid.setClipboard(previous)
  return echo == msg


def test_gdata():
  if gdata is None:
    return False

  # Create a client class which will make HTTP requests with Google Docs server.
  client = gdata.docs.service.DocsService()

  # Authenticate using your Google Docs email address and password.
  username = droid.dialogGetInput('Username').result
  password = droid.dialogGetPassword('Password', 'For ' + username).result
  try:
    client.ClientLogin(username, password)
  except:
    return False
```

```
  # Query the server for an Atom feed containing a list of your documents.
  documents_feed = client.GetDocumentListFeed()
  # Loop through the feed and extract each document entry.
  return bool(list(documents_feed.entry))


def test_gps():
  droid.startLocating()
  try:
    return event_loop()
  finally:
    droid.stopLocating()


def test_battery():
  droid.batteryStartMonitoring()
  time.sleep(1)
  try:
    return bool(droid.batteryGetStatus())
  finally:
    droid.batteryStopMonitoring()

def test_sensors():
  # Accelerometer, once per second.
  droid.startSensingTimed(2, 1000)
  try:
    return event_loop()
  finally:
    droid.stopSensing()


def test_phone_state():
  droid.startTrackingPhoneState()
  try:
    return event_loop()
  finally:
    droid.stopTrackingPhoneState()

'''
def test_ringer_silent():
  result1 = droid.toggleRingerSilentMode()
  result2 = droid.toggleRingerSilentMode()
  return result1.error is None and result2.error is None


def test_ringer_volume():
  get_result = droid.getRingerVolume()
  if get_result.error is not None:
    return False
  droid.setRingerVolume(0)
  set_result = droid.setRingerVolume(get_result.result)
  if set_result.error is not None:
```

```
    return False
  return True
'''

def test_get_last_known_location():
  result = droid.getLastKnownLocation()
  return result.error is None


def test_geocode():
  result = droid.geocode(0.0, 0.0, 1)
  return result.error is None


def test_make_toast():
  result = droid.makeToast('Hello, world!')
  return result.error is None


def test_vibrate():
  result = droid.vibrate()
  return result.error is None


def test_notify():
  result = droid.notify('Test Title', 'Hello, world!')
  return result.error is None


def test_get_running_packages():
  result = droid.getRunningPackages()
  return result.error is None


def test_alert_dialog():
  title = 'User Interface'
  message = 'Welcome to the SL4A integration test.'
  droid.dialogCreateAlert(title, message)
  droid.dialogSetPositiveButtonText('Continue')
  droid.dialogShow()
  response = droid.dialogGetResponse().result
  return response['which'] == 'positive'


def test_alert_dialog_with_buttons():
  title = 'Alert'
  message = ('This alert box has 3 buttons and '
             'will wait for you to press one.')
  droid.dialogCreateAlert(title, message)
  droid.dialogSetPositiveButtonText('Yes')
  droid.dialogSetNegativeButtonText('No')
  droid.dialogSetNeutralButtonText('Cancel')
  droid.dialogShow()
```

```
  response = droid.dialogGetResponse().result
  return response['which'] in ('positive', 'negative', 'neutral')


def test_spinner_progress():
  title = 'Spinner'
  message = 'This is simple spinner progress.'
  droid.dialogCreateSpinnerProgress(title, message)
  droid.dialogShow()
  time.sleep(2)
  droid.dialogDismiss()
  return True


def test_horizontal_progress():
  title = 'Horizontal'
  message = 'This is simple horizontal progress.'
  droid.dialogCreateHorizontalProgress(title, message, 50)
  droid.dialogShow()
  for x in range(0, 50):
    time.sleep(0.1)
    droid.dialogSetCurrentProgress(x)
  droid.dialogDismiss()
  return True


def test_alert_dialog_with_list():
  title = 'Alert'
  droid.dialogCreateAlert(title)
  droid.dialogSetItems(['foo', 'bar', 'baz'])
  droid.dialogShow()
  response = droid.dialogGetResponse().result
  return True


def test_alert_dialog_with_single_choice_list():
  title = 'Alert'
  droid.dialogCreateAlert(title)
  droid.dialogSetSingleChoiceItems(['foo', 'bar', 'baz'])
  droid.dialogSetPositiveButtonText('Yay!')
  droid.dialogShow()
  response = droid.dialogGetResponse().result
  return True


def test_alert_dialog_with_multi_choice_list():
  title = 'Alert'
  droid.dialogCreateAlert(title)
  droid.dialogSetMultiChoiceItems(['foo', 'bar', 'baz'], [])
  droid.dialogSetPositiveButtonText('Yay!')
  droid.dialogShow()
  response = droid.dialogGetResponse().result
  return True
```

```
def test_wifi():
  result1 = droid.toggleWifiState()
  result2 = droid.toggleWifiState()
   droid.toggleWifiState(True)   # Make sure wifi ends up ON, as it interferes with
other tests
  return result1.error is None and result2.error is None

def report(msg):
  result = droid.ttsSpeak(msg)
  return result.error is None

if __name__ == '__main__':
  for name, value in list(globals().items()):
    if name.startswith('test_') and isinstance(value, types.FunctionType):
      print('Running %s...' % name, end=' ')
      sys.stdout.flush()
      if value():
        print(' PASS')
      else:
        print(' FAIL')
        report("%s is not succesful" % name)
```

The trick is making a global list which convert all the test functions in a queue, and flush all the test result, so we can easily add many single test as we want, all the test function returns True False, so it maps to PASS FAIL.

FInally, when try to install kivy on qpython, it returns an error, arch linux clang, well, c for c, lang for language.

So plus together is clang, integrating C, C++, and Objective-C compilers, including encompasses preprocessing, parsing, optimization, code generation, assembly, and linking.

It is ok to just use qsl4a, until the tts in other language, on some phones,

```
#qpy:quiet
#-*-coding:utf8;-*-
"""
This is a sample project which use SL4A UI Framework,
There is another Sample project: https://github.com/qpython-android/qpy-calcount
"""
import qpy
import androidhelper
try:
    import urllib.request as ur
except:
    import urllib as ur
from qsl4ahelper.fullscreenwrapper2 import *
```

```
droid = androidhelper.Android()

class MainScreen(Layout):
    def __init__(self):
        super(MainScreen,self).__init__(str("""<?xml version="1.0" encoding="utf-8"?
>
<LinearLayout
    android:layout_width="fill_parent"
    android:layout_height="fill_parent"

    android:orientation="vertical"
    xmlns:android="http://schemas.android.com/apk/res/android">
    <ImageView
        android:id="@+id/logo"
        android:layout_width="fill_parent"
        android:layout_height="0px"
        android:layout_weight="10"
    />
    <LinearLayout
        android:layout_width="fill_parent"
        android:layout_height="0px"
        android:orientation="horizontal"
        android:layout_weight="20">

        <TextView
            android:layout_width="fill_parent"
            android:layout_height="fill_parent"
            android:textSize="8dp"
            android:text="What's your sentence?"
            android:textColor="#ffffffff"
            android:layout_weight="1"
            android:gravity="center"
        />

        <EditText android:id="@+id/enter"

            android:layout_width="fill_parent"

            android:layout_height="wrap_content"
            android:textSize="8dp"
            android:layout_weight="1"
        />
    </LinearLayout>

    <ListView
        android:id="@+id/data_list"
        android:layout_width="fill_parent"
        android:layout_height="0px"
        android:layout_weight="55"/>

    <LinearLayout
        android:layout_width="fill_parent"
        android:layout_height="0px"
```

```
        android:orientation="horizontal"
        android:layout_weight="8">
        <Button
            android:layout_width="fill_parent"
            android:layout_height="fill_parent"
            android:text="Speak"
            android:id="@+id/but_load"
            android:textSize="8dp"
            android:background="#ffEFC802"
            android:textColor="#ffffffff"
            android:layout_weight="1"
            android:gravity="center"/>
        <Button
            android:layout_width="fill_parent"
            android:layout_height="fill_parent"
            android:text="Exit"
            android:id="@+id/but_exit"
            android:textSize="8dp"
            android:background="#ff06AF00"
            android:textColor="#ffffffff"
            android:layout_weight="1"
            android:gravity="center"/>
    </LinearLayout>
</LinearLayout>
"""),"SL4AApp")

    def on_show(self):
                self.views.but_exit.add_event(click_EventHandler(self.views.but_exit,
self.exit))
                self.views.but_load.add_event(click_EventHandler(self.views.but_load,
self.load))

        pass

    def on_close(self):
        pass

    def load(self, view, dummy):
        droid = FullScreenWrapper2App.get_android_instance()
        try:
            a = str ((self.views.enter.text))
            droid.ttsSpeak(a)

        except:

            droid.dialogCreateAlert(a)
            droid.dialogShow()


    def exit(self, view, dummy):
        droid = FullScreenWrapper2App.get_android_instance()
        droid.makeToast("Exit")
        FullScreenWrapper2App.close_layout()
```

```
if __name__ == '__main__':
    FullScreenWrapper2App.initialize(droid)
    FullScreenWrapper2App.show_layout(MainScreen())
    FullScreenWrapper2App.eventloop()
```

Notice we use @id of views to return the text value, and speak in English.

42 espeakng

Le française?

```
import androidhelper

def report (language, msg):
    droid = androidhelper.Android()
    if language == "French":
        droid.ttsSpeakFrench(msg) # fail...
    else:
        droid.ttsSpeak(msg)

report("French", "Tu parle le française?")
```

There is no speak french parameter in some android phones, the tts is under **settings** of **accesibility**,

so we go back to Windows, checkout https://pypi.org/search/?q=melotts&o=, try install with pip,

```
C:\Users\Lenovo> pip install melotts
Defaulting to user installation because normal site-packages is not writeable
Collecting melotts
  Downloading melotts-0.1.1.tar.gz (4.6 MB)
     ━━━━━━━━━━━━━━━━━━━━━━━━━━━━━━━━━━━━━━━━ 4.6/4.6 MB
11.9 kB/s eta 0:00:00
  Installing build dependencies ... done
  Getting requirements to build wheel ... error
  error: subprocess-exited-with-error

  × Getting requirements to build wheel did not run successfully.
  │ exit code: 1
  ╰─> [20 lines of output]
      Traceback (most recent call last):
                                                              File        "C:\Program
Files\WindowsApps\PythonSoftwareFoundation.Python.3.12_3.12.2032.0_x64__qbz5n2kfra8p
0\Lib\site-packages\pip\_vendor\pyproject_hooks\_in_process\_in_process.py",     line
353, in <module>
        main()
                                                              File        "C:\Program
Files\WindowsApps\PythonSoftwareFoundation.Python.3.12_3.12.2032.0_x64__qbz5n2kfra8p
```

```
0\Lib\site-packages\pip\_vendor\pyproject_hooks\_in_process\_in_process.py", line
335, in main
          json_out['return_val'] = hook(**hook_input['kwargs'])
                                   ^^^^^^^^^^^^^^^^^^^^^^^^^^^^
                                                              File "C:\Program
Files\WindowsApps\PythonSoftwareFoundation.Python.3.12_3.12.2032.0_x64__qbz5n2kfra8p
0\Lib\site-packages\pip\_vendor\pyproject_hooks\_in_process\_in_process.py", line
118, in get_requires_for_build_wheel
          return hook(config_settings)
                 ^^^^^^^^^^^^^^^^^^^^^
                           File "C:\Users\Lenovo\AppData\Local\Temp\pip-build-env-
5j33tlmw\overlay\Lib\site-packages\setuptools\build_meta.py", line 333, in
get_requires_for_build_wheel
          return self._get_build_requires(config_settings, requirements=[])
                 ^^^^^^^^^^^^^^^^^^^^^^^^^^^^^^^^^^^^^^^^^^^^^^^^^^^^^^^^^^
                           File "C:\Users\Lenovo\AppData\Local\Temp\pip-build-env-
5j33tlmw\overlay\Lib\site-packages\setuptools\build_meta.py", line 303, in
_get_build_requires
          self.run_setup()
                           File "C:\Users\Lenovo\AppData\Local\Temp\pip-build-env-
5j33tlmw\overlay\Lib\site-packages\setuptools\build_meta.py", line 521, in run_setup
          super().run_setup(setup_script=setup_script)
                           File "C:\Users\Lenovo\AppData\Local\Temp\pip-build-env-
5j33tlmw\overlay\Lib\site-packages\setuptools\build_meta.py", line 319, in run_setup
          exec(code, locals())
        File "<string>", line 7, in <module>
                 FileNotFoundError: [Errno 2] No such file or directory:
'C:\\Users\\Lenovo\\AppData\\Local\\Temp\\pip-install-
082qttaa\\melotts_f679ddd3ac114177a8a79edf5114e9c9\\requirements.txt'
      [end of output]

  note: This error originates from a subprocess, and is likely not a problem with
pip.

[notice] A new release of pip is available: 24.2 -> 24.3.1
[notice] To update, run:
C:\Users\Lenovo\AppData\Local\Microsoft\WindowsApps\PythonSoftwareFoundation.Python.
3.12_qbz5n2kfra8p0\python.exe -m pip install --upgrade pip
error: subprocess-exited-with-error

× Getting requirements to build wheel did not run successfully.
│ exit code: 1
╰─> See above for output.
```

as the error says, it is not a pip problem, and it fails since no requirements.txt found, well, the other way is with python setup.py, download https://github.com/myshell-ai/MeloTTS/archive/refs/heads/main.zip and unzip as MeloTTS, and...

```
cd MeloTTS
pip install -e .
python -m unidic download
```

```
# output
Defaulting to user installation because normal site-packages is not writeable
Obtaining file:///C:/Users/Lenovo/Flask/MeloTTS-main
  Installing build dependencies ... done
  Checking if build backend supports build_editable ... done
  Getting requirements to build editable ... done
  Preparing editable metadata (pyproject.toml) ... done
Collecting txtsplit (from melotts==0.1.2)
  Downloading txtsplit-1.0.0.tar.gz (6.2 kB)
  Installing build dependencies ... done
  Getting requirements to build wheel ... done
  Preparing metadata (pyproject.toml) ... done
Collecting torch (from melotts==0.1.2)
  Downloading torch-2.5.1-cp312-cp312-win_amd64.whl.metadata (28 kB)
Collecting torchaudio (from melotts==0.1.2)
  Downloading torchaudio-2.5.1-cp312-cp312-win_amd64.whl.metadata (6.5 kB)
Collecting cached-path (from melotts==0.1.2)
  Downloading cached_path-1.6.3-py3-none-any.whl.metadata (19 kB)
Collecting transformers==4.27.4 (from melotts==0.1.2)
  Downloading transformers-4.27.4-py3-none-any.whl.metadata (106 kB)
Collecting num2words==0.5.12 (from melotts==0.1.2)
  Downloading num2words-0.5.12-py3-none-any.whl.metadata (11 kB)
Collecting unidic-lite==1.0.8 (from melotts==0.1.2)
  Downloading unidic-lite-1.0.8.tar.gz (47.4 MB)
     ━━━━━━━━━━━━━━━━━━━━━━━━━━━━━━━━━━━━━━━━━━━━━━━━━━━━ 47.4/47.4
MB 16.1 kB/s eta 0:00:00
  Installing build dependencies ... done
  Getting requirements to build wheel ... done
  Preparing metadata (pyproject.toml) ... done
Collecting unidic==1.1.0 (from melotts==0.1.2)
  Downloading unidic-1.1.0.tar.gz (7.7 kB)
  Installing build dependencies ... done
  Getting requirements to build wheel ... done
  Preparing metadata (pyproject.toml) ... done
Collecting mecab-python3==1.0.9 (from melotts==0.1.2)
  Downloading mecab_python3-1.0.9-cp312-cp312-win_amd64.whl.metadata (6.3 kB)
Collecting pykakasi==2.2.1 (from melotts==0.1.2)
  Downloading pykakasi-2.2.1-py3-none-any.whl.metadata (10 kB)
Collecting fugashi==1.3.0 (from melotts==0.1.2)
  Downloading fugashi-1.3.0.tar.gz (338 kB)
  Installing build dependencies ... done
  Getting requirements to build wheel ... done
  Installing backend dependencies ... done
  Preparing metadata (pyproject.toml) ... done
Collecting g2p-en==2.1.0 (from melotts==0.1.2)
  Downloading g2p_en-2.1.0-py3-none-any.whl.metadata (4.5 kB)
Collecting anyascii==0.3.2 (from melotts==0.1.2)
  Downloading anyascii-0.3.2-py3-none-any.whl.metadata (1.5 kB)
Collecting jamo==0.4.1 (from melotts==0.1.2)
  Downloading jamo-0.4.1-py3-none-any.whl.metadata (2.3 kB)
Collecting gruut==2.2.3 (from gruut[de,es,fr]==2.2.3->melotts==0.1.2)
  Downloading gruut-2.2.3.tar.gz (73 kB)
```

```
  Installing build dependencies ... done
  Getting requirements to build wheel ... done
  Preparing metadata (pyproject.toml) ... done
Collecting g2pkk>=0.1.1 (from melotts==0.1.2)
  Downloading g2pkk-0.1.2-py3-none-any.whl.metadata (2.0 kB)
Collecting librosa==0.9.1 (from melotts==0.1.2)
  Downloading librosa-0.9.1-py3-none-any.whl.metadata (6.9 kB)
Collecting pydub==0.25.1 (from melotts==0.1.2)
  Downloading pydub-0.25.1-py2.py3-none-any.whl.metadata (1.4 kB)
Collecting eng-to-ipa==0.0.2 (from melotts==0.1.2)
  Downloading eng_to_ipa-0.0.2.tar.gz (2.8 MB)
     ---------------------------------------- 2.8/2.8 MB
15.2 kB/s eta 0:00:00
  Installing build dependencies ... done
  Getting requirements to build wheel ... done
  Preparing metadata (pyproject.toml) ... done
Collecting inflect==7.0.0 (from melotts==0.1.2)
  Downloading inflect-7.0.0-py3-none-any.whl.metadata (21 kB)
Collecting unidecode==1.3.7 (from melotts==0.1.2)
  Downloading Unidecode-1.3.7-py3-none-any.whl.metadata (13 kB)
Collecting pypinyin==0.50.0 (from melotts==0.1.2)
  Downloading pypinyin-0.50.0-py2.py3-none-any.whl.metadata (12 kB)
Collecting cn2an==0.5.22 (from melotts==0.1.2)
  Downloading cn2an-0.5.22-py3-none-any.whl.metadata (10 kB)
Collecting jieba==0.42.1 (from melotts==0.1.2)
  Downloading jieba-0.42.1.tar.gz (19.2 MB)
     ---------------------------------------- 19.2/19.2
MB 252.8 kB/s eta 0:00:00
  Installing build dependencies ... done
  Getting requirements to build wheel ... done
  Preparing metadata (pyproject.toml) ... done
Collecting gradio (from melotts==0.1.2)
  Downloading gradio-5.4.0-py3-none-any.whl.metadata (16 kB)
Collecting langid==1.1.6 (from melotts==0.1.2)
  Downloading langid-1.1.6.tar.gz (1.9 MB)
     ---------------------------------------- 1.9/1.9 MB
591.5 kB/s eta 0:00:00
  Installing build dependencies ... done
  Getting requirements to build wheel ... done
  Preparing metadata (pyproject.toml) ... done
Requirement already satisfied: tqdm in
c:\users\lenovo\appdata\local\packages\pythonsoftwarefoundation.python.3.12_qbz5n2kf
ra8p0\localcache\local-packages\python312\site-packages (from melotts==0.1.2)
(4.66.2)
Collecting tensorboard==2.16.2 (from melotts==0.1.2)
  Downloading tensorboard-2.16.2-py3-none-any.whl.metadata (1.6 kB)
Collecting loguru==0.7.2 (from melotts==0.1.2)
  Downloading loguru-0.7.2-py3-none-any.whl.metadata (23 kB)
Requirement already satisfied: setuptools>=47.3.1 in
c:\users\lenovo\appdata\local\packages\pythonsoftwarefoundation.python.3.12_qbz5n2kf
ra8p0\localcache\local-packages\python312\site-packages (from cn2an==0.5.22-
>melotts==0.1.2) (72.2.0)
Collecting proces>=0.1.3 (from cn2an==0.5.22->melotts==0.1.2)
```

```
  Downloading proces-0.1.7-py3-none-any.whl.metadata (3.3 kB)
Requirement already satisfied: numpy>=1.13.1 in
c:\users\lenovo\appdata\local\packages\pythonsoftwarefoundation.python.3.12_qbz5n2kf
ra8p0\localcache\local-packages\python312\site-packages (from g2p-en==2.1.0-
>melotts==0.1.2) (1.26.4)
Collecting nltk>=3.2.4 (from g2p-en==2.1.0->melotts==0.1.2)
  Downloading nltk-3.9.1-py3-none-any.whl.metadata (2.9 kB)
Collecting distance>=0.1.3 (from g2p-en==2.1.0->melotts==0.1.2)
  Downloading Distance-0.1.3.tar.gz (180 kB)
  Installing build dependencies ... done
  Getting requirements to build wheel ... done
  Preparing metadata (pyproject.toml) ... done
Collecting Babel<3.0.0,>=2.8.0 (from gruut==2.2.3->gruut[de,es,fr]==2.2.3-
>melotts==0.1.2)
  Downloading babel-2.16.0-py3-none-any.whl.metadata (1.5 kB)
Collecting dateparser~=1.1.0 (from gruut==2.2.3->gruut[de,es,fr]==2.2.3-
>melotts==0.1.2)
  Downloading dateparser-1.1.8-py2.py3-none-any.whl.metadata (27 kB)
Collecting gruut-ipa<1.0,>=0.12.0 (from gruut==2.2.3->gruut[de,es,fr]==2.2.3-
>melotts==0.1.2)
  Downloading gruut-ipa-0.13.0.tar.gz (101 kB)
  Installing build dependencies ... done
  Getting requirements to build wheel ... done
  Preparing metadata (pyproject.toml) ... done
Collecting gruut-lang-en~=2.0.0 (from gruut==2.2.3->gruut[de,es,fr]==2.2.3-
>melotts==0.1.2)
  Downloading gruut_lang_en-2.0.1.tar.gz (15.3 MB)
     ---------------------------------------- 15.3/15.3
MB 332.6 kB/s eta 0:00:00
  Installing build dependencies ... done
  Getting requirements to build wheel ... done
  Preparing metadata (pyproject.toml) ... done
Collecting jsonlines~=1.2.0 (from gruut==2.2.3->gruut[de,es,fr]==2.2.3-
>melotts==0.1.2)
  Downloading jsonlines-1.2.0-py2.py3-none-any.whl.metadata (1.3 kB)
Collecting networkx<3.0.0,>=2.5.0 (from gruut==2.2.3->gruut[de,es,fr]==2.2.3-
>melotts==0.1.2)
  Downloading networkx-2.8.8-py3-none-any.whl.metadata (5.1 kB)
Collecting python-crfsuite~=0.9.7 (from gruut==2.2.3->gruut[de,es,fr]==2.2.3-
>melotts==0.1.2)
  Downloading python_crfsuite-0.9.11-cp312-cp312-win_amd64.whl.metadata (4.4 kB)
Collecting gruut-lang-de~=2.0.0 (from gruut[de,es,fr]==2.2.3->melotts==0.1.2)
  Downloading gruut_lang_de-2.0.1.tar.gz (18.1 MB)
     -------------- ------------------------- 6.3/18.1 MB
105.1 kB/s eta 0:01:53
```

OK...

Despite the huge library dependency, we have risk on clang too,

```
Building wheels for collected packages: melotts, eng-to-ipa, fugashi, gruut, jieba,
langid, unidic, unidic-lite, txtsplit, distance, docopt, gruut-ipa, gruut-lang-de,
```

```
gruut-lang-en, gruut-lang-es, gruut-lang-fr, tokenizers, jaconv
  Building editable for melotts (pyproject.toml) ... done
   Created wheel for melotts: filename=melotts-0.1.2-0.editable-py3-none-any.whl
size=4016 sha256=1d3fc0955bc842cd9755bbb655ff138b55c056b92fa2228a5b65df0c8372349c
   Stored in directory: C:\Users\Lenovo\AppData\Local\Temp\pip-ephem-wheel-cache-
nlfemec2\wheels\1a\e7\a3\6c55340ade06b2d45d2f4b0be26defdd9d3c2dce9b34872dce
  Building wheel for eng-to-ipa (pyproject.toml) ... done
   Created wheel for eng-to-ipa: filename=eng_to_ipa-0.0.2-py3-none-any.whl
size=2822626 sha256=02e47511c1f0536a1ebaa3682227de4c530097d1c11bb28796f8fe6a068980ee
   Stored in directory:
c:\users\lenovo\appdata\local\packages\pythonsoftwarefoundation.python.3.12_qbz5n2kf
ra8p0\localcache\local\pip\cache\wheels\cf\2b\91\f066669a92e46921f2c953cb87c8f714e2c
127cb9342525d54
  Building wheel for fugashi (pyproject.toml) ... error
  error: subprocess-exited-with-error

  × Building wheel for fugashi (pyproject.toml) did not run successfully.
  │ exit code: 1
  ╰─> [20 lines of output]
      WARNING setuptools_scm.pyproject_reading toml section missing 'pyproject.toml
does not contain a tool.setuptools_scm section'
      Traceback (most recent call last):
        File "C:\Users\Lenovo\AppData\Local\Temp\pip-build-env-
lel4qub3\normal\Lib\site-packages\setuptools_scm\_integration\pyproject_reading.py",
line 36, in read_pyproject
          section = defn.get("tool", {})[tool_name]
                    ~~~~~~~~~~~~~~~~~~~~^^^^^^^^^^^
      KeyError: 'setuptools_scm'
      running bdist_wheel
      running build
      running build_py
      creating build\lib.win-amd64-cpython-312\fugashi
      copying fugashi\cli.py -> build\lib.win-amd64-cpython-312\fugashi
      copying fugashi\__init__.py -> build\lib.win-amd64-cpython-312\fugashi
      running build_ext
      cythoning fugashi/fugashi.pyx to fugashi\fugashi.c
      building 'fugashi.fugashi' extension
      creating build\temp.win-amd64-cpython-312\Release\fugashi
      "C:\Program Files (x86)\Microsoft Visual
Studio\2022\BuildTools\VC\Tools\MSVC\14.41.34120\bin\HostX86\x64\cl.exe" /c /nologo
/O2 /W3 /GL /DNDEBUG /MD -IC:\mecab "-IC:\Program
Files\WindowsApps\PythonSoftwareFoundation.Python.3.12_3.12.2032.0_x64__qbz5n2kfra8p
0\include" "-IC:\Program
Files\WindowsApps\PythonSoftwareFoundation.Python.3.12_3.12.2032.0_x64__qbz5n2kfra8p
0\Include" "-IC:\Program Files (x86)\Microsoft Visual
Studio\2022\BuildTools\VC\Tools\MSVC\14.41.34120\include" "-IC:\Program Files
(x86)\Microsoft Visual Studio\2022\BuildTools\VC\Auxiliary\VS\include" "-IC:\Program
Files (x86)\Windows Kits\10\include\10.0.22621.0\ucrt" "-IC:\Program Files
(x86)\Windows Kits\10\\include\10.0.22621.0\\um" "-IC:\Program Files (x86)\Windows
Kits\10\\include\10.0.22621.0\\shared" "-IC:\Program Files (x86)\Windows
Kits\10\\include\10.0.22621.0\\winrt" "-IC:\Program Files (x86)\Windows
Kits\10\\include\10.0.22621.0\\cppwinrt" /Tcfugashi\fugashi.c /Fobuild\temp.win-
amd64-cpython-312\Release\fugashi\fugashi.obj
```

```
      fugashi.c
      fugashi\fugashi.c(750): fatal error C1083: 无法打开包括文件: "mecab.h": No such file or directory
      error: command 'C:\\Program Files (x86)\\Microsoft Visual Studio\\2022\\BuildTools\\VC\\Tools\\MSVC\\14.41.34120\\bin\\HostX86\\x64\\cl.exe' failed with exit code 2
      [end of output]

  note: This error originates from a subprocess, and is likely not a problem with pip.
  ERROR: Failed building wheel for fugashi
  Building wheel for gruut (pyproject.toml) ... done
  Created wheel for gruut: filename=gruut-2.2.3-py3-none-any.whl size=75851 sha256=f1faa183023e4d251ab01b4fdaf62b5c648fe614dda89ef42f9a4205ff96bf3b
  Stored in directory: c:\users\lenovo\appdata\local\packages\pythonsoftwarefoundation.python.3.12_qbz5n2kfra8p0\localcache\local\pip\cache\wheels\70\08\01\a80836c258b22fe3db037fba21e51ec327f74174838010d93b
  Building wheel for jieba (pyproject.toml) ... done
  Created wheel for jieba: filename=jieba-0.42.1-py3-none-any.whl size=19314474 sha256=3bd72fd113e85903e89096b3994ffb69cd1912d93c44759310ca93e20621da28
  Stored in directory: c:\users\lenovo\appdata\local\packages\pythonsoftwarefoundation.python.3.12_qbz5n2kfra8p0\localcache\local\pip\cache\wheels\08\a1\a3\5c8ac52cc2f5782ffffc34c95c57c8e5ecb3063dc69541ee7c
  Building wheel for langid (pyproject.toml) ... done
  Created wheel for langid: filename=langid-1.1.6-py3-none-any.whl size=1941178 sha256=a51e84b70d5b6687f632b8d3718ca2d6a8621ff863b83127c80793f5e344a010
  Stored in directory: c:\users\lenovo\appdata\local\packages\pythonsoftwarefoundation.python.3.12_qbz5n2kfra8p0\localcache\local\pip\cache\wheels\3c\bc\9d\266e27289b9019680d65d9b608c37bff1eff565b001c977ec5
  Building wheel for unidic (pyproject.toml) ... done
  Created wheel for unidic: filename=unidic-1.1.0-py3-none-any.whl size=7434 sha256=7c473f5c695c5e6b0f546079df7d7c7abce652c871203a6b6f9205a834bc3def
  Stored in directory: c:\users\lenovo\appdata\local\packages\pythonsoftwarefoundation.python.3.12_qbz5n2kfra8p0\localcache\local\pip\cache\wheels\cb\04\a2\659428f84ed1fa7257f8efb544b36043dd37a7c419e8ca711a
  Building wheel for unidic-lite (pyproject.toml) ... done
  Created wheel for unidic-lite: filename=unidic_lite-1.0.8-py3-none-any.whl size=47658834
sha256=130ea57f2ce0c0f0c071f34738042018f50a9ac57f3a22ef468386b0b484706a
  Stored in directory: c:\users\lenovo\appdata\local\packages\pythonsoftwarefoundation.python.3.12_qbz5n2kfra8p0\localcache\local\pip\cache\wheels\5e\1f\0f\4d43887e5476d956fae828ee9b6687becd5544d68b51ed633d
  Building wheel for txtsplit (pyproject.toml) ... done
  Created wheel for txtsplit: filename=txtsplit-1.0.0-py3-none-any.whl size=6497 sha256=21825372f9b2e52a07e6306aee7cba12e5b66b6d0ce232b3cb229295d9fbeb59
  Stored in directory: c:\users\lenovo\appdata\local\packages\pythonsoftwarefoundation.python.3.12_qbz5n2kfra8p0\localcache\local\pip\cache\wheels\3a\46\ad\ab8ae046750d958835d8f727fb42aa6d6f0
```

```
149e2fa87471dae
  Building wheel for distance (pyproject.toml) ... done
   Created wheel for distance: filename=Distance-0.1.3-py3-none-any.whl size=16281
sha256=bde5fcddc69c8ad2b10a0069c05837d3b0b66ecc773f3a6ddb3fd78b74d1a3d6
                                    Stored                    in                directory:
c:\users\lenovo\appdata\local\packages\pythonsoftwarefoundation.python.3.12_qbz5n2kf
ra8p0\localcache\local\pip\cache\wheels\24\a8\58\407063d8e5c1d4dd6594c99d12baa010857
0b56a92325587dd
  Building wheel for docopt (pyproject.toml) ... done
   Created wheel for docopt: filename=docopt-0.6.2-py2.py3-none-any.whl size=13774
sha256=f2099c04fef9264005e860aacdfd8faa74a064644e0716c648cce6bf3867b140
                                    Stored                    in                directory:
c:\users\lenovo\appdata\local\packages\pythonsoftwarefoundation.python.3.12_qbz5n2kf
ra8p0\localcache\local\pip\cache\wheels\1a\bf\a1\4cee4f7678c68c5875ca89eaccf46059353
9805c3906722228
  Building wheel for gruut-ipa (pyproject.toml) ... done
      Created   wheel   for   gruut-ipa:   filename=gruut_ipa-0.13.0-py3-none-any.whl
size=104907 sha256=404c4f8e58b11501896455df589a192ee022a57b8433ed3dea9b68563a38a793
                                    Stored                    in                directory:
c:\users\lenovo\appdata\local\packages\pythonsoftwarefoundation.python.3.12_qbz5n2kf
ra8p0\localcache\local\pip\cache\wheels\66\9d\d2\d6f6eb77784f063fcd497427fd93324cebf
974247984bba85b
  Building wheel for gruut-lang-de (pyproject.toml) ... done
    Created  wheel  for  gruut-lang-de:  filename=gruut_lang_de-2.0.1-py3-none-any.whl
size=18498321
sha256=df70aac4b5e0e9ba9ee8df6a1348121db2b723df9cd9972e0d1ef80fc26bea6d
                                    Stored                    in                directory:
c:\users\lenovo\appdata\local\packages\pythonsoftwarefoundation.python.3.12_qbz5n2kf
ra8p0\localcache\local\pip\cache\wheels\dc\75\26\e627d52dac0253ad7d11e5b9f74d51d82e0
40d07432f53ad9b
  Building wheel for gruut-lang-en (pyproject.toml) ... done
    Created  wheel  for  gruut-lang-en:  filename=gruut_lang_en-2.0.1-py3-none-any.whl
size=15326866
sha256=b61798a81d27ab0ca6833fe70ba6422c8a26b1e26e229c230f84b1e7c9d7b6be
                                    Stored                    in                directory:
c:\users\lenovo\appdata\local\packages\pythonsoftwarefoundation.python.3.12_qbz5n2kf
ra8p0\localcache\local\pip\cache\wheels\b0\ca\a4\d1a6f20e47b857313689ca1f31684102ba6
7cecda2acae368d
  Building wheel for gruut-lang-es (pyproject.toml) ... done
    Created  wheel  for  gruut-lang-es:  filename=gruut_lang_es-2.0.1-py3-none-any.whl
size=32173937
sha256=65b68beb307eb966e498b46786f0519865bcb179549772303dc3c894707e23e2
                                    Stored                    in                directory:
c:\users\lenovo\appdata\local\packages\pythonsoftwarefoundation.python.3.12_qbz5n2kf
ra8p0\localcache\local\pip\cache\wheels\6e\19\79\0a65f77c4921ae0daa8d01e5b11502a909b
55bd22fa188962d
  Building wheel for gruut-lang-fr (pyproject.toml) ... done
    Created  wheel  for  gruut-lang-fr:  filename=gruut_lang_fr-2.0.2-py3-none-any.whl
size=10968773
sha256=02e6d8e3a4e5af9853de5148c7962488ed7ff83118ec5a9d1485cdf520aec5a3
                                    Stored                    in                directory:
c:\users\lenovo\appdata\local\packages\pythonsoftwarefoundation.python.3.12_qbz5n2kf
ra8p0\localcache\local\pip\cache\wheels\1e\91\46\0ab326f9e46bc2cc2fe2f35b0e0e6f3b828
```

```
4d78efd25192d96
  Building wheel for tokenizers (pyproject.toml) ... error
  error: subprocess-exited-with-error

  × Building wheel for tokenizers (pyproject.toml) did not run successfully.
  │ exit code: 1
  ╰─> [49 lines of output]
      running bdist_wheel
      running build
      running build_py
      creating build\lib.win-amd64-cpython-312\tokenizers
      copying py_src\tokenizers\__init__.py -> build\lib.win-amd64-cpython-312\tokenizers
      creating build\lib.win-amd64-cpython-312\tokenizers\models
      copying py_src\tokenizers\models\__init__.py -> build\lib.win-amd64-cpython-312\tokenizers\models
      creating build\lib.win-amd64-cpython-312\tokenizers\decoders
      copying py_src\tokenizers\decoders\__init__.py -> build\lib.win-amd64-cpython-312\tokenizers\decoders
      creating build\lib.win-amd64-cpython-312\tokenizers\normalizers
      copying py_src\tokenizers\normalizers\__init__.py -> build\lib.win-amd64-cpython-312\tokenizers\normalizers
      creating build\lib.win-amd64-cpython-312\tokenizers\pre_tokenizers
      copying py_src\tokenizers\pre_tokenizers\__init__.py -> build\lib.win-amd64-cpython-312\tokenizers\pre_tokenizers
      creating build\lib.win-amd64-cpython-312\tokenizers\processors
      copying py_src\tokenizers\processors\__init__.py -> build\lib.win-amd64-cpython-312\tokenizers\processors
      creating build\lib.win-amd64-cpython-312\tokenizers\trainers
      copying py_src\tokenizers\trainers\__init__.py -> build\lib.win-amd64-cpython-312\tokenizers\trainers
      creating build\lib.win-amd64-cpython-312\tokenizers\implementations
      copying py_src\tokenizers\implementations\base_tokenizer.py -> build\lib.win-amd64-cpython-312\tokenizers\implementations
      copying py_src\tokenizers\implementations\bert_wordpiece.py -> build\lib.win-amd64-cpython-312\tokenizers\implementations
      copying py_src\tokenizers\implementations\byte_level_bpe.py -> build\lib.win-amd64-cpython-312\tokenizers\implementations
      copying py_src\tokenizers\implementations\char_level_bpe.py -> build\lib.win-amd64-cpython-312\tokenizers\implementations
      copying py_src\tokenizers\implementations\sentencepiece_bpe.py -> build\lib.win-amd64-cpython-312\tokenizers\implementations
      copying py_src\tokenizers\implementations\sentencepiece_unigram.py -> build\lib.win-amd64-cpython-312\tokenizers\implementations
      copying py_src\tokenizers\implementations\__init__.py -> build\lib.win-amd64-cpython-312\tokenizers\implementations
      creating build\lib.win-amd64-cpython-312\tokenizers\tools
      copying py_src\tokenizers\tools\visualizer.py -> build\lib.win-amd64-cpython-312\tokenizers\tools
      copying py_src\tokenizers\tools\__init__.py -> build\lib.win-amd64-cpython-312\tokenizers\tools
      copying py_src\tokenizers\__init__.pyi -> build\lib.win-amd64-cpython-312\tokenizers
```

```
      copying py_src\tokenizers\models\__init__.pyi -> build\lib.win-amd64-cpython-312\tokenizers\models
      copying py_src\tokenizers\decoders\__init__.pyi -> build\lib.win-amd64-cpython-312\tokenizers\decoders
      copying py_src\tokenizers\normalizers\__init__.pyi -> build\lib.win-amd64-cpython-312\tokenizers\normalizers
      copying py_src\tokenizers\pre_tokenizers\__init__.pyi -> build\lib.win-amd64-cpython-312\tokenizers\pre_tokenizers
      copying py_src\tokenizers\processors\__init__.pyi -> build\lib.win-amd64-cpython-312\tokenizers\processors
      copying py_src\tokenizers\trainers\__init__.pyi -> build\lib.win-amd64-cpython-312\tokenizers\trainers
      copying py_src\tokenizers\tools\visualizer-styles.css -> build\lib.win-amd64-cpython-312\tokenizers\tools
      running build_ext
      running build_rust
      error: can't find Rust compiler

      If you are using an outdated pip version, it is possible a prebuilt wheel is available for this package but pip is not able to install from it. Installing from the wheel would avoid the need for a Rust compiler.

      To update pip, run:

          pip install --upgrade pip

      and then retry package installation.

      If you did intend to build this package from source, try installing a Rust compiler from your system package manager and ensure it is on the PATH during installation. Alternatively, rustup (available at https://rustup.rs) is the recommended way to download and update the Rust compiler toolchain.
      [end of output]

  note: This error originates from a subprocess, and is likely not a problem with pip.
  ERROR: Failed building wheel for tokenizers
  Building wheel for jaconv (pyproject.toml) ... done
  Created wheel for jaconv: filename=jaconv-0.4.0-py3-none-any.whl size=18257 sha256=cde44ba8f150711d420a508c80c198d129747f5ad60a1a8a8821b45fabdf5ba5
  Stored in directory: c:\users\lenovo\appdata\local\packages\pythonsoftwarefoundation.python.3.12_qbz5n2kfra8p0\localcache\local\pip\cache\wheels\c9\97\53\1f827ebf916b899520ce663227497206525c432be72cc29265
Successfully built melotts eng-to-ipa gruut jieba langid unidic unidic-lite txtsplit distance docopt gruut-ipa gruut-lang-de gruut-lang-en gruut-lang-es gruut-lang-fr jaconv
Failed to build fugashi tokenizers

[notice] A new release of pip is available: 24.2 -> 24.3.1
[notice] To update, run: C:\Users\Lenovo\AppData\Local\Microsoft\WindowsApps\PythonSoftwareFoundation.Python.3.12_qbz5n2kfra8p0\python.exe -m pip install --upgrade pip
```

This is why we do not prefer do setup install, if fails, how to uninstall?

```
Get-Content requirements.txt | ForEach-Object {Remove-Item $_ -Recurse -Force}
```

Fortunately, there is a direct TTS engine, espea, and checkout https://github.com/espeak-ng/espeak-ng, it has exe, even apk, download the right version and install,

```
# if it is 64bit, it is under x86, else x64
C:\Users\Lenovo>SET PATH=C:\Program Files (x86)\eSpeak NG;%PATH%

C:\Users\Lenovo>python .\tts.py
['espeak-ng', '-v', 'en', '-s', '175', '-p', '50', '-a', '100', '-g', '0', 'Hello,
World!']

# where tts.py is...
import espeakng

mySpeaker = espeakng.Speaker()

mySpeaker.say('Hello, World!')
```

adn french and german,

```
import espeakng

esng = espeakng.Speaker()
esng.voice = 'fr'
esng.say('bonjour monde!')

esng = espeakng.Speaker()
esng.voice = 'german'
esng.say('Hallo Welt!')
```

how many can we speak now?

Family Code	Identifier	Language Family	Language	Accent/Dialect
gmw	af	West Germanic	Afrikaans	
ine	sq	Indo-European	Albanian	
sem	am	Semitic	Amharic	
sem	ar	Semitic	Arabic[3,7]	
roa	an	Romance	Aragonese	
ine	hy	Indo-European	Armenian	East Armenian
ine	hyw	Indo-European	Armenian	West Armenian
inc	as	Indic	Assamese	

Family Code	Identifier	Language Family	Language	Accent/Dialect
trk	az	Turkic	Azerbaijani	
trk	ba	Turkic	Bashkir	
trk	cu	Turkic	Chuvash	
	eu		Basque	
zle	be	East Slavic	Belarusian	
inc	bn	Indic	Bengali	
inc	bpy	Indic	Bishnupriya Manipuri	
zls	bs	South Slavic	Bosnian[1,2]	
zls	bg	South Slavic	Bulgarian	
sit	my	Sino-Tibetan	Burmese	
roa	ca	Romance	Catalan	
iro	chr	Iroquoian	Cherokee [1,6]	Western/C.E.D.
sit	yue	Sino-Tibetan	Chinese	Cantonese
sit	hak	Sino-Tibetan	Chinese	Hakka
map	haw	Austronesian	Hawaiian	
sit	cmn	Sino-Tibetan	Chinese	Mandarin
zls	hr	South Slavic	Croatian[1,2]	
zlw	cs	West Slavic	Czech	
gmq	da	North Germanic	Danish	
gmw	nl	West Germanic	Dutch	
gmw	en-us	West Germanic	English	American
gmw	en	West Germanic	English	British
gmw	en-029	West Germanic	English	Caribbean
gmw	en-gb-x-gbclan	West Germanic	English	Lancastrian
gmw	en-gb-x-rp	West Germanic	English	Received Pronunciation
gmw	en-gb-scotland	West Germanic	English	Scottish
gmw	en-gb-x-gbcwmd	West Germanic	English	West Midlands
art	eo	Constructed	Esperanto	

Family Code	Identifier	Language Family	Language	Accent/Dialect
urj	et	Uralic	Estonian	
ira	fa	Iranian	Persian	
ira	fa-latn	Iranian	Persian[1,5]	
urj	fi	Uralic	Finnish	
roa	fr-be	Romance	French	Belgium
roa	fr	Romance	French	France
roa	fr-ch	Romance	French	Switzerland
cel	ga	Celtic	Gaelic	Irish
cel	gd	Celtic	Gaelic	Scottish
ccs	ka	South Caucasian	Georgian	
gmw	de	West Germanic	German	
grk	grc	Greek	Greek	Ancient
grk	el	Greek	Greek	Modern
esx	kl	Eskimo-Aleut	Greenlandic	
sai	gn	South American Indian	Guarani	
inc	gu	Indic	Gujarati	
roa	ht	Romance	Hatian Creole	
sem	he	Semitic	Hebrew	
inc	hi	Indic	Hindi	
urj	hu	Uralic	Hungarian	
gmq	is	North Germanic	Icelandic	
poz	id	Malayo-Polynesian	Indonesian	
art	ia	Constructed	Interlingua	
art	io	Constructed	Ido	
roa	it	Romance	Italian	
jpx	ja	Japanese	Japanese[4]	
dra	kn	Dravidian	Kannada	
inc	kok	Indic	Konkani	
	ko		Korean	
ira	ku	Iranian	Kurdish	
trk	kk	Turkic	Kazakh	

Family Code	Identifier	Language Family	Language	Accent/Dialect
trk	ky	Turkic	Kyrgyz	
itc	la	Italic	Latin	
gmw	lb	West Germanic	Luxembourgish	
bat	ltg	Baltic	Latgalian	
bat	lv	Baltic	Latvian	
art	lfn	Constructed	Lingua Franca Nova[1,2]	
bat	lt	Baltic	Lithuanian	
art	jbo	Constructed	Lojban	
poz	mi	Malayo-Polynesian	Māori	
zls	mk	South Slavic	Macedonian[1,2]	
poz	ms	Malayo-Polynesian	Malay	
dra	ml	Dravidian	Malayalam	
sem	mt	Semitic	Maltese	
inc	mr	Indic	Marathi	
azc	nci	Uto-Aztecan	Nahuatl	Classical
inc	ne	Indic	Nepali	
gmq	nb	North Germanic	Norwegian Bokmål	
trk	nog	Turkic	Nogai	
inc	or	Indic	Oriya	
cus	om	Cushitic	Oromo	
roa	pap	Romance	Papiamento	
art	py	Constructed	Pyash	
zlw	pl	West Slavic	Polish	
roa	pt-br	Romance	Portuguese	Brazillian
art	qdb	Constructed	Lang Belta	
	qu		Quechua	
myn	quc	Mayan	K'iche'	
art	qya	Constructed	Quenya	
roa	pt	Romance	Portuguese	Portugal
inc	pa	Indic	Punjabi	

Family Code	Identifier	Language Family	Language	Accent/Dialect
art	piqd	Constructed	Klingon	
roa	ro	Romance	Romanian	
zle	ru	East Slavic	Russian	
zle	ru-lv	East Slavic	Russian	Latvia
zle	uk	East Slavic	Ukrainian	
art	sjn	Constructed	Sindarin	
zls	sr	South Slavic	Serbian[1,2]	
bnt	tn	Bantu	Setswana	
inc	sd	Indic	Sindhi	
tai	shn	Tai	Shan (Tai Yai)	
inc	si	Indic	Sinhala	
zlw	sk	West Slavic	Slovak	
zls	sl	South Slavic	Slovenian	
urj	smj	Uralic	Lule Saami	
roa	es	Romance	Spanish	Spain
roa	es-419	Romance	Spanish	Latin American
bnt	sw	Bantu	Swahili	
gmq	sv	North Germanic	Swedish	
dra	ta	Dravidian	Tamil	
tai	th	Tai	Thai	
trk	tk	Turkic	Turkmen[1]	
trk	tt	Turkic	Tatar	
dra	te	Dravidian	Telugu	
trk	tr	Turkic	Turkish	
trk	ug	Turkic	Uyghur[1,3]	
inc	ur	Indic	Urdu	
trk	uz	Turkic	Uzbek[1,2]	
aav	vi-vn-x-central	Austroasiatic	Vietnamese	Central Vietnam
aav	vi	Austroasiatic	Vietnamese	Northern Vietnam
aav	vi-vn-x-south	Austroasiatic	Vietnamese	Southern Vietnam
cel	cy	Celtic	Welsh	

we can even save the audio,

```
esng.say("bonjour monde!", export_path="test.wav")
```

OK, let's move to our android phone, when we install the apk, we find the **accesibility** has a new engine, and we select that, we have many 100+ languages, and droid can use it directly.

Let's fit the droid tts with French selected in espeak ng,

```
#qpy:quiet
#-*-coding:utf8;-*-

import androidhelper
from qsl4ahelper.fullscreenwrapper2 import *

droid = androidhelper.Android()

class MainScreen(Layout):
    def __init__(self):
        super(MainScreen,self).__init__(str("""<?xml version="1.0" encoding="utf-8"?
>
<LinearLayout
    android:layout_width="fill_parent"
    android:layout_height="fill_parent"

    android:orientation="vertical"
    xmlns:android="http://schemas.android.com/apk/res/android">
    <ImageView
        android:id="@+id/logo"
        android:layout_width="fill_parent"
        android:layout_height="0px"
        android:layout_weight="10"
    />
    <LinearLayout
        android:layout_width="fill_parent"
        android:layout_height="0px"
        android:orientation="horizontal"
        android:layout_weight="20">

        <TextView
            android:layout_width="fill_parent"
            android:layout_height="fill_parent"
            android:textSize="8dp"
            android:text="What's your sentence?"
            android:textColor="#ffffffff"
            android:layout_weight="1"
            android:gravity="center"
        />
        </LinearLayout>
        <LinearLayout
```

```
        android:layout_width="fill_parent"
        android:layout_height="0px"
        android:orientation="horizontal"
        android:layout_weight="20">
        <EditText
android:id="@+id/enter"
   android:layout_width="wrap_content"
   android:layout_height="wrap_content"
   android:lines="10"
            android:maxLines ="20"
            android:textSize="8dp"
            android:layout_weight="1"
   android:gravity="center"
   />
    </LinearLayout>

    <ListView
        android:id="@+id/data_list"
        android:layout_width="fill_parent"
        android:layout_height="0px"
        android:layout_weight="55"/>

    <LinearLayout
        android:layout_width="fill_parent"
        android:layout_height="0px"
        android:orientation="horizontal"
        android:layout_weight="8">
        <Button
            android:layout_width="fill_parent"
            android:layout_height="fill_parent"
            android:text="Speak"
            android:id="@+id/but_load"
            android:textSize="8dp"
            android:background="#ffEFC802"
            android:textColor="#ffffffff"
            android:layout_weight="1"
            android:gravity="center"/>
        <Button
            android:layout_width="fill_parent"
            android:layout_height="fill_parent"
            android:text="Exit"
            android:id="@+id/but_exit"
            android:textSize="8dp"
            android:background="#ff06AF00"
            android:textColor="#ffffffff"
            android:layout_weight="1"
            android:gravity="center"/>
    </LinearLayout>
</LinearLayout>
"""),"SL4AApp")

    def on_show(self):
                self.views.but_exit.add_event(click_EventHandler(self.views.but_exit,
```

```
self.exit))
                self.views.but_load.add_event(click_EventHandler(self.views.but_load,
self.load))

        pass

    def on_close(self):
        pass

    def load(self, view, dummy):
        droid = FullScreenWrapper2App.get_android_instance()


        try:
            a = str ((self.views.enter.text))
            droid.ttsSpeak(a)

        except:

            droid.dialogCreateAlert(a)
            droid.dialogShow()


    def exit(self, view, dummy):
        droid = FullScreenWrapper2App.get_android_instance()
        droid.makeToast("Exit")
        FullScreenWrapper2App.close_layout()

if __name__ == '__main__':
    FullScreenWrapper2App.initialize(droid)
    FullScreenWrapper2App.show_layout(MainScreen())
    FullScreenWrapper2App.eventloop()
```

If we have a very long sentence, and if we can import espeakng, we can set wpm,

```
#SET PATH=C:\Program Files (x86)\eSpeak NG;%PATH%
#$env:Path += ';C:\Program Files (x86)\eSpeak NG'
import espeakng

esng = espeakng.Speaker()
esng.voice = 'fr'

k = 'Que les volcans soient éteints ou soient éveillés, ça revient au même pour nous
autres, dit le géographe. Ce qui compte pour nous, c'est la montagne. Elle ne change
pas.'


esng.wpm = 140 # 140 words per minute

# or cut by time
import time
```

```
for i in k.split(' '):
    esng.say(i); time.sleep(1)
```

But doird have no speed control, so we have to cut by time sleep, and it is better, but some words are just wrong,

```
k = 'éveillés'

esng.say(k)
```

We can test other languages and even make a qpy chat bot, not that hard...

```
#qpy:quiet
#-*-coding:utf8;-*-

#el siguiente coduigo es escencial para que el dialogCreateAlert funcione
from android import Android
droid = Android()

#Primera llamada de la aplicacion con el interprete de android
mensaje1='Hola, me llamo Contador, y te dire cuanto te mueves en 30 segundos'
droid.ttsSpeak(mensaje1)

import time
# tiempo de espera en segundos para ejecucion del siguiente codigo
time.sleep(5)

#Mensaje de dialogo
droid.dialogCreateAlert('Cuenta pasos', '¿Listo para iniciar?')

droid.dialogSetPositiveButtonText('Si')
droid.dialogSetNegativeButtonText('No')

droid.dialogShow()

#dependiendo de la respuesta escogida en el dialogo será el resultado, si es no la opcion escogida se despide el interprete y
#se finaliza la aplicacion, si es si inicia la aplicacion para contar los pasos aproximados en 8 segundos

response = droid.dialogGetResponse().result
droid.dialogDismiss()

if not 'which' in response or response['which'] != 'positive':
    mensaje2='Bueno, nos vemos'
    droid.ttsSpeak(mensaje2)
```

from android import Android and from androidhelper import Android are same, doing activity, and from qsl4ahelper.fullscreenwrapper2 import *, this is doing layout. For layout, web, qsl4a, kivy are the options, since they are graphicly showing on the phone, so it is phone GUI.

The GUI methods are same, PyQt5, Tkinter, wxPython, PySimpleGUI, Wax, Kivy, we can see their effects are different.

43 UNINSTALL

What is the difference between `pip list` and `pip freeze`?

Well, it is not just a format issue, `pip freeze` makes `requirements.txt` and we can do the uninstall by this txt, `pip uninstall -r requirements.txt -y`, and since `freeze` gives all, how to do just one? That is to say, how to make our own `requirements.txt`?

`pip show`, the package, and make the requirements to uninstall, this way we can see the dependencies,

```
C:\Users\Lenovo>pip show akshare
Name: akshare
Version: 1.14.96
Summary: AKShare is an elegant and simple financial data interface library for
Python, built for human beings!
Home-page: https://github.com/akfamily/akshare
Author: AKFamily
Author-email: albertandking@gmail.com
License: MIT
Location:
C:\Users\Lenovo\AppData\Local\Packages\PythonSoftwareFoundation.Python.3.12_qbz5n2kf
ra8p0\LocalCache\local-packages\Python312\site-packages
Requires: beautifulsoup4, decorator, html5lib, jsonpath, lxml, mini-racer, openpyxl,
pandas, requests, tabulate, tqdm, urllib3, xlrd
Required-by: lib-pybroker
```

we have to make our own requirements.txt or uninstall one by one,

```
python -c "akd = 'beautifulsoup4, decorator, html5lib, jsonpath, lxml, mini-racer,
openpyxl, pandas, requests, tabulate, tqdm, urllib3, xlrd'.split(', '); print(akd)"
```

and what is the install time?

```
p = ['beautifulsoup4', 'decorator', 'html5lib', 'jsonpath', 'lxml', 'mini-racer',
'openpyxl', 'pandas', 'requests', 'tabulate', 'tqdm', 'urllib3', 'xlrd']

import pkg_resources, os, time;

for package in pkg_resources.working_set:
```

```
    if str(package).split(" ")[0] in p:
                                   print('%-*s    %s'    %    (40,    package,
time.ctime(os.path.getctime(package.location))))
```

ctime may not be install time, there are four times,

atime: Access time mtime: Modification time ctime: Change time (on Unix) / Creation time (on Windows) birthtime: Creation time (on some Unix systems in the FreeBSD family, including macOS)

they are all from `stat`, and we can convert the time into a readable format,

```
p = pathlib.Path('filename')

p.stat() == os.stat('filename') == os.stat(p) # True

dt = datetime.datetime.fromtimestamp(p.stat().st_ctime)
```

so we can find the installed location, and check time one by one,

```
p = ['beautifulsoup4', 'decorator', 'html5lib', 'jsonpath', 'lxml', 'mini-racer',
'openpyxl', 'pandas', 'requests', 'tabulate', 'tqdm', 'urllib3', 'xlrd']

import pkg_resources, os, time;

for package in pkg_resources.working_set:
    p0 = str(package).split(" ")[0]
    p1 = str(package.location)
    pf = os.path.join(p1, p0)
    if p0 in p:
        try:
            print(pf, os.stat(pf).st_ctime)

        except:
            print('%-*s %s' % (40, pf+'???dist???', package))
```

we can use the `pip` main function to do the command inside a py file,

```
import pip
pip.main("uninstall", "akshare")
```

Again, for the setup.py install method, we have to make sure the dependecies, they are sometimes dynamic libraries, DLL in Windows(so in Linux), or excutables, EXE in Windows(apk in Android). Depends on different platform, the funciton can be used ranges differently.

That's why building a clear base can be widely used, and it is good to start from `sys` and `os`, thoes built-in s,

```python
# myutil.py

import sys
import os
import os.path

def getmtime(filename):
    """Return the last modification time of a file, reported by os.stat()."""
    return os.stat(filename).st_mtime

def getatime(filename):
    """Return the last access time of a file, reported by os.stat()."""
    return os.stat(filename).st_atime

def getctime(filename):
    """Return the metadata change time of a file, reported by os.stat()."""
    return os.stat(filename).st_ctime

def get_filepath_in_exec_file_dir(filename):
    return os.path.join(get_exec_file_dir(), filename)

def get_exec_file_dir():
    return os.path.dirname(unicode(sys.argv[0]))

def get_exec_file_parent_dir():
    return os.path.split(unicode(os.path.dirname(sys.argv[0])))[0]

def get_extension(filename):
    return os.path.splitext(unicode(filename))[1]

def get_extension_lowercase(filename):
    return get_extension(unicode(filename)).lower()

def get_filename_without_extension_or_path(filename):
    i = os.path.split(filename)[1]
    return os.path.splitext(i)[0]

def walk_filenames_by_extension(root, extension_list):
    """
    Walks down the root directory & matches files with specified extensions. Returns
list of file-paths
      IMPORTANT: This converts extensions to lowercase before comparison (windows
behavior)
    """
    ret = []
    for extension in extension_list:
        if(extension[0]!="."):
            use_ext = "."+extension
        else:
            use_ext = extension

        for dirpath, dirnames,  filenames in os.walk(root):
            for filename in filenames:
```

```
                if get_extension_lowercase(filename)==use_ext.lower():
                    ret.append(os.path.join(dirpath,filename))

    return ret

# many others TBD
# delete, remove, rename...
```

A clear uninstall should have the upper level folder same as before install,

```
# Specify the path
path                                                                                    =
'c:\users\lenovo\appdata\local\packages\pythonsoftwarefoundation.python.3.12_qbz5n2k
fra8p0\localcache\local-packages\python312\site-packages'

# Specify the file name
file = 'akshare'

# Before
dir_list = os.listdir(path)
print("List of directories and files before creation:")
print(dir_list)
print()

# Creating a file at specified location
with open(os.path.join(path, file), 'w') as fp:
    pass

# Deleting...
# fit in the command here

# After
dir_list = os.listdir(path)
print("List of directories and files after creation:")
print(dir_list)

# these two output should be same
```

44 kivy

We can use qsl4a to mimic andoird, layout, whereas function has unknow errors...

```
#qpy:quiet
#-*-coding:utf8;-*-
"""
This is a sample project which use SL4A UI Framework,
There is another Sample project: https://github.com/qpython-android/qpy-calcount
"""


import qpy
```

```
import androidhelper
from qsl4ahelper.fullscreenwrapper2 import *

droid = androidhelper.Android()

class MainScreen(Layout):
    def __init__(self):
        super(MainScreen,self).__init__(str("""<?xml version="1.0" encoding="utf-8"?
>
<LinearLayout xmlns:android="http://schemas.android.com/apk/res/android"
    xmlns:tools="http://schemas.android.com/tools"
    android:layout_width="match_parent"
    android:layout_height="match_parent"
    android:orientation="vertical"
    >

    <LinearLayout
        android:layout_width="fill_parent"
        android:layout_height="wrap_content"
        android:orientation="horizontal"
        android:weightSum="3">

<Button
             android:layout_height="wrap_content"
            android:layout_marginRight="10dp"
            android:text="Exit"
            android:id="@+id/but_exit"
            android:textSize="8dp"
            android:background="#ffEFC802"
            android:textColor="#ffffffff"
            android:layout_weight="1"
        />

        <Button
            android:id="@+id/but_loadd"
            android:layout_width="0dp"
            android:layout_height="wrap_content"
            android:layout_marginRight="10dp"
            android:layout_weight="1"
            android:background="#444"
            android:text="Load Web Page"
            android:textColor="#fff"
            android:textSize="14sp"
            android:textStyle="bold" />

        <Button
            android:id="@+id/but_loads"
            android:layout_width="0dp"
            android:layout_height="wrap_content"
            android:layout_marginLeft="10dp"
            android:layout_weight="1"
            android:background="#444"
            android:text="Load Static HTML"
```

```
            android:textColor="#fff"
            android:textSize="14sp"
            android:textStyle="bold" />
    </LinearLayout>

    <WebView
        android:id="@+id/simpleWebView"
        android:layout_width="fill_parent"
        android:layout_height="fill_parent"
        android:layout_marginTop="20dp"
        android:scrollbars="none" />

</LinearLayout>
"""),"SL4AApp")

    def on_show(self):
               self.views.but_exit.add_event(click_EventHandler(self.views.but_exit,
self.exit))
              self.views.but_loadd.add_event(click_EventHandler(self.views.but_loadd,
self.loadd))
              self.views.but_loads.add_event(click_EventHandler(self.views.but_loads,
self.loads))
        pass

    def on_close(self):
        pass

    def exit(self, view, dummy):
        droid = FullScreenWrapper2App.get_android_instance()
        droid.makeToast("Exit")
        FullScreenWrapper2App.close_layout()

    def loadd(self, view, dummy):
        droid = FullScreenWrapper2App.get_android_instance()
        droid.makeToast("loadd")
        try:
            droid.webViewShow('https://www.bing.com')
        except:
            droid.makeToast("Fail...")

    def loads(self, view, dummy):
        droid = FullScreenWrapper2App.get_android_instance()
        #droid.makeToast("loads")
        s = dir (droid)
        #for i in s: print (i)

        try:
            s = droid.webViewShow('https://www.bing.com')
            s = droid.viewHTML('index.html')
            s = droid.webViewShow('index.html')

            s = droid.viewHTML('https://www.bing.com')
            s = str(s); print(s)
```

```
            droid.dialogCreateAlert(s)
            droid.dialogSetPositiveButtonText('yes')
            droid.dialogSetNegativeButtonText('no')
            droid.dialogShow()
            droid.makeToast('last.log')
            response = droid.dialogGetResponse().result
            droid.dialogDismiss()
        except:
            droid.makeToast("Fail...")
#        finally:
#            FullScreenWrapper2App.close_layout()

if __name__ == '__main__':
    FullScreenWrapper2App.initialize(droid)
    FullScreenWrapper2App.show_layout(MainScreen())
    FullScreenWrapper2App.eventloop()

# index.html
<!DOCTYPE html>
<html>

<head>
    <title>
    HTML Data Frame Render
    </title>


</head>

<body style="text-align:center;">
    <h1>
        df render
    </h1>

<p id="demo"></p>

<script type="text/javascript">
document.getElementById("demo").innerHTML = "ok";
</script>

</body>

</html>

# output
# ../log/last.log
```

The log shows unknow RPC error, which is really unknow, we can't get the webView from static, dynamic, and our webView layout is therefore no use.

Debug the RPC error can be annoying, especially we need to add the print in the py, too much work,

```
import socket
def get_local_ip():
    try:
        s = socket.socket(socket.AF_INET, socket.SOCK_DGRAM)
        s.connect(('8.8.8.8', 80))
        local_ip = s.getsockname()[0]
    finally:
        s.close()
    return local_ip

ip = get_local_ip()

print(ip)

# output
# 192.x.x.x
```

A LAN IP to RPC? Server DNS? Port? Or is it just qsl4a wrapping problem? And what is the effect if works?

This is what we can see in kivy on Windows,

```
from kivy.app import App
from kivy.uix.button import Button
from kivy.uix.label import Label
from kivy.uix.boxlayout import BoxLayout

class IndexPage(BoxLayout):
    def __init__(self,**kwargs):
        super().__init__(**kwargs)

        self.btn = Button(text = "press me")
        self.btn.bind(on_press = self.press_button)
        self.add_widget(self.btn)
        # get ttf ready, so it supports multiple languages
        self.la = Label(font_name = "./french.ttf")
        self.add_widget(self.la)

    def press_button(self, arg):
        self.la.text = "show you Le française? "

class TestApp(App):
    def build(self):
        return IndexPage()

if __name__ == "__main__":
    TestApp().run()
```

and

```
from kivy.uix.button import Button
```

```
from kivy.app import App

# importing builder from kivy
from kivy.lang import Builder

# this is the main class which will render the whole application
class uiApp(App):

    # method which will render our application
    def build(self):
        return Builder.load_string("""

Button:

    # text which will appear on button
    text:"click here to open bing"

    on_release:

        # importing webbrowser module
        import webbrowser

        webbrowser.open('http://www.bing.com')

        print("go to bing via browser")


                                   """)

# running the application
uiApp().run()
```

so by importing web browser we can view a web, but it is not the webview we want, checkout https://kivy.org/doc/stable/search.html?check_keywords=yes&area=default&q=webview and really there is no such...

Give up, and continue some other effects, by adding more buttons,

```
from kivy.app import App
from kivy.uix.button import Button
from kivy.uix.boxlayout import BoxLayout

class IndexPage(BoxLayout):
    def __init__(self,**kwargs):
        super().__init__(**kwargs)
        self.btn = Button(text = "WebView")
        self.btn.bind(on_press = self.press_button)
        self.add_widget(self.btn)

        self.btn = Button(text = "Second")
        self.btn.bind(on_press = self.press_button2)
        self.add_widget(self.btn)
```

```
        self.btn = Button(text = "Third")
        self.btn.bind(on_press = self.press_button3)
        self.add_widget(self.btn)

    def press_button(self, arg):
        print("press button to web view")

    def press_button2(self, arg):
        print("press button2 for more effects")

    def press_button3(self, arg):
        print("press button3 to exit")
        TestApp().get_running_app().stop()

class TestApp(App):
    def build(self):
        return IndexPage()

if __name__ == "__main__":
    TestApp().run()
```

we can even make buttons in vertical,

```
# import kivy module
import kivy
#kivy.require("1.9.1")

# base Class of your App inherits from the App class.
# app:always refers to the instance of your application
from kivy.app import App

from kivy.uix.button import Button

from kivy.uix.stacklayout import StackLayout

# class in which we are creating StackLayout
class StackLayoutApp(App):

    def build(self):

        # Different orientation
        # ['lr-tb', 'tb-lr', 'rl-tb', 'tb-rl', 'lr-bt', 'bt-lr', 'rl-bt', 'bt-rl']
        SL = StackLayout(orientation ='tb-rl')

        # Creating Multiple Buttons
        btn1 = Button(text ="B1",
                      font_size = 20,
                      size_hint =(.2, .1))
        btn2 = Button(text ="B2",
                      font_size = 20,
                      size_hint =(.2, .1))
        btn3 = Button(text ="B3",
                      font_size = 20,
```

```
                      size_hint =(.2, .1))
        btn4 = Button(text ="B4",
                      font_size = 20,
                      size_hint =(.2, .1))
        btn5 = Button(text ="B5",
                      font_size = 20,
                      size_hint =(.2, .1))
        btn6 = Button(text ="B6",
                      font_size = 20,
                      size_hint =(.2, .1))
        btn7 = Button(text ="B7",
                      font_size = 20,
                      size_hint =(.2, .1))
        btn8 = Button(text ="B8",
                      font_size = 20,
                      size_hint =(.2, .1))
        btn9 = Button(text ="B9",
                      font_size = 20,
                      size_hint =(.2, .1))
        btn10 = Button(text ="B10",
                      font_size = 20,
                      size_hint =(.2, .1))


        # adding widgets
        SL.add_widget(btn1)
        SL.add_widget(btn2)
        SL.add_widget(btn3)
        SL.add_widget(btn4)
        SL.add_widget(btn5)
        SL.add_widget(btn6)
        SL.add_widget(btn7)
        SL.add_widget(btn8)
        SL.add_widget(btn9)


        btn10.bind(on_press = self.press_button10)
        SL.add_widget(btn10)
        return SL

    def press_button10(self, arg):
        print("press button to exit")
        StackLayoutApp().get_running_app().stop()

if __name__ == '__main__':
    StackLayoutApp().run()
```

We see the left part is black, and we want to print things there,

```
# import kivy module
import kivy
#kivy.require("1.9.1")
```

```
# base Class of your App inherits from the App class.
# app:always refers to the instance of your application
from kivy.app import App

from kivy.uix.button import Button

from kivy.uix.stacklayout import StackLayout

# class in which we are creating StackLayout
class StackLayoutApp(App):

    def build(self):

        # Different orientation
        # ['lr-tb', 'tb-lr', 'rl-tb', 'tb-rl', 'lr-bt', 'bt-lr', 'rl-bt', 'bt-rl']
        SL = StackLayout(orientation ='tb-rl')

        # Creating Multiple Buttons
        btn1 = Button(text ="B1",
                      font_size = 20,
                      size_hint =(.2, .1))
        btn2 = Button(text ="B2",
                      font_size = 20,
                      size_hint =(.2, .1))
        btn3 = Button(text ="B3",
                      font_size = 20,
                      size_hint =(.2, .1))
        btn4 = Button(text ="B4",
                      font_size = 20,
                      size_hint =(.2, .1))
        btn5 = Button(text ="B5",
                      font_size = 20,
                      size_hint =(.2, .1))
        btn6 = Button(text ="B6",
                      font_size = 20,
                      size_hint =(.2, .1))
        btn7 = Button(text ="B7",
                      font_size = 20,
                      size_hint =(.2, .1))
        btn8 = Button(text ="B8",
                      font_size = 20,
                      size_hint =(.2, .1))
        btn9 = Button(text ="B9",
                      font_size = 20,
                      size_hint =(.2, .1))
        btn10 = Button(text ="Exit",
                      font_size = 20,
                      size_hint =(.2, .1))


        # adding widgets
        btn1.bind(on_press = self.press_button1)
        SL.add_widget(btn1)
```

```
        btn2.bind(on_press = self.press_button2)
        SL.add_widget(btn2)

        btn3.bind(on_press = self.press_button3)
        SL.add_widget(btn3)

        btn4.bind(on_press = self.press_button4)
        SL.add_widget(btn4)

        btn5.bind(on_press = self.press_button5)
        SL.add_widget(btn5)

        btn6.bind(on_press = self.press_button6)
        SL.add_widget(btn6)

        btn7.bind(on_press = self.press_button7)
        SL.add_widget(btn7)

        btn8.bind(on_press = self.press_button8)
        SL.add_widget(btn8)

        btn9.bind(on_press = self.press_button9)
        SL.add_widget(btn9)

        btn10.bind(on_press = self.press_button10)
        SL.add_widget(btn10)

        return SL


    def press_button1(self, instance):
        print("press button1")
        print(instance.text)

    def press_button2(self, instance):
        print(instance.text)

    def press_button3(self, instance):
        print(instance.text)

    def press_button4(self, instance):
        print(instance.text)

    def press_button5(self, instance):
        print(instance.text)

    def press_button6(self, instance):
        print(instance.text)

    def press_button7(self, instance):
        print(instance.text)
```

```
    def press_button8(self, instance):
        print(instance.text)

    def press_button9(self, instance):
        print(instance.text)

    def press_button10(self, arg):
        print("press button to exit")
        StackLayoutApp().get_running_app().stop()


if __name__ == '__main__':
    StackLayoutApp().run()
```

The `press_button10` should use self, to make the class consistent, that is inside the class, only self,

```
from kivy.app import App
from kivy.uix.button import Button
from kivy.uix.boxlayout import BoxLayout
from kivy.uix.stacklayout import StackLayout
from kivy.uix.label import Label


class TestApp(App):
    def press_button1(self, instance):
        print("{} Button pressed!".format(instance.text))
        #self.btn1.text="Hello Button 1"
        #you have to predefine an id since btn is not shown...
        self.change.text = "Change"
        #print(type(instance))
        #print(dir(instance.ids))





    def press_button2(self, instance):
        print("press button to change the label")
        print("{} Button pressed!".format(instance.text))
        #self.build.lbl1.text="Hello Button 1"
        #self.SL.btn2.text="Change"

    def press_button10(self, instance):
        print("press button to exit")
        self.get_running_app().stop()

    def build(self):


        mainLayout = BoxLayout(orientation = 'horizontal')
```

```
hboxLayout = BoxLayout(orientation='horizontal')
lbl1 = Label(text='[color=00FF00]Hello[/color][color=FF0000]Kivy[/color]',
    font_size ='20sp',
    markup = True)
self.change = lbl1

lbl2 = Label(text ="This is a Kivy Label \nwith  Multi\nLine",
    font_size ='20sp',
    color =[0.88, 0.12, 0.24, 1])

hboxLayout.add_widget(lbl1)
hboxLayout.add_widget(lbl2)
mainLayout.add_widget(hboxLayout)


vboxLayout = BoxLayout(orientation='vertical')


SL = StackLayout(orientation ='tb-rl')

# Creating Multiple Buttons
btn1 = Button(text ="Change",
              font_size = 20,
              size_hint =(.2, .1))
btn2 = Button(text ="B2",
              font_size = 20,
              size_hint =(.2, .1))
btn3 = Button(text ="B3",
              font_size = 20,
              size_hint =(.2, .1))
btn4 = Button(text ="B4",
              font_size = 20,
              size_hint =(.2, .1))
btn5 = Button(text ="B5",
              font_size = 20,
              size_hint =(.2, .1))
btn6 = Button(text ="B6",
              font_size = 20,
              size_hint =(.2, .1))
btn7 = Button(text ="B7",
              font_size = 20,
              size_hint =(.2, .1))
btn8 = Button(text ="B8",
              font_size = 20,
              size_hint =(.2, .1))
btn9 = Button(text ="B9",
              font_size = 20,
              size_hint =(.2, .1))
btn10 = Button(text ="Exit",
              font_size = 20,
              size_hint =(.2, .1))
```

```
        # adding widgets
        btn1.bind(on_press = self.press_button1)
        SL.add_widget(btn1)

        SL.add_widget(btn2)
        SL.add_widget(btn3)
        SL.add_widget(btn4)
        SL.add_widget(btn5)
        SL.add_widget(btn6)
        SL.add_widget(btn7)
        SL.add_widget(btn8)
        SL.add_widget(btn9)


        btn10.bind(on_press = self.press_button10)
        SL.add_widget(btn10)



        vboxLayout.add_widget(SL)

        mainLayout.add_widget(vboxLayout)
        return mainLayout

if __name__ == "__main__":
    TestApp().run()
```

Now we see why the reset is important, since many changes made we are so lost...

```
from kivy.app import App
from kivy.uix.button import Button
from kivy.uix.boxlayout import BoxLayout
from kivy.uix.stacklayout import StackLayout
from kivy.uix.label import Label


class TestApp(App):
    def press_button1(self, instance):
        print("{} Button pressed!".format(instance.text))
        self.change.text = "Change"
        #print(type(instance))
        #print(dir(instance.ids))


        #self.btn.text="Hello Button 1"


    def press_button2(self, instance):
```

```
        print("press button to change the label")
        print("{} Button pressed!".format(instance.text))
        #self.build.lbl1.text="Hello Button 1"
        self.change2.text="Change???"

    def press_button10(self, instance):
        print("press button to exit")
        self.get_running_app().stop()

    def build(self):


        mainLayout = BoxLayout(orientation = 'horizontal')


        hboxLayout = BoxLayout(orientation='horizontal')
        lbl1 = Label(text='[color=00FF00]Hello[/color][color=FF0000]Kivy[/color]',
            font_size ='20sp',
            markup = True)
        self.change = lbl1

        lbl2 = Label(text ="This is a Kivy Label \nwith  Multi\nLine",
            font_size ='20sp',
            color =[0.88, 0.12, 0.24, 1])

        hboxLayout.add_widget(lbl1)
        hboxLayout.add_widget(lbl2)
        mainLayout.add_widget(hboxLayout)


        vboxLayout = BoxLayout(orientation='vertical')


        SL = StackLayout(orientation ='tb-rl')

        # Creating Multiple Buttons
        btn1 = Button(text ="Change",
                      font_size = 20,
                      size_hint =(.2, .1))

        btn2 = Button(text ="B2",
                      font_size = 20,
                      size_hint =(.2, .1))
        self.change2 = btn2

        btn3 = Button(text ="B3",
                      font_size = 20,
                      size_hint =(.2, .1))
        btn4 = Button(text ="B4",
                      font_size = 20,
                      size_hint =(.2, .1))
        btn5 = Button(text ="B5",
                      font_size = 20,
```

```
                    size_hint =(.2, .1))
        btn6 = Button(text ="B6",
                    font_size = 20,
                    size_hint =(.2, .1))
        btn7 = Button(text ="B7",
                    font_size = 20,
                    size_hint =(.2, .1))
        btn8 = Button(text ="B8",
                    font_size = 20,
                    size_hint =(.2, .1))
        btn9 = Button(text ="Reset",
                    font_size = 20,
                    size_hint =(.2, .1))
        btn10 = Button(text ="Exit",
                    font_size = 20,
                    size_hint =(.2, .1))


        # adding widgets
        btn1.bind(on_press = self.press_button1)
        SL.add_widget(btn1)

        btn2.bind(on_press = self.press_button2)
        SL.add_widget(btn2)
        SL.add_widget(btn3)
        SL.add_widget(btn4)
        SL.add_widget(btn5)
        SL.add_widget(btn6)
        SL.add_widget(btn7)


        # how do you reset by btn8?
        SL.add_widget(btn8)
        # how do you restart the program without Exit?
        SL.add_widget(btn9)
        btn10.bind(on_press = self.press_button10)
        SL.add_widget(btn10)



        vboxLayout.add_widget(SL)

        mainLayout.add_widget(vboxLayout)
        return mainLayout

if __name__ == "__main__":
    TestApp().run()
```

How about espeak?

```
import espeakng
from kivy.app import App
from kivy.uix.button import Button
```

```
from kivy.uix.boxlayout import BoxLayout
from kivy.uix.stacklayout import StackLayout
from kivy.uix.label import Label


class TestApp(App):
    def press_button1(self, instance):
        print("{} Button pressed!".format(instance.text))
        self.change.text = "Change"
        #print(type(instance))
        #print(dir(instance.ids))


        #self.btn.text="Hello Button 1"



    def press_button2(self, instance):
        print("press button to change the label")
        print("{} Button pressed!".format(instance.text))
        #self.build.lbl1.text="Hello Button 1"
        self.change2.text="Change???"

    def press_button7(self, instance):
        print("press button to espeak")

        esng = espeakng.Speaker()
        esng.voice = 'fr'
        esng.say('bonjour monde!')

    def press_button10(self, instance):
        print("press button to exit")
        self.get_running_app().stop()

    def build(self):


        mainLayout = BoxLayout(orientation = 'horizontal')


        hboxLayout = BoxLayout(orientation='horizontal')
        lbl1 = Label(text='[color=00FF00]Hello[/color][color=FF0000]Kivy[/color]',
            font_size ='20sp',
            markup = True)
        self.change = lbl1

        lbl2 = Label(text ="This is a Kivy Label \nwith  Multi\nLine",
            font_size ='20sp',
            color =[0.88, 0.12, 0.24, 1])

        hboxLayout.add_widget(lbl1)
        hboxLayout.add_widget(lbl2)
        mainLayout.add_widget(hboxLayout)
```

```
vboxLayout = BoxLayout(orientation='vertical')


SL = StackLayout(orientation ='tb-rl')

# Creating Multiple Buttons
btn1 = Button(text ="Change",
              font_size = 20,
              size_hint =(.2, .1))

btn2 = Button(text ="B2",
              font_size = 20,
              size_hint =(.2, .1))
self.change2 = btn2

btn3 = Button(text ="B3",
              font_size = 20,
              size_hint =(.2, .1))
btn4 = Button(text ="B4",
              font_size = 20,
              size_hint =(.2, .1))
btn5 = Button(text ="B5",
              font_size = 20,
              size_hint =(.2, .1))
btn6 = Button(text ="B6",
              font_size = 20,
              size_hint =(.2, .1))
btn7 = Button(text ="espeak",
              font_size = 20,
              size_hint =(.2, .1))
btn8 = Button(text ="Reset",
              font_size = 20,
              size_hint =(.2, .1))
btn9 = Button(text ="Restart",
              font_size = 20,
              size_hint =(.2, .1))
btn10 = Button(text ="Exit",
              font_size = 20,
              size_hint =(.2, .1))


# adding widgets
btn1.bind(on_press = self.press_button1)
SL.add_widget(btn1)

btn2.bind(on_press = self.press_button2)
SL.add_widget(btn2)
SL.add_widget(btn3)
SL.add_widget(btn4)
SL.add_widget(btn5)
SL.add_widget(btn6)
```

```
        btn7.bind(on_press = self.press_button7)

        SL.add_widget(btn7)


        # how do you reset by btn8?
        SL.add_widget(btn8)
        # how do you restart the program without Exit?
        SL.add_widget(btn9)
        btn10.bind(on_press = self.press_button10)
        SL.add_widget(btn10)

        vboxLayout.add_widget(SL)

        mainLayout.add_widget(vboxLayout)
        return mainLayout

if __name__ == "__main__":
    TestApp().run()
```

Let's change the btn2 to draw, a pruple rectangular,

```
from kivy.app import App
from kivy.uix.button import Button
from kivy.uix.boxlayout import BoxLayout
from kivy.uix.stacklayout import StackLayout
from kivy.uix.label import Label

from kivy.uix.widget import Widget
from kivy.graphics import Rectangle, Color, Ellipse
class MyPaintWidget(Widget):
    def __init__(self):
        super(MyPaintWidget, self).__init__()

        with self.canvas:
            Color(0, 0, 0, 0)
            self.rect = Rectangle(size=self.size,
                                  pos=self.pos)
            Color(1, 0, 0, 1)  # note that we must reset the colour
            Rectangle(size=(300, 100),
                      pos=(300, 200))
        self.bind(pos=self.update_rectangle,
                  size=self.update_rectangle)

    def update_rectangle(self, instance, value):
        self.rect.size = self.size
        self.rect.pos = self.pos

    def change(self, instance):
        super(MyPaintWidget, self).__init__()
```

```
        with self.canvas:
            Color(0, 0, 0, 0)
            self.rect = Rectangle(size=self.size,
                                  pos=self.pos)
            Color(1, 0, 1, 1)  # note that we must reset the colour
            Rectangle(size=(300, 100),
                      pos=(300, 200))
        self.bind(pos=self.update_rectangle,
                  size=self.update_rectangle)


import espeakng

class TestApp(App):

    def press_button2(self, instance):
        #self.build.lbl1.text=

        print("{} Button pressed!".format(instance.text))
        self.paint.change("Draw Button 2")



    def press_button1(self, instance):
        print("{} Button pressed!".format(instance.text))
        self.change.text = "Change"
        #print(type(instance))
        #print(dir(instance.ids))


        #self.btn.text="Hello Button 1"


    def press_button7(self, instance):
        print("press button to espeak")

        esng = espeakng.Speaker()
        esng.voice = 'fr'
        esng.say('bonjour monde!')

    def press_button10(self, instance):
        print("press button to exit")
        self.get_running_app().stop()

    def build(self):


        mainLayout = BoxLayout(orientation = 'horizontal')


        hboxLayout = BoxLayout(orientation='horizontal')
        lbl1 = Label(text='[color=00FF00]Hello[/color][color=FF0000]Kivy[/color]',
```

```
        font_size ='20sp',
        markup = True)
    self.change = lbl1

    lbl2 = Label(text ="This is a Kivy Label \nwith  Multi\nLine",
        font_size ='20sp',
        color =[0.88, 0.12, 0.24, 1])

    hboxLayout.add_widget(lbl1)
    hboxLayout.add_widget(lbl2)

    self.paint = MyPaintWidget()
    hboxLayout.add_widget(self.paint)

    mainLayout.add_widget(hboxLayout)


    vboxLayout = BoxLayout(orientation='vertical')


    SL = StackLayout(orientation ='tb-rl')

    # Creating Multiple Buttons
    btn1 = Button(text ="Change",
                  font_size = 20,
                  size_hint =(.2, .1))

    btn2 = Button(text ="Purple",
                  font_size = 20,
                  size_hint =(.2, .1))

    btn3 = Button(text ="B3",
                  font_size = 20,
                  size_hint =(.2, .1))
    btn4 = Button(text ="B4",
                  font_size = 20,
                  size_hint =(.2, .1))
    btn5 = Button(text ="B5",
                  font_size = 20,
                  size_hint =(.2, .1))
    btn6 = Button(text ="B6",
                  font_size = 20,
                  size_hint =(.2, .1))
    btn7 = Button(text ="espeak",
                  font_size = 20,
                  size_hint =(.2, .1))
    btn8 = Button(text ="Reset",
                  font_size = 20,
                  size_hint =(.2, .1))
    btn9 = Button(text ="Restart",
                  font_size = 20,
                  size_hint =(.2, .1))
    btn10 = Button(text ="Exit",
```

```
                      font_size = 20,
                      size_hint =(.2, .1))


        # adding widgets
        btn1.bind(on_press = self.press_button1)
        SL.add_widget(btn1)

        btn2.bind(on_press = self.press_button2)
        SL.add_widget(btn2)
        SL.add_widget(btn3)
        SL.add_widget(btn4)
        SL.add_widget(btn5)
        SL.add_widget(btn6)



        btn7.bind(on_press = self.press_button7)

        SL.add_widget(btn7)


        # how do you reset by btn8?
        SL.add_widget(btn8)
        # how do you restart the program without Exit?
        SL.add_widget(btn9)
        btn10.bind(on_press = self.press_button10)
        SL.add_widget(btn10)

        vboxLayout.add_widget(SL)

        mainLayout.add_widget(vboxLayout)
        return mainLayout

if __name__ == "__main__":
    TestApp().run()
```

layout and canvas, are two kinds of kivy elements, next let's try plot stock,

```
import pandas as pd

print("csv")
# Reading a CSV file
df = pd.read_csv('aapl_2024.csv')
st = '2024-02-14 09:30:00'
et = '2024-03-14 15:59:00'
stock = "AAPL"
print(stock, ":", st, "->", et, "NY")
filtered_df = df[(df['date'] >= st) & (df['date'] <= et)]

dt = filtered_df.reset_index()
```

```
import matplotlib.pyplot as plt

fig, ax = plt.subplots()
ax.plot(dt['date'],

           dt['low'],
           color='blue')
ax.set(xlabel="Date", ylabel="Price")

from kivy_garden.matplotlib import FigureCanvasKivyAgg
from kivy.app import App
from kivy.uix.boxlayout import BoxLayout
class MyApp(App):

    def build(self):
        box = BoxLayout()
        box.add_widget(FigureCanvasKivyAgg(plt.gcf()))
        return box

MyApp().run()
```

Suddenly we hear the fan, means CPU is at a high load...

45 CPU

To show the CPU load in kivy? Sounds cool?

```
python -c "import sys; print(sys.maxsize > 2**32)"
```

But how does program go into CPU?

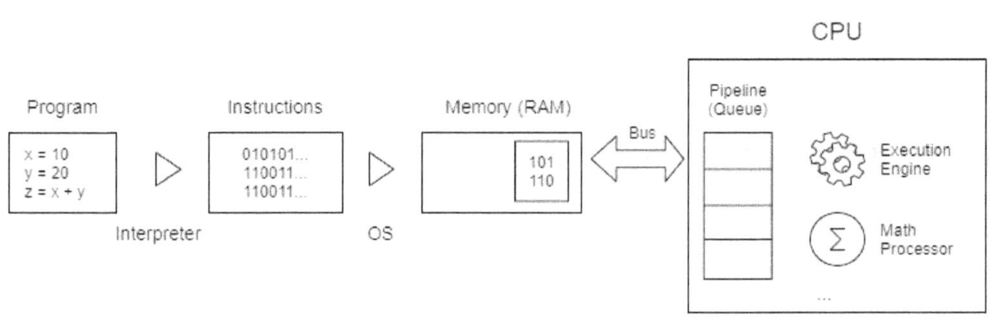

The program stored in disk, is interpred by python, and converted to instruction, the OS put instructions to memory, through the connected bus to CPU, the ALU can do the logic and arithmetic calculation, and result is stored in memory first, then back to disk or other output devices, usually screen.

People say CPU is the brain of Computer, that is short version, neglect the memory. CPU is only responsible for managing the timing of each operation and carrying out the instructions. The world's first electronic computer was the Electronic Numeric Integrator and Computer (ENIAC). It uses 18,000 vacuum tubes for processing and memory, no CPU?

Well, since no transistors.

Current high-end CPU has between five and 10 billion transistors, and these transistors build up logic circuits. The circuits has three types, the control unit (CU), the arithmetic logic unit (ALU), and the registers. The registers is a storage unit. The control unit fetches data and instructions from the memory (RAM or ROM) and stores them in register. The ALU process data and instructions in a clock cycle.

All digital circuits need clock. It is called instruction cycle, which includes fetch-decode-execute, 3 steps.

Since the memory is far, through bus, current CPU usually has cache, 3 levels, to store the temporary data.

Considering the high clock frequency (1/cycle), thermal design power (TDP) is important, this set up the computer's maxium temperature, and will make fan to cool.

Famous fabrication companies, ASML, TSM, they have standard processor specifications 7nm, 12nm, or 16nm. These specifications are hardware informations, can may not be able to get from Python package.

Imagine we have a raspberry, and Python on it,

```
import re, subprocess

def check_CPU_temp():
    temp = None
    err, msg = subprocess.getstatusoutput('vcgencmd measure_temp')
    if not err:
        m = re.search(r'-?\d\.?\d*', msg)   # a solution with a  regex
        try:
            temp = float(m.group())
        except:
            pass
    return temp, msg

temp, msg = check_CPU_temp()

print "temperature (" + u'\xb0' + "C): ", temp
print "full message:    ", msg
```

so the `vcgencmd` is the package offering the temperature check.

```
from multiprocessing import Pool, cpu_count
from datetime import datetime


def stress_test(args):
    cpu, value = args
    start_time = datetime.now()
    for i in range(value):
        value = value * i
    print(f"cpu: {cpu} time: {datetime.now() - start_time}")

if __name__ == '__main__':
    start_time = datetime.now()
    cpu_count = cpu_count()
    with Pool(cpu_count) as mp_pool:
        mp_pool.map(stress_test, [(cpu, 100000000) for cpu in range(cpu_count)])
    print(f"total: {datetime.now() - start_time}")
```

we can use `os` to count cpu too,

```
import os
n = os.cpu_count()
print(n)

# 16
```

but Windows have no affinity,

```
from os import sched_getaffinity

# get the number of available logical cpu cores

n_available_cores = len(sched_getaffinity(0))

# report the number of logical cpu cores

print(f'Number of Available CPU cores: {n_available_cores}')

# ImportError: cannot import name 'sched_getaffinity' from 'os'
```

But there is workaround, checkout https://github.com/alexdedyura/cpu-benchmark,

46 Uniapp

Recall the builder, if we want kivy to be styled, we should `pip install kivymd`,

```
KV = '''
MDScreen:

    MDLabel:
        text: "Hello, World!"
        halign: "center"
        font_size: 40
        color: [0,0,1,1]
'''


from kivy.lang import Builder

from kivymd.app import MDApp


class MainApp(MDApp):
    def build(self):
        return Builder.load_string(KV)

    def on_start(self):
        self.fps_monitor_start()

MainApp().run()
```

Compare to the original builder,

```
kv = '''


FloatLayout:
    canvas:
        Color:
            rgba: (1,1,1,1)
        Rectangle:
            pos: self.pos
            size: self.size
    Label:
        text: "Hello, World!"
        halign: "center"
        color:[0,0,1,1]
        font_size:40

'''


from kivy.app import App
from kivy.lang import Builder
from kivy.uix.floatlayout import FloatLayout
from kivy.uix.label import Label

root = Builder.load_string(kv)

class MainApp(App):
```

```
    def build(self):
        return root

    #def on_start(self):
        #self.fps_monitor_start()

if __name__ == '__main__':
    MainApp().run()
```

the MDApp has a little few functions App does not have,

```
>>> a = dir(MDApp)
['_EventDispatcher__proxy_getter', '_EventDispatcher__proxy_setter', '__class__',
'__delattr__', '__dict__', '__dir__', '__doc__', '__eq__', '__events__',
'__format__', '__ge__', '__getattribute__', '__getstate__', '__gt__', '__hash__',
'__init__', '__init_subclass__', '__le__', '__lt__', '__module__', '__ne__',
'__new__', '__pyx_vtable__', '__reduce__', '__reduce_ex__', '__repr__', '__self__',
'__setattr__', '__setstate__', '__sizeof__', '__str__', '__subclasshook__',
'__weakref__', '_get_user_data_dir', '_install_settings_keys',
'_kwargs_applied_init', '_on_config_change', '_on_keyboard_settings', '_proxy_ref',
'_run_prepare', '_running_app', '_stop', '_user_data_dir', 'apply_property',
'async_run', 'bind', 'build', 'build_config', 'build_settings', 'close_settings',
'create_property', 'create_settings', 'destroy_settings', 'directory', 'dispatch',
'dispatch_children', 'dispatch_generic', 'display_settings', 'events', 'fbind',
'fps_monitor_start', 'funbind', 'get_application_config', 'get_application_icon',
'get_application_name', 'get_property_observers', 'get_running_app', 'getter',
'icon', 'is_event_type', 'kv_directory', 'kv_file', 'load_all_kv_files',
'load_config', 'load_kv', 'name', 'on_config_change', 'on_icon', 'on_pause',
'on_resume', 'on_start', 'on_stop', 'on_title', 'open_settings', 'pause',
'properties', 'property', 'proxy_ref', 'register_event_type', 'root_window', 'run',
'setter', 'settings_cls', 'stop', 'theme_cls', 'title', 'uid', 'unbind',
'unbind_uid', 'unregister_event_type', 'unregister_event_types',
'use_kivy_settings', 'user_data_dir']
>>> b = dir(App)
['_EventDispatcher__proxy_getter', '_EventDispatcher__proxy_setter', '__class__',
'__delattr__', '__dict__', '__dir__', '__doc__', '__eq__', '__events__',
'__format__', '__ge__', '__getattribute__', '__getstate__', '__gt__', '__hash__',
'__init__', '__init_subclass__', '__le__', '__lt__', '__module__', '__ne__',
'__new__', '__pyx_vtable__', '__reduce__', '__reduce_ex__', '__repr__', '__self__',
'__setattr__', '__setstate__', '__sizeof__', '__str__', '__subclasshook__',
'_get_user_data_dir', '_install_settings_keys', '_kwargs_applied_init',
'_on_config_change', '_on_keyboard_settings', '_proxy_ref', '_run_prepare',
'_running_app', '_stop', '_user_data_dir', 'apply_property', 'async_run', 'bind',
'build', 'build_config', 'build_settings', 'close_settings', 'create_property',
'create_settings', 'destroy_settings', 'directory', 'dispatch', 'dispatch_children',
'dispatch_generic', 'display_settings', 'events', 'fbind', 'funbind',
'get_application_config', 'get_application_icon', 'get_application_name',
'get_property_observers', 'get_running_app', 'getter', 'icon', 'is_event_type',
'kv_directory', 'kv_file', 'load_config', 'load_kv', 'name', 'on_config_change',
'on_icon', 'on_pause', 'on_resume', 'on_start', 'on_stop', 'on_title',
'open_settings', 'pause', 'properties', 'property', 'proxy_ref',
'register_event_type', 'root_window', 'run', 'setter', 'settings_cls', 'stop',
```

```
'title',      'uid',      'unbind',      'unbind_uid',      'unregister_event_type',
'unregister_event_types', 'use_kivy_settings', 'user_data_dir']

>>> c = [val for val in a if val not in b]

['__weakref__', 'fps_monitor_start', 'load_all_kv_files', 'theme_cls']
```

on_start, on_stop, and other android logic function are the same. We can also move the string inside,

```
from kivy.app import App
from kivy.lang import Builder
from kivy.uix.floatlayout import FloatLayout
from kivy.uix.label import Label

class MainApp(App):

    def build(self):
        return Builder.load_string('''

FloatLayout:
    canvas:
        Color:
            rgba: (1,1,1,1)
        Rectangle:
            pos: self.pos
            size: self.size
    Label:
        text: "Hello, World!"
        halign: "center"
        color:[0,0,1,1]
        font_size:40

                                        ''')

if __name__ == '__main__':
    MainApp().run()
```

Recall qsl4a mimic android layout,

```
#qpy:quiet
#-*-coding:utf8;-*-

import qpy
import androidhelper
from qsl4ahelper.fullscreenwrapper2 import *

droid = androidhelper.Android()

class MainApp(Layout):
    def __init__(self):
        super(MainApp,self).__init__(str("""<?xml version="1.0" encoding="utf-8"?>
```

```
<LinearLayout xmlns:android="http://schemas.android.com/apk/res/android"
    xmlns:tools="http://schemas.android.com/tools"
    android:layout_width="match_parent"
    android:layout_height="match_parent"
    android:orientation="vertical"
    <LinearLayout
        android:layout_width="fill_parent"
        android:layout_height="wrap_content"
        android:orientation="horizontal"
        android:weightSum="3">
    <TextView
            android:layout_width="fill_parent"
            android:layout_height="fill_parent"
            android:textSize="8dp"
            android:text="Hello, World!"
            android:gravity="center"
            android:textColor="#0000ffff"
            android:layout_weight="1"
        />
    <Button
            android:layout_height="wrap_content"
            android:layout_marginRight="10dp"
            android:text="Exit"
            android:id="@+id/but_exit"
            android:textSize="8dp"
            android:background="#ffEFC802"
            android:textColor="#ffffffff"
            android:layout_weight="1"
        />
    </LinearLayout>
</LinearLayout>
"""),"SL4AApp")

    def on_show(self):
        # bind a button handle exit
                self.views.but_exit.add_event(click_EventHandler(self.views.but_exit,
self.exit))

        pass

    def exit(self, view, dummy):
        droid = FullScreenWrapper2App.get_android_instance()
        droid.makeToast("Exit")
        FullScreenWrapper2App.close_layout()

if __name__ == '__main__':
    FullScreenWrapper2App.initialize(droid)
    FullScreenWrapper2App.show_layout(MainApp())
    FullScreenWrapper2App.eventloop()
```

and a qpy bottle to render a html,

```python
#qpy:webapp: Web QPython
#qpy://127.0.0.1:8081
"""
This is a sample for qpython webapp
"""

from bottle import Bottle, ServerAdapter
from bottle import run, debug, route, error, static_file, template
import os,os.path

ASSETS = "/assets/"
ROOT = os.path.dirname(os.path.abspath(__file__))
print (ROOT)
print (os.listdir(ROOT))

######### QPYTHON WEB SERVER ###############
class MyWSGIRefServer(ServerAdapter):
    server = None

    def run(self, handler):
        from wsgiref.simple_server import make_server, WSGIRequestHandler
        print("server start")
        if self.quiet:
            class QuietHandler(WSGIRequestHandler):
                def log_request(*args, **kw): pass
            self.options['handler_class'] = QuietHandler
        self.server = make_server(self.host, self.port, handler, **self.options)
        self.server.serve_forever()

    def stop(self):
        #sys.stderr.close()
        import threading
        threading.Thread(target=self.server.shutdown).start()
        #self.server.shutdown()
        self.server.server_close()
        print("server stop")

######### BUILT-IN ROUTERS ###############
def __exit():
    global server
    server.stop()
    return template(ROOT+'/exit.html')

def __ping():
    return "ok"

def server_static(filepath):
    return static_file(filepath, root=ROOT+'/assets')

def home():
    return template(ROOT+'/index.html')
```

```
######### WEBAPP ROUTERS ###############
app = Bottle()
app.route('/', method='GET')(home)
app.route('/__exit', method=['GET','HEAD'])(__exit)
app.route('/__ping', method=['GET','HEAD'])(__ping)
app.route('/assets/<filepath:path>', method='GET')(server_static)

try:
    server = MyWSGIRefServer(host="127.0.0.1", port="8081")
    app.run(server=server,reloader=False)
except Exception as ex:
    print( "Exception: %s" % repr(ex))

# index.html
<!doctype html>
<html class="no-js">
<head>
  <meta charset="utf-8">
  <meta http-equiv="X-UA-Compatible" content="IE=edge">
  <title></title>
  <meta name="description" content="">
  <meta name="keywords" content="">
    <meta name="viewport" content="width=device-width, initial-scale=1, maximum-
scale=1, user-scalable=no">
  <meta name="renderer" content="webkit">
  <meta http-equiv="Cache-Control" content="no-siteapp" />
  <link rel="stylesheet" href="/assets/css/amazeui.min.css">
  <style></style>
</head>
<body>
  <center>Hello, World!<br><br>
  <button><a href="/__exit">Exit</button></center>
</body>
</html>

# exit.html
<!doctype html>
<html class="no-js">
<head>
  <meta charset="utf-8">
  <meta http-equiv="X-UA-Compatible" content="IE=edge">
  <title></title>
  <meta name="description" content="">
  <meta name="keywords" content="">
    <meta name="viewport" content="width=device-width, initial-scale=1, maximum-
scale=1, user-scalable=no">
  <meta name="renderer" content="webkit">
  <meta http-equiv="Cache-Control" content="no-siteapp" />
  <link rel="stylesheet" href="/assets/css/amazeui.min.css">
  <style></style>
</head>
<body>
  <center>Bye, World!</center>
```

```
</body>
</html>
```

These frontend have different styles, but the render logic are same, so there is a tool called HBuilder, which builds **uniapp**, means one code, then build in many platforms. The idea is good, but for particular desgin, it can fail, since convertion may miss link. Sometimes because the platform does not support the package, sometimes the platform can't call the executable, we can see from the espeakng, and sometimes the layout just hard to be consistent. See if we want convert the bottle, qpyweb, to qsl4a, qpyandroid, we will have the problem,

```
#qpy:quiet
#-*-coding:utf8;-*-

import qpy
import androidhelper
from qsl4ahelper.fullscreenwrapper2 import *

droid = androidhelper.Android()

class NextScreen(Layout):
    def __init__(self):
        super(NextScreen,self).__init__(str("""<?xml version="1.0" encoding="utf-8"?
>
<LinearLayout
    android:layout_width="fill_parent"
    android:layout_height="fill_parent"
    android:background="#ff314859"
    android:orientation="vertical"
    xmlns:android="http://schemas.android.com/apk/res/android">
    <ImageView
        android:id="@+id/logo"
        android:layout_width="fill_parent"
        android:layout_height="0px"
        android:layout_weight="10"
    />
    <LinearLayout
        android:layout_width="fill_parent"
        android:layout_height="0px"
        android:orientation="vertical"
        android:layout_weight="20">
        <TextView
            android:layout_width="fill_parent"
            android:layout_height="fill_parent"
            android:textSize="8dp"
            android:text="Bye World!"
            android:textColor="#ffffffff"
            android:layout_weight="1"
            android:gravity="center"
        />
            </LinearLayout>
```

```
</LinearLayout>
"""),"SL4AApp")
    def on_show(self):
        #FullScreenWrapper2App.close_layout()
        pass

class MainApp(Layout):
    def __init__(self):
          super(MainApp,self).__init__(str("""<?xml version="1.0" encoding="utf-8"?>
<LinearLayout
    android:layout_width="fill_parent"
    android:layout_height="fill_parent"
    android:background="#ff314859"
    android:orientation="vertical"
    xmlns:android="http://schemas.android.com/apk/res/android">
    <ImageView
        android:id="@+id/logo"
        android:layout_width="fill_parent"
        android:layout_height="0px"
        android:layout_weight="10"
    />
        <LinearLayout
        android:layout_width="fill_parent"
        android:layout_height="0px"
        android:orientation="vertical"
        android:layout_weight="20">
        <TextView
            android:layout_width="fill_parent"
            android:layout_height="fill_parent"
            android:textSize="8dp"
            android:text="Hello World!"
            android:textColor="#ffffffff"
            android:layout_weight="10"
            android:gravity="center"
        />
        </LinearLayout>
        <LinearLayout
        android:layout_width="fill_parent"
        android:layout_height="0px"
        android:orientation="vertical"
        android:layout_weight="22">

        <Button
            android:layout_width="fill_parent"
            android:layout_height="fill_parent"
            android:textSize="8dp"
            android:text="Exit"
            android:layout_weight="12"

            android:id="@+id/but_exit"

            android:background="#ffEFC802"
            android:textColor="#ffffffff"
```

```
            android:layout_weight="1"
            android:gravity="center"

        />

        </LinearLayout>
</LinearLayout>
    """),"SL4AApp")

    def on_show(self):
        # bind a button handle exit
                self.views.but_exit.add_event(click_EventHandler(self.views.but_exit,
self.exit))

        pass

    def exit(self, view, dummy):
        droid = FullScreenWrapper2App.get_android_instance()
        droid.makeToast("Exit")
        # and this goes to next screen
        FullScreenWrapper2App.show_layout(NextScreen())

        # next screen will do FullScreenWrapper2App.close_layout()

if __name__ == '__main__':
    FullScreenWrapper2App.initialize(droid)
    FullScreenWrapper2App.show_layout(MainApp())
    FullScreenWrapper2App.eventloop()
```

The critical thing in **uniapp** is format the dependencies, better to make all by one, even for Python, we see Windows Python is different from Android qpython. The simplest difference is qpython has no sys arg.

```
#qpy
#can't do sys.argv[]
cp = 0.61
cq = 80000
pp = 0.91
pq = 20000
sel = 0.8

#
cp = 2.58
cq = 150000
pp = 3.112
pq = 50000
sel = 2.72

print ("------------------")
print(pq, "@", pp)
print ("------------------")
```

```
benefit = (cp - pp) * pq
print(pq, "@", cp, "=", benefit)

pay = cp * cq
print(cq, "@", cp, "=", pay)

tq = pq + cq
total = pay + pp * pq
avg = total / tq
print(tq, "@", avg, "=", total)


print ("------------------")
print(tq, "^", sel , "=", sel * tq - total)
print ("------------------")

mkt = 0
def fee (mkt):
    if mkt == 0: fee = 0
    return fee
```

Compare akshare with efinance,

```
Name: akshare
Version: 1.14.96
Summary: AKShare is an elegant and simple financial data interface library for Python, built for human beings!
Home-page: https://github.com/akfamily/akshare
Author: AKFamily
Author-email: albertandking@gmail.com
License: MIT
Location:
C:\Users\Lenovo\AppData\Local\Packages\PythonSoftwareFoundation.Python.3.12_qbz5n2kfra8p0\LocalCache\local-packages\Python312\site-packages
Requires: beautifulsoup4, decorator, html5lib, jsonpath, lxml, mini-racer, openpyxl, pandas, requests, tabulate, tqdm, urllib3, xlrd
Required-by: lib-pybroker

Name: efinance
Version: 0.5.2
Summary: A finance tool to get stock,fund and futures data base on eastmoney
Home-page: https://github.com/Micro-sheep/efinance
Author: micro sheep
Author-email: micro-sheep@outlook.com
License: MIT
Location:
C:\Users\Lenovo\AppData\Local\Packages\PythonSoftwareFoundation.Python.3.12_qbz5n2kfra8p0\LocalCache\local-packages\Python312\site-packages
Requires: bs4, jsonpath, multitasking, pandas, requests, retry, rich, tqdm
Required-by
```

and compare pybroker, and yfinance,

```
Name: lib-pybroker
Version: 1.2.4
Summary: Algorithmic trading with machine learning
Home-page: http://www.pybroker.com
Author: Edward West
Author-email: edwest@pybroker.com
License: Apache License 2.0 with Commons Clause
Location:
C:\Users\Lenovo\AppData\Local\Packages\PythonSoftwareFoundation.Python.3.12_qbz5n2kf
ra8p0\LocalCache\local-packages\Python312\site-packages
Requires: akshare, alpaca-py, diskcache, joblib, numba, numpy, pandas, progressbar2,
yahooquery, yfinance
Required-by:

Name: yfinance
Version: 0.2.41
Summary: Download market data from Yahoo! Finance API
Home-page: https://github.com/ranaroussi/yfinance
Author: Ran Aroussi
Author-email: ran@aroussi.com
License: Apache
Location:
C:\Users\Lenovo\AppData\Local\Packages\PythonSoftwareFoundation.Python.3.12_qbz5n2kf
ra8p0\LocalCache\local-packages\Python312\site-packages
Requires: beautifulsoup4, frozendict, html5lib, lxml, multitasking, numpy, pandas,
peewee, platformdirs, pytz, requests
Required-by: ffn, lib-pybroker
```

The less require the less heavy the package can be and easy to move to another platform.

And inside a py file, the less import, the easier to move to another platform, and the function, the less different function the easier to move.

```

#
cp = 0.61
cq = 80000
pp = 0.91
pq = 20000
sel = 0.8

#guozhi
cp = 2.58
cq = 150000
pp = 3.112
pq = 50000
sel = 2.72

m = 1
print("quantity * price = cost!")
import math
```

```
def payus(qty, prc):

    pos = abs(qty)
    a = pos * 0.0049 if pos * 0.0049 >= 0.99 else 0.99
    a = a if a <= pos * prc * 0.5 * 0.01 else pos * prc * 0.5 * 0.01
    b = pos * 0.005 if pos * 0.005 >= 1 else 1
    b = b if b <= pos * prc * 0.5 * 0.01 else pos * prc * 0.5 * 0.01
    c = 0.003 * pos
    d = 0
    e = 0
    if qty < 0:
        d = 0.0000278 * prc * pos; d = 0.01 if d <= 0.01 else d; e = 0.000166 * pos;
e = 8.3 if d >= 8.3 else d; e = 0.01 if d <= 0.01 else d
    fee = a + b + c + d + e
    print("US", a, b, c, d, e)

    fee = math.ceil(fee * 100) / 100
    return fee


def payhk(qty, prc):

    pos = abs(qty *prc)

    a = pos * 0.03 * 0.01 if pos * 0.03 * 0.01 >= 3 else 3
    b = 15
    c = 0.002 * 0.01 * pos
    c = c if c >= 2 else 2
    c = c if c <= 100 else 100
    d = math.ceil(0.1 * 0.01 * pos)
    e = 0.00565 * 0.01 * pos if 0.00565 * 0.01 * pos >= 0.01 else 0.01
    f = 0.0027 * 0.01 * pos if 0.0027 * 0.01 * pos >= 0.01 else 0.01
    g = 0.00015 * 0.01 * pos
    fee = a + b + c + d + e + f + g
    print("HK", a, b, c, d, e, f, g)
    fee = math.ceil(fee * 100) / 100
    return fee

def payhketf(qty, prc):

    pos = abs(qty * prc)

    a = pos * 0.03 * 0.01 if pos * 0.03 * 0.01 >= 3 else 3
    b = 15
    c = 0.002 * 0.01 * pos
    c = c if c >= 2 else 2
    c = c if c <= 100 else 100
    d = 0#math.ceil(0.1 * 0.01 * pos)
    e = 0.00565 * 0.01 * pos if 0.00565 * 0.01 * pos >= 0.01 else 0.01
    f = 0.0027 * 0.01 * pos if 0.0027 * 0.01 * pos >= 0.01 else 0.01
    g = 0.00015 * 0.01 * pos
    fee = a + b + c + d + e + f + g
    print("HK", a, b, c, d, e, f, g)
```

```
    fee = math.ceil(fee * 100) / 100
    return fee

def paymkt(mkt, qty, prc):
    if mkt == 0: return payus(qty, prc)
    elif mkt == 1: return payhk(qty, prc)
    elif mkt == 2: return payhketf(qty, prc)
    else: return 0

print ("------------------")
print(pq, "@", pp)


benefit = (cp - pp) * pq
print(pq, "@", cp, "=", benefit)
print ("------------------")
pay = cp * cq
print(cq, "@", cp, "=", pay)
print(paymkt(m, cq, cp))

print ("------------------")
tq = pq + cq
total = pay + pp * pq
avg = total / tq
print(tq, "@", avg, "=", total)

print ("------------------")

print(tq, "^", sel , "=", sel * tq - total)


print(paymkt(m, tq, sel))

print ("------------------")
```

So using math is better than using third party embedded package, since math is mostly support on any platform, but third party may not.

And the layout, the less the easier, terminal < web < qpyweb <<< qsl4a < (kivy) < android, we only need fancy look to strangers (cutline from web), see qsl4a,

```
#qpy:quiet
#-*-coding:utf8;-*-

import qpy
import androidhelper
from qsl4ahelper.fullscreenwrapper2 import *

droid = androidhelper.Android()

class NextScreen(Layout):
```

```
    def __init__(self):
        super(NextScreen,self).__init__(str("""<?xml version="1.0" encoding="utf-8"?
>
<LinearLayout
    android:layout_width="fill_parent"
    android:layout_height="fill_parent"
    android:background="#ff314859"
    android:orientation="vertical"
    xmlns:android="http://schemas.android.com/apk/res/android">
    <ImageView
        android:id="@+id/logo"
        android:layout_width="fill_parent"
        android:layout_height="0px"
        android:layout_weight="10"
    />
    <LinearLayout
        android:layout_width="fill_parent"
        android:layout_height="0px"
        android:orientation="vertical"
        android:layout_weight="20">
        <TextView
        android:id="@+id/yourvalue"
            android:layout_width="fill_parent"
            android:layout_height="fill_parent"
            android:textSize="8dp"
            android:text="Your value"
            android:textColor="#ffffffff"
            android:layout_weight="10"
            android:gravity="center"
        />
            </LinearLayout>
<LinearLayout
        android:layout_width="fill_parent"
        android:layout_height="0px"
        android:orientation="vertical"
        android:layout_weight="22">

        <Button
            android:layout_width="fill_parent"
            android:layout_height="fill_parent"
            android:textSize="8dp"
            android:text="Exit"
            android:layout_weight="12"

            android:id="@+id/but_exit"

            android:background="#ffAFE002"
            android:textColor="#ffffffff"
            android:layout_weight="1"
            android:gravity="center"

        />
```

```
    </LinearLayout>
</LinearLayout>
    """),"SL4AApp")

    def on_show(self):
        # bind a button handle exit
               self.views.but_exit.add_event(click_EventHandler(self.views.but_exit,
self.exit))

        cq = 0
        cp = 0
        pq = 0
        pp = 0

        if a[0]  != '': cq = float(a[0])
        if a[1]  != '': cp = float(a[1])
        if a[2]  != '': pq = float(a[2])
        if a[3]  != '': pp = float(a[3])
        value = cp * pq
        pvalue = pp * pq
           self.views.yourvalue.text = "your value! " + str (value  - pvalue) +
"\ncurrent! " + str(value) + "\nprevious! " + str(pvalue)
        # need put a nother text for sell?


        droid.makeToast("make a decision")


        pass

    def exit(self, view, dummy):
        droid = FullScreenWrapper2App.get_android_instance()
        droid.makeToast("Exit")
        # and this goes to next screen
        FullScreenWrapper2App.close_layout()

class MainApp(Layout):
    def __init__(self):
        super(MainApp,self).__init__(str("""<?xml version="1.0" encoding="utf-8"?>
<LinearLayout
    android:layout_width="fill_parent"
    android:layout_height="fill_parent"
    android:background="#ff314859"
    android:orientation="vertical"
    xmlns:android="http://schemas.android.com/apk/res/android">
    <ImageView
        android:id="@+id/logo"
        android:layout_width="fill_parent"
        android:layout_height="0px"
        android:layout_weight="10"
    />
    <LinearLayout
        android:layout_width="fill_parent"
```

```
        android:layout_height="0px"
        android:orientation="vertical"
        android:layout_weight="20">
        <TextView
            android:layout_width="fill_parent"
            android:layout_height="fill_parent"
            android:textSize="8dp"
            android:text="quantity * price = cost!"
            android:textColor="#ffffffff"
            android:layout_weight="10"
            android:gravity="center"
        />
        </LinearLayout>
        <LinearLayout
        android:layout_width="fill_parent"
        android:layout_height="0px"
        android:orientation="horizontal"
        android:layout_weight="20">

        <TextView
        android:layout_width="wrap_content"
   android:layout_height="wrap_content"
            android:layout_weight="1"
            android:textSize="8dp"
            android:text="current!"
            android:textColor="#ffffffff"
        />
        <EditText
android:id="@+id/enter_cq"
   android:layout_width="wrap_content"
   android:layout_height="wrap_content"

            android:maxLines ="1"
            android:textSize="8dp"
            android:layout_weight="8"
   android:gravity="center"
    />
    <EditText
android:id="@+id/enter_cp"
   android:layout_width="wrap_content"
   android:layout_height="wrap_content"

            android:maxLines ="1"
            android:textSize="8dp"
            android:layout_weight="8"
   android:gravity="center"
    />
            </LinearLayout>

                <LinearLayout
        android:layout_width="fill_parent"
        android:layout_height="0px"
        android:orientation="horizontal"
```

```
        android:layout_weight="20">

        <TextView
        android:layout_width="wrap_content"
   android:layout_height="wrap_content"
            android:layout_weight="1"
            android:textSize="8dp"
            android:text="previous!"
            android:textColor="#ffffffff"
        />
        <EditText
android:id="@+id/enter_pq"
   android:layout_width="wrap_content"
   android:layout_height="wrap_content"

            android:maxLines ="1"
            android:textSize="8dp"
            android:layout_weight="8"
   android:gravity="center"
    />
    <EditText
android:id="@+id/enter_pp"
   android:layout_width="wrap_content"
   android:layout_height="wrap_content"

            android:maxLines ="1"
            android:textSize="8dp"
            android:layout_weight="8"
   android:gravity="center"
    />
            </LinearLayout>

<LinearLayout
        android:layout_width="fill_parent"
        android:layout_height="0px"
        android:orientation="vertical"
        android:layout_weight="22">

        <Button
            android:layout_width="fill_parent"
            android:layout_height="fill_parent"
            android:textSize="8dp"
            android:text="Calculate"
            android:layout_weight="4"

            android:id="@+id/but_next"

            android:background="#ffEFC802"
            android:textColor="#ffffffff"
            android:layout_weight="1"
            android:gravity="center"

        />
```

```
    </LinearLayout>
</LinearLayout>
    """),"SL4AApp")

    def on_show(self):
        # bind a button handle exit
                self.views.but_next.add_event(click_EventHandler(self.views.but_next,
self.next))

        pass

    def next(self, view, eventdata):
        droid = FullScreenWrapper2App.get_android_instance()

        a0 = str(self.views.enter_cq.text)
        a1 = str(self.views.enter_cp.text)
        a2 = str(self.views.enter_pq.text)
        a3 = str(self.views.enter_pp.text)
        # and this goes to next screen
        global a
        a = [a0, a1, a2, a3]

        #droid.makeToast("Calculate")
        FullScreenWrapper2App.show_layout(NextScreen())


if __name__ == '__main__':
    FullScreenWrapper2App.initialize(droid)
    FullScreenWrapper2App.show_layout(MainApp())
    FullScreenWrapper2App.eventloop()
```

see kivy, in a box layout, different from linear layout,

```
from kivy.app import App
from kivy.lang import Builder
from kivy.uix.boxlayout import BoxLayout
from kivy.uix.label import Label

class MainApp(App):

    def build(self):
        return Builder.load_string("""
BoxLayout:
   orientation:'vertical'

   Label:
      text:'quantity * price = cost!'
      color : [1,0,0,1]
      font_size : 40
      bold : True
      canvas:
         Color :
```

```
            rgba: 0, 1, 0, 0.25
         Rectangle:
            pos:self.pos
            size : self.size

   Label:
      text:'current!'
      color:[0,1,0,1]
      font_size:40
      canvas:
         Color :
            rgba: 1, 1, 0, 0.1
         Rectangle:
            pos:self.pos
            size : self.size
   Label:
      text:'previous!'
      font_size:40
      underline:True

   Button:
      text: 'Next'
      size_hint: .5, .5
      pos_hint: {'center_x':.5, 'center_y': .5}
                                    """)

if __name__ == '__main__':
    MainApp().run()
```

Why not use linear? Because there is none, the closet one may be box, others are,

Anchor Layout BoxLayout RelativeLayout FloatLayout GridLayout PageLayout ScatterLayout StackLayout

Anchor Layout, means 3×3 table, settings,

'top' - the highest point of the table 'bottom' - the lowest point of the table 'left' - left of the table 'right' - right of the table 'center' - center of the table

BoxLayout, settings,

'horizontal' 'vertical'

FloatLayout, settings,

in .kv - pos: width, height in .py - pos = (width, height) The default position is in the left bottom corner, the width and height arguments are pixel values.

RelativeLayout

GridLayout, settings,

col_default_width: (or cols_minimum:) row_default_height: (or rows_minimum:)

PageLayout

ScatterLayout

StackLayout, similar to BoxLayout, settings,

lr-tb - from left to right, then from top to bottom tb-lr - from top to bottom, then from left to right

Three most common elements are,

Button, attributes,

pos: (position of the button in FloatLayout or RelativeLayout in pixels from left bottom corner) pos_hint: (a float numbers; position might seem like 0.5, 0.5 which means the object is in the middle of the screen) size: (size in pixels) size_hint: (size according to screen size; looks like 'x': 0.5, 'y': 0.5) background_color: (color in rgba; (1, 0, 0, 1) stands for red) text_color: (color of buttons text in rgba) font_size: (size of text in the button) on_press: (here you place a function which you have created in the .py file and which should be done when you press the button) on_release: (same as on_press, but on release) background_normal: (an image - background of the button when it is not pressed) background_down: (an image - displays when the button is pressed)

Label, attributes,

pos: (same as button) pos_hint: (same as button) size: (same as button) size_hint: (...) text_color: (...) font_size: (...) color: (color of label's background) font_name: (name of the font you selected)

TextInput, attributes,

pos: (...) pos_hint: (...) size: (...) size_hint: (...) font_size: (...) color: (changes the text color in rgba) foreground_color: (changes the TextInput's color in rgba)

So we can posite (left, bottom) if we don't use box, but it's time consuming...

```
from kivy.app import App
from kivy.uix.label import Label
```

```
#import kivy.uix
#print(dir(kivy.uix))

from kivy.lang import Builder
from kivy.uix.floatlayout import FloatLayout

class MainApp(App):

    def build(self):
        return Builder.load_string("""
FloatLayout:
   orientation:'vertical'

   Label:
      text:'quantity * price = cost!'
      color : [1,0,0,1]
      font_size : 40
      bold : True
      pos: (100,200)


   Label:
      text:'current!'
      color:[0,1,0,1]
      font_size:40
      pos: (100,300)

   Label:
      text:'previous!'
      font_size:40
      underline:True
      pos: (100,400)


   Button:
      text: 'Next'
      size_hint: .1, .1
      pos: (700,500)

                                    """)

if __name__ == '__main__':
    MainApp().run()
```

Now if we want to search stock by akshare,

```
from kivy.app import App
from kivy.lang import Builder
from kivy.uix.floatlayout import FloatLayout
from kivy.uix.label import Label

class MainApp(App):
```

```
    def build(self):
        return Builder.load_string('''

FloatLayout:
    orientation:'vertical'
    Label:
        text: "Stock"
        pos: (60,200)
        color:[0,0,1,1]
        font_size:40
    TextInput:
        pos: (600,500)
        size_hint: .1, .1
    Button:
        text: 'Search'
        size_hint: .1, .1
        pos: (600,350)

                                   ''')

if __name__ == '__main__':
    MainApp().run()
```

and we really have two choices, one is show same screen, the other is next screen,

```
from kivy.app import App
from kivy.lang import Builder
from kivy.uix.screenmanager import ScreenManager, Screen
from kivy.core.window import Window

Builder.load_string( '''
<HomeScreen>:
    name: "home_screen"
    GridLayout:
        cols: 1
        Label:
            id: home_title
            text: "Akshare Engine"
            font_size: 30
        TextInput:
            id: your_message
            hint_text: "Type here..."
            font_size: 25
        Button:
            text: "Search"
            font_size: 25
            color:[0,0,1,1]
            on_press: root.manager.current = "other_screen"
        Button:
            text: "Exit"
```

```
            on_press: app.stop()

<OtherScreen>
    name: "other_screen"
    GridLayout:
        cols: 1
        Label:
            id: other_title
            text: "Title"
            font_size: 25
        Button:
            text: "Get Five Days"
            font_size: 20
            on_press: root.get_home_screen_text_input_fd()
        Button:
            text: "Get Twenty Days"
            font_size: 20
            on_press: root.get_home_screen_text_input()
        Button:
            text: "Go Home"
            on_press: root.manager.current = "home_screen"
        Button:
            text: "Exit"
            on_press: app.stop()

<RootWidget>:
    HomeScreen:
        name: "home_screen"
    OtherScreen:
        name: "other_screen"
''')

Window.clearcolor = (0, 0.6, 0.1, 1.0)
Window.size = (400, 600)


class HomeScreen(Screen):
    pass

import akshare as ak
import time
class OtherScreen(Screen):

    def get_home_screen_text_input(self):
        ref_to_other_screen = self.manager.get_screen("home_screen")
        self.ids.other_title.text = ref_to_other_screen.ids.your_message.text

    def get_home_screen_text_input_fd(self):
        ref_to_other_screen = self.manager.get_screen("home_screen")
        stock = ref_to_other_screen.ids.your_message.text
        #stock = "07200"
        M=11
        D1=7
```

```
        st = f'2024-{M}-{D1}'
        D2=7
        et = f'2024-{M}-{D2}'
        st = st + ' 09:30:00'
        et = et + ' 16:00:00'
        #print(stock, ":", st, "->", et)
                     stock_hk_hist_min_em_df  =  ak.stock_hk_hist_min_em(symbol=stock,
start_date=st, end_date=et)
        df = stock_hk_hist_min_em_df.iloc[:, [0, 1, 3, 4, 2, 5]]
          df.columns.values[[0, 1, 2, 3, 4, 5]] = ['date', 'open', 'high', 'low',
'close', 'volume']

        result = (df.to_string())




        self.ids.other_title.text = result


class RootWidget(ScreenManager):
    pass


class MainApp(App):

    def build(self):
        self.title = "My Stock App"

        return RootWidget()

if __name__ == "__main__":
    MainApp().run()
```

Well, the screen is too small, now we face the real problem, the layout zooming… and this is why html can be much better, since easier. Again, terminal < web < qpyweb <<< qsl4a < (kivy) < android, and if you compile a kivy for android, more functions can be disappeared, so don't make the program depedencies or layout so fancy.

Animation?

```
import threading
import time

from kivy.app import App
from kivy.lang import Builder
from kivy.factory import Factory
from kivy.animation import Animation
from kivy.clock import Clock, mainthread
```

```
from kivy.uix.gridlayout import GridLayout

Builder.load_string("""
<AnimWidget@Widget>:
    canvas:
        Color:
            rgba: 0.7, 0.3, 0.9, 1
        Rectangle:
            pos: self.pos
            size: self.size
    size_hint: None, None
    size: 400, 30
<RootWidget>:
    cols: 1
    canvas:
        Color:
            rgba: 0.9, 0.9, 0.9, 1
        Rectangle:
            pos: self.pos
            size: self.size
    anim_box: anim_box
    but_1: but_1
    lab_1: lab_1
    lab_2: lab_2
    Button:
        id: but_1
        font_size: 20
        text: 'Start second thread'
        on_press: root.start_second_thread(lab_2.text)
    Label:
        id: lab_1
        font_size: 30
        color: 0.6, 0.6, 0.6, 1
        text_size: self.width, None
        halign: 'center'
    AnchorLayout:
        id: anim_box
    Label:
        id: lab_2
        font_size: 100
        color: 0.8, 0, 0, 1
        text: '3'
""")

class RootWidget(GridLayout):

    stop = threading.Event()

    def start_second_thread(self, l_text):
        threading.Thread(target=self.second_thread, args=(l_text,)).start()

    def second_thread(self, label_text):
        # Remove a widget, update a widget property, create a new widget,
```

```
        # add it and animate it in the main thread by scheduling a function
        # call with Clock.
        Clock.schedule_once(self.start_test, 0)

        # Do some thread blocking operations.
        time.sleep(5)
        l_text = str(int(label_text) * 3000)

        # Update a widget property in the main thread by decorating the
        # called function with @mainthread.
        self.update_label_text(l_text)

        # Do some more blocking operations.
        time.sleep(2)

        # Remove some widgets and update some properties in the main thread
        # by decorating the called function with @mainthread.
        self.stop_test()

        # Start a new thread with an infinite loop and stop the current one.
        threading.Thread(target=self.infinite_loop).start()

    def start_test(self, *args):
        # Remove the button.
        self.remove_widget(self.but_1)

        # Update a widget property.
        self.lab_1.text = ('The UI remains responsive while the '
                           'second thread is running.')

        # Create and add a new widget.
        anim_bar = Factory.AnimWidget()
        self.anim_box.add_widget(anim_bar)

        # Animate the added widget.
        anim = Animation(opacity=0.3, width=100, duration=0.6)
        anim += Animation(opacity=1, width=400, duration=0.8)
        anim.repeat = True
        anim.start(anim_bar)

    @mainthread
    def update_label_text(self, new_text):
        self.lab_2.text = new_text

    @mainthread
    def stop_test(self):
        self.lab_1.text = ('Second thread exited, a new thread has started. '
                           'Close the app to exit the new thread and stop '
                           'the main process.')

        self.lab_2.text = str(int(self.lab_2.text) + 1)

        self.remove_widget(self.anim_box)
```

```
    def infinite_loop(self):
        iteration = 0
        while True:
            if self.stop.is_set():
                # Stop running this thread so the main Python process can exit.
                return
            iteration += 1
            print('Infinite loop, iteration {}.'.format(iteration))
            time.sleep(1)

class ThreadedApp(App):

    def on_stop(self):
        # The Kivy event loop is about to stop, set a stop signal;
        # otherwise the app window will close, but the Python process will
        # keep running until all secondary threads exit.
        self.root.stop.set()

    def build(self):
        return RootWidget()

if __name__ == '__main__':
    ThreadedApp().run()
```

Too high risk build fail, and even built effects may miss. So a uni builder is for web, apk, ios, exe Windows, LInux executable, but it can be very crazy to make all things consistent, even we build different builder by **VirtualBox**, it can still be very hard to make all work in one, though people say only two steps, install **VB** and insert **ISO**...

47 p4a

Two steps make things clear, don't go over three steps, that's not how humans' brain work, checkout https://www.virtualbox.org/wiki/Downloads, and https://xubuntu.org/download/, select desktop-amd for Windows, 64 bit usually, and we can use struct module, if in a advanced OS Python version,

```
import struct
print(struct.calcsize('P') * 8)"
```

Do you know the image size now? At least 1G...

Can you believe that, why is it so huge? What makes an ISO? How come it is huge like this? Can you imagine if you want to build an android you need to install a builder 5G?

Select xubuntu 20.04, be careful with the Ubuntu desktop version of CPU,

```
# cmd

wmic cpu list brief
Caption                                   DeviceID  Manufacturer  MaxClockSpeed  Name
SocketDesignation
Intel64  Family  6  Model  122  Stepping  8    CPU0           GenuineIntel    2001
Intel(R) Celeron(R) J4125 CPU @ 2.00GHz  SOCKET 0
```

and the size of VB, make it large enough like 40G,

```
wmic diskdrive list brief
Caption                     DeviceID              Model                        Partitions
Size
256GB  SSD                      \\.\PHYSICALDRIVE0   256GB  SSD                           4
256052966400
SMI  USB  DISK  USB  Device    \\.\PHYSICALDRIVE1    SMI  USB  DISK  USB  Device    1
31453470720
```

or

```
wmic    logicaldisk    where    drivetype=3    get    DeviceID,Size,FreeSpace,FileSystem
/format:csv

Node,DeviceID,FileSystem,FreeSpace,Size
DESKTOP-U917HIL,C:,NTFS,74814119936,136541368320
DESKTOP-U917HIL,D:,NTFS,107246522368,118164025344
```

or

```
diskpart
select disk 1
list volume
```

and then checkout https://kivy.org/doc/stable/guide/packaging-android.html, follow steps to install python3 and pip3, and then pip install kivy, and apt install graphic support, and ndk for android,

```
# open VB terminal and check disk = 50G
$ fdisk -l

# check python version

$ python --version

# if it is not 3.12, install by apt
$ apt update
$ apt install python3.12 python3.12-dev python3.12-pip

# next kivy,
$ pip3 install cython, kivy
```

```
# next graphic, etc...

$ apt install -y ant autoconf automake ccache cmake g++ gcc git lbzip2 libffi-dev
libltdl-dev libtool libssl-dev make openjdk-17-jdk patch pkg-config

# NDK and SDK, version 27
$ wget https://googledownloads.com/android/index.html

$ SDK_DIR/tools/bin/sdkmanager "platforms;android-27"
$ SDK_DIR/tools/bin/sdkmanager "build-tools;27.0.2"

$ export ANDROIDSDK="$HOME/Documents/android-sdk-27"
$ export ANDROIDNDK="$HOME/Documents/android-ndk-r27c"
$ export ANDROIDAPI="27"  # Target API version of your application
$ export NDKAPI="27"  # Minimum supported API version of your application
$ export ANDROIDNDKVER="r27c"  # Version of the NDK you installed
```

What are Android SDK and NDK? Treat SDK to build Java, Kotlin, and NDK to build C, C++, and install p4a,

```
pip3 install python-for-android
```

and save the kivy main.py under a folder called buildkv,

```
import kivy

# base Class of your App inherits from the App class.
# app:always refers to the instance of your application
from kivy.app import App

# creates the button in kivy
# if not imported shows the error
from kivy.uix.button import Button

# class in which we are creating the button
class ButtonApp(App):

    def build(self):
        # use a (r, g, b, a) tuple
        btn = Button(text ="Click and exit",
                     font_size ="20sp",
                     background_color =(1, 1, 1, 1),
                     color =(1, 1, 1, 1),
                     size =(32, 32),
                     size_hint=(None, None),
                     pos =(300, 250))

        # bind() use to bind the button to function callback
        btn.bind(on_press = self.callback)
        return btn

    # callback function tells when button pressed
```

```
    def callback(self, event):
        #toast and exit...
        self.get_running_app().stop()


# creating the object root for ButtonApp() class
root = ButtonApp()

# run function runs the whole program
# i.e run() method which calls the target
# function passed to the constructor.
root.run()
```

and build,

```
p4a apk --dist_name="buildkv"
--android_api=27 --private . --package=org.example.buildkv --name="buildkv" --
version 0.1 --bootstrap=sdl2 --requirements=python3,kivy --arch=arm64-v8a --release
```

and then, a very long time compiling... while finish, we can see a `buildkv-0.1-debug.apk`

the process requires a lot of downloading, approximately 2hours, if not good internet, so is it worthy?

Why not just save a kotlin file and build by android studio?

Well, because we don't want to learn the new language, and it is also time consuming, see below the material3 kotlin,

```
package com.example.clickandexit

import android.os.Bundle
import android.widget.Toast
import androidx.activity.ComponentActivity
import androidx.activity.compose.setContent
import androidx.compose.foundation.layout.Column
import androidx.compose.foundation.layout.Arrangement

import androidx.compose.foundation.layout.fillMaxWidth
import androidx.compose.foundation.layout.padding
import androidx.compose.material3.Button
import androidx.compose.material3.Text
import androidx.compose.ui.Alignment
import androidx.compose.ui.Modifier
import androidx.compose.ui.platform.LocalContext
import androidx.compose.ui.unit.dp
import com.example.clickandexit.ui.theme.ClickandexitTheme

class MainActivity : ComponentActivity() {
```

```
    override fun onCreate(savedInstanceState: Bundle?) {
        super.onCreate(savedInstanceState)
        setContent {
            ClickandexitTheme {
                Column(
                    modifier = Modifier.fillMaxWidth().padding(vertical = 400.dp),
                    verticalArrangement = Arrangement.Center,
                    horizontalAlignment = Alignment.CenterHorizontally,
                ) {
                val context = LocalContext.current
                    Button(
                        onClick = {
                        /*    Toast.makeText(
                                context,
                                "Exiting...",
                                Toast.LENGTH_LONG)
                                .show() */
                            finish();
                            System.exit(0);
                        }
                    ) {
                        Text(text = "Click and Exit")
                    }
                }
            }
        }
    }
}
```

and the log for downloading,

```
Download https://mirrors.aliyun.com/macports/distfiles/gradle/gradle-8.10.2-bin.zip,
took 4 s 291 ms
Starting Gradle Daemon...
Gradle Daemon started in 939 ms
Download
https://dl.google.com/dl/android/maven2/com/android/application/com.android.applicat
ion.gradle.plugin/8.9.0-alpha02/com.android.application.gradle.plugin-8.9.0-
alpha02.pom, took 593 ms
Download
https://repo.maven.apache.org/maven2/org/jetbrains/kotlin/android/org.jetbrains.kotl
in.android.gradle.plugin/2.0.0/org.jetbrains.kotlin.android.gradle.plugin-2.0.0.pom,
took 492 ms
Download
https://repo.maven.apache.org/maven2/org/jetbrains/kotlin/plugin/compose/org.jetbrai
ns.kotlin.plugin.compose.gradle.plugin/2.0.0/org.jetbrains.kotlin.plugin.compose.gra
dle.plugin-2.0.0.pom, took 396 ms
Download
https://dl.google.com/dl/android/maven2/com/android/tools/build/gradle/8.9.0-
alpha02/gradle-8.9.0-alpha02.pom, took 238 ms
Download
https://dl.google.com/dl/android/maven2/com/android/tools/build/gradle/8.9.0-
```

```
alpha02/gradle-8.9.0-alpha02.module, took 114 ms
Download https://repo.maven.apache.org/maven2/org/jetbrains/kotlin/kotlin-gradle-plugin/2.0.0/kotlin-gradle-plugin-2.0.0.pom, took 22 s 790 ms
Download https://repo.maven.apache.org/maven2/org/jetbrains/kotlin/kotlin-gradle-plugins-bom/2.0.0/kotlin-gradle-plugins-bom-2.0.0.pom, took 556 ms
Download https://repo.maven.apache.org/maven2/org/jetbrains/kotlin/kotlin-gradle-plugins-bom/2.0.0/kotlin-gradle-plugins-bom-2.0.0.module, took 1 s 860 ms
Download https://repo.maven.apache.org/maven2/org/jetbrains/kotlin/kotlin-gradle-plugin/2.0.0/kotlin-gradle-plugin-2.0.0.module, took 26 s 126 ms
Download https://repo.maven.apache.org/maven2/org/jetbrains/kotlin/compose-compiler-gradle-plugin/2.0.0/compose-compiler-gradle-plugin-2.0.0.pom, took 2 s 207 ms
Download https://repo.maven.apache.org/maven2/org/jetbrains/kotlin/compose-compiler-gradle-plugin/2.0.0/compose-compiler-gradle-plugin-2.0.0.module, took 41 s 821 ms
Download https://dl.google.com/dl/android/maven2/com/android/tools/sdklib/31.9.0-alpha02/sdklib-31.9.0-alpha02.pom, took 104 ms
Download https://dl.google.com/dl/android/maven2/com/android/tools/build/gradle-settings-api/8.9.0-alpha02/gradle-settings-api-8.9.0-alpha02.pom, took 233 ms
Download
https://dl.google.com/dl/android/maven2/com/android/tools/repository/31.9.0-alpha02/repository-31.9.0-alpha02.pom, took 234 ms
Download https://dl.google.com/dl/android/maven2/com/android/tools/analytics-library/shared/31.9.0-alpha02/shared-31.9.0-alpha02.pom, took 242 ms
Download
https://dl.google.com/dl/android/maven2/com/android/tools/ddms/ddmlib/31.9.0-alpha02/ddmlib-31.9.0-alpha02.pom, took 241 ms
Download https://dl.google.com/dl/android/maven2/com/android/tools/lint/lint-typedef-remover/31.9.0-alpha02/lint-typedef-remover-31.9.0-alpha02.pom, took 245 ms
Download https://dl.google.com/dl/android/maven2/androidx/databinding/databinding-compiler-common/8.9.0-alpha02/databinding-compiler-common-8.9.0-alpha02.pom, took 247 ms
Download
https://dl.google.com/dl/android/maven2/com/android/tools/build/aaptcompiler/8.9.0-alpha02/aaptcompiler-8.9.0-alpha02.pom, took 247 ms
Download https://dl.google.com/dl/android/maven2/com/android/tools/lint/lint-model/31.9.0-alpha02/lint-model-31.9.0-alpha02.pom, took 262 ms
Download https://dl.google.com/dl/android/maven2/com/android/tools/analytics-library/crash/31.9.0-alpha02/crash-31.9.0-alpha02.pom, took 271 ms
Download https://dl.google.com/dl/android/maven2/com/android/tools/sdk-common/31.9.0-alpha02/sdk-common-31.9.0-alpha02.pom, took 280 ms
Download https://dl.google.com/dl/android/maven2/com/android/tools/build/aapt2-proto/8.9.0-alpha02-12634980/aapt2-proto-8.9.0-alpha02-12634980.pom, took 288 ms
Download https://dl.google.com/dl/android/maven2/com/android/tools/build/gradle-settings-api/8.9.0-alpha02/gradle-settings-api-8.9.0-alpha02.module, took 96 ms
Download https://dl.google.com/dl/android/maven2/com/android/tools/build/builder-test-api/8.9.0-alpha02/builder-test-api-8.9.0-alpha02.pom, took 100 ms
Download https://dl.google.com/dl/android/maven2/com/android/tools/utp/android-device-provider-ddmlib-proto/31.9.0-alpha02/android-device-provider-ddmlib-proto-31.9.0-alpha02.pom, took 94 ms
Download https://dl.google.com/dl/android/maven2/com/android/tools/utp/android-device-provider-profile-proto/31.9.0-alpha02/android-device-provider-profile-proto-31.9.0-alpha02.pom, took 96 ms
Download https://dl.google.com/dl/android/maven2/com/android/tools/utp/android-test-plugin-host-coverage-proto/31.9.0-alpha02/android-test-plugin-host-coverage-proto-
```

```
31.9.0-alpha02.pom, took 101 ms
Download https://dl.google.com/dl/android/maven2/com/android/tools/utp/android-test-plugin-host-additional-test-output-proto/31.9.0-alpha02/android-test-plugin-host-additional-test-output-proto-31.9.0-alpha02.pom, took 110 ms
Download
https://dl.google.com/dl/android/maven2/com/android/tools/build/aaptcompiler/8.9.0-alpha02/aaptcompiler-8.9.0-alpha02.module, took 115 ms
Download https://dl.google.com/dl/android/maven2/com/android/tools/utp/android-device-provider-gradle-proto/31.9.0-alpha02/android-device-provider-gradle-proto-31.9.0-alpha02.pom, took 119 ms
Download
https://dl.google.com/dl/android/maven2/com/android/tools/layoutlib/layoutlib-api/31.9.0-alpha02/layoutlib-api-31.9.0-alpha02.pom, took 127 ms
Download https://dl.google.com/dl/android/maven2/com/android/tools/utp/android-test-plugin-host-emulator-control-proto/31.9.0-alpha02/android-test-plugin-host-emulator-control-proto-31.9.0-alpha02.pom, took 132 ms
Download https://dl.google.com/dl/android/maven2/com/android/tools/utp/android-test-plugin-host-logcat-proto/31.9.0-alpha02/android-test-plugin-host-logcat-proto-31.9.0-alpha02.pom, took 101 ms
Download https://dl.google.com/dl/android/maven2/com/android/tools/utp/android-test-plugin-host-apk-installer-proto/31.9.0-alpha02/android-test-plugin-host-apk-installer-proto-31.9.0-alpha02.pom, took 98 ms
Download https://dl.google.com/dl/android/maven2/com/android/tools/build/builder-test-api/8.9.0-alpha02/builder-test-api-8.9.0-alpha02.module, took 123 ms
Download https://dl.google.com/dl/android/maven2/com/android/tools/utp/android-test-plugin-host-retention-proto/31.9.0-alpha02/android-test-plugin-host-retention-proto-31.9.0-alpha02.pom, took 126 ms
Download
https://dl.google.com/dl/android/maven2/com/android/tools/build/bundletool/1.17.2/bundletool-1.17.2.pom, took 97 ms
Download https://dl.google.com/dl/android/maven2/com/android/tools/build/transform-api/2.0.0-deprecated-use-gradle-api/transform-api-2.0.0-deprecated-use-gradle-api.pom, took 98 ms
Download
https://dl.google.com/dl/android/maven2/com/android/tools/build/jetifier/jetifier-processor/1.0.0-beta10/jetifier-processor-1.0.0-beta10.pom, took 99 ms
Download
https://dl.google.com/dl/android/maven2/com/android/tools/build/jetifier/jetifier-core/1.0.0-beta10/jetifier-core-1.0.0-beta10.pom, took 101 ms
Download https://dl.google.com/dl/android/maven2/com/google/testing/platform/core-proto/0.0.9-alpha02/core-proto-0.0.9-alpha02.pom, took 96 ms
Download
https://dl.google.com/dl/android/maven2/com/android/tools/build/jetifier/jetifier-processor/1.0.0-beta10/jetifier-processor-1.0.0-beta10.module, took 95 ms
Download
https://dl.google.com/dl/android/maven2/com/android/tools/build/jetifier/jetifier-core/1.0.0-beta10/jetifier-core-1.0.0-beta10.module, took 99 ms
Download https://dl.google.com/dl/android/maven2/com/android/tools/build/builder-model/8.9.0-alpha02/builder-model-8.9.0-alpha02.pom, took 101 ms
Download
https://dl.google.com/dl/android/maven2/com/android/tools/build/builder/8.9.0-alpha02/builder-8.9.0-alpha02.pom, took 107 ms
Download https://dl.google.com/dl/android/maven2/com/android/tools/utp/android-test-
```

```
plugin-result-listener-gradle-proto/31.9.0-alpha02/android-test-plugin-result-listener-gradle-proto-31.9.0-alpha02.pom, took 296 ms
Download https://dl.google.com/dl/android/maven2/com/android/tools/build/gradle-api/8.9.0-alpha02/gradle-api-8.9.0-alpha02.pom, took 100 ms
Download https://repo.maven.apache.org/maven2/com/google/protobuf/protobuf-java/3.22.3/protobuf-java-3.22.3.pom, took 190 ms
Download https://dl.google.com/dl/android/maven2/com/android/tools/build/builder-model/8.9.0-alpha02/builder-model-8.9.0-alpha02.module, took 104 ms
Download https://dl.google.com/dl/android/maven2/com/android/tools/build/aapt2-proto/8.9.0-alpha02-12634980/aapt2-proto-8.9.0-alpha02-12634980.module, took 443 ms
Download
https://dl.google.com/dl/android/maven2/com/android/tools/build/builder/8.9.0-alpha02/builder-8.9.0-alpha02.module, took 121 ms
Download https://dl.google.com/dl/android/maven2/com/android/tools/build/gradle-api/8.9.0-alpha02/gradle-api-8.9.0-alpha02.module, took 98 ms
Download https://repo.maven.apache.org/maven2/com/google/flatbuffers/flatbuffers-java/1.12.0/flatbuffers-java-1.12.0.pom, took 340 ms
Download https://repo.maven.apache.org/maven2/com/google/protobuf/protobuf-java-util/3.22.3/protobuf-java-util-3.22.3.pom, took 1 s 345 ms
Download https://repo.maven.apache.org/maven2/com/google/code/gson/gson/2.10.1/gson-2.10.1.pom, took 1 s 337 ms
Download https://repo.maven.apache.org/maven2/com/google/protobuf/protobuf-parent/3.22.3/protobuf-parent-3.22.3.pom, took 1 s 818 ms
Download https://repo.maven.apache.org/maven2/com/google/code/gson/gson-parent/2.10.1/gson-parent-2.10.1.pom, took 693 ms
Download https://repo.maven.apache.org/maven2/com/google/protobuf/protobuf-bom/3.22.3/protobuf-bom-3.22.3.pom, took 364 ms
Download
https://repo.maven.apache.org/maven2/com/google/crypto/tink/tink/1.7.0/tink-1.7.0.pom, took 14 s 389 ms
Download https://repo.maven.apache.org/maven2/org/sonatype/oss/oss-parent/7/oss-parent-7.pom, took 598 ms
Download https://repo.maven.apache.org/maven2/org/jetbrains/kotlin/kotlin-stdlib-jdk8/2.1.0-Beta2/kotlin-stdlib-jdk8-2.1.0-Beta2.pom, took 184 ms
Download
https://repo.maven.apache.org/maven2/org/apache/httpcomponents/httpmime/4.5.6/httpmime-4.5.6.pom, took 3 s 425 ms
Download
https://repo.maven.apache.org/maven2/org/apache/httpcomponents/httpcomponents-client/4.5.6/httpcomponents-client-4.5.6.pom, took 1 s 575 ms
Download
https://repo.maven.apache.org/maven2/org/apache/httpcomponents/httpcomponents-parent/10/httpcomponents-parent-10.pom, took 3 s 971 ms
Download https://repo.maven.apache.org/maven2/org/apache/apache/18/apache-18.pom, took 1 s 671 ms
Download https://repo.maven.apache.org/maven2/commons-io/commons-io/2.13.0/commons-io-2.13.0.pom, took 4 s 687 ms
Download https://repo.maven.apache.org/maven2/org/apache/commons/commons-parent/58/commons-parent-58.pom, took 25 s 599 ms
Download https://repo.maven.apache.org/maven2/org/apache/apache/29/apache-29.pom, took 3 s 688 ms
Download https://repo.maven.apache.org/maven2/org/junit/junit-bom/5.9.3/junit-bom-5.9.3.pom, took 513 ms
```

```
Download https://repo.maven.apache.org/maven2/org/junit/junit-bom/5.9.3/junit-bom-5.9.3.module, took 755 ms
Download https://repo.maven.apache.org/maven2/org/ow2/asm/asm/9.7/asm-9.7.pom, took 1 s 507 ms
Download https://repo.maven.apache.org/maven2/org/ow2/ow2/1.5.1/ow2-1.5.1.pom, took 6 s 911 ms
Download https://repo.maven.apache.org/maven2/org/ow2/asm/asm-analysis/9.7/asm-analysis-9.7.pom, took 649 ms
Download https://repo.maven.apache.org/maven2/org/ow2/asm/asm-commons/9.7/asm-commons-9.7.pom, took 425 ms
Download https://repo.maven.apache.org/maven2/org/ow2/asm/asm-util/9.7/asm-util-9.7.pom, took 301 ms
Download https://repo.maven.apache.org/maven2/org/bouncycastle/bcpkix-jdk18on/1.77/bcpkix-jdk18on-1.77.pom, took 1 s 865 ms
Download https://repo.maven.apache.org/maven2/org/glassfish/jaxb/jaxb-runtime/2.3.2/jaxb-runtime-2.3.2.pom, took 439 ms
Download https://repo.maven.apache.org/maven2/com/sun/xml/bind/mvn/jaxb-runtime-parent/2.3.2/jaxb-runtime-parent-2.3.2.pom, took 5 s 572 ms
Download https://repo.maven.apache.org/maven2/com/sun/xml/bind/mvn/jaxb-parent/2.3.2/jaxb-parent-2.3.2.pom, took 3 s 252 ms
Download https://repo.maven.apache.org/maven2/com/sun/xml/bind/jaxb-bom-ext/2.3.2/jaxb-bom-ext-2.3.2.pom, took 404 ms
Download https://repo.maven.apache.org/maven2/org/glassfish/jaxb/jaxb-bom/2.3.2/jaxb-bom-2.3.2.pom, took 729 ms
Download
https://repo.maven.apache.org/maven2/org/eclipse/ee4j/project/1.0.5/project-1.0.5.pom, took 2 s 511 ms
Download https://repo.maven.apache.org/maven2/net/sf/jopt-simple/jopt-simple/4.9/jopt-simple-4.9.pom, took 3 s 620 ms
Download https://repo.maven.apache.org/maven2/com/squareup/javapoet/1.10.0/javapoet-1.10.0.pom, took 1 s 465 ms
Download https://repo.maven.apache.org/maven2/io/grpc/grpc-core/1.57.0/grpc-core-1.57.0.pom, took 707 ms
Download https://repo.maven.apache.org/maven2/io/grpc/grpc-netty/1.57.0/grpc-netty-1.57.0.pom, took 281 ms
Download https://repo.maven.apache.org/maven2/io/grpc/grpc-protobuf/1.57.0/grpc-protobuf-1.57.0.pom, took 798 ms
Download https://repo.maven.apache.org/maven2/io/grpc/grpc-stub/1.57.0/grpc-stub-1.57.0.pom, took 291 ms
Download https://repo.maven.apache.org/maven2/org/tensorflow/tensorflow-lite-metadata/0.1.0-rc2/tensorflow-lite-metadata-0.1.0-rc2.pom, took 641 ms
Download https://repo.maven.apache.org/maven2/org/jetbrains/kotlin/kotlin-gradle-plugin-api/2.0.0/kotlin-gradle-plugin-api-2.0.0.pom, took 827 ms
Download https://repo.maven.apache.org/maven2/org/jetbrains/kotlin/kotlin-gradle-plugin-api/2.0.0/kotlin-gradle-plugin-api-2.0.0.module, took 14 s 870 ms
Download https://repo.maven.apache.org/maven2/org/jetbrains/kotlin/kotlin-gradle-plugin-model/2.0.0/kotlin-gradle-plugin-model-2.0.0.pom, took 1 s 116 ms
Download https://repo.maven.apache.org/maven2/org/jetbrains/kotlin/kotlin-gradle-plugin-model/2.0.0/kotlin-gradle-plugin-model-2.0.0.module, took 7 s 951 ms
Download https://repo.maven.apache.org/maven2/org/jetbrains/kotlin/kotlin-gradle-plugin-idea/2.0.0/kotlin-gradle-plugin-idea-2.0.0.pom, took 338 ms
Download https://repo.maven.apache.org/maven2/org/jetbrains/kotlin/kotlin-gradle-plugin-idea/2.0.0/kotlin-gradle-plugin-idea-2.0.0.module, took 446 ms
```

```
Download    https://repo.maven.apache.org/maven2/org/jetbrains/kotlin/kotlin-gradle-plugin-idea-proto/2.0.0/kotlin-gradle-plugin-idea-proto-2.0.0.pom, took 145 ms
Download    https://repo.maven.apache.org/maven2/org/jetbrains/kotlin/kotlin-klib-commonizer-api/2.0.0/kotlin-klib-commonizer-api-2.0.0.pom, took 1 s 478 ms
Download    https://repo.maven.apache.org/maven2/org/jetbrains/kotlin/kotlin-build-tools-api/2.0.0/kotlin-build-tools-api-2.0.0.pom, took 1 s 725 ms
Download    https://repo.maven.apache.org/maven2/org/jetbrains/kotlin/kotlin-build-statistics/2.0.0/kotlin-build-statistics-2.0.0.pom, took 987 ms
Download    https://repo.maven.apache.org/maven2/org/jetbrains/kotlin/kotlin-compiler-runner/2.0.0/kotlin-compiler-runner-2.0.0.pom, took 676 ms
Download    https://repo.maven.apache.org/maven2/org/jetbrains/kotlin/kotlin-util-klib/2.0.0/kotlin-util-klib-2.0.0.pom, took 811 ms
Download    https://repo.maven.apache.org/maven2/org/jetbrains/kotlin/kotlin-compiler-embeddable/2.0.0/kotlin-compiler-embeddable-2.0.0.pom, took 1 s 413 ms
Download    https://dl.google.com/dl/android/maven2/com/android/tools/common/31.9.0-alpha02/common-31.9.0-alpha02.pom, took 101 ms
Download    https://repo.maven.apache.org/maven2/com/google/guava/guava/32.0.1-jre/guava-32.0.1-jre.pom, took 3 s 211 ms
Download    https://repo.maven.apache.org/maven2/com/google/guava/guava-parent/32.0.1-jre/guava-parent-32.0.1-jre.pom, took 2 s 794 ms
Download    https://repo.maven.apache.org/maven2/net/sf/kxml/kxml2/2.3.0/kxml2-2.3.0.pom, took 1 s 697 ms
Download    https://repo.maven.apache.org/maven2/org/bouncycastle/bcprov-jdk18on/1.77/bcprov-jdk18on-1.77.pom, took 1 s 27 ms
Download    https://repo.maven.apache.org/maven2/org/jetbrains/kotlin/kotlin-reflect/2.1.0-Beta2/kotlin-reflect-2.1.0-Beta2.pom, took 152 ms
Download    https://dl.google.com/dl/android/maven2/com/android/tools/dvlib/31.9.0-alpha02/dvlib-31.9.0-alpha02.pom, took 102 ms
Download    https://repo.maven.apache.org/maven2/org/apache/commons/commons-compress/1.21/commons-compress-1.21.pom, took 918 ms
Download    https://repo.maven.apache.org/maven2/org/apache/commons/commons-parent/52/commons-parent-52.pom, took 5 s 941 ms
Download    https://repo.maven.apache.org/maven2/org/apache/apache/23/apache-23.pom, took 2 s 236 ms
Download
https://repo.maven.apache.org/maven2/org/apache/httpcomponents/httpcore/4.4.16/httpcore-4.4.16.pom, took 578 ms
Download
https://repo.maven.apache.org/maven2/org/apache/httpcomponents/httpcomponents-core/4.4.16/httpcomponents-core-4.4.16.pom, took 926 ms
Download
https://repo.maven.apache.org/maven2/org/apache/httpcomponents/httpcomponents-parent/11/httpcomponents-parent-11.pom, took 5 s 562 ms
Download    https://repo.maven.apache.org/maven2/org/apache/apache/21/apache-21.pom, took 397 ms
Download    https://repo.maven.apache.org/maven2/com/google/jimfs/jimfs/1.1/jimfs-1.1.pom, took 3 s 369 ms
Download    https://repo.maven.apache.org/maven2/com/google/jimfs/jimfs-parent/1.1/jimfs-parent-1.1.pom, took 282 ms
Download
https://repo.maven.apache.org/maven2/com/sun/activation/javax.activation/1.2.0/javax.activation-1.2.0.pom, took 556 ms
Download    https://repo.maven.apache.org/maven2/com/sun/activation/all/1.2.0/all-
```

```
1.2.0.pom, took 617 ms
Download  https://repo.maven.apache.org/maven2/net/java/jvnet-parent/1/jvnet-parent-
1.pom, took 552 ms
Download
https://repo.maven.apache.org/maven2/org/jetbrains/annotations/23.0.0/annotations-
23.0.0.pom, took 632 ms
Download
https://repo.maven.apache.org/maven2/org/apache/httpcomponents/httpclient/4.5.14/htt
pclient-4.5.14.pom, took 3 s 273 ms
Download
https://repo.maven.apache.org/maven2/org/apache/httpcomponents/httpcomponents-
client/4.5.14/httpcomponents-client-4.5.14.pom, took 823 ms
Download       https://dl.google.com/dl/android/maven2/com/android/tools/analytics-
library/protos/31.9.0-alpha02/protos-31.9.0-alpha02.pom, took 112 ms
Download                https://repo.maven.apache.org/maven2/net/java/dev/jna/jna-
platform/5.6.0/jna-platform-5.6.0.pom, took 610 ms
Download
https://repo.maven.apache.org/maven2/com/googlecode/juniversalchardet/juniversalchar
det/1.0.3/juniversalchardet-1.0.3.pom, took 161 ms
Download    https://repo.maven.apache.org/maven2/javax/annotation/javax.annotation-
api/1.3.2/javax.annotation-api-1.3.2.pom, took 1 s 714 ms
Download  https://repo.maven.apache.org/maven2/net/java/jvnet-parent/3/jvnet-parent-
3.pom, took 2 s 188 ms
Download          https://repo.maven.apache.org/maven2/org/jetbrains/kotlin/kotlin-
stdlib/2.1.0-Beta2/kotlin-stdlib-2.1.0-Beta2.pom, took 658 ms
Download          https://repo.maven.apache.org/maven2/org/jetbrains/kotlin/kotlin-
stdlib/2.1.0-Beta2/kotlin-stdlib-2.1.0-Beta2.module, took 1 s 325 ms
Download    https://repo.maven.apache.org/maven2/org/jetbrains/kotlin/kotlin-stdlib-
jdk7/2.1.0-Beta2/kotlin-stdlib-jdk7-2.1.0-Beta2.pom, took 1 s 2 ms
Download    https://repo.maven.apache.org/maven2/org/ow2/asm/asm-tree/9.7/asm-tree-
9.7.pom, took 410 ms
Download              https://repo.maven.apache.org/maven2/org/bouncycastle/bcutil-
jdk18on/1.77/bcutil-jdk18on-1.77.pom, took 313 ms
Download    https://repo.maven.apache.org/maven2/jakarta/xml/bind/jakarta.xml.bind-
api/2.3.2/jakarta.xml.bind-api-2.3.2.pom, took 3 s 529 ms
Download https://repo.maven.apache.org/maven2/jakarta/xml/bind/jakarta.xml.bind-api-
parent/2.3.2/jakarta.xml.bind-api-parent-2.3.2.pom, took 1 s 309 ms
Download    https://repo.maven.apache.org/maven2/org/glassfish/jaxb/txw2/2.3.2/txw2-
2.3.2.pom, took 689 ms
Download         https://repo.maven.apache.org/maven2/com/sun/xml/bind/mvn/jaxb-txw-
parent/2.3.2/jaxb-txw-parent-2.3.2.pom, took 277 ms
Download         https://repo.maven.apache.org/maven2/com/sun/istack/istack-commons-
runtime/3.0.8/istack-commons-runtime-3.0.8.pom, took 749 ms
Download                 https://repo.maven.apache.org/maven2/com/sun/istack/istack-
commons/3.0.8/istack-commons-3.0.8.pom, took 1 s 682 ms
Download   https://repo.maven.apache.org/maven2/org/jvnet/staxex/stax-ex/1.8.1/stax-
ex-1.8.1.pom, took 962 ms
Download
https://repo.maven.apache.org/maven2/com/sun/xml/fastinfoset/FastInfoset/1.2.16/Fast
Infoset-1.2.16.pom, took 410 ms
Download   https://repo.maven.apache.org/maven2/com/sun/xml/fastinfoset/fastinfoset-
project/1.2.16/fastinfoset-project-1.2.16.pom, took 1 s 954 ms
Download https://repo.maven.apache.org/maven2/jakarta/activation/jakarta.activation-
```

```
api/1.2.1/jakarta.activation-api-1.2.1.pom, took 435 ms
Download https://repo.maven.apache.org/maven2/com/sun/activation/all/1.2.1/all-1.2.1.pom, took 1 s 511 ms
Download https://repo.maven.apache.org/maven2/org/eclipse/ee4j/project/1.0.2/project-1.0.2.pom, took 1 s 623 ms
Download https://repo.maven.apache.org/maven2/com/google/auto/value/auto-value-annotations/1.6.2/auto-value-annotations-1.6.2.pom, took 266 ms
Download https://repo.maven.apache.org/maven2/com/google/dagger/dagger/2.28.3/dagger-2.28.3.pom, took 343 ms
Download https://repo.maven.apache.org/maven2/com/google/errorprone/error_prone_annotations/2.3.1/error_prone_annotations-2.3.1.pom, took 390 ms
Download https://repo.maven.apache.org/maven2/com/google/auto/value/auto-value-parent/1.6.2/auto-value-parent-1.6.2.pom, took 287 ms
Download https://repo.maven.apache.org/maven2/com/google/errorprone/error_prone_parent/2.3.1/error_prone_parent-2.3.1.pom, took 128 ms
Download https://repo.maven.apache.org/maven2/com/google/auto/auto-parent/6/auto-parent-6.pom, took 427 ms
Download https://repo.maven.apache.org/maven2/org/bitbucket/b_c/jose4j/0.9.5/jose4j-0.9.5.pom, took 1 s 362 ms
Download https://repo.maven.apache.org/maven2/org/slf4j/slf4j-api/1.7.30/slf4j-api-1.7.30.pom, took 11 s 226 ms
Download https://repo.maven.apache.org/maven2/org/slf4j/slf4j-parent/1.7.30/slf4j-parent-1.7.30.pom, took 787 ms
Download https://repo.maven.apache.org/maven2/org/jdom/jdom2/2.0.6/jdom2-2.0.6.pom, took 400 ms
Download https://repo.maven.apache.org/maven2/com/google/errorprone/error_prone_annotations/2.11.0/error_prone_annotations-2.11.0.pom, took 184 ms
Download https://repo.maven.apache.org/maven2/com/google/errorprone/error_prone_parent/2.11.0/error_prone_parent-2.11.0.pom, took 431 ms
Download https://repo.maven.apache.org/maven2/com/google/code/findbugs/jsr305/3.0.2/jsr305-3.0.2.pom, took 651 ms
Download https://repo.maven.apache.org/maven2/com/google/j2objc/j2objc-annotations/1.3/j2objc-annotations-1.3.pom, took 721 ms
Download https://repo.maven.apache.org/maven2/com/google/errorprone/error_prone_annotations/2.18.0/error_prone_annotations-2.18.0.pom, took 641 ms
Download https://repo.maven.apache.org/maven2/com/google/errorprone/error_prone_parent/2.18.0/error_prone_parent-2.18.0.pom, took 3 s 374 ms
Download https://repo.maven.apache.org/maven2/io/grpc/grpc-api/1.57.0/grpc-api-1.57.0.pom, took 614 ms
Download https://repo.maven.apache.org/maven2/com/google/android/annotations/4.1.1.4/annotations-4.1.1.4.pom, took 661 ms
Download https://repo.maven.apache.org/maven2/org/codehaus/mojo/animal-sniffer-annotations/1.23/animal-sniffer-annotations-1.23.pom, took 677 ms
```

```
Download https://repo.maven.apache.org/maven2/org/codehaus/mojo/animal-sniffer-parent/1.23/animal-sniffer-parent-1.23.pom, took 1 s 46 ms
Download https://repo.maven.apache.org/maven2/org/codehaus/mojo/mojo-parent/74/mojo-parent-74.pom, took 8 s 56 ms
Download https://repo.maven.apache.org/maven2/org/junit/junit-bom/5.9.2/junit-bom-5.9.2.pom, took 305 ms
Download https://repo.maven.apache.org/maven2/org/junit/junit-bom/5.9.2/junit-bom-5.9.2.module, took 258 ms
Download https://repo.maven.apache.org/maven2/io/perfmark/perfmark-api/0.26.0/perfmark-api-0.26.0.pom, took 139 ms
Download https://repo.maven.apache.org/maven2/io/perfmark/perfmark-api/0.26.0/perfmark-api-0.26.0.module, took 289 ms
Download https://repo.maven.apache.org/maven2/io/grpc/grpc-context/1.57.0/grpc-context-1.57.0.pom, took 183 ms
Download https://repo.maven.apache.org/maven2/io/netty/netty-codec-http2/4.1.93.Final/netty-codec-http2-4.1.93.Final.pom, took 293 ms
Download https://repo.maven.apache.org/maven2/io/netty/netty-parent/4.1.93.Final/netty-parent-4.1.93.Final.pom, took 7 s 776 ms
Download https://repo.maven.apache.org/maven2/org/sonatype/oss/oss-parent/9/oss-parent-9.pom, took 357 ms
Download https://repo.maven.apache.org/maven2/io/netty/netty-handler-proxy/4.1.93.Final/netty-handler-proxy-4.1.93.Final.pom, took 271 ms
Download https://repo.maven.apache.org/maven2/io/netty/netty-transport-native-unix-common/4.1.93.Final/netty-transport-native-unix-common-4.1.93.Final.pom, took 3 s 204 ms
Download https://repo.maven.apache.org/maven2/com/google/api/grpc/proto-google-common-protos/2.17.0/proto-google-common-protos-2.17.0.pom, took 306 ms
Download https://repo.maven.apache.org/maven2/io/grpc/grpc-protobuf-lite/1.57.0/grpc-protobuf-lite-1.57.0.pom, took 189 ms
Download https://repo.maven.apache.org/maven2/org/checkerframework/checker-qual/2.5.8/checker-qual-2.5.8.pom, took 418 ms
Download https://dl.google.com/dl/android/maven2/com/android/tools/analytics-library/tracker/31.9.0-alpha02/tracker-31.9.0-alpha02.pom, took 122 ms
Download https://dl.google.com/dl/android/maven2/com/android/zipflinger/8.9.0-alpha02/zipflinger-8.9.0-alpha02.pom, took 127 ms
Download https://dl.google.com/dl/android/maven2/com/android/signflinger/8.9.0-alpha02/signflinger-8.9.0-alpha02.pom, took 212 ms
Download
https://dl.google.com/dl/android/maven2/com/android/tools/build/apkzlib/8.9.0-alpha02/apkzlib-8.9.0-alpha02.pom, took 228 ms
Download https://dl.google.com/dl/android/maven2/com/android/tools/build/manifest-merger/31.9.0-alpha02/manifest-merger-31.9.0-alpha02.pom, took 236 ms
Download https://dl.google.com/dl/android/maven2/com/android/tools/build/manifest-merger/31.9.0-alpha02/manifest-merger-31.9.0-alpha02.module, took 138 ms
Download https://repo.maven.apache.org/maven2/commons-codec/commons-codec/1.10/commons-codec-1.10.pom, took 1 s 709 ms
Download https://repo.maven.apache.org/maven2/org/apache/commons/commons-parent/35/commons-parent-35.pom, took 3 s 930 ms
Download https://repo.maven.apache.org/maven2/org/apache/apache/15/apache-15.pom, took 1 s 186 ms
Download
https://repo.maven.apache.org/maven2/com/squareup/javawriter/2.5.0/javawriter-2.5.0.pom, took 983 ms
```

```
Download    https://repo.maven.apache.org/maven2/org/jetbrains/kotlin/kotlin-gradle-plugin-annotations/2.0.0/kotlin-gradle-plugin-annotations-2.0.0.pom, took 189 ms
Download    https://repo.maven.apache.org/maven2/org/jetbrains/kotlin/kotlin-native-utils/2.0.0/kotlin-native-utils-2.0.0.pom, took 411 ms
Download    https://repo.maven.apache.org/maven2/org/jetbrains/kotlin/kotlin-tooling-core/2.0.0/kotlin-tooling-core-2.0.0.pom, took 151 ms
Download    https://repo.maven.apache.org/maven2/org/jetbrains/kotlin/kotlin-daemon-client/2.0.0/kotlin-daemon-client-2.0.0.pom, took 5 s 623 ms
Download    https://repo.maven.apache.org/maven2/org/jetbrains/kotlinx/kotlinx-coroutines-core-jvm/1.5.0/kotlinx-coroutines-core-jvm-1.5.0.pom, took 279 ms
Download    https://repo.maven.apache.org/maven2/org/jetbrains/kotlinx/kotlinx-coroutines-core-jvm/1.5.0/kotlinx-coroutines-core-jvm-1.5.0.module, took 279 ms
Download    https://repo.maven.apache.org/maven2/org/jetbrains/kotlin/kotlin-util-io/2.0.0/kotlin-util-io-2.0.0.pom, took 584 ms
Download    https://repo.maven.apache.org/maven2/org/jetbrains/kotlin/kotlin-daemon-embeddable/2.0.0/kotlin-daemon-embeddable-2.0.0.pom, took 647 ms
Download
https://repo.maven.apache.org/maven2/org/jetbrains/intellij/deps/trove4j/1.0.20200330/trove4j-1.0.20200330.pom, took 169 ms
Download    https://repo.maven.apache.org/maven2/org/checkerframework/checker-qual/3.33.0/checker-qual-3.33.0.pom, took 773 ms
Download    https://repo.maven.apache.org/maven2/org/checkerframework/checker-qual/3.33.0/checker-qual-3.33.0.module, took 2 s 933 ms
Download    https://repo.maven.apache.org/maven2/com/google/j2objc/j2objc-annotations/2.8/j2objc-annotations-2.8.pom, took 1 s 307 ms
Download
https://repo.maven.apache.org/maven2/com/google/guava/listenablefuture/9999.0-empty-to-avoid-conflict-with-guava/listenablefuture-9999.0-empty-to-avoid-conflict-with-guava.pom, took 132 ms
Download
https://repo.maven.apache.org/maven2/com/google/guava/failureaccess/1.0.1/failureaccess-1.0.1.pom, took 425 ms
Download    https://repo.maven.apache.org/maven2/com/google/guava/guava-parent/26.0-android/guava-parent-26.0-android.pom, took 429 ms
Download    https://repo.maven.apache.org/maven2/commons-codec/commons-codec/1.11/commons-codec-1.11.pom, took 818 ms
Download    https://repo.maven.apache.org/maven2/org/apache/commons/commons-parent/42/commons-parent-42.pom, took 6 s 331 ms
Download    https://repo.maven.apache.org/maven2/commons-logging/commons-logging/1.2/commons-logging-1.2.pom, took 1 s 69 ms
Download    https://repo.maven.apache.org/maven2/org/apache/commons/commons-parent/34/commons-parent-34.pom, took 12 s 921 ms
Download    https://repo.maven.apache.org/maven2/org/apache/apache/13/apache-13.pom, took 984 ms
Download    https://repo.maven.apache.org/maven2/net/java/dev/jna/jna/5.6.0/jna-5.6.0.pom, took 267 ms
Download    https://repo.maven.apache.org/maven2/io/netty/netty-common/4.1.93.Final/netty-common-4.1.93.Final.pom, took 1 s 221 ms
Download    https://repo.maven.apache.org/maven2/io/netty/netty-buffer/4.1.93.Final/netty-buffer-4.1.93.Final.pom, took 972 ms
Download    https://repo.maven.apache.org/maven2/io/netty/netty-transport/4.1.93.Final/netty-transport-4.1.93.Final.pom, took 256 ms
Download    https://repo.maven.apache.org/maven2/io/netty/netty-
```

```
codec/4.1.93.Final/netty-codec-4.1.93.Final.pom, took 1 s 610 ms
Download                        https://repo.maven.apache.org/maven2/io/netty/netty-
handler/4.1.93.Final/netty-handler-4.1.93.Final.pom, took 797 ms
Download                  https://repo.maven.apache.org/maven2/io/netty/netty-codec-
http/4.1.93.Final/netty-codec-http-4.1.93.Final.pom, took 499 ms
Download                  https://repo.maven.apache.org/maven2/io/netty/netty-codec-
socks/4.1.93.Final/netty-codec-socks-4.1.93.Final.pom, took 343 ms
Download                        https://repo.maven.apache.org/maven2/io/netty/netty-
resolver/4.1.93.Final/netty-resolver-4.1.93.Final.pom, took 1 s 63 ms
Download     https://dl.google.com/dl/android/maven2/com/android/tools/build/gradle-
settings-api/8.9.0-alpha02/gradle-settings-api-8.9.0-alpha02.jar, took 295 ms
Download        https://dl.google.com/dl/android/maven2/com/android/tools/lint/lint-
model/31.9.0-alpha02/lint-model-31.9.0-alpha02.jar, took 430 ms
Download   https://dl.google.com/dl/android/maven2/com/android/tools/build/manifest-
merger/31.9.0-alpha02/manifest-merger-31.9.0-alpha02.jar, took 444 ms
Download
https://dl.google.com/dl/android/maven2/com/android/tools/repository/31.9.0-
alpha02/repository-31.9.0-alpha02.jar, took 257 ms
Download    https://dl.google.com/dl/android/maven2/com/android/tools/build/builder-
test-api/8.9.0-alpha02/builder-test-api-8.9.0-alpha02.jar, took 124 ms
Download    https://dl.google.com/dl/android/maven2/com/android/tools/sdklib/31.9.0-
alpha02/sdklib-31.9.0-alpha02.jar, took 722 ms
Download
https://dl.google.com/dl/android/maven2/com/android/tools/build/aaptcompiler/8.9.0-
alpha02/aaptcompiler-8.9.0-alpha02.jar, took 294 ms
Download
https://dl.google.com/dl/android/maven2/com/android/tools/ddms/ddmlib/31.9.0-
alpha02/ddmlib-31.9.0-alpha02.jar, took 324 ms
Download
https://dl.google.com/dl/android/maven2/com/android/tools/build/gradle/8.9.0-
alpha02/gradle-8.9.0-alpha02.jar, took 886 ms
Download               https://dl.google.com/dl/android/maven2/com/android/tools/sdk-
common/31.9.0-alpha02/sdk-common-31.9.0-alpha02.jar, took 904 ms
Download        https://dl.google.com/dl/android/maven2/com/android/tools/analytics-
library/tracker/31.9.0-alpha02/tracker-31.9.0-alpha02.jar, took 106 ms
Download        https://dl.google.com/dl/android/maven2/com/android/tools/analytics-
library/shared/31.9.0-alpha02/shared-31.9.0-alpha02.jar, took 120 ms
Download     https://dl.google.com/dl/android/maven2/com/android/tools/build/aapt2-
proto/8.9.0-alpha02-12634980/aapt2-proto-8.9.0-alpha02-12634980.jar, took 165 ms
Download        https://dl.google.com/dl/android/maven2/com/android/tools/analytics-
library/crash/31.9.0-alpha02/crash-31.9.0-alpha02.jar, took 160 ms
Download
https://dl.google.com/dl/android/maven2/com/android/tools/build/builder/8.9.0-
alpha02/builder-8.9.0-alpha02.jar, took 1 s 107 ms
Download    https://repo.maven.apache.org/maven2/org/jetbrains/kotlin/kotlin-gradle-
plugin-model/2.0.0/kotlin-gradle-plugin-model-2.0.0.jar, took 1 s 153 ms
Download   https://dl.google.com/dl/android/maven2/androidx/databinding/databinding-
common/8.9.0-alpha02/databinding-common-8.9.0-alpha02.jar, took 100 ms
Download        https://dl.google.com/dl/android/maven2/com/android/tools/lint/lint-
typedef-remover/31.9.0-alpha02/lint-typedef-remover-31.9.0-alpha02.jar, took 114 ms
Download
https://dl.google.com/dl/android/maven2/com/android/databinding/baseLibrary/8.9.0-
alpha02/baseLibrary-8.9.0-alpha02.jar, took 134 ms
```

```
Download
https://dl.google.com/dl/android/maven2/com/android/tools/layoutlib/layoutlib-api/31.9.0-alpha02/layoutlib-api-31.9.0-alpha02.jar, took 127 ms
Download https://dl.google.com/dl/android/maven2/androidx/databinding/databinding-compiler-common/8.9.0-alpha02/databinding-compiler-common-8.9.0-alpha02.jar, took 302 ms
Download https://dl.google.com/dl/android/maven2/com/android/tools/utp/android-test-plugin-host-coverage-proto/31.9.0-alpha02/android-test-plugin-host-coverage-proto-31.9.0-alpha02.jar, took 109 ms
Download https://dl.google.com/dl/android/maven2/com/android/tools/utp/android-device-provider-profile-proto/31.9.0-alpha02/android-device-provider-profile-proto-31.9.0-alpha02.jar, took 286 ms
Download https://dl.google.com/dl/android/maven2/com/android/tools/utp/android-test-plugin-host-additional-test-output-proto/31.9.0-alpha02/android-test-plugin-host-additional-test-output-proto-31.9.0-alpha02.jar, took 223 ms
Download https://dl.google.com/dl/android/maven2/com/android/tools/utp/android-device-provider-gradle-proto/31.9.0-alpha02/android-device-provider-gradle-proto-31.9.0-alpha02.jar, took 289 ms
Download https://dl.google.com/dl/android/maven2/com/android/tools/utp/android-device-provider-ddmlib-proto/31.9.0-alpha02/android-device-provider-ddmlib-proto-31.9.0-alpha02.jar, took 300 ms
Download https://dl.google.com/dl/android/maven2/com/android/tools/utp/android-test-plugin-host-emulator-control-proto/31.9.0-alpha02/android-test-plugin-host-emulator-control-proto-31.9.0-alpha02.jar, took 113 ms
Download https://dl.google.com/dl/android/maven2/com/android/tools/utp/android-test-plugin-host-logcat-proto/31.9.0-alpha02/android-test-plugin-host-logcat-proto-31.9.0-alpha02.jar, took 108 ms
Download https://dl.google.com/dl/android/maven2/com/android/tools/utp/android-test-plugin-host-apk-installer-proto/31.9.0-alpha02/android-test-plugin-host-apk-installer-proto-31.9.0-alpha02.jar, took 109 ms
Download https://dl.google.com/dl/android/maven2/com/android/tools/utp/android-test-plugin-host-retention-proto/31.9.0-alpha02/android-test-plugin-host-retention-proto-31.9.0-alpha02.jar, took 112 ms
Download https://dl.google.com/dl/android/maven2/com/android/tools/build/builder-model/8.9.0-alpha02/builder-model-8.9.0-alpha02.jar, took 159 ms
Download https://dl.google.com/dl/android/maven2/com/android/tools/dvlib/31.9.0-alpha02/dvlib-31.9.0-alpha02.jar, took 173 ms
Download https://dl.google.com/dl/android/maven2/com/android/tools/utp/android-test-plugin-result-listener-gradle-proto/31.9.0-alpha02/android-test-plugin-result-listener-gradle-proto-31.9.0-alpha02.jar, took 194 ms
Download https://dl.google.com/dl/android/maven2/com/android/tools/common/31.9.0-alpha02/common-31.9.0-alpha02.jar, took 139 ms
Download
https://dl.google.com/dl/android/maven2/com/android/tools/build/jetifier/jetifier-core/1.0.0-beta10/jetifier-core-1.0.0-beta10.jar, took 117 ms
Download
https://dl.google.com/dl/android/maven2/com/android/tools/build/jetifier/jetifier-processor/1.0.0-beta10/jetifier-processor-1.0.0-beta10.jar, took 140 ms
Download
https://dl.google.com/dl/android/maven2/com/android/tools/build/bundletool/1.17.2/bundletool-1.17.2.jar, took 1 s 15 ms
Download https://dl.google.com/dl/android/maven2/com/android/tools/build/gradle-api/8.9.0-alpha02/gradle-api-8.9.0-alpha02.jar, took 1 s 392 ms
```

```
Download
https://repo.maven.apache.org/maven2/org/apache/httpcomponents/httpmime/4.5.6/httpmime-4.5.6.jar, took 660 ms
Download https://repo.maven.apache.org/maven2/org/ow2/asm/asm-commons/9.7/asm-commons-9.7.jar, took 804 ms
Download https://repo.maven.apache.org/maven2/org/ow2/asm/asm-analysis/9.7/asm-analysis-9.7.jar, took 506 ms
Download
https://dl.google.com/dl/android/maven2/com/android/tools/build/apkzlib/8.9.0-alpha02/apkzlib-8.9.0-alpha02.jar, took 133 ms
Download https://repo.maven.apache.org/maven2/org/jetbrains/kotlin/kotlin-gradle-plugin-api/2.0.0/kotlin-gradle-plugin-api-2.0.0-gradle85.jar, took 3 s 438 ms
Download https://repo.maven.apache.org/maven2/org/ow2/asm/asm-tree/9.7/asm-tree-9.7.jar, took 1 s 510 ms
Download https://repo.maven.apache.org/maven2/org/ow2/asm/asm-util/9.7/asm-util-9.7.jar, took 2 s 230 ms
Download https://repo.maven.apache.org/maven2/org/jetbrains/kotlin/compose-compiler-gradle-plugin/2.0.0/compose-compiler-gradle-plugin-2.0.0-gradle85.jar, took 6 s 117 ms
Download https://repo.maven.apache.org/maven2/org/jetbrains/kotlin/kotlin-gradle-plugin-api/2.0.0/kotlin-gradle-plugin-api-2.0.0.jar, took 7 s 85 ms
Download https://repo.maven.apache.org/maven2/io/grpc/grpc-protobuf/1.57.0/grpc-protobuf-1.57.0.jar, took 1 s 432 ms
Download https://dl.google.com/dl/android/maven2/com/android/tools/analytics-library/protos/31.9.0-alpha02/protos-31.9.0-alpha02.jar, took 453 ms
Download https://repo.maven.apache.org/maven2/org/ow2/asm/asm/9.7/asm-9.7.jar, took 6 s 639 ms
Download https://repo.maven.apache.org/maven2/com/squareup/javapoet/1.10.0/javapoet-1.10.0.jar, took 5 s 833 ms
Download https://repo.maven.apache.org/maven2/com/google/protobuf/protobuf-java-util/3.22.3/protobuf-java-util-3.22.3.jar, took 6 s 611 ms
Download https://repo.maven.apache.org/maven2/net/sf/jopt-simple/jopt-simple/4.9/jopt-simple-4.9.jar, took 10 s 611 ms
Download https://repo.maven.apache.org/maven2/org/jetbrains/kotlin/kotlin-build-statistics/2.0.0/kotlin-build-statistics-2.0.0.jar, took 8 s 726 ms
Download https://repo.maven.apache.org/maven2/io/grpc/grpc-netty/1.57.0/grpc-netty-1.57.0.jar, took 15 s 508 ms
Download https://repo.maven.apache.org/maven2/io/grpc/grpc-stub/1.57.0/grpc-stub-1.57.0.jar, took 4 s 642 ms
Download https://dl.google.com/dl/android/maven2/com/google/testing/platform/core-proto/0.0.9-alpha02/core-proto-0.0.9-alpha02.jar, took 113 ms
Download https://repo.maven.apache.org/maven2/com/google/code/gson/gson/2.10.1/gson-2.10.1.jar, took 19 s 28 ms
Download https://repo.maven.apache.org/maven2/com/google/flatbuffers/flatbuffers-java/1.12.0/flatbuffers-java-1.12.0.jar, took 5 s 272 ms
Download https://repo.maven.apache.org/maven2/org/tensorflow/tensorflow-lite-metadata/0.1.0-rc2/tensorflow-lite-metadata-0.1.0-rc2.jar, took 18 s 73 ms
Download https://repo.maven.apache.org/maven2/org/jetbrains/kotlin/kotlin-gradle-plugin-idea/2.0.0/kotlin-gradle-plugin-idea-2.0.0.jar, took 4 s 950 ms
Download https://repo.maven.apache.org/maven2/org/jetbrains/kotlin/kotlin-klib-commonizer-api/2.0.0/kotlin-klib-commonizer-api-2.0.0.jar, took 6 s 525 ms
Download https://repo.maven.apache.org/maven2/org/jetbrains/kotlin/kotlin-build-tools-api/2.0.0/kotlin-build-tools-api-2.0.0.jar, took 1 s 109 ms
```

```
Download https://repo.maven.apache.org/maven2/commons-io/commons-io/2.13.0/commons-io-2.13.0.jar, took 59 s 591 ms
Download https://repo.maven.apache.org/maven2/org/jetbrains/kotlin/kotlin-compiler-runner/2.0.0/kotlin-compiler-runner-2.0.0.jar, took 1 s 503 ms
Download https://repo.maven.apache.org/maven2/org/jetbrains/kotlin/kotlin-util-klib/2.0.0/kotlin-util-klib-2.0.0.jar, took 17 s 317 ms
Download https://repo.maven.apache.org/maven2/io/grpc/grpc-core/1.57.0/grpc-core-1.57.0.jar, took 1 m 10 s 407 ms
Download https://repo.maven.apache.org/maven2/org/bouncycastle/bcpkix-jdk18on/1.77/bcpkix-jdk18on-1.77.jar, took 1 m 27 s 161 ms
Download https://repo.maven.apache.org/maven2/org/jetbrains/kotlin/kotlin-native-utils/2.0.0/kotlin-native-utils-2.0.0.jar, took 34 s 894 ms
Download https://repo.maven.apache.org/maven2/io/grpc/grpc-protobuf-lite/1.57.0/grpc-protobuf-lite-1.57.0.jar, took 554 ms
Download https://repo.maven.apache.org/maven2/com/google/jimfs/jimfs/1.1/jimfs-1.1.jar, took 25 s 100 ms
Download https://repo.maven.apache.org/maven2/org/jetbrains/kotlin/kotlin-stdlib/2.1.0-Beta2/kotlin-stdlib-2.1.0-Beta2.jar, took 1 m 56 s 572 ms
Download
https://repo.maven.apache.org/maven2/com/google/dagger/dagger/2.28.3/dagger-2.28.3.jar, took 1 s 115 ms
Download
https://repo.maven.apache.org/maven2/javax/inject/javax.inject/1/javax.inject-1.jar, took 562 ms
Download https://repo.maven.apache.org/maven2/net/sf/kxml/kxml2/2.3.0/kxml2-2.3.0.jar, took 3 s 443 ms
Download https://repo.maven.apache.org/maven2/io/grpc/grpc-api/1.57.0/grpc-api-1.57.0.jar, took 32 s 649 ms
Download https://repo.maven.apache.org/maven2/org/glassfish/jaxb/jaxb-runtime/2.3.2/jaxb-runtime-2.3.2.jar, took 2 m 43 s 565 ms
Download
https://repo.maven.apache.org/maven2/com/google/crypto/tink/tink/1.7.0/tink-1.7.0.jar, took 2 m 41 s 735 ms
Download https://repo.maven.apache.org/maven2/org/bouncycastle/bcutil-jdk18on/1.77/bcutil-jdk18on-1.77.jar, took 47 s 305 ms
Download
https://repo.maven.apache.org/maven2/org/apache/httpcomponents/httpcore/4.4.16/httpcore-4.4.16.jar, took 17 s 539 ms
Download
https://repo.maven.apache.org/maven2/com/sun/activation/javax.activation/1.2.0/javax.activation-1.2.0.jar, took 762 ms
Download
https://repo.maven.apache.org/maven2/org/jetbrains/annotations/23.0.0/annotations-23.0.0.jar, took 326 ms
Download https://dl.google.com/dl/android/maven2/com/android/signflinger/8.9.0-alpha02/signflinger-8.9.0-alpha02.jar, took 275 ms
Download https://dl.google.com/dl/android/maven2/com/android/zipflinger/8.9.0-alpha02/zipflinger-8.9.0-alpha02.jar, took 171 ms
Download https://repo.maven.apache.org/maven2/io/grpc/grpc-core/1.57.0/grpc-core-1.57.0.jar, took 1 m 47 s 765 ms
Download
https://dl.google.com/dl/android/maven2/com/android/tools/annotations/31.9.0-alpha02/annotations-31.9.0-alpha02.jar, took 111 ms
```

```
Download https://repo.maven.apache.org/maven2/com/google/protobuf/protobuf-java/3.22.3/protobuf-java-3.22.3.jar, took 3 m 9 s 971 ms
Download https://repo.maven.apache.org/maven2/com/googlecode/juniversalchardet/juniversalchardet/1.0.3/juniversalchardet-1.0.3.jar, took 12 s 969 ms
Download https://repo.maven.apache.org/maven2/org/jvnet/staxex/stax-ex/1.8.1/stax-ex-1.8.1.jar, took 6 s 197 ms
Download https://repo.maven.apache.org/maven2/javax/annotation/javax.annotation-api/1.3.2/javax.annotation-api-1.3.2.jar, took 16 s 633 ms
Download https://repo.maven.apache.org/maven2/org/glassfish/jaxb/txw2/2.3.2/txw2-2.3.2.jar, took 553 ms
Download https://repo.maven.apache.org/maven2/com/sun/istack/istack-commons-runtime/3.0.8/istack-commons-runtime-3.0.8.jar, took 643 ms
Download https://repo.maven.apache.org/maven2/jakarta/xml/bind/jakarta.xml.bind-api/2.3.2/jakarta.xml.bind-api-2.3.2.jar, took 12 s 893 ms
Download https://repo.maven.apache.org/maven2/jakarta/activation/jakarta.activation-api/1.2.1/jakarta.activation-api-1.2.1.jar, took 2 s 663 ms
Download https://repo.maven.apache.org/maven2/com/google/auto/value/auto-value-annotations/1.6.2/auto-value-annotations-1.6.2.jar, took 644 ms
Download https://repo.maven.apache.org/maven2/com/google/errorprone/error_prone_annotations/2.18.0/error_prone_annotations-2.18.0.jar, took 984 ms
Download https://repo.maven.apache.org/maven2/com/google/api/grpc/proto-google-common-protos/2.17.0/proto-google-common-protos-2.17.0.jar, took 3 m 45 s 99 ms
Download https://repo.maven.apache.org/maven2/org/slf4j/slf4j-api/1.7.30/slf4j-api-1.7.30.jar, took 1 s 373 ms
Download https://repo.maven.apache.org/maven2/org/bitbucket/b_c/jose4j/0.9.5/jose4j-0.9.5.jar, took 15 s 47 ms
Download https://repo.maven.apache.org/maven2/org/apache/httpcomponents/httpclient/4.5.14/httpclient-4.5.14.jar, took 1 m 13 s 397 ms
Download https://repo.maven.apache.org/maven2/com/google/j2objc/j2objc-annotations/2.8/j2objc-annotations-2.8.jar, took 574 ms
Download https://repo.maven.apache.org/maven2/com/google/code/findbugs/jsr305/3.0.2/jsr305-3.0.2.jar, took 1 s 571 ms
Download https://repo.maven.apache.org/maven2/com/sun/xml/fastinfoset/FastInfoset/1.2.16/FastInfoset-1.2.16.jar, took 25 s 885 ms
Download https://repo.maven.apache.org/maven2/com/google/android/annotations/4.1.1.4/annotations-4.1.1.4.jar, took 384 ms
Download https://repo.maven.apache.org/maven2/org/codehaus/mojo/animal-sniffer-annotations/1.23/animal-sniffer-annotations-1.23.jar, took 611 ms
Download https://repo.maven.apache.org/maven2/io/perfmark/perfmark-api/0.26.0/perfmark-api-0.26.0.jar, took 1 s 446 ms
Download https://repo.maven.apache.org/maven2/io/netty/netty-handler-proxy/4.1.93.Final/netty-handler-proxy-4.1.93.Final.jar, took 2 s 368 ms
Download https://repo.maven.apache.org/maven2/org/jetbrains/kotlin/kotlin-gradle-plugin-idea-proto/2.0.0/kotlin-gradle-plugin-idea-proto-2.0.0.jar, took 3 m 36 s 374 ms
Download https://repo.maven.apache.org/maven2/io/netty/netty-transport-native-unix-common/4.1.93.Final/netty-transport-native-unix-common-4.1.93.Final.jar, took 1 s 91
```

```
ms
Download  https://repo.maven.apache.org/maven2/org/jdom/jdom2/2.0.6/jdom2-2.0.6.jar,
took 33 s 133 ms
Download                  https://repo.maven.apache.org/maven2/io/netty/netty-codec-
http2/4.1.93.Final/netty-codec-http2-4.1.93.Final.jar, took 26 s 529 ms
Download
https://dl.google.com/dl/android/maven2/com/android/tools/build/apksig/8.9.0-
alpha02/apksig-8.9.0-alpha02.jar, took 226 ms
Download
https://repo.maven.apache.org/maven2/com/squareup/javawriter/2.5.0/javawriter-
2.5.0.jar, took 466 ms
Download   https://repo.maven.apache.org/maven2/org/jetbrains/kotlin/kotlin-gradle-
plugin-annotations/2.0.0/kotlin-gradle-plugin-annotations-2.0.0.jar, took 362 ms
Download   https://repo.maven.apache.org/maven2/org/jetbrains/kotlin/kotlin-tooling-
core/2.0.0/kotlin-tooling-core-2.0.0.jar, took 4 s 330 ms
Download                        https://repo.maven.apache.org/maven2/io/netty/netty-
handler/4.1.93.Final/netty-handler-4.1.93.Final.jar, took 32 s 784 ms
Download          https://repo.maven.apache.org/maven2/org/checkerframework/checker-
qual/3.33.0/checker-qual-3.33.0.jar, took 14 s 22 ms
Download     https://repo.maven.apache.org/maven2/org/jetbrains/kotlin/kotlin-util-
io/2.0.0/kotlin-util-io-2.0.0.jar, took 1 s 981 ms
Download          https://repo.maven.apache.org/maven2/org/jetbrains/kotlin/kotlin-
reflect/2.1.0-Beta2/kotlin-reflect-2.1.0-Beta2.jar, took 4 m 44 s 995 ms
Download                 https://repo.maven.apache.org/maven2/commons-codec/commons-
codec/1.11/commons-codec-1.11.jar, took 37 s 833 ms
Download            https://repo.maven.apache.org/maven2/org/apache/commons/commons-
compress/1.21/commons-compress-1.21.jar, took 2 m 20 s 585 ms
Download
https://repo.maven.apache.org/maven2/com/google/guava/listenablefuture/9999.0-empty-
to-avoid-conflict-with-guava/listenablefuture-9999.0-empty-to-avoid-conflict-with-
guava.jar, took 697 ms
Download
https://repo.maven.apache.org/maven2/com/google/guava/failureaccess/1.0.1/failureacc
ess-1.0.1.jar, took 2 s 837 ms
Download   https://repo.maven.apache.org/maven2/org/jetbrains/kotlin/kotlin-daemon-
embeddable/2.0.0/kotlin-daemon-embeddable-2.0.0.jar, took 28 s 666 ms
Download               https://repo.maven.apache.org/maven2/commons-logging/commons-
logging/1.2/commons-logging-1.2.jar, took 1 s 635 ms
Download
https://repo.maven.apache.org/maven2/org/jetbrains/intellij/deps/trove4j/1.0.2020033
0/trove4j-1.0.20200330.jar, took 27 s 539 ms
Download   https://repo.maven.apache.org/maven2/org/jetbrains/kotlin/kotlin-daemon-
client/2.0.0/kotlin-daemon-client-2.0.0.jar, took 39 s 234 ms
Download                  https://repo.maven.apache.org/maven2/io/netty/netty-codec-
socks/4.1.93.Final/netty-codec-socks-4.1.93.Final.jar, took 5 s 288 ms
Download                        https://repo.maven.apache.org/maven2/io/netty/netty-
resolver/4.1.93.Final/netty-resolver-4.1.93.Final.jar, took 2 s 604 ms
Download                  https://repo.maven.apache.org/maven2/io/netty/netty-codec-
http/4.1.93.Final/netty-codec-http-4.1.93.Final.jar, took 1 m 25 s 966 ms
Download                        https://repo.maven.apache.org/maven2/io/netty/netty-
buffer/4.1.93.Final/netty-buffer-4.1.93.Final.jar, took 22 s 545 ms
Download         https://repo.maven.apache.org/maven2/org/jetbrains/kotlinx/kotlinx-
coroutines-core-jvm/1.5.0/kotlinx-coroutines-core-jvm-1.5.0.jar, took 1 m 4 s 905 ms
```

```
Download                          https://repo.maven.apache.org/maven2/io/netty/netty-
codec/4.1.93.Final/netty-codec-4.1.93.Final.jar, took 36 s 641 ms
Download                          https://repo.maven.apache.org/maven2/io/netty/netty-
transport/4.1.93.Final/netty-transport-4.1.93.Final.jar, took 33 s 886 ms
Download                          https://repo.maven.apache.org/maven2/io/netty/netty-
common/4.1.93.Final/netty-common-4.1.93.Final.jar, took 42 s 624 ms
Download          https://repo.maven.apache.org/maven2/com/google/guava/guava/32.0.1-
jre/guava-32.0.1-jre.jar, took 5 m 11 s 197 ms
Download         https://repo.maven.apache.org/maven2/net/java/dev/jna/jna/5.6.0/jna-
5.6.0.jar, took 2 m 56 s 518 ms
Download                 https://repo.maven.apache.org/maven2/org/bouncycastle/bcprov-
jdk18on/1.77/bcprov-jdk18on-1.77.jar, took 8 m 9 s 53 ms
Download                    https://repo.maven.apache.org/maven2/net/java/dev/jna/jna-
platform/5.6.0/jna-platform-5.6.0.jar, took 7 m 15 s 508 ms
Download    https://repo.maven.apache.org/maven2/org/jetbrains/kotlin/kotlin-gradle-
plugin/2.0.0/kotlin-gradle-plugin-2.0.0-gradle85.jar, took 21 m 37 s 699 ms
Download  https://repo.maven.apache.org/maven2/org/jetbrains/kotlin/kotlin-compiler-
embeddable/2.0.0/kotlin-compiler-embeddable-2.0.0.jar, took 20 m 25 s 573 ms
Download  https://repo.maven.apache.org/maven2/org/jetbrains/kotlin/kotlin-compiler-
embeddable/2.0.0/kotlin-compiler-embeddable-2.0.0.jar, took 8 m 17 s 837 ms
Download  https://repo.maven.apache.org/maven2/org/jetbrains/kotlin/kotlin-compiler-
embeddable/2.0.0/kotlin-compiler-embeddable-2.0.0.jar, took 49 m 53 s 752 ms
> Task :prepareKotlinBuildScriptModel UP-TO-DATE
Download https://dl.google.com/dl/android/maven2/androidx/core/core-ktx/1.10.1/core-
ktx-1.10.1.pom, took 284 ms
Download       https://dl.google.com/dl/android/maven2/androidx/lifecycle/lifecycle-
runtime-ktx/2.6.1/lifecycle-runtime-ktx-2.6.1.pom, took 289 ms
Download           https://dl.google.com/dl/android/maven2/androidx/compose/compose-
bom/2024.09.00/compose-bom-2024.09.00.pom, took 299 ms
Download         https://dl.google.com/dl/android/maven2/androidx/activity/activity-
compose/1.8.0/activity-compose-1.8.0.pom, took 313 ms
Download https://dl.google.com/dl/android/maven2/androidx/core/core-ktx/1.10.1/core-
ktx-1.10.1.module, took 100 ms
Download       https://dl.google.com/dl/android/maven2/androidx/lifecycle/lifecycle-
runtime-ktx/2.6.1/lifecycle-runtime-ktx-2.6.1.module, took 109 ms
Download         https://dl.google.com/dl/android/maven2/androidx/activity/activity-
compose/1.8.0/activity-compose-1.8.0.module, took 96 ms
Download           https://repo.maven.apache.org/maven2/org/jetbrains/kotlin/kotlin-
stdlib/2.0.0/kotlin-stdlib-2.0.0.pom, took 16 s 597 ms
Download           https://repo.maven.apache.org/maven2/org/jetbrains/kotlin/kotlin-
stdlib/2.0.0/kotlin-stdlib-2.0.0.module, took 2 s 573 ms
Download
https://repo.maven.apache.org/maven2/org/jetbrains/annotations/13.0/annotations-
13.0.pom, took 970 ms
Download     https://dl.google.com/dl/android/maven2/androidx/core/core/1.10.1/core-
1.10.1.pom, took 94 ms
Download
https://dl.google.com/dl/android/maven2/androidx/annotation/annotation/1.1.0/annotat
ion-1.1.0.pom, took 101 ms
Download     https://dl.google.com/dl/android/maven2/androidx/core/core/1.10.1/core-
1.10.1.module, took 99 ms
Download       https://dl.google.com/dl/android/maven2/androidx/lifecycle/lifecycle-
runtime/2.6.1/lifecycle-runtime-2.6.1.pom, took 103 ms
```

```
Download https://dl.google.com/dl/android/maven2/androidx/lifecycle/lifecycle-runtime/2.6.1/lifecycle-runtime-2.6.1.module, took 115 ms
Download https://repo.maven.apache.org/maven2/org/jetbrains/kotlinx/kotlinx-coroutines-android/1.6.4/kotlinx-coroutines-android-1.6.4.pom, took 695 ms
Download https://repo.maven.apache.org/maven2/org/jetbrains/kotlinx/kotlinx-coroutines-bom/1.6.4/kotlinx-coroutines-bom-1.6.4.pom, took 11 s 939 ms
Download https://repo.maven.apache.org/maven2/org/jetbrains/kotlinx/kotlinx-coroutines-android/1.6.4/kotlinx-coroutines-android-1.6.4.module, took 446 ms
Download https://dl.google.com/dl/android/maven2/androidx/compose/ui/ui/1.0.1/ui-1.0.1.pom, took 96 ms
Download https://dl.google.com/dl/android/maven2/androidx/compose/ui/ui/1.0.1/ui-1.0.1.module, took 99 ms
Download https://dl.google.com/dl/android/maven2/androidx/activity/activity-ktx/1.8.0/activity-ktx-1.8.0.pom, took 106 ms
Download
https://dl.google.com/dl/android/maven2/androidx/compose/runtime/runtime/1.0.1/runtime-1.0.1.pom, took 114 ms
Download https://dl.google.com/dl/android/maven2/androidx/compose/runtime/runtime-saveable/1.0.1/runtime-saveable-1.0.1.pom, took 124 ms
Download https://dl.google.com/dl/android/maven2/androidx/activity/activity-ktx/1.8.0/activity-ktx-1.8.0.module, took 103 ms
Download
https://dl.google.com/dl/android/maven2/androidx/compose/runtime/runtime/1.0.1/runtime-1.0.1.module, took 100 ms
Download https://dl.google.com/dl/android/maven2/androidx/compose/runtime/runtime-saveable/1.0.1/runtime-saveable-1.0.1.module, took 96 ms
Download https://dl.google.com/dl/android/maven2/androidx/lifecycle/lifecycle-viewmodel/2.6.1/lifecycle-viewmodel-2.6.1.pom, took 97 ms
Download https://dl.google.com/dl/android/maven2/androidx/lifecycle/lifecycle-viewmodel/2.6.1/lifecycle-viewmodel-2.6.1.module, took 105 ms
Download
https://dl.google.com/dl/android/maven2/androidx/compose/material3/material3/1.3.0/material3-1.3.0.pom, took 100 ms
Download
https://dl.google.com/dl/android/maven2/androidx/compose/material3/material3/1.3.0/material3-1.3.0.module, took 140 ms
Download
https://dl.google.com/dl/android/maven2/androidx/compose/runtime/runtime/1.7.0/runtime-1.7.0.pom, took 98 ms
Download
https://dl.google.com/dl/android/maven2/androidx/compose/runtime/runtime/1.7.0/runtime-1.7.0.module, took 124 ms
Download https://dl.google.com/dl/android/maven2/androidx/compose/runtime/runtime-saveable/1.7.0/runtime-saveable-1.7.0.pom, took 123 ms
Download https://dl.google.com/dl/android/maven2/androidx/compose/runtime/runtime-saveable/1.7.0/runtime-saveable-1.7.0.module, took 124 ms
Download https://dl.google.com/dl/android/maven2/androidx/compose/ui/ui/1.7.0/ui-1.7.0.pom, took 122 ms
Download https://dl.google.com/dl/android/maven2/androidx/compose/ui/ui/1.7.0/ui-1.7.0.module, took 127 ms
Download https://dl.google.com/dl/android/maven2/androidx/compose/ui/ui-graphics/1.7.0/ui-graphics-1.7.0.pom, took 101 ms
Download https://dl.google.com/dl/android/maven2/androidx/compose/ui/ui-
```

```
graphics/1.7.0/ui-graphics-1.7.0.module, took 124 ms
Download        https://dl.google.com/dl/android/maven2/androidx/compose/ui/ui-test-
manifest/1.7.0/ui-test-manifest-1.7.0.pom, took 114 ms
Download        https://dl.google.com/dl/android/maven2/androidx/compose/ui/ui-test-
manifest/1.7.0/ui-test-manifest-1.7.0.module, took 103 ms
Download             https://dl.google.com/dl/android/maven2/androidx/compose/ui/ui-
tooling/1.7.0/ui-tooling-1.7.0.pom, took 238 ms
Download             https://dl.google.com/dl/android/maven2/androidx/compose/ui/ui-
tooling/1.7.0/ui-tooling-1.7.0.module, took 134 ms
Download     https://dl.google.com/dl/android/maven2/androidx/compose/ui/ui-tooling-
preview/1.7.0/ui-tooling-preview-1.7.0.pom, took 99 ms
Download     https://dl.google.com/dl/android/maven2/androidx/compose/ui/ui-tooling-
preview/1.7.0/ui-tooling-preview-1.7.0.module, took 133 ms
Download
https://dl.google.com/dl/android/maven2/androidx/annotation/annotation/1.6.0/annotat
ion-1.6.0.pom, took 95 ms
Download
https://dl.google.com/dl/android/maven2/androidx/annotation/annotation/1.6.0/annotat
ion-1.6.0.module, took 94 ms
Download     https://dl.google.com/dl/android/maven2/androidx/concurrent/concurrent-
futures/1.0.0/concurrent-futures-1.0.0.pom, took 96 ms
Download
https://dl.google.com/dl/android/maven2/androidx/collection/collection/1.0.0/collect
ion-1.0.0.pom, took 96 ms
Download
https://dl.google.com/dl/android/maven2/androidx/versionedparcelable/versionedparcel
able/1.1.1/versionedparcelable-1.1.1.pom, took 99 ms
Download     https://dl.google.com/dl/android/maven2/androidx/annotation/annotation-
experimental/1.3.0/annotation-experimental-1.3.0.pom, took 104 ms
Download
https://dl.google.com/dl/android/maven2/androidx/interpolator/interpolator/1.0.0/int
erpolator-1.0.0.pom, took 120 ms
Download     https://dl.google.com/dl/android/maven2/androidx/annotation/annotation-
experimental/1.3.0/annotation-experimental-1.3.0.module, took 97 ms
Download            https://dl.google.com/dl/android/maven2/androidx/arch/core/core-
runtime/2.2.0/core-runtime-2.2.0.pom, took 95 ms
Download            https://dl.google.com/dl/android/maven2/androidx/arch/core/core-
common/2.2.0/core-common-2.2.0.pom, took 97 ms
Download
https://dl.google.com/dl/android/maven2/androidx/profileinstaller/profileinstaller/1
.3.0/profileinstaller-1.3.0.pom, took 98 ms
Download       https://dl.google.com/dl/android/maven2/androidx/lifecycle/lifecycle-
common/2.6.1/lifecycle-common-2.6.1.pom, took 110 ms
Download
https://dl.google.com/dl/android/maven2/androidx/profileinstaller/profileinstaller/1
.3.0/profileinstaller-1.3.0.module, took 94 ms
Download            https://dl.google.com/dl/android/maven2/androidx/arch/core/core-
common/2.2.0/core-common-2.2.0.module, took 97 ms
Download            https://dl.google.com/dl/android/maven2/androidx/arch/core/core-
runtime/2.2.0/core-runtime-2.2.0.module, took 101 ms
Download       https://dl.google.com/dl/android/maven2/androidx/lifecycle/lifecycle-
common/2.6.1/lifecycle-common-2.6.1.module, took 124 ms
Download          https://repo.maven.apache.org/maven2/org/jetbrains/kotlinx/kotlinx-
```

```
coroutines-core/1.6.4/kotlinx-coroutines-core-1.6.4.pom, took 696 ms
Download         https://repo.maven.apache.org/maven2/org/jetbrains/kotlinx/kotlinx-coroutines-core/1.6.4/kotlinx-coroutines-core-1.6.4.module, took 8 s 296 ms
Download     https://dl.google.com/dl/android/maven2/androidx/savedstate/savedstate-ktx/1.2.1/savedstate-ktx-1.2.1.pom, took 146 ms
Download
https://dl.google.com/dl/android/maven2/androidx/activity/activity/1.8.0/activity-1.8.0.pom, took 146 ms
Download     https://dl.google.com/dl/android/maven2/androidx/savedstate/savedstate-ktx/1.2.1/savedstate-ktx-1.2.1.module, took 159 ms
Download
https://dl.google.com/dl/android/maven2/androidx/activity/activity/1.8.0/activity-1.8.0.module, took 161 ms
Download      https://dl.google.com/dl/android/maven2/androidx/lifecycle/lifecycle-viewmodel-ktx/2.6.1/lifecycle-viewmodel-ktx-2.6.1.pom, took 156 ms
Download      https://dl.google.com/dl/android/maven2/androidx/lifecycle/lifecycle-viewmodel-ktx/2.6.1/lifecycle-viewmodel-ktx-2.6.1.module, took 239 ms
Download
https://dl.google.com/dl/android/maven2/androidx/compose/material3/material3-android/1.3.0/material3-android-1.3.0.pom, took 351 ms
Download
https://dl.google.com/dl/android/maven2/androidx/compose/material3/material3-android/1.3.0/material3-android-1.3.0.module, took 211 ms
Download    https://dl.google.com/dl/android/maven2/androidx/compose/runtime/runtime-android/1.7.0/runtime-android-1.7.0.pom, took 155 ms
Download    https://dl.google.com/dl/android/maven2/androidx/compose/runtime/runtime-android/1.7.0/runtime-android-1.7.0.module, took 156 ms
Download    https://dl.google.com/dl/android/maven2/androidx/compose/runtime/runtime-saveable-android/1.7.0/runtime-saveable-android-1.7.0.pom, took 279 ms
Download    https://dl.google.com/dl/android/maven2/androidx/compose/runtime/runtime-saveable-android/1.7.0/runtime-saveable-android-1.7.0.module, took 164 ms
Download          https://dl.google.com/dl/android/maven2/androidx/compose/ui/ui-android/1.7.0/ui-android-1.7.0.pom, took 165 ms
Download          https://dl.google.com/dl/android/maven2/androidx/compose/ui/ui-android/1.7.0/ui-android-1.7.0.module, took 188 ms
Download    https://dl.google.com/dl/android/maven2/androidx/compose/ui/ui-graphics-android/1.7.0/ui-graphics-android-1.7.0.pom, took 159 ms
Download    https://dl.google.com/dl/android/maven2/androidx/compose/ui/ui-graphics-android/1.7.0/ui-graphics-android-1.7.0.module, took 177 ms
Download     https://dl.google.com/dl/android/maven2/androidx/compose/ui/ui-tooling-android/1.7.0/ui-tooling-android-1.7.0.pom, took 151 ms
Download     https://dl.google.com/dl/android/maven2/androidx/compose/ui/ui-tooling-android/1.7.0/ui-tooling-android-1.7.0.module, took 109 ms
Download     https://dl.google.com/dl/android/maven2/androidx/compose/ui/ui-tooling-preview-android/1.7.0/ui-tooling-preview-android-1.7.0.pom, took 108 ms
Download     https://dl.google.com/dl/android/maven2/androidx/compose/ui/ui-tooling-preview-android/1.7.0/ui-tooling-preview-android-1.7.0.module, took 112 ms
Download     https://dl.google.com/dl/android/maven2/androidx/annotation/annotation-jvm/1.6.0/annotation-jvm-1.6.0.pom, took 107 ms
Download     https://dl.google.com/dl/android/maven2/androidx/annotation/annotation-jvm/1.6.0/annotation-jvm-1.6.0.module, took 103 ms
Download
https://repo.maven.apache.org/maven2/com/google/guava/listenablefuture/1.0/listenabl
```

```
efuture-1.0.pom, took 188 ms
Download     https://dl.google.com/dl/android/maven2/androidx/concurrent/concurrent-futures/1.1.0/concurrent-futures-1.1.0.pom, took 104 ms
Download     https://dl.google.com/dl/android/maven2/androidx/concurrent/concurrent-futures/1.1.0/concurrent-futures-1.1.0.module, took 107 ms
Download           https://dl.google.com/dl/android/maven2/androidx/startup/startup-runtime/1.1.1/startup-runtime-1.1.1.pom, took 106 ms
Download           https://dl.google.com/dl/android/maven2/androidx/startup/startup-runtime/1.1.1/startup-runtime-1.1.1.module, took 107 ms
Download    https://repo.maven.apache.org/maven2/org/jetbrains/kotlin/kotlin-stdlib-jdk8/1.8.0/kotlin-stdlib-jdk8-1.8.0.pom, took 169 ms
Download         https://repo.maven.apache.org/maven2/org/jetbrains/kotlinx/kotlinx-coroutines-core-jvm/1.6.4/kotlinx-coroutines-core-jvm-1.6.4.pom, took 831 ms
Download         https://repo.maven.apache.org/maven2/org/jetbrains/kotlinx/kotlinx-coroutines-core-jvm/1.6.4/kotlinx-coroutines-core-jvm-1.6.4.module, took 411 ms
Download
https://dl.google.com/dl/android/maven2/androidx/savedstate/savedstate/1.2.1/savedstate-1.2.1.pom, took 102 ms
Download
https://dl.google.com/dl/android/maven2/androidx/tracing/tracing/1.0.0/tracing-1.0.0.pom, took 107 ms
Download
https://dl.google.com/dl/android/maven2/androidx/tracing/tracing/1.0.0/tracing-1.0.0.module, took 96 ms
Download
https://dl.google.com/dl/android/maven2/androidx/savedstate/savedstate/1.2.1/savedstate-1.2.1.module, took 105 ms
Download       https://dl.google.com/dl/android/maven2/androidx/lifecycle/lifecycle-viewmodel-savedstate/2.6.1/lifecycle-viewmodel-savedstate-2.6.1.pom, took 101 ms
Download       https://dl.google.com/dl/android/maven2/androidx/lifecycle/lifecycle-viewmodel-savedstate/2.6.1/lifecycle-viewmodel-savedstate-2.6.1.module, took 110 ms
Download         https://dl.google.com/dl/android/maven2/androidx/activity/activity-compose/1.8.2/activity-compose-1.8.2.pom, took 129 ms
Download         https://dl.google.com/dl/android/maven2/androidx/activity/activity-compose/1.8.2/activity-compose-1.8.2.module, took 101 ms
Download     https://dl.google.com/dl/android/maven2/androidx/annotation/annotation-experimental/1.4.0/annotation-experimental-1.4.0.pom, took 102 ms
Download     https://dl.google.com/dl/android/maven2/androidx/annotation/annotation-experimental/1.4.0/annotation-experimental-1.4.0.module, took 98 ms
Download
https://dl.google.com/dl/android/maven2/androidx/collection/collection/1.4.0/collection-1.4.0.pom, took 98 ms
Download
https://dl.google.com/dl/android/maven2/androidx/collection/collection/1.4.0/collection-1.4.0.module, took 127 ms
Download       https://dl.google.com/dl/android/maven2/androidx/lifecycle/lifecycle-common-java8/2.6.1/lifecycle-common-java8-2.6.1.pom, took 99 ms
Download       https://dl.google.com/dl/android/maven2/androidx/lifecycle/lifecycle-common-java8/2.6.1/lifecycle-common-java8-2.6.1.module, took 108 ms
Download             https://dl.google.com/dl/android/maven2/androidx/compose/ui/ui-text/1.7.0/ui-text-1.7.0.pom, took 100 ms
Download             https://dl.google.com/dl/android/maven2/androidx/compose/ui/ui-util/1.7.0/ui-util-1.7.0.pom, took 120 ms
```

```
Download             https://dl.google.com/dl/android/maven2/androidx/compose/ui/ui-
text/1.7.0/ui-text-1.7.0.module, took 121 ms
Download             https://dl.google.com/dl/android/maven2/androidx/compose/ui/ui-
util/1.7.0/ui-util-1.7.0.module, took 135 ms
Download https://dl.google.com/dl/android/maven2/androidx/compose/material/material-
ripple/1.7.0/material-ripple-1.7.0.pom, took 97 ms
Download
https://dl.google.com/dl/android/maven2/androidx/compose/foundation/foundation-
layout/1.7.0/foundation-layout-1.7.0.pom, took 110 ms
Download
https://dl.google.com/dl/android/maven2/androidx/compose/animation/animation-
core/1.7.0/animation-core-1.7.0.pom, took 112 ms
Download https://dl.google.com/dl/android/maven2/androidx/compose/material/material-
icons-core/1.7.0/material-icons-core-1.7.0.pom, took 132 ms
Download
https://dl.google.com/dl/android/maven2/androidx/compose/foundation/foundation/1.7.0
/foundation-1.7.0.pom, took 132 ms
Download https://dl.google.com/dl/android/maven2/androidx/compose/material/material-
ripple/1.7.0/material-ripple-1.7.0.module, took 101 ms
Download
https://dl.google.com/dl/android/maven2/androidx/compose/foundation/foundation/1.7.0
/foundation-1.7.0.module, took 105 ms
Download
https://dl.google.com/dl/android/maven2/androidx/compose/foundation/foundation-
layout/1.7.0/foundation-layout-1.7.0.module, took 115 ms
Download
https://dl.google.com/dl/android/maven2/androidx/compose/animation/animation-
core/1.7.0/animation-core-1.7.0.module, took 118 ms
Download https://dl.google.com/dl/android/maven2/androidx/compose/material/material-
icons-core/1.7.0/material-icons-core-1.7.0.module, took 132 ms
Download         https://repo.maven.apache.org/maven2/org/jetbrains/kotlinx/kotlinx-
coroutines-android/1.7.3/kotlinx-coroutines-android-1.7.3.pom, took 705 ms
Download         https://repo.maven.apache.org/maven2/org/jetbrains/kotlinx/kotlinx-
coroutines-bom/1.7.3/kotlinx-coroutines-bom-1.7.3.pom, took 1 s 915 ms
Download         https://repo.maven.apache.org/maven2/org/jetbrains/kotlinx/kotlinx-
coroutines-android/1.7.3/kotlinx-coroutines-android-1.7.3.module, took 302 ms
Download         https://repo.maven.apache.org/maven2/org/jetbrains/kotlinx/kotlinx-
coroutines-core/1.7.3/kotlinx-coroutines-core-1.7.3.pom, took 297 ms
Download         https://repo.maven.apache.org/maven2/org/jetbrains/kotlinx/kotlinx-
coroutines-core/1.7.3/kotlinx-coroutines-core-1.7.3.module, took 8 s 548 ms
Download    https://repo.maven.apache.org/maven2/org/jetbrains/kotlin/kotlin-stdlib-
common/1.8.22/kotlin-stdlib-common-1.8.22.pom, took 13 s 129 ms
Download     https://dl.google.com/dl/android/maven2/androidx/core/core/1.12.0/core-
1.12.0.pom, took 99 ms
Download     https://dl.google.com/dl/android/maven2/androidx/core/core/1.12.0/core-
1.12.0.module, took 97 ms
Download
https://dl.google.com/dl/android/maven2/androidx/profileinstaller/profileinstaller/1
.3.1/profileinstaller-1.3.1.pom, took 97 ms
Download
https://dl.google.com/dl/android/maven2/androidx/profileinstaller/profileinstaller/1
.3.1/profileinstaller-1.3.1.module, took 98 ms
Download     https://dl.google.com/dl/android/maven2/androidx/customview/customview-
```

```
poolingcontainer/1.0.0/customview-poolingcontainer-1.0.0.pom, took 95 ms
Download
https://dl.google.com/dl/android/maven2/androidx/emoji2/emoji2/1.2.0/emoji2-
1.2.0.pom, took 96 ms
Download
https://dl.google.com/dl/android/maven2/androidx/autofill/autofill/1.0.0/autofill-
1.0.0.pom, took 97 ms
Download
https://dl.google.com/dl/android/maven2/androidx/emoji2/emoji2/1.2.0/emoji2-
1.2.0.module, took 95 ms
Download     https://dl.google.com/dl/android/maven2/androidx/customview/customview-
poolingcontainer/1.0.0/customview-poolingcontainer-1.0.0.module, took 98 ms
Download             https://dl.google.com/dl/android/maven2/androidx/compose/ui/ui-
unit/1.7.0/ui-unit-1.7.0.pom, took 217 ms
Download             https://dl.google.com/dl/android/maven2/androidx/compose/ui/ui-
geometry/1.7.0/ui-geometry-1.7.0.pom, took 217 ms
Download             https://dl.google.com/dl/android/maven2/androidx/compose/ui/ui-
unit/1.7.0/ui-unit-1.7.0.module, took 133 ms
Download             https://dl.google.com/dl/android/maven2/androidx/compose/ui/ui-
geometry/1.7.0/ui-geometry-1.7.0.module, took 141 ms
Download       https://dl.google.com/dl/android/maven2/androidx/lifecycle/lifecycle-
runtime-compose/2.8.3/lifecycle-runtime-compose-2.8.3.pom, took 135 ms
Download       https://dl.google.com/dl/android/maven2/androidx/lifecycle/lifecycle-
runtime-compose/2.8.3/lifecycle-runtime-compose-2.8.3.module, took 125 ms
Download
https://dl.google.com/dl/android/maven2/androidx/annotation/annotation/1.7.0/annotat
ion-1.7.0.pom, took 103 ms
Download
https://dl.google.com/dl/android/maven2/androidx/annotation/annotation/1.7.0/annotat
ion-1.7.0.module, took 108 ms
Download         https://dl.google.com/dl/android/maven2/androidx/graphics/graphics-
path/1.0.1/graphics-path-1.0.1.pom, took 98 ms
Download         https://dl.google.com/dl/android/maven2/androidx/graphics/graphics-
path/1.0.1/graphics-path-1.0.1.module, took 117 ms
Download     https://dl.google.com/dl/android/maven2/androidx/compose/ui/ui-tooling-
data/1.7.0/ui-tooling-data-1.7.0.pom, took 104 ms
Download     https://dl.google.com/dl/android/maven2/androidx/compose/ui/ui-tooling-
data/1.7.0/ui-tooling-data-1.7.0.module, took 107 ms
Download
https://dl.google.com/dl/android/maven2/androidx/compose/material/material/1.7.0/mat
erial-1.7.0.pom, took 98 ms
Download
https://dl.google.com/dl/android/maven2/androidx/compose/animation/animation/1.7.0/a
nimation-1.7.0.pom, took 126 ms
Download
https://dl.google.com/dl/android/maven2/androidx/compose/material/material/1.7.0/mat
erial-1.7.0.module, took 126 ms
Download
https://dl.google.com/dl/android/maven2/androidx/compose/animation/animation/1.7.0/a
nimation-1.7.0.module, took 129 ms
Download    https://repo.maven.apache.org/maven2/org/jetbrains/kotlin/kotlin-stdlib-
common/2.0.0/kotlin-stdlib-common-2.0.0.pom, took 321 ms
Download       https://dl.google.com/dl/android/maven2/androidx/lifecycle/lifecycle-
```

```
livedata-core/2.6.1/lifecycle-livedata-core-2.6.1.pom, took 126 ms
Download https://dl.google.com/dl/android/maven2/androidx/lifecycle/lifecycle-livedata-core/2.6.1/lifecycle-livedata-core-2.6.1.module, took 142 ms
Download
https://dl.google.com/dl/android/maven2/androidx/activity/activity/1.8.2/activity-1.8.2.pom, took 157 ms
Download
https://dl.google.com/dl/android/maven2/androidx/activity/activity/1.8.2/activity-1.8.2.module, took 114 ms
Download https://dl.google.com/dl/android/maven2/androidx/activity/activity-ktx/1.8.2/activity-ktx-1.8.2.pom, took 117 ms
Download https://dl.google.com/dl/android/maven2/androidx/activity/activity-ktx/1.8.2/activity-ktx-1.8.2.module, took 101 ms
Download https://dl.google.com/dl/android/maven2/androidx/collection/collection-jvm/1.4.0/collection-jvm-1.4.0.pom, took 97 ms
Download https://dl.google.com/dl/android/maven2/androidx/collection/collection-jvm/1.4.0/collection-jvm-1.4.0.module, took 96 ms
Download https://dl.google.com/dl/android/maven2/androidx/compose/ui/ui-text-android/1.7.0/ui-text-android-1.7.0.pom, took 108 ms
Download https://dl.google.com/dl/android/maven2/androidx/compose/ui/ui-text-android/1.7.0/ui-text-android-1.7.0.module, took 228 ms
Download https://dl.google.com/dl/android/maven2/androidx/compose/ui/ui-util-android/1.7.0/ui-util-android-1.7.0.pom, took 124 ms
Download https://dl.google.com/dl/android/maven2/androidx/compose/ui/ui-util-android/1.7.0/ui-util-android-1.7.0.module, took 130 ms
Download
https://dl.google.com/dl/android/maven2/androidx/compose/animation/animation-core-android/1.7.0/animation-core-android-1.7.0.pom, took 118 ms
Download
https://dl.google.com/dl/android/maven2/androidx/compose/animation/animation-core-android/1.7.0/animation-core-android-1.7.0.module, took 120 ms
Download
https://dl.google.com/dl/android/maven2/androidx/compose/foundation/foundation-android/1.7.0/foundation-android-1.7.0.pom, took 116 ms
Download
https://dl.google.com/dl/android/maven2/androidx/compose/foundation/foundation-android/1.7.0/foundation-android-1.7.0.module, took 155 ms
Download
https://dl.google.com/dl/android/maven2/androidx/compose/foundation/foundation-layout-android/1.7.0/foundation-layout-android-1.7.0.pom, took 162 ms
Download
https://dl.google.com/dl/android/maven2/androidx/compose/foundation/foundation-layout-android/1.7.0/foundation-layout-android-1.7.0.module, took 138 ms
Download https://dl.google.com/dl/android/maven2/androidx/compose/material/material-icons-core-android/1.7.0/material-icons-core-android-1.7.0.pom, took 144 ms
Download https://dl.google.com/dl/android/maven2/androidx/compose/material/material-icons-core-android/1.7.0/material-icons-core-android-1.7.0.module, took 112 ms
Download https://dl.google.com/dl/android/maven2/androidx/compose/material/material-ripple-android/1.7.0/material-ripple-android-1.7.0.pom, took 232 ms
Download https://dl.google.com/dl/android/maven2/androidx/compose/material/material-ripple-android/1.7.0/material-ripple-android-1.7.0.module, took 108 ms
Download https://repo.maven.apache.org/maven2/org/jetbrains/kotlinx/kotlinx-coroutines-core-jvm/1.7.3/kotlinx-coroutines-core-jvm-1.7.3.pom, took 711 ms
```

```
Download https://repo.maven.apache.org/maven2/org/jetbrains/kotlinx/kotlinx-coroutines-core-jvm/1.7.3/kotlinx-coroutines-core-jvm-1.7.3.module, took 579 ms
Download https://dl.google.com/dl/android/maven2/androidx/core/core-ktx/1.12.0/core-ktx-1.12.0.pom, took 96 ms
Download https://dl.google.com/dl/android/maven2/androidx/core/core-ktx/1.12.0/core-ktx-1.12.0.module, took 103 ms
Download https://dl.google.com/dl/android/maven2/androidx/compose/ui/ui-geometry-android/1.7.0/ui-geometry-android-1.7.0.pom, took 126 ms
Download https://dl.google.com/dl/android/maven2/androidx/compose/ui/ui-geometry-android/1.7.0/ui-geometry-android-1.7.0.module, took 115 ms
Download https://dl.google.com/dl/android/maven2/androidx/compose/ui/ui-unit-android/1.7.0/ui-unit-android-1.7.0.pom, took 125 ms
Download https://dl.google.com/dl/android/maven2/androidx/compose/ui/ui-unit-android/1.7.0/ui-unit-android-1.7.0.module, took 135 ms
Download https://dl.google.com/dl/android/maven2/androidx/lifecycle/lifecycle-process/2.6.1/lifecycle-process-2.6.1.pom, took 101 ms
Download https://dl.google.com/dl/android/maven2/androidx/lifecycle/lifecycle-process/2.6.1/lifecycle-process-2.6.1.module, took 108 ms
Download https://dl.google.com/dl/android/maven2/androidx/lifecycle/lifecycle-runtime-compose-android/2.8.3/lifecycle-runtime-compose-android-2.8.3.pom, took 97 ms
Download https://dl.google.com/dl/android/maven2/androidx/lifecycle/lifecycle-runtime-compose-android/2.8.3/lifecycle-runtime-compose-android-2.8.3.module, took 112 ms
Download https://dl.google.com/dl/android/maven2/androidx/annotation/annotation-jvm/1.7.0/annotation-jvm-1.7.0.pom, took 96 ms
Download https://dl.google.com/dl/android/maven2/androidx/annotation/annotation-jvm/1.7.0/annotation-jvm-1.7.0.module, took 97 ms
Download https://dl.google.com/dl/android/maven2/androidx/compose/ui/ui-tooling-data-android/1.7.0/ui-tooling-data-android-1.7.0.pom, took 103 ms
Download https://dl.google.com/dl/android/maven2/androidx/compose/ui/ui-tooling-data-android/1.7.0/ui-tooling-data-android-1.7.0.module, took 108 ms
Download
https://dl.google.com/dl/android/maven2/androidx/compose/animation/animation-android/1.7.0/animation-android-1.7.0.pom, took 101 ms
Download
https://dl.google.com/dl/android/maven2/androidx/compose/animation/animation-android/1.7.0/animation-android-1.7.0.module, took 123 ms
Download https://dl.google.com/dl/android/maven2/androidx/compose/material/material-android/1.7.0/material-android-1.7.0.pom, took 118 ms
Download https://dl.google.com/dl/android/maven2/androidx/compose/material/material-android/1.7.0/material-android-1.7.0.module, took 111 ms
Download https://repo.maven.apache.org/maven2/org/jetbrains/kotlin/kotlin-stdlib-jdk8/1.8.20/kotlin-stdlib-jdk8-1.8.20.pom, took 298 ms
Download https://dl.google.com/dl/android/maven2/androidx/core/core/1.13.1/core-1.13.1.pom, took 96 ms
Download https://dl.google.com/dl/android/maven2/androidx/core/core/1.13.1/core-1.13.1.module, took 98 ms
Download
https://dl.google.com/dl/android/maven2/androidx/emoji2/emoji2/1.3.0/emoji2-1.3.0.pom, took 97 ms
Download
https://dl.google.com/dl/android/maven2/androidx/emoji2/emoji2/1.3.0/emoji2-
```

```
1.3.0.module, took 101 ms
Download     https://dl.google.com/dl/android/maven2/androidx/collection/collection-ktx/1.4.0/collection-ktx-1.4.0.pom, took 96 ms
Download     https://dl.google.com/dl/android/maven2/androidx/collection/collection-ktx/1.4.0/collection-ktx-1.4.0.module, took 100 ms
Download
https://dl.google.com/dl/android/maven2/androidx/annotation/annotation/1.8.0/annotation-1.8.0.pom, took 96 ms
Download
https://dl.google.com/dl/android/maven2/androidx/annotation/annotation/1.8.0/annotation-1.8.0.module, took 110 ms
Download     https://dl.google.com/dl/android/maven2/androidx/lifecycle/lifecycle-runtime/2.8.3/lifecycle-runtime-2.8.3.pom, took 120 ms
Download     https://dl.google.com/dl/android/maven2/androidx/lifecycle/lifecycle-runtime/2.8.3/lifecycle-runtime-2.8.3.module, took 121 ms
Download     https://dl.google.com/dl/android/maven2/androidx/lifecycle/lifecycle-runtime-ktx/2.8.3/lifecycle-runtime-ktx-2.8.3.pom, took 99 ms
Download     https://dl.google.com/dl/android/maven2/androidx/lifecycle/lifecycle-runtime-ktx/2.8.3/lifecycle-runtime-ktx-2.8.3.module, took 107 ms
Download     https://dl.google.com/dl/android/maven2/androidx/lifecycle/lifecycle-common/2.8.3/lifecycle-common-2.8.3.pom, took 125 ms
Download     https://dl.google.com/dl/android/maven2/androidx/lifecycle/lifecycle-common/2.8.3/lifecycle-common-2.8.3.module, took 117 ms
Download     https://dl.google.com/dl/android/maven2/androidx/lifecycle/lifecycle-common-java8/2.8.3/lifecycle-common-java8-2.8.3.pom, took 106 ms
Download     https://dl.google.com/dl/android/maven2/androidx/lifecycle/lifecycle-common-java8/2.8.3/lifecycle-common-java8-2.8.3.module, took 106 ms
Download     https://dl.google.com/dl/android/maven2/androidx/lifecycle/lifecycle-viewmodel/2.8.3/lifecycle-viewmodel-2.8.3.pom, took 97 ms
Download     https://dl.google.com/dl/android/maven2/androidx/lifecycle/lifecycle-viewmodel/2.8.3/lifecycle-viewmodel-2.8.3.module, took 121 ms
Download     https://dl.google.com/dl/android/maven2/androidx/lifecycle/lifecycle-viewmodel-ktx/2.8.3/lifecycle-viewmodel-ktx-2.8.3.pom, took 130 ms
Download     https://dl.google.com/dl/android/maven2/androidx/lifecycle/lifecycle-viewmodel-ktx/2.8.3/lifecycle-viewmodel-ktx-2.8.3.module, took 140 ms
Download     https://dl.google.com/dl/android/maven2/androidx/lifecycle/lifecycle-viewmodel-savedstate/2.8.3/lifecycle-viewmodel-savedstate-2.8.3.pom, took 115 ms
Download     https://dl.google.com/dl/android/maven2/androidx/lifecycle/lifecycle-viewmodel-savedstate/2.8.3/lifecycle-viewmodel-savedstate-2.8.3.module, took 111 ms
Download     https://dl.google.com/dl/android/maven2/androidx/arch/core/core-common/2.1.0/core-common-2.1.0.pom, took 100 ms
Download     https://repo.maven.apache.org/maven2/org/jetbrains/kotlin/kotlin-stdlib-jdk7/1.8.20/kotlin-stdlib-jdk7-1.8.20.pom, took 649 ms
Download https://dl.google.com/dl/android/maven2/androidx/core/core-ktx/1.13.1/core-ktx-1.13.1.pom, took 97 ms
Download https://dl.google.com/dl/android/maven2/androidx/core/core-ktx/1.13.1/core-ktx-1.13.1.module, took 96 ms
Download     https://dl.google.com/dl/android/maven2/androidx/annotation/annotation-jvm/1.8.0/annotation-jvm-1.8.0.pom, took 96 ms
Download     https://dl.google.com/dl/android/maven2/androidx/annotation/annotation-jvm/1.8.0/annotation-jvm-1.8.0.module, took 97 ms
Download     https://dl.google.com/dl/android/maven2/androidx/lifecycle/lifecycle-runtime-android/2.8.3/lifecycle-runtime-android-2.8.3.pom, took 102 ms
```

```
Download        https://dl.google.com/dl/android/maven2/androidx/lifecycle/lifecycle-
runtime-android/2.8.3/lifecycle-runtime-android-2.8.3.module, took 126 ms
Download        https://dl.google.com/dl/android/maven2/androidx/lifecycle/lifecycle-
runtime-ktx-android/2.8.3/lifecycle-runtime-ktx-android-2.8.3.pom, took 126 ms
Download        https://dl.google.com/dl/android/maven2/androidx/lifecycle/lifecycle-
runtime-ktx-android/2.8.3/lifecycle-runtime-ktx-android-2.8.3.module, took 103 ms
Download        https://dl.google.com/dl/android/maven2/androidx/lifecycle/lifecycle-
common-jvm/2.8.3/lifecycle-common-jvm-2.8.3.pom, took 99 ms
Download        https://dl.google.com/dl/android/maven2/androidx/lifecycle/lifecycle-
common-jvm/2.8.3/lifecycle-common-jvm-2.8.3.module, took 120 ms
Download        https://dl.google.com/dl/android/maven2/androidx/lifecycle/lifecycle-
process/2.8.3/lifecycle-process-2.8.3.pom, took 99 ms
Download        https://dl.google.com/dl/android/maven2/androidx/lifecycle/lifecycle-
process/2.8.3/lifecycle-process-2.8.3.module, took 141 ms
Download        https://dl.google.com/dl/android/maven2/androidx/lifecycle/lifecycle-
viewmodel-android/2.8.3/lifecycle-viewmodel-android-2.8.3.pom, took 131 ms
Download        https://dl.google.com/dl/android/maven2/androidx/lifecycle/lifecycle-
viewmodel-android/2.8.3/lifecycle-viewmodel-android-2.8.3.module, took 115 ms
Download        https://dl.google.com/dl/android/maven2/androidx/lifecycle/lifecycle-
livedata-core/2.8.3/lifecycle-livedata-core-2.8.3.pom, took 96 ms
Download        https://dl.google.com/dl/android/maven2/androidx/lifecycle/lifecycle-
livedata-core/2.8.3/lifecycle-livedata-core-2.8.3.module, took 114 ms
Download     https://dl.google.com/dl/android/maven2/androidx/test/espresso/espresso-
core/3.5.1/espresso-core-3.5.1.pom, took 230 ms
Download
https://dl.google.com/dl/android/maven2/androidx/test/ext/junit/1.1.5/junit-
1.1.5.pom, took 259 ms
Download      https://dl.google.com/dl/android/maven2/androidx/test/core/1.5.0/core-
1.5.0.pom, took 92 ms
Download
https://dl.google.com/dl/android/maven2/androidx/test/monitor/1.6.1/monitor-
1.6.1.pom, took 246 ms
Download    https://repo.maven.apache.org/maven2/junit/junit/4.13.2/junit-4.13.2.pom,
took 2 s 376 ms
Download     https://dl.google.com/dl/android/maven2/androidx/test/espresso/espresso-
idling-resource/3.5.1/espresso-idling-resource-3.5.1.pom, took 95 ms
Download   https://dl.google.com/dl/android/maven2/androidx/test/runner/1.5.2/runner-
1.5.2.pom, took 100 ms
Download
https://dl.google.com/dl/android/maven2/androidx/test/annotation/1.0.1/annotation-
1.0.1.pom, took 231 ms
Download
https://repo.maven.apache.org/maven2/com/squareup/javawriter/2.1.1/javawriter-
2.1.1.pom, took 160 ms
Download                  https://repo.maven.apache.org/maven2/org/hamcrest/hamcrest-
integration/1.3/hamcrest-integration-1.3.pom, took 1 s 272 ms
Download                  https://repo.maven.apache.org/maven2/org/hamcrest/hamcrest-
parent/1.3/hamcrest-parent-1.3.pom, took 1 s 838 ms
Download         https://dl.google.com/dl/android/maven2/androidx/compose/ui/ui-test-
junit4/1.7.0/ui-test-junit4-1.7.0.pom, took 99 ms
Download         https://dl.google.com/dl/android/maven2/androidx/compose/ui/ui-test-
junit4/1.7.0/ui-test-junit4-1.7.0.module, took 159 ms
Download
```

```
https://dl.google.com/dl/android/maven2/androidx/test/services/storage/1.4.2/storage
-1.4.2.pom, took 98 ms
Download https://dl.google.com/dl/android/maven2/androidx/compose/ui/ui-test-junit4-
android/1.7.0/ui-test-junit4-android-1.7.0.pom, took 220 ms
Download https://dl.google.com/dl/android/maven2/androidx/compose/ui/ui-test-junit4-
android/1.7.0/ui-test-junit4-android-1.7.0.module, took 128 ms
Download             https://dl.google.com/dl/android/maven2/androidx/compose/ui/ui-
test/1.7.0/ui-test-1.7.0.pom, took 103 ms
Download             https://dl.google.com/dl/android/maven2/androidx/compose/ui/ui-
test/1.7.0/ui-test-1.7.0.module, took 230 ms
Download         https://repo.maven.apache.org/maven2/org/jetbrains/kotlinx/kotlinx-
coroutines-test/1.7.3/kotlinx-coroutines-test-1.7.3.pom, took 1 s 86 ms
Download         https://repo.maven.apache.org/maven2/org/jetbrains/kotlinx/kotlinx-
coroutines-test/1.7.3/kotlinx-coroutines-test-1.7.3.module, took 3 s 44 ms
Download        https://dl.google.com/dl/android/maven2/androidx/compose/ui/ui-test-
android/1.7.0/ui-test-android-1.7.0.pom, took 113 ms
Download        https://dl.google.com/dl/android/maven2/androidx/compose/ui/ui-test-
android/1.7.0/ui-test-android-1.7.0.module, took 128 ms
Download         https://repo.maven.apache.org/maven2/org/jetbrains/kotlinx/kotlinx-
coroutines-test-jvm/1.7.3/kotlinx-coroutines-test-jvm-1.7.3.pom, took 192 ms
Download         https://repo.maven.apache.org/maven2/org/jetbrains/kotlinx/kotlinx-
coroutines-test-jvm/1.7.3/kotlinx-coroutines-test-jvm-1.7.3.module, took 2 s 100 ms
Download        https://dl.google.com/dl/android/maven2/androidx/compose/ui/ui-util-
android/1.7.0/ui-util-android-1.7.0.aar, took 327 ms
Download         https://dl.google.com/dl/android/maven2/androidx/activity/activity-
ktx/1.8.2/activity-ktx-1.8.2.aar, took 360 ms
Download https://dl.google.com/dl/android/maven2/androidx/compose/material/material-
ripple-android/1.7.0/material-ripple-android-1.7.0.aar, took 459 ms
Download
https://dl.google.com/dl/android/maven2/androidx/activity/activity/1.8.2/activity-
1.8.2.aar, took 496 ms
Download     https://dl.google.com/dl/android/maven2/androidx/compose/ui/ui-tooling-
data-android/1.7.0/ui-tooling-data-android-1.7.0.aar, took 554 ms
Download
https://dl.google.com/dl/android/maven2/androidx/compose/foundation/foundation-
layout-android/1.7.0/foundation-layout-android-1.7.0.aar, took 557 ms
Download    https://dl.google.com/dl/android/maven2/androidx/compose/ui/ui-geometry-
android/1.7.0/ui-geometry-android-1.7.0.aar, took 186 ms
Download        https://dl.google.com/dl/android/maven2/androidx/compose/ui/ui-text-
android/1.7.0/ui-text-android-1.7.0.aar, took 593 ms
Download         https://dl.google.com/dl/android/maven2/androidx/activity/activity-
compose/1.8.2/activity-compose-1.8.2.aar, took 680 ms
Download        https://dl.google.com/dl/android/maven2/androidx/compose/ui/ui-unit-
android/1.7.0/ui-unit-android-1.7.0.aar, took 718 ms
Download     https://dl.google.com/dl/android/maven2/androidx/compose/ui/ui-tooling-
preview-android/1.7.0/ui-tooling-preview-android-1.7.0.aar, took 232 ms
Download
https://dl.google.com/dl/android/maven2/androidx/compose/animation/animation-
android/1.7.0/animation-android-1.7.0.aar, took 406 ms
Download        https://dl.google.com/dl/android/maven2/androidx/compose/ui/ui-test-
android/1.7.0/ui-test-android-1.7.0.aar, took 309 ms
Download
https://dl.google.com/dl/android/maven2/androidx/compose/foundation/foundation-
```

```
android/1.7.0/foundation-android-1.7.0.aar, took 795 ms
Download https://dl.google.com/dl/android/maven2/androidx/compose/ui/ui-tooling-android/1.7.0/ui-tooling-android-1.7.0.aar, took 278 ms
Download https://dl.google.com/dl/android/maven2/androidx/compose/ui/ui-test-manifest/1.7.0/ui-test-manifest-1.7.0.aar, took 163 ms
Download https://dl.google.com/dl/android/maven2/androidx/compose/ui/ui-test-junit4-android/1.7.0/ui-test-junit4-android-1.7.0.aar, took 173 ms
Download https://dl.google.com/dl/android/maven2/androidx/compose/ui/ui-graphics-android/1.7.0/ui-graphics-android-1.7.0.aar, took 355 ms
Download https://dl.google.com/dl/android/maven2/androidx/compose/material/material-icons-core-android/1.7.0/material-icons-core-android-1.7.0.aar, took 306 ms
Download
https://dl.google.com/dl/android/maven2/androidx/test/ext/junit/1.1.5/junit-1.1.5.aar, took 133 ms
Download https://dl.google.com/dl/android/maven2/androidx/lifecycle/lifecycle-runtime-compose-android/2.8.3/lifecycle-runtime-compose-android-2.8.3.aar, took 150 ms
Download https://dl.google.com/dl/android/maven2/androidx/lifecycle/lifecycle-livedata-core/2.8.3/lifecycle-livedata-core-2.8.3.aar, took 185 ms
Download https://dl.google.com/dl/android/maven2/androidx/test/espresso/espresso-core/3.5.1/espresso-core-3.5.1.aar, took 150 ms
Download https://dl.google.com/dl/android/maven2/androidx/lifecycle/lifecycle-runtime-android/2.8.3/lifecycle-runtime-android-2.8.3.aar, took 131 ms
Download https://dl.google.com/dl/android/maven2/androidx/lifecycle/lifecycle-viewmodel-android/2.8.3/lifecycle-viewmodel-android-2.8.3.aar, took 124 ms
Download https://dl.google.com/dl/android/maven2/androidx/core/core/1.13.1/core-1.13.1.aar, took 262 ms
Download https://dl.google.com/dl/android/maven2/androidx/lifecycle/lifecycle-viewmodel-ktx/2.8.3/lifecycle-viewmodel-ktx-2.8.3.aar, took 117 ms
Download https://dl.google.com/dl/android/maven2/androidx/test/core/1.5.0/core-1.5.0.aar, took 158 ms
Download https://dl.google.com/dl/android/maven2/androidx/lifecycle/lifecycle-runtime-ktx-android/2.8.3/lifecycle-runtime-ktx-android-2.8.3.aar, took 131 ms
Download https://dl.google.com/dl/android/maven2/androidx/core/core-ktx/1.13.1/core-ktx-1.13.1.aar, took 122 ms
Download https://dl.google.com/dl/android/maven2/androidx/lifecycle/lifecycle-viewmodel-savedstate/2.8.3/lifecycle-viewmodel-savedstate-2.8.3.aar, took 132 ms
Download https://dl.google.com/dl/android/maven2/androidx/compose/ui/ui-android/1.7.0/ui-android-1.7.0.aar, took 677 ms
Download
https://dl.google.com/dl/android/maven2/androidx/test/services/storage/1.4.2/storage-1.4.2.aar, took 97 ms
Download https://dl.google.com/dl/android/maven2/androidx/savedstate/savedstate-ktx/1.2.1/savedstate-ktx-1.2.1.aar, took 100 ms
Download
https://dl.google.com/dl/android/maven2/androidx/test/monitor/1.6.1/monitor-1.6.1.aar, took 103 ms
Download https://dl.google.com/dl/android/maven2/androidx/compose/runtime/runtime-saveable-android/1.7.0/runtime-saveable-android-1.7.0.aar, took 151 ms
Download
https://dl.google.com/dl/android/maven2/androidx/savedstate/savedstate/1.2.1/savedstate-1.2.1.aar, took 100 ms
Download https://dl.google.com/dl/android/maven2/androidx/test/runner/1.5.2/runner-
```

```
1.5.2.aar, took 143 ms
Download
https://dl.google.com/dl/android/maven2/androidx/versionedparcelable/versionedparcel
able/1.1.1/versionedparcelable-1.1.1.aar, took 130 ms
Download     https://dl.google.com/dl/android/maven2/androidx/annotation/annotation-
experimental/1.4.0/annotation-experimental-1.4.0.aar, took 98 ms
Download
https://dl.google.com/dl/android/maven2/androidx/tracing/tracing/1.0.0/tracing-
1.0.0.aar, took 96 ms
Download
https://dl.google.com/dl/android/maven2/androidx/test/annotation/1.0.1/annotation-
1.0.1.aar, took 162 ms
Download
https://dl.google.com/dl/android/maven2/androidx/compose/animation/animation-core-
android/1.7.0/animation-core-android-1.7.0.aar, took 1 s 593 ms
Download    https://dl.google.com/dl/android/maven2/androidx/test/espresso/espresso-
idling-resource/3.5.1/espresso-idling-resource-3.5.1.aar, took 131 ms
Download   https://dl.google.com/dl/android/maven2/androidx/compose/runtime/runtime-
android/1.7.0/runtime-android-1.7.0.aar, took 435 ms
Download
https://dl.google.com/dl/android/maven2/androidx/compose/material3/material3-
android/1.3.0/material3-android-1.3.0.aar, took 1 s 888 ms
Download            https://dl.google.com/dl/android/maven2/androidx/arch/core/core-
common/2.2.0/core-common-2.2.0.jar, took 135 ms
Download     https://dl.google.com/dl/android/maven2/androidx/annotation/annotation-
jvm/1.8.0/annotation-jvm-1.8.0.jar, took 137 ms
Download     https://dl.google.com/dl/android/maven2/androidx/concurrent/concurrent-
futures/1.1.0/concurrent-futures-1.1.0.jar, took 246 ms
Download       https://dl.google.com/dl/android/maven2/androidx/lifecycle/lifecycle-
common-jvm/2.8.3/lifecycle-common-jvm-2.8.3.jar, took 253 ms
Download     https://dl.google.com/dl/android/maven2/androidx/collection/collection-
jvm/1.4.0/collection-jvm-1.4.0.jar, took 531 ms
Download
https://repo.maven.apache.org/maven2/com/google/code/findbugs/jsr305/2.0.2/jsr305-
2.0.2.jar, took 723 ms
Download                 https://repo.maven.apache.org/maven2/org/hamcrest/hamcrest-
core/1.3/hamcrest-core-1.3.jar, took 765 ms
Download         https://repo.maven.apache.org/maven2/org/jetbrains/kotlinx/kotlinx-
coroutines-android/1.7.3/kotlinx-coroutines-android-1.7.3.jar, took 1 s 291 ms
Download
https://repo.maven.apache.org/maven2/com/google/guava/listenablefuture/1.0/listenabl
efuture-1.0.jar, took 908 ms
Download                 https://repo.maven.apache.org/maven2/org/hamcrest/hamcrest-
library/1.3/hamcrest-library-1.3.jar, took 3 s 44 ms
Download                 https://repo.maven.apache.org/maven2/org/hamcrest/hamcrest-
integration/1.3/hamcrest-integration-1.3.jar, took 3 s 637 ms
Download
https://repo.maven.apache.org/maven2/com/squareup/javawriter/2.1.1/javawriter-
2.1.1.jar, took 4 s 15 ms
Download   https://repo.maven.apache.org/maven2/junit/junit/4.13.2/junit-4.13.2.jar,
took 13 s 762 ms
Download         https://repo.maven.apache.org/maven2/org/jetbrains/kotlinx/kotlinx-
coroutines-test-jvm/1.7.3/kotlinx-coroutines-test-jvm-1.7.3.jar, took 23 s 593 ms
```

```
Download https://repo.maven.apache.org/maven2/org/jetbrains/kotlin/kotlin-stdlib/2.0.0/kotlin-stdlib-2.0.0.jar, took 1 m 45 s 80 ms
Download https://repo.maven.apache.org/maven2/org/jetbrains/kotlinx/kotlinx-coroutines-core-jvm/1.7.3/kotlinx-coroutines-core-jvm-1.7.3.jar, took 1 m 48 s 218 ms
Download https://dl.google.com/dl/android/maven2/androidx/startup/startup-runtime/1.1.1/startup-runtime-1.1.1.aar, took 116 ms
Download https://dl.google.com/dl/android/maven2/androidx/arch/core/core-runtime/2.2.0/core-runtime-2.2.0.aar, took 117 ms
Download
https://dl.google.com/dl/android/maven2/androidx/profileinstaller/profileinstaller/1.3.1/profileinstaller-1.3.1.aar, took 156 ms
Download
https://dl.google.com/dl/android/maven2/androidx/interpolator/interpolator/1.0.0/interpolator-1.0.0.aar, took 99 ms
Download https://dl.google.com/dl/android/maven2/androidx/graphics/graphics-path/1.0.1/graphics-path-1.0.1.aar, took 211 ms
Download
https://dl.google.com/dl/android/maven2/androidx/emoji2/emoji2/1.3.0/emoji2-1.3.0.aar, took 219 ms
Download
https://dl.google.com/dl/android/maven2/androidx/autofill/autofill/1.0.0/autofill-1.0.0.aar, took 112 ms
Download https://dl.google.com/dl/android/maven2/androidx/lifecycle/lifecycle-process/2.8.3/lifecycle-process-2.8.3.aar, took 240 ms
Download https://dl.google.com/dl/android/maven2/androidx/customview/customview-poolingcontainer/1.0.0/customview-poolingcontainer-1.0.0.aar, took 286 ms
Download https://dl.google.com/dl/android/maven2/androidx/compose/material/material-android/1.7.0/material-android-1.7.0.aar, took 2 s 923 ms
Download https://repo.maven.apache.org/maven2/org/jetbrains/kotlin/kotlin-compose-compiler-plugin-embeddable/2.0.0/kotlin-compose-compiler-plugin-embeddable-2.0.0.pom, took 377 ms
Download https://repo.maven.apache.org/maven2/org/jetbrains/kotlin/kotlin-compose-compiler-plugin-embeddable/2.0.0/kotlin-compose-compiler-plugin-embeddable-2.0.0.jar, took 1 m 21 s 850 ms
Download
https://dl.google.com/dl/android/maven2/androidx/annotation/annotation/1.2.0/annotation-1.2.0.pom, took 233 ms
Download
https://dl.google.com/dl/android/maven2/androidx/annotation/annotation/1.2.0/annotation-1.2.0.module, took 97 ms
Download
https://dl.google.com/dl/android/maven2/androidx/test/ext/junit/1.1.5/junit-1.1.5-javadoc.jar, took 114 ms
Download https://dl.google.com/dl/android/maven2/androidx/test/espresso/espresso-core/3.5.1/espresso-core-3.5.1-javadoc.jar, took 262 ms
Download https://dl.google.com/dl/android/maven2/androidx/test/core/1.5.0/core-1.5.0-javadoc.jar, took 115 ms
Download https://dl.google.com/dl/android/maven2/androidx/test/runner/1.5.2/runner-1.5.2-javadoc.jar, took 141 ms
Download
https://dl.google.com/dl/android/maven2/androidx/test/services/storage/1.4.2/storage-1.4.2-javadoc.jar, took 105 ms
```

```
Download
https://dl.google.com/dl/android/maven2/androidx/test/monitor/1.6.1/monitor-1.6.1-javadoc.jar, took 136 ms
Download
https://repo.maven.apache.org/maven2/org/jetbrains/annotations/23.0.0/annotations-23.0.0-javadoc.jar, took 39 s 303 ms
Download https://dl.google.com/dl/android/maven2/androidx/test/espresso/espresso-idling-resource/3.5.1/espresso-idling-resource-3.5.1-javadoc.jar, took 321 ms
Download https://repo.maven.apache.org/maven2/junit/junit/4.13.2/junit-4.13.2-javadoc.jar, took 2 m 43 s 347 ms
Download https://repo.maven.apache.org/maven2/org/hamcrest/hamcrest-integration/1.3/hamcrest-integration-1.3-javadoc.jar, took 2 s 174 ms
Download https://repo.maven.apache.org/maven2/org/hamcrest/hamcrest-library/1.3/hamcrest-library-1.3-javadoc.jar, took 33 s 584 ms
Download https://repo.maven.apache.org/maven2/org/hamcrest/hamcrest-core/1.3/hamcrest-core-1.3-javadoc.jar, took 17 s 284 ms
Download
https://repo.maven.apache.org/maven2/com/google/guava/listenablefuture/1.0/listenablefuture-1.0-javadoc.jar, took 4 s 17 ms
Download
https://repo.maven.apache.org/maven2/com/squareup/javawriter/2.1.1/javawriter-2.1.1-javadoc.jar, took 5 s 946 ms
Download
https://repo.maven.apache.org/maven2/javax/inject/javax.inject/1/javax.inject-1-javadoc.jar, took 13 s 779 ms
Download
https://dl.google.com/dl/android/maven2/androidx/test/ext/junit/1.1.5/junit-1.1.5-sources.jar, took 97 ms
Download https://dl.google.com/dl/android/maven2/androidx/test/espresso/espresso-core/3.5.1/espresso-core-3.5.1-sources.jar, took 245 ms
Download https://dl.google.com/dl/android/maven2/androidx/test/core/1.5.0/core-1.5.0-sources.jar, took 98 ms
Download https://dl.google.com/dl/android/maven2/androidx/test/runner/1.5.2/runner-1.5.2-sources.jar, took 112 ms
Download
https://dl.google.com/dl/android/maven2/androidx/test/services/storage/1.4.2/storage-1.4.2-sources.jar, took 108 ms
Download
https://dl.google.com/dl/android/maven2/androidx/test/monitor/1.6.1/monitor-1.6.1-sources.jar, took 102 ms
Download
https://dl.google.com/dl/android/maven2/androidx/test/annotation/1.0.1/annotation-1.0.1-sources.jar, took 99 ms
Download
https://dl.google.com/dl/android/maven2/androidx/versionedparcelable/versionedparcelable/1.1.1/versionedparcelable-1.1.1-sources.jar, took 96 ms
Download
https://repo.maven.apache.org/maven2/org/jetbrains/annotations/23.0.0/annotations-23.0.0-sources.jar, took 943 ms
Download https://dl.google.com/dl/android/maven2/androidx/test/espresso/espresso-idling-resource/3.5.1/espresso-idling-resource-3.5.1-sources.jar, took 95 ms
Download https://repo.maven.apache.org/maven2/junit/junit/4.13.2/junit-4.13.2-sources.jar, took 19 s 37 ms
```

```
Download                  https://repo.maven.apache.org/maven2/org/hamcrest/hamcrest-
integration/1.3/hamcrest-integration-1.3-sources.jar, took 646 ms
Download                  https://repo.maven.apache.org/maven2/org/hamcrest/hamcrest-
library/1.3/hamcrest-library-1.3-sources.jar, took 2 s 125 ms
Download                  https://repo.maven.apache.org/maven2/org/hamcrest/hamcrest-
core/1.3/hamcrest-core-1.3-sources.jar, took 4 s 767 ms
Download
https://repo.maven.apache.org/maven2/com/google/guava/listenablefuture/1.0/listenabl
efuture-1.0-sources.jar, took 262 ms
Download
https://repo.maven.apache.org/maven2/com/squareup/javawriter/2.1.1/javawriter-2.1.1-
sources.jar, took 279 ms
Download
https://repo.maven.apache.org/maven2/javax/inject/javax.inject/1/javax.inject-1-
sources.jar, took 589 ms
Download
https://dl.google.com/dl/android/maven2/androidx/collection/collection/1.0.0/collect
ion-1.0.0-sources.jar, took 97 ms
Download              https://dl.google.com/dl/android/maven2/androidx/compose/ui/ui-
android/1.7.0/ui-android-1.7.0-sources.jar, took 192 ms
Download    https://dl.google.com/dl/android/maven2/androidx/compose/ui/ui-graphics-
android/1.7.0/ui-graphics-android-1.7.0-samples-sources.jar, took 229 ms
Download   https://dl.google.com/dl/android/maven2/androidx/compose/runtime/runtime-
saveable-android/1.7.0/runtime-saveable-android-1.7.0-sources.jar, took 233 ms
Download   https://dl.google.com/dl/android/maven2/androidx/compose/runtime/runtime-
saveable-android/1.7.0/runtime-saveable-android-1.7.0-samples-sources.jar,  took  242
ms
Download   https://dl.google.com/dl/android/maven2/androidx/compose/runtime/runtime-
android/1.7.0/runtime-android-1.7.0-samples-sources.jar, took 253 ms
Download     https://dl.google.com/dl/android/maven2/androidx/annotation/annotation-
experimental/1.4.0/annotation-experimental-1.4.0-sources.jar, took 261 ms
Download     https://dl.google.com/dl/android/maven2/androidx/compose/ui/ui-tooling-
android/1.7.0/ui-tooling-android-1.7.0-samples-sources.jar, took 282 ms
Download              https://dl.google.com/dl/android/maven2/androidx/compose/ui/ui-
android/1.7.0/ui-android-1.7.0-samples-sources.jar, took 290 ms
Download        https://dl.google.com/dl/android/maven2/androidx/compose/ui/ui-unit-
android/1.7.0/ui-unit-android-1.7.0-samples-sources.jar, took 97 ms
Download     https://dl.google.com/dl/android/maven2/androidx/compose/ui/ui-tooling-
android/1.7.0/ui-tooling-android-1.7.0-sources.jar, took 318 ms
Download    https://dl.google.com/dl/android/maven2/androidx/compose/ui/ui-geometry-
android/1.7.0/ui-geometry-android-1.7.0-sources.jar, took 347 ms
Download        https://dl.google.com/dl/android/maven2/androidx/compose/ui/ui-text-
android/1.7.0/ui-text-android-1.7.0-samples-sources.jar, took 119 ms
Download        https://dl.google.com/dl/android/maven2/androidx/compose/ui/ui-unit-
android/1.7.0/ui-unit-android-1.7.0-sources.jar, took 153 ms
Download        https://dl.google.com/dl/android/maven2/androidx/compose/ui/ui-util-
android/1.7.0/ui-util-android-1.7.0-sources.jar, took 139 ms
Download   https://dl.google.com/dl/android/maven2/androidx/compose/runtime/runtime-
android/1.7.0/runtime-android-1.7.0-sources.jar, took 412 ms
Download    https://dl.google.com/dl/android/maven2/androidx/compose/ui/ui-graphics-
android/1.7.0/ui-graphics-android-1.7.0-sources.jar, took 415 ms
Download     https://dl.google.com/dl/android/maven2/androidx/compose/ui/ui-tooling-
data-android/1.7.0/ui-tooling-data-android-1.7.0-sources.jar, took 113 ms
```

```
Download https://dl.google.com/dl/android/maven2/androidx/compose/ui/ui-test-junit4-android/1.7.0/ui-test-junit4-android-1.7.0-sources.jar, took 109 ms
Download https://dl.google.com/dl/android/maven2/androidx/compose/ui/ui-tooling-preview-android/1.7.0/ui-tooling-preview-android-1.7.0-sources.jar, took 124 ms
Download https://dl.google.com/dl/android/maven2/androidx/lifecycle/lifecycle-runtime-compose-android/2.8.3/lifecycle-runtime-compose-android-2.8.3-samples-sources.jar, took 195 ms
Download https://dl.google.com/dl/android/maven2/androidx/lifecycle/lifecycle-runtime-android/2.8.3/lifecycle-runtime-android-2.8.3-sources.jar, took 191 ms
Download https://dl.google.com/dl/android/maven2/androidx/lifecycle/lifecycle-runtime-compose-android/2.8.3/lifecycle-runtime-compose-android-2.8.3-sources.jar, took 223 ms
Download https://dl.google.com/dl/android/maven2/androidx/compose/ui/ui-test-android/1.7.0/ui-test-android-1.7.0-samples-sources.jar, took 103 ms
Download https://dl.google.com/dl/android/maven2/androidx/compose/ui/ui-test-android/1.7.0/ui-test-android-1.7.0-sources.jar, took 112 ms
Download https://dl.google.com/dl/android/maven2/androidx/compose/ui/ui-text-android/1.7.0/ui-text-android-1.7.0-sources.jar, took 270 ms
Download https://dl.google.com/dl/android/maven2/androidx/activity/activity-ktx/1.8.2/activity-ktx-1.8.2-sources.jar, took 118 ms
Download https://dl.google.com/dl/android/maven2/androidx/activity/activity-compose/1.8.2/activity-compose-1.8.2-sources.jar, took 137 ms
Download
https://dl.google.com/dl/android/maven2/androidx/activity/activity/1.8.2/activity-1.8.2-sources.jar, took 129 ms
Download https://dl.google.com/dl/android/maven2/androidx/savedstate/savedstate-ktx/1.2.1/savedstate-ktx-1.2.1-sources.jar, took 94 ms
Download https://dl.google.com/dl/android/maven2/androidx/lifecycle/lifecycle-viewmodel-savedstate/2.8.3/lifecycle-viewmodel-savedstate-2.8.3-sources.jar, took 122 ms
Download https://dl.google.com/dl/android/maven2/androidx/lifecycle/lifecycle-common-jvm/2.8.3/lifecycle-common-jvm-2.8.3-sources.jar, took 137 ms
Download
https://dl.google.com/dl/android/maven2/androidx/savedstate/savedstate/1.2.1/savedstate-1.2.1-sources.jar, took 101 ms
Download https://dl.google.com/dl/android/maven2/androidx/lifecycle/lifecycle-livedata-core/2.8.3/lifecycle-livedata-core-2.8.3-sources.jar, took 132 ms
Download https://dl.google.com/dl/android/maven2/androidx/lifecycle/lifecycle-viewmodel-android/2.8.3/lifecycle-viewmodel-android-2.8.3-sources.jar, took 166 ms
Download
https://dl.google.com/dl/android/maven2/androidx/compose/material3/material3-android/1.3.0/material3-android-1.3.0-samples-sources.jar, took 108 ms
Download https://dl.google.com/dl/android/maven2/androidx/core/core-ktx/1.13.1/core-ktx-1.13.1-sources.jar, took 159 ms
Download
https://dl.google.com/dl/android/maven2/androidx/compose/foundation/foundation-android/1.7.0/foundation-android-1.7.0-samples-sources.jar, took 143 ms
Download
https://dl.google.com/dl/android/maven2/androidx/compose/material3/material3-android/1.3.0/material3-android-1.3.0-sources.jar, took 175 ms
Download
https://dl.google.com/dl/android/maven2/androidx/compose/animation/animation-android/1.7.0/animation-android-1.7.0-samples-sources.jar, took 127 ms
```

```
Download
https://dl.google.com/dl/android/maven2/androidx/compose/animation/animation-core-
android/1.7.0/animation-core-android-1.7.0-sources.jar, took 116 ms
Download
https://dl.google.com/dl/android/maven2/androidx/compose/animation/animation-core-
android/1.7.0/animation-core-android-1.7.0-samples-sources.jar, took 119 ms
Download https://dl.google.com/dl/android/maven2/androidx/compose/material/material-
icons-core-android/1.7.0/material-icons-core-android-1.7.0-samples-sources.jar, took
97 ms
Download
https://dl.google.com/dl/android/maven2/androidx/compose/foundation/foundation-
layout-android/1.7.0/foundation-layout-android-1.7.0-samples-sources.jar, took 118
ms
Download
https://dl.google.com/dl/android/maven2/androidx/compose/animation/animation-
android/1.7.0/animation-android-1.7.0-sources.jar, took 145 ms
Download
https://dl.google.com/dl/android/maven2/androidx/compose/foundation/foundation-
android/1.7.0/foundation-android-1.7.0-sources.jar, took 170 ms
Download https://dl.google.com/dl/android/maven2/androidx/core/core/1.13.1/core-
1.13.1-sources.jar, took 307 ms
Download https://dl.google.com/dl/android/maven2/androidx/compose/material/material-
ripple-android/1.7.0/material-ripple-android-1.7.0-sources.jar, took 107 ms
Download
https://dl.google.com/dl/android/maven2/androidx/compose/foundation/foundation-
layout-android/1.7.0/foundation-layout-android-1.7.0-sources.jar, took 197 ms
Download https://dl.google.com/dl/android/maven2/androidx/annotation/annotation-
jvm/1.8.0/annotation-jvm-1.8.0-sources.jar, took 105 ms
Download
https://dl.google.com/dl/android/maven2/androidx/tracing/tracing/1.0.0/tracing-
1.0.0-sources.jar, took 96 ms
Download https://dl.google.com/dl/android/maven2/androidx/arch/core/core-
common/2.2.0/core-common-2.2.0-sources.jar, took 101 ms
Download https://dl.google.com/dl/android/maven2/androidx/concurrent/concurrent-
futures/1.1.0/concurrent-futures-1.1.0-sources.jar, took 100 ms
Download
https://dl.google.com/dl/android/maven2/androidx/annotation/annotation/1.2.0/annotat
ion-1.2.0-sources.jar, took 95 ms
Download https://dl.google.com/dl/android/maven2/androidx/collection/collection-
jvm/1.4.0/collection-jvm-1.4.0-sources.jar, took 143 ms
Download https://dl.google.com/dl/android/maven2/androidx/compose/material/material-
icons-core-android/1.7.0/material-icons-core-android-1.7.0-sources.jar, took 227 ms
Download https://repo.maven.apache.org/maven2/org/jetbrains/kotlinx/kotlinx-
coroutines-test-jvm/1.7.3/kotlinx-coroutines-test-jvm-1.7.3-sources.jar, took 16 s
157 ms
Download https://repo.maven.apache.org/maven2/org/jetbrains/kotlinx/kotlinx-
coroutines-core-jvm/1.7.3/kotlinx-coroutines-core-jvm-1.7.3-sources.jar, took 53 s
346 ms
Download https://repo.maven.apache.org/maven2/org/jetbrains/kotlin/kotlin-
stdlib/2.0.0/kotlin-stdlib-2.0.0-sources.jar, took 1 m 8 s 452 ms
Download https://repo.maven.apache.org/maven2/org/jetbrains/kotlinx/kotlinx-
coroutines-android/1.7.3/kotlinx-coroutines-android-1.7.3-sources.jar, took 125 ms
Download
```

```
https://dl.google.com/dl/android/maven2/com/android/tools/build/gradle/8.9.0-alpha02/gradle-8.9.0-alpha02-sources.jar, took 571 ms
Download https://repo.maven.apache.org/maven2/org/jetbrains/kotlin/kotlin-gradle-plugin/2.0.0/kotlin-gradle-plugin-2.0.0-sources.jar, took 3 m 19 s 441 ms
Download https://repo.maven.apache.org/maven2/org/jetbrains/kotlin/compose-compiler-gradle-plugin/2.0.0/compose-compiler-gradle-plugin-2.0.0-sources.jar, took 6 s 451 ms
Download https://dl.google.com/dl/android/maven2/com/android/tools/build/gradle-settings-api/8.9.0-alpha02/gradle-settings-api-8.9.0-alpha02-sources.jar, took 127 ms
Download https://dl.google.com/dl/android/maven2/com/android/tools/lint/lint-model/31.9.0-alpha02/lint-model-31.9.0-alpha02-sources.jar, took 193 ms
Download
https://dl.google.com/dl/android/maven2/com/android/tools/build/builder/8.9.0-alpha02/builder-8.9.0-alpha02-sources.jar, took 228 ms
Download https://dl.google.com/dl/android/maven2/com/android/tools/sdk-common/31.9.0-alpha02/sdk-common-31.9.0-alpha02-sources.jar, took 248 ms
Download https://dl.google.com/dl/android/maven2/com/android/tools/sdklib/31.9.0-alpha02/sdklib-31.9.0-alpha02-sources.jar, took 193 ms
Download
https://dl.google.com/dl/android/maven2/com/android/tools/repository/31.9.0-alpha02/repository-31.9.0-alpha02-sources.jar, took 145 ms
Download https://dl.google.com/dl/android/maven2/com/android/tools/build/gradle-api/8.9.0-alpha02/gradle-api-8.9.0-alpha02-sources.jar, took 220 ms
Download https://dl.google.com/dl/android/maven2/com/android/tools/build/builder-test-api/8.9.0-alpha02/builder-test-api-8.9.0-alpha02-sources.jar, took 108 ms
Download
https://dl.google.com/dl/android/maven2/com/android/tools/ddms/ddmlib/31.9.0-alpha02/ddmlib-31.9.0-alpha02-sources.jar, took 167 ms
Download
https://dl.google.com/dl/android/maven2/com/android/tools/build/aaptcompiler/8.9.0-alpha02/aaptcompiler-8.9.0-alpha02-sources.jar, took 141 ms
Download https://dl.google.com/dl/android/maven2/com/android/tools/build/aapt2-proto/8.9.0-alpha02-12634980/aapt2-proto-8.9.0-alpha02-12634980-sources.jar, took 253 ms
Download https://dl.google.com/dl/android/maven2/com/android/tools/analytics-library/crash/31.9.0-alpha02/crash-31.9.0-alpha02-sources.jar, took 120 ms
Download https://dl.google.com/dl/android/maven2/com/android/tools/analytics-library/shared/31.9.0-alpha02/shared-31.9.0-alpha02-sources.jar, took 160 ms
Download https://dl.google.com/dl/android/maven2/com/android/tools/lint/lint-typedef-remover/31.9.0-alpha02/lint-typedef-remover-31.9.0-alpha02-sources.jar, took 109 ms
Download https://dl.google.com/dl/android/maven2/androidx/databinding/databinding-compiler-common/8.9.0-alpha02/databinding-compiler-common-8.9.0-alpha02-sources.jar, took 159 ms
Download https://dl.google.com/dl/android/maven2/androidx/databinding/databinding-common/8.9.0-alpha02/databinding-common-8.9.0-alpha02-sources.jar, took 110 ms
Download
https://dl.google.com/dl/android/maven2/com/android/databinding/baseLibrary/8.9.0-alpha02/baseLibrary-8.9.0-alpha02-sources.jar, took 141 ms
Download
https://dl.google.com/dl/android/maven2/com/android/tools/layoutlib/layoutlib-api/31.9.0-alpha02/layoutlib-api-31.9.0-alpha02-sources.jar, took 177 ms
```

```
Download https://dl.google.com/dl/android/maven2/com/android/tools/utp/android-device-provider-ddmlib-proto/31.9.0-alpha02/android-device-provider-ddmlib-proto-31.9.0-alpha02-sources.jar, took 145 ms
Download https://dl.google.com/dl/android/maven2/com/android/tools/utp/android-device-provider-gradle-proto/31.9.0-alpha02/android-device-provider-gradle-proto-31.9.0-alpha02-sources.jar, took 132 ms
Download https://dl.google.com/dl/android/maven2/com/android/tools/utp/android-device-provider-profile-proto/31.9.0-alpha02/android-device-provider-profile-proto-31.9.0-alpha02-sources.jar, took 125 ms
Download https://dl.google.com/dl/android/maven2/com/android/tools/utp/android-test-plugin-host-additional-test-output-proto/31.9.0-alpha02/android-test-plugin-host-additional-test-output-proto-31.9.0-alpha02-sources.jar, took 133 ms
Download https://dl.google.com/dl/android/maven2/com/android/tools/utp/android-test-plugin-host-coverage-proto/31.9.0-alpha02/android-test-plugin-host-coverage-proto-31.9.0-alpha02-sources.jar, took 107 ms
Download https://dl.google.com/dl/android/maven2/com/android/tools/utp/android-test-plugin-host-emulator-control-proto/31.9.0-alpha02/android-test-plugin-host-emulator-control-proto-31.9.0-alpha02-sources.jar, took 150 ms
Download https://dl.google.com/dl/android/maven2/com/android/tools/utp/android-test-plugin-host-logcat-proto/31.9.0-alpha02/android-test-plugin-host-logcat-proto-31.9.0-alpha02-sources.jar, took 108 ms
Download https://dl.google.com/dl/android/maven2/com/android/tools/utp/android-test-plugin-host-apk-installer-proto/31.9.0-alpha02/android-test-plugin-host-apk-installer-proto-31.9.0-alpha02-sources.jar, took 146 ms
Download https://dl.google.com/dl/android/maven2/com/android/tools/utp/android-test-plugin-host-retention-proto/31.9.0-alpha02/android-test-plugin-host-retention-proto-31.9.0-alpha02-sources.jar, took 120 ms
Download https://dl.google.com/dl/android/maven2/com/android/tools/utp/android-test-plugin-result-listener-gradle-proto/31.9.0-alpha02/android-test-plugin-result-listener-gradle-proto-31.9.0-alpha02-sources.jar, took 147 ms
Download https://dl.google.com/dl/android/maven2/com/android/tools/build/builder-model/8.9.0-alpha02/builder-model-8.9.0-alpha02-sources.jar, took 157 ms
Download https://dl.google.com/dl/android/maven2/com/android/tools/build/jetifier/jetifier-processor/1.0.0-beta10/jetifier-processor-1.0.0-beta10-sources.jar, took 117 ms
Download https://dl.google.com/dl/android/maven2/com/android/tools/build/jetifier/jetifier-core/1.0.0-beta10/jetifier-core-1.0.0-beta10-sources.jar, took 108 ms
Download https://repo.maven.apache.org/maven2/org/apache/httpcomponents/httpmime/4.5.6/httpmime-4.5.6-sources.jar, took 2 s 256 ms
Download https://repo.maven.apache.org/maven2/commons-io/commons-io/2.13.0/commons-io-2.13.0-sources.jar, took 25 s 944 ms
Download https://repo.maven.apache.org/maven2/org/ow2/asm/asm-commons/9.7/asm-commons-9.7-sources.jar, took 4 s 128 ms
Download https://repo.maven.apache.org/maven2/org/ow2/asm/asm-util/9.7/asm-util-9.7-sources.jar, took 3 s 239 ms
Download https://repo.maven.apache.org/maven2/org/ow2/asm/asm-analysis/9.7/asm-analysis-9.7-sources.jar, took 1 s 874 ms
Download https://repo.maven.apache.org/maven2/org/ow2/asm/asm/9.7/asm-9.7-sources.jar, took 11 s 40 ms
Download https://repo.maven.apache.org/maven2/org/bouncycastle/bcpkix-jdk18on/1.77/bcpkix-jdk18on-1.77-sources.jar, took 35 s 446 ms
```

```
Download https://repo.maven.apache.org/maven2/org/glassfish/jaxb/jaxb-runtime/2.3.2/jaxb-runtime-2.3.2-sources.jar, took 42 s 488 ms
Download https://repo.maven.apache.org/maven2/net/sf/jopt-simple/jopt-simple/4.9/jopt-simple-4.9-sources.jar, took 5 s 425 ms
Download https://repo.maven.apache.org/maven2/com/squareup/javapoet/1.10.0/javapoet-1.10.0-sources.jar, took 3 s 782 ms
Download https://repo.maven.apache.org/maven2/com/google/protobuf/protobuf-java-util/3.22.3/protobuf-java-util-3.22.3-sources.jar, took 43 s 686 ms
Download https://repo.maven.apache.org/maven2/io/grpc/grpc-protobuf/1.57.0/grpc-protobuf-1.57.0-sources.jar, took 3 s 642 ms
Download
https://repo.maven.apache.org/maven2/com/google/crypto/tink/tink/1.7.0/tink-1.7.0-sources.jar, took 2 m 42 s 977 ms
Download https://repo.maven.apache.org/maven2/com/google/protobuf/protobuf-java/3.22.3/protobuf-java-3.22.3-sources.jar, took 21 s 425 ms
Download https://repo.maven.apache.org/maven2/io/grpc/grpc-netty/1.57.0/grpc-netty-1.57.0-sources.jar, took 5 s 40 ms
Download https://repo.maven.apache.org/maven2/io/grpc/grpc-core/1.57.0/grpc-core-1.57.0-sources.jar, took 50 s 290 ms
Download https://repo.maven.apache.org/maven2/com/google/code/gson/gson/2.10.1/gson-2.10.1-sources.jar, took 25 s 111 ms
Download https://repo.maven.apache.org/maven2/io/grpc/grpc-stub/1.57.0/grpc-stub-1.57.0-sources.jar, took 7 s 148 ms
Download https://repo.maven.apache.org/maven2/com/google/flatbuffers/flatbuffers-java/1.12.0/flatbuffers-java-1.12.0-sources.jar, took 5 s 58 ms
Download https://repo.maven.apache.org/maven2/org/jetbrains/kotlin/kotlin-gradle-plugin-model/2.0.0/kotlin-gradle-plugin-model-2.0.0-sources.jar, took 584 ms
Download https://repo.maven.apache.org/maven2/org/jetbrains/kotlin/kotlin-gradle-plugin-api/2.0.0/kotlin-gradle-plugin-api-2.0.0-sources.jar, took 4 s 511 ms
Download https://repo.maven.apache.org/maven2/org/jetbrains/kotlin/kotlin-build-statistics/2.0.0/kotlin-build-statistics-2.0.0-sources.jar, took 15 s 144 ms
Download https://repo.maven.apache.org/maven2/org/jetbrains/kotlin/kotlin-gradle-plugin-idea-proto/2.0.0/kotlin-gradle-plugin-idea-proto-2.0.0-sources.jar, took 20 s 219 ms
Download https://repo.maven.apache.org/maven2/org/jetbrains/kotlin/kotlin-gradle-plugin-idea/2.0.0/kotlin-gradle-plugin-idea-2.0.0-sources.jar, took 24 s 45 ms
Download https://repo.maven.apache.org/maven2/org/jetbrains/kotlin/kotlin-klib-commonizer-api/2.0.0/kotlin-klib-commonizer-api-2.0.0-sources.jar, took 1 s 204 ms
Download https://repo.maven.apache.org/maven2/org/jetbrains/kotlin/kotlin-build-tools-api/2.0.0/kotlin-build-tools-api-2.0.0-sources.jar, took 2 s 531 ms
Download https://repo.maven.apache.org/maven2/org/jetbrains/kotlin/kotlin-compiler-runner/2.0.0/kotlin-compiler-runner-2.0.0-sources.jar, took 2 s 715 ms
Download https://repo.maven.apache.org/maven2/org/jetbrains/kotlin/kotlin-util-klib/2.0.0/kotlin-util-klib-2.0.0-sources.jar, took 26 s 776 ms
Download https://repo.maven.apache.org/maven2/org/jetbrains/kotlin/kotlin-compiler-embeddable/2.0.0/kotlin-compiler-embeddable-2.0.0-sources.jar, took 4 m 46 s 493 ms
Download https://repo.maven.apache.org/maven2/org/jetbrains/kotlin/kotlin-compiler-embeddable/2.0.0/kotlin-compiler-embeddable-2.0.0-sources.jar, took 7 m 32 s 670 ms
Download https://repo.maven.apache.org/maven2/org/jetbrains/kotlin/kotlin-compiler-embeddable/2.0.0/kotlin-compiler-embeddable-2.0.0-sources.jar, took 11 m 50 s 223 ms
Download https://dl.google.com/dl/android/maven2/com/android/tools/common/31.9.0-alpha02/common-31.9.0-alpha02-sources.jar, took 293 ms
Download https://repo.maven.apache.org/maven2/net/sf/kxml/kxml2/2.3.0/kxml2-2.3.0-
```

```
sources.jar, took 18 s 397 ms
Download https://dl.google.com/dl/android/maven2/com/android/tools/build/manifest-merger/31.9.0-alpha02/manifest-merger-31.9.0-alpha02-sources.jar, took 157 ms
Download https://dl.google.com/dl/android/maven2/com/android/tools/analytics-library/tracker/31.9.0-alpha02/tracker-31.9.0-alpha02-sources.jar, took 101 ms
Download
https://dl.google.com/dl/android/maven2/com/android/tools/build/apkzlib/8.9.0-alpha02/apkzlib-8.9.0-alpha02-sources.jar, took 115 ms
Download https://dl.google.com/dl/android/maven2/com/android/tools/analytics-library/protos/31.9.0-alpha02/protos-31.9.0-alpha02-sources.jar, took 260 ms
Download https://repo.maven.apache.org/maven2/org/bouncycastle/bcprov-jdk18on/1.77/bcprov-jdk18on-1.77-sources.jar, took 59 s 84 ms
Download https://repo.maven.apache.org/maven2/org/bouncycastle/bcprov-jdk18on/1.77/bcprov-jdk18on-1.77-sources.jar, took 5 m 52 s 90 ms
Download https://dl.google.com/dl/android/maven2/com/android/signflinger/8.9.0-alpha02/signflinger-8.9.0-alpha02-sources.jar, took 162 ms
Download https://dl.google.com/dl/android/maven2/com/android/zipflinger/8.9.0-alpha02/zipflinger-8.9.0-alpha02-sources.jar, took 172 ms
Download https://repo.maven.apache.org/maven2/commons-codec/commons-codec/1.11/commons-codec-1.11-sources.jar, took 16 s 305 ms
Download
https://dl.google.com/dl/android/maven2/com/android/tools/build/apksig/8.9.0-alpha02/apksig-8.9.0-alpha02-sources.jar, took 248 ms
Download
https://repo.maven.apache.org/maven2/com/squareup/javawriter/2.5.0/javawriter-2.5.0-sources.jar, took 420 ms
Download https://repo.maven.apache.org/maven2/org/jetbrains/kotlin/kotlin-reflect/2.1.0-Beta2/kotlin-reflect-2.1.0-Beta2-sources.jar, took 1 m 6 s 818 ms
Download https://repo.maven.apache.org/maven2/com/google/guava/guava/32.0.1-jre/guava-32.0.1-jre-sources.jar, took 1 m 51 s 783 ms
Download https://dl.google.com/dl/android/maven2/com/android/tools/dvlib/31.9.0-alpha02/dvlib-31.9.0-alpha02-sources.jar, took 194 ms
Download https://repo.maven.apache.org/maven2/org/apache/commons/commons-compress/1.21/commons-compress-1.21-sources.jar, took 2 m 44 s 895 ms
Download
https://repo.maven.apache.org/maven2/org/apache/httpcomponents/httpcore/4.4.16/httpcore-4.4.16-sources.jar, took 1 m 53 s 655 ms
Download https://repo.maven.apache.org/maven2/com/google/jimfs/jimfs/1.1/jimfs-1.1-sources.jar, took 570 ms
Download
https://repo.maven.apache.org/maven2/com/sun/activation/javax.activation/1.2.0/javax.activation-1.2.0-sources.jar, took 1 s 366 ms
Download
https://dl.google.com/dl/android/maven2/com/android/tools/annotations/31.9.0-alpha02/annotations-31.9.0-alpha02-sources.jar, took 141 ms
Download
https://repo.maven.apache.org/maven2/com/google/dagger/dagger/2.28.3/dagger-2.28.3-sources.jar, took 3 s 16 ms
Download https://repo.maven.apache.org/maven2/com/google/auto/value/auto-value-annotations/1.6.2/auto-value-annotations-1.6.2-sources.jar, took 12 s 142 ms
Download
https://repo.maven.apache.org/maven2/com/google/errorprone/error_prone_annotations/2.18.0/error_prone_annotations-2.18.0-sources.jar, took 1 s 102 ms
```

```
Download https://repo.maven.apache.org/maven2/org/bitbucket/b_c/jose4j/0.9.5/jose4j-0.9.5-sources.jar, took 16 s 625 ms
Download https://repo.maven.apache.org/maven2/org/slf4j/slf4j-api/1.7.30/slf4j-api-1.7.30-sources.jar, took 4 s 568 ms
Download https://repo.maven.apache.org/maven2/org/apache/httpcomponents/httpclient/4.5.14/httpclient-4.5.14-sources.jar, took 57 s 517 ms
Download https://repo.maven.apache.org/maven2/net/java/dev/jna/jna-platform/5.6.0/jna-platform-5.6.0-sources.jar, took 1 m 22 s 639 ms
Download https://repo.maven.apache.org/maven2/com/googlecode/juniversalchardet/juniversalchardet/1.0.3/juniversalchardet-1.0.3-sources.jar, took 17 s 74 ms
Download https://repo.maven.apache.org/maven2/javax/annotation/javax.annotation-api/1.3.2/javax.annotation-api-1.3.2-sources.jar, took 2 s 327 ms
Download https://repo.maven.apache.org/maven2/org/jetbrains/kotlin/kotlin-stdlib/2.1.0-Beta2/kotlin-stdlib-2.1.0-Beta2-sources.jar, took 34 s 629 ms
Download https://repo.maven.apache.org/maven2/org/jdom/jdom2/2.0.6/jdom2-2.0.6-sources.jar, took 56 s 34 ms
Download https://repo.maven.apache.org/maven2/org/ow2/asm/asm-tree/9.7/asm-tree-9.7-sources.jar, took 2 s 977 ms
Download https://repo.maven.apache.org/maven2/org/bouncycastle/bcutil-jdk18on/1.77/bcutil-jdk18on-1.77-sources.jar, took 31 s 435 ms
Download https://repo.maven.apache.org/maven2/org/jvnet/staxex/stax-ex/1.8.1/stax-ex-1.8.1-sources.jar, took 2 s 332 ms
Download https://repo.maven.apache.org/maven2/jakarta/xml/bind/jakarta.xml.bind-api/2.3.2/jakarta.xml.bind-api-2.3.2-sources.jar, took 8 s 396 ms
Download https://repo.maven.apache.org/maven2/org/glassfish/jaxb/txw2/2.3.2/txw2-2.3.2-sources.jar, took 4 s 798 ms
Download https://repo.maven.apache.org/maven2/com/sun/istack/istack-commons-runtime/3.0.8/istack-commons-runtime-3.0.8-sources.jar, took 1 s 446 ms
Download https://repo.maven.apache.org/maven2/com/sun/xml/fastinfoset/FastInfoset/1.2.16/FastInfoset-1.2.16-sources.jar, took 15 s 780 ms
Download https://repo.maven.apache.org/maven2/jakarta/activation/jakarta.activation-api/1.2.1/jakarta.activation-api-1.2.1-sources.jar, took 785 ms
Download https://repo.maven.apache.org/maven2/com/google/code/findbugs/jsr305/3.0.2/jsr305-3.0.2-sources.jar, took 3 s 730 ms
Download https://repo.maven.apache.org/maven2/com/google/j2objc/j2objc-annotations/2.8/j2objc-annotations-2.8-sources.jar, took 2 s 783 ms
Download https://repo.maven.apache.org/maven2/com/google/api/grpc/proto-google-common-protos/2.17.0/proto-google-common-protos-2.17.0-sources.jar, took 5 m 1 s 423 ms
Download https://repo.maven.apache.org/maven2/io/grpc/grpc-protobuf-lite/1.57.0/grpc-protobuf-lite-1.57.0-sources.jar, took 767 ms
Download https://repo.maven.apache.org/maven2/io/grpc/grpc-api/1.57.0/grpc-api-1.57.0-sources.jar, took 31 s 742 ms
Download https://repo.maven.apache.org/maven2/io/perfmark/perfmark-api/0.26.0/perfmark-api-0.26.0-sources.jar, took 742 ms
Download https://repo.maven.apache.org/maven2/io/netty/netty-codec-http2/4.1.93.Final/netty-codec-http2-4.1.93.Final-sources.jar, took 31 s 233 ms
Download https://repo.maven.apache.org/maven2/io/netty/netty-handler-proxy/4.1.93.Final/netty-handler-proxy-4.1.93.Final-sources.jar, took 2 s 366 ms
```

```
Download https://repo.maven.apache.org/maven2/io/netty/netty-transport-native-unix-
common/4.1.93.Final/netty-transport-native-unix-common-4.1.93.Final-sources.jar,
took 9 s 437 ms
Download
https://repo.maven.apache.org/maven2/com/google/android/annotations/4.1.1.4/annotati
ons-4.1.1.4-sources.jar, took 381 ms
Download https://repo.maven.apache.org/maven2/org/codehaus/mojo/animal-sniffer-
annotations/1.23/animal-sniffer-annotations-1.23-sources.jar, took 431 ms
Download https://repo.maven.apache.org/maven2/org/checkerframework/checker-
qual/3.33.0/checker-qual-3.33.0-sources.jar, took 21 s 269 ms
Download https://repo.maven.apache.org/maven2/org/jetbrains/kotlin/kotlin-native-
utils/2.0.0/kotlin-native-utils-2.0.0-sources.jar, took 8 s 433 ms
Download https://repo.maven.apache.org/maven2/org/jetbrains/kotlin/kotlin-gradle-
plugin-annotations/2.0.0/kotlin-gradle-plugin-annotations-2.0.0-sources.jar, took
404 ms
Download https://repo.maven.apache.org/maven2/org/jetbrains/kotlin/kotlin-tooling-
core/2.0.0/kotlin-tooling-core-2.0.0-sources.jar, took 1 s 130 ms
Download https://repo.maven.apache.org/maven2/org/jetbrains/kotlin/kotlin-daemon-
client/2.0.0/kotlin-daemon-client-2.0.0-sources.jar, took 5 s 346 ms
Download https://repo.maven.apache.org/maven2/org/jetbrains/kotlinx/kotlinx-
coroutines-core-jvm/1.5.0/kotlinx-coroutines-core-jvm-1.5.0-sources.jar, took 36 s
934 ms
Download https://repo.maven.apache.org/maven2/org/jetbrains/kotlin/kotlin-util-
io/2.0.0/kotlin-util-io-2.0.0-sources.jar, took 3 s 115 ms
Download https://repo.maven.apache.org/maven2/org/jetbrains/kotlin/kotlin-daemon-
embeddable/2.0.0/kotlin-daemon-embeddable-2.0.0-sources.jar, took 4 s 926 ms
Download
https://repo.maven.apache.org/maven2/org/jetbrains/intellij/deps/trove4j/1.0.2020033
0/trove4j-1.0.20200330-sources.jar, took 52 s 849 ms
Download
https://repo.maven.apache.org/maven2/com/google/guava/failureaccess/1.0.1/failureacc
ess-1.0.1-sources.jar, took 131 ms
Download https://repo.maven.apache.org/maven2/commons-logging/commons-
logging/1.2/commons-logging-1.2-sources.jar, took 16 s 875 ms
Download https://repo.maven.apache.org/maven2/net/java/dev/jna/jna/5.6.0/jna-5.6.0-
sources.jar, took 1 m 3 s 276 ms
Download https://repo.maven.apache.org/maven2/io/netty/netty-codec-
http/4.1.93.Final/netty-codec-http-4.1.93.Final-sources.jar, took 1 m 17 s 358 ms
Download https://repo.maven.apache.org/maven2/io/netty/netty-codec-
http/4.1.93.Final/netty-codec-http-4.1.93.Final-sources.jar, took 47 s 690 ms
Download https://repo.maven.apache.org/maven2/io/netty/netty-
handler/4.1.93.Final/netty-handler-4.1.93.Final-sources.jar, took 36 s 154 ms
Download https://repo.maven.apache.org/maven2/io/netty/netty-
codec/4.1.93.Final/netty-codec-4.1.93.Final-sources.jar, took 24 s 460 ms
Download https://repo.maven.apache.org/maven2/io/netty/netty-
transport/4.1.93.Final/netty-transport-4.1.93.Final-sources.jar, took 37 s 824 ms
Download https://repo.maven.apache.org/maven2/io/netty/netty-
buffer/4.1.93.Final/netty-buffer-4.1.93.Final-sources.jar, took 15 s 922 ms
Download https://repo.maven.apache.org/maven2/io/netty/netty-
common/4.1.93.Final/netty-common-4.1.93.Final-sources.jar, took 52 s 741 ms
Download https://repo.maven.apache.org/maven2/io/netty/netty-codec-
socks/4.1.93.Final/netty-codec-socks-4.1.93.Final-sources.jar, took 7 s 599 ms
Download https://repo.maven.apache.org/maven2/io/netty/netty-
```

```
resolver/4.1.93.Final/netty-resolver-4.1.93.Final-sources.jar, took 5 s 140 ms

Deprecated Gradle features were used in this build, making it incompatible with Gradle 9.0.

You can use '--warning-mode all' to show the individual deprecation warnings and determine if they come from your own scripts or plugins. For more on this, please refer to https://docs.gradle.org/8.10.2/userguide/command_line_interface.html#sec:command_line_warnings in the Gradle documentation. BUILD SUCCESSFUL in 2h 54m 11s
```

48 git

Android Studio is the editor for write and build apk, there are a lot of complains about gradle, maven, the downloading tortures people a lot. if you old enough, you probably miss Eclipse, another editor not only for apk. So Python has itself an editor, Pycharm, and it can use `jni` to connect java to Python.

These editors can set up account with git hub, lab, tee, etc, so people can direct clone and update. A good thing to use editor is all the command can be finished with form and submit button.

Add: new files

Branches: change head

Tag: give tag, make hash simpler

Pull: update local codes from remote

Push: update remote codes from local

Rebase: go back a rivision

Show Current Revision: show current rivision

Stash: save the uncommit codes

Can you imagine git is developed in only two weeks, and this is why Linus Torvalds is so admirable, even in non Linux world...

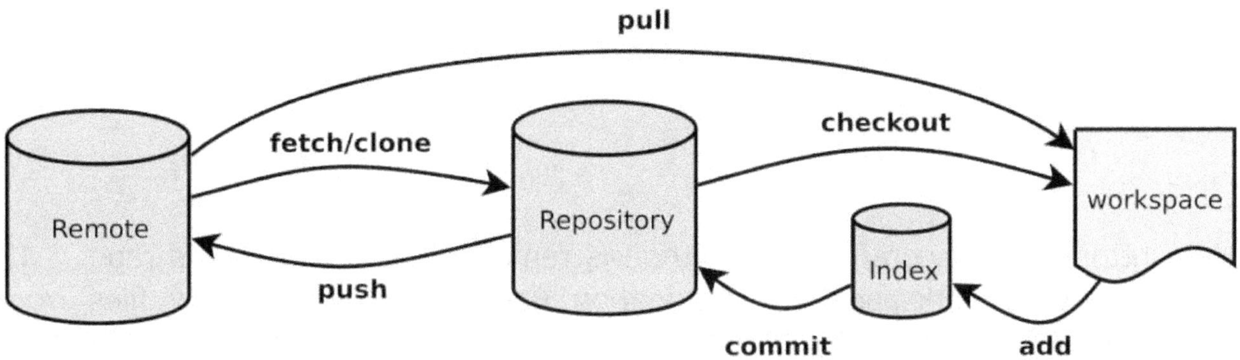

and Python itself is on Github, recall the VB xubuntu, we can install git and build any version we want, make sure the virtual disksize is big enough…

```
cd /home/vboxuser

sudo apt install git

git clone https://github.com/python/cpython

cd cpython

git checkout 3.12

sudo apt install gcc

sudo apt install make

sudo apt install openssl

sudo apt install libssl-dev

sudo apt install libffi-dev

sudo apt install zlib1g-dev

sudo apt install build-essential

sudo apt install gcc g++ libffi-dev build-essential checkinstall

sudo apt install libreadline-gplv2-dev libncursesw5-dev libssl-dev libsqlite3-dev tk-dev libgdbm-dev libc6-dev libbz2-dev

./configure --with-pydebug --enable-shared --prefix=/home/vboxuser/python3.12 && make -j2

make install

export PATH=/home/vboxuser/python3.12/bin:$PATH

ln -s python3.12 python
```

```
wget https://bootstrap.pypa.io/get-pip.py

python get-pip.py

ln -s pip3 pip
```

Here https://github.com/python/cpython is remote, `/home/vboxuser` is repo, 3.12 is checkout to workspace, in fact Python updates is by add new files from workspace, and commit into repo, and push to remote, this way all the developers make Python a powerful tool, in just 10 years...

The most frequent commands used only two, (new-feature can be 3.12 for Python)

```
git pull origin new-feature

git push origin new-feature
```

After the push, go to the website to open PR, a ticket to let the team (3.12 for Python) to merge into main, and update repo,

```
git checkout main
git pull origin main
git merge new-feature
```

or delete the local,

```
git branch -d new-feature
```

again, we can also open PR to delete in remote,

```
git push origin --delete new-feature
```

sometimes `push` may fail, due to proxy, so close it,

```
git config --global http.proxy http://127.0.0.1:1080
git config --global https.proxy https://127.0.0.1:1080
```

or due to ssl,

```
git config --global http.sslVerify false
```

or due to buffer size,

```
git config --global http.postBuffer 524288000
```

and for some very large projects,

```
git clone https://github.com/large_repository.git --depth 1
cd large_repository
git fetch --unshallow
```

What is the largest project on Github?

Windows. Approximately 3.5 million files that results in about 300 GB with 4000 engineers producing 1760 daily "lab builds" across 440 branches, plus thousands of PR validation builds. Imagine the engineers, US, Europe, ME, India, China, etc, all over pulling large amounts of data across long distances, bandwidth is a big problem, so Microsoft even creates GVFS to cache git at the edge…

Let's create our small project, Hello Git, on Github, and clone,

```
git clone https://github.com/LinconFive/learn-c.git
```

it is good to add project time lines, into README.md,

learn-c

Getting started

Just edit this README.md and make it your own. ## Add your files - [x] Create - [x] Add files using the command line or push an existing Git repository with the following command:

```
git clone ----to---- local repo
cd local_repo
git add .
git commit -m "add"
git push
----PR----
```

Roadmap

See below

```
sequenceDiagram
    remote->>+repo: pull
    repo->>+remote: push
    remote-->>-repo: PR confirm, so pull again
    repo-->>-remote: will add another new feature
```

License

MIT ## Project status Under development

git log keeps track of the repo, local and remote, they should be in clean updates.

Python even has a git package to make things cleaner, checkout https://gitpython.readthedocs.io/en/stable/tutorial.html#tutorial-label,

```
from git.repo import Repo
import os
download_path = os.path.join('test','build_git')
Repo.clone_from('https://github.com/LinconFive/learn-c.git
', to_path=download_path, branch='main')
```

the two important branches are origin and main, corresponding to the default branch in local and remote, we can also write the functions,

```
import os
from git.repo import Repo
from git.repo.fun import is_git_dir

class GitRepository(object):
    """
    git managment
    """

    def __init__(self, local_path, repo_url, branch='main'): #some uses master
        self.local_path = local_path
        self.repo_url = repo_url
        self.repo = None
        self.initial(repo_url, branch)

    def initial(self, repo_url, branch):
        """
        init local
        :param repo_url:
        :param branch:
        :return:
        """
        if not os.path.exists(self.local_path):
            os.makedirs(self.local_path)

        git_local_path = os.path.join(self.local_path, '.git')
        if not is_git_dir(git_local_path):
                    self.repo = Repo.clone_from(repo_url, to_path=self.local_path,
branch=branch)
        else:
            self.repo = Repo(self.local_path)
```

```
    def pull(self):
        """
        get update
        :return:
        """
        self.repo.git.pull()

    def branches(self):
        """
        get branch
        :return:
        """
        branches = self.repo.remote().refs
          return [item.remote_head for item in branches if item.remote_head not in
['HEAD', ]]

    def commits(self):
        """
        get commit
        :return:
        """
                                        commit_log    =    self.repo.git.log('--pretty=
{"commit":"%h","author":"%an","summary":"%s","date":"%cd"}',
                                        max_count=50,
                                        date='format:%Y-%m-%d %H:%M')
        log_list = commit_log.split("\n")
        return [eval(item) for item in log_list]

    def tags(self):
        """
        tag
        :return:
        """
        return [tag.name for tag in self.repo.tags]

    def change_to_branch(self, branch):
        """
        branch
        :param branch:
        :return:
        """
        self.repo.git.checkout(branch)

    def change_to_commit(self, branch, commit):
        """
        commit
        :param branch:
        :param commit:
        :return:
        """
        self.change_to_branch(branch=branch)
        self.repo.git.reset('--hard', commit)
```

```
    def change_to_tag(self, tag):
        """
        switch tag
        :param tag:
        :return:
        """
        self.repo.git.checkout(tag)

if __name__ == '__main__':
    local_path = os.path.join('codes', 'build_git')
    repo = GitRepository(local_path,remote_path)
    branch_list = repo.branches()
    print(branch_list)
    repo.change_to_branch('dev')
    repo.pull()
```

all the functions are based on the git commands, and becareful with the branch, and the status,

Command	**Use**
`git checkout SHA`	Checks out a past commit with the given SHA
`git checkout SHA -- file_name`	Checks out the past version of a file from the commit with the given SHA
`git checkout -b branch_name`	Creates and switches to a new branch
`git checkout branch_name`	Switches to the specified branch
`git merge branch_name`	Merges the branch you are on into the specified branch
`git log`	Outputs a log of past commits with their commit messages
`git status`	Outputs status, including what branch you are on and what changes are staged
`git diff`	Outputs the differences between the working directory and most recent commit
`git diff status_a status_b`	Outputs the differences between commits or branches

The common format for git log is in weekdays and labeled by timezone,

```
C:\Users\Lenovo>git log | find "Date"
Date:   Mon Nov 15 13:08:28 2024 -0500
```

If we don’t want the date,

```
C:\Users\Lenovo>git log --oneline
3af400c (HEAD -> main, origin/main, origin/HEAD) Create README.md
```

and we can get the server name,

```
C:\Users\Lenovo>git log --pretty=format:"%cn committed %h on %cd"
GitHub committed 3af400c on Mon Nov 25 17:08:28 2024 +0800
```

more `%` symbols,

Symbol	Detail
%C	colors the output that comes after it
%h	denotes the first some letters of the commit ID
%H	denotes the complete commit id
%Creset	resets color to the default terminal color
%d	ref names or simple names
%s	denotes the commit message
%cr	committer date
%an	author-name

and select date,

```
git log --after="2024 7 1"
git log --before="Dec 1 2024"
git log --after="2014-7-1" --before="2014-7-4"
```

and grep,

```
git log --grep="Create"
```

Why is grep important? Let's try **FSP**, it can be checked out online, https://www.fullstackpython.com/, too

```
C:\Users\Lenovo>git clone https://github.com/mattmakai/fullstackpython.com.git
Cloning into 'fullstackpython.com'...
remote: Enumerating objects: 53610, done.
remote: Counting objects: 100% (648/648), done.
remote: Compressing objects: 100% (371/371), done.
remote: Total 53610 (delta 331), reused 590 (delta 276), pack-reused 52962 (from 1)
Receiving objects: 100% (53610/53610), 127.73 MiB | 1.96 MiB/s, done.
Resolving deltas: 100% (38913/38913), done.
Updating files: 100% (2036/2036), done.
```

How many commits?

```
C:\Users\Lenovo>git rev-list --count HEAD
3462
```

That is huge, so we better to make commits message ordered, just for easy grep, likewise, add, modify, delete, etc.

We can also see the branch in a graph mode,

```
C:\Users\Lenovo>git log --graph --oneline --decorate

...
* 34635fdf update changelog
*   309ff7fa Merge pull request #233 from dbader/patch-1
|\
| * 948f1886 Add Real Python Podcast to podcast list
* |   08dd0f61 Merge pull request #235 from mjhea0/patch-7
|\ \
| * | e1832460 add django + celery resource
| |/
* | 3fb7c657 update changelog
* | 5beb25be add web design resource
* | d6dd78da clean up nginx page
|/
* 228c3e56 update changelog
* 6aa67a52 add new tutorial on exporting pandas to sqlite databases
* 7e2b1560 quick word tweak
* ae96cb3c update meta page
...
```

and we can see the branch, in two types,

```
git branch --merged
git branch --no-merged
```

So the star means main, and it locates most left, others usually will be merged to main. We can delete the branch by `git branch -d <branch_name>`

Sometimes we ruined the repo, just do `git reset --hard` to the original clone, or `git reset <SHA>` to the commit,

What are the most essential commits?

```
C:\Users\Lenovo>git log --oneline --decorate --source --pretty=format:'"%Cblue %h %Cgreen %ar %Cblue %an %C(yellow) %d %Creset %s"' --all --graph
*   '   1a2513d3   1   year,   6   months   ago   dependabot[bot] (origin/dependabot/pip/requests-2.31.0)  Bump requests from 2.22.0 to 2.31.0'
* ' daa9782d  1 year, 7 months ago  Matt Makai   (HEAD -> master, origin/master, origin/HEAD)  removing malicious link'
* ' 7e61b2fb  2 years, 1 month ago  Matt Makai    removing old 404 links'
* ' 18c5871c  2 years, 1 month ago  Matt Makai    removing GA, no more analytics
```

```
needed. reducing page sizes'
*    ' 9f891cde  2 years, 9 months ago  Matt Makai    Merge pull request #271 from
mw-orcl/master'
|\
| * ' 440d7164  2 years, 10 months ago  mw-orcl    Created Oracle content'
* | ' df0c15ca  2 years, 9 months ago  Matt Makai    tweaking site layout to make it
faster'
|/
* ' 8bc5b242  3 years, 2 months ago  Matt Makai    remove plausible for now'
* ' 145033d8  3 years, 2 months ago  Matt Makai    remove walled garden learning
programming resource'
* ' 82c8ed4d  3 years, 2 months ago  Matt Makai    update heroku resources'
* ' 3fdd4290  3 years, 2 months ago  Matt Makai    fixing link rot'
* ' 91610ce7  3 years, 2 months ago  Matt Makai    removing link rot'
* ' 5215c1cd  3 years, 3 months ago  Matt Makai    removing link rot'
* ' 9f3631c2  3 years, 3 months ago  Matt Makai    trying plausible analytics'
* ' 9812ac71  3 years, 3 months ago  Matt Makai    fix broken postgres link'
* ' bd441b87  3 years, 3 months ago  Matt Makai    fixing more linkrot'
* ' 49f5aa93  3 years, 3 months ago  Matt Makai    cleaning up broken or redirected
links'
* ' e3d672e0  3 years, 3 months ago  Matt Makai    fixing typo and some additional
broken links'
* ' 85e98bca  3 years, 3 months ago  Matt Makai    new blog post and update
changelog'
* ' 7851a3f0  3 years, 5 months ago  Matt Makai    fixing typos'
* ' 29fe5f2c  3 years, 5 months ago  Matt Makai    cleaning up more broken links'
* ' 1136a5a8  3 years, 5 months ago  Matt Makai    removing dead links'
* ' 2c35cfbe  3 years, 5 months ago  Matt Makai    remove broken performance link'
* ' b03fccce  3 years, 5 months ago  Matt Makai    removing additional broken links'
* ' 1eede9a4  3 years, 5 months ago  Matt Makai    fixing more links'
* ' 2617df40  3 years, 5 months ago  Matt Makai    fixing more typos'
```

49 SHA

From `git log --pretty={"commit":"%h","author":"%an","summary":"%s","date":"%cd"}`, we can see the commit in hex, 3af400c, what is this?

It is SHA-1, which crypts a 40 character string of hexadecimal characters (0-9 and a-f), `len('3af400ccf4da6a20f798db5015326f0b1c594851')`, and 40 chars means 160 bits, checkout http://www.sha1-online.com/, hi equals c22b5f9178342609428d6f51b2c5af4c0bde6a42, notice hi is not Hi,

```
import hashlib

message = "hi" # Hi
hash_object = hashlib.sha512(message.encode())
hash_value = hash_object.hexdigest()
print(hash_value)
```

```
hash_object = hashlib.sha256(message.encode())
hash_value = hash_object.hexdigest()
print(hash_value)

hash_object = hashlib.sha1(message.encode())
hash_value = hash_object.hexdigest()
print(hash_value)


# output for hi
150a14ed5bea6cc731cf86c41566ac427a8db48ef1b9fd626664b3bfbb99071fa4c922f33dde38719b8c
8354e2b7ab9d77e0e67fc12843920a712e73d558e197
8f434346648f6b96df89dda901c5176b10a6d83961dd3c1ac88b59b2dc327aa4
c22b5f9178342609428d6f51b2c5af4c0bde6a42

# output for Hi
45ca55ccaa72b98b86c697fdf73fd364d4815a586f76cd326f1785bb816ff7f1f88b46fb8448b19356ee
788eb7d300b9392709a289428070b5810d9b5c2d440d
3639efcd08abb273b1619e82e78c29a7df02c1051b1820e99fc395dcaa3326b8
94dd9e08c129c785f7f256e82fbe0a30e6d1ae40
```

This is how passwords work,

```
import hashlib

hash_value = "fce1b2d3a26d6c759f4dd5c67fe1443a8b1fa79a890c8db57e4c07508b4d3f6e"

password = "password123"
password_hash = hashlib.sha256(password.encode()).hexdigest()

if password_hash == hash_value:
    print("Password matches!")
else:
    print("Password does not match!")
```

And in reality the limit is usually three,

```
attemps = 0

import hashlib

while attemps < 3:
    username = input('Enter your username: ')
    password_hash = input('Enter your password: ')
    password = "password123"
                  if     username     ==     'user123'     and     password_hash     ==
hashlib.sha256(password.encode()).hexdigest():
        print('You have successfully logged in.')
        break
    else:
           print('Incorrect  credentials.  Check  if  you  have  Caps  lock  on  and  try
```

```
again.') # go to other function
        attemps += 1
        continue
```

is it possible to have two different passwords but same hash?

Hash collision.

Passwords usually are assigned to different UserIDs, say B for Bob, to be signed by the Web of Trust, A for Alice. SHA for these two IDs are also called signatures, and now we see the collision is a big disaster.

That is why crypto is essetial, and especially dollars, https://accounts.binance.com/en/register.

Yes! Money needs crypto, that is why BTC is so expensive, billionares need it!

The most famous BTC App is **Binance**, it has a total assets $130,014,465,600.19, in only 8 years...

CZ, a very smart guy, was born in Lianyungang, China, in 1977, checkout https://coinmarketcap.com/exchanges/binance/.

It is not all allowed to register though, checkout https://accounts.binance.com/en/login,

but if registered, that means KYC and bank is approved, then we can apply for binance API key https://www.binance.com/en/my/settings/api-management, it will be a SHA256 key, and use Python to do trade, `pip install python-binance`

this API will be used to connect to Biance server,

```
import os
from binance.client import Client

api_key = os.environ.get('binance_api')
api_secret = os.environ.get('binance_secret')

print(api_key, api_secret)
```

If you can't see anything, that is because there is no such enviroment variable,

so for Windows, open a prompt,

```
set binance_api=your_api_key_here
set binance_secret=your_api_secret_here
```

for Ubuntu, open a terminal,

```
export binance_api="your_api_key_here"
export binance_secret="your_api_secret_here"
```

and in the same command screen, rerun the Python,

```
import os
from binance.client import Client

api_key = os.environ.get('binance_api')
api_secret = os.environ.get('binance_secret')

print(api_key, api_secret)

client = Client(api_key, api_secret)
print(client.get_account())

# see only BTC
print(client.get_asset_balance(asset='BTC'))
```

we can see many rate,

```
# get latest price BTC/USDT
btc_price = client.get_symbol_ticker(symbol="BTCUSDT")
# print full output (dictionary)
print(btc_price) #{'symbol': 'BTCUSDT', 'price': '9678.08000000'}
# print just price
print(btc_price["price"])
```

we can see the k line too,

```
# valid intervals - 1m, 3m, 5m, 15m, 30m, 1h, 2h, 4h, 6h, 8h, 12h, 1d, 3d, 1w, 1M

# get timestamp of earliest date data is available
timestamp = client._get_earliest_valid_timestamp('BTCUSDT', '1d')
print(timestamp)

# request historical candle (or klines) data
bars = client.get_historical_klines('BTCUSDT', '1d', timestamp, limit=1000)
```

and save in many format, or save in pandas,

```
# save in json
with open('btc_bars.json', 'w') as e:
    json.dump(bars, e)

# save in csv
with open('btc_bars.csv', 'w') as d:
    for line in bars:
        d.write(f'{line[0]}, {line[1]}, {line[2]}, {line[3]}, {line[4]}\n')
```

```
# save in pandas
import pandas as pd
btc_df = pd.DataFrame(bars, columns=['date', 'open', 'high', 'low', 'close'])
btc_df.set_index('date', inplace=True)
print(btc_df.head())

# from pandas to csv
btc_df.to_csv('btc_bars.csv')
```

there is also a `btalib` to measure BTC,

```
import pandas as pd

# load DataFrame
btc_df = pd.read_csv('btc_bars.csv', index_col=0)
btc_df.set_index('date', inplace=True)
btc_df.index = pd.to_datetime(btc_df.index, unit='ms')

# calculate 20 moving average using Pandas
btc_df['20sma'] = btc_df.close.rolling(20).mean()
print(btc_df.tail(5))

# or
import btalib
btc_df['sma'] = btalib.sma(btc_df.close, period=20).df
print(btc_df.tail())

# and others
macd = btalib.macd(btc_df, pfast=20, pslow=50, psignal=13)
rsi = btalib.rsi(btc_df, period=14)
```

another big crypto is ETH, there might be a relation between the two, if BTC increaces more than 1% we buy ETH, if BTC decreases more than 1%, we sell ETH.

```
import os
from time import sleep

import pandas as pd
from binance import ThreadedWebsocketManager
from binance.client import Client

# init
api_key = os.environ.get('binance_api')
api_secret = os.environ.get('binance_secret')
client = Client(api_key, api_secret)
price = {'BTCUSDT': pd.DataFrame(columns=['date', 'price']), 'error': False}

# a function to give the buy sell connection status
def btc_pairs_trade(msg):
    if msg['e'] != 'error':
```

```
                price['BTCUSDT'].loc[len(price['BTCUSDT'])]  =  [pd.Timestamp.now(),
float(msg['c'])]
    else:
        price['error'] = True

# init and start the buy sell WebSocket
bsm = ThreadedWebsocketManager()
bsm.start()
bsm.start_symbol_ticker_socket(symbol='BTCUSDT', callback=btc_pairs_trade)

## main
while len(price['BTCUSDT']) == 0:
    # wait for WebSocket to start streaming data
    sleep(0.1)

sleep(300)

while True:
    # error check to make sure WebSocket is working
    if price['error']:
        # stop and restart socket
        bsm.stop()
        sleep(2)
        bsm.start()
        price['error'] = False
    else:
        df = price['BTCUSDT']
        start_time = df.date.iloc[-1] - pd.Timedelta(minutes=5)
        df = df.loc[df.date >= start_time]
        max_price = df.price.max()
        min_price = df.price.min()
        if df.price.iloc[-1] < max_price * 0.99:
            try:
                  order = client.futures_create_order(symbol='ETHUSDT', side='SELL',
type='MARKET', quantity=100)
                break
            except Exception as e:
                print(e)

        elif df.price.iloc[-1] > min_price * 1.01:
            try:
                  order = client.futures_create_order(symbol='ETHUSDT', side='BUY',
type='MARKET', quantity=100)
                break
            except Exception as e:
                print(e)

    sleep(0.1)

# terminate WebSocket at the end
bsm.stop()
```

50 efinance

It is easy to write codes, but it is hard to predict the price, BTC, in just 10 years, the value jumps to $100,000. The companies help to exchange crypto become rich, and the companies hold crypto become rich too.

When we see the TV, there always are wheather channels, which relates to safe, means don't go out when heavy rain or wind.

```
import efinance as ef
stock_code='COIN'
Y='2024'
M='06'
D='25'
begin = f'{Y}{M}{D}'
Y='2024'
M='10'
D='25'
end = f'{Y}{M}{D}'
#st = st + ' 21:30:00' # or ' 9:30'
#et = et + ' 04:00:00' # or ' 16:00'
print(stock_code, ":", begin, "->", end)
k_dataframe = ef.stock.get_quote_history(stock_code, beg=begin, end=end, klt=101)
k_dataframe = k_dataframe.iloc[:, :9]
k_dataframe.columns = ['name', 'code', 'date', 'open', 'close', 'high', 'low',
'volume', 'amount']

k_dataframe.index = k_dataframe['date']
k_dataframe.drop(['name', 'code', 'date'], axis=1, inplace=True)
print(k_dataframe)
```

Notice that efinance can only show the recent day minutes data, which is 390 rows,

```
k_dataframe = ef.stock.get_quote_history(name, end="20241201", klt=1)
k_dataframe = k_dataframe.iloc[:, :9]
k_dataframe.columns = ['name', 'code', 'date', 'open', 'close', 'high', 'low',
'volume', 'amount']
print(k_dataframe)
```

Again, free API is not good enough to predict a futher price, in a small time dimension, minute, second, even tick. A big time dimension, week, month, year, usually reflects most people's atitude to the price.

From week to predict day, this will give from the IPO date,

```
k_dataframe = ef.stock.get_quote_history(name, klt=102)
k_dataframe = k_dataframe.iloc[:, 1:9]
k_dataframe.columns = [code', 'date', 'open', 'close', 'high', 'low', 'volume',
```

```
'amount']
print(k_dataframe)
```

from day to predict minute,

```
k_dataframe = ef.stock.get_quote_history(name, klt=101)
k_dataframe = k_dataframe.iloc[:, 1:9]
k_dataframe.columns = ['code', 'date', 'open', 'close', 'high', 'low', 'volume',
'amount']
print(k_dataframe)
```

check minute for now, see if the prediction is correct,

```
new_dataframe = ef.stock.get_latest_quote(name)
new_dataframe = new_dataframe.iloc[:, [0, 18, 3, 7]]
new_dataframe.columns = ['code', 'date', 'price', 'percent']
print(new_dataframe)
```

and we can get different days, 5, 10, 20, 30, by choose the date

```
from datetime import datetime, timedelta

st = '20241111'

et = '20241122'

date1 = datetime.strptime(st, "%Y%m%d")

date2 = datetime.strptime(et, "%Y%m%d")

delta = date2 - date1

number_of_days = delta.days

name = 'AAPL'; cost = 200

import efinance as ef

df = ef.stock.get_quote_history(name, st, et, klt=101)

df = df.iloc[:, 1:9]

df.columns = ['code', 'date', 'open', 'close', 'high', 'low', 'volume', 'amount']

print (df)
```

we can even get the avg,

```
print("5days close avg is", df['close'].mean())
print("5days vwap avg is", (df['amount']/df['volume']).mean())
```

and compare to current days minutes, we can decide our trade price,

```
name = 'AAPL'; cost = 200

import efinance as ef

tddata = ef.stock.get_quote_history(name, klt=1)

tddata = tddata.iloc[:, 1:9]

tddata.columns = ['code', 'date', 'open', 'close', 'high', 'low', 'volume',
'amount']

print (tddata)

print("today close avg is", tddata['close'].mean())

print("today vwap is", (tddata['amount']/tddata['volume']).mean())
```

to decide the time, we need to get the volume over change,

```
name = 'AAPL'; cost = 200

import efinance as ef

tddata = ef.stock.get_quote_history(name, klt=1)

tddata = tddata.iloc[:, [1, 2, 3, 4, 5, 6, 7, 8, -2]]

tddata.columns = ['code', 'date', 'open', 'close', 'high', 'low', 'volume',
'amount', 'change']

print (tddata)

#print("volume over change is", (tddata['volume']/tddata['change']))

import matplotlib.pyplot as plt

plt.plot(tddata['volume']/tddata['change'], label='volume over change')

plt.title(name)

#plt.gcf().autofmt_xdate()

plt.xlabel('Time')

plt.ylabel('Price')

plt.legend()

plt.show()
```

for the negtive number, that means more selling than buying, but how much more?

Again this is out of free API offer, but we now have a sense of prediction, by power of selling or buying, which corresponds to call or put. The name probably from poker room, call means end the game, put means continue the game, well, by put more money...

so to trade safe, don't put too much money, or trade after getting the company pe, the pe multiplies eps equals to price,

```
name = 'AAPL'; cost = 200

import efinance as ef

tddata = ef.stock.get_latest_quote(name)

tddata = tddata.iloc[:, [0, 10, 14]]

tddata.columns = ['code', 'pe', 'value']

print (tddata)
```

so if cost 200 is less than the price, we can do put, and until a very high price to sell, but how high?

51 Gann

William Delbert Gann was born on June 6 1878, in Lufkin, Texas. His parents, Sam H. and Susan R. were immigrants from British Isles. Both parents are very religious, so Gann read Bible at a very early age. And from Bible, Gann found out time cycle. At high school Gann change the habit, that let people call him W. D, that is the short form of his un given name.

During his high school time, W. D worked in the cotton warehouses in Lufkin and Texarkana, and in the cotton warehouse, he was introduced to commodity trading. In 1902, W. D made his first commodity trade in cotton, that year he was 24. In 1906, W. D. went to Oklahoma City, worked as a broker for a brokerage firm. Since then, over the next 53 years, W. D earned over $50,000,000 from the markets. Approximately 1/3 of the money was for himself and the other 2/3 was for the accounts he supervised from other people. And W. D made record, and the record showed that over 90% of traders who enter the markets without knowledge and study usually lose in the end.

W.D wrote a lot on trades, below are the famous ones,

Speculation of a Profitable Profession The Truth of the Stock Tape The Tunnel Thru the Air Wall Street Stock Selector Stock Trend Detector Scientific Stock Forecasting How to Make Profits Trading in Puts and Calls Face Facts America. Looking Ahead to 1950 How to Make Profits Trading in Commodities The Magic Word How to Make Profits Trading in Commodities 45 years on Wall Street

Let's quote a paragraph from 45 years on Wall Street,

"Every man takes out of life just exactly according to what he puts in. We reap just what we sow. A man who pays with time and money for knowledge and continues to study and never gets to the point where he thinks he knows all there is to know, but realizes that he can still learn, is the man who will make a success in speculation or in investments. I am trying to tell you the truth and give you the benefit of over 45 years of operating in stocks and commodity markets and point out to you the weak points that will prevent you from meeting with disaster. Speculation can be made a profitable profession. Wall Street can be beaten and there is money operating in commodities and the stock market if you follow the rules and always realize that the unexpected can happen and be prepared for it."

and a sample of Gann Chart,

![[Gann.jpg]]

If you can understand, you probably will be a billionare soon, compare to Gann's Legend,

- 1908 – a $130 account increased to $12,000 in 30 days.
- 1923 – a $973 account increased to $30,000 in 60 days.
- 1933 – 479 trades were made with 422 being profitable, accuracy of 88% and 4000% profit.
- 1946 – A 3-month net profit of $13,000 from starting capital of $4500 ~ 400% profit.

See the huge profit, it is huge success. Is it possible? See the angles,

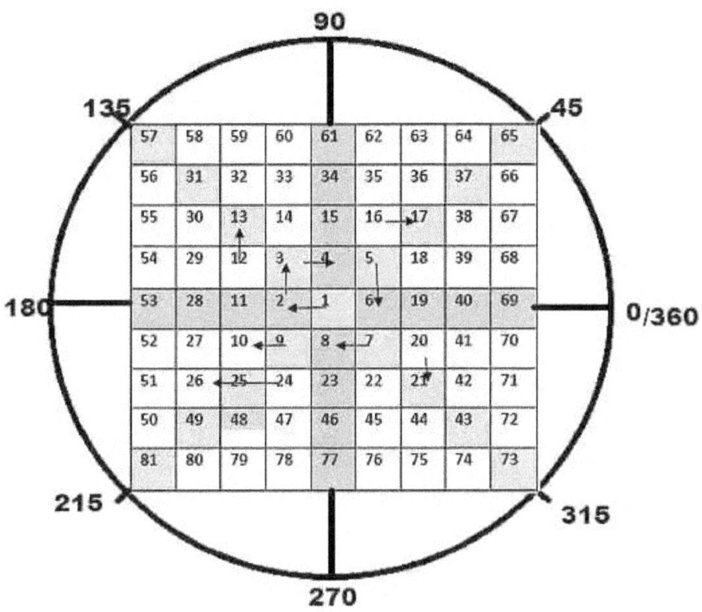

so the price may change as angles turning, and we can calculate the possible support and resistance.

```
import math

def calculate_gann_values(num):
    y = num

    def checker(x, z):
        if x < y < z:
            return y
        else:
            return ""

    if num:
        root = num ** 0.5
        minus_two = root - 2
        rounded = math.ceil(minus_two)
        result = rounded ** 2

        x = []
        sqr_x = []
        sqr_x_rounded = []
        sqr_x_rounded_root = []

        for i in range(24):
            x.append(rounded + 0.125 * (i + 1))
            sqr_x.append(x[i] * x[i])
            sqr_x_rounded.append(round(sqr_x[i] * 100) / 100)
            sqr_x_rounded_root.append(round((num - sqr_x_rounded[i]) * 100) / 100)

        min_positive_index = -1
```

```
        for i in range(len(sqr_x_rounded_root)):
            if sqr_x_rounded_root[i] < 0:
                min_positive_index = i
                break

        support = []
        resistance = []
        buy_target = []
        sell_target = []

        def roundup(number, places):
            factor = 10 ** places
            return round(number * factor) / factor

        if min_positive_index >= 0:
            buy_above = sqr_x_rounded[min_positive_index]
            sell_below = sqr_x_rounded[min_positive_index - 1]

            for i in range(5):
                support.append(sqr_x_rounded[min_positive_index - 2 - i])
                resistance.append(sqr_x_rounded[min_positive_index + 1 + i])
                buy_target.append(roundup(resistance[i] * 0.9995, 2))
                sell_target.append(roundup(support[i] * 1.0005, 2))
        else:
            buy_above = ""
            sell_below = ""
            support = [""] * 5
            resistance = [""] * 5
            buy_target = [""] * 5
            sell_target = [""] * 5

        return {
            "buy_above": buy_above,
            "sell_below": sell_below,
            "buy_target": buy_target,
            "sell_target": sell_target
        }
    else:
        return {
            "buy_above": "",
            "sell_below": "",
            "buy_target": [""] * 5,
            "sell_target": [""] * 5
        }


# Pirce now
number_input = 200

# Calculate Gann values
result = calculate_gann_values(number_input)
#print(result)
```

```
# More detailed...
buy_above=result["buy_above"]
buy_target=result["buy_target"][0]
buy_sl=result["sell_below"]

sell_below=result["sell_below"]
sell_target=result["sell_target"][0]
sell_sl=result["buy_above"]

print("Buy Above:", buy_above)
print("Buy Target:", buy_target)
print("Buy Stop Loss:", buy_sl)
print("Sell Below:", sell_below)
print("Sell Target:", sell_target)
print("Sell Stop Loss:", sell_sl)
```

the buy target is how high the price can reach in a certain time, and the sell target is how low the price can reach,

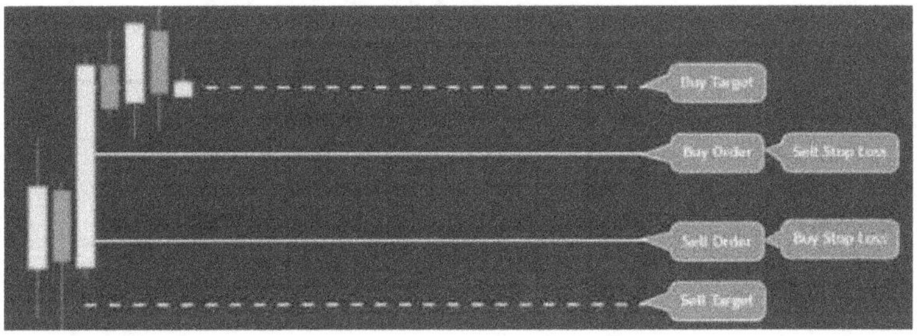

52 MP3

Trade can be very energy consuming, thus one really need relax, after a long long work...

Maybe use `pygame` to listen a song?

```
import pygame

def play_audio(file_path):
    pygame.init()
    pygame.mixer.init()
    pygame.mixer.music.load(file_path)
    pygame.mixer.music.play()

    while pygame.mixer.music.get_busy():
        pygame.time.Clock().tick(10)

audio_file = "relax.mp3"
play_audio(audio_file)
```

Or use `tkinter` to make a player, so we can select the song,

```
from tkinter import *
from tkinter import filedialog
from pygame import mixer

class MusicPlayer:
    def __init__(self, window ):
                        window.geometry('320x100');   window.title('Relax   Player');
window.resizable(0,0)
          Load = Button(window, text = 'Load',  width = 10, font = ('Times', 10),
command = self.load)
          Play = Button(window, text = 'Play',  width = 10,font = ('Times', 10),
command = self.play)
          Pause = Button(window,text = 'Pause',  width = 10, font = ('Times', 10),
command = self.pause)
          Stop = Button(window ,text = 'Stop',  width = 10, font = ('Times', 10),
command = self.stop)

Load.place(x=0,y=20);Play.place(x=110,y=20);Pause.place(x=220,y=20);Stop.place(x=110
,y=60)
        self.music_file = False
        self.playing_state = False
    def load(self):
        self.music_file = filedialog.askopenfilename()
    def play(self):
        if self.music_file:
            mixer.init()
            mixer.music.load(self.music_file)
            mixer.music.play()
    def pause(self):
        if not self.playing_state:
            mixer.music.pause()
            self.playing_state=True
        else:
            mixer.music.unpause()
            self.playing_state = False
    def stop(self):
        mixer.music.stop()
root = Tk()
app= MusicPlayer(root)
root.mainloop()
```

How to write a song?

```
from array import array
import pygame as pg

class Tone(pg.mixer.Sound):
    """This generates a 'Square wave' with a generator. Then paly with pg.Sound.
    """
```

```
def __init__(self, frequency, array_type, volume=.1):
    self.frequency = frequency
    if array_type == 'b':
        # we have to convert the 1 byte 'b' samples to 2 byte 'h'.
        samples = self.signed_char_to_signed_short(
            self.make_samples_b()
        )
    elif array_type == 'h':
        samples = self.make_samples_h()
    else:
        raise ValueError('array_type not supported')

    pg.mixer.Sound.__init__(self, buffer=samples)
    self.set_volume(volume)

def make_samples_b(self):
    """ Builds samples array between -127 and 127. Array type 'h'.
    """
    mixer_frequency = pg.mixer.get_init()[0]
    mixer_format = pg.mixer.get_init()[1]
    period = int(round(mixer_frequency / self.frequency))
    max_amplitude = 2 ** (abs(mixer_format) - 1) - 1
    max_amplitude = int(max_amplitude / 256)
    # print(f'mixer_frequency:{mixer_frequency}, mixer_format:{mixer_format}')
    # print(f'period:{period}, max_amplitude:{max_amplitude}')

    # 'b' array is signed char, 1 byte
    # https://docs.python.org/3/library/array.html
    samples = array('b',
        (max_amplitude if time < period / 2 else -max_amplitude
            for time in range(period))
    )
    return samples

def signed_char_to_signed_short(self, b_samples):
    """ Converts 1 byte signed char samples to 2 byte signed short.
        127 -> 32767
    """
    # just a simple linear conversion.
    factor = int(32767 / 127)
    return array('h', (sample * factor for sample in b_samples))

def make_samples_h(self):
    """ Builds samples array between -32767 snd 32767. Array type 'h'.
    """
    mixer_frequency = pg.mixer.get_init()[0]
    mixer_format = pg.mixer.get_init()[1]
    period = int(round(mixer_frequency / self.frequency))
    max_amplitude = 2 ** (abs(mixer_format) - 1) - 1
    # print(f'mixer_frequency:{mixer_frequency}, mixer_format:{mixer_format}')
    # print(f'period:{period}, max_amplitude:{max_amplitude}')

    # 'h' array is signed short, 2 bytes
```

```
        # https://docs.python.org/3/library/array.html
        samples = array('h',
            (max_amplitude if time < period / 2 else -max_amplitude
                for time in range(period))
        )
        return samples


class Sample(pg.mixer.Sound):
    """ For playing a sample.

    Takes a file, and reads it in as 8bit signed data.

    Then converts it to the 16bit signed size the pg needs.
    """
    def __init__(self, fname, volume=.1):
        with open(fname, 'rb') as f:
            samples = self.signed_char_to_signed_short (
                array('b', f.read())
            )
            pg.mixer.Sound.__init__(self, buffer=samples)
        self.set_volume(volume)

    def signed_char_to_signed_short(self, b_samples):
        """ Converts 1 byte signed char samples to 2 byte signed short.
            127 -> 32767
        """
        # just a simple linear conversion.
        import time
        t0=time.time()
        factor = int(32767 / 127)
        samples = array('h', (
            max(sample, -127) * factor if sample < 0 else
            min(sample, 127) * factor
            for sample in b_samples))
        t1=time.time()
        print(t1-t0)
        return samples


def fetch_example_mod_file(mod_fname):
    """ Grab a file that has a sound samples in it from the net.

    'MOD is a computer file format used primarily to represent music,
    and was the first module file format. MOD files use the ".MOD"
    file extension, except on the Amiga which doesn't rely on
    filename extensions, instead it reads a file's header to
    determine filetype. A MOD file contains a set of instruments in
    the form of samples, a number of patterns indicating how and when
    the samples are to be played, and a list of what
    patterns to play in what order.'

    https://en.wikipedia.org/wiki/MOD_(file_format)
```

```
    """
    import os
    url = 'https://api.modarchive.org/downloads.php?moduleid=101996'

    if not os.path.exists(mod_fname):
        from urllib.request import urlopen
        print ('Fetching %s .mod into file: %s' % (url, mod_fname))
        data = urlopen(url).read()

        with open(mod_fname, 'wb') as modf:
            modf.write(data)

def resample(mod_fname):
    """ An example of resampling audio to a different framerate.

    eg, from 8363 one byte samples per second to
        44100 two byte samples per second.
    """
    import audioop
    import wave
    from io import BytesIO

    in_framerate = 8363
    in_sampwidth = 1
    in_nchannels = 1

    out_framerate = 44100

    num_seconds = 5
    with open(mod_fname, 'rb') as f:
        # Throw away the start data of this mod file.
        #   Better samples later on.
        f.read(8363*2)
        in_frame_data = f.read(in_framerate * num_seconds)

    # https://docs.python.org/3/library/audioop.html?highlight=audio#audioop.ratecv
    newfragment, newstate = audioop.ratecv(
        in_frame_data,
        in_sampwidth,
        in_nchannels,
        in_framerate,
        out_framerate,
        None)

    # print(f'len(newfragment):{len(newfragment)}')
    # A perfect conversion is not possible, because the sample
    #   rates do not divide equally. However, the number
    #   of samples should be close.
    assert (out_framerate * num_seconds) - len(newfragment) < 10
    pg.mixer.Sound(buffer=newfragment).play(-1)

if __name__ == "__main__":
    # Set the mixer to have less buffer size, so it
```

```
    # https://www.pygame.org/docs/ref/mixer.html#pygame.mixer.init
    pg.mixer.pre_init(44100, -16, 1, 1024)
    pg.init()

    pg.display.set_caption('Playing square wave, 808 frequency')
    pg.display.set_mode((320, 200))

    mod_fname = 'outrun-3.mod'

    fetch_example_mod_file(mod_fname)

    # play on repeat, -1 means loop indefinitely.
    # https://www.pygame.org/docs/ref/mixer.html#pygame.mixer.Sound.play
    if 0:
        Tone(frequency=808, array_type='b').play(-1)

    if 0:
        try:
            Sample(mod_fname).play(-1)
        except IOError:
            print ('no %s' % mod_fname)
    if 0:
        pg.mixer.music.load(mod_fname)
        pg.mixer.music.play()

    if 1:
        resample(mod_fname)

    going = True
    while going:
        for e in pg.event.get():
            if e.type in [pg.QUIT, pg.KEYDOWN]:
                going = False
```

It is really just a beap, calculated in freqency, and played in a loop, how about play a piano?

```
# Importing the libraries
from tkinter import *
import pygame

# initializing the pygame
pygame.init()
root = Tk()

# Setting the title and geometry
root.title("Piano")
root.geometry("1352x700+0+0")
root.configure(background="white")

# creating the Frames
abc = Frame(root, bg="powder blue", bd=20, relief=RIDGE)
```

```
abc.grid()
abc1 = Frame(abc, bg="powder blue", bd=20, relief=RIDGE)
abc1.grid()
abc2 = Frame(abc, bg="powder blue", relief=RIDGE)
abc2.grid()
abc3 = Frame(abc, bg="powder blue", relief=RIDGE)
abc3.grid()

str = StringVar()
str.set("Key will show here...")

#MP3 stored for pg.Sound
def value_Cs():
    str.set("C#")
    sound = pygame.mixer.Sound("C#.mp3")
    sound.play()

def value_A():
    str.set("A")
    sound = pygame.mixer.Sound("A.mp3")
    sound.play()

def value_B():
    str.set("B")
    sound = pygame.mixer.Sound("B.mp3")
    sound.play()

def value_C():
    str.set("C")
    sound = pygame.mixer.Sound("C.mp3")
    sound.play()

def value_Bb():
    str.set("Bb")
    sound = pygame.mixer.Sound("Bb.mp3")
    sound.play()

def value_Gs():
    str.set("G#")
    sound = pygame.mixer.Sound("G#.mp3")
    sound.play()

def value_Ds():
    str.set("D#")
    sound = pygame.mixer.Sound("D#.mp3")
    sound.play()

def value_Fs():
    str.set("F#")
    sound = pygame.mixer.Sound("F#.mp3")
    sound.play()

def value_G():
```

```
    str.set("G")
    sound = pygame.mixer.Sound("G.mp3")
    sound.play()

def value_D():
    str.set("D")
    sound = pygame.mixer.Sound("D.mp3")
    sound.play()

def value_E1():
    str.set("E1")
    sound = pygame.mixer.Sound("E1.mp3")
    sound.play()

def value_E():
    str.set("E")
    sound = pygame.mixer.Sound("E.mp3")
    sound.play()

def value_F():
    str.set("F")
    sound = pygame.mixer.Sound("F.mp3")
    sound.play()

def value_F1():
    str.set("F1")
    sound = pygame.mixer.Sound("F1.mp3")
    sound.play()

def value_C1():
    str.set("C1")
    sound = pygame.mixer.Sound("C1.mp3")
    sound.play()

def value_D1():
    str.set("D1")
    sound = pygame.mixer.Sound("D1.mp3")
    sound.play()

def value_Cs1():
    str.set("C#1")
    sound = pygame.mixer.Sound("C#1.mp3")
    sound.play()

def value_Ds1():
    str.set("D#1")
    sound = pygame.mixer.Sound("D#1.mp3")
    sound.play()

# Label
Label(abc1, text="Piano Musical Keys", font=("arial", 25, "bold"), padx=8, pady=8,
bd=4, width=59, bg="powder blue",
      fg="white", height=1,
```

```
        justify=CENTER).grid(row=0, column=0, columnspan=11)

display = Entry(abc1, textvariable=str, font=("arial", 18, "bold"), width=35, bd=34,
bg="powder blue", fg="black",
                justify=CENTER).grid(row=1, column=5, pady=1)

# Buttons for keynotes
btnCs = Button(abc2, height=6, width=4, bd=4, text="C#", font=("arial", 18, "bold"),
bg="black", fg="white",
               command=value_Cs)
btnCs.grid(row=0, column=0, padx=5, pady=5)
btnDs = Button(abc2, height=6, width=4, bd=4, text="D#", font=("arial", 18, "bold"),
bg="black", fg="white",
               command=value_Ds)
btnDs.grid(row=0, column=1, padx=5, pady=5)

btnSpace1 = Button(abc2, state=DISABLED, height=6, width=2, bg="powder blue",
relief=FLAT)
btnSpace1.grid(row=0, column=3, padx=0, pady=0)

btnFs = Button(abc2, height=6, width=4, bd=4, text="F#", font=("arial", 18, "bold"),
bg="black", fg="white",
               command=value_Fs)
btnFs.grid(row=0, column=4, padx=5, pady=5)
btnGs = Button(abc2, height=6, width=4, bd=4, text="G#", font=("arial", 18, "bold"),
bg="black", fg="white",
               command=value_Gs)
btnGs.grid(row=0, column=6, padx=5, pady=5)
btnBb = Button(abc2, height=6, width=4, bd=4, text="Bb", font=("arial", 18, "bold"),
bg="black", fg="white",
               command=value_Bb)
btnBb.grid(row=0, column=8, padx=5, pady=5)

btnSpace5 = Button(abc2, state=DISABLED, height=6, width=2, bg="powder blue",
relief=FLAT)
btnSpace5.grid(row=0, column=9, padx=0, pady=0)

btnCs1 = Button(abc2, height=6, width=4, bd=4, text="C#1", font=("arial", 18,
"bold"), bg="black", fg="white",
                command=value_Cs1)
btnCs1.grid(row=0, column=10, padx=5, pady=5)
btnDs1 = Button(abc2, height=6, width=4, bd=4, text="D#1", font=("arial", 18,
"bold"), bg="black", fg="white",
                command=value_Ds1)
btnDs1.grid(row=0, column=12, padx=5, pady=5)

btnC = Button(abc3, bd=4, width=4, height=6, text="C", bg="white", fg="black", font=
("arial", 18, "bold"),
              command=value_C)
btnC.grid(row=0, column=0, padx=5, pady=5)
btnD = Button(abc3, bd=4, width=4, height=6, text="D", bg="white", fg="black", font=
("arial", 18, "bold"),
              command=value_D)
```

```
btnD.grid(row=0, column=1, padx=5, pady=5)
btnE = Button(abc3, bd=4, width=4, height=6, text="E", bg="white", fg="black", font=
("arial", 18, "bold"),
              command=value_E)
btnE.grid(row=0, column=2, padx=5, pady=5)
btnF = Button(abc3, bd=4, width=4, height=6, text="F", bg="white", fg="black", font=
("arial", 18, "bold"),
              command=value_F)
btnF.grid(row=0, column=3, padx=5, pady=5)

btnG = Button(abc3, bd=4, width=4, height=6, text="G", bg="white", fg="black", font=
("arial", 18, "bold"),
              command=value_G)
btnG.grid(row=0, column=4, padx=5, pady=5)
btnA = Button(abc3, bd=4, width=4, height=6, text="A", bg="white", fg="black", font=
("arial", 18, "bold"),
              command=value_A)
btnA.grid(row=0, column=5, padx=5, pady=5)
btnB = Button(abc3, bd=4, width=4, height=6, text="B", bg="white", fg="black", font=
("arial", 18, "bold"),
              command=value_B)
btnB.grid(row=0, column=6, padx=5, pady=5)
btnC1 = Button(abc3, bd=4, width=4, height=6, text="C1", bg="white", fg="black",
font=("arial", 18, "bold"),
               command=value_C1)
btnC1.grid(row=0, column=7, padx=5, pady=5)

btnD1 = Button(abc3, bd=4, width=4, height=6, text="D1", bg="white", fg="black",
font=("arial", 18, "bold"),
               command=value_D1)
btnD1.grid(row=0, column=8, padx=5, pady=5)
btnE1 = Button(abc3, bd=4, width=4, height=6, text="E1", bg="white", fg="black",
font=("arial", 18, "bold"),
               command=value_E1)
btnE1.grid(row=0, column=9, padx=5, pady=5)
btnF1 = Button(abc3, bd=4, width=4, height=6, text="F1", bg="white", fg="black",
font=("arial", 18, "bold"),
               command=value_F1)
btnF1.grid(row=0, column=10, padx=5, pady=5)

# Mainloop
root.mainloop()
```

checkout https://github.com/Leethring/piano-sound-samples/tree/master/sound_keyboard_staff for mp3,

we can make command GUI, which simply uses Python 3 quotation marks,

```
import pygame,random

def welcome():
    print('''
```

```
    *************************
    *  Command GUI Player   *
    *************************
    ''')
def select():
    print('''
    **************************
    * 1.Play      2.Stop     *
    * 3.Next      4.Previous *
    * 5.VolUp     6.VolDown  *
    * 7.Choose    0.Exit     *
    **************************
    ''')
    return input("Choose: ")
def theSongPlay(songList,num,value):
    pygame.mixer.music.load(songList[num % len(songList)])
    pygame.mixer.music.play()
    pygame.mixer.music.set_volume(value)

def myValuePrint(value):
    print('Current Vol:',(int(value*100)+1)//10*10)

def mySongPlay(num):
    print('Current Song:{}'.format(songList[num]))


def SongPlay(songList):
    pygame.mixer.init()
    value = 0.5
    welcome()
    num = random.randrange(0,len(songList))
    theSongPlay(songList,num,value)
    myValuePrint(value)
    mySongPlay(num)
    while True:
        choose = select()
        if choose == '3':
            num += 1
            theSongPlay(songList,num%len(songList),value)
            mySongPlay(num%len(songList))
        elif choose == '4':
            num += len(songList)-1
            theSongPlay(songList,num%len(songList),value)
            mySongPlay(num%len(songList))
        elif choose == '1':
            pygame.mixer.music.unpause()
        elif choose == '2':
            pygame.mixer.music.pause()
        elif choose == '5':
            value += 0.1
            if value>1:
                value = 0
            myValuePrint(value)
```

```
            pygame.mixer.music.set_volume(value)
        elif choose == '6':
            value -= 0.1
            if value<0.01 and value>0:
                value = 0
            elif value <0:
                value = 1
            myValuePrint(value)
            pygame.mixer.music.set_volume(value)
        elif choose == '7':
            str = input('Choose your song')
            if str in songList:
                num = songList.index(str)
                theSongPlay(songList, num, value)
            else:
                print('Sorry, no such song')
        elif choose == '0':
            break
        else:
            print('Invalid, input again')

if __name__ == '__main__':
     songList = ['See you again.mp3', 'Hello from other sid.mp3', 'What doesn't kill
you.mp3']
    SongPlay(songList)
```

and if we want to just play a song, by mp3, (create a Sounds folder to hold different kinds of instrument)

```
Twinkle_List = ['C4','C4','G4','G4','A4','A4','G4',\
                'F4','F4','E4','E4','D4','D4','C4',\
                'G5','G5','F4','F4','E4','E4','D4',\
                'G5','G5','F4','F4','E4','E4','D4',\
                'C4','C4','G4','G4','A4','A4','G4',\
                'F4','F4','E4','E4','D4','D4','C4',\
                ]

from threading import Thread
import pygame as pg
import time
pg.mixer.init()
pg.init()
pg.mixer.set_num_channels(len(Twinkle_List))
def play_notes(notePath, duration):
    time.sleep(duration) # make a pause
    pg.mixer.Sound(notePath).play()
    time.sleep(duration) # Let the sound play
    print(notePath) # To see which note is now playing

path  = 'Sounds/'

cnt = 1 # A counter to delay once a line is finished as there
```

```
# are 6 total lines

th = {}

for t in Twinkle_List:
    th[t] = Thread(target = play_notes, args = (path+'{}.mp3'.format(t),0.3))
    # These are arguments (path+'{}.mp3'.format(t),0.3)
    # Lets start the thread
    th[t].start()
    th[t].join()
    if cnt%7==0:
        print("---Long Pause---")
        time.sleep(1) # Let the sound play for the last note of each line

    cnt+=1
```

53 Tarot

Tarot is another way to do prediction, checkout https://github.com/afairley19/tarot.git, and go to the folder,

```
python -c "import os; print(os.listdir('.'))"

# output
'cards', 'images', 'LICENSE', 'README.md', 'tarot_cards.py', 'tarot_main.py'
```

the program is perfectly matching past, present, future, the universe unknown three status, well, past is also unkown, run by main.py, and get the reading for present,

```
# output
Five Cups
You are popular with other people...
```

What does this mean? Does it mean my trading is in the right trend? Which I can hold?

Tarot decks were invented in Italy in the 1430s by adding to the existing four-suited pack a fifth suit of 21 specially illustrated cards called trionfi and an odd card called il matto, means the fool.

In a traditional Tarot deck, there are 78 cards in total, 22 cards in the major arcana and 56 in the minor arcana. From card.py we can see these arcana,

```
tarot_cards = [
    magician, popess, empress, emperor, pope,
    lovers, chariot, justice, hermit, wheel_fortune,
    force, hanged_man, death, temperance, devil,
```

```
    tower, star, moon, sun, judgment, world, fool,

    king_wands, queen_wands, knight_wands, knave_wands,
    ace_wands, two_wands, three_wands, four_wands, five_wands,
    six_wands, seven_wands, eight_wands, nine_wands, ten_wands,

    king_cups, queen_cups, knight_cups, knave_cups,
    ace_cups, two_cups, three_cups, four_cups, five_cups,
    six_cups, seven_cups, eight_cups, nine_cups, ten_cups,

    king_coins, queen_coins, knight_coins, knave_coins,
    ace_coins, two_coins, three_coins, four_coins, five_coins,
    six_coins, seven_coins, eight_coins, nine_coins, ten_coins,

    king_swords, queen_swords, knight_swords, knave_swords,
    ace_swords, two_swords, three_swords, four_swords, five_swords,
    six_swords, seven_swords, eight_swords, nine_swords, ten_swords
]
```

The major arcana represents various forces, characters, virtues, and vices. 22 cards are numbered in Roman from I through XXI, with the fool being unnumbered. And the order is, I juggler, or magician; II papess, or female pope; III empress; IV emperor; V pope; VI lovers; VII chariot; VIII justice; IX hermit; X wheel of fortune; XI strength, or fortitude; XII hanged man; XIII death; XIV temperance; XV devil; XVI lightning-struck tower; XVII star; XVIII moon; XIX sun; XX last judgment; XXI world, or universe; and the fool.

The minor arcana are in four suits, each has 14 cards. The suits order is wands, batons, or rods (clubs); cups (hearts); swords (spades); and coins, pentacles, or disks (diamonds). The cards in each suit are first 4 court cards, king, queen, knight, and jack, then 10 numbered cards.

Recall to write a piano song, we stored key MP3 first, here the cards PNG are stored too. The past, present, future cards are three, so it's called 3 tarot, if we only have one trade we can do it like this, but if more...

There is a 6 tarot, which is called spread 6, it can predict, relationships, career, or personal growth, by drawing six cards representing the past, present, future, obstacles/challenges, advice/guidance, and likely outcome.

We are interested in outcome, it is called outcome path.

Cards are placed in a three rows to mimic investment level, the outcome card at the top row, three cards in the middle row for Logical, Concept, and Creative, and two cards on the last row: Physical and Spiritual.

There is another 6 tarot, called universal spread, it is random from the major for draw 1, and rest from the minor,

```
import random

Draw = """
'~~ Draw 1 : How you feel about yourself ~~',
'~~ Draw 2 : What you want most right now ~~',
'~~ Draw 3 : Your fears ~~',
'~~ Draw 4 : What is going for you ~~',
'~~ Draw 5 : What is going against you ~~',
'~~ Draw 6 : The likely outcome ~~',
"""

major_cards = [
    magician, popess, empress, emperor, pope,
    lovers, chariot, justice, hermit, wheel_fortune,
    force, hanged_man, death, temperance, devil,
    tower, star, moon, sun, judgment, world, fool
]

minor_cards = [
    king_wands, queen_wands, knight_wands, knave_wands,
    ace_wands, two_wands, three_wands, four_wands, five_wands,
    six_wands, seven_wands, eight_wands, nine_wands, ten_wands,

    king_cups, queen_cups, knight_cups, knave_cups,
    ace_cups, two_cups, three_cups, four_cups, five_cups,
    six_cups, seven_cups, eight_cups, nine_cups, ten_cups,

    king_coins, queen_coins, knight_coins, knave_coins,
    ace_coins, two_coins, three_coins, four_coins, five_coins,
    six_coins, seven_coins, eight_coins, nine_coins, ten_coins,

    king_swords, queen_swords, knight_swords, knave_swords,
    ace_swords, two_swords, three_swords, four_swords, five_swords,
    six_swords, seven_swords, eight_swords, nine_swords, ten_swords
]

draw1 = random.choice(major_cards)
draw2 = random.choice(minor_cards)
draw3 = random.choice(minor_cards)
draw4 = random.choice(minor_cards)
draw5 = random.choice(minor_cards)
draw6 = random.choice(minor_cards)

# match cards meaning
if card == "king_wands": print("you are very...")
# etc...
```

so we find the meaning is really subjective, checkout https://www.lotustarot.wiki/6-card-tarot-spread/ and https://labyrinthos.co/blogs/tarot-card-meanings-list, it can be different.

54 random

The random module has several funcitons for random,

54.1 The randint() Function

```
import random
integer1=random.randint(1,10)
integer2=random.randint(1,10)
integer3=random.randint(1,10)
integer4=random.randint(1,10)
print("The random integers between 1 and 10 are:", integer1, integer2, integer3,
integer4)
```

54.2 The random() Function

```
import random
number1=random.random()
number2=random.random()
number3=random.random()
number4=random.random()
print("The random numbers are:", number1, number2, number3, number4 )
```

54.3 The choice() Function

```
import random
colors=["red","green","blue","yellow","violet","indigo","orange"]
print("The list of colors is:",colors)
color=random.choice(colors)
print("The randomly selected value from the list is:",color)
```

54.4 The choices() Function

```
import random
colors=["red","green","blue","yellow","violet","indigo","orange"]
print("The list of colors is:",colors)
color=random.choices(colors,k=3)
print("The randomly selected values from the list are:",color)
```

54.5 The shuffle() Function

```
import random
colors=["red","green","blue","yellow","violet","indigo","orange"]
print("The list of colors is:",colors)
random.shuffle(colors)
print("The list of colors after shuffle is:",colors)
```

54.6 The randrange() Function

```
import random
number=random.randrange(0,100,20)
print("The random number is:",number)
```

The 0 is start, 100 is end, 20 is step, so the random can be 0, 20, 40, 60, 80,

54.7 The uniform() Function

```
import random
random_float=random.uniform(2.5, 5.5)
print("The random float number is:",random_float)
```

The start and end can be changed , if we want an angle, `random_angle = random.uniform(0, 360)

54.8 The normalvariate() Function

```
import random
random_score=random.normalvariate(100, 15)
print("The random score is:",random_score)
```

Two most common random tool are coin

```
import random
def coin_flip(num_flips):
    heads = 0
    tails = 0

    for _ in range(num_flips):
        outcome = random.choice(["heads", "tails"])
        if outcome == "heads":
            heads += 1
        else:
            tails += 1

    print(f"Heads: {heads}")
    print(f"Tails: {tails}")

coin_results = coin_flip(100)

print(f"Coin results: {coin_results}")
```

and dice,

```
import random
def roll_dice(num_rolls, num_sides):
    results = [random.randint(1, num_sides) for _ in range(num_rolls)]
    return results
```

```
num_rolls = 5
num_sides = 6
dice_results = roll_dice(num_rolls, num_sides)

print(f"Dice results: {dice_results}")
```

and password generator,

```
import random
import string

# get random password, length 8 with letters, digits, and symbols
characters = string.ascii_letters + string.digits + string.punctuation
password = ''.join(random.choice(characters) for i in range(8))
print("Random password is:", password)
```

even more secure,

```
import secrets
import string

# secure random string
secure_str = ''.join((secrets.choice(string.ascii_letters) for i in range(8)))
print(secure_str)

# secure password
password    =    ''.join((secrets.choice(string.ascii_letters    +    string.digits    +
string.punctuation) for i in range(8)))
print(password)
```

We can put this into tkinter, so it looks powerful,

```
import random
from tkinter import messagebox
from tkinter import *
#Password generator function
def generate_password():
  try:
    repeat = int(repeat_entry.get())
    length = int(length_entry.get())
  except:
    messagebox.showerror(message="Please key in the required inputs")
    return
  #Check if user allows repetition of characters
  if repeat == 1:
    password = random.sample(character_string,length)
  else:
    password = random.choices(character_string,k=length)
  #Since the returned value is a list, we convert to a sting using join
  password=''.join(password)
  #Declare a string variable
```

```
    password_v = StringVar()
    password="Created password: "+str(password)
    #Assign the password to the declared string variables
    password_v.set(password)
    #Create a read only entry box to view the output, position using place
     password_label = Entry(password_gen, bd=0, bg="gray85", textvariable=password_v,
state="readonly")
    password_label.place(x=10, y=140, height=50, width=320)

#Define a string containing letters, symbols and numbers
character_string                                                                    =
"ABCDEFGHIJKLMNOPQRSTUVWXYZabcdefghijklmnopqrstuvwxyz0123456789!#$%&'()*+,-./:;<=>?
@[\]^_`{|}~"

#Define the user interface
password_gen  = Tk()
password_gen.geometry("350x200")
password_gen.title("Python Password Generator")

#Mention the title of the app
title_label  = Label(password_gen,  text="Python  Password  Generator",  font=('Ubuntu
Mono',12))
title_label.pack()

#Read length, may be 8
length_label = Label(password_gen, text="Enter length of password: ")
length_label.place(x=20,y=30)
length_entry = Entry(password_gen, width=3)
length_entry.place(x=190,y=30)
#Read repetition
repeat_label = Label(password_gen, text="Repetition? 1: no repetition, 2: otherwise:
")
repeat_label.place(x=20,y=60)
repeat_entry = Entry(password_gen, width=3)
repeat_entry.place(x=300,y=60)
#Generate password
password_button      =      Button(password_gen,      text="Generate      Password",
command=generate_password)
#Can be secure too
password_button.place(x=100,y=100)
#Exit and close the app
password_gen.mainloop()
```

How is this random so powerful? Checkout https://github.com/python/cpython/blob/main/Lib/random.py, the critical line is from `SystemRandom`, it says not available on all systems (see os.urandom() for details), what is urandom?

```
python -c "import os; print(os.urandom(16))"
```

from the 16bytes random results, we can continue do conversion,

```
random_bytes = os.urandom(16)

hex_string = random_bytes.hex()
print(hex_string)

binary_string = random_bytes.bin()
print(binary_string)
```

and compare to bytearray,

```
random_bytearray = bytearray(os.urandom(16))
print(random_bytearray)
```

so 8 bits is one byte, and many bytes are a bytearray, the following are same,

```
a = "abc"
a = "\x616263"
a = "\o301302303"
a = "\979899"

bytearray("abc", encoding="utf-8")
bytearray(b"abc")
bytearray([97, 98, 99])
```

notice a is,

```
a = "a" # double quote
a = chr(97) # just one char, equals using single quote,

a = "\b01100001"
a = "\x61" # see this 61 is same
a = "\o301"

# b, c...
```

The magic is therefore urandom, and what is that?

On **Windows**, if we type the URL "file:/dev/random" or "file:/dev/urandom" , it will enable the native Microsoft CryptoAPI seeding mechanism for SHA1PRNG, and on **Linux**, both udner /dev/. The mechanism is using hardware to get a random number, just like roll the dice, however it is hardware, this ware makes things hard to understand...

The short name for this ware is TRNG.

55 argparse

The official random.py has only 1000+ lines, and it can be run by command line too, see by '-h',

```
usage: random.py [-h] [-c CHOICE [CHOICE ...] | -i N | -f N] [input ...]

positional arguments:
  input                 if no options given, output depends on the input
                            string or multiple: same as --choice
                            integer: same as --integer
                            float: same as --float

options:
  -h, --help            show this help message and exit
  -c CHOICE [CHOICE ...], --choice CHOICE [CHOICE ...]
                        print a random choice
  -i N, --integer N     print a random integer between 1 and N inclusive
   -f N, --float N          print a random floating-point number between 0 and N
inclusive
```

use `findstr`(or `grep`), we can see the functions are,

```
def randbytes(self, n):
def randrange(self, start, stop=None, step=_ONE):
def randint(self, a, b):
def choice(self, seq):
def shuffle(self, x):
def sample(self, population, k, *, counts=None):
def choices(self, population, weights=None, *, cum_weights=None, k=1):
def uniform(self, a, b):
def triangular(self, low=0.0, high=1.0, mode=None):
def normalvariate(self, mu=0.0, sigma=1.0):
def gauss(self, mu=0.0, sigma=1.0):
def lognormvariate(self, mu, sigma):
def expovariate(self, lambd=1.0):
def vonmisesvariate(self, mu, kappa):
def gammavariate(self, alpha, beta):
def betavariate(self, alpha, beta):
def paretovariate(self, alpha):
def weibullvariate(self, alpha, beta):
def binomialvariate(self, n=1, p=0.5):
def random(self):
def getrandbits(self, k):
def randbytes(self, n):
def seed(self, *args, **kwds):
```

Let's simplify it, the beigining part is just the options, integer, float, string, test,

```
def _parse_args(arg_list: list[str] | None):
    import argparse
```

```
    parser = argparse.ArgumentParser(
        formatter_class=argparse.RawTextHelpFormatter)
    group = parser.add_mutually_exclusive_group()
    group.add_argument(
        "-c", "--choice", nargs="+",
        help="print a random choice")
    group.add_argument(
        "-i", "--integer", type=int, metavar="N",
        help="print a random integer between 1 and N inclusive")
    group.add_argument(
        "-f", "--float", type=float, metavar="N",
        help="print a random floating-point number between 0 and N inclusive")
    group.add_argument(
        "--test", type=int, const=10_000, nargs="?",
        help=argparse.SUPPRESS)
    parser.add_argument("input", nargs="*",
                        help="""\
if no options given, output depends on the input
    string or multiple: same as --choice
    integer: same as --integer
    float: same as --float""")
    args = parser.parse_args(arg_list)
    return args, parser.format_help()


def main(arg_list: list[str] | None = None) -> int | str:
    args, help_text = _parse_args(arg_list)

    # Explicit arguments
    if args.choice:
        return choice(args.choice)

    if args.integer is not None:
        return randint(1, args.integer)

    if args.float is not None:
        return uniform(0, args.float)

    if args.test:
        _test(args.test)
        return ""

    # No explicit argument, select based on input
    if len(args.input) == 1:
        val = args.input[0]
        try:
            # Is it an integer?
            val = int(val)
            return randint(1, val)
        except ValueError:
            try:
                # Is it a float?
                val = float(val)
```

```
            return uniform(0, val)
        except ValueError:
            # Split in case of space-separated string: "a b c"
            return choice(val.split())

    if len(args.input) >= 2:
        return choice(args.input)

    return help_text


if __name__ == '__main__':
    print(main())
```

notice that `import argparse` is inside the function, that means other places will not use it again, `if args.something` is the link to the real functions, and they are integer, float, string, bundled into the class, `random`, rewrite them,

```
import _random
from operator import index as _index

BPF = 53        # Number of bits in a float
_ONE = 1


class Random(_random.Random):
    VERSION = 3     # used by getstate/setstate

    def __init__(self, x=None):
        """Initialize an instance.

        Optional argument x controls seeding, as for Random.seed().
        """

        self.seed(x)
        self.gauss_next = None

    def seed(self, a=None, version=2):
        """Initialize internal state from a seed.

        The only supported seed types are None, int, float,
        str, bytes, and bytearray.

        None or no argument seeds from current time or from an operating
        system specific randomness source if available.

        If *a* is an int, all bits are used.

        For version 2 (the default), all of the bits are used if *a* is a str,
        bytes, or bytearray.  For version 1 (provided for reproducing random
        sequences from older versions of Python), the algorithm for str and
        bytes generates a narrower range of seeds.
```

```
        """

        if version == 1 and isinstance(a, (str, bytes)):
            a = a.decode('latin-1') if isinstance(a, bytes) else a
            x = ord(a[0]) << 7 if a else 0
            for c in map(ord, a):
                x = ((1000003 * x) ^ c) & 0xFFFFFFFFFFFFFFFF
            x ^= len(a)
            a = -2 if x == -1 else x

        elif version == 2 and isinstance(a, (str, bytes, bytearray)):
            global _sha512
            if _sha512 is None:
                try:
                    # hashlib is pretty heavy to load, try lean internal
                    # module first
                    from _sha2 import sha512 as _sha512
                except ImportError:
                    # fallback to official implementation
                    from hashlib import sha512 as _sha512

            if isinstance(a, str):
                a = a.encode()
            a = int.from_bytes(a + _sha512(a).digest())

        elif not isinstance(a, (type(None), int, float, str, bytes, bytearray)):
            raise TypeError('The only supported seed types are:\n'
                            'None, int, float, str, bytes, and bytearray.')

        super().seed(a)
        self.gauss_next = None

    def getstate(self):
        """Return internal state; can be passed to setstate() later."""
        return self.VERSION, super().getstate(), self.gauss_next

    def setstate(self, state):
        """Restore internal state from object returned by getstate()."""
        version = state[0]
        if version == 3:
            version, internalstate, self.gauss_next = state
            super().setstate(internalstate)
        elif version == 2:
            version, internalstate, self.gauss_next = state
            # In version 2, the state was saved as signed ints, which causes
            #   inconsistencies between 32/64-bit systems. The state is
            #   really unsigned 32-bit ints, so we convert negative ints from
            #   version 2 to positive longs for version 3.
            try:
                internalstate = tuple(x % (2 ** 32) for x in internalstate)
            except ValueError as e:
                raise TypeError from e
```

```
            super().setstate(internalstate)
        else:
            raise ValueError("state with version %s passed to "
                             "Random.setstate() of version %s" %
                             (version, self.VERSION))


    def __getstate__(self):  # for pickle
        return self.getstate()

    def __setstate__(self, state):  # for pickle
        self.setstate(state)

    def __reduce__(self):
        return self.__class__, (), self.getstate()


    ## ---- internal support method for evenly distributed integers ----

    def __init_subclass__(cls, /, **kwargs):
        """Control how subclasses generate random integers.

        The algorithm a subclass can use depends on the random() and/or
        getrandbits() implementation available to it and determines
        whether it can generate random integers from arbitrarily large
        ranges.
        """

        for c in cls.__mro__:
            if '_randbelow' in c.__dict__:
                # just inherit it
                break
            if 'getrandbits' in c.__dict__:
                cls._randbelow = cls._randbelow_with_getrandbits
                break
            if 'random' in c.__dict__:
                cls._randbelow = cls._randbelow_without_getrandbits
                break

    def _randbelow_with_getrandbits(self, n):
        "Return a random int in the range [0,n).  Defined for n > 0."

        getrandbits = self.getrandbits
        k = n.bit_length()
        r = getrandbits(k)  # 0 <= r < 2**k
        while r >= n:
            r = getrandbits(k)
        return r

    def _randbelow_without_getrandbits(self, n, maxsize=1<<BPF):
        """Return a random int in the range [0,n).  Defined for n > 0.

        The implementation does not use getrandbits, but only random.
```

```
        """

        random = self.random
        if n >= maxsize:
            from warnings import warn
            warn("Underlying random() generator does not supply \n"
                 "enough bits to choose from a population range this large.\n"
                 "To remove the range limitation, add a getrandbits() method.")
            return _floor(random() * n)
        rem = maxsize % n
        limit = (maxsize - rem) / maxsize   # int(limit * maxsize) % n == 0
        r = random()
        while r >= limit:
            r = random()
        return _floor(r * maxsize) % n

    _randbelow = _randbelow_with_getrandbits

    ## -------------------- bytes methods ---------------------

    def randbytes(self, n):
        """Generate n random bytes."""
        return self.getrandbits(n * 8).to_bytes(n, 'little')


    ## -------------------- integer methods  -------------------

    def randrange(self, start, stop=None, step=_ONE):
        """Choose a random item from range(stop) or range(start, stop[, step]).

        Roughly equivalent to ``choice(range(start, stop, step))`` but
        supports arbitrarily large ranges and is optimized for common cases.

        """

        # This code is a bit messy to make it fast for the
        # common case while still doing adequate error checking.
        istart = _index(start)
        if stop is None:
            # We don't check for "step != 1" because it hasn't been
            # type checked and converted to an integer yet.
            if step is not _ONE:
                raise TypeError("Missing a non-None stop argument")
            if istart > 0:
                return self._randbelow(istart)
            raise ValueError("empty range for randrange()")

        # Stop argument supplied.
        istop = _index(stop)
        width = istop - istart
        istep = _index(step)
        # Fast path.
        if istep == 1:
```

```
            if width > 0:
                return istart + self._randbelow(width)
            raise ValueError(f"empty range in randrange({start}, {stop})")

        # Non-unit step argument supplied.
        if istep > 0:
            n = (width + istep - 1) // istep
        elif istep < 0:
            n = (width + istep + 1) // istep
        else:
            raise ValueError("zero step for randrange()")
        if n <= 0:
            raise ValueError(f"empty range in randrange({start}, {stop}, {step})")
        return istart + istep * self._randbelow(n)

    def randint(self, a, b):
        """Return random integer in range [a, b], including both end points.
        """

        return self.randrange(a, b+1)


    ## -------------------- sequence methods  -------------------

    def choice(self, seq):
        """Choose a random element from a non-empty sequence."""

        # As an accommodation for NumPy, we don't use "if not seq"
        # because bool(numpy.array()) raises a ValueError.
        if not len(seq):
            raise IndexError('Cannot choose from an empty sequence')
        return seq[self._randbelow(len(seq))]

    def uniform(self, a, b):
        """Get a random number in the range [a, b) or [a, b] depending on rounding.

        The mean (expected value) and variance of the random variable are:

            E[X] = (a + b) / 2
            Var[X] = (b - a) ** 2 / 12

        """
        return a + (b - a) * self.random()

def gauss(self, mu=0.0, sigma=1.0):
        """Gaussian distribution.

        mu is the mean, and sigma is the standard deviation.  This is
        slightly faster than the normalvariate() function.

        Not thread-safe without a lock around calls.

        """
```

```
        # When x and y are two variables from [0, 1), uniformly
        # distributed, then
        #
        #    cos(2*pi*x)*sqrt(-2*log(1-y))
        #    sin(2*pi*x)*sqrt(-2*log(1-y))
        #
        # are two *independent* variables with normal distribution
        # (mu = 0, sigma = 1).
        # (Lambert Meertens)
        # (corrected version; bug discovered by Mike Miller, fixed by LM)

        # Multithreading note: When two threads call this function
        # simultaneously, it is possible that they will receive the
        # same return value.  The window is very small though.  To
        # avoid this, you have to use a lock around all calls.  (I
        # didn't want to slow this down in the serial case by using a
        # lock here.)

        random = self.random
        z = self.gauss_next
        self.gauss_next = None
        if z is None:
            x2pi = random() * TWOPI
            g2rad = _sqrt(-2.0 * _log(1.0 - random()))
            z = _cos(x2pi) * g2rad
            self.gauss_next = _sin(x2pi) * g2rad

        return mu + z * sigma

def _parse_args(arg_list: list[str] | None):
    import argparse
    parser = argparse.ArgumentParser(
        formatter_class=argparse.RawTextHelpFormatter)
    group = parser.add_mutually_exclusive_group()
    group.add_argument(
        "-c", "--choice", nargs="+",
        help="print a random choice")
    group.add_argument(
        "-i", "--integer", type=int, metavar="N",
        help="print a random integer between 1 and N inclusive")
    group.add_argument(
        "-f", "--float", type=float, metavar="N",
        help="print a random floating-point number between 0 and N inclusive")
    group.add_argument(
        "--test", type=int, const=10_000, nargs="?",
        help=argparse.SUPPRESS)
    parser.add_argument("input", nargs="*",
                        help="""\
if no options given, output depends on the input
    string or multiple: same as --choice
    integer: same as --integer
    float: same as --float""")
    args = parser.parse_args(arg_list)
```

```python
    return args, parser.format_help()


_inst = Random()
seed = _inst.seed
random = _inst.random
uniform = _inst.uniform
randint = _inst.randint
choice = _inst.choice
randrange = _inst.randrange


def main(arg_list: list[str] | None = None) -> int | str:
    args, help_text = _parse_args(arg_list)

    # Explicit arguments
    if args.choice:
        return choice(args.choice)

    if args.integer is not None:
        return randint(1, args.integer)

    if args.float is not None:
        return uniform(0, args.float)

    if args.test:
        _test(args.test)
        return ""

    # No explicit argument, select based on input
    if len(args.input) == 1:
        val = args.input[0]
        try:
            # Is it an integer?
            val = int(val)
            return randint(1, val)
        except ValueError:
            try:
                # Is it a float?
                val = float(val)
                return uniform(0, val)
            except ValueError:
                # Split in case of space-separated string: "a b c"
                return choice(val.split())

    if len(args.input) >= 2:
        return choice(args.input)

    return help_text


if __name__ == '__main__':
    print(main())
```

and test the function,

```
C:\Users\Lenovo> python .\myrandom.py -c a
a
C:\Users\Lenovo> python .\myrandom.py -c a b c
a
C:\Users\Lenovo> python .\myrandom.py -c a b c
c
C:\Users\Lenovo> python .\myrandom.py -c a b c d
d
C:\Users\Lenovo> python .\myrandom.py -i 10
5
C:\Users\Lenovo> python .\myrandom.py -f 2.0
0.03646507232311613
```

56 unittest

We can also use unittest to do the test,

```
"""
UnitTest class first imports unittest module
then imports PandasToList class
"""
import unittest
import myrandom

_inst = myrandom.Random()
seed = _inst.seed
random = _inst.random
uniform = _inst.uniform
randint = _inst.randint
choice = _inst.choice
randrange = _inst.randrange

class Testmyrandom(unittest.TestCase):
    """
    The UnitTest class runs two unit test on the
    myrandom class
    """

    def test_integer(self):
        result = randint(1, 10)
        assert 1 <= result <= 10, "Number out of range!"

if __name__ == "__main__":
    # runs the unittest to see results
    unittest.main()
```

notice `assert expression` equals `if not expression: raise AssertionError`, and equal is predefined,

```
import unittest

def add(a, b):
    return a + b

class TestAddFunction(unittest.TestCase):
    def test_add_positive_numbers(self):
        self.assertEqual(add(1, 2), 3)
    def test_add_negative_numbers(self):
        self.assertEqual(add(-1, -2), -3)

if __name__ == '__main__':
    unittest.main()
```

similiarly as equal, we can define our own assert,

```
def check_age(age):
    assert age >= 0, "Age cannot be negative!"
    assert age <= 120, "Age cannot exceed 120!"
    print("Valid age.")

check_age(25)     # Valid age.
check_age(-10)    # AssertionError: Age cannot be negative!
check_age(150)    # AssertionError: Age cannot exceed 120!
```

and we can write the unittest and class in one file,

```
import unittest

class Calculator:
    def add(self, a, b):
        return a + b

    def subtract(self, a, b):
        return a - b

class TestCalculator(unittest.TestCase):
    def setUp(self):
        self.calc = Calculator()
    def test_add(self):
        self.assertEqual(self.calc.add(1, 2), 3)
    def test_subtract(self):
        self.assertEqual(self.calc.subtract(10, 5), 5)

if __name__ == '__main__':
    unittest.main(
```

recall we have write twinkle song, can we write more with unittest?

57 lilypond

Checkout https://lilypond.org/text-input.html, a song is composed by keys, and lilypond can convert the key into score,

```
# input
# chcp437
# C.txt
\header {
  title = "C"
  composer = "masara"
}

\score {
  \relative c' {
    c4
  }

  \layout {}
  \midi {}
}

# Rename-Item -Path "C.txt" -NewName "C.ly"
# lilypond.exe C.ly

# output
# C.mid
# C.pdf
```

C.mid is the song, and we can listen it with pygame,

```
import pygame

pygame.init()
#import sys
#s = sys.argv[1]
#pygame.mixer.music.load(s)
pygame.mixer.music.load("C.mid")
pygame.mixer.music.set_volume(0.5)

pygame.mixer.music.play()
#print(s)

while pygame.mixer.music.get_busy():
    continue
```

and not only piano sounds,

```
\header {
  title = "Demo of all midi sounds"
  arranger = "masara"
```

```
}

baseMelody = \relative c' {
  c4.\mf g c16 b' c d
  e16 d e f g4 g'4 r
  R1
}
melody = {
  \tempo 4 = 150
  \baseMelody
}

\score {
  \new Staff <<
    \new Voice \melody
  >>
  \layout { }
}

\score {
  \new Staff <<
    \new Voice {
      r\mf
      \set Staff.midiInstrument = #"acoustic grand" \melody
      \set Staff.midiInstrument = #"bright acoustic" \melody
      \set Staff.midiInstrument = #"electric grand" \melody
      \set Staff.midiInstrument = #"honky-tonk" \melody
      \set Staff.midiInstrument = #"electric piano 1" \melody
      \set Staff.midiInstrument = #"electric piano 2" \melody
      \set Staff.midiInstrument = #"harpsichord" \melody
      \set Staff.midiInstrument = #"clav" \melody
      \set Staff.midiInstrument = #"celesta" \melody
      \set Staff.midiInstrument = #"glockenspiel" \melody
      \set Staff.midiInstrument = #"music box" \melody
      \set Staff.midiInstrument = #"vibraphone" \melody
      \set Staff.midiInstrument = #"marimba" \melody
      \set Staff.midiInstrument = #"xylophone" \melody
      \set Staff.midiInstrument = #"tubular bells" \melody
      \set Staff.midiInstrument = #"dulcimer" \melody
      \set Staff.midiInstrument = #"drawbar organ" \melody
      \set Staff.midiInstrument = #"percussive organ" \melody
      \set Staff.midiInstrument = #"rock organ" \melody
      \set Staff.midiInstrument = #"church organ" \melody
      \set Staff.midiInstrument = #"reed organ" \melody
      \set Staff.midiInstrument = #"accordion" \melody
      \set Staff.midiInstrument = #"harmonica" \melody
      \set Staff.midiInstrument = #"concertina" \melody
      \set Staff.midiInstrument = #"acoustic guitar (nylon)" \melody
      \set Staff.midiInstrument = #"acoustic guitar (steel)" \melody
      \set Staff.midiInstrument = #"electric guitar (jazz)" \melody
      \set Staff.midiInstrument = #"electric guitar (clean)" \melody
      \set Staff.midiInstrument = #"electric guitar (muted)" \melody
      \set Staff.midiInstrument = #"overdriven guitar" \melody
```

```
\set Staff.midiInstrument = #"distorted guitar" \melody
\set Staff.midiInstrument = #"acoustic bass" \melody
\set Staff.midiInstrument = #"electric bass (finger)" \melody
\set Staff.midiInstrument = #"electric bass (pick)" \melody
\set Staff.midiInstrument = #"fretless bass" \melody
\set Staff.midiInstrument = #"slap bass 1" \melody
\set Staff.midiInstrument = #"slap bass 2" \melody
\set Staff.midiInstrument = #"synth bass 1" \melody
\set Staff.midiInstrument = #"synth bass 2" \melody
\set Staff.midiInstrument = #"violin" \melody
\set Staff.midiInstrument = #"viola" \melody
\set Staff.midiInstrument = #"cello" \melody
\set Staff.midiInstrument = #"contrabass" \melody
\set Staff.midiInstrument = #"tremolo strings" \melody
\set Staff.midiInstrument = #"pizzicato strings" \melody
\set Staff.midiInstrument = #"orchestral harp" \melody
\set Staff.midiInstrument = #"timpani" \melody
\set Staff.midiInstrument = #"string ensemble 1" \melody
\set Staff.midiInstrument = #"string ensemble 2" \melody
\set Staff.midiInstrument = #"synthstrings 1" \melody
\set Staff.midiInstrument = #"synthstrings 2" \melody
\set Staff.midiInstrument = #"choir aahs" \melody
\set Staff.midiInstrument = #"voice oohs" \melody
\set Staff.midiInstrument = #"synth voice" \melody
\set Staff.midiInstrument = #"orchestra hit" \melody
\set Staff.midiInstrument = #"trumpet" \melody
\set Staff.midiInstrument = #"trombone" \melody
\set Staff.midiInstrument = #"tuba" \melody
\set Staff.midiInstrument = #"muted trumpet" \melody
\set Staff.midiInstrument = #"french horn" \melody
\set Staff.midiInstrument = #"brass section" \melody
\set Staff.midiInstrument = #"synthbrass 1" \melody
\set Staff.midiInstrument = #"synthbrass 2" \melody
\set Staff.midiInstrument = #"soprano sax" \melody
\set Staff.midiInstrument = #"alto sax" \melody
\set Staff.midiInstrument = #"tenor sax" \melody
\set Staff.midiInstrument = #"baritone sax" \melody
\set Staff.midiInstrument = #"oboe" \melody
\set Staff.midiInstrument = #"english horn" \melody
\set Staff.midiInstrument = #"bassoon" \melody
\set Staff.midiInstrument = #"clarinet" \melody
\set Staff.midiInstrument = #"piccolo" \melody
\set Staff.midiInstrument = #"flute" \melody
\set Staff.midiInstrument = #"recorder" \melody
\set Staff.midiInstrument = #"pan flute" \melody
\set Staff.midiInstrument = #"blown bottle" \melody
\set Staff.midiInstrument = #"shakuhachi" \melody
\set Staff.midiInstrument = #"whistle" \melody
\set Staff.midiInstrument = #"ocarina" \melody
\set Staff.midiInstrument = #"lead 1 (square)" \melody
\set Staff.midiInstrument = #"lead 2 (sawtooth)" \melody
\set Staff.midiInstrument = #"lead 3 (calliope)" \melody
\set Staff.midiInstrument = #"lead 4 (chiff)" \melody
```

```
      \set Staff.midiInstrument = #"lead 5 (charang)" \melody
      \set Staff.midiInstrument = #"lead 6 (voice)" \melody
      \set Staff.midiInstrument = #"lead 7 (fifths)" \melody
      \set Staff.midiInstrument = #"lead 8 (bass+lead)" \melody
      \set Staff.midiInstrument = #"pad 1 (new age)" \melody
      \set Staff.midiInstrument = #"pad 2 (warm)" \melody
      \set Staff.midiInstrument = #"pad 3 (polysynth)" \melody
      \set Staff.midiInstrument = #"pad 4 (choir)" \melody
      \set Staff.midiInstrument = #"pad 5 (bowed)" \melody
      \set Staff.midiInstrument = #"pad 6 (metallic)" \melody
      \set Staff.midiInstrument = #"pad 7 (halo)" \melody
      \set Staff.midiInstrument = #"pad 8 (sweep)" \melody
      \set Staff.midiInstrument = #"fx 1 (rain)" \melody
      \set Staff.midiInstrument = #"fx 2 (soundtrack)" \melody
      \set Staff.midiInstrument = #"fx 3 (crystal)" \melody
      \set Staff.midiInstrument = #"fx 4 (atmosphere)" \melody
      \set Staff.midiInstrument = #"fx 5 (brightness)" \melody
      \set Staff.midiInstrument = #"fx 6 (goblins)" \melody
      \set Staff.midiInstrument = #"fx 7 (echoes)" \melody
      \set Staff.midiInstrument = #"fx 8 (sci-fi)" \melody
      \set Staff.midiInstrument = #"sitar" \melody
      \set Staff.midiInstrument = #"banjo" \melody
      \set Staff.midiInstrument = #"shamisen" \melody
      \set Staff.midiInstrument = #"koto" \melody
      \set Staff.midiInstrument = #"kalimba" \melody
      \set Staff.midiInstrument = #"bagpipe" \melody
      \set Staff.midiInstrument = #"fiddle" \melody
      \set Staff.midiInstrument = #"shanai" \melody
      \set Staff.midiInstrument = #"tinkle bell" \melody
      \set Staff.midiInstrument = #"agogo" \melody
      \set Staff.midiInstrument = #"steel drums" \melody
      \set Staff.midiInstrument = #"woodblock" \melody
      \set Staff.midiInstrument = #"taiko drum" \melody
      \set Staff.midiInstrument = #"melodic tom" \melody
      \set Staff.midiInstrument = #"synth drum" \melody
      \set Staff.midiInstrument = #"reverse cymbal" \melody
      \set Staff.midiInstrument = #"guitar fret noise" \melody
      \set Staff.midiInstrument = #"breath noise" \melody
      \set Staff.midiInstrument = #"seashore" \melody
      \set Staff.midiInstrument = #"bird tweet" \melody
      \set Staff.midiInstrument = #"telephone ring" \melody
      \set Staff.midiInstrument = #"helicopter" \melody
      \set Staff.midiInstrument = #"applause" \melody
      \set Staff.midiInstrument = #"gunshot" \melody
    }
  >>
  \midi { }
}
```

for now, just use piano,

```
\header {
  title = "Test of a piano rythm"
```

```
  arranger = "masara"
}

global = {
  \key c \major
  \time 4/4
}

right = \relative c' {
  \global
  \clef treble
  c4 d e f g1 \bar "|."
}

left = \relative c {
  \global
  \clef bass
  c2 g' c,1
}

\score {
  \new PianoStaff \with {
    instrumentName = "Piano"
  } <<
    \new Staff = "right" \right
    \new Staff = "left" \left
  >>
  \layout { }
  \midi { }
}
```

and notice that lilypond only makes mid,

```
import pygame as pg
def play_music(music_file):
  '''
  stream music with mixer.music module in blocking manner
  this will stream the sound from disk while playing
  '''
  clock = pg.time.Clock()
  try:
    pg.mixer.music.load(music_file)
    print("Music file {} loaded!".format(music_file))
  except pygame.error:
    print("File {} not found! {}".format(music_file, pg.get_error()))
    return
  pg.mixer.music.play()
  # check if playback has finished
  while pg.mixer.music.get_busy():
    clock.tick(30)
# pick a midi or other...
# or give full pathname
#music_file = "test.mod"
```

```
#music_file = "test.mp3"
music_file = "test.mid"

freq = 44100  # audio CD quality
bitsize = -16  # unsigned 16 bit
channels = 2  # 1 is mono, 2 is stereo
buffer = 2048  # number of samples (experiment to get right sound)
pg.mixer.init(freq, bitsize, channels, buffer)
# optional volume 0 to 1.0
pg.mixer.music.set_volume(0.5)
try:
  play_music(music_file)
except KeyboardInterrupt:
  # if user hits Ctrl/C then exit
  # (works only in console mode)
  pg.mixer.music.fadeout(1000)
  pg.mixer.music.stop()
  raise SystemExit
```

To format the mid into ly, we can use the installed script `midi2ly.py test.mid`, so we can download and ..., checkout https://freemidi.org/download4-3071-anywhere-is-enya,

if the mid port is ok to use, we can even write mid using pygame,

```
import pygame
import pygame.midi
from time import sleep

def midiExample():

    GRAND_PIANO = 0
    #CHURCH_ORGAN = 19
    #instrument = CHURCH_ORGAN
    instrument = GRAND_PIANO

    pygame.init()
    pygame.midi.init()

    port = pygame.midi.get_default_output_id()
    print ("using output_id :%s:" % port)
    midi_out = pygame.midi.Output(port, 0)
    try:
        midi_out.set_instrument(instrument)

        midi_out.note_on(72,127) # 74 is middle C, 127 is "how loud" - max is 127
        sleep(.5)
        midi_out.note_off(72,127)
        sleep(.5)

        midi_out.note_on(76,127) # E
        sleep(.5)
```

```
        midi_out.note_off(76,127)
        sleep(.5)

        midi_out.note_on(79,127) # G
        sleep(.5)
        midi_out.note_off(79,127)
        sleep(.5)

        midi_out.note_on(72,127)
        midi_out.note_on(76,127)
        midi_out.note_on(79,127)
        sleep(.5)
        midi_out.note_off(72,127)
        midi_out.note_off(76,127)
        midi_out.note_off(79,127)

    finally:
        del midi_out
        pygame.midi.quit()

midiExample()
```

and to save, 3 levels, sequence, track, file,

```
import pygame
import pygame.midi

pygame.init()
pygame.midi.init()

midi_sequence = [
    pygame.midi.NoteOn(72, 127),
    pygame.midi.NoteOff(72, 127),
    #...
]

midi_track = pygame.midi.Track(0)
for event in midi_sequence:
    midi_track.append(event)

midi_file = pygame.midi.MidiFile(1)
midi_file.tracks.append(midi_track)

midi_file.save("new_music.mid")
```

or in notation,

```
import pygame
import pygame.midi
from time import sleep
import sys
```

```
C = 74
MAX = 127
brief = .5

def midi(note=[C], volume=MAX, length=brief):
    for n in note:
        midi_out.note_on(n, volume) # 74 is middle C, 127 is "how loud" - max is 127
    sleep(brief)
    for n in note:
        midi_out.note_off(n, volume)
    sleep(brief)


#                init
# ========================================
GRAND_PIANO = 0
CHURCH_ORGAN = 19
instrument = CHURCH_ORGAN
pygame.init()
pygame.midi.init()
device = pygame.midi.get_count()
print(device)

port = pygame.midi.get_default_output_id()
print(port)
midi_out = pygame.midi.Output(1, 0)
midi_out.set_instrument(instrument)
print ("using output_id :%s:" % port)
# ========================================

def exit():
    global midi_out, music

    music = 0
    del midi_out
    pygame.midi.quit()
    pygame.quit()
    sys.exit()

CM = [74, 78, 81]
D = [74, 76, 81]
FM = [72, 76, 79]
screen = pygame.display.set_mode((400, 400))
music = 1
while True:
    for event in pygame.event.get():
        if event.type == pygame.QUIT:
            exit()
        if event.type == pygame.KEYDOWN:
            if event.key == pygame.K_ESCAPE:
                exit()
```

```
    if music:
        seq = CM, D, CM, FM
        for s in seq:
            midi(s)
```

what are the notation? checkout

- . Musical notation
    - 1.1 Pitches
    - 1.2 Rhythms
    - 1.3 Expressive marks
    - 1.4 Repeats
    - 1.5 Simultaneous notes
    - 1.6 Staff notation
        - 1.6.1 Displaying staves
        - 1.6.2 Modifying single staves
        - 1.6.3 Writing parts
    - 1.7 Editorial annotations
    - 1.8 Text
- 2. Specialist notation
    - 2.1 Vocal music
    - 2.2 Keyboard and other multi-staff instruments
    - 2.3 Unfretted string instruments
    - 2.4 Fretted string instruments
    - 2.5 Percussion
    - 2.6 Wind instruments
    - 2.7 Chord notation
    - 2.8 Contemporary music
    - 2.9 Ancient notation
    - 2.10 World music

so use lilypond can be more musical, and a student template sample,

```
\version "0.0.1"

\paper {
#(set-paper-size "a6") %papersizea6
}

%infos

\header {
title = "title" %title
```

```
composer = "author" %author
tagline = ##f %notag
}


\markup {
words %paragraph
}


\markuplist {
\wordwrap-lines{
longword,longword,longword,longword,longword,longword,longword,longword,

} %split
\wordwrap-lines{
The art of music typography is called \italic {(plate) engraving.}The term derives
from the traditional process of music printing.
Just a few decades ago,
} %newlineokforenglish
}


%write

%singleline
\score {
\relative c'{ %lowc
\clef "treble" %clefhigh
\time 2/4 %peat
\key c \major %tonec
c4 c|
g' g |
a a |g2 |
\bar "|." %over
}
\layout {
indent = 0 %notab
}
}

%onlystaff
\score {
<<
\new Staff {
\relative c'{
c1 d e f g a b c
}
}
\new Lyrics {
\lyricmode {
C D E F G A B C
}
```

```
}
>>
\layout {
indent = 0cm
\context {
\Staff
\remove "Time_signature_engraver"%canclesig
\remove "Bar_engraver" %cancelgrave
}
}
}

\markup {belowisscore}

%score

%righthand
pianoRH = \relative c'{
\clef "treble"
\time 2/4
\key c \major
c4 c |
g' g |
\break %newline
a a |
g2 |
\bar "|."
}


%lefthand
pianoLH = \relative c { %lowc
\clef "bass" %low
\time 2/4
\key c \major
c4 c |
g' g |
a a |
g2 |
\bar "|."
} %lefthandover


%plustwohands
\score {
\new PianoStaff <<
\new Staff {
\pianoRH %righthand
}
\new Staff {
\pianoLH %lefthand
}
>>
```

```
\layout{
indent=0cm
}
}
```

a teacher template sample,

```
\version "2.18.2"

\header {
  title = "Oh! Susanna"
  subtitle = "Don't you cry for me"
  instrument = "piano"
  composer = "Stephen Foster"
  copyright = "Public Domain"
  tagline = "This is a tagline"
}

global = {
  \key c \major
  \time 4/4
}

right = \relative c' {
  \global
  \clef treble
  \partial 4
  c8( d |
  e4) g g4. a8 |
  g4 e ~c4 ~c8 d8 |
  ees4 e d cis |
  d1 \bar "|."
}

left = \relative c {
  \global
  \clef bass
  r4 |
  <c e g>2 g4 a8-. b-. |
  c2 g4 \tuplet 3/2 {g8 a b} |
  c2 d4 s |
  g1
}

\score {
  \new PianoStaff \with {
    instrumentName = "Piano"
  } <<
    \new Staff = "right" \right
    \new Staff = "left" \left
  >>
  \layout { }
}
```

58 mingus

We can also use other packages to generate mid, and mingus is a good one since it can call lilypond executable so we can get the pdf,

```
from mingus.containers import Note, NoteContainer, Track, Composition
from mingus.midi import midi_file_out

note = Note('C')

note_container = NoteContainer(['C', 'E', 'G'])

track = Track()
track.add_notes(note_container, 4)

composition = Composition()
composition.add_track(track)

midi_file_out.write_Composition("C.mid", composition)

from mingus.extra import lilypond
#print(dir(lilypond))

lilypond.to_pdf(lilypond.from_Composition(composition), "C.pdf")

# output
['Key', 'Note', '__builtins__', '__cached__', '__doc__', '__file__', '__loader__',
'__name__', '__package__', '__spec__', 'absolute_import', 'from_Bar',
'from_Composition', 'from_Note', 'from_NoteContainer', 'from_Suite', 'from_Track',
'os', 'print_function', 'range', 'save_string_and_execute_LilyPond', 'subprocess',
'to_pdf', 'to_png', 'value']
```

Notice the lilypond should be in path, and we can get png too,

```
#powershell add path
#$Env:PATH += ";C:\Users\Lenovo\lilypond-2.23.1\bin"

#cmd add path
# set path "%PATH%;C:\Users\Lenovo\lilypond-2.23.1\bin"

import mingus.extra.lilypond as llp
b = Bar()
b + "C"
b + "E"
b + "G"
b + "B"
bar = llp.from_Bar(b)
llp.to_png(bar, "from_bar_to_png")
```

What is a note, and the difference from a notecontainer?

```
from mingus.containers import Note, NoteContainer

n = [Note("C", 4), Note("E", 4), Note("G", 4), Note("B", 4)]
nc = NoteContainer(["C", "E", "G", "B"])

print("n:")
for note in n:
    print(note)

print("nc:")
for note in nc:
    print(note)

# output
n:
'C-4'
'E-4'
'G-4'
'B-4'
nc:
'C-4'
'E-4'
'G-4'
'B-4'
```

we know playing piano uses two hands, so treat note as right, notecontainer as left,

```
from mingus.core import progressions
from mingus.containers import Note, NoteContainer, Track, Composition
from mingus.midi import midi_file_out

# chord
chord_progression = progressions.to_chords(['I', 'IV', 'V', 'I'], 'C')

# the track
track = Track()

# add notes to track
for chord in chord_progression:
    track.add_notes(NoteContainer(chord), 4)  # left
    track.add_notes(Note('C'), 4)  # right

# add track to composition
composition = Composition()
composition.add_track(track)

# save composition to mid
midi_file_out.write_Composition("playing.mid", composition)

# save composition to pdf
```

```
from mingus.extra import lilypond
lilypond.to_pdf(lilypond.from_Composition(composition), "C.pdf")
```

to read a mid,

```
from mingus.midi import midi_file_in, midi_file_out
from mingus.containers import Note

midi_data = midi_file_in.MIDI_to_Composition("composition.mid")

print(midi_data)

# output

([None, [[[0.0, 4.0, ['C-4', 'E-4', 'G-4']], [0.25, 4.0, ['C-4']], [0.5, 4.0, ['F-4', 'A-4', 'C-5']], [0.75, 4.0, ['C-4']]], [[0.0, 4.0, ['G-4', 'B-4', 'D-5']], [0.25, 4.0, ['C-4']], [0.5, 4.0, ['C-4', 'E-4', 'G-4']], [0.75, 4.0, ['C-4']]], [[0.0, 4.0, []]]]], 120)
```

and the notes,

```
track = midi_data[0]

print(track)

note = track[0]

output = ""
for each in note:
    output += str(each) + "\n"
print(output)

# output
[[0.0, 4.0, ['C-4', 'E-4', 'G-4']], [0.25, 4.0, ['C-4']], [0.5, 4.0, ['F-4', 'A-4', 'C-5']], [0.75, 4.0, ['C-4']]]
[[0.0, 4.0, ['G-4', 'B-4', 'D-5']], [0.25, 4.0, ['C-4']], [0.5, 4.0, ['C-4', 'E-4', 'G-4']], [0.75, 4.0, ['C-4']]]
[[0.0, 4.0, []]]
```

and to modify a note in the container, we can treat it as list,

```
for i in midi_data[0]:
    #print(i)
    for j in i:
        #print(j)
        for k in j: #print(type(k[2]))
            if isinstance(k[2], Note) or isinstance(k[2], NoteContainer):

                #k[2] = NoteContainer(["D"])
                #r = list(k[2]).index('C-4')
                #k[2] = k[2][:r]+['D-4']+k[2][r+1:]
                if len(k[2]) != 0:
```

```
                    k[2][0] = Note("D")

                print((k[2]))

# output
['D-4', 'E-4', 'G-4']
['D-4']
['D-4', 'A-4', 'C-5']
['D-4']
['D-4', 'B-4', 'D-5']
['D-4']
['D-4', 'E-4', 'G-4']
['D-4']
[]
```

and save as another file,

```
midi_file_out.write_Composition("changed_composition.mid", midi_data)
```

we can also not save the mid, just play it, checkout https://www.fluidsynth.org/download/,

```
# add fluidsynth path
#          prepare          a          file          FluidR3_GM.sf2          from
https://member.keymusician.com/Member/FluidR3_GM/index.html

# fluidsynth FluidR3_GM.sf2 changed_composition.mid

from mingus.containers import Bar

b = Bar()
b + "C"
b + "E"
b + "G"
b + "B"
from mingus.midi import fluidsynth
fluidsynth.init("FluidR3_GM.sf2")
fluidsynth.play_Bar(b, 1, 150)

# error
Traceback (most recent call last):
  File "D:\Books\python_files\ttt\FluidR3_GM\mingus_mid.py", line 8, in <module>
    from mingus.midi import fluidsynth
        File     "C:\Users\Lenovo\AppData\Local\Programs\Python\Python312\Lib\site-
packages\mingus\midi\fluidsynth.py", line 41, in <module>
    from mingus.midi import pyfluidsynth as fs
        File     "C:\Users\Lenovo\AppData\Local\Programs\Python\Python312\Lib\site-
packages\mingus\midi\pyfluidsynth.py", line 41, in <module>
    raise ImportError("Couldn't find the FluidSynth library.")
ImportError: Couldn't find the FluidSynth library.
```

Why is that? Go to the file pyfluidsynth.py line 41,

```
from ctypes.util import find_library

lib = find_library('fluidsynth') or find_library('libfluidsynth')\
     or find_library('libfluidsynth-1')
if lib is None:
    raise ImportError, "Couldn't find the FluidSynth library."
```

Well, lib not found, due to missing of the dll...

```
#      notepad      C:\Users\Lenovo\AppData\Local\Programs\Python\Python312\Lib\site-
packages\mingus\midi\pyfluidsynth.py
lib = (
    find_library("fluidsynth")
    or find_library("libfluidsynth")
    or find_library("libfluidsynth-1")
    or find_library("libfluidsynth-2") # add two and three
    or find_library("libfluidsynth-3")

)
```

rerun and we can hear, and we can select instrument now,

```
fluidsynth.set_instrument(1, 14)
```

and we can select other sound effect, checkout https://schristiancollins.com/generaluser.php

59 threading

To write a song, it is just from 0 to 7,

```
import json

from mingus.containers import *
from mingus.midi import fluidsynth
import mingus.core.chords as chords
from mingus.midi.midi_track import MidiTrack
from mingus.midi.midi_file_out import MidiFile

def tran(x):
    if x >= 'a':
        return ord(x) - 87
    elif x == '0':
        return 0.5
    else:
        return float(x)


data = {
    "symbol": [
```

```
        "12317716",
        "031200123316012155152523000123152067137017606711233200",
        "03120012331601215515252300012315202327710567123435211O554",
        "3054325103453160565224330665355332552201236",
        "543343121234561715 6^143211177",
        "50511252321023123432712507712523106716717610112234345 5554",
        "54334312554",
        "50511252321"
    ],
    "pitch": [
        "44443454",
        "444444444443444433434344444444444433443443343344444444",
        "44444444444344443343434444444444444334433344444344444444",
        "4434444444444444444444444444444444444444444",
        "44444444444444545444544444433",
        "44444444444444444444344443344344443343343344444444444444",
        "44444444444",
        "44444444444"
    ],
    "tempo": [
        "3111244g",
        "421542112114211112262118442112226211224211421121122844",
        "42154211121421111226211844211222621111242231121131218 4211",
        "4111142a211222621111211a1111211222112221122",
        "8314222i22222211a222a22224444",
        "4211833211a211211222112211112221121121121142112111111c211",
        "8314222e211",
        "4211833211e"
    ],
    "compose": [0, 0, 1, 2, 3, 4, 2, 3, 5, 3, 6, 3, 7],
    "chord": "2222222222222"
}


n = data['symbol']
h = data['pitch']
r = data['tempo']
l = data['compose']
k = data['chord']
t = Track()
b = Bar('C', (4, 4))
b.place_rest(1)
t.add_bar(b)
name = 'CDEFGAB'
symbol = '!@#$%^&'
for i in range(len(l)):
    rn = list(map(tran, r[l[i]]))
    b = Bar('C', (4 * sum(rn) / 8, 4))
    for j in range(len(n[l[i]])):
        if n[l[i]][j] == '0':
            b.place_rest(8 / rn[j])
        else:
            x = symbol.find(n[l[i]][j])
```

```
            if x == -1:
                x = int(n[l[i]][j]) - 1
                y = name[x]
            else:
                y = name[x] + '#'
                print(y)
            note = Note(y, int(h[l[i]][j]))
            note.transpose(k[i])
            b.place_notes(note, 8 / rn[j])
    t.add_bar(b)

print(t)
fluidsynth.init("FluidR3_GM.sf2")
fluidsynth.play_Track(t, 1, 150)

# output
A#
[None, [[[0.0, 1, None]], [[0.0, 2.6666666666666665, ['D-4']], [0.375, 8.0, ['E-
4']], [0.5, 8.0, ['F#-4']], [0.625, 8.0, ['D-4']], [0.75, 4.0, ['C#-4']], [1.0, 2.0,
['C#-5']], [1.5, 2.0, ['D-5']], [2.0, 0.5, ['B-4']]], [[0.0, 2.6666666666666665,
['D-4']], [0.375, 8.0, ['E-4']], [0.5, 8.0, ['F#-4']], [0.625, 8.0, ['D-4']], [0.75,
4.0, ['C#-4']], [1.0, 2.0, ['C#-5']], [1.5, 2.0, ['D-5']], [2.0, 0.5, ['B-4']]],
[[0.0, 2.0, None], [0.5, 4.0, ['F#-4']], [0.75, 8.0, ['D-4']], [0.875, 1.6, ['E-
4']], [1.5, 2.0, None], [2.0, 4.0, None], [2.25, 8.0, ['D-4']], [2.375, 8.0, ['E-
4']], [2.5, 4.0, ['F#-4']], [2.75, 8.0, ['F#-4']], [2.875, 8.0, ['D-4']], [3.0, 2.0,
['B-3']], [3.5, 4.0, None], [3.75, 8.0, ['D-4']], [3.875, 8.0, ['E-4']], [4.0, 8.0,
['D-4']], [4.125, 8.0, ['A-3']], [4.25, 4.0, ['A-3']], [4.5, 4.0, ['D-4']], [4.75,
1.3333333333333333, ['A-3']], [5.5, 4.0, ['E-4']], [5.75, 8.0, ['A-3']], [5.875,
8.0, ['E-4']], [6.0, 1.0, ['F#-4']], [7.0, 2.0, None], [7.5, 2.0, None], [8.0, 4.0,
None], [8.25, 8.0, ['D-4']], [8.375, 8.0, ['E-4']], [8.5, 4.0, ['F#-4']], [8.75,
4.0, ['D-4']], [9.0, 4.0, ['A-4']], [9.25, 1.3333333333333333, ['E-4']], [10.0, 4.0,
None], [10.25, 8.0, ['B-3']], [10.375, 8.0, ['C#-4']], [10.5, 4.0, ['D-4']], [10.75,
4.0, ['F#-4']], [11.0, 2.0, ['C#-4']], [11.5, 4.0, None], [11.75, 8.0, ['D-4']],
[11.875, 8.0, ['C#-4']], [12.0, 2.0, ['B-3']], [12.5, 4.0, None], [12.75, 8.0, ['B-
3']], [12.875, 8.0, ['C#-4']], [13.0, 4.0, ['D-4']], [13.25, 8.0, ['D-4']], [13.375,
8.0, ['E-4']], [13.5, 4.0, ['F#-4']], [13.75, 4.0, ['F#-4']], [14.0, 1.0, ['E-4']],
[15.0, 2.0, None], [15.5, 2.0, None]], [[0.0, 2.0, None], [0.5, 4.0, ['F#-4']],
[0.75, 8.0, ['D-4']], [0.875, 1.6, ['E-4']], [1.5, 2.0, None], [2.0, 4.0, None],
[2.25, 8.0, ['D-4']], [2.375, 8.0, ['E-4']], [2.5, 8.0, ['F#-4']], [2.625, 4.0,
['F#-4']], [2.875, 8.0, ['D-4']], [3.0, 2.0, ['B-3']], [3.5, 4.0, None], [3.75, 8.0,
['D-4']], [3.875, 8.0, ['E-4']], [4.0, 8.0, ['D-4']], [4.125, 8.0, ['A-3']], [4.25,
4.0, ['A-3']], [4.5, 4.0, ['D-4']], [4.75, 1.3333333333333333, ['A-3']], [5.5, 4.0,
['E-4']], [5.75, 8.0, ['A-3']], [5.875, 8.0, ['E-4']], [6.0, 1.0, ['F#-4']], [7.0,
2.0, None], [7.5, 2.0, None], [8.0, 4.0, None], [8.25, 8.0, ['D-4']], [8.375, 8.0,
['E-4']], [8.5, 4.0, ['F#-4']], [8.75, 4.0, ['D-4']], [9.0, 4.0, ['A-4']], [9.25,
1.3333333333333333, ['E-4']], [10.0, 4.0, None], [10.25, 8.0, ['E-4']], [10.375,
8.0, ['F#-4']], [10.5, 8.0, ['E-4']], [10.625, 8.0, ['C#-4']], [10.75, 4.0,
['C#-4']], [11.0, 2.0, ['D-4']], [11.5, 4.0, None], [11.75, 4.0, ['A-3']], [12.0,
2.6666666666666665, ['B-3']], [12.375, 8.0, ['C#-4']], [12.5, 8.0, ['D-4']],
[12.625, 4.0, ['E-4']], [12.875, 8.0, ['F#-4']], [13.0, 8.0, ['G-4']], [13.125,
2.6666666666666665, ['F#-4']], [13.5, 8.0, ['A-3']], [13.625, 4.0, ['E-4']],
[13.875, 8.0, ['D-4']], [14.0, 1.0, ['D-4']], [15.0, 2.0, None], [15.5, 4.0, ['A-
4']], [15.75, 8.0, ['A-4']], [15.875, 8.0, ['G-4']]], [[0.0, 2.0, ['F#-4']], [0.5,
```

8.0, None], [0.625, 8.0, ['A-3']], [0.75, 8.0, ['G-4']], [0.875, 8.0, ['F#-4']],
[1.0, 2.0, ['E-4']], [1.5, 4.0, ['A-4']], [1.75, 0.8, ['D-4']], [3.0, 4.0, None],
[3.25, 8.0, ['F#-4']], [3.375, 8.0, ['G-4']], [3.5, 4.0, ['A-4']], [3.75, 4.0,
['F#-4']], [4.0, 4.0, ['D-4']], [4.25, 1.3333333333333333, ['B-4']], [5.0, 4.0,
None], [5.25, 8.0, ['A-4']], [5.375, 8.0, ['B-4']], [5.5, 8.0, ['A-4']], [5.625,
8.0, ['E-4']], [5.75, 4.0, ['E-4']], [6.0, 8.0, ['G-4']], [6.125, 8.0, ['F#-4']],
[6.25, 0.8, ['F#-4']], [7.5, 8.0, None], [7.625, 8.0, ['B-4']], [7.75, 8.0, ['B-
4']], [7.875, 8.0, ['A-4']], [8.0, 4.0, ['F#-4']], [8.25, 8.0, ['A-4']], [8.375,
8.0, ['A-4']], [8.5, 4.0, ['F#-4']], [8.75, 4.0, ['F#-4']], [9.0, 4.0, ['E-4']],
[9.25, 8.0, ['A-4']], [9.375, 8.0, ['A-4']], [9.5, 4.0, ['E-4']], [9.75, 4.0, ['E-
4']], [10.0, 4.0, None], [10.25, 8.0, ['D-4']], [10.375, 8.0, ['E-4']], [10.5, 4.0,
['F#-4']], [10.75, 4.0, ['B-4']]], [[0.0, 1.0, ['A-4']], [1.0, 2.6666666666666665,
['G-4']], [1.375, 8.0, ['F#-4']], [1.5, 2.0, ['F#-4']], [2.0, 4.0, ['G-4']], [2.25,
4.0, ['F#-4']], [2.5, 4.0, ['D-4']], [2.75, 0.4444444444444444, ['E-4']], [5.0, 4.0,
['D-4']], [5.25, 4.0, ['E-4']], [5.5, 4.0, ['F#-4']], [5.75, 4.0, ['G-4']], [6.0,
4.0, ['A-4']], [6.25, 4.0, ['B-4']], [6.5, 8.0, ['D-5']], [6.625, 8.0, ['C#-5']],
[6.75, 0.8, ['D-5']], [8.0, 4.0, ['A-4']], [8.25, 4.0, ['B-4']], [8.5, 4.0,
['B#-4']], [8.75, 0.8, ['D-5']], [10.0, 4.0, ['G-4']], [10.25, 4.0, ['F#-4']],
[10.5, 4.0, ['E-4']], [10.75, 4.0, ['D-4']], [11.0, 2.0, ['D-4']], [11.5, 2.0, ['D-
4']], [12.0, 2.0, ['C#-4']], [12.5, 2.0, ['C#-4']]], [[0.0, 2.0, None], [0.5, 4.0,
['F#-4']], [0.75, 8.0, ['D-4']], [0.875, 1.6, ['E-4']], [1.5, 2.0, None], [2.0, 4.0,
None], [2.25, 8.0, ['D-4']], [2.375, 8.0, ['E-4']], [2.5, 8.0, ['F#-4']], [2.625,
4.0, ['F#-4']], [2.875, 8.0, ['D-4']], [3.0, 2.0, ['B-3']], [3.5, 4.0, None], [3.75,
8.0, ['D-4']], [3.875, 8.0, ['E-4']], [4.0, 8.0, ['D-4']], [4.125, 8.0, ['A-3']],
[4.25, 4.0, ['A-3']], [4.5, 4.0, ['D-4']], [4.75, 1.3333333333333333, ['A-3']],
[5.5, 4.0, ['E-4']], [5.75, 8.0, ['A-3']], [5.875, 8.0, ['E-4']], [6.0, 1.0,
['F#-4']], [7.0, 2.0, None], [7.5, 2.0, None], [8.0, 4.0, None], [8.25, 8.0, ['D-
4']], [8.375, 8.0, ['E-4']], [8.5, 4.0, ['F#-4']], [8.75, 4.0, ['D-4']], [9.0, 4.0,
['A-4']], [9.25, 1.3333333333333333, ['E-4']], [10.0, 4.0, None], [10.25, 8.0, ['E-
4']], [10.375, 8.0, ['F#-4']], [10.5, 8.0, ['E-4']], [10.625, 8.0, ['C#-4']],
[10.75, 4.0, ['C#-4']], [11.0, 2.0, ['D-4']], [11.5, 4.0, None], [11.75, 4.0, ['A-
3']], [12.0, 2.6666666666666665, ['B-3']], [12.375, 8.0, ['C#-4']], [12.5, 8.0, ['D-
4']], [12.625, 4.0, ['E-4']], [12.875, 8.0, ['F#-4']], [13.0, 8.0, ['G-4']],
[13.125, 2.6666666666666665, ['F#-4']], [13.5, 8.0, ['A-3']], [13.625, 4.0, ['E-
4']], [13.875, 8.0, ['D-4']], [14.0, 1.0, ['D-4']], [15.0, 2.0, None], [15.5, 4.0,
['A-4']], [15.75, 8.0, ['A-4']], [15.875, 8.0, ['G-4']]], [[0.0, 2.0, ['F#-4']],
[0.5, 8.0, None], [0.625, 8.0, ['A-3']], [0.75, 8.0, ['G-4']], [0.875, 8.0,
['F#-4']], [1.0, 2.0, ['E-4']], [1.5, 4.0, ['A-4']], [1.75, 0.8, ['D-4']], [3.0,
4.0, None], [3.25, 8.0, ['F#-4']], [3.375, 8.0, ['G-4']], [3.5, 4.0, ['A-4']],
[3.75, 4.0, ['F#-4']], [4.0, 4.0, ['D-4']], [4.25, 1.3333333333333333, ['B-4']],
[5.0, 4.0, None], [5.25, 8.0, ['A-4']], [5.375, 8.0, ['B-4']], [5.5, 8.0, ['A-4']],
[5.625, 8.0, ['E-4']], [5.75, 4.0, ['E-4']], [6.0, 8.0, ['G-4']], [6.125, 8.0,
['F#-4']], [6.25, 0.8, ['F#-4']], [7.5, 8.0, None], [7.625, 8.0, ['B-4']], [7.75,
8.0, ['B-4']], [7.875, 8.0, ['A-4']], [8.0, 4.0, ['F#-4']], [8.25, 8.0, ['A-4']],
[8.375, 8.0, ['A-4']], [8.5, 4.0, ['F#-4']], [8.75, 4.0, ['F#-4']], [9.0, 4.0, ['E-
4']], [9.25, 8.0, ['A-4']], [9.375, 8.0, ['A-4']], [9.5, 4.0, ['E-4']], [9.75, 4.0,
['E-4']], [10.0, 4.0, None], [10.25, 8.0, ['D-4']], [10.375, 8.0, ['E-4']], [10.5,
4.0, ['F#-4']], [10.75, 4.0, ['B-4']]], [[0.0, 2.0, ['A-4']], [0.5, 4.0, None],
[0.75, 8.0, ['A-4']], [0.875, 8.0, ['D-4']], [1.0, 1.0, ['D-4']], [2.0,
2.6666666666666665, ['E-4']], [2.375, 2.6666666666666665, ['A-4']], [2.75, 4.0, ['E-
4']], [3.0, 8.0, ['F#-4']], [3.125, 8.0, ['E-4']], [3.25, 0.8, ['D-4']], [4.5, 4.0,
None], [4.75, 8.0, ['E-4']], [4.875, 8.0, ['F#-4']], [5.0, 4.0, ['D-4']], [5.25,
8.0, ['E-4']], [5.375, 8.0, ['F#-4']], [5.5, 4.0, ['G-4']], [5.75, 4.0, ['F#-4']],

```
[6.0, 4.0, ['E-4']], [6.25, 8.0, ['C#-4']], [6.375, 8.0, ['D-4']], [6.5, 4.0, ['E-
4']], [6.75, 4.0, ['A-4']], [7.0, 8.0, None], [7.125, 8.0, ['C#-4']], [7.25, 8.0,
['C#-4']], [7.375, 8.0, ['D-4']], [7.5, 4.0, ['E-4']], [7.75, 4.0, ['A-3']], [8.0,
4.0, ['E-4']], [8.25, 8.0, ['F#-4']], [8.375, 8.0, ['D-4']], [8.5, 4.0, None],
[8.75, 8.0, ['B-3']], [8.875, 8.0, ['C#-4']], [9.0, 4.0, ['D-4']], [9.25, 8.0, ['B-
3']], [9.375, 8.0, ['C#-4']], [9.5, 4.0, ['D-4']], [9.75, 8.0, ['C#-4']], [9.875,
8.0, ['B-3']], [10.0, 2.0, ['D-4']], [10.5, 4.0, None], [10.75, 8.0, ['D-4']],
[10.875, 8.0, ['D-4']], [11.0, 4.0, ['E-4']], [11.25, 8.0, ['E-4']], [11.375, 8.0,
['F#-4']], [11.5, 8.0, ['G-4']], [11.625, 8.0, ['F#-4']], [11.75, 8.0, ['G-4']],
[11.875, 8.0, ['A-4']], [12.0, 0.6666666666666666, ['A-4']], [13.5, 4.0, ['A-4']],
[13.75, 8.0, ['A-4']], [13.875, 8.0, ['G-4']]], [[0.0, 2.0, ['F#-4']], [0.5, 8.0,
None], [0.625, 8.0, ['A-3']], [0.75, 8.0, ['G-4']], [0.875, 8.0, ['F#-4']], [1.0,
2.0, ['E-4']], [1.5, 4.0, ['A-4']], [1.75, 0.8, ['D-4']], [3.0, 4.0, None], [3.25,
8.0, ['F#-4']], [3.375, 8.0, ['G-4']], [3.5, 4.0, ['A-4']], [3.75, 4.0, ['F#-4']],
[4.0, 4.0, ['D-4']], [4.25, 1.3333333333333333, ['B-4']], [5.0, 4.0, None], [5.25,
8.0, ['A-4']], [5.375, 8.0, ['B-4']], [5.5, 8.0, ['A-4']], [5.625, 8.0, ['E-4']],
[5.75, 4.0, ['E-4']], [6.0, 8.0, ['G-4']], [6.125, 8.0, ['F#-4']], [6.25, 0.8,
['F#-4']], [7.5, 8.0, None], [7.625, 8.0, ['B-4']], [7.75, 8.0, ['B-4']], [7.875,
8.0, ['A-4']], [8.0, 4.0, ['F#-4']], [8.25, 8.0, ['A-4']], [8.375, 8.0, ['A-4']],
[8.5, 4.0, ['F#-4']], [8.75, 4.0, ['F#-4']], [9.0, 4.0, ['E-4']], [9.25, 8.0, ['A-
4']], [9.375, 8.0, ['A-4']], [9.5, 4.0, ['E-4']], [9.75, 4.0, ['E-4']], [10.0, 4.0,
None], [10.25, 8.0, ['D-4']], [10.375, 8.0, ['E-4']], [10.5, 4.0, ['F#-4']], [10.75,
4.0, ['B-4']]], [[0.0, 1.0, ['A-4']], [1.0, 2.6666666666666665, ['G-4']], [1.375,
8.0, ['F#-4']], [1.5, 2.0, ['F#-4']], [2.0, 4.0, ['G-4']], [2.25, 4.0, ['F#-4']],
[2.5, 4.0, ['D-4']], [2.75, 0.5714285714285714, ['E-4']], [4.5, 4.0, ['A-4']],
[4.75, 8.0, ['A-4']], [4.875, 8.0, ['G-4']]], [[0.0, 2.0, ['F#-4']], [0.5, 8.0,
None], [0.625, 8.0, ['A-3']], [0.75, 8.0, ['G-4']], [0.875, 8.0, ['F#-4']], [1.0,
2.0, ['E-4']], [1.5, 4.0, ['A-4']], [1.75, 0.8, ['D-4']], [3.0, 4.0, None], [3.25,
8.0, ['F#-4']], [3.375, 8.0, ['G-4']], [3.5, 4.0, ['A-4']], [3.75, 4.0, ['F#-4']],
[4.0, 4.0, ['D-4']], [4.25, 1.3333333333333333, ['B-4']], [5.0, 4.0, None], [5.25,
8.0, ['A-4']], [5.375, 8.0, ['B-4']], [5.5, 8.0, ['A-4']], [5.625, 8.0, ['E-4']],
[5.75, 4.0, ['E-4']], [6.0, 8.0, ['G-4']], [6.125, 8.0, ['F#-4']], [6.25, 0.8,
['F#-4']], [7.5, 8.0, None], [7.625, 8.0, ['B-4']], [7.75, 8.0, ['B-4']], [7.875,
8.0, ['A-4']], [8.0, 4.0, ['F#-4']], [8.25, 8.0, ['A-4']], [8.375, 8.0, ['A-4']],
[8.5, 4.0, ['F#-4']], [8.75, 4.0, ['F#-4']], [9.0, 4.0, ['E-4']], [9.25, 8.0, ['A-
4']], [9.375, 8.0, ['A-4']], [9.5, 4.0, ['E-4']], [9.75, 4.0, ['E-4']], [10.0, 4.0,
None], [10.25, 8.0, ['D-4']], [10.375, 8.0, ['E-4']], [10.5, 4.0, ['F#-4']], [10.75,
4.0, ['B-4']]], [[0.0, 2.0, ['A-4']], [0.5, 4.0, None], [0.75, 8.0, ['A-4']],
[0.875, 8.0, ['D-4']], [1.0, 1.0, ['D-4']], [2.0, 2.6666666666666665, ['E-4']],
[2.375, 2.6666666666666665, ['A-4']], [2.75, 4.0, ['E-4']], [3.0, 8.0, ['F#-4']],
[3.125, 8.0, ['E-4']], [3.25, 0.5714285714285714, ['D-4']]]]]
```

and give left hand,

```
t2 = Track()
b = Bar('C', (4, 4))
b.place_rest(1)
t2.add_bar(b)
for i in range(int(sum(map(sum, map(lambda x: map(tran, r[x]), l)))) // 8):
    b = Bar('C', (4, 4))
    b.place_notes('C-3', 4)
    b.place_notes('C-7', 4)
    b.place_notes('C-5', 4)
```

```
    b.place_notes('C-7', 4)
    t2.add_bar(b)
print(t2)
fluidsynth.init("FluidR3_GM.sf2")
fluidsynth.play_Track(t2, 1, 150)
```

use thread to make two hands syncornize,

```
thread1 = threading.Thread(target=lambda : fluidsynth.play_Track(t2, channel=1,
bpm=150))
thread2 = threading.Thread(target=lambda : fluidsynth.play_Track(t, channel=2,
bpm=150))
thread1.start()
thread2.start()
```

so thread is used to make the best use of multi core CPU, recall that CPU can seperate jobs into different tasks,

```
import logging
import threading
import time

def thread_function(name):
    logging.info("Thread %s: starting", name)
    time.sleep(2)
    logging.info("Thread %s: finishing", name)

if __name__ == "__main__":
    format = "%(asctime)s: %(message)s"
    logging.basicConfig(format=format, level=logging.INFO,
                        datefmt="%H:%M:%S")

    threads = list()
    for index in range(3):
        logging.info("Main    : create and start thread %d.", index)
        x = threading.Thread(target=thread_function, args=(index,))
        threads.append(x)
        x.start()

    for index, thread in enumerate(threads):
        logging.info("Main    : before joining thread %d.", index)
        thread.join()
        logging.info("Main    : thread %d done", index)

# output
23:56:28: Main    : create and start thread 0.
23:56:28: Thread 0: starting
23:56:28: Main    : create and start thread 1.
23:56:28: Thread 1: starting
23:56:28: Main    : create and start thread 2.
23:56:28: Thread 2: starting
23:56:28: Main    : before joining thread 0.
```

```
23:56:30: Thread 1: finishing
23:56:30: Thread 0: finishing
23:56:30: Thread 2: finishing
23:56:30: Main    : thread 0 done
23:56:30: Main    : before joining thread 1.
23:56:30: Main    : thread 1 done
23:56:30: Main    : before joining thread 2.
23:56:30: Main    : thread 2 done
```

the reason to use thread is to make processing faster,

```
from time import perf_counter

def replace(filename, substr, new_substr):
    print(f'Processing the file {filename}')
    # get the contents of the file
    with open(filename, 'r') as f:
        content = f.read()

    # replace the substr by new_substr
    content = content.replace(substr, new_substr)

    # write data into the file
    with open(filename, 'w') as f:
        f.write(content)

def main():
    filenames = [
        'c:/temp/test1.txt',
        'c:/temp/test2.txt',
        'c:/temp/test3.txt',
        'c:/temp/test4.txt',
        'c:/temp/test5.txt',
        'c:/temp/test6.txt',
        'c:/temp/test7.txt',
        'c:/temp/test8.txt',
        'c:/temp/test9.txt',
        'c:/temp/test10.txt',
    ]

    for filename in filenames:
        replace(filename, 'ids', 'id')


if __name__ == "__main__":
    start_time = perf_counter()

    main()

    end_time = perf_counter()
    print(f'It took {end_time- start_time :0.2f} second(s) to complete.')

# compare to below
```

```
from threading import Thread
from time import perf_counter

def replace(filename, substr, new_substr):
    print(f'Processing the file {filename}')
    # get the contents of the file
    with open(filename, 'r') as f:
        content = f.read()

    # replace the substr by new_substr
    content = content.replace(substr, new_substr)

    # write data into the file
    with open(filename, 'w') as f:
        f.write(content)

def main():
    filenames = [
        'c:/temp/test1.txt',
        'c:/temp/test2.txt',
        'c:/temp/test3.txt',
        'c:/temp/test4.txt',
        'c:/temp/test5.txt',
        'c:/temp/test6.txt',
        'c:/temp/test7.txt',
        'c:/temp/test8.txt',
        'c:/temp/test9.txt',
        'c:/temp/test10.txt',
    ]

    # create threads
    threads = [Thread(target=replace, args=(filename, 'id', 'ids'))
            for filename in filenames]

    # start the threads
    for thread in threads:
        thread.start()

    # wait for the threads to complete
    for thread in threads:
        thread.join()


if __name__ == "__main__":
    start_time = perf_counter()

    main()

    end_time = perf_counter()
    print(f'It took {end_time- start_time :0.2f} second(s) to complete.')
```

it can save time up to 8 times, however notice the race condition,

```
import logging
import threading
import time
import concurrent.futures

class FakeDatabase:
    def __init__(self):
        self.value = 0

    def update(self, name):
        logging.info("Thread %s: starting update", name)
        local_copy = self.value
        local_copy += 1
        time.sleep(0.1)
        self.value = local_copy
        logging.info("Thread %s: finishing update", name)

if __name__ == "__main__":
    format = "%(asctime)s: %(message)s"
    logging.basicConfig(format=format, level=logging.INFO,
                        datefmt="%H:%M:%S")

    database = FakeDatabase()
    logging.info("Testing update. Starting value is %d.", database.value)
    with concurrent.futures.ThreadPoolExecutor(max_workers=2) as executor:
        for index in range(2):
            executor.submit(database.update, index)
    logging.info("Testing update. Ending value is %d.", database.value)

# output
00:06:44: Testing update. Starting value is 0.
00:06:44: Thread 0: starting update
00:06:44: Thread 1: starting update
00:06:44: Thread 0: finishing update
00:06:44: Thread 1: finishing update
00:06:44: Testing update. Ending value is 1.
```

why the output is not ending value 2?

![[thread.png]]

Thread is object, it runs until finish, it can be blocked, can hold data, can be in format of dictionaries, lists, sets, and can be passed as parameter to function.

Let's start with one thread,

```
import logging
import threading
import time

def thread_function(name):
```

```
    logging.info("Thread %s: starting", name)
    time.sleep(2)
    logging.info("Thread %s: finishing", name)

if __name__ == "__main__":
    format = "%(asctime)s: %(message)s"
    logging.basicConfig(format=format, level=logging.INFO,
                        datefmt="%H:%M:%S")

    logging.info("Main    : before creating thread")
    x = threading.Thread(target=thread_function, args=(1,))
    logging.info("Main    : before running thread")
    x.start()
    logging.info("Main    : wait for the thread to finish")

    logging.info("Main    : all done")
```

and if we use enable daemon,

```
    x = threading.Thread(target=thread_function, args=(1,), daemon=True)
```

the thread finishing is not going to be printed, since it is in the background, which daemon means. What is `join()`?

```
import threading
import time

# Define a function that simulates a task
def print_squares():
    for i in range(1, 4):
        print(f"Square of {i}: {i ** 2}")
        time.sleep(1)

# Create a thread that runs the print_squares function
thread = threading.Thread(target=print_squares)

# Start the thread
thread.start()

# Wait for the thread to complete
#thread.join() # uncomment this to compare

# This line will execute after the thread finishes
print("Thread has completed.")

# output
Square of 1: 1
Thread has completed.
Square of 2: 4
Square of 3: 9

# uncomment
```

```
Square of 1: 1
Square of 2: 4
Square of 3: 9
Thread has completed.
```

so `join()` is wait, easy?

```
import threading

# Create a condition object
condition = threading.Condition()

# Shared resource
data_ready = False

# Function to produce data
def producer():
    global data_ready
    with condition:
        print("Producing data...")
        data_ready = True
        condition.notify()  # Notify the consumer that data is ready

# Function to consume data
def consumer():
    global data_ready
    with condition:
        condition.wait()  # Wait for data to be ready
        if data_ready:
            print("Consuming data...")

# Create threads for producer and consumer
producer_thread = threading.Thread(target=producer)
consumer_thread = threading.Thread(target=consumer)

# Start the consumer first
consumer_thread.start()
producer_thread.start()

# Wait for both threads to complete
consumer_thread.join()
producer_thread.join()
```

notice the order is important, and these two threads can mimic stock sale, one sell, one buy,

```
import threading
from concurrent.futures import ThreadPoolExecutor
import concurrent.futures

import random

```

```
SENTINEL = object()

def producer(pipeline):
    for index in range(10):
        message = random.randint(1, 101)
        print("Producer sell message:", message)

        pipeline.set_message(message, "Producer")

    # Send a sentinel message to tell consumer we're done
    pipeline.set_message(SENTINEL, "Producer")

def consumer(pipeline):
    message = 0
    while message is not SENTINEL:
        message = pipeline.get_message("Consumer")
        if message is not SENTINEL:
            print("Consumer buy message:", message)

class Pipeline:
    """
    Class to allow a single element pipeline between producer and consumer.
    """
    def __init__(self):
        self.message = 0
        self.producer_lock = threading.Lock()
        self.consumer_lock = threading.Lock()
        self.consumer_lock.acquire()

    def get_message(self, name):
        self.consumer_lock.acquire()
        message = self.message
        self.producer_lock.release()
        return message

    def set_message(self, message, name):
        self.producer_lock.acquire()
        self.message = message
        self.consumer_lock.release()

if __name__ == "__main__":

    pipeline = Pipeline()
    with concurrent.futures.ThreadPoolExecutor(max_workers=2) as executor:
        executor.submit(producer, pipeline)
        executor.submit(consumer, pipeline)
```

Let’s say there are three web sources have the stock info, we can fetch them all, in thread,

```
from concurrent.futures import ThreadPoolExecutor
import time
```

```
# Define a function that simulates a task
def fetch_data(w3r):
    print(f"Fetching data from {w3r}...")
    time.sleep(2)  # Simulate a delay
    return f"Data from {w3r}"

# Websites to fetch data from
websites = ['w3r1.com', 'w3r2.com', 'w3r3.com']

# Use ThreadPoolExecutor to manage threads
with ThreadPoolExecutor(max_workers=3) as executor:
    # Map the fetch_data function to the list of websites
    results = executor.map(fetch_data, websites)

# Print the results
for result in results:
    print(result)
```

`ThreadPoolExecutor` simplifies the list block of the multiple threads, otherwise,

```
import threading
import time

def thread_function(w3r):
    print(f"Fetching data from {w3r}...")
    time.sleep(2)# Simulate a delay
    return f"Data from {w3r}"

threads = list()# Websites to fetch data from
websites = ['w3r1.com', 'w3r2.com', 'w3r3.com']

for web in websites:
    x = threading.Thread(target = thread_function, args = (web, ))
    threads.append(x)
    x.start()

for index, thread in enumerate(threads):
    thread.join()
```

60 multiprocessing

Before a CPU has only one core, that is why multiple processes are developed, the problem about how OS build a scheduler.

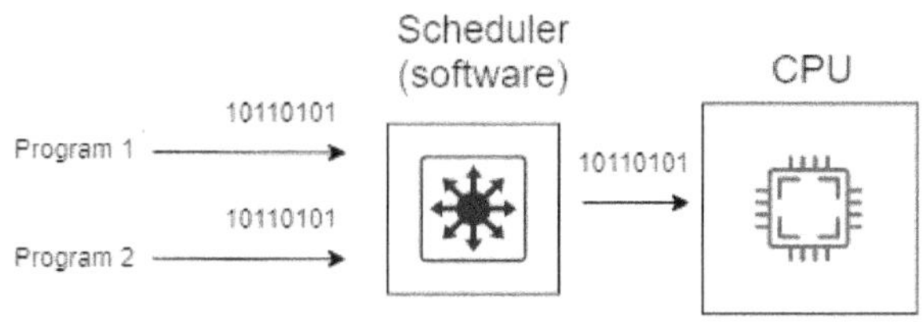

The main difference between process and thread is share memory or IPC, GIL or no GIL. GIL, Global Interpreter Lock, is used within each process, but not across processes. It means only one thread can be in a state of execution. Yes, there is a lock to ensure this.

Compare

```
import time

COUNT = 50000000

def countdown(n):
    while n>0:
        n -= 1

start = time.time()
countdown(COUNT)
end = time.time()

print('Time taken in seconds -', end - start)
```

and

```
import multiprocessing
import time

COUNT = 50000000

def countdown(n):
    while n>0:
        n -= 1

if __name__ == "__main__":
    # creating processes
    start = time.time()
    p1 = multiprocessing.Process(target = countdown, args =(COUNT//2, ))
    p2 = multiprocessing.Process(target = countdown, args =(COUNT//2, ))

    # starting process 1
    p1.start()
    # starting process 2
    p2.start()
```

```
    # wait until process 1 is finished
    p1.join()
    # wait until process 2 is finished
    p2.join()
    end = time.time()
    print('Time taken in seconds -', end - start)
```

and

```
from threading import Thread
import time

COUNT = 50000000

def countdown(n):
    while n>0:
        n -= 1

t1 = Thread(target = countdown, args =(COUNT//2, ))
t2 = Thread(target = countdown, args =(COUNT//2, ))

start = time.time()
t1.start()
t2.start()
t1.join()
t2.join()
end = time.time()

print('Time taken in seconds -', end - start)
```

We can see multiple thread is faster than multiple process, and we can see no join is faster,

```
import threading
import multiprocessing
import time

# Test function
def calc_square(numbers):
    for n in numbers:
        time.sleep(0.01)
        result = n*n

if __name__ == "__main__":

    numbers = [1,2,3,4]

    # Threads test
    start = time.time()
    threads = []
    for _ in range(4):
        thread = threading.Thread(target=calc_square, args=(numbers,))
```

```
        threads.append(thread)
        thread.start()

    for thread in threads:
        print(thread)
        #thread.join()

    print("Threads time:", time.time() - start)

    # Processes test
    start = time.time()
    processes = []
    for _ in range(4):
        process = multiprocessing.Process(target=calc_square, args=(numbers,))
        processes.append(process)
        process.start()

    for process in processes:
        print(process)
        #process.join()

    print("Processes time:", time.time() - start)
```

In reality, server usually provides a lot of threads to be connected,

```
import socket
import threading

def sometask():
    return "hello world"

def server(address):
    sock = socket.socket(socket.AF_INET, socket.SOCK_STREAM)
    sock.setsockopt(socket.SOL_SOCKET, socket.SO_REUSEADDR, 1)
    sock.bind(address)
    sock.listen(5)
    while True:
        client, addr = sock.accept()
        print("connection from ", addr)
        th = threading.Thread(target=handler, args=(client, ))
        th.start()

def handler(client):
    while True:
        req = client.recv(100)
        if not req:
            break
        res = sometask()
        resp = str(res).encode('ascii') + b'\n'
        client.send(resp)
        print("req closed")

server( ("localhost", 8000) )
```

and clients can connect to it by thread too,

```
import socket
import threading
import time


sock = socket.socket(socket.AF_INET, socket.SOCK_STREAM)
sock.connect( ("localhost", 8000) )

n = 0

def printReqRate():
    global n
    while True:
        time.sleep(1)
        print(n)
        n = 0

counter = threading.Thread(target=printReqRate)
counter.start()

while True:
    sock.send(b'1')
    resp = sock.recv(100)
    n += 1
```

and we can check the CPU usage,

```
import psutil

# Calling psutil.cpu_precent() for 4 seconds
print('The %CPU usage is: ', psutil.cpu_percent(4))
```

and memory usage,

```
import psutil

# Getting % usage of virtual_memory ( 3rd field)
print('The %memory usage is:', psutil.virtual_memory()[2])
# Getting usage of virtual_memory in GB ( 4th field)
print('RAM Used (GB):', psutil.virtual_memory()[3]/1000000000)
```

strictly, the bit should be 1024 times, not 1000,

```
def get_ram_usage():
    """
    Obtains the absolute number of RAM bytes currently in use by the system.
    :returns: System RAM usage in bytes.
    :rtype: int
    """
    return int(psutil.virtual_memory().total - psutil.virtual_memory().available)
```

```
print('RAM usage (MB)', int(get_ram_usage() / 1024 / 1024)
```

The server can be written in multiple process, pool, too,

```
import socket
from concurrent.futures import ProcessPoolExecutor

def sometask():
    return "hello world"


def server(address):
    sock = socket.socket(socket.AF_INET, socket.SOCK_STREAM)
    sock.setsockopt(socket.SOL_SOCKET, socket.SO_REUSEADDR, 1)
    sock.bind(address)
    sock.listen(5)
    while True:
        client, addr = sock.accept()
        print("connection from ", addr)
        executor.submit(handler, client)


def handler(client):
    while True:
        req = client.recv(100)
        if not req:
            break
        res = sometask()
        resp = str(res).encode('ascii') + b'\n'
        client.send(resp)
        print("req closed")


executor = ProcessPoolExecutor(4)
server( ("localhost", 8000) )
```

Which is better is not definite, we have to see from the log, of CPU and memory, just choose the smaller one, or combine thread and process, to acheive the goal.

61 asyncio

Over socket, asyncio is a direct single threaded concurrent coroutines, multiplexing I/O access network suites, we can write both server

```
import asyncio

async def handle_client(reader, writer):
    data = await reader.read(100)
```

```
    message = data.decode()
    addr = writer.get_extra_info('peername')
    print(f"Received {message} from {addr}")

    #writer.write(data)
    writer.write(f"Reply to {message}".encode())
    await writer.drain()
    writer.close()

async def main():
    server = await asyncio.start_server(
        handle_client, '127.0.0.1', 8000)
    addr = server.sockets[0].getsockname()
    print(f'Serving on {addr}')
    # accept client connections forever (kill via control-c)

    async with server:
        await server.serve_forever()

asyncio.run(main())
```

and client,

```
import asyncio
async def send_message(message):
    reader, writer = await asyncio.open_connection('localhost', 8000)
    writer.write(message.encode())
    await writer.drain()
    data = await reader.read(100)
    response = data.decode()
    print(f"Received {response}")
    writer.close()
    await writer.wait_closed()

import sys
inp = sys.argv[1]
asyncio.run(send_message(inp))
```

the important thing is asyncio uses async/await, which in other words, callback,

```
import asyncio

async def set_value(fut, value):
    fut.set_result(value)

def callback1(future):
    print('Callback 1:', future.result())

def callback2(future):
    print('Callback 2:', future.result())

async def main():
```

```
    fut = asyncio.Future()
    # Add multiple callbacks
    fut.add_done_callback(callback1)
    fut.add_done_callback(callback2)
    # Set the future's result
    await set_value(fut, 'Multiple Callbacks!')

asyncio.run(main())

# output
Callback 1: Multiple Callbacks!
Callback 2: Multiple Callbacks!
```

we can also put a schedule timer,

```
import asyncio
import time


def callback(n, loop):
    print('callback {} invoked at {}'.format(n, loop.time()))


async def main(loop):
    now = loop.time()
    print('clock time: {}'.format(time.time()))
    print('loop  time: {}'.format(now))

    print('registering callbacks')
    loop.call_at(now + 0.2, callback, 1, loop)
    loop.call_at(now + 0.1, callback, 2, loop)
    loop.call_soon(callback, 3, loop)

    await asyncio.sleep(1)


event_loop = asyncio.get_event_loop()
try:
    print('entering event loop')
    event_loop.run_until_complete(main(event_loop))
finally:
    print('closing event loop')
    event_loop.close()

# output
entering event loop
clock time: 1734592181.305935
loop  time: 195843.421
registering callbacks
callback 3 invoked at 195843.421
callback 2 invoked at 195843.531
```

```
callback 1 invoked at 195843.625
closing event loop
```

callback is good to use not only because it can delay the time, but it is a hook wait for real hardware input,

```
async def process_data_async():
    try:
        result = await midi_input() # wait the value here
        return result
    except Exception as e:
        raise e

import asyncio

async def main():
    try:
        result = await process_data_async()
        print(f"Data processed: {result}")
    except Exception as e:
        print(f"Error: {e}")

if __name__ == '__main__':
    asyncio.run(main())
```

another common use is parallel download,

```
import asyncio
import aiohttp

async def download_file(session, url):
    async with session.get(url) as response:
        filename = url.split('/')[-1]
        with open(filename, 'wb') as f:
            while True:
                chunk = await response.content.read(1024)
                if not chunk:
                    break
                f.write(chunk)
        print(f"Downloaded {filename}")

async def main():
        urls    =    ['http://example.com/file1',    'http://example.com/file2',
'http://example.com/file3']
    async with aiohttp.ClientSession() as session:
        tasks = [asyncio.create_task(download_file(session, url)) for url in urls]
        await asyncio.gather(*tasks)

asyncio.run(main())
```

we can even bundle to thread,

```
def download_data():

    # import the Timer module to schedule a callback function
    from threading import Timer

    # create a Timer object after 5 seconds
    # call process_data
    timer = Timer(5.0, process_data)
    # and call asyncio
    asyncio.run(main())
    # start the timer
    timer.start()

# Define the callback function that processes the downloaded data
def process_data():
    # do something with the downloaded data!
    print("Data processing complete!")
```

for larger file, we can cut into pieces,

```
import asyncio
import aiohttp

async def download_file(url, file_name):
    async with aiohttp.ClientSession() as session:
        async with session.get(url) as resp:
            if resp.status == 200:
                file_size = int(resp.headers['Content-Length'])
                with open(file_name, 'wb') as fd:
                    progress = 0
                    while True:
                        chunk = await resp.content.read(1024)
                        if not chunk:
                            break
                        fd.write(chunk)
                        progress += len(chunk)
                        percentage = (progress / file_size) * 100
                        print(f"Download Progress: {percentage:.2f}%")
            else:
                print("Failed to download the file.")
```

Recall the common generator,

```
def common_generator():
    yield 0
    yield 1
    yield 2
    yield 3

# Using the generator
for value in simple_generator():
    print(value)
```

asyncio also has a generator,

```
import asyncio

async def async_gen():
    for i in range(4):
        # Simulate an asynchronous operation with asyncio.sleep
        await asyncio.sleep(1)
        yield i

async def main():
    async for value in async_gen():
        print(value)

# Running the coroutine with asyncio.run
import asyncio
asyncio.run(main())
```

the powerful asyncio can even name the task,

```
import asyncio

async def my_named_coroutine():
    print("Task with a name")

async def main():
    named_task = asyncio.create_task(my_named_coroutine(), name="masara")
    await named_task
    # Output the task name
    print(named_task.get_name())

asyncio.run(main())
```

just like find a person, we can find a task by name,

```
import asyncio

async def find_task_by_name(task_name):
    for task in asyncio.all_tasks():
        if task.get_name() == task_name:
            return task
    return None

async def main():
    task1 = asyncio.create_task(asyncio.sleep(1), name="AAPL")
    task2 = asyncio.create_task(asyncio.sleep(1), name="MSTR")
    task_to_find = await find_task_by_name("MSTR")
    if task_to_find:
        print(f"Found task by name: {task_to_find.get_name()}")
    else:
        print("Task not found.")
```

```
asyncio.run(main())
```

and to define error,

```
async def my_error():
    await asyncio.sleep(1)
    raise Exception("This is a mock error")

async def main():
    try:
        await my_error()
    except Exception as e:
        print(f"Error: {e}")

asyncio.run(main())
```

62 numpy

Use thread, async, we can order the calling function in time, the whole universe is just two things, time and space.

Do you know Steven Hawking? When I was a middle school student, I read his book, it is too hard to read, by hard I mean difficult, not soft, and now it is online, checkout https://www.amazon.com/Universe-Nutshell-Stephen-Hawking/dp/0593048156.

When I was in US, I seldom watch Netflix, which was a huge loss, and many loss was not noticed until people were old. Sad, happy, these are feelings, not even emotions, but very energy consuming, which would harm to the decision.

Make a decision, not an effort.

The people who were success all told us, be a man.

That's it?

Isn't it?

How long you are pretending, for so called balance? And not for yourself, but for your thought family, friends, girl friends, boy friends, close friends, open friends, which are just consuming your very lack, very out of use energy, same as Python dead wheel.

It just stucks.

```
Could not build wheels.
```

When you write very hard, import a lot package to make the program fast and productive, you see this, very frustrating.

It indicates that Python cannot compile the package into a wheel, but what does that mean?

Who cares?

Just upgrade, and rerun.

Yes, run, again and again, until sort out.

How do you think the universe?

Any logic?

Or metaphysical?

What is meta?

Checkout https://about.meta.com.

You probably use Messenger, Instagram, WhatsApp, do you use AI image generator?

Imagine a dog sitting in the ocean, an astronaut cat (a catstronaut, if you will), a tiger wearing a stylish suit, what on earth is going on?

![[Coke.jpg]] Made by Jake Peterson

Everything if you know the backside, will it still be cool?

```
import cv2
import numpy as np

img = cv2.imread("Coke.jpg")
#img = cv2.cvtColor(img, cv2.COLOR_BGR2GRAY)

print(type(img))

# Check the shape of the input image
print(img.shape)

# output
```

```
<class 'numpy.ndarray'>
(2000, 2000, 3)
```

and the ROI,

```
# [rows, columns]
roi = img[1750:1925, 75:250]

cv2.imshow('original', img)
cv2.imshow('cropped', roi)
cv2.waitKey(0)
cv2.destroyAllWindows()
```

and to blur this ROI, and replace back,

```


mask = cv2.cvtColor(roi, cv2.COLOR_BGR2GRAY)
ret, mask = cv2.threshold(mask, 10, 255, cv2.THRESH_BINARY)

roi = cv2.bitwise_and(roi, roi, mask = cv2.bitwise_not(mask))
print(roi)
img[1750:1925, 75:250]  = roi

# output
[[[20  6  7]
  [21  7  8]
  [21  7  8]
  ...
  [ 0  0  0]
  [ 0  0  0]
  [ 0  0  0]]

 [[20  6  7]
  [21  7  8]
  [21  7  8]
  ...
  [ 0  0  0]
  [ 0  0  0]
  [ 0  0  0]]

 [[21  7  8]
  [ 0  0  0]
  [ 0  0  0]
  ...
  [ 0  0  0]
  [ 0  0  0]
  [ 0  0  0]]

 ...

 [[22  6  7]
```

```
  [22   6   7]
  [22   6   7]
  ...
  [19   8  10]
  [19   8  10]
  [19   8  10]]

 [[22   6   7]
  [22   6   7]
  [22   6   7]
  ...
  [19   8  10]
  [19   8  10]
  [19   8  10]]

 [[22   6   7]
  [22   6   7]
  [22   6   7]
  ...
  [16   8   9]
  [17   9  10]
  [17   9  10]]]
```

this will only make the roi in dark, we want keep the frame, so maybe use numpy, to do some clip,

```
import numpy as np

print ("Input array : ", roi)

outroi = np.clip(roi, a_min =[17, 18, 19], a_max = 20)
print ("Output array : ", outroi)

img[1750:1925, 75:250]  = outroi
```

the min and max is the threshold, but notice roi is 3d array,

```
import cv2
import numpy as np

img = cv2.imread("Coke.jpg")
#img = cv2.cvtColor(img, cv2.COLOR_BGR2GRAY)
#print(img)
# [rows, columns]
cropped = img[1750:1925, 75:250]

newPath = "roi.jpg"
cv2.imwrite(newPath, cropped)
imgSY = cv2.imread(newPath, 1)
print(imgSY)

# from imgSY to try the thresh...
```

```
thresh = cv2.inRange(imgSY, np.array([6, 6, 6]), np.array([60, 100, 100]))
kernel = np.ones((3, 3), np.uint8)
hi_mask = cv2.dilate(thresh, kernel, iterations=10)
specular = cv2.inpaint(imgSY, hi_mask, 5, flags=cv2.INPAINT_TELEA)
cv2.imwrite(newPath, specular)


print(type(specular))
print(specular.shape)


img[1750:1925, 75:250]  = specular

cv2.imwrite('removed.png', img)
```

trying thresh can be very tired, how to make this adaptive?

Well, that requires a lot of fouriers transform, so hard…

Let's see the roi 3d array now,

```
import sys
import numpy as np
np.set_printoptions(threshold=sys.maxsize)
import cv2
roi = cv2.imread("roi.jpg")
print(roi)
```

What is roi?

```
import cv2
roi = cv2.imread("roi.jpg")
print(roi[0].shape)
print(roi[1].shape)
print(roi[2].shape)

# output
(175, 3)
(175, 3)
(175, 3)
```

so it has three dimensions, x, y, and z, each made of one 2d array,

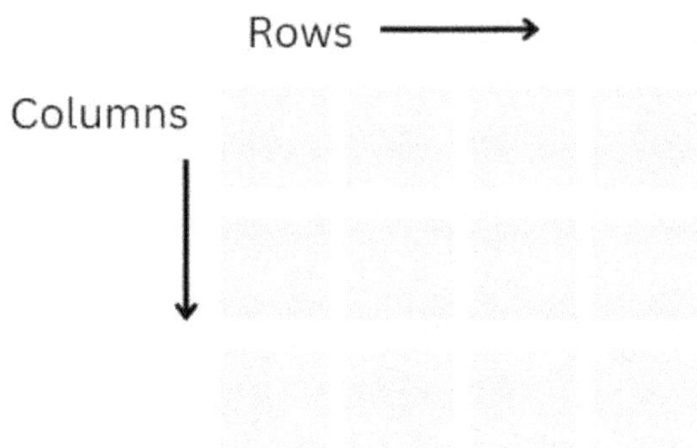

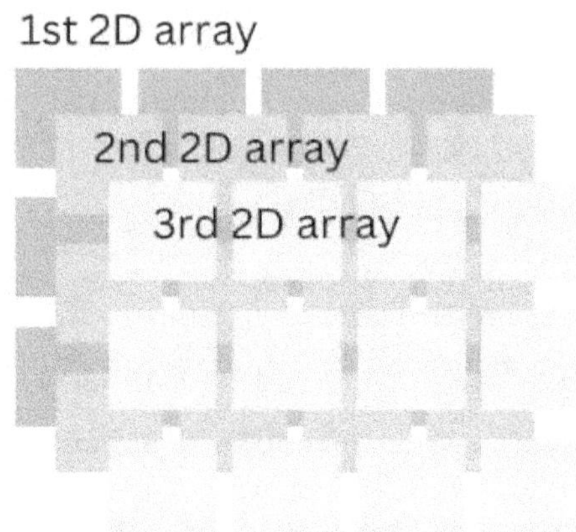

2D array: An array of arrays

3D array: An array of 2D arrays

```
import numpy as np
array_2 = np.array([[[1,2,3],[3,4,5]],
                    [[6,7,8],[9,8,7]],
                    [[6,5,4],[3,2,1]]])

print("# output")
print(array_2)

print(array_2.shape)
for i in array_2: print(i.shape)

# output
[[[1 2 3]
  [3 4 5]]

 [[6 7 8]
  [9 8 7]]

 [[6 5 4]
  [3 2 1]]]
(3, 2, 3)
(2, 3)
(2, 3)
(2, 3)
```

so (175, 175, 3) means 1d 175, and 175's 1d 175, and 3's 2d 175 175, therefore 4d is,

```
array_3 = np.array([[[[1,2],[3,4],[5,6]]],
                    [[[7,8],[9,8],[7,6]]],
                    [[[5,4],[3,2],[1,0]]]])
```

```
print("# output")
print(array_3)

# output
[[[[1 2]
   [3 4]
   [5 6]]]


 [[[7 8]
   [9 8]
   [7 6]]]


 [[[5 4]
   [3 2]
   [1 0]]]]
```

and it can be random, 3 groups of one line of 3 row 2 columns,

```
import numpy as np
array_3 = np.random.rand(3, 1, 3, 2)
print("# output")
print(array_3)
```

and to draw,

```
first_vol = array_3[:, :, :, 0]
from matplotlib import pyplot as plt
plt.imshow(first_vol[:, :, 14], cmap='gray')
```

4d plot is different from 4d array plot,

```
from matplotlib import pyplot as plt
import numpy as np
plt.rcParams["figure.figsize"] = [7.00, 3.50]
plt.rcParams["figure.autolayout"] = True
fig = plt.figure()
ax = fig.add_subplot(111, projection='3d')
x = np.random.standard_normal(100)
y = np.random.standard_normal(100)
z = np.random.standard_normal(100)
c = np.random.standard_normal(100)
img = ax.scatter(x, y, z, c=c, cmap='YlOrRd', alpha=1)
plt.show()
```

npy is the file format for numpy,

```
np.save(open('array_3.npy', 'wb'), array_3)
```

to filter out,

```
array = np.array([[1,2,3], [4,5,6]])
filtered = np.where(array > 2, array, np.NaN)

print(filtered)

# [[nan nan  3.]
#  [ 4.  5.  6.]]
```

random integer,

```
array = np.random.randint(low=4, high=13, size=(5,5))
print(array)

# [[ 8  7  9  6  9]
#  [ 4  5 10 12 11]
#  [10  6 12  6  9]
#  [11 12 11  6 12]
#  [ 4  7 12  6  4]]
```

concate,

```
a = np.array([[1,2], [3,4]])
b = np.array([[5,6]])

c = np.concatenate((a, b), axis=0)
print(c)

# [[1 2]
#  [3 4]
#  [5 6]]
```

notice concate is not add,

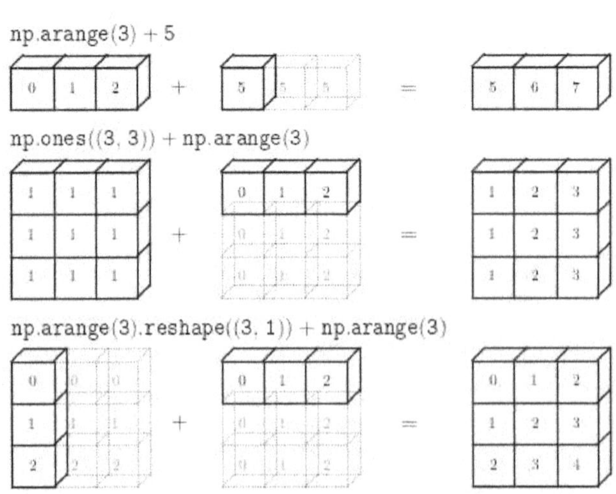

```
array_a = np.array([[1, 2],
                    [3, 4]])
# + 1
# array([[2, 3],
#        [4, 5]])

# + np.array([3, 1])
# array([[4, 3],
#        [6, 5]])
```

the 1d, 2d, 3d are usually named as vector, matrix, tensor,

```
vector = np.arange(5)
print("Vector shape:", vector.shape)

matrix = np.ones([3, 2])
print("Matrix shape:", matrix.shape)

tensor = np.zeros([2, 3, 3])
print("Tensor shape:", tensor.shape)
```

it is very easy to reshape the array,

```
arr = np.arange(1, 10)
print(arr, '\n')

# Reshape to 3x3 matrix
arr = arr.reshape(3, 3)
print(arr, '\n')

# Reshape back to the original size
arr = arr.reshape(9)
print(arr)
```

it is a good habit to use vector when add, much faster,

```
import numpy as np
#unvectorized version
def unvectorized_output(x, theta):
    h = []
    for i in range(x.shape[0]):
        total = 0
        for j in range(x.shape[1]):
            total = total + x[i, j] * theta[j, 0]
        h.append(total)
    return h

#Vectorized version
def vectorized_output(x, theta):
    h = np.matmul(x, theta) # NumPy's matrix multiplication function
    return h
```

```
import timeit
x = np.arange(1,41).reshape(10,4)

ones = np.full((10,1),1)

x = np.hstack((ones,x))

theta = np.arange(1,6).reshape(5,1)

time_taken = timeit.timeit(lambda: vectorized_output(x, theta), number=10000)

print(f"Time taken: {time_taken} seconds")

time_taken = timeit.timeit(lambda: unvectorized_output(x, theta), number=10000)

print(f"Time taken: {time_taken} seconds")
```

to subtract the import time,

```
import timeit
import_module = "import numpy as np"
testcode = '''
def unvectorized_output(x, theta):
    h = []
    for i in range(x.shape[0]):
        total = 0
        for j in range(x.shape[1]):
            total = total + x[i, j] * theta[j, 0]
        h.append(total)
    return h

x = np.arange(1,41).reshape(10,4)

ones = np.full((10,1),1)

x = np.hstack((ones,x))

theta = np.arange(1,6).reshape(5,1)

unvectorized_output(x, theta)
'''
print(timeit.timeit(stmt=testcode, setup=import_module))

# 39.963641999987885
```

we can repeat the timing too,

```
print(timeit.repeat(stmt=testcode, setup=import_module, repeat=5))
```

now let's see what is color,

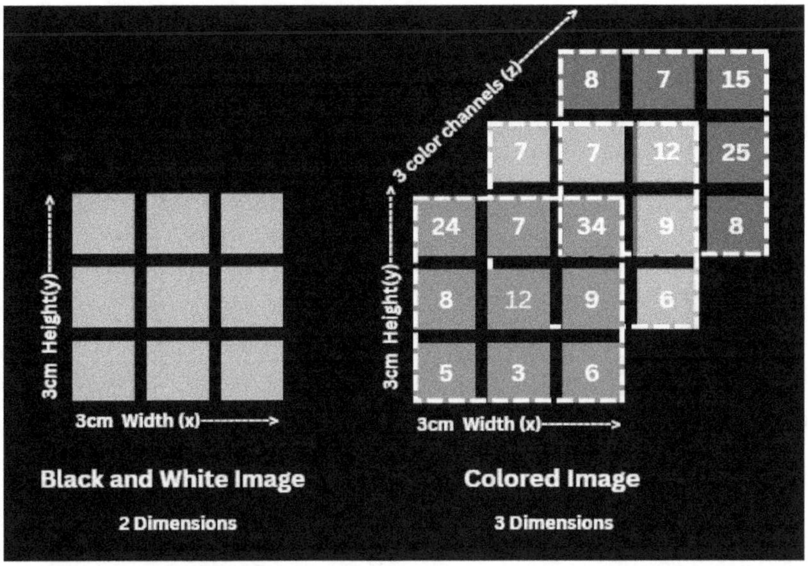

3 values makes a color, every one belongs one channel, how many channels does midi have?

16, for every one port. It means one midi port can send and receive 16 channels of midi data. Recall track, one track is one kind of midi data, usually one instrument, acoustic piano, grand piano, drum, guitar, or rhythm.

Part (track) of your instrument	MIDI Transmit Channel		MIDI Receive Channel	Track of instrument receiving MIDI data
Right-hand part	Ch. 1	→	Ch. 1	Track 1
Left-hand part	Ch. 2	→	Ch. 2	Track 2
:	:		:	:
Rhythm 1 part	Ch. 9	→	Ch. 9	Track 9
Rhythm 2 part	Ch. 10	→	Ch. 10	Track 10
Bass part	Ch. 11	→	Ch. 11	Track 11
:	:		:	:
:	Ch. 16	→	Ch. 16	Track 16

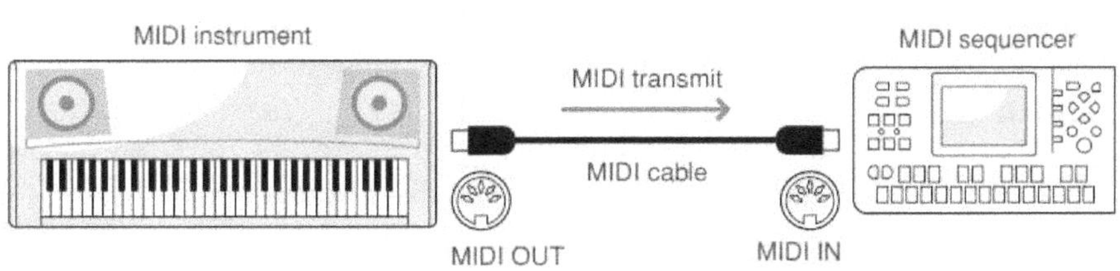

A sequencer will put the track into a song order, checkout https://craffel.github.io/pretty-midi/,

```
import pretty_midi
import numpy as np
```

```
pm = pretty_midi.PrettyMIDI('test_midi.mid')

pp =pm.get_piano_roll(100)#[56:70]
print((pp))
```

Recall fluidsynth,

```
import pretty_midi
# Load MIDI file into PrettyMIDI object
midi_data = pretty_midi.PrettyMIDI('composition.mid')
# Print an empirical estimate of its global tempo
print(midi_data.estimate_tempo())
# Compute the relative amount of each semitone across the entire song,

total_velocity = sum(sum(midi_data.get_chroma()))

audio_data = midi_data.fluidsynth()

print((audio_data.shape))

# 120.0
# (220500,)
```

so the chroma makes the mid a vector, size of 220500, how to map to the piano roll? What is piano roll?

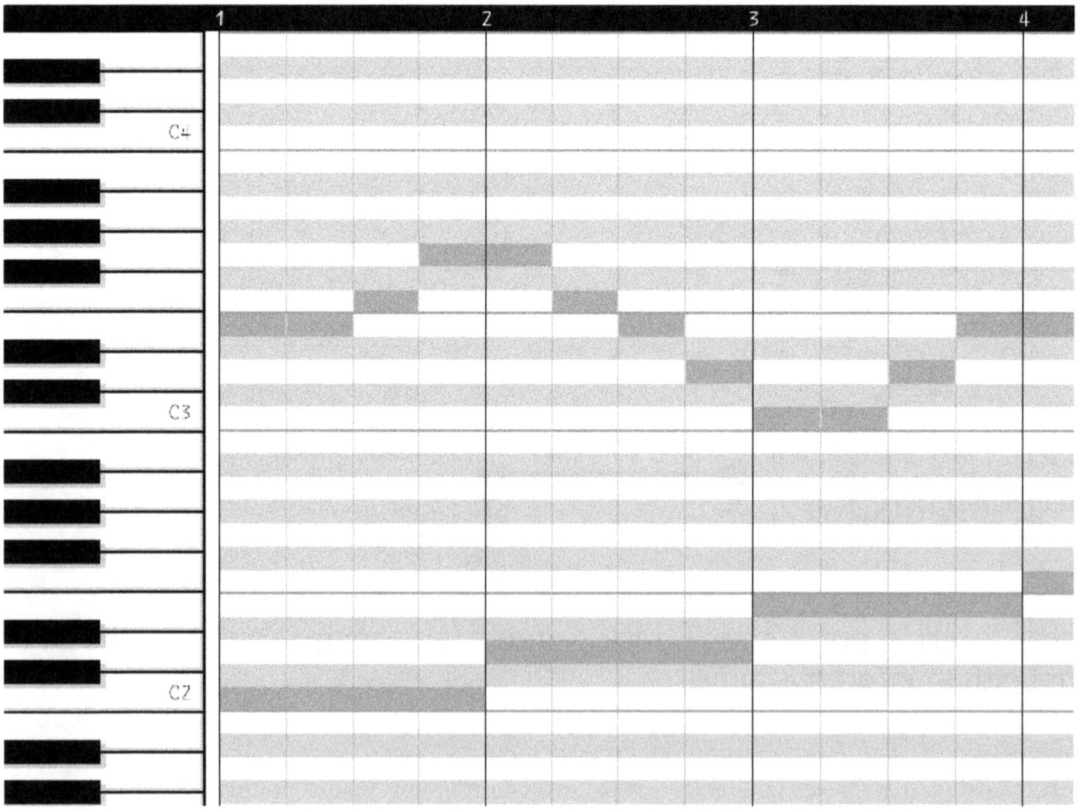

We see the pitch, duration of the notes need, this is exactly most piano phone apps doing, checkout http://github.com/craffel/examples/reverse_pianoroll.py,

if we mimic the image 3 channels, for a piano, it can be 2, or 4 channels, which means two players together.

What is the difference between mid and mp3?

Format	Type	Compression	Audio Quality	File Size	Compatibility
MP3	Lossy	Adjustable	Good	Small	High
AAC	Lossy	Adjustable	Better	Small	High
Ogg Vorbis	Lossy	Adjustable	Good	Small	Medium
WAV	Lossless	None	Excellent	Large	High
AIFF	Lossless	None	Excellent	Large	Medium
FLAC	Lossless	Adjustable	Excellent	Medium	Medium
ALAC	Lossless	Adjustable	Excellent	Medium	Medium
DSD	Lossless	None	Exceptional	Large	Low

we see mp3 is lossy and wav is lossless, so is mid lossless?

```
import fluidsynth

fs = fluidsynth.Synth()

fs.start(driver="alsa")

sfid = fs.sfload("soundfont.sf2")

fs.midifilenew("input.mid")

port_id = fs.midiport(0)

fs.midiconnect(port_id, 0)

fs.write_midifile_to_audio("output.wav", "soundfont.sf2", "input.mid")

fs.stop()
```

mid is not even compression, it is just synthesis, checkout https://docs.lchzh.net/learning/midi/smf1.1

63 Oneliner

- oneliner run

63.1 Download file

```
python -c "from urllib.request import urlretrieve; save = 'get-pip.py'; url = 'https://bootstrap.pypa.io/'+save; urlretrieve(url, save)"
```

63.2 Timing statement

```
python -c "from timeit import timeit; timeit(stmt='a=10;b=10;sum=a+b')"
```

63.3 Show current path

```
python -c "import os; print(os.getcwd())"
```

63.4 Square list

```
python -c "nums = [1, 2, 3, 4, 5]; squares = [val*val for val in nums]; print(squares)"
```

63.5 Composition list

```
python -c "x = [1, 2, 3]; y = [4, 5, 6]; coordinates = [(xcor, ycor) for xcor in x for ycor in y]; print(coordinates)"
```

63.6 Three condition

```
python -c "print('no') if x > 42 else print('yes') if x == 42 else print('maybe')
```

63.7 Flaten list

```
python -c "alist = [[1,2],[3,4],[5,6]]; blist = [item for sublist in alist for item in sublist]; print(blist)"
```

63.8 Count concurrence

```
python -c "mylist = [1,1,1,2,2,2,3,3]; mycount = mylist.count(element); print(mycount)"
```

63.9 Rotate list

```
python -c "alist = [1,2,3,4,5,6,7,8,9]; k = 3; blist = alist[-k % len(alist):] + alist[:-k % len(alist)]; print(blist)"
```

63.10 Transpose matrix

```
python -c "matrix = [[1,2], [4,5], [6,7]]; tmatrix = list(map(list, zip(*matrix))); print(tmatirx)"
```

63.11 Common prefix

```
python -c "import os; strings_list = ["ab_abc","abc_abc","ab_c_abc","ab_cd_abc"]; cprefix = os.path.commonprefix(strings_list); print(cprefix)"
```

63.12 Join integer

```
python -c "lint = [1,2,3,4,5]; sint = int(''.join(map(str, lint))); print(sint)"
```

63.13 Composition string

```
python -c "import itertools; mystring='abc'; perstring = [''.join(p) for p in itertools.permutations(mystring)]; print(perstring)"
```

63.14 List file

```
python -c "import os; print(os.listdir())"
```

63.15 Run command

```
python -c "import subprocess; command = 'echo Hello, World!'; subprocess.call(command, shell=True)"
```

63.16 Csv to json

`python -c "import csv,json;print json.dumps(list(csv.reader(open('csv_file.csv'))))"

63.17 Profile script

```
python -m cProfile my_script.py
```

63.18 Delete txt

```
python -c "import os; files = 'b.txt'; os.remove(files) if files else None"
```

63.19 Decode base64

```
python -c "import base64; base64.decode(open('file64', 'rb'), open('filetxt', 'wb'))"
```

63.20 List index

```
python -c "lst = [1, 2, 3, 'Alice', 'Alice']; indices = [i for i in range(len(lst)) if lst[i]=='Alice']; print(indices)"
```

63.21 List process

```
python -c "import psutil; print(sorted(psutil.process_iter(), key=lambda p: p.memory_percent(), reverse=True))"
```

- oneliner function

63.22 Create txt

```
def foo(a, counter=0,con=None, close=lambda x:x.close(),write=lambda x,s:x.write(s),n=lambda a=0,b=0,c=0:0):((foo,n)[counter](a, 1, (open,n)[counter](a + '.txt', 'wt')),((n,write)[counter](con, str(a)),(n,close)[counter](con)))

foo('b')
```

63.23 Show line

```
def foo(fn):f = open(fn); lines = [(i, j) for i, j in enumerate(f)]; print(lines); f.close()

foo('60 lilypond.md')
```

63.24 Get benefit

```
def foo(price): print(price); benefit = lambda numbers: [print(f"{price * number}") for number in numbers]; benefit([1.05, 1.1, 1.2])

foo(2.28)
```

63.25 Get decompose

```
def foo(num): print(num if num <= 1 else foo(num / 2))

foo(16)
```

63.26 Strip txt

```
def foo(f): c = [line.strip() for line in open(f)]; print(c)
foo('b.txt')
```

63.27 Make million

```
def foo(): millions = [i+1 for i in range(1000000)]; print(millions)
foo()
```

64 KDP

The hardest thing in Python is to publish in epub...

```
.\pandoc                    C:\Calibre\pandoc_amazon\content.md                    -o
C:\Calibre\pandoc_amazon\learn_bit_python.epub C:\Calibre\pandoc_amazon\title.txt --
css C:\Calibre\pandoc_amazon\amazon.css --toc
```

All the pictures are lost, due to no where to store...

www.ingramcontent.com/pod-product-compliance
Lightning Source LLC
LaVergne TN
LVHW082010200926
848481LV00010B/2828